X WINDOW SYSTEM

The Complete Reference to Xlib, X Protocol, ICCCM, XLFD

Digital Press X and Motif Series

Motif Programming

The Essentials . . . and More

Marshall Brain

X Window System Toolkit

The Complete Programmer's Guide and Specification

Paul J. Asente and Ralph R. Swick

X and Motif Quick Reference Guide

Randi J. Rost

X Window System

The Complete Reference to Xlib, X Protocol, ICCCM, XLFD
Third Edition

Robert W. Scheifler and James Gettys
With Jim Flowers, David Rosenthal

X WINDOW SYSTEM

The Complete Reference to Xlib, X Protocol, ICCCM, XLFD

Third Edition

X VERSION 11, RELEASE 5

Robert W. Scheifler   James Gettys

with Jim Flowers, David Rosenthal

and contributions from Chuck Adams, Vania Joloboff, Bill McMahon, Al Mento, Rod Newman, Al Tabayoyon, Glenn Widener

Digital Press

digital™

Printed in the United States of America

9 8 7 6 5 4 3 2

Order number EY-J802E-DP

The publisher offers discounts on bulk orders of this book. For information, please write:

Special Sales Department
Digital Press
One Burlington Woods Drive
Burlington, MA 01803

Trademarks mentioned in this book are listed on page 1000.

Library of Congress Cataloging-in-Publication Data

Scheifler, Robert W., 1954–
X Window System : the complete reference to Xlib, X Protocol ICCCM, XLFD / Robert W. Scheifler, James Gettys; with Jim Flowers David Rosenthal. – 3rd ed.
p. cm. – (Digital Press X and Motif series)
"X version 11, release 5"
Includes index.
ISBN 1-55558-088-2
1. X Window System (Computer System) I. Gettys, James, 1953–
II. Title. III. Series.
QA76.76.W56S34 1992
005.4'3—dc20 91-42753
CIP

Contents

Chapter 10. Events 247

Acknowledgments

X Window System, Version 11

The design and implementation of the first ten versions of X were primarily the work of three individuals: Robert Scheifler of the MIT Laboratory for Computer Science and Jim Gettys of Digital Equipment Corporation and Ron Newman of MIT, both at MIT Project Athena. X version 11, however, is the result of the efforts of dozens of individuals at almost as many locations and organizations. At the risk of offending some of the players by exclusion, we would like to acknowledge some of the people who deserve special credit and recognition for their work on Xlib. Our apologies to anyone inadvertently overlooked.

Xlib – C Library X Interface
Release 1

Our thanks goes to Ron Newman (MIT Project Athena), who contributed substantially to the design and implementation of the Version 11 Xlib interface.

Our thanks also goes to Ralph Swick (Project Athena and Digital) who kept it all together for us during the early releases. He handled literally thousands of requests from people everywhere and saved the sanity of at least one of us. His calm good cheer was a foundation on which we could build.

Our thanks also goes to Todd Brunhoff (Tektronix) who was "loaned" to Project Athena at exactly the right moment to provide very capable and much-needed assistance during the alpha and beta releases. He was responsible for the successful integration of sources from multiple sites; we would not have had a release without him.

Our thanks also goes to Al Mento and Al Wojtas of Digital's ULTRIX Documentation Group. With good humor and cheer, they took a rough draft and made it an infinitely better and more useful document. The work they have done will help many everywhere. We also would like to thank Hal Murray (Digital SRC) and Peter George (Digital VMS) who contributed much by proofreading the early drafts of this document.

Our thanks also goes to Jeff Dike (Digital UEG), Tom Benson, Jackie Granfield, and Vince Orgovan (Digital VMS) who helped with the library utilities implementation; to Hania Gajewska (Digital UEG-WSL) who, along with Ellis Cohen (CMU and Siemens), was instrumental in the semantic design of the window manager properties; and to Dave Rosenthal (Sun Microsystems) who also contributed to the protocol and provided the sample generic color frame buffer device-dependent code.

The alpha and beta test participants deserve special recognition and thanks as well. It is significant that the bug reports (and many fixes) during alpha and beta test came almost exclusively from just a few of the alpha testers, mostly hardware vendors working on product implementations of X. The continued public contribution of vendors and universities is certainly to the benefit of the entire X community.

Special thanks must go to Sam Fuller, Vice-President of Corporate Research at Digital, who has remained committed to the widest public availability of X and who made it possible to greatly supplement MIT's resources with the Digital staff in order to make version 11 a reality. Many of the people mentioned here are part of the Western Software Laboratory (Digital UEG-WSL) of the ULTRIX Engineering Group and work for Smokey Wallace, who has been vital to the project's success. Others not mentioned here worked on the toolkit and are acknowledged in the X Toolkit documentation.

Of course, we must particularly thank Paul Asente, formerly of Stanford University and now of Digital UEG-WSL, who wrote W, the predecessor to X, and Brian Reid, formerly of Stanford University and now of Digital WRL, who had much to do with W's design.

Finally, our thanks goes to MIT, Digital Equipment Corporation, and IBM for providing the environment where it could happen.

Release 4

Our thanks go to Jim Fulton (MIT X Consortium) for designing and specifying the new Xlib functions for Inter-Client Communication Conventions (ICCCM) support.

We also thank Al Mento of Digital for his continued effort in maintaining this document and Jim Fulton and Donna Converse (MIT X Consortium) for their much-appreciated efforts in reviewing the changes.

Release 5

The principal authors of the Input Method facilities are Vania Joloboff (OSF) and Bill McMahon (HP). The principal author of the rest of the internationalization facilities is Glenn Widener (Tektronix). Our thanks to them for keeping their sense of humor through a long and sometimes difficult design process. Although the words and much of the design are due to them, many others have contributed substantially to the design and implementation. Tom McFarland (HP) and Frank Rojas (IBM) deserve particular recognition for their contributions. Other contributors were Tim Anderson (Motorola), Alka Badshah (OSF), Gabe Beged-Dov (HP), Chih-Chung Ko (III), Vera Cheng (III), Michael Collins (Digital), Walt Daniels (IBM), Noritoshi Demizu (OMRON), Keisuke Fukui (Fujitsu), Hitoshoi Fukumoto (Nihon Sun), Tim Greenwood (Digital), John Harvey (IBM), Fred Horman (AT&T), Norikazu Kaiya (Fujitsu), Yuji Kamata (IBM), Yutaka Kataoka (Waseda University), Ranee Khubchandani (Sun), Akari Kon (NEC), Hiroshi Kuribayashi (OMRON), Teruhiko Kurosaka (Sun), Seiji Kuwari (OMRON), Sandra Martin (OSF), Masato Morisaki (NTT), Nelson Ng (Sun), Takashi Nishimura (NTT America), Makato Nishino (IBM), Akira Ohsone (Nihon Sun), Chris Peterson (MIT), Sam Shteingart (AT&T), Manish Sheth (AT&T), Muneiyoshi Suzuki (NTT), Cori Mehring (Digital), Shoji Sugiyama (IBM), and Eiji Tosa (IBM).

We are deeply indebted to Tatsuya Kato (NTT), Hiroshi Kuribayashi (OMRON), Seiji Kuwari (OMRON), Muneiyoshi Suzuki (NTT), and Li Yuhong (OMRON) for producing the first complete sample implementation of the internationalization facilities. We are also very much indebted to Masato Morisaki (NTT) for coordinating the integration, testing, and release of this implementation. We also thank Michael Collins for his design of the pluggable layer inside Xlib.

The principal authors (design and implementation) of the Xcms color management facilities are Al Tabayoyon (Tektronix) and Chuck Adams (Tektronix). Joann Taylor (Tektronix), Bob Toole (Tektronix), and Keith Packard (MIT X Consortium) also contributed significantly to the design. Others who contributed are Harold Boll (Kodak), Ken Bronstein (HP), Nancy Cam (SGI), Donna Converse (MIT X Consortium), Elias Israel (ISC), Deron Johnson (Sun), Jim King (Adobe), Ricardo Motta (HP), Keith Packard (MIT), Chuck Peek (IBM), Wil Plouffe (IBM), Dave Sternlicht (MIT X Consortium), Kumar Talluri (AT&T), and Richard Verberg (IBM).

We also once again thank Al Mento of Digital for his work in formatting and reformatting text for this manual and for producing manpages. Thanks also to Clive Feather (IXI) for proofreading and finding a number of small errors.

X Window System Protocol

The primary contributers to the X11 protocol are Dave Carver (Digital HPW), Branko Gerovac (Digital HPW), Jim Gettys (MIT/Project Athena, Digital), Phil Karlton (Digital WSL), Scott McGregor (Digital SSG), Ram Rao (Digital UEG), David Rosenthal (Sun), and Dave Winchell (Digital UEG).

The implementors of initial server who provided useful input are Susan Angebranndt (Digital), Raymond Drewry (Digital), and Todd Newman (Digital).

The invited reviewers who provided useful input are Andrew Cherenson (Berkeley), Burns Fisher (Digital), Dan Garfinkel (HP), Leo Hourvitz (Next), Brock Krizan (HP), David Laidlaw (Stellar), Dave Mellinger (Interleaf), Ron Newman (MIT), John Ousterhout (Berkeley), Andrew Palay (ITC CMU), Ralph Swick (MIT), Craig Taylor (Sun), and Jeffery Vroom (Stellar).

Thanks go to Al Mento of Digital for formatting this document.

Inter-Client Communication Conventions Manual

David Rosenthal had overall architectural responsibility for the conventions defined in this document; he wrote most of the text and edited the document, but its development has been a communal effort. The details were thrashed out in meetings at the January 1988 MIT X Conference and at the 1988 Summer Usenix conference, and through months (and megabytes) of argument on the `wmtalk` mail alias. Thanks are due to everyone who contributed, and especially to the following people.

For the Selection section, thanks go to Jerry Farrell (Sun), Phil Karlton (Digital), Loretta Guarino Reid (Digital), Mark Manasse (Digital), and Bob Scheifler (MIT).

For the Cut Buffer section, thanks go to Andrew Palay (CMU).

For the Window and Session Manager sections, thanks go to Todd Brunhoff (Tektronix), Ellis Cohen (Siemens), Jim Fulton (MIT), Hania Gajewska (Digital), Jordan Hubbard (Ardent), Kerry Kimbrough (TI), Audrey Ishizaki (HP), Matt Landau (BBN), Mark Manasse (Digital), Bob Scheifler (MIT), Ralph Swick (Project Athena and Digital), Mike Wexler (Wyse), and Glenn Widener (Tektronix).

For the Device Color Characterization section, thanks go to Keith Packard (MIT).

In addition, thanks are due to those who contributed to the public review: Gary Combs (Tektronix), Errol Crary (Tektronix), Nancy Cyprych (Digital), John Diamant (HP), Clive Feather (IXI), Burns Fisher (Digital), Richard Greco (Tektronix), Tim Greenwood (Digital), Kee Hinckley (Apollo), Brian Holt (Apollo), John Interrante (Stanford), John Irwin (Franz Inc.), Vania Joloboff (INRIA), John Laporta (Apollo), Ken Lee (Daisy), Stuart Marks (Sun), Alan Mimms (Apple), Colas Nahaboo (INRIA), Mark Patrick (Ardent), Steve Pitschke (Stellar), Brad Reed (EDS), and John Thomas (Tektronix).

X Logical Font Description

Our thanks go to Jim Flowers (Digital), who had architectural and editorial responsibility for the conventions defined in this X Consortium Standard; he drafted the initial proposal during the final stages of X11 development and guided it through the year-long internal and external review process.

In addition, a number of Consortium members provided critical input and comments on the proposal, especially Bob Scheifler (MIT), Phil Karlton (Digital), Glenn Widener (Tektronix), and Daniel Dardailler (Bull).

Jim Gettys
Cambridge Research Laboratory
Digital Equipment Corporation

Robert W. Scheifler
Laboratory for Computer Science
Massachusetts Institute of Technology

X WINDOW SYSTEM

The Complete Reference to Xlib, X Protocol, ICCCM, XLFD

Introduction

The X Window System, or X, is a network-transparent window system. With X, multiple applications can run simultaneously in windows, generating text and graphics in monochrome or color on a bitmap display. Network transparency means that application programs can run on machines scattered throughout the network. Because X permits applications to be device-independent, applications need not be rewritten, recompiled, or even relinked to work with new display hardware.

X provides facilities for generating multifont text and two-dimensional graphics (such as points, lines, arcs, and polygons) in a hierarchy of rectangular windows. Every window can be thought of as a "virtual screen" and can contain subwindows within it, to an arbitrary depth. Windows can overlap each other like stacks of papers on a desk and can be moved, resized, and restacked dynamically. Windows are inexpensive resources; applications using several hundred subwindows are common. For example, windows are often used to implement individual user interface components such as scroll bars, menus, buttons, and so forth.

Although users typically think of themselves as clients of the system, X applications, in terms of the network, are the clients that use the network services of the window system. A program running on the machine with the display hardware provides these services and so is called the X server. The X server acts as an intermediary between applications and the display, handling output from the clients to the display and forwarding input (entered with a keyboard or mouse) to the appropriate clients for processing.

Clients and servers use some form of interprocess communication to exchange information. The syntax and semantics of this conversation are defined by a communication protocol. This protocol is the foundation of the X Window System. Clients use the protocol to send requests to the server to create and manipulate windows, to generate text and graphics, to control input from the user, and to communicate with other clients. The server uses the protocol to send information back to the client in response to various requests and to forward keyboard and other user input on to the appropriate clients.

Because a network round-trip is an expensive operation relative to basic request execution, the protocol is primarily asynchronous, and data can be in transit in both directions (client to server and server to client) simultaneously. After generating a request, a client typically does not wait for the server to execute the request before generating a new request. Instead, the client generates a stream of requests that are eventually received by the server and executed. The server does not acknowledge receipt of a request and, in most cases, does not acknowledge execution of a request. (This is possible because the underlying transport is reliable.)

The protocol is designed explicitly to minimize the need to query the window system for information. Clients should not depend on the server to obtain information that the clients initially supplied. In addition, clients do not poll for input by sending requests to the server. Instead, clients use requests to register interest in various events, and the server sends event notifications asynchronously. Asynchronous operation may be one of the most significant differences between X and other window systems.

For the best performance, when the client and the server reside on the same machine, communication between them often is implemented using shared memory. When the client and the server reside on different machines, communication can take place over any network transport layer that provides reliable, in-order delivery of data in both directions (usually called a reliable duplex byte stream). For example, TCP (in the Internet protocol family) and DECnet streams are two commonly used transport layers. To support distributed computing in a heterogeneous environment, the communication protocol is designed to be independent of the operating system, programming language, and processor hardware. Thus, a single display can display applications written in multiple languages under multiple operating systems on multiple hardware architectures simultaneously.

Although X is fundamentally defined by a network protocol, most application programmers do not want to think about bits, bytes, and message formats. Therefore, X has an interface library. This library provides a familiar procedural interface that masks the details of the protocol encoding and transport interactions and automatically handles the buffering of requests for efficient transport to the server, much as the C standard I/O library buffers output to minimize system calls. The library also provides various utility functions that are not directly related to the protocol but are nevertheless important in building applications. The exact interface for this library differs for each programming language. Xlib is the library for the C programming language.

The accompanying figure shows a block diagram of a complete X environment. Each X server controls one or more screens, a keyboard, and a pointing device (typically a mouse) with one or more buttons on it. There can be many X servers; often there is one for every workstation on the network. Applications can run on any machine, even those without X servers. An application might communicate with multiple servers simultaneously (for example, to support computer conferencing between individuals in different locations). Multiple applications can be active at the same time on a single server.

In X, many facilities that are built into other window systems are provided by client libraries. The X protocol does not specify menus, scroll bars, and dialog boxes or how an application should respond to user input. The protocol and X library avoid mandating such policy decisions as much as possible and should be viewed as a construction kit that provides a rich set of mechanisms that can implement a variety of user interface policies. Toolkits (providing menus, scroll bars, dialog boxes, and so on), higher-level graphics libraries (which might transform abstract object descriptions into graphics requests, for example), and user interface management systems (UIMS) can all be implemented on top of the X library. Although the X library provides the foundation, the expectation is that applications will be written using these higher-level facilities in conjunction with the facilities of the X library, rather than solely on the "bare bones" of the X library.

A user interface can be viewed as having two primary components: the interaction with the user that is logically internal to an application (for example, typing text into a text editor or changing a cell's contents in a spreadsheet) and the interaction that is logically external to an application (for

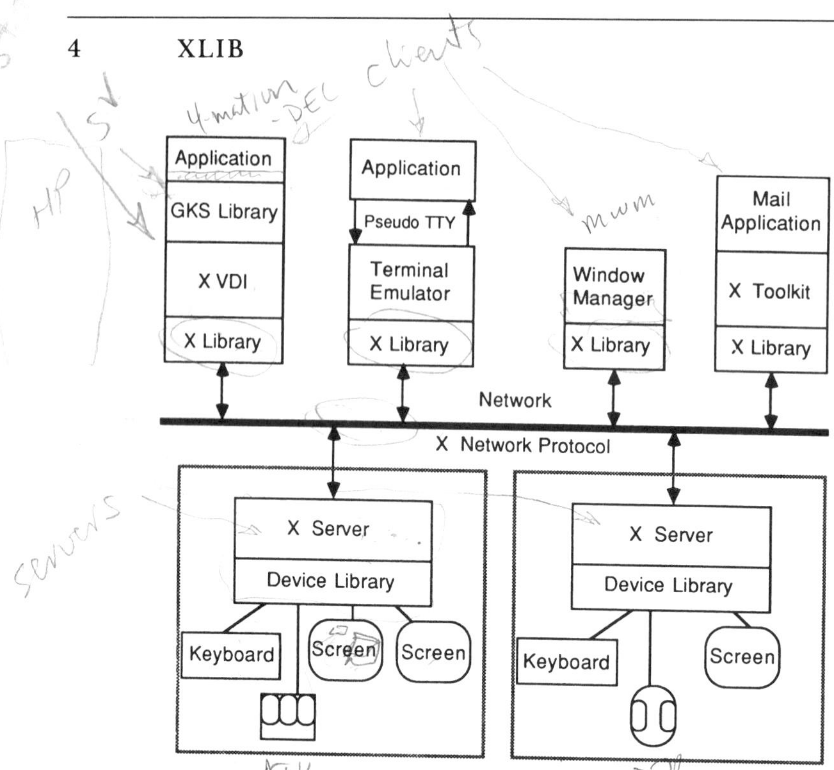

Figure 1. X window system block diagram

example, moving or resizing an application window or turning an application window into an icon). The external user interface is built into many other window systems, but this is not the case with X. The X protocol does not define an external user interface at all. Rather, the protocol provides mechanisms with which a variety of external user interfaces can be built. These mechanisms are designed so that a single client, called a window manager, can provide the external user interface independent of all the other clients.

A window manager can enforce a strict window layout policy if it desires (for example, "tiling" the screen so that application windows never overlap) as well as can automatically provide the following:

- Title bars, borders, and other window decorations for each application
- Uniform icons for applications
- A uniform means of moving and resizing windows
- A uniform interface for switching the keyboard between applications

With a suitable set of conventions, which have been standardized and are called the Inter-Client Communications Convention (see part III), applications are insensitive to the external user interface provided by a window manager and run correctly unmodified in multiple environments.

Because the protocol can deal with such a broad spectrum of user interfaces, no single program, toolkit, UIMS, or window manager is likely to use all the facilities the protocol and the X library provide.

Principles

Early in the development of X, we argued about what should and should not be implemented in the server. For example, we did not know if menus or terminal emulators could be implemented in the client with adequate performance or whether "rubber-banding" (dynamically stretching a simple figure in response to movement of the pointing device) would be acceptable when performed across a network. Experimentation during the first months showed us that more was possible than we had first believed.

These observations hardened into the following principles, which guided us through the early X design:

- Do not add new functionality unless an implementor cannot complete a real application without it.
- It is as important to decide what a system is not as to decide what it is. Do not serve all the world's needs; rather, make the system extensible so that additional needs can be met in an upwardly compatible fashion.
- The only thing worse than generalizing from one example is generalizing from no examples at all.
- If a problem is not completely understood, it is probably best to provide no solution at all.
- If you can get 90 percent of the desired effect for 10 percent of the work, use the simpler solution.
- Isolate complexity as much as possible.
- Provide mechanism rather than policy. In particular, place user interface policy in the clients' hands.

The first principle kept the wish list under control. Just because someone wanted something in the server, we did not feel obligated to add it. This kept us focused on the important issues that made real applications work. This principle was a somewhat more difficult touchstone to use during the design of the present version of X, given its appreciably larger audience. We modified the principle to be "know of some real application that will require it."

At each iteration of the X design, there was always more to do than time allowed. We therefore focused on mechanisms with the broadest applicability and for which consensus in the group could easily be achieved. For example, we focused on two-dimensional graphics, explicitly deferring three-dimensional graphics.

At the same time, to avoid obsolescence, we designed the present version of X to be extensible at both the protocol and library interfaces and without requiring incompatible changes to existing applications. Examples of extensions that we had in mind were additional graphics models (such as GKS, PHIGS, and PostScript), real-time video, and general programmability in the server. (We view programmability as simply one example of an extension, not as the sole mechanism for extensibility; mere programmability does not give support for video or high-performance support for graphics.)

During the design and implementation process, we generally suspected that any problems were just the tips of large icebergs. Expending effort to solve an immediate problem without first trying to generalize the problem is usually a mistake; a few related examples often make a whole class of problems clear. This is not to say that we ignored the first instance of a problem; often there were adequate solutions using existing mechanisms.

We attempted to avoid solutions to problems we did not fully understand. For example, the preliminary design for the present version of X supported multiple input devices (more than just a single keyboard and mouse). As we worked through the design, we realized it had flaws that would take a lot of time and experimentation to correct. As a result, we removed this support from the system, knowing that correct support could be added later through the extension mechanism.

We also tried to avoid winning a complexity merit badge. If we could get most of what we needed with less complexity than a complete solution would require, we were willing to compromise our goals. Only history will decide if these trade-offs were successful.

Much of the existing complexity is a result of providing support for external window management; most programmers need not be concerned with this, particularly those using an X toolkit. We expected that toolkits would hide various forms of tedium from the programmer. For example, a program that displays "Hello World" with configurable colors and font and obeys window management conventions is about 150 lines of code when written using only the facilities of the X library. An equivalent program written using a toolkit can have fewer than a dozen lines of code. Thus, it is important to keep in mind that the X library is only one layer in a complete X programming environment.

Isolation of complexity is necessary in large systems. A system in which every component is intimately related to every other becomes difficult to change as circumstances change. We therefore attempted to build as much as possible into client programs, introducing only the minimum mechanisms required in the server.

Deciding what a system is not is as important as deciding what it is. For example, at various times people urged that remote execution and general inter-client remote procedure calls be integral parts of X. They felt there were no established standards in these areas, and they wanted X to be a self-contained environment. As is often the case, solving the immediate problem by adding to the existing framework rather than by integrating into a larger framework is less work, but the result is not satisfactory for long. The X protocol is correctly viewed as just one component in an overall distributed systems architecture, not as the complete architecture by itself.

User interface design is difficult and currently quite diverse. Although global user interface standards might someday be possible, we believed it prudent to promote the cooperative coexistence of a variety of user interface styles and to support diverse user communities and ongoing research activities. By separating window management functions from the server and from normal applications and by layering user interface policy in higher-level libraries on top of the X library, we allowed for experimentation without forcing all users to be guinea pigs. As a result, many existing user interfaces have been imported into the X environment. Having a "pick one or roll your own" policy instead of a "love it or leave it" one has drawbacks; applications developers must choose a user interface style and user community. The X library and the protocol should be remembered not as an end but a foundation.

As might have been predicted, X not only has become a fertile ground for experimentation in user interfaces but also has become a source of market competition. Two major user interface toolkits and window managers (with quite different look-and-feels) are Motif[1] and Open Look.[2] Applications using either can coexist simultaneously (although they provide quite different results to the end user).

Significant research toolkits include InterViews, written in C++ at Stanford, the Andrew system of CMU, several Common Lisp toolkits, and a dozen major window managers. There are a number of user interface management systems and other application builders for X.

All of this, of course, is to enable applications to be built easily and cheaply. These are now appearing in quantity for X. It is by these that we must judge the success of X; by this metric, we have only succeeded in attaining our goals in 1989.

History

X was born of necessity in 1984. Bob Scheifler was working at MIT's Laboratory for Computer Science (LCS) on the Argus distributed system and was in need of a decent display environment for debugging multiple distributed processes. Jim Gettys, a Digital engineer, was assigned to MIT Project Athena, an undergraduate education program sponsored by Digital and IBM that would ultimately populate the MIT campus with thousands of workstations.

Neither Digital nor IBM had a workstation product with a bitmap display in 1984. The closest simulacrum available was from Digital—a VS100 display attached to a VAX. Both Athena and LCS had VAX-11/750s, and Athena was in the process of acquiring about 70 VS100s. VS100s were in field test at the time, and the firmware for them was unreliable. Athena lent one of the first VS100s to LCS in exchange for cooperative work on the software. Our immediate goal was clear: we needed to build a window system environment running under UNIX on VS100s for ourselves and the groups we worked for. We had little thought of anything beyond these goals but wondered where to begin. Little software was available elsewhere that was not encumbered by license or portability.

[1] Motif, a registered trademark of the Open Software Foundation, is based on technology from Hewlett-Packard and Digital Equipment Corporation.

[2] Open Look, a registered trademark of AT&T, is based on technology from AT&T and Sun Microsystems.

Paul Asente and Brian Reid, then both at Stanford University, had developed a prototype window system, called W, to run under Stanford's V operating system. W used a network protocol and supported "dumb terminal" windows and "transparent graphics" windows with display lists maintained in the server. In the summer of 1983, Paul Asente and Chris Kent, summer students at Digital's Western Research Laboratory, ported W to the VS100 under UNIX and were kind enough to give us a copy.

The V system has reasonably fast synchronous remote procedure call, and W in the V environment was designed with a synchronous protocol. The port to UNIX retained the synchronous communication even though communication in UNIX was easily five times slower than in V. The combination of prototype VS100s with unreliable firmware and W using slow communication was not encouraging, to say the least; one could easily type faster than the terminal window could echo characters.

In May 1984, we received reliable VS100 hardware and firmware. That summer, Bob Scheifler replaced the synchronous protocol of W with an asynchronous protocol and replaced the display lists with immediate mode graphics. The result was sufficiently different from W that continuing to call it W was inappropriate and would have caused confusion, as W was in some limited use at Athena. With no particular thought about the name and because the familial resemblance to W was still strong at that date, Bob called the result X. Much later, when the name became a serious issue, X had already stuck and was used by too many people to permit a change.

Development was rapid during the next eight months. The first terminal emulator (VT52) and window manager were written in the CLU programming language, the language of choice in the research group where Bob worked. Bob continued development of the server and the protocol, which went from version 1 to version 6 during this period (the version number was incremented each time an incompatible change was made). Mark Vandevoorde at Athena wrote a new VT100 terminal emulator in C, and Jim Gettys worked on the X library and the UNIX support for starting the window system. Late in 1984, we received faster VS100 firmware, causing the first round of performance analysis and optimization. Within a few weeks, we were again hardware limited but had a much better understanding of performance issues.

By early 1985, many people inside Digital were using X, and plans were under way for the first Digital UNIX workstation product, which was based on the MicroVAX-II. At that time, support for UNIX in Digital was limited, and there was no chance of getting any other window system except X on Digital hardware. Other systems were either nonportable or were unavailable because of licensing problems (as was the case with Andrew). X was the logical candidate. We had ported X version 6 to the QVSS display on the MicroVAX. Ron Newman joined Project Athena at this time and worked on documenting the X library, which was already in its third major revision.

We redesigned X to support color during the second quarter of 1985, with Digital's eventual VAXstation-II/GPX as the intended target. Although MIT had licensed version 6 to a few outside groups for a brief time at nominal charge, a key decision was made in the summer of 1985 not to license future versions of X. Instead, it would be available to anyone at the cost of production. In September 1985, version 9 of X was made publicly available, and the field test of the VAXstation-II/GPX began. During that fall, Brown University and MIT started porting X to the IBM RT/PC, which was in field test at those universities. A problem with reading unaligned data on the RT forced an incompatible change to the protocol; this was the only difference between version 9 and version 10.

During the fall, the first significant outside contributions of code to X started to appear from several universities and from Digital. In January 1986, Digital announced the VAXstation-II/GPX, which was the first commercial X implementation. Release 3 of X (X10R3) was available in February and was a major watershed in X development. Although we were happy to see a major corporation incorporate X into its product line, we knew the design was limited to the taste and needs of a small group of people. It could solve just the problems we faced, and its hardware origins were still obvious in key aspects of the design. We knew version 10 had inherent limitations that would force major redesign within a few years, although it was certainly adequate for developing many interesting applications.

Over the next few months, a strange phenomenon occurred. Many other corporations, such as Hewlett-Packard, were basing products on version 10, and groups at universities and elsewhere were porting X to other displays and systems, including Apollo Computer and Sun Microsystems workstations. The server was even ported to the IBM PC/AT. Somewhat later, Hewlett-Packard contributed their toolkit to the MIT distribution.

We grew tired of hearing comments such as "We like X, but there is this one thing you ought to change." People were already declaring it a standard, which was, to our thinking, premature. Before long, however, we were confronted with a fundamental decision about X's future. We seriously considered doing nothing; after all, X did almost everything we needed it to, and what it did not do could be added without difficulty. Unfortunately, this would leave many people using an inadequate platform for their work. In the long run, X would either die because of its inadequacies, or it would spawn wildly incompatible variations. Alternatively, based on feedback from users and developers, we could undertake a second major redesign of X.

Although we were willing to do the design work, we knew that the resulting design would be ambitious and would require much more implementation work than our meager resources at MIT would permit. Fortunately, Digital's Western Software Laboratory (DECWSL) was between projects. This group had the required expertise, including people who had contributed to pioneering Xerox window systems. More importantly, these people were intimately familiar with X. Smokey Wallace, DECWSL's manager, and Jim Gettys proposed the implementation of version 11, which would then be given back to MIT for public distribution without a license. Digital management quickly approved the proposal.

We started intensive protocol design in May 1986. No proprietary information was used in the design process. Key contributors included Phil Karlton and Scott McGregor of Digital. Dave Rosenthal of Sun Microsystems was invited to join Digital engineers on the design team, and Bob Scheifler acted as the chief architect. At the first design meeting, we decided it was not feasible to design a protocol that would be upwardly compatible with version 10 and still provide the functionality essential for the range of display hardware that had to be supported. With some reluctance, we abandoned compatibility with version 10 (although Todd Brunhoff of Tektronix has since shown that one can build a reasonable "compatibility server" to display version 10 applications on a version 11 server).

We carried out most of the actual design work using the electronic mail facilities of the DARPA Internet, which connects hundreds of networks around the country, including MIT's campus network and Digital's engineering network. The entire group held only three day-long meetings during the design process. During these meetings, we reached a consensus on issues we could not resolve by mail. Even with group members on opposite coasts, responses to most design issues were only a few minutes away. A printed copy of all the messages exchanged during this time would be a stack of paper several feet high. Without electronic mail, the design simply would not have been possible.

Once we had completed a preliminary protocol design, we invited people from other companies and universities to review the specification. By August, we had a design ready for public review, which was again carried out using electronic mail, courtesy of the Internet. Design of the sample server implementation started at this time. Phil Karlton and Susan Angebranndt of DECWSL designed and implemented the device-independent parts of the server, and Raymond Drewry and Todd Newman implemented the portable, machine-independent graphics library. Jim Gettys acted as the the X library architect and with Ron Newman at MIT worked on the redesign and implementation of the X library. Many other contributions came from DECWSL as well, such as rewriting version 10 clients and the Xt toolkit intrinsics (another story in itself).

During the fall of 1986, Digital decided to base its entire desktop workstation strategy for ULTRIX, VMS, and MS-DOS on X. Although this was gratifying to us, it also meant we had even more people to talk to. This resulted in some delay, but, in the end, it also resulted in a better design. Ralph Swick of Digital joined Project Athena during this period and played a vital role thoughout version 11's development. The last version 10 release was made available in December 1986.

In January 1987, approximately 250 people attended the first X technical conference, which was held at MIT. During the conference, eleven major computer hardware and software vendors announced their support for X version 11 at an unprecedented press conference.

Alpha testing of version 11 started in February 1988, and beta testing started three months later at over 100 sites. Server back-ends and other code contributions came from Apollo, Digital, Hewlett-Packard, IBM, Sun, and the University of California at Berkeley. Tektronix lent Todd Brunhoff to MIT to help coordinate testing and integration, which was a godsend to us all. Texas Instruments provided an implementation of a Common Lisp interface library, based on an interface specification by Bob Scheifler. We made the first release of version 11 (V11R1) available on September 15, 1987.

The MIT X Consortium

Toward the end of the design phase of the version 11 protocol, the MIT principals were feeling that perhaps it was time to relinquish control of X and let the industry take over, although we had only vague ideas about what that might mean. Window system design was something we had fallen into. We did not think of it as our real occupation, and it seemed there was sufficient industry momentum for X to succeed. We made our feelings known at the first X Technical Conference in January 1987 and during a few protocol design sessions.

We were somewhat surprised by the reaction, but this was just another instance of underestimating the impact of X. Representatives of nine major computer vendors collectively called for a meeting with MIT, held in June 1987; their consistent position was that it could be fatal to X if MIT relinquished control. They argued that a vendor-neutral architect was a key factor in the success of X. To make UNIX successful, it was necessary to encourage application development by independent software vendors (ISVs). Prior to X, ISVs saw the UNIX marketplace as fragmented with multiple proprietary graphics and windowing systems. X was bringing coherence to the marketplace. However, without continued vendor-neutral control, different segments of the industry would surely take divergent paths, and interoperability would again be lost.

From this meeting came the idea of a more formal organization for controlling the evolution of X, with MIT at the helm, and in January 1988 the MIT X Consortium was born, with Bob Scheifler as its director. The goal of the Consortium is to promote cooperation within the computer industry in the creation of standard software interfaces at all layers in the X Window System environment. MIT's role is to provide the vendor-neutral architectural and administrative leadership required to make this work. The Consortium is financially self-supporting from membership fees with membership open to any organization. At present, over 95 companies as well as several universities and research organizations (which represent the bulk of the US and a considerable segment of the international computer industries) belong to the X Consortium.

The X Consortium hosted its fifth annual X conference in January 1991 (approximately 1200 people attended). The fifth release of version 11 was available September 5, 1991.

The director of the X Consortium acts as the chief architect for all X specifications and software and is the final authority for standards. The activities of the Consortium are overseen by an MIT Steering Committee, which includes the director and one associate director of LCS. The Steering Committee helps set policy and establish goals as well as provides strategic guidance and review of the Consortium's activities. An Advisory Committee, which is made up of member representatives, meets regularly to review the Consortium's plans, assess its progress, and suggest future directions.

The interests of the Consortium, which are quite broad, include the following:

- Incorporating three-dimensional graphics functionality (such as that provided by the PHIGS international graphics standard)
- Incorporating live and still video display and control
- Incorporating scalable/outline font technology
- Incorporating security mechanisms in support of both commercial and government requirements
- Incorporating digital image processing functionality
- Developing high-level toolkits to support the rapid construction of high-quality user interfaces and to support the reuse of user interface components across applications
- Developing conventions to allow applications to operate reasonably under a variety of externally controlled window management policies and to allow independent applications to exchange meaningful data in a cooperative fashion
- Developing programming interfaces to simplify building internationalized applications that are capable of being tailored to a variety of languages and keyboard input methods
- Developing control protocols and support services for X terminals (network-based graphics terminals designed specifically to run the X server)
- Developing and maintaining software test suites for major system components
- Sponsoring an annual conference, open to the public, to promote the exchange of technical information about X

The Consortium's activities take place almost exclusively using electronic mail with occasional meetings only when required. As designs and specifications take shape, interest groups are formed from experts in the participating organizations. Typically, a small multi-organization architecture team leads the design with others acting as close observers and reviewers. Once a complete specification is produced, it is submitted for formal technical review by the Consortium as a proposed standard. The standards process includes public review outside the Consortium and a demonstration of proof of concept. Proof of concept typically requires a complete, public, portable implementation of the specification. The MIT staff of the Consortium maintains a software and documentation collection containing implementations of Consortium standards and a wide variety of user-contributed software. It also makes periodic distributions of this collection available to the public without license and for a minimal fee.

Various formal standards bodies have now taken an interest in X. The specification of the X protocol is progressing toward the status of a national standard under the auspices of the American National Standards Institute (ANSI), and the International Standards Organization (ISO) has indicated its desire to review the resulting specification for international standardization. The Institute of Electrical and Electronics Engineers (IEEE) is currently considering several industry-sponsored X toolkits for review toward standardization.

The Structure of This Book

This book consists of four main parts, each a standard specification produced by the MIT X Consortium:

- Part I, "Xlib – C Library X Interface," is a reference manual for Xlib, the lowest level C language X programming interface to the X Window System. It has been reorganized for greater ease-of-use in Release 5. Chapter 1 provides a basic overview and establishes conventions used throughout Part I. Chapter 2 deals with opening and closing connections and obtaining basic information about the connected display. Chapters 3 and 4 describe how to create and manipulate windows. Chapter 5 discusses the pixmap and cursor functions. Chapter 6 discusses the color management functions. Chapters 7 and 8 describe Xlib's graphics capabilities. Chapter 9 explains the window and session manager functions. Chapters 10 and 11 discuss events and the event-handling functions. Chapter 12 describes the input device functions. Chapter 13 discusses the internationalization facilities and functions. Chapter 14 describes the inter-client communication functions. Chapter 15 explains the resource manager functions. Finally, chapter 16 describes a variety of utility functions for keyboard input, region arithmetic, and image manipulation.

- Part II, "X Window System Protocol," is the concise, precise specification of the X protocol semantics. The protocol specification is independent of any particular programming language, and as such, is an appropriate starting point for creating interface libraries for other programming languages. C programmers will prefer the Xlib reference to the protocol descriptions, although the protocol's alternative description may clarify points of confusion.
- Part III, "Inter-Client Communication Conventions Manual," also known as the ICCCM, discusses the conventions that govern inter-client communication. These conventions are language-independent, do not impose any one user interface, and cover the following areas: the selection mechanism, cut buffers, window managers, session managers, and the manipulation of colormaps and input devices.
- Part IV, "X Logical Font Description," also known as the XLFD, discusses the conventions for font names and font properties, which when followed allow clients to query and access fonts across X server implementations.

In addition, this book contains a glossary and a number of appendices. The glossary provides definitions of the basic terminology used specifically in Parts I and II but that also are relevant to Parts III and IV. Appendix A provides cross-reference information between protocol requests and library functions. Appendix B provides the standard predefined cursor shapes in Xlib. Appendix C provides information required to build Xlib interfaces to protocol extensions. Appendix D provides information about those X11 and X10 Xlib functions that have been superseded by newer X11 functions but are provided for compatibility reasons. Appendix E provides the predefined keyboard symbol (KEYSYM) encodings. Appendix F provides the bit and byte description of the X protocol. Appendix G provides a list of the CharSet names that have been registered with the X Consortium. Appendix H provides the Bitmap Distribution Format (BDF) standard for font interchange. Appendix I provides the Compound Text standard for text interchange.

Part I. XLib—C Language X Interface

Chapter 1

Introduction to Xlib

The X Window System is a network-transparent window system that was designed at MIT. X display servers run on computers with either monochrome or color bitmap display hardware. The server distributes user input to and accepts output requests from various client programs located either on the same machine or elsewhere in the network. Xlib is a C subroutine library that application programs (clients) use to interface with the window system by means of a stream connection. Although a client usually runs on the same machine as the X server it is talking to, this need not be the case.

Part I, "Xlib – C Language X Interface," is a reference guide to the low-level C language interface to the X Window System protocol. It is neither a tutorial nor a user's guide to programming the X Window System. Rather, it provides a detailed description of each function in the library as well as a discussion of the related background information. It assumes a basic understanding of a graphics window system and of the C programming language. Other higher-level abstractions (for example, those provided by the toolkits for X) are built on top of the Xlib library. For further information about these higher-level libraries, see the appropriate toolkit documentation. Part II, "X Window System Protocol," provides the definitive word on the behavior of X. Although additional information appears here, the protocol document is the ruling document.

To provide an introduction to X programming, this chapter discusses:

- Overview of the X Window System
- Errors

- Standard header files
- Naming and argument conventions
- Programming considerations
- Formatting conventions

1.1 Overview of the X Window System

Some of the terms used in this book are unique to X, and other terms that are common to other window systems have different meanings in X. You may find it helpful to refer to the glossary, which is located at the end of the book.

The X Window System supports one or more screens containing overlapping windows or subwindows. A screen is a physical monitor and hardware, which can be either color, grayscale, or monochrome. There can be multiple screens for each display or workstation. A single X server can provide display services for any number of screens. A set of screens for a single user with one keyboard and one pointer (usually a mouse) is called a display.

All the windows in an X server are arranged in strict hierarchies. At the top of each hierarchy is a root window, which covers each of the display screens. Each root window is partially or completely covered by child windows. All windows, except for root windows, have parents. There is usually at least one window for each application program. Child windows may in turn have their own children. In this way, an application program can create an arbitrarily deep tree on each screen. X provides graphics, text, and raster operations for windows.

A child window can be larger than its parent. That is, part or all of the child window can extend beyond the boundaries of the parent, but all output to a window is clipped by its parent. If several children of a window have overlapping locations, one of the children is considered to be on top of or raised over the others thus obscuring them. Output to areas covered by other windows is suppressed by the window system unless the window has backing store. If a window is obscured by a second window, the second window obscures only those ancestors of the second window, which are also ancestors of the first window.

A window has a border zero or more pixels in width, which can be any pattern (pixmap) or solid color you like. A window usually but not always has a background pattern, which will be repainted by the window system when

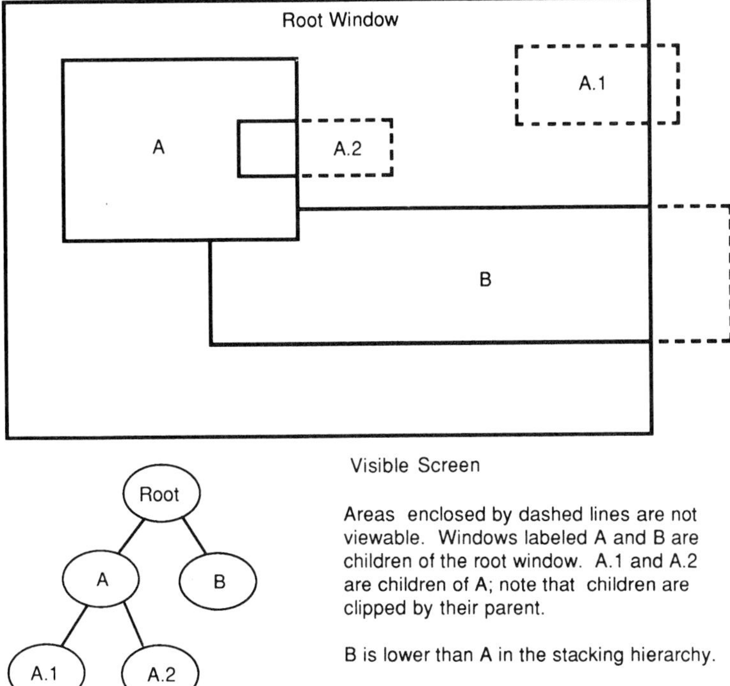

Figure 1.1. Window hierarchy

uncovered. Child windows obscure their parents, and graphic operations in the parent window usually are clipped by the children.

Each window and pixmap has its own coordinate system. The coordinate system has the X axis horizontal and the Y axis vertical with the origin [0, 0] at the upper-left corner. Coordinates are integral, in terms of pixels, and coincide with pixel centers. For a window, the origin is inside the border at the inside, upper-left corner.

X does not guarantee to preserve the contents of windows. When part or all of a window is hidden and then brought back onto the screen, its contents may be lost. The server then sends the client program an `Expose` event to notify it that part or all of the window needs to be repainted. Programs must be prepared to regenerate the contents of windows on demand.

X also provides off-screen storage of graphics objects, called pixmaps. Single plane (depth 1) pixmaps are sometimes referred to as bitmaps. Pixmaps can be used in most graphics functions interchangeably with windows and are used in various graphics operations to define patterns or tiles. Windows and pixmaps together are referred to as drawables.

Most of the functions in Xlib just add requests to an output buffer. These requests later execute asynchronously on the X server. Functions that return values of information stored in the server do not return (that is, they block) until an explicit reply is received or an error occurs. You can provide an error handler, which will be called when the error is reported.

If a client does not want a request to execute asynchronously, it can follow the request with a call to `XSync`, which blocks until all previously buffered asynchronous events have been sent and acted on. As an important side effect, the output buffer in Xlib is always flushed by a call to any function that returns a value from the server or waits for input.

Many Xlib functions will return an integer resource ID, which allows you to refer to objects stored on the X server. These can be of type `Window`, `Font`, `Pixmap`, `Colormap`, `Cursor`, and `GContext`, as defined in the file `<X11/X.h>`. These resources are created by requests and are destroyed (or freed) by requests or when connections are closed. Most of these resources are potentially sharable between applications, and in fact, windows are manipulated explicitly by window manager programs. Fonts and cursors are shared automatically across multiple screens. Fonts are loaded and unloaded as needed and are shared by multiple clients. Fonts are often cached in the server. Xlib provides no support for sharing graphics contexts between applications.

Client programs are informed of events. Events may either be side effects of a request (for example, restacking windows generates `Expose` events) or completely asynchronous (for example, from the keyboard). A client program asks to be informed of events. Because other applications can send events to your application, programs must be prepared to handle (or ignore) events of all types.

Input events (for example, a key pressed or the pointer moved) arrive asynchronously from the server and are queued until they are requested by an explicit call (for example, `XNextEvent` or `XWindowEvent`). In addition, some library functions (for example, `XRaiseWindow`) generate `Expose` and

ConfigureRequest events. These events also arrive asynchronously, but the client may wish to explicitly wait for them by calling XSync after calling a function that can cause the server to generate events.

1.2 Errors

Some functions return Status, an integer error indication. If the function fails, it returns a zero. If the function returns a status of zero, it has not updated the return arguments. Because C does not provide multiple return values, many functions must return their results by writing into client-passed storage. By default, errors are handled either by a standard library function or by one that you provide. Functions that return pointers to strings return NULL pointers if the string does not exist.

The X server reports protocol errors at the time that it detects them. If more than one error could be generated for a given request, the server can report any of them.

Because Xlib usually does not transmit requests to the server immediately (that is, it buffers them), errors can be reported much later than they actually occur. For debugging purposes, however, Xlib provides a mechanism for forcing synchronous behavior (see section 11.8.1). When synchronization is enabled, errors are reported as they are generated.

When Xlib detects an error, it calls an error handler, which your program can provide. If you do not provide an error handler, the error is printed, and your program terminates.

1.3 Standard Header Files

The following include files are part of the Xlib standard:

- <X11/Xlib.h>
  This is the main header file for Xlib. The majority of all Xlib symbols are declared by including this file. This file also contains the preprocessor symbol XlibSpecificationRelease. This symbol is defined to have the value 5 in this release of the standard. (Earlier releases of Xlib did not have this symbol.)
- <X11/X.h>
  This file declares types and constants for the X protocol that are to be used by applications. It is included automatically from <X11/Xlib.h>, so application code should never need to reference this file directly.

- `<X11/Xcms.h>`
  This file contains symbols for much of the color management facilities described in chapter 6. All functions, types, and symbols with the prefix "Xcms", plus the Color Conversion Contexts macros, are declared in this file. `<X11/Xlib.h>` must be included before including this file.
- `<X11/Xutil.h>`
  This file declares various functions, types, and symbols used for inter-client communication and application utility functions, which are described in chapters 14 and 16. `<X11/Xlib.h>` must be included before including this file.
- `<X11/Xresource.h>`
  This file declares all functions, types, and symbols for the resource manager facilities, which are described in chapter 15. `<X11/Xlib.h>` must be included before including this file.
- `<X11/Xatom.h>`
  This file declares all predefined atoms, which are symbols with the prefix "XA_".
- `<X11/cursorfont.h>`
  This file declares the cursor symbols for the standard cursor font, which are listed in appendix B. All cursor symbols have the prefix "XC_".
- `<X11/keysymdef.h>`
  This file declares all standard KeySym values, which are symbols with the prefix "XK_". The KeySyms are arranged in groups, and a preprocessor symbol controls inclusion of each group. The preprocessor symbol must be defined prior to inclusion of the file to obtain the associated values. The preprocessor symbols are XK_MISCELLANY, XK_LATIN1, XK_LATIN2, XK_LATIN3, XK_LATIN4, XK_KATAKANA, XK_ARABIC, XK_CYRILLIC, XK_GREEK, XK_TECHNICAL, XK_SPECIAL, XK_PUBLISHING, XK_APL, and XK_HEBREW.
- `<X11/keysym.h>`
  This file defines the preprocessor symbols XK_MISCELLANY, XK_LATIN1, XK_LATIN2, XK_LATIN3, XK_LATIN4, and XK_GREEK and then includes `<X11/keysymdef.h>`.
- `<X11/Xlibint.h>`
  This file declares all the functions, types, and symbols used for extensions, which are described in appendix C. This file automatically includes `<X11/Xlib.h>`.
- `<X11/Xproto.h>`
  This file declares types and symbols for the basic X protocol, for use in implementing extensions. It is included automatically from `<X11/Xlibint.h>`, so application and extension code should never need to reference this file directly.

- `<X11/Xprotostr.h>`
  This file declares types and symbols for the basic X protocol, for use in implementing extensions. It is included automatically from `<X11/Xproto.h>`, so application and extension code should never need to reference this file directly.
- `<X11/X10.h>`
  This file declares all the functions, types, and symbols used for the X10 compatibility functions, which are described in appendix D.

1.4 Generic Values and Types

The following symbols are defined by Xlib and used throughout part I:

- Xlib defines the type `Bool` and the Boolean values `True` and `False`.
- `None` is the universal null resource ID or atom.
- The type `XID` is used for generic resource IDs.
- The type `XPointer` is defined to be char* and is used as a generic opaque pointer to data.

1.5 Naming and Argument Conventions within Xlib

Xlib follows a number of conventions for the naming and syntax of the functions. Given that you remember what information the function requires, these conventions are intended to make the syntax of the functions more predictable.

The major naming conventions are:

- To differentiate the X symbols from the other symbols, the library uses mixed case for external symbols. It leaves lowercase for variables and all uppercase for user macros, as per existing convention.
- All Xlib functions begin with a capital X.
- The beginnings of all function names and symbols are capitalized.
- All user-visible data structures begin with a capital X. More generally, anything that a user might dereference begins with a capital X.
- Macros and other symbols do not begin with a capital X. To distinguish them from all user symbols, each word in the macro is capitalized.
- All elements of or variables in a data structure are in lowercase. Compound words, where needed, are constructed with underscores (_).
- The display argument, where used, is always first in the argument list.

- All resource objects, where used, occur at the beginning of the argument list immediately after the display argument.
- When a graphics context is present together with another type of resource (most commonly, a drawable), the graphics context occurs in the argument list after the other resource. Drawables outrank all other resources.
- Source arguments always precede the destination arguments in the argument list.
- The x argument always precedes the y argument in the argument list.
- The width argument always precedes the height argument in the argument list.
- Where the x, y, width, and height arguments are used together, the x and y arguments always precede the width and height arguments.
- Where a mask is accompanied with a structure, the mask always precedes the pointer to the structure in the argument list.

1.6 Programming Considerations

The major programming considerations are:

- Coordinates and sizes in X are actually 16-bit quantities. This decision was made to minimize the bandwidth required for a given level of performance. Coordinates usually are declared as an `int` in the interface. Values larger than 16 bits are truncated silently. Sizes (width and height) are declared as unsigned quantities.
- Keyboards are the greatest variable between different manufacturers' workstations. If you want your program to be portable, you should be particularly conservative here.
- Many display systems have limited amounts of off-screen memory. If you can, you should minimize use of pixmaps and backing store.
- The user should have control of his screen real estate. Therefore, you should write your applications to react to window management rather than presume control of the entire screen. What you do inside of your top-level window, however, is up to your application. For further information, see chapter 14 and part III, "Inter-Client Communication Conventions Manual."

1.7 Character Sets and Encodings

Some of the Xlib functions make reference to specific character sets and character encodings. The following are the most common:

- X Portable Character Set
  A basic set of 97 characters, which are assumed to exist in all locales supported by Xlib. This set contains the following characters:

a..z A..Z 0..9
!"#$%&'()*+,-./:;<=>?@[\]^_`{|}~
<space>, <tab>, and <newline>

This set is the left/lower half of the graphic character set of ISO8859-1 plus space, tab, and newline. It is also the set of graphic characters in 7-bit ASCII plus the same three control characters. The actual encoding of these characters on the host is system dependent.

- Host Portable Character Encoding
  The encoding of the X Portable Character Set on the host. The encoding itself is not defined by this standard, but the encoding must be the same in all locales supported by Xlib on the host. If a string is said to be in the Host Portable Character Encoding, then it only contains characters from the X Portable Character Set, in the host encoding.
- Latin-1
  The coded character set defined by the ISO8859-1 standard.
- Latin Portable Character Encoding
  The encoding of the X Portable Character Set using the Latin-1 codepoints plus ASCII control characters. If a string is said to be in the Latin Portable Character Encoding, then it only contains characters from the X Portable Character Set, not all of Latin-1.
- STRING Encoding
  Latin-1, plus tab and newline.
- POSIX Portable Filename Character Set
  The set of 65 characters, which can be used in naming files on a POSIX-compliant host, that are correctly processed in all locales. The set is:

  a..z A..Z 0..9 ._-

1.8 Formatting Conventions

The following conventions are used throughout part I:

- Global symbols are printed in `this special font`. These can be either function names, symbols defined in include files, or structure names. When declared and defined, function arguments are printed in *italics*. In the explanatory text that follows, they usually are printed in regular type.
- Each function is introduced by a general discussion that distinguishes it from other functions. The function declaration itself follows, and each argument is specifically explained. Although ANSI C function prototype syntax is not used, Xlib header files normally declare functions using function prototypes in ANSI C environments. General discussion of the function, if any is required, follows the arguments. Where applicable,

the last paragraph of the explanation lists the possible Xlib error codes that the function can generate. For a complete discussion of the Xlib error codes, see section 11.8.2.

- To eliminate any ambiguity between those arguments that you pass and those that a function returns to you, the explanations for all arguments that you pass start with the word *specifies* or, in the case of multiple arguments, the word *specify*. The explanations for all arguments that are returned to you start with the word *returns* or, in the case of multiple arguments, the word *return*. The explanations for all arguments that you can pass and are returned start with the words *specifies and returns*.
- Any pointer to a structure that is used to return a value is designated as such by the *_return* suffix as part of its name. All other pointers passed to these functions are used for reading only. A few arguments use pointers to structures that are used for both input and output and are indicated by using the *_in_out* suffix.

Chapter 2

Display Functions

Before your program can use a display, you must establish a connection to the X server. Once you have established a connection, you then can use the Xlib macros and functions discussed in this chapter to return information about the display. This chapter discusses how to:

- Open (connect to) the display
- Obtain information about the display, image format, and screen
- Free client-created data
- Close (disconnect from) a display

The chapter concludes with a general discussion of what occurs when the connection to the X server is closed.

2.1 Opening the Display

To open a connection to the X server that controls a display, use `XOpenDisplay`.

Display *XOpenDisplay (*display_name*)
    char **display_name*;

display_name Specifies the hardware display name, which determines the display and communications domain to be used. On a POSIX-conformant system, if the display_name is NULL, it defaults to the value of the DISPLAY environment variable.

The encoding and interpretation of the display name is implementation dependent. Strings in the Host Portable Character Encoding are supported; support for other characters is implementation dependent. On POSIX-conformant systems, the display name or DISPLAY environment variable can be a string in the format:

hostname: *number*. *screen_number*

hostname Specifies the name of the host machine on which the display is physically attached. You follow the hostname with either a single colon (:) or a double colon (::).

number Specifies the number of the display server on that host machine. You may optionally follow this display number with a period (.). A single CPU can have more than one display. Multiple displays are usually numbered starting with zero.

screen_number Specifies the screen to be used on that server. Multiple screens can be controlled by a single X server. The screen_number sets an internal variable that can be accessed by using the `XDefaultScreen` macro or the `XDefaultScreen` function if you are using languages other than C (see section 2.2.1).

For example, the following would specify screen 1 of display 0 on the machine named "dual-headed":

dual-headed:0.1

The `XOpenDisplay` function returns a `Display` structure that serves as the connection to the X server and that contains all the information about that X server. `XOpenDisplay` connects your application to the X server through TCP or DECnet communications protocols, or through some local inter-process communication protocol. If the hostname is a host machine name and a single colon (:) separates the hostname and display number, `XOpenDisplay` connects using TCP streams. If the hostname is not specified, Xlib uses whatever it believes is the fastest transport. If the hostname is a host machine name and a double colon (::) separates the hostname and display number, `XOpenDisplay` connects using DECnet. A single X server can support any or all of these transport mechanisms simultaneously. A particular Xlib implementation can support many more of these transport mechanisms.

If successful, `XOpenDisplay` returns a pointer to a `Display` structure, which is defined in `<X11/Xlib.h>`. If `XOpenDisplay` does not succeed, it returns

NULL. After a successful call to `XOpenDisplay`, all of the screens in the display can be used by the client. The screen number specified in the display_name argument is returned by the `DefaultScreen` macro (or the `XDefaultScreen` function). You can access elements of the `Display` and `Screen` structures only by using the information macros or functions. For information about using macros and functions to obtain information from the `Display` structure, see section 2.2.1.

X servers may implement various types of access control mechanisms (see section 9.8).

2.2 Obtaining Information about the Display, Image Formats, or Screens

The Xlib library provides a number of useful macros and corresponding functions that return data from the `Display` structure. The macros are used for C programming, and their corresponding function equivalents are for other language bindings. This section discusses the:

- Display macros
- Image format macros
- Screen macros

All other members of the `Display` structure (that is, those for which no macros are defined) are private to Xlib and must not be used. Applications must never directly modify or inspect these private members of the `Display` structure.

Note The `XDisplayWidth`, `XDisplayHeight`, `XDisplayCells`, `XDisplayPlanes`, `XDisplayWidthMM`, and `XDisplayHeightMM` functions in the next sections are misnamed. These functions really should be named Screen*whatever* and XScreen*whatever*, not Display*whatever* or XDisplay*whatever*. Our apologies for the resulting confusion.

2.2.1 Display Macros

Applications should not directly modify any part of the `Display` and `Screen` structures. The members should be considered read-only, although they may change as the result of other operations on the display.

The following lists the C language macros, their corresponding function equivalents that are for other language bindings, and what data they both can return.

AllPlanes

unsigned long XAllPlanes( )

Both return a value with all bits set to 1 suitable for use in a plane argument to a procedure.

Both `BlackPixel` and `WhitePixel` can be used in implementing a monochrome application. These pixel values are for permanently allocated entries in the default colormap. The actual RGB (red, green, and blue) values are settable on some screens and, in any case, may not actually be black or white. The names are intended to convey the expected relative intensity of the colors.

BlackPixel (*display*, *screen_number*)

unsigned long XBlackPixel (*display*, *screen_number*)
  Display **display*;
  int *screen_number*;

display Specifies the connection to the X server.
screen_number Specifies the appropriate screen number on the host server.

Both return the black pixel value for the specified screen.

WhitePixel (*display*, *screen_number*)

unsigned long XWhitePixel (*display*, *screen_number*)
  Display **display*;
  int *screen_number*;

display Specifies the connection to the X server.
screen_number Specifies the appropriate screen number on the host server.

Both return the white pixel value for the specified screen.

ConnectionNumber (*display*)

int XConnectionNumber (*display*)
  Display **display*;

display Specifies the connection to the X server.

Both return a connection number for the specified display. On a POSIX-conformant system, this is the file descriptor of the connection.

```
DefaultColormap ( display, screen_number)

Colormap XDefaultColormap ( display, screen_number)
    Display *display;
    int screen_number;
```

display Specifies the connection to the X server.

screen_number Specifies the appropriate screen number on the host server.

Both return the default colormap ID for allocation on the specified screen. Most routine allocations of color should be made out of this colormap.

```
DefaultDepth ( display, screen_number)

int XDefaultDepth ( display, screen_number)
    Display *display;
    int screen_number;
```

display Specifies the connection to the X server.

screen_number Specifies the appropriate screen number on the host server.

Both return the depth (number of planes) of the default root window for the specified screen. Other depths may also be supported on this screen (see `XMatchVisualInfo`).

To determine the number of depths that are available on a given screen, use `XListDepths`.

```
int *XListDepths ( display, screen_number, count_return)
    Display *display;
    int screen_number;
    int *count_return;
```

display Specifies the connection to the X server.

screen_number Specifies the appropriate screen number on the host server.

count_return Returns the number of depths.

The `XListDepths` function returns the array of depths that are available on the specified screen. If the specified screen_number is valid and sufficient memory for the array can be allocated, `XListDepths` sets count_return to the number of available depths. Otherwise, it does not set count_return and returns NULL. To release the memory allocated for the array of depths, use `XFree`.

```
DefaultGC ( display, screen_number)

GC XDefaultGC ( display, screen_number)
    Display *display;
```

```
   int screen_number;
```

display Specifies the connection to the X server.

screen_number Specifies the appropriate screen number on the host server.

Both return the default graphics context for the root window of the specified screen. This GC is created for the convenience of simple applications and contains the default GC components with the foreground and background pixel values initialized to the black and white pixels for the screen, respectively. You can modify its contents freely because it is not used in any Xlib function. This GC should never be freed.

```
DefaultRootWindow (display)

Window XDefaultRootWindow (display)
   Display *display;
```

display Specifies the connection to the X server.

Both return the root window for the default screen.

```
DefaultScreenOfDisplay (display)

Screen *XDefaultScreenOfDisplay (display)
   Display *display;
```

display Specifies the connection to the X server.

Both return a pointer to the default screen.

```
ScreenOfDisplay (display, screen_number)

Screen *XScreenOfDisplay (display, screen_number)
   Display *display;
   int screen_number;
```

display Specifies the connection to the X server.

screen_number Specifies the appropriate screen number on the host server.

Both return a pointer to the indicated screen.

```
DefaultScreen (display)

int XDefaultScreen (display)
   Display *display;
```

display Specifies the connection to the X server.

Both return the default screen number referenced by the `XOpenDisplay` function. This macro or function should be used to retrieve the screen number in applications that will use only a single screen.

DefaultVisual (*display*, *screen_number*)

Visual *XDefaultVisual (*display*, *screen_number*)
  Display **display*;
  int *screen_number*;

display Specifies the connection to the X server.
screen_number Specifies the appropriate screen number on the host server.

Both return the default visual type for the specified screen. For further information about visual types, see section 3.1.

DisplayCells (*display*, *screen_number*)

int XDisplayCells (*display*, *screen_number*)
  Display **display*;
  int *screen_number*;

display Specifies the connection to the X server.
screen_number Specifies the appropriate screen number on the host server.

Both return the number of entries in the default colormap.

DisplayPlanes (*display*, *screen_number*)

int XDisplayPlanes (*display*, *screen_number*)
  Display **display*;
  int *screen_number*;

display Specifies the connection to the X server.
screen_number Specifies the appropriate screen number on the host server.

Both return the depth of the root window of the specified screen. For an explanation of depth, see the glossary.

DisplayString (*display*)

char *XDisplayString (*display*)
  Display **display*;

display Specifies the connection to the X server.

Both return the string that was passed to `XOpenDisplay` when the current display was opened. On POSIX-conformant systems, if the passed string was

NULL, these return the value of the DISPLAY environment variable when the current display was opened. These are useful to applications that invoke the `fork` system call and want to open a new connection to the same display from the child process as well as for printing error messages.

long XMaxRequestSize(*display*)
  Display **display*;

display Specifies the connection to the X server.

The `XMaxRequestSize` function returns the maximum request size (in 4-byte units) supported by the server. Single protocol requests to the server can be no longer than this size. The protocol guarantees the size to be no smaller than 4096 units (16384 bytes). Xlib automatically breaks data up into multiple protocol requests as necessary for the following functions: `XDrawPoints`, `XDrawRectangles`, `XDrawSegments`, `XFillArcs`, `XFillRectangles`, and `XPutImage`.

LastKnownRequestProcessed (*display*)

unsigned long XLastKnownRequestProcessed (*display*)
  Display **display*;

display Specifies the connection to the X server.

Both extract the full serial number of the last request known by Xlib to have been processed by the X server. Xlib automatically sets this number when replies, events, and errors are received.

NextRequest (*display*)

unsigned long XNextRequest (*display*)
  Display **display*;

display Specifies the connection to the X server.

Both extract the full serial number that is to be used for the next request. Serial numbers are maintained separately for each display connection.

ProtocolVersion (*display*)

int XProtocolVersion (*display*)
  Display **display*;

display Specifies the connection to the X server.

Both return the major version number (11) of the X protocol associated with the connected display.

ProtocolRevision (*display*)

int XProtocolRevision (*display*)
 Display **display*;

display Specifies the connection to the X server.

Both return the minor protocol revision number of the X server.

QLength (*display*)

int XQLength (*display*)
 Display **display*;

display Specifies the connection to the X server.

Both return the length of the event queue for the connected display. Note that there may be more events that have not been read into the queue yet (see `XEventsQueued`).

RootWindow (*display*, *screen_number*)

Window XRootWindow (*display*, *screen_number*)
 Display **display*;
 int *screen_number*;

display Specifies the connection to the X server.
screen_number Specifies the appropriate screen number on the host server.

Both return the root window. These are useful with functions that need a drawable of a particular screen and for creating top-level windows.

ScreenCount (*display*)

int XScreenCount (*display*)
 Display **display*;

display Specifies the connection to the X server.

Both return the number of available screens.

ServerVendor (*display*)

char *XServerVendor (*display*)
 Display **display*;

display Specifies the connection to the X server.

Both return a pointer to a null-terminated string that provides some identification of the owner of the X server implementation. If the data returned by the server is in the Latin Portable Character Encoding, then the string is in the Host Portable Character Encoding. Otherwise, the contents of the string are implementation dependent.

VendorRelease (*display*)

int XVendorRelease (*display*)
  Display **display*;

display Specifies the connection to the X server.

Both return a number related to a vendor's release of the X server.

2.2.2 Image Format Functions and Macros

Applications are required to present data to the X server in a format that the server demands. To help simplify applications, most of the work required to convert the data is provided by Xlib (see sections 8.7 and 16.8).

The `XPixmapFormatValues` structure provides an interface to the pixmap format information that is returned at the time of a connection setup. It contains:

```
typedef struct {
    int depth;
    int bits_per_pixel;
    int scanline_pad;
} XPixmapFormatValues;
```

To obtain the pixmap format information for a given display, use `XListPixmapFormats`.

XPixmapFormatValues *XListPixmapFormats (*display, count_return*)
  Display **display*;
  int **count_return*;

display Specifies the connection to the X server.

count_return Returns the number of pixmap formats that are supported by the display.

The `XListPixmapFormats` function returns an array of `XPixmapFormatValues` structures that describe the types of Z format images supported by the specified display. If insufficient memory is available, `XListPixmapFormats` returns NULL. To free the allocated storage for the `XPixmapFormatValues` structures, use `XFree`.

The following lists the C language macros, their corresponding function equivalents that are for other language bindings, and what data they both return for the specified server and screen. These are often used by toolkits as well as by simple applications.

ImageByteOrder (*display*)

int XImageByteOrder (*display*)
Display **display*;

display Specifies the connection to the X server.

Both specify the required byte order for images for each scanline unit in XY format (bitmap) or for each pixel value in Z format. The macro or function can return either `LSBFirst` or `MSBFirst`.

BitmapUnit (*display*)

int XBitmapUnit (*display*)
Display **display*;

display Specifies the connection to the X server.

Both return the size of a bitmap's scanline unit in bits. The scanline is calculated in multiples of this value.

BitmapBitOrder (*display*)

int XBitmapBitOrder (*display*)
Display **display*;

display Specifies the connection to the X server.

Within each bitmap unit, the left-most bit in the bitmap as displayed on the screen is either the least-significant or most-significant bit in the unit. This macro or function can return `LSBFirst` or `MSBFirst`.

BitmapPad (*display*)

int XBitmapPad (*display*)
Display **display*;

display Specifies the connection to the X server.

Each scanline must be padded to a multiple of bits returned by this macro or function.

```
DisplayHeight(display, screen_number)

int XDisplayHeight(display, screen_number)
    Display *display;
    int screen_number;
```

display Specifies the connection to the X server.

screen_number Specifies the appropriate screen number on the host server.

Both return an integer that describes the height of the screen in pixels.

```
DisplayHeightMM(display, screen_number)

int XDisplayHeightMM(display, screen_number)
    Display *display;
    int screen_number;
```

display Specifies the connection to the X server.

screen_number Specifies the appropriate screen number on the host server.

Both return the height of the specified screen in millimeters.

```
DisplayWidth(display, screen_number)

int XDisplayWidth(display, screen_number)
    Display *display;
    int screen_number;
```

display Specifies the connection to the X server.

screen_number Specifies the appropriate screen number on the host server.

Both return the width of the screen in pixels.

```
DisplayWidthMM(display, screen_number)

int XDisplayWidthMM(display, screen_number)
    Display *display;
    int screen_number;
```

display Specifies the connection to the X server.

screen_number Specifies the appropriate screen number on the host server.

Both return the width of the specified screen in millimeters.

2.2.3 Screen Information Macros

The following lists the C language macros, their corresponding function equivalents that are for other language bindings, and what data they both can return. These macros or functions all take a pointer to the appropriate screen structure.

BlackPixelOfScreen (*screen*)

unsigned long XBlackPixelOfScreen (*screen*)
  Screen **screen*;

screen Specifies the appropriate `Screen` structure.

Both return the black pixel value of the specified screen.

WhitePixelOfScreen (*screen*)

unsigned long XWhitePixelOfScreen (*screen*)
  Screen **screen*;

screen Specifies the appropriate `Screen` structure.

Both return the white pixel value of the specified screen.

CellsOfScreen (*screen*)

int XCellsOfScreen (*screen*)
  Screen **screen*;

screen Specifies the appropriate `Screen` structure.

Both return the number of colormap cells in the default colormap of the specified screen.

DefaultColormapOfScreen (*screen*)

Colormap XDefaultColormapOfScreen (*screen*)
  Screen **screen*;

screen Specifies the appropriate `Screen` structure.

Both return the default colormap of the specified screen.

DefaultDepthOfScreen (*screen*)

int XDefaultDepthOfScreen (*screen*)
  Screen **screen*;

screen Specifies the appropriate `Screen` structure.

Both return the depth of the root window.

DefaultGCOfScreen (*screen*)

GC XDefaultGCOfScreen (*screen*)
  Screen **screen*;

screen Specifies the appropriate `Screen` structure.

Both return a default graphics context (GC) of the specified screen, which has the same depth as the root window of the screen. The GC must never be freed.

DefaultVisualOfScreen (*screen*)

Visual *XDefaultVisualOfScreen (*screen*)
  Screen **screen*;

screen Specifies the appropriate `Screen` structure.

Both return the default visual of the specified screen. For information on visual types, see section 3.1.

DoesBackingStore (*screen*)

int XDoesBackingStore (*screen*)
  Screen **screen*;

screen Specifies the appropriate `Screen` structure.

Both return a value indicating whether the screen supports backing stores. The value returned can be one of `WhenMapped`, `NotUseful`, or `Always` (see section 3.2.4).

DoesSaveUnders (*screen*)

Bool XDoesSaveUnders (*screen*)
  Screen **screen*;

screen Specifies the appropriate `Screen` structure.

Both return a Boolean value indicating whether the screen supports save unders. If `True`, the screen supports save unders. If `False`, the screen does not support save unders (see section 3.2.5).

DisplayOfScreen (*screen*)

Display *XDisplayOfScreen (*screen*)
  Screen **screen*;

screen Specifies the appropriate `Screen` structure.

Both return the display of the specified screen.

```
int XScreenNumberOfScreen (screen)
    Screen *screen;
```

screen Specifies the appropriate `Screen` structure.

The `XScreenNumberOfScreen` function returns the screen index number of the specified screen.

```
EventMaskOfScreen (screen)

long XEventMaskOfScreen (screen)
    Screen *screen;
```

screen Specifies the appropriate `Screen` structure.

Both return the event mask of the root window for the specified screen at connection setup time.

```
WidthOfScreen (screen)

int XWidthOfScreen (screen)
    Screen *screen;
```

screen Specifies the appropriate `Screen` structure.

Both return the width of the specified screen in pixels.

```
HeightOfScreen (screen)

int XHeightOfScreen (screen)
    Screen *screen;
```

screen Specifies the appropriate `Screen` structure.

Both return the height of the specified screen in pixels.

```
WidthMMOfScreen (screen)

int XWidthMMOfScreen (screen)
    Screen *screen;
```

screen Specifies the appropriate `Screen` structure.

Both return the width of the specified screen in millimeters.

```
HeightMMOfScreen (screen)

int XHeightMMOfScreen (screen)
    Screen *screen;
```

screen Specifies the appropriate `Screen` structure.

Both return the height of the specified screen in millimeters.

```
MaxCmapsOfScreen (screen)

int XMaxCmapsOfScreen (screen)
    Screen *screen;
```

screen Specifies the appropriate `Screen` structure.

Both return the maximum number of installed colormaps supported by the specified screen (see section 9.3).

```
MinCmapsOfScreen (screen)

int XMinCmapsOfScreen (screen)
    Screen *screen;
```

screen Specifies the appropriate `Screen` structure.

Both return the minimum number of installed colormaps supported by the specified screen (see section 9.3).

```
PlanesOfScreen (screen)

int XPlanesOfScreen (screen)
    Screen *screen;
```

screen Specifies the appropriate `Screen` structure.

Both return the depth of the root window.

```
RootWindowOfScreen (screen)

Window XRootWindowOfScreen (screen)
    Screen *screen;
```

screen Specifies the appropriate `Screen` structure.

Both return the root window of the specified screen.

2.3 Generating a NoOperation Protocol Request

To execute a `NoOperation` protocol request, use `XNoOp`.

```
XNoOp (display)
    Display *display;
```

display Specifies the connection to the X server.

The `XNoOp` function sends a `NoOperation` protocol request to the X server, thereby exercising the connection.

2.4 Freeing Client-Created Data

To free in-memory data that was created by an Xlib function, use `XFree`.

XFree (*data*)
  void **data*;

data Specifies the data that is to be freed.

The `XFree` function is a general-purpose Xlib routine that frees the specified data. You must use it to free any objects that were allocated by Xlib, unless an alternate function is explicitly specified for the object.

2.5 Closing the Display

To close a display or disconnect from the X server, use `XCloseDisplay`.

XCloseDisplay (*display*)
  Display **display*;

display Specifies the connection to the X server.

The `XCloseDisplay` function closes the connection to the X server for the display specified in the `Display` structure and destroys all windows, resource IDs (`Window`, `Font`, `Pixmap`, `Colormap`, `Cursor`, and `GContext`), or other resources that the client has created on this display, unless the close-down mode of the resource has been changed (see `XSetCloseDownMode`). Therefore, these windows, resource IDs, and other resources should never be referenced again or an error will be generated. Before exiting, you should call `XCloseDisplay` explicitly so that any pending errors are reported as `XCloseDisplay` performs a final `XSync` operation.

`XCloseDisplay` can generate a `BadGC` error.

Xlib provides a function to permit the resources owned by a client to survive after the client's connection is closed. To change a client's close-down mode, use `XSetCloseDownMode`.

XSetCloseDownMode (*display*, *close_mode*)
  Display **display*;
  int *close_mode*;

display Specifies the connection to the X server.

close_mode Specifies the client close-down mode. You can pass `DestroyAll`, `RetainPermanent`, or `RetainTemporary`.

The `XSetCloseDownMode` defines what will happen to the client's resources at connection close. A connection starts in `DestroyAll` mode. For information on what happens to the client's resources when the close_mode argument is `RetainPermanent` or `RetainTemporary`, see section 2.6.

`XSetCloseDownMode` can generate a `BadValue` error.

2.6 X Server Connection Close Operations

When the X server's connection to a client is closed either by an explicit call to `XCloseDisplay` or by a process that exits, the X server performs the following automatic operations:

- It disowns all selections owned by the client (see `XSetSelectionOwner`).
- It performs an `XUngrabPointer` and `XUngrabKeyboard` if the client has actively grabbed the pointer or the keyboard.
- It performs an `XUngrabServer` if the client has grabbed the server.
- It releases all passive grabs made by the client.
- It marks all resources (including colormap entries) allocated by the client either as permanent or temporary, depending on whether the close-down mode is `RetainPermanent` or `RetainTemporary`. However, this does not prevent other client applications from explicitly destroying the resources (see `XSetCloseDownMode`).

When the close-down mode is `DestroyAll`, the X server destroys all of a client's resources as follows:

- It examines each window in the client's save-set to determine if it is an inferior (subwindow) of a window created by the client. (The save-set is a list of other clients' windows, which are referred to as save-set windows.) If so, the X server reparents the save-set window to the closest ancestor so that the save-set window is not an inferior of a window created by the client. The reparenting leaves unchanged the absolute coordinates (with respect to the root window) of the upper-left outer corner of the save-set window.
- It performs a `MapWindow` request on the save-set window if the save-set window is unmapped. The X server does this even if the save-set window was not an inferior of a window created by the client.
- It destroys all windows created by the client.
- It performs the appropriate free request on each nonwindow resource created by the client in the server (for example, `Font`, `Pixmap`, `Cursor`, `Colormap`, and `GContext`).
- It frees all colors and colormap entries allocated by a client application.

Additional processing occurs when the last connection to the X server closes. An X server goes through a cycle of having no connections and having some connections. When the last connection to the X server closes as a result of a connection closing with the close_mode of `DestroyAll`, the X server does the following:

- It resets its state as if it had just been started. The X server begins by destroying all lingering resources from clients that have terminated in `RetainPermanent` or `RetainTemporary` mode.
- It deletes all but the predefined atom identifiers.
- It deletes all properties on all root windows (see section 4.3).
- It resets all device maps and attributes (for example, key click, bell volume, and acceleration) as well as the access control list.
- It restores the standard root tiles and cursors.
- It restores the default font path.
- It restores the input focus to state `PointerRoot`.

However, the X server does not reset if you close a connection with a close-down mode set to `RetainPermanent` or `RetainTemporary`.

Chapter 3

Window Functions

In the X Window System, a window is a rectangular area on the screen that lets you view graphic output. Client applications can display overlapping and nested windows on one or more screens that are driven by X servers on one or more machines. Clients who want to create windows must first connect their program to the X server by calling `XOpenDisplay`. This chapter begins with a discussion of visual types and window attributes. The chapter continues with a discussion of the Xlib functions you can use to:

- Create windows
- Destroy windows
- Map windows
- Unmap windows
- Configure windows
- Change the stacking order
- Change window attributes

This chapter also identifies the window actions that may generate events.

Note that it is vital that your application conform to the established conventions for communicating with window managers for it to work well with the various window managers in use (see section 14.1). Toolkits generally adhere to these conventions for you, relieving you of the burden. Toolkits also often supersede many functions in this chapter with versions of their own. Refer to the documentation for the toolkit you are using for more information.

3.1 Visual Types

On some display hardware, it may be possible to deal with color resources in more than one way. For example, you may be able to deal with a screen of either 12-bit depth with arbitrary mapping of pixel to color (pseudo-color) or 24-bit depth with 8 bits of the pixel dedicated to each of red, green, and blue. These different ways of dealing with the visual aspects of the screen are called visuals. For each screen of the display, there may be a list of valid visual types supported at different depths of the screen. Because default windows and visual types are defined for each screen, most simple applications need not deal with this complexity. Xlib provides macros and functions that return the default root window, the default depth of the default root window, and the default visual type (see sections 2.2.1 and 16.7).

Xlib uses an opaque `Visual` structure that contains information about the possible color mapping. The visual utility functions (see section 16.7) use an `XVisualInfo` structure to return this information to an application. The members of this structure pertinent to this discussion are class, red_mask, green_mask, blue_mask, bits_per_rgb, and colormap_size. The class member specifies one of the possible visual classes of the screen and can be `StaticGray`, `StaticColor`, `TrueColor`, `GrayScale`, `PseudoColor`, or `DirectColor`.

The following concepts may serve to make the explanation of visual types clearer. The screen can be color or grayscale, can have a colormap that is writable or read-only, and can also have a colormap whose indices are decomposed into separate RGB pieces, provided one is not on a grayscale screen. This leads to the following diagram:

	Color		GrayScale	
	R/O	R/W	R/O	R/W
Undecomposed Colormap	Static Color	Pseudo Color	Static Gray	Gray Scale
Decomposed Colormap	True Color	Direct Color		

Conceptually, as each pixel is read out of video memory for display on the screen, it goes through a look-up stage by indexing into a colormap. Colormaps can be manipulated arbitrarily on some hardware, in limited ways on other hardware, and not at all on other hardware. The visual types affect the colormap and the RGB values in the following ways:

- For `PseudoColor`, a pixel value indexes a colormap to produce independent RGB values, and the RGB values can be changed dynamically.
- `GrayScale` is treated the same way as `PseudoColor` except that the primary that drives the screen is undefined. Thus, the client should always store the same value for red, green, and blue in the colormaps.
- For `DirectColor`, a pixel value is decomposed into separate RGB subfields, and each subfield separately indexes the colormap for the corresponding value. The RGB values can be changed dynamically.
- `TrueColor` is treated the same way as `DirectColor` except that the colormap has predefined, read-only RGB values. These RGB values are server-dependent but provide linear or near-linear ramps in each primary.
- `StaticColor` is treated the same way as `PseudoColor` except that the colormap has predefined, read-only, server-dependent RGB values.
- `StaticGray` is treated the same way as `StaticColor` except that the RGB values are equal for any single pixel value, thus resulting in shades of gray. `StaticGray` with a two-entry colormap can be thought of as monochrome.

The red_mask, green_mask, and blue_mask members are only defined for `DirectColor` and `TrueColor`. Each has one contiguous set of bits with no intersections. The bits_per_rgb member specifies the log base 2 of the number of distinct color values (individually) of red, green, and blue. Actual RGB values are unsigned 16-bit numbers. The colormap_size member defines

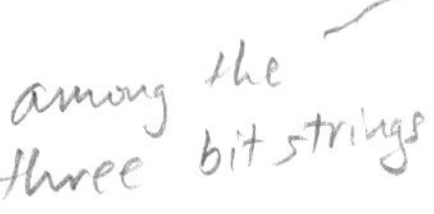

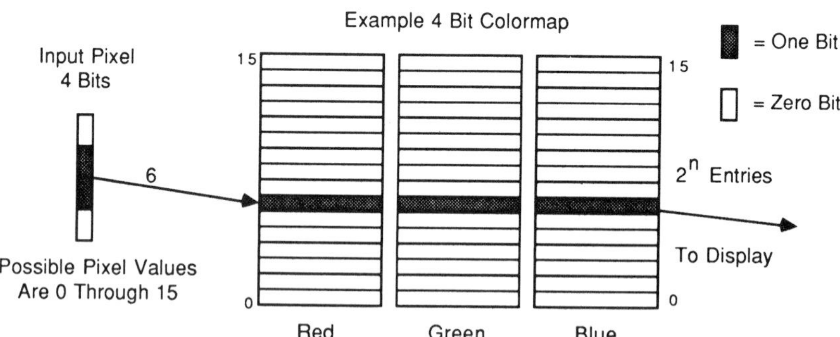

Figure 3.1. Pseudo color, gray scale, static color or static gray

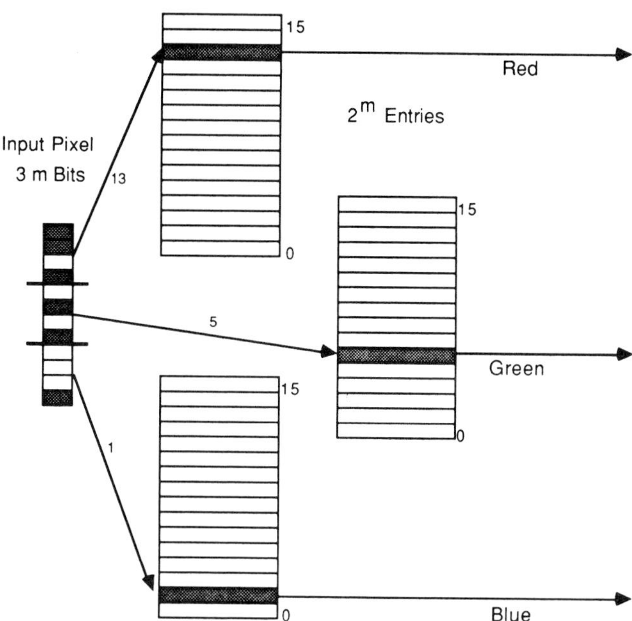

Figure 3.2. Direct color

the number of available colormap entries in a newly created colormap. For `DirectColor` and `TrueColor`, this is the size of an individual pixel subfield.

To obtain the visual ID from a `Visual`, use `XVisualIDFromVisual`.

```
VisualID XVisualIDFromVisual ( visual)
      Visual * visual;
```

visual Specifies the visual type.

The `XVisualIDFromVisual` function returns the visual ID for the specified visual type.

3.2 Window Attributes

All `InputOutput` windows have a border width of zero or more pixels, an optional background, an event suppression mask (which suppresses propagation of events from children), and a property list (see section 4.3). The window border and background can be a solid color or a pattern, called a tile. All windows except the root have a parent and are clipped by their parent. If a window is stacked on top of another window, it obscures that other window for the purpose of input. If a window has a background (almost all do), it obscures the other window for purposes of output. Attempts to output to the obscured area do nothing, and no input events (for example, pointer motion) are generated for the obscured area.

Windows also have associated property lists (see section 4.3).

Both `InputOutput` and `InputOnly` windows have the following common attributes, which are the only attributes of an `InputOnly` window:

- win-gravity
- event-mask
- do-not-propagate-mask
- override-redirect
- cursor

If you specify any other attributes for an `InputOnly` window, a `BadMatch` error results.

`InputOnly` windows are used for controlling input events in situations where `InputOutput` windows are unnecessary. `InputOnly` windows are invisible; can only be used to control such things as cursors, input event generation, and grabbing; and cannot be used in any graphics requests. Note that `InputOnly` windows cannot have `InputOutput` windows as inferiors.

Windows have borders of a programmable width and pattern as well as a background pattern or tile. Pixel values can be used for solid colors. The background and border pixmaps can be destroyed immediately after creating the window if no further explicit references to them are to be made. The pattern can either be relative to the parent or absolute. If `ParentRelative`, the parent's background is used.

When windows are first created, they are not visible (not mapped) on the screen. Any output to a window that is not visible on the screen and that does not have backing store will be discarded. An application may wish to create a window long before it is mapped to the screen. When a window is eventually mapped to the screen (using `XMapWindow`), the X server generates an `Expose` event for the window if backing store has not been maintained.

A window manager can override your choice of size, border width, and position for a top-level window. Your program must be prepared to use the actual size and position of the top window. It is not acceptable for a client application to resize itself unless in direct response to a human command to do so. Instead, either your program should use the space given to it, or if the space is too small for any useful work, your program might ask the user to resize the window. The border of your top-level window is considered fair game for window managers.

To set an attribute of a window, set the appropriate member of the `XSetWindowAttributes` structure and OR in the corresponding value bitmask in your subsequent calls to `XCreateWindow` and `XChangeWindowAttributes`, or use one of the other convenience functions that set the appropriate attribute. The symbols for the value mask bits and the `XSetWindowAttributes` structure are:

```
/* Window attribute value mask bits */
#define CWBackPixmap          (1L<<0)
#define CWBackPixel           (1L<<1)
#define CWBorderPixmap        (1L<<2)
#define CWBorderPixel         (1L<<3)
#define CWBitGravity          (1L<<4)
#define CWWinGravity          (1L<<5)
#define CWBackingStore        (1L<<6)
#define CWBackingPlanes       (1L<<7)
#define CWBackingPixel        (1L<<8)
#define CWOverrideRedirect    (1L<<9)
#define CWSaveUnder           (1L<<10)
#define CWEventMask           (1L<<11)
#define CWDontPropagate       (1L<<12)
#define CWColormap            (1L<<13)
#define CWCursor              (1L<<14)
/* Values */
typedef struct {
    Pixmap background_pixmap;          /* background, None, or ParentRelative */
    unsigned long background_pixel;    /* background pixel */
    Pixmap border_pixmap;              /* border of the window or CopyFrom-
                                          Parent */
```

```
    unsigned long border_pixel;       /* border pixel value */
    int bit_gravity;                  /* one of bit gravity values */
    int win_gravity;                  /* one of the window gravity values */
    int backing_store;                /* NotUseful,WhenMapped,Always */
    unsigned long backing_planes;     /* planes to be preserved if possible */
    unsigned long backing_pixel;      /* value to use in restoring planes */
    Bool save_under;                  /* should bits under be saved? (popups) */
    long event_mask;                  /* set of events that should be saved */
    long do_not_propagate_mask;       /* set of events that should not propagate */
    Bool override_redirect;           /* boolean value for override_redirect */
    Colormap colormap;                /* color map to be associated with
                                         window */

    Cursor cursor;                    /* cursor to be displayed (or None) */
} XSetWindowAttributes;
```

The following lists the defaults for each window attribute and indicates whether the attribute is applicable to `InputOutput` and `InputOnly` windows:

Attribute	*Default*	*InputOutput*	*InputOnly*
background-pixmap	`None`	Yes	No
background-pixel	Undefined	Yes	No
border-pixmap	`CopyFromParent`	Yes	No
border-pixel	Undefined	Yes	No
bit-gravity	`ForgetGravity`	Yes	No
win-gravity	`NorthWestGravity`	Yes	Yes
backing-store	`NotUseful`	Yes	No
backing-planes	All ones	Yes	No
backing-pixel	zero	Yes	No
save-under	`False`	Yes	No
event-mask	empty set	Yes	Yes
do-not-propagate-mask	empty set	Yes	Yes
override-redirect	`False`	Yes	Yes
colormap	`CopyFromParent`	Yes	No
cursor	`None`	Yes	Yes

3.2.1 Background Attribute

Only `InputOutput` windows can have a background. You can set the background of an `InputOutput` window by using a pixel or a pixmap.

The background-pixmap attribute of a window specifies the pixmap to be used for a window's background. This pixmap can be of any size, although some sizes may be faster than others. The background-pixel attribute of a window specifies a pixel value used to paint a window's background in a single color.

You can set the background-pixmap to a pixmap, `None` (default), or `ParentRelative`. You can set the background-pixel of a window to any pixel value (no default). If you specify a background-pixel, it overrides either the default background-pixmap or any value you may have set in the background-pixmap. A pixmap of an undefined size that is filled with the background-pixel is used for the background. Range checking is not performed on the background pixel; it simply is truncated to the appropriate number of bits.

If you set the background-pixmap, it overrides the default. The background-pixmap and the window must have the same depth, or a `BadMatch` error results. If you set background-pixmap to `None`, the window has no defined background. If you set the background-pixmap to `ParentRelative`:

- The parent window's background-pixmap is used. The child window, however, must have the same depth as its parent, or a `BadMatch` error results.
- If the parent window has a background-pixmap of `None`, the window also has a background-pixmap of `None`.
- A copy of the parent window's background-pixmap is not made. The parent's background-pixmap is examined each time the child window's background-pixmap is required.
- The background tile origin always aligns with the parent window's background tile origin. If the background-pixmap is not `ParentRelative`, the background tile origin is the child window's origin.

Setting a new background, whether by setting background-pixmap or background-pixel, overrides any previous background. The background-pixmap can be freed immediately if no further explicit reference is made to it (the X server will keep a copy to use when needed). If you later draw into the pixmap used for the background, what happens is undefined because the X implementation is free to make a copy of the pixmap or to use the same pixmap.

When no valid contents are available for regions of a window and either the regions are visible or the server is maintaining backing store, the server automatically tiles the regions with the window's background unless the window has a background of None. If the background is None, the previous screen contents from other windows of the same depth as the window are simply left in place as long as the contents come from the parent of the window or an inferior of the parent. Otherwise, the initial contents of the exposed regions are undefined. Expose events are then generated for the regions, even if the background-pixmap is None (see section 10.9).

3.2.2 Border Attribute

Only InputOutput windows can have a border. You can set the border of an InputOutput window by using a pixel or a pixmap.

The border-pixmap attribute of a window specifies the pixmap to be used for a window's border. The border-pixel attribute of a window specifies a pixmap of undefined size filled with that pixel be used for a window's border. Range checking is not performed on the background pixel; it simply is truncated to the appropriate number of bits. The border tile origin is always the same as the background tile origin.

You can also set the border-pixmap to a pixmap of any size (some may be faster than others) or to CopyFromParent (default). You can set the border-pixel to any pixel value (no default).

If you set a border-pixmap, it overrides the default. The border-pixmap and the window must have the same depth, or a BadMatch error results. If you set the border-pixmap to CopyFromParent, the parent window's border-pixmap is copied. Subsequent changes to the parent window's border attribute do not affect the child window. However, the child window must have the same depth as the parent window, or a BadMatch error results.

The border-pixmap can be freed immediately if no further explicit reference is made to it. If you later draw into the pixmap used for the border, what happens is undefined because the X implementation is free either to make a copy of the pixmap or to use the same pixmap. If you specify a border-pixel, it overrides either the default border-pixmap or any value you may have set in the border-pixmap. All pixels in the window's border will be set to the border-pixel. Setting a new border, whether by setting border-pixel or by setting border-pixmap, overrides any previous border.

Output to a window is always clipped to the inside of the window. Therefore, graphics operations never affect the window border.

3.2.3 Gravity Attributes

The bit gravity of a window defines which region of the window should be retained when an `InputOutput` window is resized. The default value for the bit-gravity attribute is `ForgetGravity`. The window gravity of a window allows you to define how the `InputOutput` or `InputOnly` window should be repositioned if its parent is resized. The default value for the win-gravity attribute is `NorthWestGravity`.

If the inside width or height of a window is not changed and if the window is moved or its border is changed, then the contents of the window are not lost but move with the window. Changing the inside width or height of the window causes its contents to be moved or lost (depending on the bit-gravity of the window) and causes children to be reconfigured (depending on their win-gravity). For a change of width and height, the (x, y) pairs are defined:

Gravity Direction	*Coordinates*
`NorthWestGravity`	(0, 0)
`NorthGravity`	(Width/2, 0)
`NorthEastGravity`	(Width, 0)
`WestGravity`	(0, Height/2)
`CenterGravity`	(Width/2, Height/2)
`EastGravity`	(Width, Height/2)
`SouthWestGravity`	(0, Height)
`SouthGravity`	(Width/2, Height)
`SouthEastGravity`	(Width, Height)

When a window with one of these bit-gravity values is resized, the corresponding pair defines the change in position of each pixel in the window. When a window with one of these win-gravities has its parent window resized, the corresponding pair defines the change in position of the window within the parent. When a window is so repositioned, a `GravityNotify` event is generated (see section 10.10.5).

A bit-gravity of `StaticGravity` indicates that the contents or origin should not move relative to the origin of the root window. If the change in size of the window is coupled with a change in position (x, y), then for bit-gravity the change in position of each pixel is (−x, −y), and for win-gravity the change in position of a child when its parent is so resized is (−x, −y). Note that

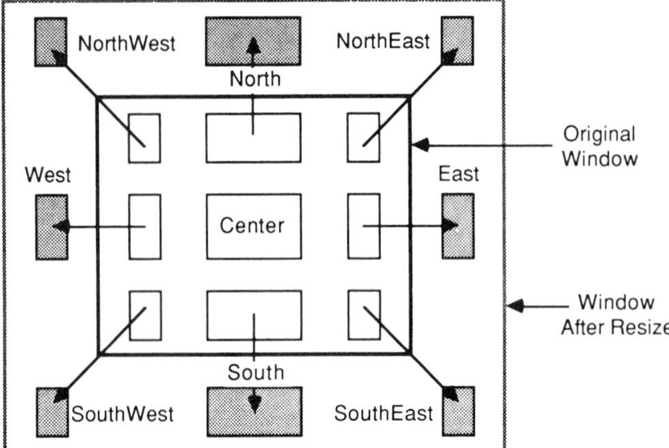

Figure 3.3. Window gravity

`StaticGravity` still only takes effect when the width or height of the window is changed, not when the window is moved.

A bit-gravity of `ForgetGravity` indicates that the window's contents are always discarded after a size change, even if a backing store or save under has been requested. The window is tiled with its background and zero or more `Expose` events are generated. If no background is defined, the existing screen contents are not altered. Some X servers may also ignore the specified bit-gravity and always generate `Expose` events.

The contents and borders of inferiors are not affected by their parent's bit-gravity. A server is permitted to ignore the specified bit-gravity and use `Forget` instead.

A win-gravity of `UnmapGravity` is like `NorthWestGravity` (the window is not moved), except the child is also unmapped when the parent is resized, and an `UnmapNotify` event is generated.

3.2.4 Backing Store Attribute

Some implementations of the X server may choose to maintain the contents of `InputOutput` windows. If the X server maintains the contents of a window, the off-screen saved pixels are known as backing store. The backing store advises the X server on what to do with the contents of a window. The backing-store attribute can be set to `NotUseful` (default), `WhenMapped`, or `Always`.

A backing-store attribute of `NotUseful` advises the X server that maintaining contents is unnecessary, although some X implementations may still choose to maintain contents and, therefore, not generate `Expose` events. A backing-store attribute of `WhenMapped` advises the X server that maintaining contents of obscured regions when the window is mapped would be beneficial. In this case, the server may generate an `Expose` event when the window is created. A backing-store attribute of `Always` advises the X server that maintaining contents even when the window is unmapped would be beneficial. Even if the window is larger than its parent, this is a request to the X server to maintain complete contents, not just the region within the parent window boundaries. While the X server maintains the window's contents, `Expose` events normally are not generated, but the X server may stop maintaining contents at any time.

When the contents of obscured regions of a window are being maintained, regions obscured by noninferior windows are included in the destination of graphics requests (and source, when the window is the source). However, regions obscured by inferior windows are not included.

3.2.5 Save Under Flag

Some server implementations may preserve contents of `InputOutput` windows under other `InputOutput` windows. This is not the same as preserving the contents of a window for you. You may get better visual appeal if transient windows (for example, pop-up menus) request that the system preserve the screen contents under them, so the temporarily obscured applications do not have to repaint.

You can set the save-under flag to `True` or `False` (default). If save-under is `True`, the X server is advised that, when this window is mapped, saving the contents of windows it obscures would be beneficial.

3.2.6 Backing Planes and Backing Pixel Attributes

You can set backing planes to indicate (with bits set to 1) which bit planes of an `InputOutput` window hold dynamic data that must be preserved in backing store and during save unders. The default value for the backing-planes attribute is all bits set to 1. You can set backing pixel to specify what bits to use in planes not covered by backing planes. The default value for the backing-pixel attribute is all bits set to 0. The X server is free to save only the specified bit planes in the backing store or the save under and is free to regenerate the remaining planes with the specified pixel value. Any extraneous bits in these values (that is, those bits beyond the specified depth of the window) may be simply ignored. If you request backing store or save unders, you should use these members to minimize the amount of off-screen memory required to store your window.

3.2.7 Event Mask and Do Not Propagate Mask Attributes

The event mask defines which events the client is interested in for this InputOutput or InputOnly window (or, for some event types, inferiors of this window). The event mask is the bitwise inclusive OR of zero or more of the valid event mask bits. You can specify that no maskable events are reported by setting NoEventMask (default).

The do-not-propagate-mask attribute defines which events should not be propagated to ancestor windows when no client has the event type selected in this InputOutput or InputOnly window. The do-not-propagate-mask is the bitwise inclusive OR of zero or more of the following masks: KeyPress, KeyRelease, ButtonPress, ButtonRelease, PointerMotion, Button1Motion, Button2Motion, Button3Motion, Button4Motion, Button5Motion, and ButtonMotion. You can specify that all events are propagated by setting NoEventMask (default).

3.2.8 Override Redirect Flag

To control window placement or to add decoration, a window manager often needs to intercept (redirect) any map or configure request. Pop-up windows, however, often need to be mapped without a window manager getting in the way. To control whether an InputOutput or InputOnly window is to ignore these structure control facilities, use the override-redirect flag.

The override-redirect flag specifies whether map and configure requests on this window should override a SubstructureRedirectMask on the parent. You can set the override-redirect flag to True or False (default). Window managers use this information to avoid tampering with pop-up windows (see also chapter 14).

3.2.9 Colormap Attribute

The colormap attribute specifies which colormap best reflects the true colors of the `InputOutput` window. The colormap must have the same visual type as the window, or a `BadMatch` error results. X servers capable of supporting multiple hardware colormaps can use this information, and window managers can use it for calls to `XInstallColormap`. You can set the colormap attribute to a colormap or to `CopyFromParent` (default).

If you set the colormap to `CopyFromParent`, the parent window's colormap is copied and used by its child. However, the child window must have the same visual type as the parent, or a `BadMatch` error results. The parent window must not have a colormap of `None`, or a `BadMatch` error results. The colormap is copied by sharing the colormap object between the child and parent, not by making a complete copy of the colormap contents. Subsequent changes to the parent window's colormap attribute do not affect the child window.

3.2.10 Cursor Attribute

The cursor attribute specifies which cursor is to be used when the pointer is in the `InputOutput` or `InputOnly` window. You can set the cursor to a cursor or `None` (default).

If you set the cursor to `None`, the parent's cursor is used when the pointer is in the `InputOutput` or `InputOnly` window, and any change in the parent's cursor will cause an immediate change in the displayed cursor. By calling `XFreeCursor`, the cursor can be freed immediately as long as no further explicit reference to it is made.

3.3 Creating Windows

Xlib provides basic ways for creating windows, and toolkits often supply higher-level functions specifically for creating and placing top-level windows, which are discussed in the appropriate toolkit documentation. If you do not use a toolkit, however, you must provide some standard information or hints for the window manager by using the Xlib inter-client communication functions (see chapter 14).

If you use Xlib to create your own top-level windows (direct children of the root window), you must observe the following rules so that all applications interact reasonably across the different styles of window management:

- You must never fight with the window manager for the size or placement of your top-level window.
- You must be able to deal with whatever size window you get, even if this means that your application just prints a message like "Please make me bigger" in its window.
- You should only attempt to resize or move top-level windows in direct response to a user request. If a request to change the size of a top-level window fails, you must be prepared to live with what you get. You are free to resize or move the children of top-level windows as necessary. (Toolkits often have facilities for automatic relayout.)
- If you do not use a toolkit that automatically sets standard window properties, you should set these properties for top-level windows before mapping them.

For further information, see chapter 14 and part III, "Inter-Client Communication Conventions Manual."

`XCreateWindow` is the more general function that allows you to set specific window attributes when you create a window. `XCreateSimpleWindow` creates a window that inherits its attributes from its parent window.

The X server acts as if `InputOnly` windows do not exist for the purposes of graphics requests, exposure processing, and `VisibilityNotify` events. An `InputOnly` window cannot be used as a drawable (that is, as a source or destination for graphics requests). `InputOnly` and `InputOutput` windows act identically in other respects (properties, grabs, input control, and so on). Extension packages can define other classes of windows.

To create an unmapped window and set its window attributes, use `XCreateWindow`.

```
Window XCreateWindow ( display, parent, x, y, width, height, border_width, depth, class,
                        visual, valuemask, attributes)
    Display *display;
    Window parent;
    int x, y;
    unsigned int width, height;
    unsigned int border_width;
    int depth;
    unsigned int class;
    Visual *visual
    unsigned long valuemask;
    XSetWindowAttributes *attributes;
```

display	Specifies the connection to the X server.
parent	Specifies the parent window.

x
y — Specify the x and y coordinates, which are the top-left outside corner of the created window's borders and are relative to the inside of the parent window's borders.

width
height — Specify the width and height, which are the created window's inside dimensions and do not include the created window's borders. The dimensions must be nonzero, or a `BadValue` error results.

border_width — Specifies the width of the created window's border in pixels.

depth — Specifies the window's depth. A depth of `CopyFromParent` means the depth is taken from the parent.

class — Specifies the created window's class. You can pass `InputOutput`, `InputOnly`, or `CopyFromParent`. A class of `CopyFromParent` means the class is taken from the parent.

visual — Specifies the visual type. A visual of `CopyFromParent` means the visual type is taken from the parent.

valuemask — Specifies which window attributes are defined in the attributes argument. This mask is the bitwise inclusive OR of the valid attribute mask bits. If valuemask is zero, the attributes are ignored and are not referenced.

attributes — Specifies the structure from which the values (as specified by the value mask) are to be taken. The value mask should have the appropriate bits set to indicate which attributes have been set in the structure.

The `XCreateWindow` function creates an unmapped subwindow for a specified parent window, returns the window ID of the created window, and causes the X server to generate a `CreateNotify` event. The created window is placed on top in the stacking order with respect to siblings.

The coordinate system has the X axis horizontal and the Y axis vertical with the origin [0, 0] at the upper-left corner. Coordinates are integral, in terms of pixels, and coincide with pixel centers. Each window and pixmap has its own coordinate system. For a window, the origin is inside the border at the inside, upper-left corner.

The border_width for an `InputOnly` window must be zero, or a `BadMatch` error results. For class `InputOutput`, the visual type and depth must be a combination supported for the screen, or a `BadMatch` error results. The depth need not be the same as the parent, but the parent must not be a window of class `InputOnly`, or a `BadMatch` error results. For an `InputOnly` window, the depth must be zero, and the visual must be one supported by the screen. If either condition is not met, a `BadMatch` error results. The parent window, however, may have any depth and class. If you specify any invalid window attribute for a window, a BadMatch error results.

The created window is not yet displayed (mapped) on the user's display. To display the window, call XMapWindow. The new window initially uses the same cursor as its parent. A new cursor can be defined for the new window by calling XDefineCursor. The window will not be visible on the screen unless it and all of its ancestors are mapped and it is not obscured by any of its ancestors.

XCreateWindow can generate BadAlloc, BadColor, BadCursor, BadMatch, BadPixmap, BadValue, and BadWindow errors.

To create an unmapped InputOutput subwindow of a given parent window, use XCreateSimpleWindow.

```
Window XCreateSimpleWindow ( display, parent, x, y, width, height, border_width,
                             border, background)
    Display *display;
    Window parent;
    int x, y;
    unsigned int width, height;
    unsigned int border_width;
    unsigned long border;
    unsigned long background;
```

display	Specifies the connection to the X server.
parent	Specifies the parent window.
x	
y	Specify the x and y coordinates, which are the top-left outside corner of the new window's borders and are relative to the inside of the parent window's borders.
width	
height	Specify the width and height, which are the created window's inside dimensions and do not include the created window's borders. The dimensions must be nonzero, or a BadValue error results.
border_width	Specifies the width of the created window's border in pixels.
border	Specifies the border pixel value of the window.
background	Specifies the background pixel value of the window.

The XCreateSimpleWindow function creates an unmapped InputOutput subwindow for a specified parent window, returns the window ID of the created window, and causes the X server to generate a CreateNotify event. The created window is placed on top in the stacking order with respect to siblings.

Any part of the window that extends outside its parent window is clipped. The border_width for an `InputOnly` window must be zero, or a `BadMatch` error results. `XCreateSimpleWindow` inherits its depth, class, and visual from its parent. All other window attributes, except background and border, have their default values.

`XCreateSimpleWindow` can generate `BadAlloc`, `BadMatch`, `BadValue`, and `BadWindow` errors.

3.4 Destroying Windows

Xlib provides functions that you can use to destroy a window or destroy all subwindows of a window.

To destroy a window and all of its subwindows, use `XDestroyWindow`.

```
XDestroyWindow(display, w)
    Display *display;
    Window w;
```

display Specifies the connection to the X server.

w Specifies the window.

The `XDestroyWindow` function destroys the specified window as well as all of its subwindows and causes the X server to generate a `DestroyNotify` event for each window. The window should never be referenced again. If the window specified by the w argument is mapped, it is unmapped automatically. The ordering of the `DestroyNotify` events is such that for any given window being destroyed, `DestroyNotify` is generated on any inferiors of the window before being generated on the window itself. The ordering among siblings and across subhierarchies is not otherwise constrained. If the window you specified is a root window, no windows are destroyed. Destroying a mapped window will generate `Expose` events on other windows that were obscured by the window being destroyed.

`XDestroyWindow` can generate a `BadWindow` error.

To destroy all subwindows of a specified window, use `XDestroySubwindows`.

```
XDestroySubwindows(display, w)
    Display *display;
```

```
    Window w;
```

display Specifies the connection to the X server.

w Specifies the window.

The `XDestroySubwindows` function destroys all inferior windows of the specified window, in bottom-to-top stacking order. It causes the X server to generate a `DestroyNotify` event for each window. If any mapped subwindows were actually destroyed, `XDestroySubwindows` causes the X server to generate `Expose` events on the specified window. This is much more efficient than deleting many windows one at a time because much of the work need be performed only once for all of the windows, rather than for each window. The subwindows should never be referenced again.

`XDestroySubwindows` can generate a `BadWindow` error.

3.5 Mapping Windows

A window is considered mapped if an `XMapWindow` call has been made on it. It may not be visible on the screen for one of the following reasons:

- It is obscured by another opaque window.
- One of its ancestors is not mapped.
- It is entirely clipped by an ancestor.

`Expose` events are generated for the window when part or all of it becomes visible on the screen. A client receives the `Expose` events only if it has asked for them. Windows retain their position in the stacking order when they are unmapped.

A window manager may want to control the placement of subwindows. If `SubstructureRedirectMask` has been selected by a window manager on a parent window (usually a root window), a map request initiated by other clients on a child window is not performed, and the window manager is sent a `MapRequest` event. However, if the override-redirect flag on the child had been set to `True` (usually only on pop-up menus), the map request is performed.

A tiling window manager might decide to reposition and resize other clients' windows and then decide to map the window to its final location. A window manager that wants to provide decoration might reparent the child into a frame first. For further information, see section 3.2.8 and section 10.10. Only a single client at a time can select for `SubstructureRedirectMask`.

Similarly, a single client can select for `ResizeRedirectMask` on a parent window. Then, any attempt to resize the window by another client is suppressed, and the client receives a `ResizeRequest` event.

To map a given window, use `XMapWindow`.

```
XMapWindow(display, w)
    Display *display;
    Window w;
```

display Specifies the connection to the X server.

w Specifies the window.

The `XMapWindow` function maps the window and all of its subwindows that have had map requests. Mapping a window that has an unmapped ancestor does not display the window but marks it as eligible for display when the ancestor becomes mapped. Such a window is called unviewable. When all its ancestors are mapped, the window becomes viewable and will be visible on the screen if it is not obscured by another window. This function has no effect if the window is already mapped.

If the override-redirect of the window is `False` and if some other client has selected `SubstructureRedirectMask` on the parent window, then the X server generates a `MapRequest` event, and the `XMapWindow` function does not map the window. Otherwise, the window is mapped, and the X server generates a `MapNotify` event.

If the window becomes viewable and no earlier contents for it are remembered, the X server tiles the window with its background. If the window's background is undefined, the existing screen contents are not altered, and the X server generates zero or more `Expose` events. If backing-store was maintained while the window was unmapped, no `Expose` events are generated. If backing-store will now be maintained, a full-window exposure is always generated. Otherwise, only visible regions may be reported. Similar tiling and exposure take place for any newly viewable inferiors.

If the window is an `InputOutput` window, `XMapWindow` generates `Expose` events on each `InputOutput` window that it causes to be displayed. If the client maps and paints the window and if the client begins processing events, the window is painted twice. To avoid this, first ask for `Expose` events and then map the window, so the client processes input events as usual. The event list will include `Expose` for each window that has appeared on the screen. The client's normal response to an `Expose` event should be to repaint the window. This method usually leads to simpler programs and to proper interaction with window managers.

`XMapWindow` can generate a `BadWindow` error.

To map and raise a window, use `XMapRaised`.

```
XMapRaised ( display, w)
    Display *display;
    Window w;
```

display Specifies the connection to the X server.

w Specifies the window.

The `XMapRaised` function essentially is similar to `XMapWindow` in that it maps the window and all of its subwindows that have had map requests. However, it also raises the specified window to the top of the stack. For additional information, see `XMapWindow`.

`XMapRaised` can generate multiple `BadWindow` errors.

To map all subwindows for a specified window, use `XMapSubwindows`.

```
XMapSubwindows ( display, w)
    Display *display;
    Window w;
```

display Specifies the connection to the X server.

w Specifies the window.

The `XMapSubwindows` function maps all subwindows for a specified window in top-to-bottom stacking order. The X server generates `Expose` events on each newly displayed window. This may be much more efficient than mapping many windows one at a time because the server needs to perform much of the work only once, for all of the windows, rather than for each window.

`XMapSubwindows` can generate a `BadWindow` error.

3.6 Unmapping Windows

Xlib provides functions that you can use to unmap a window or all subwindows.

To unmap a window, use `XUnmapWindow`.

```
XUnmapWindow ( display, w)
    Display *display;
    Window w;
```

display Specifies the connection to the X server.
w Specifies the window.

The `XUnmapWindow` function unmaps the specified window and causes the X server to generate an `UnmapNotify` event. If the specified window is already unmapped, `XUnmapWindow` has no effect. Normal exposure processing on formerly obscured windows is performed. Any child window will no longer be visible until another map call is made on the parent. In other words, the subwindows are still mapped but are not visible until the parent is mapped. Unmapping a window will generate `Expose` events on windows that were formerly obscured by it.

`XUnmapWindow` can generate a `BadWindow` error.

To unmap all subwindows for a specified window, use `XUnmapSubwindows`.

```
XUnmapSubwindows ( display, w)
    Display *display;
    Window w;
```

display Specifies the connection to the X server.
w Specifies the window.

The `XUnmapSubwindows` function unmaps all subwindows for the specified window in bottom-to-top stacking order. It causes the X server to generate an `UnmapNotify` event on each subwindow and `Expose` events on formerly obscured windows. Using this function is much more efficient than unmapping multiple windows one at a time because the server needs to perform much of the work only once, for all of the windows, rather than for each window.

`XUnmapSubwindows` can generate a `BadWindow` error.

3.7 Configuring Windows

Xlib provides functions that you can use to move a window, resize a window, move and resize a window, or change a window's border width. To change one of these parameters, set the appropriate member of the `XWindowChanges` structure and OR in the corresponding value mask in subsequent calls to `XConfigureWindow`. The symbols for the value mask bits and the `XWindowChanges` structure are:

```
/* Configure window value mask bits */
#define CWX              (1<<0)
#define CWY              (1<<1)
#define CWWidth          (1<<2)
#define CWHeight         (1<<3)
#define CWBorderWidth    (1<<4)
#define CWSibling        (1<<5)
#define CWStackMode      (1<<6)
/* Values */
typedef struct {
    int x, y;
    int width, height;
    int border_width;
    Window sibling;
    int stack_mode;
} XWindowChanges;
```

The x and y members are used to set the window's x and y coordinates, which are relative to the parent's origin and indicate the position of the upper-left outer corner of the window. The width and height members are used to set the inside size of the window, not including the border, and must be nonzero, or a `BadValue` error results. Attempts to configure a root window have no effect.

The border_width member is used to set the width of the border in pixels. Note that setting just the border width leaves the outer-left corner of the window in a fixed position but moves the absolute position of the window's origin. If you attempt to set the border-width attribute of an `InputOnly` window nonzero, a `BadMatch` error results.

The sibling member is used to set the sibling window for stacking operations. The stack_mode member is used to set how the window is to be restacked and can be set to `Above`, `Below`, `TopIf`, `BottomIf`, or `Opposite`.

If the override-redirect flag of the window is `False` and if some other client has selected `SubstructureRedirectMask` on the parent, the X server generates a `ConfigureRequest` event, and no further processing is performed. Otherwise, if some other client has selected `ResizeRedirectMask` on the window and the inside width or height of the window is being changed, a `ResizeRequest` event is generated, and the current inside width and height are used instead. Note that the override-redirect flag of the window has no effect on ResizeRedirectMask and that SubstructureRedirectMask on the parent has precedence over ResizeRedirectMask on the window.

When the geometry of the window is changed as specified, the window is restacked among siblings, and a ConfigureNotify event is generated if the state of the window actually changes. GravityNotify events are generated after ConfigureNotify events. If the inside width or height of the window has actually changed, children of the window are affected as specified.

If a window's size actually changes, the window's subwindows move according to their window gravity. Depending on the window's bit gravity, the contents of the window also may be moved (see section 3.2.3).

If regions of the window were obscured but now are not, exposure processing is performed on these formerly obscured windows, including the window itself and its inferiors. As a result of increasing the width or height, exposure processing is also performed on any new regions of the window and any regions where window contents are lost.

The restack check (specifically, the computation for BottomIf, TopIf, and Opposite) is performed with respect to the window's final size and position (as controlled by the other arguments of the request), not its initial position. If a sibling is specified without a stack_mode, a BadMatch error results.

If a sibling and a stack_mode are specified, the window is restacked as follows:

Above	The window is placed just above the sibling.
Below	The window is placed just below the sibling.
TopIf	If the sibling occludes the window, the window is placed at the top of the stack.
BottomIf	If the window occludes the sibling, the window is placed at the bottom of the stack.
Opposite	If the sibling occludes the window, the window is placed at the top of the stack. If the window occludes the sibling, the window is placed at the bottom of the stack.

If a stack_mode is specified but no sibling is specified, the window is restacked as follows:

Above	The window is placed at the top of the stack.
Below	The window is placed at the bottom of the stack.

`TopIf`	If any sibling occludes the window, the window is placed at the top of the stack.
`BottomIf`	If the window occludes any sibling, the window is placed at the bottom of the stack.
`Opposite`	If any sibling occludes the window, the window is placed at the top of the stack. If the window occludes any sibling, the window is placed at the bottom of the stack.

Attempts to configure a root window have no effect.

To configure a window's size, location, stacking, or border, use `XConfigureWindow`.

```
XConfigureWindow(display, w, value_mask, values)
    Display *display;
    Window w;
    unsigned int value_mask;
    XWindowChanges *values;
```

display	Specifies the connection to the X server.
w	Specifies the window to be reconfigured.
value_mask	Specifies which values are to be set using information in the values structure. This mask is the bitwise inclusive OR of the valid configure window values bits.
values	Specifies the `XWindowChanges` structure.

The `XConfigureWindow` function uses the values specified in the `XWindowChanges` structure to reconfigure a window's size, position, border, and stacking order. Values not specified are taken from the existing geometry of the window.

If a sibling is specified without a stack_mode or if the window is not actually a sibling, a `BadMatch` error results. Note that the computations for `BottomIf`, `TopIf`, and `Opposite` are performed with respect to the window's final geometry (as controlled by the other arguments passed to `XConfigureWindow`), not its initial geometry. Any backing store contents of the window, its inferiors, and other newly visible windows are either discarded or changed to reflect the current screen contents (depending on the implementation).

`XConfigureWindow` can generate `BadMatch`, `BadValue`, and `BadWindow` errors.

To move a window without changing its size, use `XMoveWindow`.

```
XMoveWindow(display, w, x, y)
    Display *display;
    Window w;
    int x, y;
```

display Specifies the connection to the X server.

w Specifies the window to be moved.

x

y Specify the x and y coordinates, which define the new location of the top-left pixel of the window's border or the window itself if it has no border.

The `XMoveWindow` function moves the specified window to the specified x and y coordinates, but it does not change the window's size, raise the window, or change the mapping state of the window. Moving a mapped window may or may not lose the window's contents depending on if the window is obscured by nonchildren and if no backing store exists. If the contents of the window are lost, the X server generates `Expose` events. Moving a mapped window generates `Expose` events on any formerly obscured windows.

If the override-redirect flag of the window is `False` and some other client has selected `SubstructureRedirectMask` on the parent, the X server generates a `ConfigureRequest` event, and no further processing is performed. Otherwise, the window is moved.

`XMoveWindow` can generate a `BadWindow` error.

To change a window's size without changing the upper-left coordinate, use `XResizeWindow`.

```
XResizeWindow(display, w, width, height)
    Display *display;
    Window w;
    unsigned int width, height;
```

display Specifies the connection to the X server.

w Specifies the window.

width

height Specify the width and height, which are the interior dimensions of the window after the call completes.

The `XResizeWindow` function changes the inside dimensions of the specified window, not including its borders. This function does not change the window's upper-left coordinate or the origin and does not restack the window. Changing the size of a mapped window may lose its contents and generate

Expose events. If a mapped window is made smaller, changing its size generates Expose events on windows that the mapped window formerly obscured.

If the override-redirect flag of the window is False and some other client has selected SubstructureRedirectMask on the parent, the X server generates a ConfigureRequest event, and no further processing is performed. If either width or height is zero, a BadValue error results.

XResizeWindow can generate BadValue and BadWindow errors.

To change the size and location of a window, use XMoveResizeWindow.

```
XMoveResizeWindow(display, w, x, y, width, height)
    Display *display;
    Window w;
    int x, y;
    unsigned int width, height;
```

display Specifies the connection to the X server.

w Specifies the window to be reconfigured.

x
y Specify the x and y coordinates, which define the new position of the window relative to its parent.

width
height Specify the width and height, which define the interior size of the window.

The XMoveResizeWindow function changes the size and location of the specified window without raising it. Moving and resizing a mapped window may generate an Expose event on the window. Depending on the new size and location parameters, moving and resizing a window may generate Expose events on windows that the window formerly obscured.

If the override-redirect flag of the window is False and some other client has selected SubstructureRedirectMask on the parent, the X server generates a ConfigureRequest event, and no further processing is performed. Otherwise, the window size and location are changed.

XMoveResizeWindow can generate BadValue and BadWindow errors.

To change the border width of a given window, use XSetWindowBorderWidth.

```
XSetWindowBorderWidth(display, w, width)
    Display *display;
```

Window *w*;
unsigned int *width*;

display Specifies the connection to the X server.
w Specifies the window.
width Specifies the width of the window border.

The XSetWindowBorderWidth function sets the specified window's border width to the specified width.

XSetWindowBorderWidth can generate a BadWindow error.

3.8 Changing Window Stacking Order

Xlib provides functions that you can use to raise, lower, circulate, or restack windows.

To raise a window so that no sibling window obscures it, use XRaiseWindow.

XRaiseWindow (*display*, *w*)
Display **display*;
Window *w*;

display Specifies the connection to the X server.
w Specifies the window.

The XRaiseWindow function raises the specified window to the top of the stack so that no sibling window obscures it. If the windows are regarded as overlapping sheets of paper stacked on a desk, then raising a window is analogous to moving the sheet to the top of the stack but leaving its x and y location on the desk constant. Raising a mapped window may generate Expose events for the window and any mapped subwindows that were formerly obscured.

If the override-redirect attribute of the window is False and some other client has selected SubstructureRedirectMask on the parent, the X server generates a ConfigureRequest event, and no processing is performed. Otherwise, the window is raised.

XRaiseWindow can generate a BadWindow error.

To lower a window so that it does not obscure any sibling windows, use XLowerWindow.

XLowerWindow (*display*, *w*)
Display **display*;

Window *w*;

display Specifies the connection to the X server.

w Specifies the window.

The XLowerWindow function lowers the specified window to the bottom of the stack so that it does not obscure any sibling windows. If the windows are regarded as overlapping sheets of paper stacked on a desk, then lowering a window is analogous to moving the sheet to the bottom of the stack but leaving its x and y location on the desk constant. Lowering a mapped window will generate Expose events on any windows it formerly obscured.

If the override-redirect attribute of the window is False and some other client has selected SubstructureRedirectMask on the parent, the X server generates a ConfigureRequest event, and no processing is performed. Otherwise, the window is lowered to the bottom of the stack.

XLowerWindow can generate a BadWindow error.

To circulate a subwindow up or down, use XCirculateSubwindows.

XCirculateSubwindows (*display*, *w*, *direction*)
Display **display*;
Window *w*;
int *direction*;

display Specifies the connection to the X server.

w Specifies the window.

direction Specifies the direction (up or down) that you want to circulate the window. You can pass RaiseLowest or LowerHighest.

The XCirculateSubwindows function circulates children of the specified window in the specified direction. If you specify RaiseLowest, XCirculateSubwindows raises the lowest mapped child (if any) that is occluded by another child to the top of the stack. If you specify LowerHighest, XCirculateSubwindows lowers the highest mapped child (if any) that occludes another child to the bottom of the stack. Exposure processing is then performed on formerly obscured windows. If some other client has selected SubstructureRedirectMask on the window, the X server generates a CirculateRequest event, and no further processing is performed. If a child is actually restacked, the X server generates a CirculateNotify event.

XCirculateSubwindows can generate BadValue and BadWindow errors.

To raise the lowest mapped child of a window that is partially or completely occluded by another child, use `XCirculateSubwindowsUp`.

```
XCirculateSubwindowsUp ( display, w)
    Display *display;
    Window w;
```

display Specifies the connection to the X server.
w Specifies the window.

The `XCirculateSubwindowsUp` function raises the lowest mapped child of the specified window that is partially or completely occluded by another child. Completely unobscured children are not affected. This is a convenience function equivalent to `XCirculateSubwindows` with `RaiseLowest` specified.

`XCirculateSubwindowsUp` can generate a `BadWindow` error.

To lower the highest mapped child of a window that partially or completely occludes another child, use `XCirculateSubwindowsDown`.

```
XCirculateSubwindowsDown ( display, w)
    Display *display;
    Window w;
```

display Specifies the connection to the X server.
w Specifies the window.

The `XCirculateSubwindowsDown` function lowers the highest mapped child of the specified window that partially or completely occludes another child. Completely unobscured children are not affected. This is a convenience function equivalent to `XCirculateSubwindows` with `LowerHighest` specified.

`XCirculateSubwindowsDown` can generate a `BadWindow` error.

To restack a set of windows from top to bottom, use `XRestackWindows`.

```
XRestackWindows ( display, windows, nwindows);
    Display *display;
    Window windows[];
    int nwindows;
```

display Specifies the connection to the X server.
windows Specifies an array containing the windows to be restacked.
nwindows Specifies the number of windows to be restacked.

The XRestackWindows function restacks the windows in the order specified, from top to bottom. The stacking order of the first window in the windows array is unaffected, but the other windows in the array are stacked underneath the first window, in the order of the array. The stacking order of the other windows is not affected. For each window in the window array that is not a child of the specified window, a BadMatch error results.

If the override-redirect attribute of a window is False and some other client has selected SubstructureRedirectMask on the parent, the X server generates ConfigureRequest events for each window whose override-redirect flag is not set, and no further processing is performed. Otherwise, the windows will be restacked in top to bottom order.

XRestackWindows can generate a BadWindow error.

3.9 Changing Window Attributes

Xlib provides functions that you can use to set window attributes. XChangeWindowAttributes is the more general function that allows you to set one or more window attributes provided by the XSetWindowAttributes structure. The other functions described in this section allow you to set one specific window attribute, such as a window's background.

To change one or more attributes for a given window, use XChangeWindowAttributes.

```
XChangeWindowAttributes(display, w, valuemask, attributes)
    Display *display;
    Window w;
    unsigned long valuemask;
    XSetWindowAttributes *attributes;
```

display Specifies the connection to the X server.

w Specifies the window.

valuemask Specifies which window attributes are defined in the attributes argument. This mask is the bitwise inclusive OR of the valid attribute mask bits. If valuemask is zero, the attributes are ignored and are not referenced. The values and restrictions are the same as for XCreateWindow.

attributes Specifies the structure from which the values (as specified by the value mask) are to be taken. The value mask should have the appropriate bits set to indicate which attributes have been set in the structure (see section 3.2).

Depending on the valuemask, the `XChangeWindowAttributes` function uses the window attributes in the `XSetWindowAttributes` structure to change the specified window attributes. Changing the background does not cause the window contents to be changed. To repaint the window and its background, use `XClearWindow`. Setting the border or changing the background such that the border tile origin changes causes the border to be repainted. Changing the background of a root window to `None` or `ParentRelative` restores the default background pixmap. Changing the border of a root window to `CopyFromParent` restores the default border pixmap. Changing the win-gravity does not affect the current position of the window. Changing the backing-store of an obscured window to `WhenMapped` or `Always`, or changing the backing-planes, backing-pixel, or save-under of a mapped window may have no immediate effect. Changing the colormap of a window (that is, defining a new map, not changing the contents of the existing map) generates a `ColormapNotify` event. Changing the colormap of a visible window may have no immediate effect on the screen because the map may not be installed (see `XInstallColormap`). `None` restores the default cursor. Whenever possible, you are encouraged to share colormaps.

Multiple clients can select input on the same window. Their event masks are maintained separately. When an event is generated, it is reported to all interested clients. However, only one client at a time can select for `SubstructureRedirectMask`, `ResizeRedirectMask`, and `ButtonPressMask`. If a client attempts to select any of these event masks and some other client has already selected one, a `BadAccess` error results. There is only one do-not-propagate-mask for a window, not one per client.

`XChangeWindowAttributes` can generate `BadAccess`, `BadColor`, `BadCursor`, `BadMatch`, `BadPixmap`, `BadValue`, and `BadWindow` errors.

To set the background of a window to a given pixel, use `XSetWindowBackground`.

XSetWindowBackground (*display*, *w*, *background_pixel*)
 Display **display*;
 Window *w*;
 unsigned long *background_pixel*;

display Specifies the connection to the X server.

w	Specifies the window.
background_pixel	Specifies the pixel that is to be used for the background.

The XSetWindowBackground function sets the background of the window to the specified pixel value. Changing the background does not cause the window contents to be changed. XSetWindowBackground uses a pixmap of undefined size filled with the pixel value you passed. If you try to change the background of an InputOnly window, a BadMatch error results.

XSetWindowBackground can generate BadMatch and BadWindow errors.

To set the background of a window to a given pixmap, use XSetWindowBackgroundPixmap.

```
XSetWindowBackgroundPixmap ( display, w, background_pixmap)
    Display *display;
    Window w;
    Pixmap background_pixmap;
```

display	Specifies the connection to the X server.
w	Specifies the window.
background_pixmap	Specifies the background pixmap, ParentRelative, or None.

The XSetWindowBackgroundPixmap function sets the background pixmap of the window to the specified pixmap. The background pixmap can immediately be freed if no further explicit references to it are to be made. If ParentRelative is specified, the background pixmap of the window's parent is used, or on the root window, the default background is restored. If you try to change the background of an InputOnly window, a BadMatch error results. If the background is set to None, the window has no defined background.

XSetWindowBackgroundPixmap can generate BadMatch, BadPixmap, and BadWindow errors.

Note XSetWindowBackground and XSetWindowBackgroundPixmap do not change the current contents of the window.

To change and repaint a window's border to a given pixel, use XSetWindowBorder.

```
XSetWindowBorder ( display, w, border_pixel)
    Display *display;
```

```
   Window w;
   unsigned long border_pixel;
```

display Specifies the connection to the X server.
w Specifies the window.
border_pixel Specifies the entry in the colormap.

The `XSetWindowBorder` function sets the border of the window to the pixel value you specify. If you attempt to perform this on an `InputOnly` window, a `BadMatch` error results.

`XSetWindowBorder` can generate `BadMatch` and `BadWindow` errors.

To change and repaint the border tile of a given window, use `XSetWindowBorderPixmap`.

```
XSetWindowBorderPixmap ( display, w, border_pixmap)
   Display *display;
   Window w;
   Pixmap border_pixmap;
```

display Specifies the connection to the X server.
w Specifies the window.
border_pixmap Specifies the border pixmap or `CopyFromParent`.

The `XSetWindowBorderPixmap` function sets the border pixmap of the window to the pixmap you specify. The border pixmap can be freed immediately if no further explicit references to it are to be made. If you specify `CopyFromParent`, a copy of the parent window's border pixmap is used. If you attempt to perform this on an `InputOnly` window, a `BadMatch` error results.

`XSetWindowBorderPixmap` can generate `BadMatch`, `BadPixmap`, and `BadWindow` errors.

To set the colormap of a given window, use `XSetWindowColormap`.

```
XSetWindowColormap ( display, w, colormap)
   Display *display;
   Window w;
   Colormap colormap;
```

display Specifies the connection to the X server.
w Specifies the window.
colormap Specifies the colormap.

The `XSetWindowColormap` function sets the specified colormap of the specified window. The colormap must have the same visual type as the window, or a `BadMatch` error results.

`XSetWindowColormap` can generate `BadColor`, `BadMatch`, and `BadWindow` errors.

To define which cursor will be used in a window, use `XDefineCursor`.

```
XDefineCursor (display, w, cursor)
    Display *display;
    Window w;
    Cursor cursor;
```

display Specifies the connection to the X server.

w Specifies the window.

cursor Specifies the cursor that is to be displayed or `None`.

If a cursor is set, it will be used when the pointer is in the window. If the cursor is `None`, it is equivalent to `XUndefineCursor`.

`XDefineCursor` can generate `BadCursor` and `BadWindow` errors.

To undefine the cursor in a given window, use `XUndefineCursor`.

```
XUndefineCursor (display, w)
    Display *display;
    Window w;
```

display Specifies the connection to the X server.

w Specifies the window.

The `XUndefineCursor` function undoes the effect of a previous `XDefineCursor` for this window. When the pointer is in the window, the parent's cursor will now be used. On the root window, the default cursor is restored.

`XUndefineCursor` can generate a `BadWindow` error.

Chapter 4

Window Information Functions

After you connect the display to the X server and create a window, you can use the Xlib window information functions to:

- Obtain information about a window
- Translate screen coordinates
- Manipulate property lists
- Obtain and change window properties
- Manipulate selections

4.1 Obtaining Window Information

Xlib provides functions that you can use to obtain information about the window tree, the window's current attributes, the window's current geometry, or the current pointer coordinates. Because they are most frequently used by window managers, these functions all return a status to indicate whether the window still exists.

To obtain the parent, a list of children, and number of children for a given window, use `XQueryTree`.

Status XQueryTree (*display*, *w*, *root_return*, *parent_return*, *children_return*,
nchildren_return)
  Display **display*;
  Window *w*;

Window **root_return*;
Window **parent_return*;
Window ***children_return*;
unsigned int **nchildren_return*;

display	Specifies the connection to the X server.
w	Specifies the window whose list of children, root, parent, and number of children you want to obtain.
root_return	Returns the root window.
parent_return	Returns the parent window.
children_return	Returns the list of children.
nchildren_return	Returns the number of children.

The `XQueryTree` function returns the root ID, the parent window ID, a pointer to the list of children windows, and the number of children in the list for the specified window. The children are listed in current stacking order, from bottommost (first) to topmost (last). `XQueryTree` returns zero if it fails and nonzero if it succeeds. To free this list when it is no longer needed, use `XFree`.

`XQueryTree` can generate a `BadWindow` error.

To obtain the current attributes of a given window, use `XGetWindowAttributes`.

Status XGetWindowAttributes (*display*, *w*, *window_attributes_return*)
Display **display*;
Window *w*;
XWindowAttributes **window_attributes_return*;

display	Specifies the connection to the X server.
w	Specifies the window whose current attributes you want to obtain.
window_attributes_return	Returns the specified window's attributes in the `XWindowAttributes` structure.

The `XGetWindowAttributes` function returns the current attributes for the specified window to an `XWindowAttributes` structure.

```
typedef struct {
    int x, y;                    /* location of window */
    int width, height;           /* width and height of window */
    int border_width;            /* border width of window */
    int depth;                   /* depth of window */
    Visual *visual;              /* the associated visual structure */
```

```
	Window root;                          /* root of screen containing window */
	int class;                            /* InputOutput, InputOnly */
	int bit_gravity;                      /* one of the bit gravity values */
	int win_gravity;                      /* one of the window gravity values */
	int backing_store;                    /* NotUseful, WhenMapped, Always */
	unsigned long backing_planes;         /* planes to be preserved if possible */
	unsigned long backing_pixel;          /* value to be used when restoring planes */
	Bool save_under;                      /* boolean, should bits under be saved? */
	Colormap colormap;                    /* color map to be associated with window */
	Bool map_installed;                   /* boolean, is color map currently installed*/
	int map_state;                        /* IsUnmapped, IsUnviewable, IsViewable */
	long all_event_masks;                 /* set of events all people have interest in*/
	long your_event_mask;                 /* my event mask */
	long do_not_propagate_mask;           /* set of events that should not propagate */
	Bool override_redirect;               /* boolean value for override-redirect */
	Screen *screen;                       /* back pointer to correct screen */
} XWindowAttributes;
```

The x and y members are set to the upper-left outer corner relative to the parent window's origin. The width and height members are set to the inside size of the window, not including the border. The border_width member is set to the window's border width in pixels. The depth member is set to the depth of the window (that is, bits per pixel for the object). The visual member is a pointer to the screen's associated `Visual` structure. The root member is set to the root window of the screen containing the window. The class member is set to the window's class and can be either `InputOutput` or `InputOnly`.

The bit_gravity member is set to the window's bit gravity and can be one of the following:

```
ForgetGravity          EastGravity
NorthWestGravity       SouthWestGravity
NorthGravity           SouthGravity
NorthEastGravity       SouthEastGravity
WestGravity            StaticGravity
CenterGravity
```

The win_gravity member is set to the window's window gravity and can be one of the following:

```
UnmapGravity           EastGravity
NorthWestGravity       SouthWestGravity
```

```
NorthGravity          SouthGravity
NorthEastGravity      SouthEastGravity
WestGravity           StaticGravity
CenterGravity
```

For additional information on gravity, see section 3.3.

The backing_store member is set to indicate how the X server should maintain the contents of a window and can be `WhenMapped`, `Always`, or `NotUseful`. The backing_planes member is set to indicate (with bits set to 1) which bit planes of the window hold dynamic data that must be preserved in backing_stores and during save_unders. The backing_pixel member is set to indicate what values to use for planes not set in backing_planes.

The save_under member is set to `True` or `False`. The colormap member is set to the colormap for the specified window and can be a colormap ID or `None`. The map_installed member is set to indicate whether the colormap is currently installed and can be `True` or `False`. The map_state member is set to indicate the state of the window and can be `IsUnmapped`, `IsUnviewable`, or `IsViewable`. `IsUnviewable` is used if the window is mapped but some ancestor is unmapped.

The all_event_masks member is set to the bitwise inclusive OR of all event masks selected on the window by all clients. The your_event_mask member is set to the bitwise inclusive OR of all event masks selected by the querying client. The do_not_propagate_mask member is set to the bitwise inclusive OR of the set of events that should not propagate.

The override_redirect member is set to indicate whether this window overrides structure control facilities and can be `True` or `False`. Window manager clients should ignore the window if this member is `True`.

The screen member is set to a screen pointer that gives you a back pointer to the correct screen. This makes it easier to obtain the screen information without having to loop over the root window fields to see which field matches.

`XGetWindowAttributes` can generate `BadDrawable` and `BadWindow` errors.

To obtain the current geometry of a given drawable, use `XGetGeometry`.

Status XGetGeometry (*display*, *d*, *root_return*, *x_return*, *y_return*, *width_return*, *height_return*, *border_width_return*, *depth_return*)
Display **display*;
Drawable *d*;
Window **root_return*;
int **x_return*, **y_return*;

```
    unsigned int *width_return, *height_return;
    unsigned int *border_width_return;
    unsigned int *depth_return;
```

display	Specifies the connection to the X server.
d	Specifies the drawable, which can be a window or a pixmap.
root_return	Returns the root window.
x_return *y_return*	Return the x and y coordinates that define the location of the drawable. For a window, these coordinates specify the upper-left outer corner relative to its parent's origin. For pixmaps, these coordinates are always zero.
width_return *height_return*	Return the drawable's dimensions (width and height). For a window, these dimensions specify the inside size, not including the border.
border_width_return	Returns the border width in pixels. If the drawable is a pixmap, it returns zero.
depth_return	Returns the depth of the drawable (bits per pixel for the object).

The `XGetGeometry` function returns the root window and the current geometry of the drawable. The geometry of the drawable includes the x and y coordinates, width and height, border width, and depth. These are described in the argument list. It is legal to pass to this function a window whose class is `InputOnly`.

`XGetGeometry` can generate a `BadDrawable` error.

4.2 Translating Screen Coordinates

Applications sometimes need to perform a coordinate transformation from the coordinate space of one window to another window or need to determine which window the pointing device is in. `XTranslateCoordinates` and `XQueryPointer` fulfill these needs (and avoid any race conditions) by asking the X server to perform these operations.

To translate a coordinate in one window to the coordinate space of another window, use `XTranslateCoordinates`.

```
Bool XTranslateCoordinates (display, src_w, dest_w, src_x, src_y, dest_x_return,
                            dest_y_return, child_return)
    Display *display;
    Window src_w, dest_w;
```

int *src_x*, *src_y*;
int **dest_x_return*, **dest_y_return*;
Window **child_return*;

display Specifies the connection to the X server.
src_w Specifies the source window.
dest_w Specifies the destination window.
src_x
src_y Specify the x and y coordinates within the source window.
dest_x_return
dest_y_return Return the x and y coordinates within the destination window.
child_return Returns the child if the coordinates are contained in a mapped child of the destination window.

If `XTranslateCoordinates` returns `True`, it takes the src_x and src_y coordinates relative to the source window's origin and returns these coordinates to dest_x_return and dest_y_return relative to the destination window's origin. If `XTranslateCoordinates` returns `False`, src_w and dest_w are on different screens, and dest_x_return and dest_y_return are zero. If the coordinates are contained in a mapped child of dest_w, that child is returned to child_return. Otherwise, child_return is set to `None`.

`XTranslateCoordinates` can generate a `BadWindow` error.

To obtain the screen coordinates of the pointer or to determine the pointer coordinates relative to a specified window, use `XQueryPointer`.

Bool XQueryPointer (*display*, *w*, *root_return*, *child_return*, *root_x_return*, *root_y_return*, *win_x_return*, *win_y_return*, *mask_return*)
Display **display*;
Window *w*;
Window **root_return*, **child_return*;
int **root_x_return*, **root_y_return*;
int **win_x_return*, **win_y_return*;
unsigned int **mask_return*;

display Specifies the connection to the X server.
w Specifies the window.
root_return Returns the root window that the pointer is in.
child_return Returns the child window that the pointer is located in, if any.
root_x_return
root_y_return Return the pointer coordinates relative to the root window's origin.

win_x_return
win_y_return Return the pointer coordinates relative to the specified window.
mask_return Returns the current state of the modifier keys and pointer buttons.

The `XQueryPointer` function returns the root window the pointer is logically on and the pointer coordinates relative to the root window's origin. If `XQueryPointer` returns `False`, the pointer is not on the same screen as the specified window, and `XQueryPointer` returns `None` to child_return and zero to win_x_return and win_y_return. If `XQueryPointer` returns `True`, the pointer coordinates returned to win_x_return and win_y_return are relative to the origin of the specified window. In this case, `XQueryPointer` returns the child that contains the pointer, if any, or else `None` to child_return.

`XQueryPointer` returns the current logical state of the keyboard buttons and the modifier keys in mask_return. It sets mask_return to the bitwise inclusive OR of one or more of the button or modifier key bitmasks to match the current state of the mouse buttons and the modifier keys.

Note that the logical state of a device (as seen through Xlib) may lag the physical state if device event processing is frozen (see section 12.1).

`XQueryPointer` can generate a `BadWindow` error.

4.3 Properties and Atoms

A property is a collection of named, typed data. The window system has a set of predefined properties (for example, the name of a window, size hints, and so on), and users can define any other arbitrary information and associate it with windows. Each property has a name, which is an ISO Latin-1 string. For each named property, a unique identifier (atom) is associated with it. A property also has a type, for example, string or integer. These types are also indicated using atoms, so arbitrary new types can be defined. Data of only one type may be associated with a single property name. Clients can store and retrieve properties associated with windows. For efficiency reasons, an atom is used rather than a character string. `XInternAtom` can be used to obtain the atom for property names.

A property is also stored in one of several possible formats. The X server can store the information as 8-bit quantities, 16-bit quantities, or 32-bit quantities. This permits the X server to present the data in the byte order that the client expects.

Note If you define further properties of complex type, you must encode and decode them yourself. These functions must be carefully written if they are to be portable. For further information about how to write a library extension, see appendix C.

The type of a property is defined by an atom, which allows for arbitrary extension in this type scheme.

Certain property names are predefined in the server for commonly used functions. The atoms for these properties are defined in `<X11/Xatom.h>`. To avoid name clashes with user symbols, the `#define` name for each atom has the XA_ prefix. For definitions of these properties, see section 4.3. For an explanation of the functions that let you get and set much of the information stored in these predefined properties, see chapter 14.

The core protocol imposes no semantics on these property names, but semantics are specified in other X Consortium standards, such as the ''Inter-Client Communication Conventions Manual'' and the ''X Logical Font Description Conventions,'' which make up parts III and IV of this book.

You can use properties to communicate other information between applications. The functions described in this section let you define new properties and get the unique atom IDs in your applications.

Although any particular atom can have some client interpretation within each of the name spaces, atoms occur in five distinct name spaces within the protocol:

- Selections
- Property names
- Property types
- Font properties
- Type of a `ClientMessage` event (none are built into the X server)

The built-in selection property names are:

PRIMARY
SECONDARY

The built-in property names are:

CUT_BUFFER0	RESOURCE_MANAGER
CUT_BUFFER1	WM_CLASS
CUT_BUFFER2	WM_CLIENT_MACHINE
CUT_BUFFER3	WM_COLORMAP_WINDOWS
CUT_BUFFER4	WM_COMMAND
CUT_BUFFER5	WM_HINTS
CUT_BUFFER6	WM_ICON_NAME
CUT_BUFFER7	WM_ICON_SIZE
RGB_BEST_MAP	WM_NAME
RGB_BLUE_MAP	WM_NORMAL_HINTS
RGB_DEFAULT_MAP	WM_PROTOCOLS
RGB_GRAY_MAP	WM_STATE
RGB_GREEN_MAP	WM_TRANSIENT_FOR
RGB_RED_MAP	WM_ZOOM_HINTS

The built-in property types are:

ARC	POINT
ATOM	RGB_COLOR_MAP
BITMAP	RECTANGLE
CARDINAL	STRING
COLORMAP	VISUALID
CURSOR	WINDOW
DRAWABLE	WM_HINTS
FONT	WM_SIZE_HINTS
INTEGER	
PIXMAP	

The built-in font property names are:

MIN_SPACE	STRIKEOUT_DESCENT
NORM_SPACE	STRIKEOUT_ASCENT
MAX_SPACE	ITALIC_ANGLE
END_SPACE	X_HEIGHT
SUPERSCRIPT_X	QUAD_WIDTH
SUPERSCRIPT_Y	WEIGHT
SUBSCRIPT_X	POINT_SIZE
SUBSCRIPT_Y	RESOLUTION

UNDERLINE_POSITION	COPYRIGHT
UNDERLINE_THICKNESS	NOTICE
FONT_NAME	FAMILY_NAME
FULL_NAME	CAP_HEIGHT

For further information about font properties, see section 8.5.

To return an atom for a given name, use `XInternAtom`.

```
Atom XInternAtom ( display, atom_name, only_if_exists)
    Display *display;
    char *atom_name;
    Bool only_if_exists;
```

display Specifies the connection to the X server.

atom_name Specifies the name associated with the atom you want returned.

only_if_exists Specifies a Boolean value that indicates whether `XInternAtom` creates the atom.

The `XInternAtom` function returns the atom identifier associated with the specified atom_name string. If only_if_exists is `False`, the atom is created if it does not exist. Therefore, `XInternAtom` can return `None`. If the atom name is not in the Host Portable Character Encoding, the result is implementation dependent. Uppercase and lowercase matter; the strings "thing", "Thing", and "thinG" all designate different atoms. The atom will remain defined even after the client's connection closes. It will become undefined only when the last connection to the X server closes.

`XInternAtom` can generate `BadAlloc` and `BadValue` errors.

To return a name for a given atom identifier, use `XGetAtomName`.

```
char *XGetAtomName ( display, atom)
    Display *display;
    Atom atom;
```

display Specifies the connection to the X server.

atom Specifies the atom for the property name you want returned.

The `XGetAtomName` function returns the name associated with the specified atom. If the data returned by the server is in the Latin Portable Character Encoding, then the returned string is in the Host Portable Character Encoding. Otherwise, the result is implementation dependent. To free the resulting string, call `XFree`.

`XGetAtomName` can generate a `BadAtom` error.

4.4 Obtaining and Changing Window Properties

You can attach a property list to every window. Each property has a name, a type, and a value (see section 4.3). The value is an array of 8-bit, 16-bit, or 32-bit quantities, whose interpretation is left to the clients.

Xlib provides functions that you can use to obtain, change, update, or interchange window properties. In addition, Xlib provides other utility functions for inter-client communication (see chapter 14).

To obtain the type, format, and value of a property of a given window, use `XGetWindowProperty`.

```
int XGetWindowProperty ( display, w, property, long_offset, long_length, delete, req_type,
                         actual_type_return, actual_format_return, nitems_return,
                         bytes_after_return, prop_return)
    Display *display;
    Window w;
    Atom property;
    long long_offset, long_length;
    Bool delete;
    Atom req_type;
    Atom *actual_type_return;
    int *actual_format_return;
    unsigned long *nitems_return;
    unsigned long *bytes_after_return;
    unsigned char **prop_return;
```

display	Specifies the connection to the X server.
w	Specifies the window whose property you want to obtain.
property	Specifies the property name.
long_offset	Specifies the offset in the specified property (in 32-bit quantities) where the data is to be retrieved.
long_length	Specifies the length in 32-bit multiples of the data to be retrieved.
delete	Specifies a Boolean value that determines whether the property is deleted.
req_type	Specifies the atom identifier associated with the property type or `AnyPropertyType`.

actual_type_return	Returns the atom identifier that defines the actual type of the property.
actual_format_return	Returns the actual format of the property.
nitems_return	Returns the actual number of 8-bit, 16-bit, or 32-bit items stored in the prop_return data.
bytes_after_return	Returns the number of bytes remaining to be read in the property if a partial read was performed.
prop_return	Returns the data in the specified format.

The `XGetWindowProperty` function returns the actual type of the property; the actual format of the property; the number of 8-bit, 16-bit, or 32-bit items transferred; the number of bytes remaining to be read in the property; and a pointer to the data actually returned. `XGetWindowProperty` sets the return arguments as follows:

- If the specified property does not exist for the specified window, `XGetWindowProperty` returns `None` to actual_type_return and the value zero to actual_format_return and bytes_after_return. The nitems_return argument is empty. In this case, the delete argument is ignored.
- If the specified property exists but its type does not match the specified type, `XGetWindowProperty` returns the actual property type to actual_type_return, the actual property format (never zero) to actual_format_return, and the property length in bytes (even if the actual_format_return is 16 or 32) to bytes_after_return. It also ignores the delete argument. The nitems_return argument is empty.
- If the specified property exists and either you assign `AnyPropertyType` to the req_type argument or the specified type matches the actual property type, `XGetWindowProperty` returns the actual property type to actual_type_return and the actual property format (never zero) to actual_format_return. It also returns a value to bytes_after_return and nitems_return, by defining the following values:

  N = actual length of the stored property in bytes
  (even if the format is 16 or 32)
  I = 4 * long_offset
  T = N – I
  L = MINIMUM(T, 4 * long_length)
  A = N – (I + L)

The returned value starts at byte index I in the property (indexing from zero), and its length in bytes is L. If the value for long_offset causes L to be negative, a `BadValue` error results. The value of bytes_after_return is A, giving the number of trailing unread bytes in the stored property.

XGetWindowProperty always allocates one extra byte in prop_return (even if the property is zero length) and sets it to ASCII null so that simple properties consisting of characters do not have to be copied into yet another string before use. If delete is True and bytes_after_return is zero, XGetWindowProperty deletes the property from the window and generates a PropertyNotify event on the window.

The function returns Success if it executes successfully. To free the resulting data, use XFree.

XGetWindowProperty can generate BadAtom, BadValue, and BadWindow errors.

To obtain a given window's property list, use XListProperties.

Atom *XListProperties (*display*, *w*, *num_prop_return*)
  Display **display*;
  Window *w*;
  int **num_prop_return*;

display	Specifies the connection to the X server.
w	Specifies the window whose property list you want to obtain.
num_prop_return	Returns the length of the properties array.

The XListProperties function returns a pointer to an array of atom properties that are defined for the specified window or returns NULL if no properties were found. To free the memory allocated by this function, use XFree.

XListProperties can generate a BadWindow error.

To change a property of a given window, use XChangeProperty.

XChangeProperty (*display*, *w*, *property*, *type*, *format*, *mode*, *data*, *nelements*)
  Display **display*;
  Window *w*;
  Atom *property*, *type*;
  int *format*;
  int *mode*;
  unsigned char **data*;
  int *nelements*;

display	Specifies the connection to the X server.
w	Specifies the window whose property you want to change.

property Specifies the property name.
type Specifies the type of the property. The X server does not interpret the type but simply passes it back to an application that later calls XGetWindow-Property.
format Specifies whether the data should be viewed as a list of 8-bit, 16-bit, or 32-bit quantities. Possible values are 8, 16, and 32. This information allows the X server to correctly perform byte-swap operations as necessary. If the format is 16-bit or 32-bit, you must explicitly cast your data pointer to an (unsigned char *) in the call to XChangeProperty.
mode Specifies the mode of the operation. You can pass PropModeReplace, PropModePrepend, or PropModeAppend.
data Specifies the property data.
nelements Specifies the number of elements of the specified data format.

The XChangeProperty function alters the property for the specified window and causes the X server to generate a PropertyNotify event on that window. XChangeProperty performs the following:

- If mode is PropModeReplace, XChangeProperty discards the previous property value and stores the new data.
- If mode is PropModePrepend or PropModeAppend, XChangeProperty inserts the specified data before the beginning of the existing data or onto the end of the existing data, respectively. The type and format must match the existing property value, or a BadMatch error results. If the property is undefined, it is treated as defined with the correct type and format with zero-length data.

The lifetime of a property is not tied to the storing client. Properties remain until explicitly deleted, until the window is destroyed, or until the server resets. For a discussion of what happens when the connection to the X server is closed, see section 2.6. The maximum size of a property is server dependent and can vary dynamically depending on the amount of memory the server has available. (If there is insufficient space, a BadAlloc error results.)

XChangeProperty can generate BadAlloc, BadAtom, BadMatch, BadValue, and BadWindow errors.

To rotate a window's property list, use XRotateWindowProperties.

XRotateWindowProperties (*display, w, properties, num_prop, npositions*)
  Display **display*;
  Window *w*;

```
   Atom properties[];
   int num_prop;
   int npositions;
```

display Specifies the connection to the X server.
w Specifies the window.
properties Specifies the array of properties that are to be rotated.
num_prop Specifies the length of the properties array.
npositions Specifies the rotation amount.

The `XRotateWindowProperties` function allows you to rotate properties on a window and causes the X server to generate `PropertyNotify` events. If the property names in the properties array are viewed as being numbered starting from zero and if there are num_prop property names in the list, then the value associated with property name I becomes the value associated with property name (I + npositions) mod N for all I from zero to N – 1. The effect is to rotate the states by npositions places around the virtual ring of property names (right for positive npositions, left for negative npositions). If npositions mod N is nonzero, the X server generates a `PropertyNotify` event for each property in the order that they are listed in the array. If an atom occurs more than once in the list or no property with that name is defined for the window, a `BadMatch` error results. If a `BadAtom` or `BadMatch` error results, no properties are changed.

`XRotateWindowProperties` can generate `BadAtom`, `BadMatch`, and `BadWindow` errors.

To delete a property on a given window, use `XDeleteProperty`.

```
XDeleteProperty(display, w, property)
   Display *display;
   Window w;
   Atom property;
```

display Specifies the connection to the X server.
w Specifies the window whose property you want to delete.
property Specifies the property name.

The `XDeleteProperty` function deletes the specified property only if the property was defined on the specified window and causes the X server to generate a `PropertyNotify` event on the window unless the property does not exist.

`XDeleteProperty` can generate `BadAtom` and `BadWindow` errors.

4.5 Selections

Selections are one method used by applications to exchange data. By using the property mechanism, applications can exchange data of arbitrary types and can negotiate the type of the data. A selection can be thought of as an indirect property with a dynamic type. That is, rather than having the property stored in the X server, the property is maintained by some client (the owner). A selection is global in nature (considered to belong to the user but be maintained by clients) rather than being private to a particular window subhierarchy or a particular set of clients.

Xlib provides functions that you can use to set, get, or request conversion of selections. This allows applications to implement the notion of current selection, which requires that notification be sent to applications when they no longer own the selection. Applications that support selection often highlight the current selection and so must be informed when another application has acquired the selection so that they can unhighlight the selection.

When a client asks for the contents of a selection, it specifies a selection target type. This target type can be used to control the transmitted representation of the contents. For example, if the selection is "the last thing the user clicked on" and that is currently an image, then the target type might specify whether the contents of the image should be sent in XY format or Z format.

The target type can also be used to control the class of contents transmitted, for example, asking for the "looks" (fonts, line spacing, indentation, and so forth) of a paragraph selection, not the text of the paragraph. The target type can also be used for other purposes. The protocol does not constrain the semantics.

To set the selection owner, use `XSetSelectionOwner`.

XSetSelectionOwner(*display*, *selection*, *owner*, *time*)
  Display **display*;
  Atom *selection*;
  Window *owner*;
  Time *time*;

display Specifies the connection to the X server.

selection Specifies the selection atom.

owner Specifies the owner of the specified selection atom. You can pass a window or `None`.

time Specifies the time. You can pass either a timestamp or `CurrentTime`.

The `XSetSelectionOwner` function changes the owner and last-change time for the specified selection and has no effect if the specified time is earlier than the current last-change time of the specified selection or is later than the current X server time. Otherwise, the last-change time is set to the specified time, with `CurrentTime` replaced by the current server time. If the owner window is specified as `None`, then the owner of the selection becomes `None` (that is, no owner). Otherwise, the owner of the selection becomes the client executing the request.

If the new owner (whether a client or `None`) is not the same as the current owner of the selection and the current owner is not `None`, the current owner is sent a `SelectionClear` event. If the client that is the owner of a selection is later terminated (that is, its connection is closed) or if the owner window it has specified in the request is later destroyed, the owner of the selection automatically reverts to `None`, but the last-change time is not affected. The selection atom is uninterpreted by the X server. `XGetSelectionOwner` returns the owner window, which is reported in `SelectionRequest` and `SelectionClear` events. Selections are global to the X server.

`XSetSelectionOwner` can generate `BadAtom` and `BadWindow` errors.

To return the selection owner, use `XGetSelectionOwner`.

```
Window XGetSelectionOwner(display, selection)
    Display *display;
    Atom selection;
```

display Specifies the connection to the X server.

selection Specifies the selection atom whose owner you want returned.

The `XGetSelectionOwner` function returns the window ID associated with the window that currently owns the specified selection. If no selection was specified, the function returns the constant `None`. If `None` is returned, there is no owner for the selection.

`XGetSelectionOwner` can generate a `BadAtom` error.

To request conversion of a selection, use `XConvertSelection`.

```
XConvertSelection(display, selection, target, property, requestor, time)
    Display *display;
    Atom selection, target;
```

```
    Atom property;
    Window requestor;
    Time time;
```

display Specifies the connection to the X server.
selection Specifies the selection atom.
target Specifies the target atom.
property Specifies the property name. You also can pass `None`.
requestor Specifies the requestor.
time Specifies the time. You can pass either a timestamp or `CurrentTime`.

`XConvertSelection` requests that the specified selection be converted to the specified target type:

- If the specified selection has an owner, the X server sends a `SelectionRequest` event to that owner.
- If no owner for the specified selection exists, the X server generates a `Selection-Notify` event to the requestor with property `None`.

The arguments are passed on unchanged in either of the events. There are two predefined selection atoms: PRIMARY and SECONDARY.

`XConvertSelection` can generate `BadAtom` and `BadWindow` errors.

Chapter 5

Pixmap and Cursor Functions

Once you have connected to an X server, you can use the Xlib functions to:

- Create and free pixmaps
- Create, recolor, and free cursors

5.1 Creating and Freeing Pixmaps

Pixmaps can only be used on the screen on which they were created. Pixmaps are off-screen resources that are used for various operations, for example, defining cursors as tiling patterns or as the source for certain raster operations. Most graphics requests can operate either on a window or on a pixmap. A bitmap is a single bit-plane pixmap.

To create a pixmap of a given size, use `XCreatePixmap`.

Pixmap XCreatePixmap (*display*, *d*, *width*, *height*, *depth*)
  Display **display*;
  Drawable *d*;
  unsigned int *width*, *height*;
  unsigned int *depth*;

display Specifies the connection to the X server.
d Specifies which screen the pixmap is created on.

width
height Specify the width and height, which define the dimensions of the pixmap.
depth Specifies the depth of the pixmap.

The `XCreatePixmap` function creates a pixmap of the width, height, and depth you specified and returns a pixmap ID that identifies it. It is valid to pass an `InputOnly` window to the drawable argument. The width and height arguments must be nonzero, or a `BadValue` error results. The depth argument must be one of the depths supported by the screen of the specified drawable, or a `BadValue` error results.

The server uses the specified drawable to determine on which screen to create the pixmap. The pixmap can be used only on this screen and only with other drawables of the same depth (see `XCopyPlane` for an exception to this rule). The initial contents of the pixmap are undefined.

`XCreatePixmap` can generate `BadAlloc`, `BadDrawable`, and `BadValue` errors.

To free all storage associated with a specified pixmap, use `XFreePixmap`.

```
XFreePixmap ( display, pixmap)
    Display *display;
    Pixmap pixmap;
```

display Specifies the connection to the X server.
pixmap Specifies the pixmap.

The `XFreePixmap` function first deletes the association between the pixmap ID and the pixmap. Then, the X server frees the pixmap storage when there are no references to it. The pixmap should never be referenced again.

`XFreePixmap` can generate a `BadPixmap` error.

5.2 Creating, Recoloring, and Freeing Cursors

Each window can have a different cursor defined for it. Whenever the pointer is in a visible window, it is set to the cursor defined for that window. If no cursor was defined for that window, the cursor is the one defined for the parent window.

From X's perspective, a cursor consists of a cursor source, mask, colors, and a hotspot. The mask pixmap determines the shape of the cursor and must be a depth of one. The source pixmap must have a depth of one, and the colors determine the colors of the source. The hotspot defines the point on the cursor that is reported when a pointer event occurs. There may be limitations imposed by the hardware on cursors as to size and whether a mask is implemented. `XQueryBestCursor` can be used to find out what sizes are possible. There is a standard font for creating cursors, but Xlib provides functions that you can use to create cursors from an arbitrary font or from bitmaps.

To create a cursor from the standard cursor font, use `XCreateFontCursor`.

```
#include <X11/cursorfont.h>
Cursor XCreateFontCursor ( display, shape)
    Display *display;
    unsigned int shape;
```

display Specifies the connection to the X server.
shape Specifies the shape of the cursor.

X provides a set of standard cursor shapes in a special font named cursor. Applications are encouraged to use this interface for their cursors because the font can be customized for the individual display type. The shape argument specifies which glyph of the standard fonts to use.

The hotspot comes from the information stored in the cursor font. The initial colors of a cursor are a black foreground and a white background (see `XRecolorCursor`). For further information about cursor shapes, see appendix B.

`XCreateFontCursor` can generate `BadAlloc` and `BadValue` errors.

To create a cursor from font glyphs, use `XCreateGlyphCursor`.

```
Cursor XCreateGlyphCursor ( display, source_font, mask_font, source_char, mask_char,
                            foreground_color, background_color)
    Display *display;
    Font source_font, mask_font;
    unsigned int source_char, mask_char;
    XColor *foreground_color;
    XColor *background_color;
```

display Specifies the connection to the X server.
source_font Specifies the font for the source glyph.
mask_font Specifies the font for the mask glyph or `None`.
source_char Specifies the character glyph for the source.

mask_char	Specifies the glyph character for the mask.
foreground_color	Specifies the RGB values for the foreground of the source.
background_color	Specifies the RGB values for the background of the source.

The `XCreateGlyphCursor` function is similar to `XCreatePixmapCursor` except that the source and mask bitmaps are obtained from the specified font glyphs. The source_char must be a defined glyph in source_font, or a `BadValue` error results. If mask_font is given, mask_char must be a defined glyph in mask_font, or a `BadValue` error results. The mask_font and character are optional. The origins of the source_char and mask_char (if defined) glyphs are positioned coincidently and define the hotspot. The source_char and mask_char need not have the same bounding box metrics, and there is no restriction on the placement of the hotspot relative to the bounding boxes. If no mask_char is given, all pixels of the source are displayed. You can free the fonts immediately by calling `XFreeFont` if no further explicit references to them are to be made.

For 2-byte matrix fonts, the 16-bit value should be formed with the byte1 member in the most-significant byte and the byte2 member in the least-significant byte.

`XCreateGlyphCursor` can generate `BadAlloc`, `BadFont`, and `BadValue` errors.

To create a cursor from two bitmaps, use `XCreatePixmapCursor`.

```
Cursor XCreatePixmapCursor ( display, source, mask, foreground_color,
                             background_color, x, y)
   Display *display;
   Pixmap source;
   Pixmap mask;
   XColor *foreground_color;
   XColor *background_color;
   unsigned int x, y;
```

display	Specifies the connection to the X server.
source	Specifies the shape of the source cursor.
mask	Specifies the cursor's source bits to be displayed or `None`.
foreground_color	Specifies the RGB values for the foreground of the source.
background_color	Specifies the RGB values for the background of the source.
x	
y	Specify the x and y coordinates which indicate the hotspot relative to the source's origin.

The XCreatePixmapCursor function creates a cursor and returns the cursor ID associated with it. The foreground and background RGB values must be specified using foreground_color and background_color, even if the X server only has a StaticGray or GrayScale screen. The foreground color is used for the pixels set to 1 in the source, and the background color is used for the pixels set to 0. Both source and mask, if specified, must have depth one (or a BadMatch error results) but can have any root. The mask argument defines the shape of the cursor. The pixels set to 1 in the mask define which source pixels are displayed, and the pixels set to 0 define which pixels are ignored. If no mask is given, all pixels of the source are displayed. The mask, if present, must be the same size as the pixmap defined by the source argument, or a BadMatch error results. The hotspot must be a point within the source, or a BadMatch error results.

The components of the cursor can be transformed arbitrarily to meet display limitations. The pixmaps can be freed immediately if no further explicit references to them are to be made. Subsequent drawing in the source or mask pixmap has an undefined effect on the cursor. The X server might or might not make a copy of the pixmap.

XCreatePixmapCursor can generate BadAlloc and BadPixmap errors.

To determine useful cursor sizes, use XQueryBestCursor.

Status XQueryBestCursor (*display, d, width, height, width_return, height_return*)
Display **display*;
Drawable *d*;
unsigned int *width, height*;
unsigned int **width_return, *height_return*;

display	Specifies the connection to the X server.
d	Specifies the drawable, which indicates the screen.
width *height*	Specify the width and height of the cursor that you want the size information for.
width_return *height_return*	Return the best width and height that is closest to the specified width and height.

Some displays allow larger cursors than other displays. The XQueryBestCursor function provides a way to find out what size cursors are actually possible on the display. It returns the largest size that can be displayed. Applications should be prepared to use smaller cursors on displays that cannot support large ones.

XQueryBestCursor can generate a BadDrawable error.

To change the color of a given cursor, use XRecolorCursor.

XRecolorCursor (*display, cursor, foreground_color, background_color*)
  Display **display*;
  Cursor *cursor*;
  XColor **foreground_color*, **background_color*;

display	Specifies the connection to the X server.
cursor	Specifies the cursor.
foreground_color	Specifies the RGB values for the foreground of the source.
background_color	Specifies the RGB values for the background of the source.

The XRecolorCursor function changes the color of the specified cursor, and if the cursor is being displayed on a screen, the change is visible immediately. The pixel members of the XColor structures are ignored: only the RGB values are used.

XRecolorCursor can generate a BadCursor error.

To free (destroy) a given cursor, use XFreeCursor.

XFreeCursor (*display, cursor*)
  Display **display*;
  Cursor *cursor*;

display	Specifies the connection to the X server.
cursor	Specifies the cursor.

The XFreeCursor function deletes the association between the cursor resource ID and the specified cursor. The cursor storage is freed when no other resource references it. The specified cursor ID should not be referred to again.

XFreeCursor can generate a BadCursor error.

Chapter 6

Color Management Functions

Each X window always has an associated colormap that provides a level of indirection between pixel values and colors displayed on the screen. Xlib provides functions that you can use to manipulate a colormap. The X protocol defines colors using values in the RGB color space. The RGB color space is device-dependent; rendering an RGB value on differing output devices typically results in different colors. Xlib also provides a means for clients to specify color using device-independent color spaces for consistent results across devices. Xlib supports device-independent color spaces derivable from the CIE XYZ color space. This includes the CIE XYZ, xyY, L*u*v*, and L*a*b* color spaces as well as the TekHVC color space.

This chapter discusses how to:

- Create, copy, and destroy a colormap
- Specify colors by name or value
- Allocate, modify, and free color cells
- Read entries in a colormap
- Convert between color spaces
- Control aspects of color conversion
- Query the color gamut of a screen
- Add new color spaces

All functions, types, and symbols in this chapter with the prefix "Xcms" are defined in `<X11/Xcms.h>`. The remaining functions and types are defined in `<X11/Xlib.h>`.

Functions in this chapter manipulate the representation of color on the screen. For each possible value that a pixel can take in a window, there is a color cell in the colormap. For example, if a window is four bits deep, pixel values 0 through 15 are defined. A colormap is a collection of color cells. A color cell consists of a triple of red, green, and blue values. The hardware imposes limits on the number of significant bits in these values. As each pixel is read out of display memory, the pixel is looked up in a colormap. The RGB value of the cell determines what color is displayed on the screen. On a grayscale display with a black-and-white monitor, the values are combined to determine the brightness on the screen.

Typically, an application allocates color cells or sets of color cells to obtain the desired colors. The client can allocate read-only cells. In which case, the pixel values for these colors can be shared among multiple applications, and the RGB value of the cell cannot be changed. If the client allocates read/write cells, they are exclusively owned by the client, and the color associated with the pixel value can be changed at will. Cells must be allocated (and, if read/write, initialized with an RGB value) by a client to obtain desired colors. The use of a pixel value for an unallocated cell results in an undefined color.

Because colormaps are associated with windows, X supports displays with multiple colormaps and, indeed, different types of colormaps. If there are insufficient colormap resources in the display, some windows will display in their true colors, and others will display with incorrect colors. A window manager usually controls which windows are displayed in their true colors if more than one colormap is required for the color resources the applications are using. At any time, there is a set of installed colormaps for a screen. Windows using one of the installed colormaps display with true colors, and windows using other colormaps generally display with incorrect colors. You control the set of installed colormaps by using `XInstallColormap` and `XUninstallColormap`.

Colormaps are local to a particular screen. Screens always have a default colormap, and programs typically allocate cells out of this colormap. Generally, you should not write applications that monopolize color resources. Although some hardware supports multiple colormaps installed at one time, many of the hardware displays built today support only a single installed colormap, so the primitives are written to encourage sharing of colormap entries between applications.

The `DefaultColormap` macro returns the default colormap. The `DefaultVisual` macro returns the default visual type for the specified screen. Possible visual types are `StaticGray`, `GrayScale`, `StaticColor`, `PseudoColor`, `TrueColor`, or `DirectColor` (see section 3.1).

6.1 Color Structures

Functions that operate only on RGB color space values use an `XColor` structure, which contains:

```
typedef struct {
    unsigned long pixel;                /* pixel value */
    unsigned short red, green, blue;    /* rgb values */
    char flags;                         /* DoRed, DoGreen, DoBlue */
    char pad;
} XColor;
```

The red, green, and blue values are always in the range 0 to 65535 inclusive, independent of the number of bits actually used in the display hardware. The server scales these values down to the range used by the hardware. Black is represented by (0,0,0), and white is represented by (65535,65535,65535). In some functions, the flags member controls which of the red, green, and blue members is used and can be the inclusive OR of zero or more of `DoRed`, `DoGreen`, and `DoBlue`.

Functions that operate on all color space values use an `XcmsColor` structure. This structure contains a union of substructures, each supporting color specification encoding for a particular color space. Like the `XColor` structure, the `XcmsColor` structure contains pixel and color specification information (the spec member in the `XcmsColor` structure).

```
typedef unsigned long XcmsColorFormat;      /* Color Specification Format */
typedef struct {
    union {
            XcmsRGB RGB;
            XcmsRGBi RGBi;
            XcmsCIEXYZ CIEXYZ;
            XcmsCIEuvY CIEuvY;
```

```
                XcmsCIExyY CIExyY;
                XcmsCIELab CIELab;
                XcmsCIELuv CIELuv;
                XcmsTekHVC TekHVC;
                XcmsPad Pad;
        } spec;
        XcmsColorFormat format;
        unsigned long pixel;
} XcmsColor;                    /* Xcms Color Structure */
```

Because the color specification can be encoded for the various color spaces, encoding for the spec member is identified by the format member, which is of type `XcmsColorFormat`. The following macros define standard formats.

```
#define XcmsUndefinedFormat    0x00000000
#define XcmsCIEXYZFormat       0x00000001      /* CIE XYZ */
#define XcmsCIEuvYFormat       0x00000002      /* CIE u'v'Y*/
#define XcmsCIExyYFormat       0x00000003      /* CIE xyY*/
#define XcmsCIELabFormat       0x00000004      /* CIE L*a*b* */
#define XcmsCIELuvFormat       0x00000005      /* CIE L*u*v* */
#define XcmsTekHVCFormat       0x00000006      /* TekHVC */
#define XcmsRGBFormat          0x80000000      /* RGB Device */
#define XcmsRGBiFormat         0x80000001      /* RGB Intensity */
```

Note that formats for device-independent color spaces are distinguishable from those for device-dependent spaces by the 32nd bit. If this bit is set, it indicates that the color specification is in a device-dependent form; otherwise, it is in a device-independent form. If the 31st bit is set, this indicates that the color space has been added to Xlib at run time (see section 6.12.4). The format value for a color space added at run time may be different each time the program is executed. If references to such a color space must be made outside the client (for example, storing a color specification in a file), then reference should be made by color space string prefix (see `XcmsFormatOfPrefix` and `XcmsPrefixOfFormat`).

Data types that describe the color specification encoding for the various color spaces are defined as follows:

```
typedef double XcmsFloat;

typedef struct {
        unsigned short red;     /* 0x0000 to 0xffff */
```

```
        unsigned short green;       /* 0x0000 to 0xffff */
        unsigned short blue;        /* 0x0000 to 0xffff */
} XcmsRGB;                          /* RGB Device */

typedef struct {
        XcmsFloat red;              /* 0.0 to 1.0 */
        XcmsFloat green;            /* 0.0 to 1.0 */
        XcmsFloat blue;             /* 0.0 to 1.0 */
} XcmsRGBi;                         /* RGB Intensity */

typedef struct {
        XcmsFloat X;
        XcmsFloat Y;                /* 0.0 to 1.0 */
        XcmsFloat Z;
} XcmsCIEXYZ;                       /* CIE XYZ */

typedef struct {
        XcmsFloat u_prime;          /* 0.0 to ~0.6 */
        XcmsFloat v_prime;          /* 0.0 to ~0.6 */
        XcmsFloat Y;                /* 0.0 to 1.0 */
} XcmsCIEuvY;                       /* CIE u'v'Y */

typedef struct {
        XcmsFloat x;                /* 0.0 to ~.75 */
        XcmsFloat y;                /* 0.0 to ~.85 */
        XcmsFloat Y;                /* 0.0 to 1.0 */
} XcmsCIExyY;                       /* CIE xyY */

typedef struct {
        XcmsFloat L_star;           /* 0.0 to 100.0 */
        XcmsFloat a_star;
        XcmsFloat b_star;
} XcmsCIELab;                       /* CIE L*a*b* */

typedef struct {
        XcmsFloat L_star;           /* 0.0 to 100.0 */
        XcmsFloat u_star;
        XcmsFloat v_star;
} XcmsCIELuv;                       /* CIE L*u*v* */
```

```
typedef struct {
    XcmsFloat H;            /* 0.0 to 360.0 */
    XcmsFloat V;            /* 0.0 to 100.0 */
    XcmsFloat C;            /* 0.0 to 100.0 */
} XcmsTekHVC;               /* TekHVC */

typedef struct {
    XcmsFloat pad0;
    XcmsFloat pad1;
    XcmsFloat pad2;
    XcmsFloat pad3;
} XcmsPad;                  /* four doubles */
```

The device-dependent formats provided allow color specification in:

- RGB Intensity (`XcmsRGBi`)
  Red, green, and blue linear intensity values, floating-point values from 0.0 to 1.0, where 1.0 indicates full intensity, 0.5 half intensity, and so on.
- RGB Device (`XcmsRGB`)
  Red, green, and blue values appropriate for the specified output device. `XcmsRGB` values are of type unsigned short, scaled from 0 to 65535 inclusive, and are interchangeable with the red, green, and blue values in an `XColor` structure.

It is important to note that RGB Intensity values are not gamma corrected values. In contrast, RGB Device values generated as a result of converting color specifications are always gamma corrected, and RGB Device values acquired as a result of querying a colormap or passed in by the client are assumed by Xlib to be gamma corrected. The term *RGB value* in this book always refers to an RGB Device value.

6.2 Color Strings

Xlib provides a mechanism for using string names for colors. A color string may either contain an abstract color name or a numerical color specification. Color strings are case-insensitive.

Color strings are used in the following functions:

- `XAllocNamedColor`
- `XcmsAllocNamedColor`
- `XLookupColor`
- `XcmsLookupColor`

- `XParseColor`
- `XStoreNamedColor`

Xlib supports the use of abstract color names, for example, red or blue. A value for this abstract name is obtained by searching one or more color name databases. Xlib first searches zero or more client-side databases; the number, location, and content of these databases is implementation dependent and might depend on the current locale. If the name is not found, Xlib then looks for the color in the X server's database. If the color name is not in the Host Portable Character Encoding the result is implementation dependent.

A numerical color specification consists of a color space name and a set of values in the following syntax:

<color_space_name>:<value>/.../<value>

The following are examples of valid color strings.

"CIEXYZ:0.3227/0.28133/0.2493"
"RGBi:1.0/0.0/0.0"
"rgb:00/ff/00"
"CIELuv:50.0/0.0/0.0"

The syntax and semantics of numerical specifications are given for each standard color space in the following sections.

6.2.1 RGB Device String Specification

An RGB Device specification is identified by the prefix "rgb:" and conforms to the following syntax:

rgb:*<red>/<green>/<blue>*

<red>, *<green>*, *<blue>* := *h* | *hh* | *hhh* | *hhhh*
h := single hexadecimal digits (case insignificant)

Note that *h* indicates the value scaled in 4 bits, *hh* the value scaled in 8 bits, *hhh* the value scaled in 12 bits, and *hhhh* the value scaled in 16 bits, respectively.

Typical examples are the strings "rgb:ea/75/52" and "rgb:ccc/320/320", but mixed numbers of hexadecimal digit strings ("rgb:ff/a5/0" and "rgb:ccc/32/0") are also allowed.

For backward compatibility, an older syntax for RGB Device is supported, but its continued use is not encouraged. The syntax is an initial sharp sign character followed by a numeric specification, in one of the following formats:

```
#RGB              (4 bits each)
#RRGGBB           (8 bits each)
#RRRGGGBBB        (12 bits each)
#RRRRGGGGBBBB     (16 bits each)
```

The R, G, and B represent single hexadecimal digits. When fewer than 16 bits each are specified, they represent the most-significant bits of the value (unlike the "rgb:" syntax, in which values are scaled). For example, the string "#3a7" is the same as "#3000a0007000".

6.2.2 RGB Intensity String Specification

An RGB intensity specification is identified by the prefix "rgbi:" and conforms to the following syntax:

```
rgbi:<red>/<green>/<blue>
```

Note that red, green, and blue are floating-point values between 0.0 and 1.0, inclusive. The input format for these values is an optional sign, a string of numbers possibly containing a decimal point, and an optional exponent field containing an E or e followed by a possibly signed integer string.

6.2.3 Device-Independent String Specifications

The standard device-independent string specifications have the following syntax:

```
CIEXYZ:<X>/<Y>/<Z>
CIEuvY:<u>/<v>/<Y>
CIExyY:<x>/<y>/<Y>
CIELab:<L>/<a>/<b>
CIELuv:<L>/<u>/<v>
TekHVC:<H>/<V>/<C>
```

All of the values (C, H, V, X, Y, Z, a, b, u, v, y, x) are floating-point values. The syntax for these values is an optional plus or minus sign, a string of digits possibly containing a decimal point, and an optional exponent field consisting of the character "E" or "e" followed by an optional plus or minus sign followed by a string of digits.

6.3 Color Conversion Contexts and Gamut Mapping

When Xlib converts device-independent color specifications into device-dependent specifications and vice-versa, it uses knowledge about the color limitations of the screen hardware. This information, typically called the device profile, is available in a Color Conversion Context (CCC).

Because a specified color may be outside the color gamut of the target screen and the white point associated with the color specification may differ from the white point inherent to the screen, Xlib applies gamut mapping when it encounters certain conditions:

- Gamut compression occurs when conversion of device-independent color specifications to device-dependent color specifications results in a color out of the target screen's gamut.
- White adjustment occurs when the inherent white point of the screen differs from the white point assumed by the client.

Gamut handling methods are stored as callbacks in the CCC, which in turn are used by the color space conversion routines. Client data is also stored in the CCC for each callback. The CCC also contains the white point the client assumes to be associated with color specifications (that is, the Client White Point). The client can specify the gamut handling callbacks and client data as well as the Client White Point. Note that Xlib does not preclude the X client from performing other forms of gamut handling (for example, gamut expansion); however, Xlib does not provide direct support for gamut handling other than white adjustment and gamut compression.

Associated with each colormap is an initial CCC transparently generated by Xlib. Therefore, when you specify a colormap as an argument to an Xlib function, you are indirectly specifying a CCC. There is a default CCC associated with each screen. Newly created CCCs inherit attributes from the default CCC, so the default CCC attributes can be modified to affect new CCCs.

Xcms functions in which gamut mapping can occur return `Status` and have specific status values defined for them, as follows:

- `XcmsFailure` indicates that the function failed.
- `XcmsSuccess` indicates that the function succeeded. In addition, if the function performed any color conversion, the colors did not need to be compressed.
- `XcmsSuccessWithCompression` indicates the function performed color conversion and at least one of the colors needed to be compressed. The gamut compression method is determined by the gamut compression procedure in the CCC that is specified directly as a function argument or in the CCC indirectly specified by means of the colormap argument.

6.4 Creating, Copying, and Destroying Colormaps

To create a colormap for a screen, use `XCreateColormap`.

```
Colormap XCreateColormap ( display, w, visual, alloc)
    Display *display;
    Window w;
    Visual *visual;
    int alloc;
```

display Specifies the connection to the X server.

w Specifies the window on whose screen you want to create a colormap.

visual Specifies a visual type supported on the screen. If the visual type is not one supported by the screen, a `BadMatch` error results.

alloc Specifies the colormap entries to be allocated. You can pass `AllocNone` or `AllocAll`.

The `XCreateColormap` function creates a colormap of the specified visual type for the screen on which the specified window resides and returns the colormap ID associated with it. Note that the specified window is only used to determine the screen.

The initial values of the colormap entries are undefined for the visual classes `GrayScale`, `PseudoColor`, and `DirectColor`. For `StaticGray`, `StaticColor`, and `TrueColor`, the entries have defined values, but those values are specific to the visual and are not defined by X. For `StaticGray`, `StaticColor`, and `TrueColor`, alloc must be `AllocNone`, or a `BadMatch` error results. For the other visual classes, if alloc is `AllocNone`, the colormap initially has no allocated entries, and clients can allocate them. For information about the visual types, see section 3.1.

If alloc is `AllocAll`, the entire colormap is allocated writable. The initial values of all allocated entries are undefined. For `GrayScale` and `PseudoColor`, the effect is as if an XAllocColorCells call returned all pixel values from zero to N − 1, where N is the colormap entries value in the specified visual. For DirectColor, the effect is as if an XAllocColorPlanes call returned a pixel value of zero and red_mask, green_mask, and blue_mask values containing the same bits as the corresponding masks in the specified visual. However, in all cases, none of these entries can be freed by using XFreeColors.

XCreateColormap can generate BadAlloc, BadMatch, BadValue, and BadWindow errors.

To create a new colormap when the allocation out of a previously shared colormap has failed because of resource exhaustion, use XCopyColormapAndFree.

```
Colormap XCopyColormapAndFree ( display, colormap)
    Display *display;
    Colormap colormap;
```

display Specifies the connection to the X server.

colormap Specifies the colormap.

The XCopyColormapAndFree function creates a colormap of the same visual type and for the same screen as the specified colormap and returns the new colormap ID. It also moves all of the client's existing allocation from the specified colormap to the new colormap with their color values intact and their read-only or writable characteristics intact and frees those entries in the specified colormap. Color values in other entries in the new colormap are undefined. If the specified colormap was created by the client with alloc set to AllocAll, the new colormap is also created with AllocAll, all color values for all entries are copied from the specified colormap, and then all entries in the specified colormap are freed. If the specified colormap was not created by the client with AllocAll, the allocations to be moved are all those pixels and planes that have been allocated by the client using XAllocColor, XAllocNamedColor, XAllocColorCells, or XAllocColorPlanes and that have not been freed since they were allocated.

XCopyColormapAndFree can generate BadAlloc and BadColor errors.

To destroy a colormap, use XFreeColormap.

```
XFreeColormap ( display, colormap)
    Display *display;
```

```
   Colormap colormap;
display     Specifies the connection to the X server.
colormap    Specifies the colormap that you want to destroy.
```

The XFreeColormap function deletes the association between the colormap resource ID and the colormap and frees the colormap storage. However, this function has no effect on the default colormap for a screen. If the specified colormap is an installed map for a screen, it is uninstalled (see XUninstallColormap). If the specified colormap is defined as the colormap for a window (by XCreateWindow, XSetWindowColormap, or XChangeWindowAttributes), XFreeColormap changes the colormap associated with the window to None and generates a ColormapNotify event. X does not define the colors displayed for a window with a colormap of None.

XFreeColormap can generate a BadColor error.

6.5 Mapping Color Names to Values

To map a color name to an RGB value, use XLookupColor.

```
Status XLookupColor (display, colormap, color_name, exact_def_return, screen_def_return)
   Display *display;
   Colormap colormap;
   char *color_name;
   XColor *exact_def_return, *screen_def_return;
display            Specifies the connection to the X server.
colormap           Specifies the colormap.
color_name         Specifies the color name string (for example, red) whose color
                   definition structure you want returned.
exact_def_return   Returns the exact RGB values.
screen_def_return  Returns the closest RGB values provided by the hardware.
```

The XLookupColor function looks up the string name of a color with respect to the screen associated with the specified colormap. It returns both the exact color values and the closest values provided by the screen with respect to the visual type of the specified colormap. If the color name is not in the Host Portable Character Encoding, the result is implementation dependent. Use of uppercase or lowercase does not matter. XLookupColor returns nonzero if the name is resolved; otherwise, it returns zero.

XLookupColor can generate a BadColor error.

To map a color name to the exact RGB value, use `XParseColor`.

```
Status XParseColor ( display, colormap, spec, exact_def_return)
    Display *display;
    Colormap colormap;
    char *spec;
    XColor *exact_def_return;
```

display	Specifies the connection to the X server.
colormap	Specifies the colormap.
spec	Specifies the color name string; case is ignored.
exact_def_return	Returns the exact color value for later use and sets the `DoRed`, `DoGreen`, and `DoBlue` flags.

The `XParseColor` function looks up the string name of a color with respect to the screen associated with the specified colormap. It returns the exact color value. If the color name is not in the Host Portable Character Encoding, the result is implementation dependent. Use of uppercase or lowercase does not matter. `XParseColor` returns nonzero if the name is resolved; otherwise, it returns zero.

`XParseColor` can generate a `BadColor` error.

To map a color name to a value in an arbitrary color space, use `XcmsLookupColor`.

```
Status XcmsLookupColor ( display, colormap, color_string, color_exact_return,
                         color_screen_return, result_format)
    Display *display;
    Colormap colormap;
    char *color_string;
    XcmsColor *color_exact_return, *color_screen_return;
    XcmsColorFormat result_format;
```

display	Specifies the connection to the X server.
colormap	Specifies the colormap.
color_string	Specifies the color string.
color_exact_return	Returns the color specification parsed from the color string or parsed from the corresponding string found in a color name database.
color_screen_return	Returns the color that can be reproduced on the screen .
result_format	Specifies the color format for the returned color specifications (color_screen_return and color_exact_return arguments). If the

format is XcmsUndefinedFormat and the color string contains a numerical color specification, the specification is returned in the format used in that numerical color specification. If the format is XcmsUndefinedFormat and the color string contains a color name, the specification is returned in the format used to store the color in the database.

The XcmsLookupColor function looks up the string name of a color with respect to the screen associated with the specified colormap. It returns both the exact color values and the closest values provided by the screen with respect to the visual type of the specified colormap. The values are returned in the format specified by result_format. If the color name is not in the Host Portable Character Encoding, the result is implementation dependent. Use of uppercase or lowercase does not matter. XcmsLookupColor returns XcmsSuccess or XcmsSuccessWithCompression if the name is resolved; otherwise, it returns XcmsFailure. If XcmsSuccessWithCompression is returned, the color specification returned in color_screen_return is the result of gamut compression.

6.6 Allocating and Freeing Color Cells

There are two ways of allocating color cells: explicitly as read-only entries, one pixel value at a time, or read/write, where you can allocate a number of color cells and planes simultaneously. A read-only cell has its RGB value set by the server. Read/write cells do not have defined colors initially; functions described in the next section must be used to store values into them. Although it is possible for any client to store values into a read/write cell allocated by another client, read/write cells normally should be considered private to the client that allocated them.

Read-only colormap cells are shared among clients. The server counts each allocation and free of the cell by clients. When the last client frees a shared cell, the cell is finally deallocated. If a single client allocates the same read-only cell multiple times, the server counts each such allocation, not just the first one.

To allocate a read-only color cell with an RGB value, use XAllocColor.

Status XAllocColor (*display*, *colormap*, *screen_in_out*)
   Display **display*;

Colormap *colormap*;
XColor **screen_in_out*;

display	Specifies the connection to the X server.
colormap	Specifies the colormap.
screen_in_out	Specifies and returns the values actually used in the colormap.

The `XAllocColor` function allocates a read-only colormap entry corresponding to the closest RGB value supported by the hardware. `XAllocColor` returns the pixel value of the color closest to the specified RGB elements supported by the hardware and returns the RGB value actually used. The corresponding colormap cell is read-only. In addition, `XAllocColor` returns nonzero if it succeeded or zero if it failed. Multiple clients that request the same effective RGB value can be assigned the same read-only entry, thus allowing entries to be shared. When the last client deallocates a shared cell, it is deallocated. `XAllocColor` does not use or affect the flags in the `XColor` structure.

`XAllocColor` can generate a `BadColor` error.

To allocate a read-only color cell with a color in arbitrary format, use `XcmsAllocColor`.

Status XcmsAllocColor (*display*, *colormap*, *color_in_out*, *result_format*)
Display **display*;
Colormap *colormap*;
XcmsColor **color_in_out*;
XcmsColorFormat *result_format*;

display	Specifies the connection to the X server.
colormap	Specifies the colormap.
color_in_out	Specifies the color to allocate and returns the pixel and color that is actually used in the colormap.
result_format	Specifies the color format for the returned color specification.

The `XcmsAllocColor` function is similar to `XAllocColor` except the color can be specified in any format. The `XcmsAllocColor` function ultimately calls `XAllocColor` to allocate a read-only color cell (colormap entry) with the specified color. `XcmsAllocColor` first converts the color specified to an RGB value and then passes this to `XAllocColor`. `XcmsAllocColor` returns the pixel value of the color cell and the color specification actually allocated. This returned color specification is the result of converting the RGB value returned by `XAllocColor` into the format specified with the result_format argument. If there is no interest in a returned color specification, unnecessary computation can be bypassed if result_format is set to XcmsRGBFormat. The corresponding colormap cell is read-only. If this routine returns XcmsFailure, the color_in_out color specification is left unchanged.

XcmsAllocColor can generate a BadColor error.

To allocate a read-only color cell using a color name and return the closest color supported by the hardware in RGB format, use XAllocNamedColor.

Status XAllocNamedColor (*display*, *colormap*, *color_name*, *screen_def_return*, *exact_def_return*)
   Display **display*;
   Colormap *colormap*;
   char **color_name*;
   XColor **screen_def_return*, **exact_def_return*;

display	Specifies the connection to the X server.
colormap	Specifies the colormap.
color_name	Specifies the color name string (for example, red) whose color definition structure you want returned.
screen_def_return	Returns the closest RGB values provided by the hardware.
exact_def_return	Returns the exact RGB values.

The XAllocNamedColor function looks up the named color with respect to the screen that is associated with the specified colormap. It returns both the exact database definition and the closest color supported by the screen. The allocated color cell is read-only. The pixel value is returned in screen_def_return. If the color name is not in the Host Portable Character Encoding, the result is implementation dependent. Use of uppercase or lowercase does not matter. XAllocNamedColor returns nonzero if a cell is allocated; otherwise, it returns zero. XAllocNamedColor can generate a BadColor error.

To allocate a read-only color cell using a color name and return the closest color supported by the hardware in an arbitrary format, use XcmsAllocNamedColor.

Status XcmsAllocNamedColor (*display*, *colormap*, *color_string*, *color_screen_return*, *color_exact_return*, *result_format*)
   Display **display*;
   Colormap *colormap*;
   char **color_string*;

XcmsColor **color_screen_return*;
XcmsColor **color_exact_return*;
XcmsColorFormat *result_format*;

display	Specifies the connection to the X server.
colormap	Specifies the colormap.
color_string	Specifies the color string whose color definition structure is to be returned.
color_screen_return	Returns the pixel value of the color cell and color specification that actually is stored for that cell.
color_exact_return	Returns the color specification parsed from the color string or parsed from the corresponding string found in a color name database.
result_format	Specifies the color format for the returned color specifications (color_screen_return and color_exact_return arguments). If format is `XcmsUndefinedFormat` and the color string contains a numerical color specification, the specification is returned in the format used in that numerical color specification. If format is `XcmsUndefinedFormat` and the color string contains a color name, the specification is returned in the format used to store the color in the database.

The `XcmsAllocNamedColor` function is similar to `XAllocNamedColor` except the color returned can be in any format specified. This function ultimately calls `XAllocColor` to allocate a read-only color cell with the color specified by a color string. The color string is parsed into an `XcmsColor` structure (see `XcmsLookupColor`), converted to an RGB value, and finally passed to the `XAllocColor`. If the color name is not in the Host Portable Character Encoding, the result is implementation dependent. Use of uppercase or lowercase does not matter.

This function returns both the color specification as a result of parsing (exact specification) and the actual color specification stored (screen specification). This screen specification is the result of converting the RGB value returned by `XAllocColor` into the format specified in result_format. If there is no interest in a returned color specification, unnecessary computation can be bypassed if result_format is set to `XcmsRGBFormat`.

`XcmsAllocNamedColor` can generate a `BadColor` error.

To allocate read/write color cell and color plane combinations for a `PseudoColor` model, use `XAllocColorCells`.

```
Status XAllocColorCells ( display, colormap, contig, plane_masks_return, nplanes,
                          pixels_return, npixels)
    Display *display;
    Colormap colormap;
    Bool contig;
    unsigned long plane_masks_return[ ];
    unsigned int nplanes;
    unsigned long pixels_return[ ];
    unsigned int npixels;
```

display	Specifies the connection to the X server.
colormap	Specifies the colormap.
contig	Specifies a Boolean value that indicates whether the planes must be contiguous.
plane_mask_return	Returns an array of plane masks.
nplanes	Specifies the number of plane masks that are to be returned in the plane masks array.
pixels_return	Returns an array of pixel values.
npixels	Specifies the number of pixel values that are to be returned in the pixels_return array.

The `XAllocColorCells` function allocates read/write color cells. The number of colors must be positive and the number of planes nonnegative, or a `BadValue` error results. If ncolors and nplanes are requested, then ncolors pixels and nplane plane masks are returned. No mask will have any bits set to 1 in

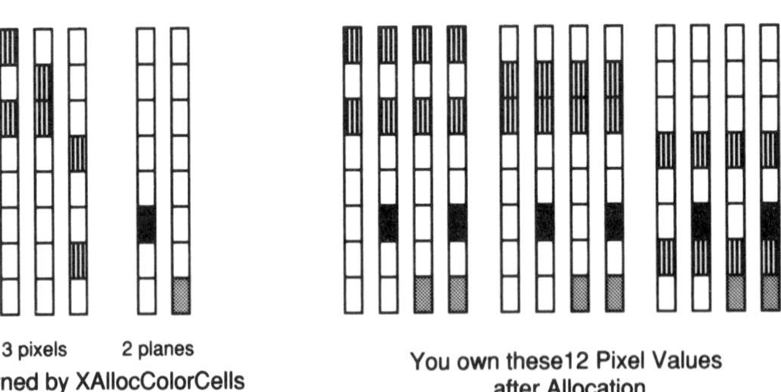

Figure 6.1. Request of 3 cells and 2 planes

common with any other mask or with any of the pixels. By ORing together each pixel with zero or more masks, ncolors * $2^{nplanes}$ distinct pixels can be produced. All of these are allocated writable by the request. For `GrayScale` or `PseudoColor`, each mask has exactly one bit set to 1. For `DirectColor`, each has exactly three bits set to 1. If contig is `True` and if all masks are ORed together, a single contiguous set of bits set to 1 will be formed for `GrayScale` or `PseudoColor` and three contiguous sets of bits set to 1 (one within each pixel subfield) for `DirectColor`. The RGB values of the allocated entries are undefined. `XAllocColorCells` returns nonzero if it succeeded or zero if it failed.

`XAllocColorCells` can generate `BadColor` and `BadValue` errors.

To allocate read/write color resources for a `DirectColor` model, use `XAllocColorPlanes`.

Status XAllocColorPlanes (*display, colormap, contig, pixels_return, ncolors, nreds, ngreens, nblues, rmask_return, gmask_return, bmask_return*)
    Display **display*;
    Colormap *colormap*;
    Bool *contig*;
    unsigned long *pixels_return*[ ];
    int *ncolors*;
    int *nreds, ngreens, nblues*;
    unsigned long **rmask_return*, **gmask_return*, **bmask_return*;

display	Specifies the connection to the X server.
colormap	Specifies the colormap.
contig	Specifies a Boolean value that indicates whether the planes must be contiguous.
pixels_return	Returns an array of pixel values. `XAllocColorPlanes` returns the pixel values in this array.
ncolors	Specifies the number of pixel values that are to be returned in the pixels_return array.
nreds *ngreens* *nblues*	Specify the number of red, green, and blue planes. The value you pass must be nonnegative.
rmask_return *gmask_return* *bmask_return*	Return bit masks for the red, green, and blue planes.

The specified ncolors must be positive; and nreds, ngreens, and nblues must be nonnegative, or a BadValue error results. If ncolors colors, nreds reds, ngreens greens, and nblues blues are requested, ncolors pixels are returned; and the masks have nreds, ngreens, and nblues bits set to 1, respectively. If contig is True, each mask will have a contiguous set of bits set to 1. No mask will have any bits set to 1 in common with any other mask or with any of the pixels. For DirectColor, each mask will lie within the corresponding pixel subfield. By ORing together subsets of masks with each pixel value, ncolors * $2^{(nreds+ngreens+nblues)}$ distinct pixel values can be produced. All of these are allocated by the request. However, in the colormap, there are only ncolors * 2^{nreds} independent red entries, ncolors * $2^{ngreens}$ independent green entries, and ncolors * 2^{nblues} independent blue entries. This is true even for PseudoColor. When the colormap entry of a pixel value is changed (using XStoreColors, XStoreColor, or XStoreNamedColor), the pixel is decomposed according to the masks, and the corresponding independent entries are updated. XAllocColorPlanes returns nonzero if it succeeded or zero if it failed.

XAllocColorPlanes can generate BadColor and BadValue errors.

To free colormap cells, use XFreeColors.

```
XFreeColors(display, colormap, pixels, npixels, planes)
    Display *display;
    Colormap colormap;
    unsigned long pixels[];
    int npixels;
    unsigned long planes;
```

display Specifies the connection to the X server.

colormap Specifies the colormap.

pixels Specifies an array of pixel values that map to the cells in the specified colormap.

npixels Specifies the number of pixels.

planes Specifies the planes you want to free.

The XFreeColors function frees the cells represented by pixels whose values are in the pixels array. The planes argument should not have any bits set to 1 in common with any of the pixels. The set of all pixels is produced by ORing together subsets of the planes argument with the pixels. The request frees all of these pixels that were allocated by the client (using XAllocColor, XAllocNamedColor, XAllocColorCells, and XAllocColorPlanes). Note that freeing an individual pixel obtained from XAllocColorPlanes may not actually allow it to be reused until all of its related pixels are also freed. Similarly, a read-only entry is not actually freed until it has been freed by all clients, and if a client allocates the same read-only entry multiple times, it must free the entry that many times before the entry is actually freed.

All specified pixels that are allocated by the client in the colormap are freed, even if one or more pixels produce an error. If a specified pixel is not a valid index into the colormap, a `BadValue` error results. If a specified pixel is not allocated by the client (that is, is unallocated or is only allocated by another client) or if the colormap was created with all entries writable (by passing `AllocAll` to `XCreateColormap`), a `BadAccess` error results. If more than one pixel is in error, the one that gets reported is arbitrary.

`XFreeColors` can generate `BadAccess`, `BadColor`, and `BadValue` errors.

6.7 Modifying and Querying Colormap Cells

To store an RGB value in a single colormap cell, use `XStoreColor`.

```
XStoreColor ( display, colormap, color)
    Display *display;
    Colormap colormap;
    XColor *color;
```

display	Specifies the connection to the X server.
colormap	Specifies the colormap.
color	Specifies the pixel and RGB values.

The `XStoreColor` function changes the colormap entry of the pixel value specified in the pixel member of the `XColor` structure. You specified this value in the pixel member of the `XColor` structure. This pixel value must be a read/write cell and a valid index into the colormap. If a specified pixel is not a valid index into the colormap, a `BadValue` error results. `XStoreColor` also changes the red, green, and/or blue color components. You specify which color components are to be changed by setting `DoRed`, `DoGreen`, and/or `DoBlue` in the flags member of the `XColor` structure. If the colormap is an installed map for its screen, the changes are visible immediately.

`XStoreColor` can generate `BadAccess`, `BadColor`, and `BadValue` errors.

To store multiple RGB values in multiple colormap cells, use `XStoreColors`.

```
XStoreColors ( display, colormap, color, ncolors)
    Display *display;
```

Colormap *colormap*;
XColor *color*[ ];
int *ncolors*;

display Specifies the connection to the X server.
colormap Specifies the colormap.
color Specifies an array of color definition structures to be stored.
ncolors Specifies the number of XColor structures in the color definition array.

The XStoreColors function changes the colormap entries of the pixel values specified in the pixel members of the XColor structures. You specify which color components are to be changed by setting DoRed, DoGreen, and/or DoBlue in the flags member of the XColor structures. If the colormap is an installed map for its screen, the changes are visible immediately. XStoreColors changes the specified pixels if they are allocated writable in the colormap by any client, even if one or more pixels generates an error. If a specified pixel is not a valid index into the colormap, a BadValue error results. If a specified pixel either is unallocated or is allocated read-only, a BadAccess error results. If more than one pixel is in error, the one that gets reported is arbitrary.

XStoreColors can generate BadAccess, BadColor, and BadValue errors.

To store a color of arbitrary format in a single colormap cell, use XcmsStoreColor.

Status XcmsStoreColor (*display*, *colormap*, *color*)
Display **display*;
Colormap *colormap*;
XcmsColor **color*;

display Specifies the connection to the X server.
colormap Specifies the colormap.
color Specifies the color cell and the color to store. Values specified in this XcmsColor structure remain unchanged upon return.

The XcmsStoreColor function converts the color specified in the XcmsColor structure into RGB values. It then uses this RGB specification in an XColor structure, whose three flags (DoRed, DoGreen, and DoBlue) are set, in a call to XStoreColor to change the color cell specified by the pixel member of the XcmsColor structure. This pixel value must be a valid index for the specified colormap, and the color cell specified by the pixel value must be a read/write cell. If the pixel value is not a valid index, a `BadValue` error results. If the color cell is unallocated or is allocated read-only, a `BadAccess` error results. If the colormap is an installed map for its screen, the changes are visible immediately.

Note that `XStoreColor` has no return value; therefore, an `XcmsSuccess` return value from this function indicates that the conversion to RGB succeeded and the call to `XStoreColor` was made. To obtain the actual color stored, use `XcmsQueryColor`. Due to the screen's hardware limitations or gamut compression, the color stored in the colormap may not be identical to the color specified.

`XcmsStoreColor` can generate `BadAccess`, `BadColor`, and `BadValue` errors.

To store multiple colors of arbitrary format in multiple colormap cells, use `XcmsStoreColors`.

```
Status XcmsStoreColors ( display, colormap, colors, ncolors, compression_flags_return)
   Display *display;
   Colormap colormap;
   XcmsColor colors[ ];
   int ncolors;
   Bool compression_flags_return[ ];
```

display	Specifies the connection to the X server.
colormap	Specifies the colormap.
colors	Specifies the color specification array of `XcmsColor` structures, each specifying a color cell and the color to store in that cell. Values specified in the array remain unchanged upon return.
ncolors	Specifies the number of `XcmsColor` structures in the color specification array.
compression_flags_return	Returns an array of Boolean values for returning compression status. If a non-NULL pointer is supplied, each element of the array is set to `True` if the corresponding color was compressed and `False` otherwise. Pass NULL if the compression status is not useful.

The `XcmsStoreColors` function converts the colors specified in the array of `XcmsColor` structures into RGB values and then uses these RGB specifications in `XColor` structures, whose three flags (`DoRed`, `DoGreen`, and `DoBlue`) are set, in a call to `XStoreColors` to change the color cells specified by the pixel member of the corresponding XcmsColor structure. Each pixel value must be a valid index for the specified colormap, and the color cell specified by each pixel value must be a read/write cell. If a pixel value is not a valid index, a BadValue error results. If a color cell is unallocated or is allocated read-only, a BadAccess error results. If more than one pixel is in error, the one that gets reported is arbitrary. If the colormap is an installed map for its screen, the changes are visible immediately.

Note that XStoreColors has no return value; therefore, an XcmsSuccess return value from this function indicates that conversions to RGB succeeded and the call to XStoreColors was made. To obtain the actual colors stored, use XcmsQueryColors. Due to the screen's hardware limitations or gamut compression, the colors stored in the colormap may not be identical to the colors specified.

XcmsStoreColors can generate BadAccess, BadColor, and BadValue errors.

To store a color specified by name in a single colormap cell, use XStoreNamedColor.

XStoreNamedColor (*display*, *colormap*, *color*, *pixel*, *flags*)
 Display **display*;
 Colormap *colormap*;
 char * *color*;
 unsigned long *pixel*;
 int *flags*;

display	Specifies the connection to the X server.
colormap	Specifies the colormap.
color	Specifies the color name string (for example, red).
pixel	Specifies the entry in the colormap.
flags	Specifies which red, green, and blue components are set.

The XStoreNamedColor function looks up the named color with respect to the screen associated with the colormap and stores the result in the specified colormap. The pixel argument determines the entry in the colormap. The flags argument determines which of the red, green, and blue components are set. You can set this member to the bitwise inclusive OR of the bits DoRed, DoGreen, and DoBlue. If the color name is not in the Host Portable Character Encoding, the result is implementation dependent. Use of uppercase or lowercase does not matter. If the specified pixel is not a valid index into the colormap, a BadValue error results. If the specified pixel either is unallocated or is allocated read-only, a BadAccess error results.

XStoreNamedColor can generate BadAccess, BadColor, BadName, and BadValue errors.

The XQueryColor and XQueryColors functions take pixel values in the pixel member of XColor structures and store in the structures the RGB values for those pixels from the specified colormap. The values returned for an unallocated entry are undefined. These functions also set the flags member in the XColor structure to all three colors. If a pixel is not a valid index into the specified colormap, a BadValue error results. If more than one pixel is in error, the one that gets reported is arbitrary.

To query the RGB value of a single colormap cell, use XQueryColor.

XQueryColor (*display*, *colormap*, *def_in_out*)
  Display **display*;
  Colormap *colormap*;
  XColor **def_in_out*;

display	Specifies the connection to the X server.
colormap	Specifies the colormap.
def_in_out	Specifies and returns the RGB values for the pixel specified in the structure.

The XQueryColor function returns the current RGB value for the pixel in the XColor structure and sets the DoRed, DoGreen, and DoBlue flags.

XQueryColor can generate BadColor and BadValue errors.

To query the RGB values of multiple colormap cells, use XQueryColors.

XQueryColors (*display*, *colormap*, *defs_in_out*, *ncolors*)
  Display **display*;
  Colormap *colormap*;
  XColor *defs_in_out*[ ];
  int *ncolors*;

display	Specifies the connection to the X server.
colormap	Specifies the colormap.
defs_in_out	Specifies and returns an array of color definition structures for the pixel specified in the structure.
ncolors	Specifies the number of XColor structures in the color definition array.

The XQueryColors function returns the RGB value for each pixel in each XColor structure and sets the DoRed, DoGreen, and DoBlue flags in each structure.

XQueryColors can generate BadColor and BadValue errors.

To query the color of a single colormap cell in an arbitrary format, use XcmsQueryColor.

```
Status XcmsQueryColor ( display, colormap, color_in_out, result_format)
    Display *display;
    Colormap colormap;
    XcmsColor *color_in_out;
    XcmsColorFormat result_format;
```

display Specifies the connection to the X server.

colormap Specifies the colormap.

color_in_out Specifies the pixel member that indicates the color cell to query. The color specification stored for the color cell is returned in this XcmsColor structure.

result_format Specifies the color format for the returned color specification.

The XcmsQueryColor function obtains the RGB value for the pixel value in the pixel member of the specified XcmsColor structure and then converts the value to the target format as specified by the result_format argument. If the pixel is not a valid index in the specified colormap, a BadValue error results.

XcmsQueryColor can generate BadColor and BadValue errors.

To query the color of multiple colormap cells in an arbitrary format, use XcmsQueryColors.

```
Status XcmsQueryColors ( display, colormap, colors_in_out, ncolors, result_format)
    Display *display;
    Colormap colormap;
    XcmsColor colors_in_out[ ];
    unsigned int ncolors;
    XcmsColorFormat result_format;
```

display Specifies the connection to the X server.

colormap Specifies the colormap.

colors_in_out Specifies an array of XcmsColor structures, each pixel member indicating the color cell to query. The color specifications for the color cells are returned in these structures.

ncolors Specifies the number of `XcmsColor` structures in the color specification array.

result_format Specifies the color format for the returned color specification.

The `XcmsQueryColors` function obtains the RGB values for pixel values in the pixel members of `XcmsColor` structures and then converts the values to the target format as specified by the result_format argument. If a pixel is not a valid index into the specified colormap, a `BadValue` error results. If more than one pixel is in error, the one that gets reported is arbitrary.

`XcmsQueryColors` can generate `BadColor` and `BadValue` errors.

6.8 Color Conversion Context Functions

This section describes functions to create, modify, and query CCCs.

Associated with each colormap is an initial CCC transparently generated by Xlib. Therefore, when you specify a colormap as an argument to a function, you are indirectly specifying a CCC. The CCC attributes that can be modified by the X client are:

- Client White Point
- Gamut compression procedure and client data
- White point adjustment procedure and client data

The initial values for these attributes are implementation specific. The CCC attributes for subsequently created CCCs can be defined by changing the CCC attributes of the default CCC. There is a default CCC associated with each screen.

6.8.1 Getting and Setting the Color Conversion Context of a Colormap

To obtain the CCC associated with a colormap, use `XcmsCCCOfColormap`.

```
XcmsCCC XcmsCCCOfColormap ( display, colormap)
    Display *display;
    Colormap colormap;
```

display Specifies the connection to the X server.

colormap Specifies the colormap.

The `XcmsCCCOfColormap` function returns the CCC associated with the specified colormap. Once obtained, the CCC attributes can be queried or modified. Unless the CCC associated with the specified colormap is changed with XcmsSetCCCOfColormap, this CCC is used when the specified colormap is used as an argument to color functions.

To change the CCC associated with a colormap, use XcmsSetCCCOf-Colormap.

```
XcmsCCC XcmsSetCCCOfColormap(display, colormap, ccc)
    Display *display;
    Colormap colormap;
    XcmsCCC ccc;
```

display Specifies the connection to the X server.
colormap Specifies the colormap.
ccc Specifies the CCC.

The XcmsSetCCCOfColormap function changes the CCC associated with the specified colormap. It returns the CCC previously associated with the colormap. If they are not used again in the application, CCCs should be freed by calling XcmsFreeCCC.

6.8.2 Obtaining the Default Color Conversion Context

You can change the default CCC attributes for subsequently created CCCs by changing the CCC attributes of the default CCC. A default CCC is associated with each screen.

To obtain the default CCC for a screen, use XcmsDefaultCCC.

```
XcmsCCC XcmsDefaultCCC(display, screen_number)
    Display *display;
    int screen_number;
```

display Specifies the connection to the X server.
screen_number Specifies the appropriate screen number on the host server.

The XcmsDefaultCCC function returns the default CCC for the specified screen. Its visual is the default visual of the screen. Its initial gamut compression and white point adjustment procedures as well as the associated client data are implementation specific.

6.8.3 Color Conversion Context Macros

Applications should not directly modify any part of the XcmsCCC. The following lists the C language macros, their corresponding function equivalents for other language bindings, and what data they both can return.

```
DisplayOfCCC (ccc)
   XcmsCCC ccc;

Display *XcmsDisplayOfCCC (ccc)
   XcmsCCC ccc;
```

ccc Specifies the CCC.

Both return the display associated with the specified CCC.

```
VisualOfCCC (ccc)
   XcmsCCC ccc;

Visual *XcmsVisualOfCCC (ccc)
   XcmsCCC ccc;
```

ccc Specifies the CCC.

Both return the visual associated with the specified CCC.

```
ScreenNumberOfCCC (ccc)
   XcmsCCC ccc;

int XcmsScreenNumberOfCCC (ccc)
   XcmsCCC ccc;
```

ccc Specifies the CCC.

Both return the number of the screen associated with the specified CCC.

```
ScreenWhitePointOfCCC (ccc)
   XcmsCCC ccc;

XcmsColor *XcmsScreenWhitePointOfCCC (ccc)
   XcmsCCC ccc;
```

ccc Specifies the CCC.

Both return the white point of the screen associated with the specified CCC.

```
ClientWhitePointOfCCC (ccc)
   XcmsCCC ccc;

XcmsColor *XcmsClientWhitePointOfCCC (ccc)
   XcmsCCC ccc;
```

ccc Specifies the CCC.

Both return the Client White Point of the specified CCC.

6.8.4 Modifying Attributes of a Color Conversion Context

To set the Client White Point in the CCC, use XcmsSetWhitePoint.

```
Status XcmsSetWhitePoint (ccc, color)
    XcmsCCC ccc;
    XcmsColor *color;
```

ccc Specifies the CCC.

color Specifies the new Client White Point.

The XcmsSetWhitePoint function changes the Client White Point in the specified CCC. Note that the pixel member is ignored and that the color specification is left unchanged upon return. The format for the new white point must be XcmsCIEXYZFormat, XcmsCIEuvYFormat, XcmsCIExyYFormat, or XcmsUndefinedFormat. If the color argument is NULL, this function sets the format component of the Client White Point specification to XcmsUndefined-Format, indicating that the Client White Point is assumed to be the same as the Screen White Point.

To set the gamut compression procedure and corresponding client data in a specified CCC, use XcmsSetCompressionProc.

```
XcmsCompressionProc XcmsSetCompressionProc (ccc, compression_proc, client_data)
    XcmsCCC ccc;
    XcmsCompressionProc compression_proc;
    XPointer client_data;
```

ccc Specifies the CCC.

compression_proc Specifies the gamut compression procedure that is to be applied when a color lies outside the screen's color gamut. If NULL is specified and a function using this CCC must convert a color specification to a device-dependent format and encounters a color that lies outside the screen's color gamut, that function will return XcmsFailure.

client_data Specifies client data for the gamut compression procedure or NULL.

The XcmsSetCompressionProc function first sets the gamut compression procedure and client data in the specified CCC with the newly specified procedure and client data and then returns the old procedure.

To set the white point adjustment procedure and corresponding client data in a specified CCC, use `XcmsSetWhiteAdjustProc`.

```
XcmsWhiteAdjustProc XcmsSetWhiteAdjustProc (ccc, white_adjust_proc, client_data)
    XcmsCCC ccc;
    XcmsWhiteAdjustProc white_adjust_proc;
    XPointer client_data;
```

ccc	Specifies the CCC.
white_adjust_proc	Specifies the white point adjustment procedure.
client_data	Specifies client data for the white point adjustment procedure or NULL.

The `XcmsSetWhiteAdjustProc` function first sets the white point adjustment procedure and client data in the specified CCC with the newly specified procedure and client data and then returns the old procedure.

6.8.5 Creating and Freeing a Color Conversion Context

You can explicitly create a CCC within your application by calling `XcmsCreateCCC`. These created CCCs can then be used by those functions that explicitly call for a CCC argument. Old CCCs that will not be used by the application should be freed using `XcmsFreeCCC`.

To create a CCC, use `XcmsCreateCCC`.

```
XcmsCCC XcmsCreateCCC ( display, screen_number, visual, client_white_point,
                        compression_proc, compression_client_data,
                        white_adjust_proc, white_adjust_client_data)
    Display *display;
    int screen_number;
    Visual *visual;
    XcmsColor *client_white_point;
    XcmsCompressionProc compression_proc;
    XPointer compression_client_data;
    XcmsWhiteAdjustProc white_adjust_proc;
    XPointer white_adjust_client_data;
```

display	Specifies the connection to the X server.
screen_number	Specifies the appropriate screen number on the host server.
visual	Specifies the visual type.
client_white_point	Specifies the Client White Point. If NULL is specified, the Client White Point is to be assumed to be the same as the Screen White Point. Note that the pixel member is ignored.

compression_proc	Specifies the gamut compression procedure that is to be applied when a color lies outside the screen's color gamut. If NULL is specified and a function using this CCC must convert a color specification to a device-dependent format and encounters a color that lies outside the screen's color gamut, that function will return `XcmsFailure`.
compression_client_data	Specifies client data for use by the gamut compression procedure or NULL.
white_adjust_proc	Specifies the white adjustment procedure that is to be applied when the Client White Point differs from the Screen White Point. NULL indicates that no white point adjustment is desired.
white_adjust_client_data	Specifies client data for use with the white point adjustment procedure or NULL.

The `XcmsCreateCCC` function creates a CCC for the specified display, screen, and visual.

To free a CCC, use `XcmsFreeCCC`.

void XcmsFreeCCC (*ccc*)
XcmsCCC *ccc*;

ccc Specifies the CCC.

The `XcmsFreeCCC` function frees the memory used for the specified CCC. Note that default CCCs and those currently associated with colormaps are ignored.

6.9 Converting Between Color Spaces

To convert an array of color specifications in arbitrary color formats to a single destination format, use `XcmsConvertColors`.

Status XcmsConvertColors (*ccc*, *colors_in_out*, *ncolors*, *target_format*, *compression_flags_return*)
XcmsCCC *ccc*;
XcmsColor *colors_in_out*[ ];
unsigned int *ncolors*;
XcmsColorFormat *target_format*;
Bool *compression_flags_return*[ ];

ccc Specifies the CCC. If conversion is between device-independent color spaces only (for example, TekHVC to

	CIELuv), the CCC is necessary only to specify the Client White Point.
colors_in_out	Specifies an array of color specifications. Pixel members are ignored and remain unchanged upon return.
ncolors	Specifies the number of `XcmsColor` structures in the color specification array.
target_format	Specifies the target color specification format.
compression_flags_return	Returns an array of Boolean values for returning compression status. If a non-NULL pointer is supplied, each element of the array is set to `True` if the corresponding color was compressed and `False` otherwise. Pass NULL if the compression status is not useful.

The `XcmsConvertColors` function converts the color specifications in the specified array of `XcmsColor` structures from their current format to a single target format, using the specified CCC. When the return value is `XcmsFailure`, the contents of the color specification array are left unchanged.

The array may contain a mixture of color specification formats (for example, 3 CIE XYZ, 2 CIE Luv, and so on). When the array contains both device-independent and device-dependent color specifications and the target_format argument specifies a device-dependent format (for example, `XcmsRGBiFormat`, `XcmsRGBFormat`), all specifications are converted to CIE XYZ format and then to the target device-dependent format.

6.10 Callback Functions

This section describes the gamut compression and white point adjustment callbacks.

The gamut compression procedure specified in the CCC is called when an attempt to convert a color specification from `XcmsCIEXYZ` to a device-dependent format (typically `XcmsRGBi`) results in a color that lies outside the screen's color gamut. If the gamut compression procedure requires client data, this data is passed via the gamut compression client data in the CCC.

During color specification conversion between device-independent and device-dependent color spaces, if a white point adjustment procedure is specified in the CCC, it is triggered when the Client White Point and Screen White Point differ. If required, the client data is obtained from the CCC.

6.10.1 Prototype Gamut Compression Procedure

The gamut compression callback interface must adhere to the following:

```
typedef Status (*XcmsCompressionProc) (ccc, colors_in_out, ncolors, index,
                                        compression_flags_return)
    XcmsCCC ccc;
    XcmsColor colors_in_out[];
    unsigned int ncolors;
    unsigned int index;
    Bool compression_flags_return[];
```

ccc	Specifies the CCC.
colors_in_out	Specifies an array of color specifications. Pixel members are ignored and remain unchanged upon return.
ncolors	Specifies the number of `XcmsColor` structures in the color specification array.
index	Specifies the index into the array of `XcmsColor` structures for the encountered color specification that lies outside the screen's color gamut. Valid values are 0 (for the first element) to ncolors – 1.
compression_flags_return	Returns an array of Boolean values for returning compression status. If a non-NULL pointer is supplied and a color at a given index is compressed, `True` should be stored at the corresponding index in this array.

When implementing a gamut compression procedure, consider the following rules and assumptions:

- The gamut compression procedure can attempt to compress one or multiple specifications at a time.
- When called, elements 0 to index – 1 in the color specification array can be assumed to fall within the screen's color gamut. In addition, these color specifications are already in some device-dependent format (typically `XcmsRGBi`). If any modifications are made to these color specifications, they must be in their initial device-dependent format upon return.
- When called, the element in the color specification array specified by the index argument contains the color specification outside the screen's color gamut encountered by the calling routine. In addition, this color specification can be assumed to be in `XcmsCIEXYZ`. Upon return, this color specification must be in `XcmsCIEXYZ`.
- When called, elements from index to ncolors – 1 in the color specification array may or may not fall within the screen's color gamut. In addition, these color specifications

can be assumed to be in `XcmsCIEXYZ`. If any modifications are made to these color specifications, they must be in `XcmsCIEXYZ` upon return.

- The color specifications passed to the gamut compression procedure have already been adjusted to the Screen White Point. This means that at this point the color specification's white point is the Screen White Point.
- If the gamut compression procedure uses a device-independent color space not initially accessible for use in the color management system, use `XcmsAddColorSpace` to insure that it is added.

6.10.2 Supplied Gamut Compression Procedures

The following equations are useful in describing gamut compression functions:

$$\textit{CIELab Psychometric Chroma} = sqrt\,(a\_star^2 + b\_star^2)$$

$$\textit{CIELab Psychometric Hue} = \tan^{-1}\left[\frac{b\_star}{a\_star}\right]$$

$$\textit{CIELuv Psychometric Chroma} = sqrt\,(u\_star^2 + v\_star^2)$$

$$\textit{CIELuv Psychometric Hue} = \tan^{-1}\left[\frac{v\_star}{u\_star}\right]$$

The gamut compression callback procedures provided by Xlib are as follows:

- `XcmsCIELabClipL`
  This brings the encountered out-of-gamut color specification into the screen's color gamut by reducing or increasing CIE metric lightness (L*) in the CIE L*a*b* color space until the color is within the gamut. If the Psychometric Chroma of the color specification is beyond maximum for the Psychometric Hue Angle, then, while maintaining the same Psychometric Hue Angle, the color will be clipped to the CIE L*a*b* coordinates of maximum Psychometric Chroma. See `XcmsCIELabQueryMaxC`. No client data is necessary.
- `XcmsCIELabClipab`
  This brings the encountered out-of-gamut color specification into the screen's color gamut by reducing Psychometric Chroma, while maintaining Psychometric Hue Angle, until the color is within the gamut. No client data is necessary.

- `XcmsCIELabClipLab`
  This brings the encountered out-of-gamut color specification into the screen's color gamut by replacing it with CIE L*a*b* coordinates that fall within the color gamut while maintaining the original Psychometric Hue Angle and whose vector to the original coordinates is the shortest attainable. No client data is necessary.
- `XcmsCIELuvClipL`
  This brings the encountered out-of-gamut color specification into the screen's color gamut by reducing or increasing CIE metric lightness (L*) in the CIE L*u*v* color space until the color is within the gamut. If the Psychometric Chroma of the color specification is beyond maximum for the Psychometric Hue Angle, then, while maintaining the same Psychometric Hue Angle, the color will be clipped to the CIE L*u*v* coordinates of maximum Psychometric Chroma. See `XcmsCIELuvQueryMaxC`. No client data is necessary.
- `XcmsCIELuvClipuv`
  This brings the encountered out-of-gamut color specification into the screen's color gamut by reducing Psychometric Chroma, while maintaining Psychometric Hue Angle, until the color is within the gamut. No client data is necessary.
- `XcmsCIELuvClipLuv`
  This brings the encountered out-of-gamut color specification into the screen's color gamut by replacing it with CIE L*u*v* coordinates that fall within the color gamut while maintaining the original Psychometric Hue Angle and whose vector to the original coordinates is the shortest attainable. No client data is necessary.
- `XcmsTekHVCClipV`
  This brings the encountered out-of-gamut color specification into the screen's color gamut by reducing or increasing the Value dimension in the TekHVC color space until the color is within the gamut. If Chroma of the color specification is beyond maximum for the particular Hue, then, while maintaining the same Hue, the color will be clipped to the Value and Chroma coordinates that represent maximum Chroma for that particular Hue. No client data is necessary.
- `XcmsTekHVCClipC`
  This brings the encountered out-of-gamut color specification into the screen's color gamut by reducing the Chroma dimension in the TekHVC color space until the color is within the gamut. No client data is necessary.
- `XcmsTekHVCClipVC`
  This brings the encountered out-of-gamut color specification into the screen's color gamut by replacing it with TekHVC coordinates that fall within the color gamut while maintaining the original Hue and whose vector to the original coordinates is the shortest attainable. No client data is necessary.

6.10.3 Prototype White Point Adjustment Procedure

The white point adjustment procedure interface must adhere to the following:

```
typedef Status (*XcmsWhiteAdjustProc) ( ccc, initial_white_point, target_white_point,
                                        target_format, colors_in_out, ncolors,
                                        compression_flags_return)
    XcmsCCC ccc;
    XcmsColor *initial_white_point;
    XcmsColor *target_white_point;
    XcmsColorFormat target_format;
    XcmsColor colors_in_out[];
    unsigned int ncolors;
    Bool compression_flags_return[];
```

ccc	Specifies the CCC.
initial_white_point	Specifies the initial white point.
target_white_point	Specifies the target white point.
target_format	Specifies the target color specification format.
colors_in_out	Specifies an array of color specifications. Pixel members are ignored and remain unchanged upon return.
ncolors	Specifies the number of `XcmsColor` structures in the color specification array.
compression_flags_return	Returns an array of Boolean values for returning compression status. If a non-NULL pointer is supplied and a color at a given index is compressed, `True` should be stored at the corresponding index in this array.

6.10.4 Supplied White Point Adjustment Procedures

White point adjustment procedures provided by Xlib are as follows:

- `XcmsCIELabWhiteShiftColors`
  This uses the CIE L*a*b* color space for adjusting the chromatic character of colors to compensate for the chromatic differences between the source and destination white points. This procedure simply converts the color specifications to `XcmsCIELab` using the source white point and then converts to the target specification format using the destinations white point. No client data is necessary.

- `XcmsCIELuvWhiteShiftColors`
  This uses the CIE L*u*v* color space for adjusting the chromatic character of colors to compensate for the chromatic differences between the source and destination

white points. This procedure simply converts the color specifications to XcmsCIELuv using the source white point and then converts to the target specification format using the destinations white point. No client data is necessary.

- XcmsTekHVCWhiteShiftColors
  This uses the TekHVC color space for adjusting the chromatic character of colors to compensate for the chromatic differences between the source and destination white points. This procedure simply converts the color specifications to XcmsTekHVC using the source white point and then converts to the target specification format using the destinations white point. An advantage of this procedure over those previously described is an attempt to minimize hue shift. No client data is necessary.

From an implementation point of view, these white point adjustment procedures convert the color specifications to a device-independent but white-point-dependent color space (for example, CIE L*u*v*, CIE L*a*b*, TekHVC) using one white point and then converting those specifications to the target color space using another white point. In other words, the specification goes in the color space with one white point but comes out with another white point, resulting in a chromatic shift based on the chromatic displacement between the initial white point and target white point. The CIE color spaces that are assumed to be white-point-independent are CIE u'v'Y, CIE XYZ, and CIE xyY. When developing a custom white point adjustment procedure that uses a device-independent color space not initially accessible for use in the color management system, use XcmsAddColorSpace to insure that it is added.

As an example, if the CCC specifies a white point adjustment procedure and if the Client White Point and Screen White Point differ, the XcmsAllocColor function will use the white point adjustment procedure twice:

- Once to convert to XcmsRGB
- A second time to convert from XcmsRGB

For example, assume the specification is in XcmsCIEuvY and the adjustment procedure is XcmsCIELuvWhiteShiftColors. During conversion to XcmsRGB, the call to XcmsAllocColor results in the following series of color specification conversions:

- From XcmsCIEuvY to XcmsCIELuv using the Client White Point
- From XcmsCIELuv to XcmsCIEuvY using the Screen White Point

- From XcmsCIEuvY to XcmsCIEXYZ (CIE u'v'Y and XYZ are white-point-independent color spaces)
- From XcmsCIEXYZ to XcmsRGBi
- From XcmsRGBi to XcmsRGB

The resulting RGB specification is passed to XAllocColor, and the RGB specification returned by XAllocColor is converted back to XcmsCIEuvY by reversing the color conversion sequence.

6.11 Gamut Querying Functions

This section describes the gamut querying functions that Xlib provides. These functions allow the client to query the boundary of the screen's color gamut in terms of the CIE L*a*b*, CIE L*u*v*, and TekHVC color spaces. Functions are also provided that allow you to query the color specification of:

- White (full intensity red, green, and blue)
- Red (full intensity red while green and blue are zero)
- Green (full intensity green while red and blue are zero)
- Blue (full intensity blue while red and green are zero)
- Black (zero intensity red, green, and blue)

The white point associated with color specifications passed to and returned from these gamut querying functions is assumed to be the Screen White Point. This is a reasonable assumption, because the client is trying to query the screen's color gamut.

The following naming convention is used for the Max and Min functions:

Xcms<*color_space*>QueryMax<*dimensions*>

Xcms<*color_space*>QueryMin<*dimensions*>

The <dimensions> consists of a letter or letters that identify the dimensions of the color space that are not fixed. For example, XcmsTekHVCQueryMaxC is given a fixed Hue and Value for which maximum Chroma is found.

6.11.1 Red, Green, and Blue Queries

To obtain the color specification for black (zero intensity red, green, and blue), use XcmsQueryBlack.

```
Status XcmsQueryBlack (ccc, target_format, color_return)
    XcmsCCC ccc;
    XcmsColorFormat target_format;
    XcmsColor *color_return;
```

ccc Specifies the CCC. The CCC's Client White Point and white point adjustment procedures are ignored.

target_format Specifies the target color specification format.

color_return Returns the color specification in the specified target format for zero intensity red, green, and blue. The white point associated with the returned color specification is the Screen White Point. The value returned in the pixel member is undefined.

The `XcmsQueryBlack` function returns the color specification in the specified target format for zero intensity red, green, and blue.

To obtain the color specification for blue (full intensity blue while red and green are zero), use `XcmsQueryBlue`.

```
Status XcmsQueryBlue (ccc, target_format, color_return)
    XcmsCCC ccc;
    XcmsColorFormat target_format;
    XcmsColor *color_return;
```

ccc Specifies the CCC. The CCC's Client White Point and white point adjustment procedures are ignored.

target_format Specifies the target color specification format.

color_return Returns the color specification in the specified target format for full intensity blue while red and green are zero. The white point associated with the returned color specification is the Screen White Point. The value returned in the pixel member is undefined.

The `XcmsQueryBlue` function returns the color specification in the specified target format for full intensity blue while red and green are zero.

To obtain the color specification for green (full intensity green while red and blue are zero), use `XcmsQueryGreen`.

```
Status XcmsQueryGreen (ccc, target_format, color_return)
    XcmsCCC ccc;
    XcmsColorFormat target_format;
    XcmsColor *color_return;
```

ccc Specifies the CCC. The CCC's Client White Point and white point adjustment procedures are ignored.

target_format Specifies the target color specification format.

color_return Returns the color specification in the specified target format for full intensity green while red and blue are zero. The white point associated with the returned color specification is the Screen White Point. The value returned in the pixel member is undefined.

The `XcmsQueryGreen` function returns the color specification in the specified target format for full intensity green while red and blue are zero.

To obtain the color specification for red (full intensity red while green and blue are zero), use `XcmsQueryRed`.

Status XcmsQueryRed (*ccc*, *target_format*, *color_return*)
  XcmsCCC *ccc*;
  XcmsColorFormat *target_format*;
  XcmsColor **color_return*;

ccc Specifies the CCC. The CCC's Client White Point and white point adjustment procedures are ignored.

target_format Specifies the target color specification format.

color_return Returns the color specification in the specified target format for full intensity red while green and blue are zero. The white point associated with the returned color specification is the Screen White Point. The value returned in the pixel member is undefined.

The `XcmsQueryRed` function returns the color specification in the specified target format for full intensity red while green and blue are zero.

To obtain the color specification for white (full intensity red, green, and blue), use `XcmsQueryWhite`.

Status XcmsQueryWhite (*ccc*, *target_format*, *color_return*)
  XcmsCCC *ccc*;
  XcmsColorFormat *target_format*;
  XcmsColor **color_return*;

ccc Specifies the CCC. The CCC's Client White Point and white point adjustment procedures are ignored.

target_format Specifies the target color specification format.

color_return Returns the color specification in the specified target format for full intensity red, green, and blue. The white point associated with the returned color specification is the Screen White Point. The value returned in the pixel member is undefined.

The `XcmsQueryWhite` function returns the color specification in the specified target format for full intensity red, green, and blue.

6.11.2 CIELab Queries

The following equations are useful in describing the CIELab query functions:

$$CIELab\ Psychometric\ Chroma = sqrt(a\_star^2 + b\_star^2)$$

$$CIELab\ Psychometric\ Hue = \tan^{-1}\left[\frac{b\_star}{a\_star}\right]$$

To obtain the CIE L*a*b* coordinates of maximum Psychometric Chroma for a given Psychometric Hue Angle and CIE metric lightness (L*), use `XcmsCIELabQueryMaxC`.

```
Status XcmsCIELabQueryMaxC (ccc, hue_angle, L_star, color_return)
    XcmsCCC ccc;
    XcmsFloat hue_angle;
    XcmsFloat L_star;
    XcmsColor *color_return;
```

ccc Specifies the CCC. The CCC's Client White Point and white point adjustment procedures are ignored.

hue_angle Specifies the hue angle (in degrees) at which to find maximum chroma.

L_star Specifies the lightness (L*) at which to find maximum chroma.

color_return Returns the CIE L*a*b* coordinates of maximum chroma displayable by the screen for the given hue angle and lightness. The white point associated with the returned color specification is the Screen White Point. The value returned in the pixel member is undefined.

The `XcmsCIELabQueryMaxC` function, given a hue angle and lightness, finds the point of maximum chroma displayable by the screen. It returns this point in CIE L*a*b* coordinates.

To obtain the CIE L*a*b* coordinates of maximum CIE metric lightness (L*) for a given Psychometric Hue Angle and Psychometric Chroma, use `XcmsCIELabQueryMaxL`.

Status XcmsCIELabQueryMaxL (*ccc, hue_angle, chroma, color_return*)
  XcmsCCC *ccc*;
  XcmsFloat *hue_angle*;
  XcmsFloat *chroma*;
  XcmsColor **color_return*;

ccc Specifies the CCC. The CCC's Client White Point and white point adjustment procedures are ignored.

hue_angle Specifies the hue angle (in degrees) at which to find maximum lightness.

chroma Specifies the chroma at which to find maximum lightness.

color_return Returns the CIE L*a*b* coordinates of maximum lightness displayable by the screen for the given hue angle and chroma. The white point associated with the returned color specification is the Screen White Point. The value returned in the pixel member is undefined.

The `XcmsCIELabQueryMaxL` function, given a hue angle and chroma, finds the point in CIE L*a*b* color space of maximum lightness (L*) displayable by the screen. It returns this point in CIE L*a*b* coordinates. An `XcmsFailure` return value usually indicates that the given chroma is beyond maximum for the given hue angle.

To obtain the CIE L*a*b* coordinates of maximum Psychometric Chroma for a given Psychometric Hue Angle, use `XcmsCIELabQueryMaxLC`.

Status XcmsCIELabQueryMaxLC (*ccc, hue_angle, color_return*)
  XcmsCCC *ccc*;
  XcmsFloat *hue_angle*;
  XcmsColor **color_return*;

ccc Specifies the CCC. The CCC's Client White Point and white point adjustment procedures are ignored.

hue_angle Specifies the hue angle (in degrees) at which to find maximum chroma.

color_return Returns the CIE L*a*b* coordinates of maximum chroma displayable by the screen for the given hue angle. The white point associated with the returned color specification is the Screen White Point. The value returned in the pixel member is undefined.

The `XcmsCIELabQueryMaxLC` function, given a hue angle, finds the point of maximum chroma displayable by the screen. It returns this point in CIE L*a*b* coordinates.

To obtain the CIE L*a*b* coordinates of minimum CIE metric lightness (L*) for a given Psychometric Hue Angle and Psychometric Chroma, use `XcmsCIELabQueryMinL`.

```
Status XcmsCIELabQueryMinL (ccc, hue_angle, chroma, color_return)
    XcmsCCC ccc;
    XcmsFloat hue_angle;
    XcmsFloat chroma;
    XcmsColor *color_return;
```

ccc Specifies the CCC. The CCC's Client White Point and white point adjustment procedures are ignored.

hue_angle Specifies the hue angle (in degrees) at which to find minimum lightness.

chroma Specifies the chroma at which to find minimum lightness.

color_return Returns the CIE L*a*b* coordinates of minimum lightness displayable by the screen for the given hue angle and chroma. The white point associated with the returned color specification is the Screen White Point. The value returned in the pixel member is undefined.

The `XcmsCIELabQueryMinL` function, given a hue angle and chroma, finds the point of minimum lightness (L*) displayable by the screen. It returns this point in CIE L*a*b* coordinates. An `XcmsFailure` return value usually indicates that the given chroma is beyond maximum for the given hue angle.

6.11.3 CIELuv Queries

The following equations are useful in describing the CIELuv query functions:

$$\mathit{CIELuv\ Psychometric\ Chroma} = sqrt(u\_star^2 + v\_star^2)$$

$$\mathit{CIELuv\ Psychometric\ Hue} = \tan^{-1}\left[\frac{v\_star}{u\_star}\right]$$

To obtain the CIE L*u*v* coordinates of maximum Psychometric Chroma for a given Psychometric Hue Angle and CIE metric lightness (L*), use `XcmsCIELuvQueryMaxC`.

```
Status XcmsCIELuvQueryMaxC (ccc, hue_angle, L_star, color_return)
    XcmsCCC ccc;
    XcmsFloat hue_angle;
```

XcmsFloat *L_star*;
XcmsColor **color_return*;

ccc Specifies the CCC. The CCC's Client White Point and white point adjustment procedures are ignored.

hue_angle Specifies the hue angle (in degrees) at which to find maximum chroma.

L_star Specifies the lightness (L*) at which to find maximum chroma.

color_return Returns the CIE L*u*v* coordinates of maximum chroma displayable by the screen for the given hue angle and lightness. The white point associated with the returned color specification is the Screen White Point. The value returned in the pixel member is undefined.

The `XcmsCIELuvQueryMaxC` function, given a hue angle and lightness, finds the point of maximum chroma displayable by the screen. It returns this point in CIE L*u*v* coordinates.

To obtain the CIE L*u*v* coordinates of maximum CIE metric lightness (L*) for a given Psychometric Hue Angle and Psychometric Chroma, use `XcmsCIELuvQueryMaxL`.

Status XcmsCIELuvQueryMaxL (*ccc*, *hue_angle*, *chroma*, *color_return*)
XcmsCCC *ccc*;
XcmsFloat *hue_angle*;
XcmsFloat *chroma*;
XcmsColor **color_return*;

ccc Specifies the CCC. The CCC's Client White Point and white point adjustment procedures are ignored.

hue_angle Specifies the hue angle (in degrees) at which to find maximum lightness.

L_star Specifies the lightness (L*) at which to find maximum lightness.

color_return Returns the CIE L*u*v* coordinates of maximum lightness displayable by the screen for the given hue angle and chroma. The white point associated with the returned color specification is the Screen White Point. The value returned in the pixel member is undefined.

The `XcmsCIELuvQueryMaxL` function, given a hue angle and chroma, finds the point in CIE L*u*v* color space of maximum lightness (L*) displayable by the screen. It returns this point in CIE L*u*v* coordinates. An `XcmsFailure` return value usually indicates that the given chroma is beyond maximum for the given hue angle.

To obtain the CIE L*u*v* coordinates of maximum Psychometric Chroma for a given Psychometric Hue Angle, use `XcmsCIELuvQueryMaxLC`.

```
Status XcmsCIELuvQueryMaxLC (ccc, hue_angle, color_return)
   XcmsCCC ccc;
   XcmsFloat hue_angle;
   XcmsColor *color_return;
```

ccc Specifies the CCC. The CCC's Client White Point and white point adjustment procedures are ignored.

hue_angle Specifies the hue angle (in degrees) at which to find maximum chroma.

color_return Returns the CIE L*u*v* coordinates of maximum chroma displayable by the screen for the given hue angle. The white point associated with the returned color specification is the Screen White Point. The value returned in the pixel member is undefined.

The `XcmsCIELuvQueryMaxLC` function, given a hue angle, finds the point of maximum chroma displayable by the screen. It returns this point in CIE L*u*v* coordinates.

To obtain the CIE L*u*v* coordinates of minimum CIE metric lightness (L*) for a given Psychometric Hue Angle and Psychometric Chroma, use `XcmsCIELuvQueryMinL`.

```
Status XcmsCIELuvQueryMinL (ccc, hue_angle, chroma, color_return)
   XcmsCCC ccc;
   XcmsFloat hue_angle;
   XcmsFloat chroma;
   XcmsColor *color_return;
```

ccc Specifies the CCC. The CCC's Client White Point and white point adjustment procedures are ignored.

hue_angle Specifies the hue angle (in degrees) at which to find minimum lightness.

chroma Specifies the chroma at which to find minimum lightness.

color_return Returns the CIE L*u*v* coordinates of minimum lightness displayable by the screen for the given hue angle and chroma. The white point associated with the returned color specification is the Screen White Point. The value returned in the pixel member is undefined.

The `XcmsCIELuvQueryMinL` function, given a hue angle and chroma, finds the point of minimum lightness (L*) displayable by the screen. It returns this point in CIE L*u*v* coordinates. An `XcmsFailure` return value usually indicates that the given chroma is beyond maximum for the given hue angle.

6.11.4 TekHVC Queries

To obtain the maximum Chroma for a given Hue and Value, use `XcmsTekHVCQueryMaxC`.

```
Status XcmsTekHVCQueryMaxC (ccc, hue, value, color_return)
    XcmsCCC ccc;
    XcmsFloat hue;
    XcmsFloat value;
    XcmsColor *color_return;
```

ccc Specifies the CCC. The CCC's Client White Point and white point adjustment procedures are ignored.

hue Specifies the Hue in which to find the maximum Chroma.

value Specifies the Value in which to find the maximum Chroma.

color_return Returns the maximum Chroma along with the actual Hue and Value at which the maximum Chroma was found. The white point associated with the returned color specification is the Screen White Point. The value returned in the pixel member is undefined.

The `XcmsTekHVCQueryMaxC` function, given a Hue and Value, determines the maximum Chroma in TekHVC color space displayable by the screen. It returns the maximum Chroma along with the actual Hue and Value at which the maximum Chroma was found.

To obtain the maximum Value for a given Hue and Chroma, use `XcmsTekHVCQueryMaxV`.

```
Status XcmsTekHVCQueryMaxV (ccc, hue, chroma, color_return)
    XcmsCCC ccc;
    XcmsFloat hue;
    XcmsFloat chroma;
    XcmsColor *color_return;
```

ccc Specifies the CCC. The CCC's Client White Point and white point adjustment procedures are ignored.

hue Specifies the Hue in which to find the maximum Value.

chroma Specifies the chroma at which to find maximum Value.

color_return Returns the maximum Value along with the Hue and Chroma at which the maximum Value was found. The white point associated with the returned color specification is the Screen White Point. The value returned in the pixel member is undefined.

The XcmsTekHVCQueryMaxV function, given a Hue and Chroma, determines the maximum Value in TekHVC color space displayable by the screen. It returns the maximum Value and the actual Hue and Chroma at which the maximum Value was found.

To obtain the maximum Chroma and Value at which it is reached for a specified Hue, use XcmsTekHVCQueryMaxVC.

```
Status XcmsTekHVCQueryMaxVC (ccc, hue, color_return)
   XcmsCCC ccc;
   XcmsFloat hue;
   XcmsColor *color_return;
```

ccc Specifies the CCC. The CCC's Client White Point and white point adjustment procedures are ignored.

hue Specifies the Hue in which to find the maximum Chroma.

color_return Returns the color specification in XcmsTekHVC for the maximum Chroma, the Value at which that maximum Chroma is reached, and the actual Hue at which the maximum Chroma was found. The white point associated with the returned color specification is the Screen White Point. The value returned in the pixel member is undefined.

The XcmsTekHVCQueryMaxVC function, given a Hue, determines the maximum Chroma in TekHVC color space displayable by the screen and the Value at which that maximum Chroma is reached. It returns the maximum Chroma, the Value at which that maximum Chroma is reached, and the actual Hue for which the maximum Chroma was found.

To obtain a specified number of TekHVC specifications such that they contain maximum Values for a specified Hue and the Chroma at which the maximum Values are reached, use XcmsTekHVCQueryMaxVSamples.

```
Status XcmsTekHVCQueryMaxVSamples (ccc, hue, colors_return, nsamples)
   XcmsCCC ccc;
   XcmsFloat hue;
   XcmsColor colors_return[];
   unsigned int nsamples;
```

ccc Specifies the CCC. The CCC's Client White Point and white point adjustment procedures are ignored.

hue Specifies the Hue for maximum Chroma/Value samples.

nsamples Specifies the number of samples.

colors_in_out Returns nsamples of color specifications in `XcmsTekHVC` such that the Chroma is the maximum attainable for the Value and Hue. The white point associated with the returned color specification is the Screen White Point. The value returned in the pixel member is undefined.

The `XcmsTekHVCQueryMaxVSamples` returns nsamples of maximum Value, the Chroma at which that maximum Value is reached, and the actual Hue for which the maximum Chroma was found. These sample points may then be used to plot the maximum Value/Chroma boundary of the screen's color gamut for the specified Hue in TekHVC color space.

To obtain the minimum Value for a given Hue and Chroma, use `XcmsTekHVCQueryMinV`.

Status XcmsTekHVCQueryMinV (*ccc, hue, chroma, color_return*)
  XcmsCCC *ccc*;
  XcmsFloat *hue*;
  XcmsFloat *chroma*;
  XcmsColor **color_return*;

ccc Specifies the CCC. The CCC's Client White Point and white point adjustment procedures are ignored.

hue Specifies the Hue in which to find the minimum Value.

value Specifies the Value in which to find the minimum Value.

color_return Returns the minimum Value and the actual Hue and Chroma at which the minimum Value was found. The white point associated with the returned color specification is the Screen White Point. The value returned in the pixel member is undefined.

The `XcmsTekHVCQueryMinV` function, given a Hue and Chroma, determines the minimum Value in TekHVC color space displayable by the screen. It returns the minimum Value and the actual Hue and Chroma at which the minimum Value was found.

6.12 Color Management Extensions

The Xlib color management facilities can be extended in two ways:

- Device-Independent Color Spaces
  Device-independent color spaces that are derivable to CIE XYZ space can be added using the `XcmsAddColorSpace` function.

- Color Characterization Function Set
  A Color Characterization Function Set consists of device-dependent color spaces and their functions that convert between these color spaces and the CIE XYZ color space, bundled together for a specific class of output devices. A function set can be added using the `XcmsAddFunctionSet` function.

6.12.1 Color Spaces

The CIE XYZ color space serves as the hub for all conversions between device-independent and device-dependent color spaces. Therefore, the knowledge to convert an `XcmsColor` structure to and from CIE XYZ format is associated with each color space. For example, conversion from CIE L*u*v* to RGB requires the knowledge to convert from CIE L*u*v* to CIE XYZ and from CIE XYZ to RGB. This knowledge is stored as an array of functions that, when applied in series, will convert the `XcmsColor` structure to or from CIE XYZ format. This color specification conversion mechanism facilitates the addition of color spaces.

Of course, when converting between only device-independent color spaces or only device-dependent color spaces, shortcuts are taken whenever possible. For example, conversion from TekHVC to CIE L*u*v* is performed by intermediate conversion to CIE u*v*Y and then to CIE L*u*v*, thus bypassing conversion between CIE u*v*Y and CIE XYZ.

6.12.2 Adding Device-Independent Color Spaces

To add a device-independent color space, use `XcmsAddColorSpace`.

Status XcmsAddColorSpace (*color_space*)
    XcmsColorSpace **color_space*;

color_space Specifies the device-independent color space to add.

The `XcmsAddColorSpace` function makes a device-independent color space (actually an `XcmsColorSpace` structure) accessible by the color management system. Because format values for unregistered color spaces are assigned at run time, they should be treated as private to the client. If references to an unregistered color space must be made outside the client (for example, storing color specifications in a file using the unregistered color space), then reference should be made by color space prefix (see `XcmsFormatOfPrefix` and `XcmsPrefixOfFormat`).

If the `XcmsColorSpace` structure is already accessible in the color management system, `XcmsAddColorSpace` returns `XcmsSuccess`.

Note that added `XcmsColorSpaces` must be retained for reference by Xlib.

6.12.3 Querying Color Space Format and Prefix

To obtain the format associated with the color space associated with a specified color string prefix, use `XcmsFormatOfPrefix`.

XcmsColorFormat XcmsFormatOfPrefix (*prefix*)
  char **prefix*;

prefix Specifies the string that contains the color space prefix.

The `XcmsFormatOfPrefix` function returns the format for the specified color space prefix (for example, the string "CIEXYZ"). The prefix is case-insensitive. If the color space is not accessible in the color management system, `XcmsFormatOfPrefix` returns `XcmsUndefinedFormat`.

To obtain the color string prefix associated with the color space specified by a color format, use `XcmsPrefixOfFormat`.

char *XcmsPrefixOfFormat (*format*)
  XcmsColorFormat *format*;

format Specifies the color specification format.

The `XcmsPrefixOfFormat` function returns the string prefix associated with the color specification encoding specified by the format argument. Otherwise, if no encoding is found, it returns NULL. The returned string must be treated as read-only.

6.12.4 Creating Additional Color Spaces

Color space specific information necessary for color space conversion and color string parsing is stored in an `XcmsColorSpace` structure. Therefore, a new structure containing this information is required for each additional color space. In the case of device-independent color spaces, a handle to this new structure (that is, by means of a global variable) is usually made accessible to the client program for use with the `XcmsAddColorSpace` function.

If a new XcmsColorSpace structure specifies a color space not registered with the X Consortium, they should be treated as private to the client because format values for unregistered color spaces are assigned at run time. If references to an unregistered color space must be made outside the client (for example, storing color specifications in a file using the unregistered color space), then reference should be made by color space prefix (see XcmsFormatOfPrefix and XcmsPrefixOfFormat).

```
typedef (*XcmsConversionProc) ();
typedef XcmsConversionProc *XcmsFuncListPtr;
    /* A NULL terminated list of function pointers*/

typedef struct _XcmsColorSpace {
    char *prefix;
    XcmsColorFormat format;
    XcmsParseStringProc parseString;
    XcmsFuncListPtr to_CIEXYZ;
    XcmsFuncListPtr from_CIEXYZ;
    int inverse_flag;
} XcmsColorSpace;
```

The prefix member specifies the prefix that indicates a color string is in this color space's string format. For example, the strings "ciexyz" or "CIEXYZ" for CIE XYZ, and "rgb" or "RGB" for RGB. The prefix is case-insensitive. The format member specifies the color specification format. Formats for unregistered color spaces are assigned at run time. The parseString member contains a pointer to the function that can parse a color string into an XcmsColor structure. This function returns an integer (int): nonzero if it succeeded and zero otherwise. The to_CIEXYZ and from_CIEXYZ members contain pointers, each to a NULL terminated list of function pointers. When the list of functions is executed in series, it will convert the color specified in an XcmsColor structure from/to the current color space format to/from the CIE XYZ format. Each function returns an integer (int): nonzero if it succeeded and zero otherwise. The white point to be associated with the colors is specified explicitly, even though white points can be found in the Color Conversion Context. The inverse_flag member, if nonzero, specifies that for each function listed in to_CIEXYZ, its inverse function can be found in from_CIEXYZ such that:

Given: n = number of functions in each list

for each i, such that 0 <= i < n
from_CIEXYZ[n - i - 1] is the inverse of to_CIEXYZ[i].

This allows Xlib to use the shortest conversion path, thus bypassing CIE XYZ if possible (for example, TekHVC to CIE L*u*v*).

6.12.5 Parse String Callback

The callback in the `XcmsColorSpace` structure for parsing a color string for the particular color space must adhere to the following software interface specification:

typedef int (*XcmsParseStringProc) (*color_string*, *color_return*)
char **color_string*;
XcmsColor **color_return*;

color_string	Specifies the color string to parse.
color_return	Returns the color specification in the color space's format.

6.12.6 Color Specification Conversion Callback

Callback functions in the `XcmsColorSpace` structure for converting a color specification between device-independent spaces must adhere to the following software interface specification:

Status ConversionProc (*ccc*, *white_point*, *colors_in_out*, *ncolors*)
XcmsCCC *ccc*;
XcmsColor **white_point*;
XcmsColor **colors_in_out*;
unsigned int *ncolors*;

ccc	Specifies the CCC.
white_point	Specifies the white point associated with color specifications. The pixel member is ignored, and the color specification is left unchanged upon return.
colors_in_out	Specifies an array of color specifications. Pixel members are ignored and remain unchanged upon return.
ncolors	Specifies the number of `XcmsColor` structures in the color specification array.

Callback functions in the `XcmsColorSpace` structure for converting a color specification to or from a device-dependent space must adhere to the following software interface specification:

Status ConversionProc (*ccc, colors_in_out, ncolors, compression_flags_return*)
XcmsCCC *ccc*;
XcmsColor **colors_in_out*;
unsigned int *ncolors*;
Bool *compression_flags_return* [ ];

ccc	Specifies the CCC.
colors_in_out	Specifies an array of color specifications. Pixel members are ignored and remain unchanged upon return.
ncolors	Specifies the number of `XcmsColor` structures in the color specification array.
compression_flags_return	Returns an array of Boolean values for returning compression status. If a non-NULL pointer is supplied and a color at a given index is compressed, `True` should be stored at the corresponding index in this array.

Conversion functions are available globally for use by other color spaces. The conversion functions provided by Xlib are:

Function	*Converts from*	*Converts to*
`XcmsCIELabToCIEXYZ`	`XcmsCIELabFormat`	`XcmsCIEXYZFormat`
`XcmsCIELuvToCIEuvY`	`XcmsCIELuvFormat`	`XcmsCIEuvYFormat`
`XcmsCIEXYZToCIELab`	`XcmsCIEXYZFormat`	`XcmsCIELabFormat`
`XcmsCIEXYZToCIEuvY`	`XcmsCIEXYZFormat`	`XcmsCIEuvYFormat`
`XcmsCIEXYZToCIExyY`	`XcmsCIEXYZFormat`	`XcmsCIExyYFormat`
`XcmsCIEXYZToRGBi`	`XcmsCIEXYZFormat`	`XcmsRGBiFormat`
`XcmsCIEuvYToCIELuv`	`XcmsCIEuvYFormat`	`XcmsCIELabFormat`
`XcmsCIEuvYToCIEXYZ`	`XcmsCIEuvYFormat`	`XcmsCIEXYZFormat`
`XcmsCIEuvYToTekHVC`	`XcmsCIEuvYFormat`	`XcmsTekHVCFormat`
`XcmsCIExyYToCIEXYZ`	`XcmsCIExyYFormat`	`XcmsCIEXYZFormat`
`XcmsRGBToRGBi`	`XcmsRGBFormat`	`XcmsRGBiFormat`
`XcmsRGBiToCIEXYZ`	`XcmsRGBiFormat`	`XcmsCIEXYZFormat`
`XcmsRGBiToRGB`	`XcmsRGBiFormat`	`XcmsRGBFormat`
`XcmsTekHVCToCIEuvY`	`XcmsTekHVCFormat`	`XcmsCIEuvYFormat`

6.12.7 Function Sets

Functions to convert between device-dependent color spaces and CIE XYZ may differ for different classes of output devices (for example, color versus gray monitors). Therefore, the notion of a Color Characterization Function Set has been developed. A function set consists of device-dependent color spaces and the functions that convert color specifications between these device-dependent color spaces and the CIE XYZ color space appropriate for a particular class of output devices. The function set also contains a function that reads color characterization data off root window properties. It is this characterization data that will differ between devices within a class of output devices. For details about how color characterization data is stored in root window properties, see the section on Device Color Characterization in part III, "Inter-Client Communication Conventions Manual."

The LINEAR_RGB function set is provided by Xlib and will support most color monitors. Function sets may require data that differs from those needed for the LINEAR_RGB function set. In that case, its corresponding data may be stored on different root window properties.

6.12.8 Adding Function Sets

To add a function set, use `XcmsAddFunctionSet`.

```
Status XcmsAddFunctionSet (function_set)
    XcmsFunctionSet *function_set;
```

function_set Specifies the function set to add.

The `XcmsAddFunctionSet` adds a function set to the color management system. If the function set uses device-dependent `XcmsColorSpace` structures not accessible in the color management system, `XcmsAddFunctionSet` adds them. If an added `XcmsColorSpace` structure is for a device-dependent color space not registered with the X Consortium, they should be treated as private to the client because format values for unregistered color spaces are assigned at run time. If references to an unregistered color space must be made outside the client (for example, storing color specifications in a file using the unregistered color space), then reference should be made by color space prefix (see `XcmsFormatOfPrefix` and `XcmsPrefixOfFormat`).

Additional function sets should be added before any calls to other Xlib routines are made. If not, the XcmsPerScrnInfo member of a previously created XcmsCCC does not have the opportunity to initialize with the added function set.

6.12.9 Creating Additional Function Sets

The creation of additional function sets should be required only when an output device does not conform to existing function sets or when additional device-dependent color spaces are necessary. A function set consists primarily of a collection of device-dependent XcmsColorSpace structures and a means to read and store a screen's color characterization data. This data is stored in an XcmsFunctionSet structure. A handle to this structure (that is, by means of global variable) is usually made accessible to the client program for use with XcmsAddFunctionSet.

If a function set uses new device-dependent XcmsColorSpace structures, they will be transparently processed into the color management system. Function sets can share an XcmsColorSpace structure for a device-dependent color space. In addition, multiple XcmsColorSpace structures are allowed for a device-dependent color space; however, a function set can reference only one of them. These XcmsColorSpace structures will differ in the functions to convert to and from CIE XYZ, thus tailored for the specific function set.

```
typedef struct _XcmsFunctionSet {
    XcmsColorSpace **DDColorSpaces;
    XcmsScreenInitProc screenInitProc;
    XcmsScreenFreeProc screenFreeProc;
} XcmsFunctionSet;
```

The DDColorSpaces member is a pointer to a NULL terminated list of pointers to XcmsColorSpace structures for the device-dependent color spaces that are supported by the function set. The screenInitProc member is set to the callback procedure (see the following interface specification) that initializes the XcmsPerScrnInfo structure for a particular screen.

The screen initialization callback must adhere to the following software interface specification:

```
typedef Status (*XcmsScreenInitProc) (display, screen_number, screen_info)
    Display *display;
    int screen_number;
    XcmsPerScrnInfo *screen_info;
```

display Specifies the connection to the X server.

screen_number Specifies the appropriate screen number on the host server.

screen_info Specifies the `XcmsPerScrnInfo` structure, which contains the per screen information.

The screen initialization callback in the `XcmsFunctionSet` structure fetches the color characterization data (device profile) for the specified screen, typically off properties on the screen's root window. It then initializes the specified `XcmsPerScrnInfo` structure. If successful, the procedure fills in the `XcmsPerScrnInfo` structure as follows:

- It sets the screenData member to the address of the created device profile data structure (contents known only by the function set).
- It next sets the screenWhitePoint member.
- It next sets the functionSet member to the address of the `XcmsFunctionSet` structure.
- It then sets the state member to `XcmsInitSuccess` and finally returns `XcmsSuccess`.

If unsuccessful, the procedure sets the state member to `XcmsInitFailure` and returns `XcmsFailure`.

The `XcmsPerScrnInfo` structure contains:

```
typedef struct _XcmsPerScrnInfo {
    XcmsColor screenWhitePoint;
    XPointer functionSet;
    XPointer screenData;
    unsigned char state;
    char pad[3];
} XcmsPerScrnInfo;
```

The screenWhitePoint member specifies the white point inherent to the screen. The functionSet member specifies the appropriate function set. The screenData member specifies the device profile. The state member is set to one of the following:

- `XcmsInitNone` indicates initialization has not been previously attempted.
- `XcmsInitFailure` indicates initialization has been previously attempted but failed.
- `XcmsInitSuccess` indicates initialization has been previously attempted and succeeded.

The screen free callback must adhere to the following software interface specification:

typedef void (*XcmsScreenFreeProc) (*screenData*)
  XPointer *screenData*;

screenData Specifies the data to be freed.

This function is called to free the screenData stored in an `XcmsPerScrnInfo` structure.

Chapter 7

Graphics Context Functions

A number of resources are used when performing graphics operations in X. Most information about performing graphics (for example, foreground color, background color, line style, and so on) is stored in resources called graphics contexts (GC). Most graphics operations (see chapter 8) take a GC as an argument. Although in theory the X protocol permits sharing of GCs between applications, it is expected that applications will use their own GCs when performing operations. Sharing of GCs is highly discouraged because the library may cache GC state.

Graphics operations can be performed to either windows or pixmaps, which collectively are called drawables. Each drawable exists on a single screen. A GC is created for a specific screen and drawable depth and can only be used with drawables of matching screen and depth.

This chapter discusses how to:

- Manipulate graphics context/state
- Use GC convenience functions

7.1 Manipulating Graphics Context/State

Most attributes of graphics operations are stored in Graphic Contexts (GCs). These include line width, line style, plane mask, foreground, background, tile, stipple, clipping region, end style, join style, and so on. Graphics operations (for example, drawing lines) use these values to determine the actual drawing operation. Extensions to X may add additional components to GCs. The contents of a GC are private to Xlib.

Xlib implements a write-back cache for all elements of a GC that are not resource IDs to allow Xlib to implement the transparent coalescing of changes to GCs. For example, a call to `XSetForeground` of a GC followed by a call to `XSetLineAttributes` results in only a single-change GC protocol request to the server. GCs are neither expected nor encouraged to be shared between client applications, so this write-back caching should present no problems. Applications cannot share GCs without external synchronization. Therefore, sharing GCs between applications is highly discouraged.

To set an attribute of a GC, set the appropriate member of the `XGCValues` structure and OR in the corresponding value bitmask in your subsequent calls to `XCreateGC`. The symbols for the value mask bits and the `XGCValues` structure are:

```
/* GC attribute value mask bits */
#define GCFunction              (1L<<0)
#define GCPlaneMask             (1L<<1)
#define GCForeground            (1L<<2)
#define GCBackground            (1L<<3)
#define GCLineWidth             (1L<<4)
#define GCLineStyle             (1L<<5)
#define GCCapStyle              (1L<<6)
#define GCJoinStyle             (1L<<7)
#define GCFillStyle             (1L<<8)
#define GCFillRule              (1L<<9)
#define GCTile                  (1L<<10)
#define GCStipple               (1L<<11)
#define GCTileStipXOrigin       (1L<<12)
#define GCTileStipYOrigin       (1L<<13)
#define GCFont                  (1L<<14)
#define GCSubwindowMode         (1L<<15)
#define GCGraphicsExposures     (1L<<16)
#define GCClipXOrigin           (1L<<17)
#define GCClipYOrigin           (1L<<18)
#define GCClipMask              (1L<<19)
#define GCDashOffset            (1L<<20)
#define GCDashList              (1L<<21)
#define GCArcMode               (1L<<22)
```

```
/* Values */
typedef struct {
    int function;                    /* logical operation */
    unsigned long plane_mask;        /* plane mask */
    unsigned long foreground;        /* foreground pixel */
    unsigned long background;        /* background pixel */
    int line_width;                  /* line width (in pixels) */
    int line_style;                  /* LineSolid, LineOnOffDash,
                                        LineDoubleDash */
    int cap_style;                   /* CapNotLast, CapButt, CapRound,
                                        CapProjecting */
    int join_style;                  /* JoinMiter, JoinRound, JoinBevel */
    int fill_style;                  /* FillSolid, FillTiled,
                                        FillStippled, FillOpaqueStippled*/
    int fill_rule;                   /* EvenOddRule, WindingRule */
    int arc_mode;                    /* ArcChord, ArcPieSlice */
    Pixmap tile;                     /* tile pixmap for tiling operations */
    Pixmap stipple;                  /* stipple 1 plane pixmap for stippling */
    int ts_x_origin;                 /* offset for tile or stipple operations */
    int ts_y_origin;
    Font font;                       /* default text font for text operations */
    int subwindow_mode;              /* ClipByChildren, IncludeInferiors */
    Bool graphics_exposures;         /* boolean, should exposures be generated */
    int clip_x_origin;               /* origin for clipping */
    int clip_y_origin;
    Pixmap clip_mask;                /* bitmap clipping; other calls for rects */
    int dash_offset;                 /* patterned/dashed line information */
    char dashes;
} XGCValues;
```

The default GC values are:

Component	*Default*
function	GXcopy
plane_mask	All ones
foreground	0
background	1
line_width	0
line_style	LineSolid
cap_style	CapButt

Component	*Default*
join_style	JoinMiter
fill_style	FillSolid
fill_rule	EvenOddRule
arc_mode	ArcPieSlice
tile	Pixmap of unspecified size filled with foreground pixel (that is, client specified pixel if any, else 0) (subsequent changes to foreground do not affect this pixmap)
stipple	Pixmap of unspecified size filled with ones
ts_x_origin	0
ts_y_origin	0
font	<implementation dependent>
subwindow_mode	ClipByChildren
graphics_exposures	True
clip_x_origin	0
clip_y_origin	0
clip_mask	None
dash_offset	0
dashes	4 (that is, the list [4, 4])

Note that foreground and background are not set to any values likely to be useful in a window.

The function attributes of a GC are used when you update a section of a drawable (the destination) with bits from somewhere else (the source). The function in a GC defines how the new destination bits are to be computed from the source bits and the old destination bits. GXcopy is typically the most useful because it will work on a color display, but special applications may use other functions, particularly in concert with particular planes of a color display. The 16 GC functions, defined in <X11/X.h>, are:

Function Name	*Value*	*Operation*
GXclear	0x	0
GXand	0x1	src AND dst
GXandReverse	0x2	src AND NOT dst
GXcopy	0x3	src
GXandInverted	0x4	(NOT src) AND dst

Function Name	*Value*	*Operation*
`GXnoop`	0x5	dst
`GXxor`	0x6	src XOR dst
`GXor`	0x7	src OR dst
`GXnor`	0x8	(NOT src) AND (NOT dst)
`GXequiv`	0x9	(NOT src) XOR dst
`GXinvert`	0xa	NOT dst
`GXorReverse`	0xb	src OR (NOT dst)
`GXcopyInverted`	0xc	NOT src
`GXorInverted`	0xd	(NOT src) OR dst
`GXnand`	0xe	(NOT src) OR (NOT dst)
`GXset`	0xf	1

Many graphics operations depend on either pixel values or planes in a GC. The planes attribute is of type long, and it specifies which planes of the destination are to be modified, one bit per plane. A monochrome display has only one plane and will be the least-significant bit of the word. As planes are added to the display hardware, they will occupy more significant bits in the plane mask.

In graphics operations, given a source and destination pixel, the result is computed bitwise on corresponding bits of the pixels. That is, a Boolean operation is performed in each bit plane. The plane_mask restricts the operation to a subset of planes. A macro constant `AllPlanes` can be used to refer to all planes of the screen simultaneously. The result is computed by the following:

((src FUNC dst) AND plane-mask) OR (dst AND (NOT plane-mask))

Range checking is not performed on the values for foreground, background, or plane_mask. They are simply truncated to the appropriate number of bits. The line-width is measured in pixels and either can be greater than or equal to one (wide line) or can be the special value zero (thin line).

Wide lines are drawn centered on the path described by the graphics request. Unless otherwise specified by the join-style or cap-style, the bounding box of a wide line with endpoints [x1, y1], [x2, y2] and width w is a rectangle with vertices at the following real coordinates:

[x1 – (w*sn/2), y1 + (w*cs/2)], [x1 + (w*sn/2), y1 – (w*cs/2)],
[x2 – (w*sn/2), y2 + (w*cs/2)], [x2 + (w*sn/2), y2 – (w*cs/2)]

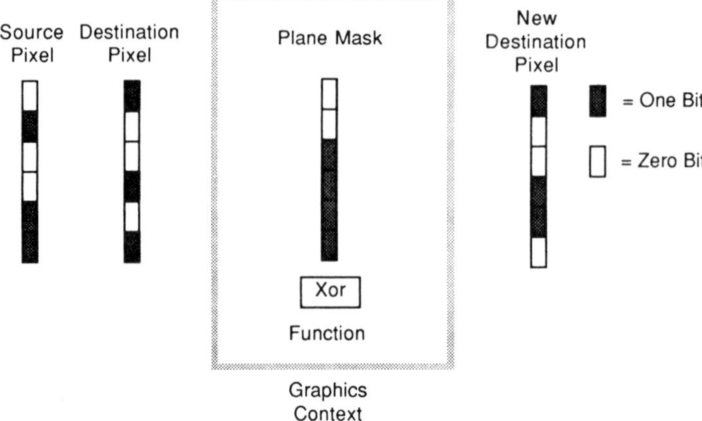

Figure 7.1. Example graphics operation using function and plane mask (4 bits/pixel)

Here sn is the sine of the angle of the line, and cs is the cosine of the angle of the line. A pixel is part of the line and so is drawn if the center of the pixel is fully inside the bounding box (which is viewed as having infinitely thin edges). If the center of the pixel is exactly on the bounding box, it is part of the line if and only if the interior is immediately to its right (x increasing direction). Pixels with centers on a horizontal edge are a special case and are part of the line if and only if the interior or the boundary is immediately below (y increasing direction) and the interior or the boundary is immediately to the right (x increasing direction).

Thin lines (zero line-width) are one-pixel-wide lines drawn using an unspecified, device-dependent algorithm. There are only two constraints on this algorithm.

1. If a line is drawn unclipped from [x1,y1] to [x2,y2] and if another line is drawn unclipped from [x1+dx,y1+dy] to [x2+dx,y2+dy], a point [x,y] is touched by drawing the first line if and only if the point [x+dx,y+dy] is touched by drawing the second line.
2. The effective set of points comprising a line cannot be affected by clipping. That is, a point is touched in a clipped line if and only if the point lies inside the clipping region and the point would be touched by the line when drawn unclipped.

A wide line drawn from [x1,y1] to [x2,y2] always draws the same pixels as a wide line drawn from [x2,y2] to [x1,y1], not counting cap-style and join-style. It is recommended that this property be true for thin lines, but this is not required. A line-width of zero may differ from a line-width of one in which pixels are drawn. This permits the use of many manufacturers' line drawing hardware, which may run many times faster than the more precisely specified wide lines.

In general, drawing a thin line will be faster than drawing a wide line of width one. However, because of their different drawing algorithms, thin lines may not mix well aesthetically with wide lines. If it is desirable to obtain precise and uniform results across all displays, a client should always use a line-width of one rather than a line-width of zero.

The line-style defines which sections of a line are drawn:

`LineSolid`	The full path of the line is drawn.
`LineDoubleDash`	The full path of the line is drawn, but the even dashes are filled differently than the odd dashes (see fill-style) with `CapButt` style used where even and odd dashes meet.
`LineOnOffDash`	Only the even dashes are drawn, and cap-style applies to all internal ends of the individual dashes, except `CapNotLast` is treated as `CapButt`.

The cap-style defines how the endpoints of a path are drawn:

`CapNotLast`	This is equivalent to `CapButt` except that for a line-width of zero the final endpoint is not drawn.
`CapButt`	The line is square at the endpoint (perpendicular to the slope of the line) with no projection beyond.
`CapRound`	The line has a circular arc with the diameter equal to the line-width, centered on the endpoint. (This is equivalent to `CapButt` for line-width of zero).
`CapProjecting`	The line is square at the end, but the path continues beyond the endpoint for a distance equal to half the line-width. (This is equivalent to `CapButt` for line-width of zero).

The join-style defines how corners are drawn for wide lines:

`JoinMiter`	The outer edges of two lines extend to meet at an angle. However, if the angle is less than 11 degrees, then a `JoinBevel` join-style is used instead.

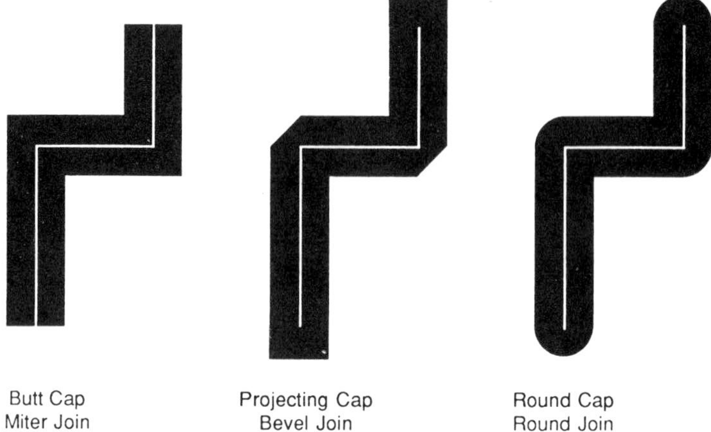

Figure 7.2. Wide line cap and join styles

`JoinRound`	The corner is a circular arc with the diameter equal to the line-width, centered on the joinpoint.
`JoinBevel`	The corner has `CapButt` endpoint styles with the triangular notch filled.

For a line with coincident endpoints (x1=x2, y1=y2), when the cap-style is applied to both endpoints, the semantics depends on the line-width and the cap-style:

`CapNotLast`	thin	The results are device-dependent, but the desired effect is that nothing is drawn.
`CapButt`	thin	The results are device-dependent, but the desired effect is that a single pixel is drawn.
`CapRound`	thin	The results are the same as for `CapButt`/thin.
`CapProjecting`	thin	The results are the same as for `CapButt`/thin.
`CapButt`	wide	Nothing is drawn.
`CapRound`	wide	The closed path is a circle, centered at the endpoint, and with the diameter equal to the line-width.
`CapProjecting`	wide	The closed path is a square, aligned with the coordinate axes, centered at the endpoint, and with the sides equal to the line-width.

For a line with coincident endpoints (x1 = x2, y1 = y2), when the join-style is applied at one or both endpoints, the effect is as if the line was removed from the overall path. However, if the total path consists of or is reduced to a single point joined with itself, the effect is the same as when the cap-style is applied at both endpoints.

The tile/stipple represents an infinite two-dimensional plane, with the tile/stipple replicated in all dimensions. When that plane is superimposed on the drawable for use in a graphics operation, the upper-left corner of some instance of the tile/stipple is at the coordinates within the drawable specified by the tile/stipple origin. The tile/stipple and clip origins are interpreted relative to the origin of whatever destination drawable is specified in a graphics request. The tile pixmap must have the same root and depth as the GC, or a `BadMatch` error results. The stipple pixmap must have depth one and must have the same root as the GC, or a `BadMatch` error results. For stipple operations where the fill-style is `FillStippled` but not `FillOpaqueStippled`, the stipple pattern is tiled in a single plane and acts as an additional clip mask to be ANDed with the clip-mask. Although some sizes may be faster to use than others, any size pixmap can be used for tiling or stippling.

The fill-style defines the contents of the source for line, text, and fill requests. For all text and fill requests (for example, `XDrawText`, `XDrawText16`, `XFillRectangle`, `XFillPolygon`, and `XFillArc`); for line requests with line-style `LineSolid` (for example, `XDrawLine`, `XDrawSegments`, `XDrawRectangle`, `XDrawArc`); and for the even dashes for line requests with line-style `LineOnOffDash` or `LineDoubleDash`, the following apply:

`FillSolid`	Foreground
`FillTiled`	Tile
`FillOpaqueStippled`	A tile with the same width and height as stipple, but with background everywhere stipple has a zero and with foreground everywhere stipple has a one
`FillStippled`	Foreground masked by stipple

When drawing lines with line-style `LineDoubleDash`, the odd dashes are controlled by the fill-style in the following manner:

`FillSolid`	Background
`FillTiled`	Same as for even dashes
`FillOpaqueStippled`	Same as for even dashes
`FillStippled`	Background masked by stipple

Storing a pixmap in a GC might or might not result in a copy being made. If the pixmap is later used as the destination for a graphics request, the change might or might not be reflected in the GC. If the pixmap is used simultaneously in a graphics request both as a destination and as a tile or stipple, the results are undefined.

For optimum performance, you should draw as much as possible with the same GC (without changing its components). The costs of changing GC components relative to using different GCs depend upon the display hardware and the server implementation. It is quite likely that some amount of GC information will be cached in display hardware and that such hardware can only cache a small number of GCs.

The dashes value is actually a simplified form of the more general patterns that can be set with `XSetDashes`. Specifying a value of N is equivalent to specifying the two-element list [N, N] in `XSetDashes`. The value must be nonzero, or a `BadValue` error results.

The clip-mask restricts writes to the destination drawable. If the clip-mask is set to a pixmap, it must have depth one and have the same root as the GC, or a `BadMatch` error results. If clip-mask is set to `None`, the pixels are always drawn regardless of the clip origin. The clip-mask also can be set by calling the `XSetClipRectangles` or `XSetRegion` functions. Only pixels where the clip-mask has a bit set to 1 are drawn. Pixels are not drawn outside the area covered by the clip-mask or where the clip-mask has a bit set to 0. The clip-mask affects all graphics requests. The clip-mask does not clip sources. The clip-mask origin is interpreted relative to the origin of whatever destination drawable is specified in a graphics request.

You can set the subwindow-mode to `ClipByChildren` or `IncludeInferiors`. For `ClipByChildren`, both source and destination windows are additionally clipped by all viewable `InputOutput` children. For `IncludeInferiors`, neither source nor destination window is clipped by inferiors. This will result in including subwindow contents in the source and drawing through subwindow boundaries of the destination. The use of `IncludeInferiors` on a window of one depth with mapped inferiors of differing depth is not illegal, but the semantics are undefined by the core protocol.

The fill-rule defines what pixels are inside (drawn) for paths given in `XFillPolygon` requests and can be set to `EvenOddRule` or `WindingRule`. For `EvenOddRule`, a point is inside if an infinite ray with the point as origin crosses

Figure 7.3. Fill rule

the path an odd number of times. For `WindingRule`, a point is inside if an infinite ray with the point as origin crosses an unequal number of clockwise and counterclockwise directed path segments. A clockwise directed path segment is one that crosses the ray from left to right as observed from the point. A counterclockwise segment is one that crosses the ray from right to left as observed from the point. The case where a directed line segment is coincident with the ray is uninteresting because you can simply choose a different ray that is not coincident with a segment.

For both `EvenOddRule` and `WindingRule`, a point is infinitely small, and the path is an infinitely thin line. A pixel is inside if the center point of the pixel is inside and the center point is not on the boundary. If the center point is on the boundary, the pixel is inside if and only if the polygon interior is immediately to its right (x increasing direction). Pixels with centers on a horizontal edge are a special case and are inside if and only if the polygon interior is immediately below (y increasing direction).

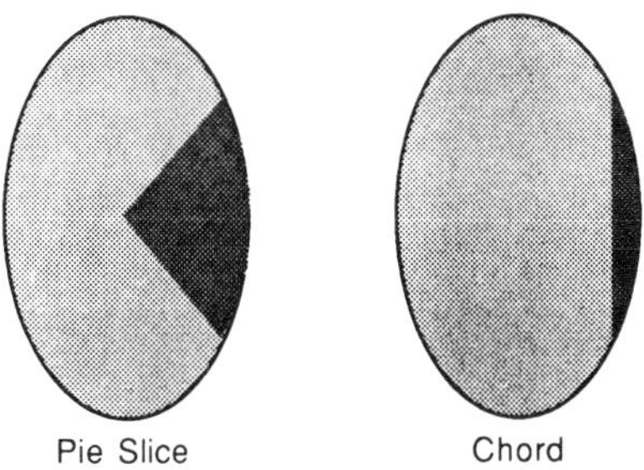

Figure 7.4. Arc mode

The arc-mode controls filling in the XFillArcs function and can be set to ArcPieSlice or ArcChord. For ArcPieSlice, the arcs are pie-slice filled. For ArcChord, the arcs are chord filled.

The graphics-exposure flag controls GraphicsExpose event generation for XCopyArea and XCopyPlane requests (and any similar requests defined by extensions).

To create a new GC that is usable on a given screen with a depth of drawable, use XCreateGC.

```
GC XCreateGC(display, d, valuemask, values)
    Display *display;
    Drawable d;
    unsigned long valuemask;
    XGCValues *values;
```

display Specifies the connection to the X server.

d Specifies the drawable.

valuemask Specifies which components in the GC are to be set using the information in the specified values structure. This argument is the bitwise inclusive OR of zero or more of the valid GC component mask bits.

values Specifies any values as specified by the valuemask.

The XCreateGC function creates a graphics context and returns a GC. The GC can be used with any destination drawable having the same root and depth as the specified drawable. Use with other drawables results in a BadMatch error.

XCreateGC can generate BadAlloc, BadDrawable, BadFont, BadMatch, BadPixmap, and BadValue errors.

To copy components from a source GC to a destination GC, use XCopyGC.

```
XCopyGC(display, src, valuemask, dest)
    Display *display;
    GC src, dest;
    unsigned long valuemask;
```

display Specifies the connection to the X server.

src Specifies the components of the source GC.

valuemask Specifies which components in the GC are to be copied to the destination GC. This argument is the bitwise inclusive OR of zero or more of the valid GC component mask bits.

dest Specifies the destination GC.

The `XCopyGC` function copies the specified components from the source GC to the destination GC. The source and destination GCs must have the same root and depth, or a `BadMatch` error results. The valuemask specifies which component to copy, as for `XCreateGC`.

`XCopyGC` can generate `BadAlloc`, `BadGC`, and `BadMatch` errors.

To change the components in a given GC, use `XChangeGC`.

```
XChangeGC ( display, gc, valuemask, values)
    Display *display;
    GC gc;
    unsigned long valuemask;
    XGCValues *values;
```

display Specifies the connection to the X server.

gc Specifies the GC.

valuemask Specifies which components in the GC are to be changed using information in the specified values structure. This argument is the bitwise inclusive OR of zero or more of the valid GC component mask bits.

values Specifies any values as specified by the valuemask.

The `XChangeGC` function changes the components specified by valuemask for the specified GC. The values argument contains the values to be set. The values and restrictions are the same as for `XCreateGC`. Changing the clip-mask overrides any previous `XSetClipRectangles` request on the context. Changing the dash-offset or dash-list overrides any previous `XSetDashes` request on the context. The order in which components are verified and altered is server-dependent. If an error is generated, a subset of the components may have been altered.

`XChangeGC` can generate `BadAlloc`, `BadFont`, `BadGC`, `BadMatch`, `BadPixmap`, and `BadValue` errors.

To obtain components of a given GC, use `XGetGCValues`.

```
Status XGetGCValues ( display, gc, valuemask, values_return)
    Display *display;
    GC gc;
    unsigned long valuemask;
    XGCValues *values_return;
```

display Specifies the connection to the X server.

gc Specifies the GC.

valuemask Specifies which components in the GC are to be returned in the values_return argument. This argument is the bitwise inclusive OR of zero or more of the valid GC component mask bits.

values_return Returns the GC values in the specified `XGCValues` structure.

The `XGetGCValues` function returns the components specified by valuemask for the specified GC. If the valuemask contains a valid set of GC mask bits (`GCFunction`, `GCPlaneMask`, `GCForeground`, `GCBackground`, `GCLineWidth`, `GCLineStyle`, `GCCapStyle`, `GCJoinStyle`, `GCFillStyle`, `GCFillRule`, `GCTile`, `GCStipple`, `GCTileStipXOrigin`, `GCTileStipYOrigin`, `GCFont`, `GCSubwindowMode`, `GCGraphicsExposures`, `GCClipXOrigin`, `GCCLipYOrigin`, `GCDashOffset`, or `GCArcMode`) and no error occurs, `XGetGCValues` sets the requested components in values_return and returns a nonzero status. Otherwise, it returns a zero status. Note that the clip-mask and dash-list (represented by the `GCClipMask` and `GCDashList` bits, respectively, in the valuemask) cannot be requested. Also note that an invalid resource ID (with one or more of the three most-significant bits set to 1) will be returned for `GCFont`, `GCTile`, and `GCStipple` if the component has never been explicitly set by the client.

To free a given GC, use `XFreeGC`.

XFreeGC (*display*, *gc*)
  Display **display*;
  GC *gc*;

display Specifies the connection to the X server.

gc Specifies the GC.

The `XFreeGC` function destroys the specified GC as well as all the associated storage.

`XFreeGC` can generate a `BadGC` error.

To obtain the `GContext` resource ID for a given GC, use `XGContextFromGC`.

GContext XGContextFromGC (*gc*)
  GC *gc*;

gc Specifies the GC for which you want the resource ID.

Xlib usually defers sending changes to the components of a GC to the server until a graphics function is actually called with that GC. This permits batching of component changes into a single server request. In some circumstances, however, it may be necessary for the client to explicitly force sending the changes to the server. An example might be when a protocol extension uses the GC indirectly, in such a way that the extension interface cannot know what GC will be used. To force sending GC component changes, use `XFlushGC`.

```
void XFlushGC ( display, gc)
    Display *display;
    GC gc;
```

display Specifies the connection to the X server.

gc Specifies the GC.

7.2 Using GC Convenience Routines

This section discusses how to set the:

- Foreground, background, plane mask, or function components
- Line attributes and dashes components
- Fill style and fill rule components
- Fill tile and stipple components
- Font component
- Clip region component
- Arc mode, subwindow mode, and graphics exposure components

7.2.1 Setting the Foreground, Background, Function, or Plane Mask

To set the foreground, background, plane mask, and function components for a given GC, use `XSetState`.

```
XSetState ( display, gc, foreground, background, function, plane_mask)
    Display *display;
    GC gc;
    unsigned long foreground, background;
    int function;
    unsigned long plane_mask;
```

display Specifies the connection to the X server.

gc Specifies the GC.

foreground Specifies the foreground you want to set for the specified GC.

background Specifies the background you want to set for the specified GC.
function Specifies the function you want to set for the specified GC.
plane_mask Specifies the plane mask.

`XSetState` can generate `BadAlloc`, `BadGC`, and `BadValue` errors.

To set the foreground of a given GC, use `XSetForeground`.

XSetForeground (*display, gc, foreground*)
  Display **display*;
  GC *gc*;
  unsigned long *foreground*;

display Specifies the connection to the X server.
gc Specifies the GC.
foreground Specifies the foreground you want to set for the specified GC.

`XSetForeground` can generate `BadAlloc` and `BadGC` errors.

To set the background of a given GC, use `XSetBackground`.

XSetBackground (*display, gc, background*)
  Display **display*;
  GC *gc*;
  unsigned long *background*;

display Specifies the connection to the X server.
gc Specifies the GC.
background Specifies the background you want to set for the specified GC.

`XSetBackground` can generate `BadAlloc` and `BadGC` errors.

To set the display function in a given GC, use `XSetFunction`.

XSetFunction (*display, gc, function*)
  Display **display*;
  GC *gc*;
  int *function*;

display Specifies the connection to the X server.
gc Specifies the GC.
function Specifies the function you want to set for the specified GC.

`XSetFunction` can generate `BadAlloc`, `BadGC`, and `BadValue` errors.

To set the plane mask of a given GC, use `XSetPlaneMask`.

```
XSetPlaneMask ( display, gc, plane_mask)
    Display *display;
    GC gc;
    unsigned long plane_mask;
```

display Specifies the connection to the X server.

gc Specifies the GC.

plane_mask Specifies the plane mask.

`XSetPlaneMask` can generate `BadAlloc` and `BadGC` errors.

7.2.2 Setting the Line Attributes and Dashes

To set the line drawing components of a given GC, use `XSetLineAttributes`.

```
XSetLineAttributes ( display, gc, line_width, line_style, cap_style, join_style)
    Display *display;
    GC gc;
    unsigned int line_width;
    int line_style;
    int cap_style;
    int join_style;
```

display Specifies the connection to the X server.

gc Specifies the GC.

line_width Specifies the line-width you want to set for the specified GC.

line_style Specifies the line-style you want to set for the specified GC. You can pass `LineSolid`, `LineOnOffDash`, or `LineDoubleDash`.

cap_style Specifies the line-style and cap-style you want to set for the specified GC. You can pass `CapNotLast`, `CapButt`, `CapRound`, or `CapProjecting`.

join_style Specifies the line join-style you want to set for the specified GC. You can pass `JoinMiter`, `JoinRound`, or `JoinBevel`.

`XSetLineAttributes` can generate `BadAlloc`, `BadGC`, and `BadValue` errors.

To set the dash-offset and dash-list for dashed line styles of a given GC, use `XSetDashes`.

```
XSetDashes ( display, gc, dash_offset, dash_list, n)
    Display *display;
    GC gc;
```

```
    int dash_offset;
    char dash_list[];
    int n;
```

display Specifies the connection to the X server.

gc Specifies the GC.

dash_offset Specifies the phase of the pattern for the dashed line-style you want to set for the specified GC.

dash_list Specifies the dash-list for the dashed line-style you want to set for the specified GC.

n Specifies the number of elements in dash_list.

The `XSetDashes` function sets the dash-offset and dash-list attributes for dashed line styles in the specified GC. There must be at least one element in the specified dash_list, or a `BadValue` error results. The initial and alternating elements (second, fourth, and so on) of the dash_list are the even dashes, and the others are the odd dashes. Each element specifies a dash length in pixels. All of the elements must be nonzero, or a `BadValue` error results. Specifying an odd-length list is equivalent to specifying the same list concatenated with itself to produce an even-length list.

The dash-offset defines the phase of the pattern, specifying how many pixels into the dash-list the pattern should actually begin in any single graphics request. Dashing is continuous through path elements combined with a join-style but is reset to the dash-offset between each sequence of joined lines.

The unit of measure for dashes is the same for the ordinary coordinate system. Ideally, a dash length is measured along the slope of the line, but imple-

Figure 7.5. Dashes: 20 50 40 50 60 50 80 50 160 50

mentations are only required to match this ideal for horizontal and vertical lines. Failing the ideal semantics, it is suggested that the length be measured along the major axis of the line. The major axis is defined as the x axis for lines drawn at an angle of between −45 and +45 degrees or between 135 and 225 degrees from the x axis. For all other lines, the major axis is the y axis.

`XSetDashes` can generate `BadAlloc`, `BadGC`, and `BadValue` errors.

7.2.3 Setting the Fill Style and Fill Rule

To set the fill-style of a given GC, use `XSetFillStyle`.

XSetFillStyle (*display, gc, fill_style*)
Display **display*;
GC *gc*;
int *fill_style*;

display Specifies the connection to the X server.

gc Specifies the GC.

fill_style Specifies the fill-style you want to set for the specified GC. You can pass `FillSolid`, `FillTiled`, `FillStippled`, or `FillOpaqueStippled`.

`XSetFillStyle` can generate `BadAlloc`, `BadGC`, and `BadValue` errors.

To set the fill-rule of a given GC, use `XSetFillRule`.

XSetFillRule (*display, gc, fill_rule*)
Display **display*;
GC *gc*;
int *fill_rule*;

display Specifies the connection to the X server.

gc Specifies the GC.

fill_rule Specifies the fill-rule you want to set for the specified GC. You can pass `EvenOddRule` or `WindingRule`.

`XSetFillRule` can generate `BadAlloc`, `BadGC`, and `BadValue` errors.

7.2.4 Setting the Fill Tile and Stipple

Some displays have hardware support for tiling or stippling with patterns of specific sizes. Tiling and stippling operations that restrict themselves to those specific sizes run much faster than such operations with arbitrary size patterns.

Xlib provides functions that you can use to determine the best size, tile, or stipple for the display as well as to set the tile or stipple shape and the tile or stipple origin.

To obtain the best size of a tile, stipple, or cursor, use `XQueryBestSize`.

```
Status XQueryBestSize ( display, class, which_screen, width, height, width_return,
                        height_return)
    Display *display;
    int class;
    Drawable which_screen;
    unsigned int width, height;
    unsigned int *width_return, *height_return;
```

display	Specifies the connection to the X server.
class	Specifies the class that you are interested in. You can pass `TileShape`, `CursorShape`, or `StippleShape`.
which_screen	Specifies any drawable on the screen.
width *height*	Specify the width and height.
width_return *height_return*	Return the width and height of the object best supported by the display hardware.

The `XQueryBestSize` function returns the best or closest size to the specified size. For `CursorShape`, this is the largest size that can be fully displayed on the screen specified by which_screen. For `TileShape`, this is the size that can be tiled fastest. For `StippleShape`, this is the size that can be stippled fastest. For `CursorShape`, the drawable indicates the desired screen. For `TileShape` and `StippleShape`, the drawable indicates the screen and possibly the window class and depth. An `InputOnly` window cannot be used as the drawable for `TileShape` or `StippleShape`, or a `BadMatch` error results.

`XQueryBestSize` can generate `BadDrawable`, `BadMatch`, and `BadValue` errors.

To obtain the best fill tile shape, use `XQueryBestTile`.

```
Status XQueryBestTile ( display, which_screen, width, height, width_return, height_return)
    Display *display;
    Drawable which_screen;
```

```
    unsigned int width, height;
    unsigned int *width_return, *height_return;
```

display Specifies the connection to the X server.

which_screen Specifies any drawable on the screen.

width
height Specify the width and height.

width_return
height_return Return the width and height of the object best supported by the display hardware.

The `XQueryBestTile` function returns the best or closest size, that is, the size that can be tiled fastest on the screen specified by which_screen. The drawable indicates the screen and possibly the window class and depth. If an `InputOnly` window is used as the drawable, a `BadMatch` error results.

`XQueryBestTile` can generate `BadDrawable` and `BadMatch` errors.

To obtain the best stipple shape, use `XQueryBestStipple`.

```
Status XQueryBestStipple (display, which_screen, width, height, width_return, height_return)
    Display *display;
    Drawable which_screen;
    unsigned int width, height;
    unsigned int *width_return, *height_return;
```

display Specifies the connection to the X server.

which_screen Specifies any drawable on the screen.

width
height Specify the width and height.

width_return
height_return Return the width and height of the object best supported by the display hardware.

The `XQueryBestStipple` function returns the best or closest size, that is, the size that can be stippled fastest on the screen specified by which_screen. The drawable indicates the screen and possibly the window class and depth. If an `InputOnly` window is used as the drawable, a `BadMatch` error results.

`XQueryBestStipple` can generate `BadDrawable` and `BadMatch` errors.

To set the fill tile of a given GC, use `XSetTile`.

```
XSetTile (display, gc, tile)
    Display *display;
    GC gc;
```

```
   Pixmap tile;
```

display Specifies the connection to the X server.

gc Specifies the GC.

tile Specifies the fill tile you want to set for the specified GC.

The tile and GC must have the same depth, or a `BadMatch` error results.

`XSetTile` can generate `BadAlloc`, `BadGC`, `BadMatch`, and `BadPixmap` errors.

To set the stipple of a given GC, use `XSetStipple`.

```
XSetStipple (display, gc, stipple)
   Display *display;
   GC gc;
   Pixmap stipple;
```

display Specifies the connection to the X server.

gc Specifies the GC.

stipple Specifies the stipple you want to set for the specified GC.

The stipple must have a depth of one, or a `BadMatch` error results.

`XSetStipple` can generate `BadAlloc`, `BadGC`, `BadMatch`, and `BadPixmap` errors.

To set the tile or stipple origin of a given GC, use `XSetTSOrigin`.

```
XSetTSOrigin (display, gc, ts_x_origin, ts_y_origin)
   Display *display;
   GC gc;
   int ts_x_origin, ts_y_origin;
```

display Specifies the connection to the X server.

gc Specifies the GC.

ts_x_origin
ts_y_origin Specify the x and y coordinates of the tile and stipple origin.

When graphics requests call for tiling or stippling, the parent's origin will be interpreted relative to whatever destination drawable is specified in the graphics request.

`XSetTSOrigin` can generate `BadAlloc` and `BadGC` error.

7.2.5 Setting the Current Font

To set the current font of a given GC, use `XSetFont`.

```
XSetFont(display, gc, font)
    Display *display;
    GC gc;
    Font font;
```

display	Specifies the connection to the X server.
gc	Specifies the GC.
font	Specifies the font.

`XSetFont` can generate `BadAlloc`, `BadFont`, and `BadGC` errors.

7.2.6 Setting the Clip Region

Xlib provides functions that you can use to set the clip-origin and the clip-mask or set the clip-mask to a list of rectangles.

To set the clip-origin of a given GC, use `XSetClipOrigin`.

```
XSetClipOrigin(display, gc, clip_x_origin, clip_y_origin)
    Display *display;
    GC gc;
    int clip_x_origin, clip_y_origin;
```

display	Specifies the connection to the X server.
gc	Specifies the GC.
clip_x_origin	
clip_y_origin	Specify the x and y coordinates of the clip-mask origin.

The clip-mask origin is interpreted relative to the origin of whatever destination drawable is specified in the graphics request.

`XSetClipOrigin` can generate `BadAlloc` and `BadGC` errors.

To set the clip-mask of a given GC to the specified pixmap, use `XSetClipMask`.

```
XSetClipMask(display, gc, pixmap)
    Display *display;
    GC gc;
    Pixmap pixmap;
```

display Specifies the connection to the X server.
gc Specifies the GC.
pixmap Specifies the pixmap or None.

If the clip-mask is set to None, the pixels are are always drawn (regardless of the clip-origin).

XSetClipMask can generate BadAlloc, BadGC, BadMatch, and BadPixmap errors.

To set the clip-mask of a given GC to the specified list of rectangles, use XSetClipRectangles.

```
XSetClipRectangles(display, gc, clip_x_origin, clip_y_origin, rectangles, n, ordering)
    Display *display;
    GC gc;
    int clip_x_origin, clip_y_origin;
    XRectangle rectangles[];
    int n;
    int ordering;
```

display Specifies the connection to the X server.
gc Specifies the GC.
clip_x_origin
clip_y_origin Specify the x and y coordinates of the clip-mask origin.
rectangles Specifies an array of rectangles that define the clip-mask.
n Specifies the number of rectangles.
ordering Specifies the ordering relations on the rectangles. You can pass Unsorted, YSorted, YXSorted, or YXBanded.

The XSetClipRectangles function changes the clip-mask in the specified GC to the specified list of rectangles and sets the clip origin. The output is clipped to remain contained within the rectangles. The clip-origin is interpreted relative to the origin of whatever destination drawable is specified in a graphics request. The rectangle coordinates are interpreted relative to the clip-origin. The rectangles should be nonintersecting, or the graphics results will be undefined. Note that the list of rectangles can be empty, which effectively disables output. This is the opposite of passing None as the clip-mask in XCreateGC, XChangeGC, and XSetClipMask.

If known by the client, ordering relations on the rectangles can be specified with the ordering argument. This may provide faster operation by the server. If an incorrect ordering is specified, the X server may generate a BadMatch error, but it is not required to do so. If no error is generated, the graphics results are undefined. Unsorted means the rectangles are in arbitrary order. YSorted means that the rectangles are nondecreasing in their Y origin. YXSorted additionally constrains YSorted order in that all rectangles with an equal Y origin are nondecreasing in their X origin. YXBanded additionally constrains YXSorted by requiring that, for every possible Y scanline, all rectangles that include that scanline have an identical Y origins and Y extents.

XSetClipRectangles can generate BadAlloc, BadGC, BadMatch, and BadValue errors.

Xlib provides a set of basic functions for performing region arithmetic. For information about these functions, see section 16.5.

7.2.7 Setting the Arc Mode, Subwindow Mode, and Graphics Exposure

To set the arc mode of a given GC, use XSetArcMode.

```
XSetArcMode (display, gc, arc_mode)
    Display *display;
    GC gc;
    int arc_mode;
```

display Specifies the connection to the X server.

gc Specifies the GC.

arc_mode Specifies the arc mode. You can pass ArcChord or ArcPieSlice.

XSetArcMode can generate BadAlloc, BadGC, and BadValue errors.

To set the subwindow mode of a given GC, use XSetSubwindowMode.

```
XSetSubwindowMode (display, gc, subwindow_mode)
    Display *display;
    GC gc;
    int subwindow_mode;
```

display Specifies the connection to the X server.

gc Specifies the GC.

subwindow_mode Specifies the subwindow mode. You can pass ClipByChildren or IncludeInferiors.

XSetSubwindowMode can generate BadAlloc, BadGC, and BadValue errors.

To set the graphics-exposures flag of a given GC, use `XSetGraphicsExposures`.

```
XSetGraphicsExposures ( display, gc, graphics_exposures)
    Display *display;
    GC gc;
    Bool graphics_exposures;
```

display Specifies the connection to the X server.

gc Specifies the GC.

graphics_exposures Specifies a Boolean value that indicates whether you want `GraphicsExpose` and `NoExpose` events to be reported when calling `XCopyArea` and `XCopyPlane` with this GC.

`XSetGraphicsExposures` can generate `BadAlloc`, `BadGC`, and `BadValue` errors.

Chapter 8

Graphics Functions

Once you have established a connection to a display, you can use the Xlib graphics functions to:

- Clear and copy areas
- Draw points, lines, rectangles, and arcs
- Fill areas
- Manipulate fonts
- Draw text
- Transfer images between clients and the server

If the same drawable and GC is used for each call, Xlib batches back-to-back calls to `XDrawPoint`, `XDrawLine`, `XDrawRectangle`, `XFillArc`, and `XFillRectangle`. Note that this reduces the total number of requests sent to the server.

8.1 Clearing Areas

Xlib provides functions that you can use to clear an area or the entire window. Because pixmaps do not have defined backgrounds, they cannot be filled by using the functions described in this section. Instead, to accomplish an analogous operation on a pixmap, you should use `XFillRectangle`, which sets the pixmap to a known value.

To clear a rectangular area of a given window, use `XClearArea`.

```
XClearArea ( display, w, x, y, width, height, exposures)
    Display *display;
    Window w;
    int x, y;
    unsigned int width, height;
    Bool exposures;
```

display	Specifies the connection to the X server.
w	Specifies the window.
x	
y	Specify the x and y coordinates, which are relative to the origin of the window and specify the upper-left corner of the rectangle.
width	
height	Specify the width and height, which are the dimensions of the rectangle.
exposures	Specifies a Boolean value that indicates if `Expose` events are to be generated.

The `XClearArea` function paints a rectangular area in the specified window according to the specified dimensions with the window's background pixel or pixmap. The subwindow-mode effectively is `ClipByChildren`. If width is zero, it is replaced with the current width of the window minus x. If height is zero, it is replaced with the current height of the window minus y. If the window has a defined background tile, the rectangle clipped by any children is filled with this tile. If the window has background `None`, the contents of the window are not changed. In either case, if exposures is `True`, one or more `Expose` events are generated for regions of the rectangle that are either visible or are being retained in a backing store. If you specify a window whose class is `InputOnly`, a `BadMatch` error results.

`XClearArea` can generate `BadMatch`, `BadValue`, and `BadWindow` errors.

To clear the entire area in a given window, use `XClearWindow`.

```
XClearWindow ( display, w)
    Display *display;
    Window w;
```

display	Specifies the connection to the X server.
w	Specifies the window.

The XClearWindow function clears the entire area in the specified window and is equivalent to XClearArea(display, w, 0, 0, 0, 0, False). If the window has a defined background tile, the rectangle is tiled with a plane-mask of all ones and GXcopy function. If the window has background None, the contents of the window are not changed. If you specify a window whose class is InputOnly, a BadMatch error results.

XClearWindow can generate BadMatch and BadWindow errors.

8.2 Copying Areas

Xlib provides functions that you can use to copy an area or a bit plane.

To copy an area between drawables of the same root and depth, use XCopyArea.

XCopyArea (*display, src, dest, gc, src_x, src_y, width, height, dest_x, dest_y*)
  Display **display*;
  Drawable *src, dest*;
  GC *gc*;
  int *src_x, src_y*;
  unsigned int *width, height*;
  int *dest_x, dest_y*;

display Specifies the connection to the X server.

src
dest Specify the source and destination rectangles to be combined.

gc Specifies the GC.

src_x
src_y Specify the x and y coordinates, which are relative to the origin of the source rectangle and specify its upper-left corner.

width
height Specify the width and height, which are the dimensions of both the source and destination rectangles.

dest_x
dest_y Specify the x and y coordinates, which are relative to the origin of the destination rectangle and specify its upper-left corner.

The XCopyArea function combines the specified rectangle of src with the specified rectangle of dest. The drawables must have the same root and depth, or a BadMatch error results.

If regions of the source rectangle are obscured and have not been retained in backing store or if regions outside the boundaries of the source drawable are specified, those regions are not copied. Instead, the following occurs on all corresponding destination regions that are either visible or are retained in backing store. If the destination is a window with a background other than `None`, corresponding regions of the destination are tiled with that background (with plane-mask of all ones and `GXcopy` function). Regardless of tiling or whether the destination is a window or a pixmap, if graphics-exposures is `True`, then `GraphicsExpose` events for all corresponding destination regions are generated. If graphics-exposures is `True` but no `GraphicsExpose` events are generated, a `NoExpose` event is generated. Note that by default graphics-exposures is `True` in new GCs.

This function uses these GC components: function, plane-mask, subwindow-mode, graphics-exposures, clip-x-origin, clip-y-origin, and clip-mask.

`XCopyArea` can generate `BadDrawable`, `BadGC`, and `BadMatch` errors.

To copy a single bit plane of a given drawable, use `XCopyPlane`.

XCopyPlane (*display*, *src*, *dest*, *gc*, *src_x*, *src_y*, *width*, *height*, *dest_x*, *dest_y*, *plane*)
  Display **display*;
  Drawable *src*, *dest*;
  GC *gc*;
  int *src_x*, *src_y*;
  unsigned int *width*, *height*;
  int *dest_x*, *dest_y*;
  unsigned long *plane*;

display Specifies the connection to the X server.

src
dest Specify the source and destination rectangles to be combined.

gc Specifies the GC.

src_x
src_y Specify the x and y coordinates, which are relative to the origin of the source rectangle and specify its upper-left corner.

width
height Specify the width and height, which are the dimensions of both the source and destination rectangles.

dest_x
dest_y Specify the x and y coordinates, which are relative to the origin of the destination rectangle and specify its upper-left corner.
plane Specifies the bit plane. You must set exactly one bit to 1.

The `XCopyPlane` function uses a single bit plane of the specified source rectangle combined with the specified GC to modify the specified rectangle of dest. The drawables must have the same root but need not have the same depth. If the drawables do not have the same root, a `BadMatch` error results. If plane does not have exactly one bit set to 1 and the values of planes must be less than 2^n, where n is the depth of src, a `BadValue` error results.

Effectively, `XCopyPlane` forms a pixmap of the same depth as the rectangle of dest and with a size specified by the source region. It uses the foreground/background pixels in the GC (foreground everywhere the bit plane in src contains a bit set to 1, background everywhere the bit plane in src contains a bit set to 0) and the equivalent of a `CopyArea` protocol request is performed with all the same exposure semantics. This can also be thought of as using the specified region of the source bit plane as a stipple with a fill-style of `FillOpaqueStippled` for filling a rectangular area of the destination.

This function uses these GC components: function, plane-mask, foreground, background, subwindow-mode, graphics-exposures, clip-x-origin, clip-y-origin, and clip-mask.

`XCopyPlane` can generate `BadDrawable`, `BadGC`, `BadMatch`, and `BadValue` errors.

8.3 Drawing Points, Lines, Rectangles, and Arcs

Xlib provides functions that you can use to draw:

- A single point or multiple points
- A single line or multiple lines
- A single rectangle or multiple rectangles
- A single arc or multiple arcs

Some of the functions described in the following sections use these structures:

```
typedef struct {
    short x1, y1, x2, y2;
} XSegment;
```

```
typedef struct {
      short x, y;
} XPoint;

typedef struct {
      short x, y;
      unsigned short width, height;
} XRectangle;

typedef struct {
      short x, y;
      unsigned short width, height;
      short angle1, angle2;              /* Degrees * 64 */
} XArc;
```

All x and y members are signed integers. The width and height members are 16-bit unsigned integers. You should be careful not to generate coordinates and sizes out of the 16-bit ranges, because the protocol only has 16-bit fields for these values.

8.3.1 Drawing Single and Multiple Points

To draw a single point in a given drawable, use `XDrawPoint`.

```
XDrawPoint ( display, d, gc, x, y)
   Display *display;
   Drawable d;
   GC gc;
   int x, y;
```

display Specifies the connection to the X server.

d Specifies the drawable.

gc Specifies the GC.

x

y Specify the x and y coordinates where you want the point drawn.

To draw multiple points in a given drawable, use `XDrawPoints`.

```
XDrawPoints ( display, d, gc, points, npoints, mode)
   Display *display;
   Drawable d;
   GC gc;
   XPoint *points;
   int npoints;
   int mode;
```

display Specifies the connection to the X server.
d Specifies the drawable.
gc Specifies the GC.
points Specifies an array of points.
npoints Specifies the number of points in the array.
mode Specifies the coordinate mode. You can pass `CoordModeOrigin` or `CoordModePrevious`.

The `XDrawPoint` function uses the foreground pixel and function components of the GC to draw a single point into the specified drawable; `XDrawPoints` draws multiple points this way. `CoordModeOrigin` treats all coordinates as relative to the origin, and `CoordModePrevious` treats all coordinates after the first as relative to the previous point. `XDrawPoints` draws the points in the order listed in the array.

Both functions use these GC components: function, plane-mask, foreground, subwindow-mode, clip-x-origin, clip-y-origin, and clip-mask.

`XDrawPoint` can generate `BadDrawable`, `BadGC`, and `BadMatch` errors. `XDrawPoints` can generate `BadDrawable`, `BadGC`, `BadMatch`, and `BadValue` errors.

8.3.2 Drawing Single and Multiple Lines

To draw a single line between two points in a given drawable, use `XDrawLine`.

```
XDrawLine (display, d, gc, x1, y1, x2, y2)
    Display *display;
    Drawable d;
    GC gc;
    int x1, y1, x2, y2;
```

display Specifies the connection to the X server.
d Specifies the drawable.
gc Specifies the GC.
x1
y1
x2
y2 Specify the points (x1, y1) and (x2, y2) to be connected.

To draw multiple lines in a given drawable, use `XDrawLines`.

```
XDrawLines (display, d, gc, points, npoints, mode)
    Display *display;
```

```
    Drawable d;
    GC gc;
    XPoint *points;
    int npoints;
    int mode;
```

display Specifies the connection to the X server.

d Specifies the drawable.

gc Specifies the GC.

points Specifies an array of points.

npoints Specifies the number of points in the array.

mode Specifies the coordinate mode. You can pass `CoordModeOrigin` or `CoordModePrevious`.

To draw multiple, unconnected lines in a given drawable, use `XDrawSegments`.

```
XDrawSegments (display, d, gc, segments, nsegments)
    Display *display;
    Drawable d;
    GC gc;
    XSegment *segments;
    int nsegments;
```

display Specifies the connection to the X server.

d Specifies the drawable.

gc Specifies the GC.

segments Specifies an array of segments.

nsegments Specifies the number of segments in the array.

The `XDrawLine` function uses the components of the specified GC to draw a line between the specified set of points (x1, y1) and (x2, y2). It does not perform joining at coincident endpoints. For any given line, `XDrawLine` does not draw a pixel more than once. If lines intersect, the intersecting pixels are drawn multiple times.

The `XDrawLines` function uses the components of the specified GC to draw npoints–1 lines between each pair of points (point[i], point[i+1]) in the array of `XPoint` structures. It draws the lines in the order listed in the array. The lines join correctly at all intermediate points, and if the first and last points coincide, the first and last lines also join correctly. For any given line, `XDrawLines` does not draw a pixel more than once. If thin (zero line-width) lines intersect, the intersecting pixels are drawn multiple times. If wide lines intersect, the intersecting pixels are drawn only once, as though the entire

`PolyLine` protocol request were a single, filled shape. `CoordModeOrigin` treats all coordinates as relative to the origin, and `CoordModePrevious` treats all coordinates after the first as relative to the previous point.

The `XDrawSegments` function draws multiple, unconnected lines. For each segment, `XDrawSegments` draws a line between (x1, y1) and (x2, y2). It draws the lines in the order listed in the array of `XSegment` structures and does not perform joining at coincident endpoints. For any given line, `XDrawSegments` does not draw a pixel more than once. If lines intersect, the intersecting pixels are drawn multiple times.

All three functions use these GC components: function, plane-mask, line-width, line-style, cap-style, fill-style, subwindow-mode, clip-x-origin, clip-y-origin, and clip-mask. The `XDrawLines` function also uses the join-style GC component. All three functions also use these GC mode-dependent components: foreground, background, tile, stipple, tile-stipple-x-origin, tile-stipple-y-origin, dash-offset, and dash-list.

`XDrawLine`, `XDrawLines`, and `XDrawSegments` can generate `BadDrawable`, `BadGC`, and `BadMatch` errors. `XDrawLines` also can generate `BadValue` errors.

8.3.3 Drawing Single and Multiple Rectangles

To draw the outline of a single rectangle in a given drawable, use `XDrawRectangle`.

XDrawRectangle (*display*, *d*, *gc*, *x*, *y*, *width*, *height*)
  Display **display*;
  Drawable *d*;
  GC *gc*;
  int *x*, *y*;
  unsigned int *width*, *height*;

display Specifies the connection to the X server.

d Specifies the drawable.

gc Specifies the GC.

x
y Specify the x and y coordinates which specify the upper-left corner of the rectangle.

width
height Specify the width and height, which specify the dimensions of the rectangle.

To draw the outline of multiple rectangles in a given drawable, use `XDrawRectangles`.

```
XDrawRectangles (display, d, gc, rectangles, nrectangles)
    Display *display;
    Drawable d;
    GC gc;
    XRectangle rectangles[ ];
    int nrectangles;
```

display	Specifies the connection to the X server.
d	Specifies the drawable.
gc	Specifies the GC.
rectangles	Specifies an array of rectangles.
nrectangles	Specifies the number of rectangles in the array.

The `XDrawRectangle` and `XDrawRectangles` functions draw the outlines of the specified rectangle or rectangles as if a five-point `PolyLine` protocol request were specified for each rectangle:

[x,y] [x+width,y] [x+width,y+height] [x,y+height] [x,y]

For the specified rectangle or rectangles, these functions do not draw a pixel more than once. `XDrawRectangles` draws the rectangles in the order listed in the array. If rectangles intersect, the intersecting pixels are drawn multiple times.

Both functions use these GC components: function, plane-mask, line-width, line-style, cap-style, join-style, fill-style, subwindow-mode, clip-x-origin, clip-y-origin, and clip-mask. They also use these GC mode-dependent components: foreground, background, tile, stipple, tile-stipple-x-origin, tile-stipple-y-origin, dash-offset, and dash-list.

`XDrawRectangle` and `XDrawRectangles` can generate `BadDrawable`, `BadGC`, and `BadMatch` errors.

8.3.4 Drawing Single and Multiple Arcs

To draw a single arc in a given drawable, use `XDrawArc`.

```
XDrawArc (display, d, gc, x, y, width, height, angle1, angle2)
    Display *display;
    Drawable d;
```

```
    GC gc;
    int x, y;
    unsigned int width, height;
    int angle1, angle2;
```

display Specifies the connection to the X server.
d Specifies the drawable.
gc Specifies the GC.
x
y Specify the x and y coordinates, which are relative to the origin of the drawable and specify the upper-left corner of the bounding rectangle.
width
height Specify the width and height, which are the major and minor axes of the arc.
angle1 Specifies the start of the arc relative to the three-o'clock position from the center, in units of degrees * 64.
angle2 Specifies the path and extent of the arc relative to the start of the arc, in units of degrees * 64.

To draw multiple arcs in a given drawable, use `XDrawArcs`.

```
XDrawArcs ( display, d, gc, arcs, narcs)
    Display *display;
    Drawable d;
    GC gc;
    XArc *arcs;
    int narcs;
```

display Specifies the connection to the X server.
d Specifies the drawable.
gc Specifies the GC.
arcs Specifies an array of arcs.
narcs Specifies the number of arcs in the array.

`XDrawArc` draws a single circular or elliptical arc, and `XDrawArcs` draws multiple circular or elliptical arcs. Each arc is specified by a rectangle and two angles. The center of the circle or ellipse is the center of the rectangle, and the major and minor axes are specified by the width and height. Positive angles indicate counterclockwise motion, and negative angles indicate clockwise motion. If the magnitude of angle2 is greater than 360 degrees, `XDrawArc` or `XDrawArcs` truncates it to 360 degrees.

For an arc specified as [*x*, *y*, *width*, *height*, *angle*1, *angle*2], the origin of the major and minor axes is at $[x+\frac{width}{2}, y+\frac{height}{2}]$, and the infinitely thin path describing the entire circle or ellipse intersects the horizontal axis at $[x, y+\frac{height}{2}]$ and $[x+width, y+\frac{height}{2}]$ and intersects the vertical axis at $[x+\frac{width}{2}, y]$ and $[x+\frac{width}{2}, y+height]$. These coordinates can be fractional and so are not truncated to discrete coordinates. The path should be defined by the ideal mathematical path. For a wide line with line-width lw, the bounding outlines for filling are given by the two infinitely thin paths consisting of all points whose perpendicular distance from the path of the circle/ellipse is equal to lw/2 (which may be a fractional value). The cap-style and join-style are applied the same as for a line corresponding to the tangent of the circle/ellipse at the endpoint.

For an arc specified as [*x*, *y*, *width*, *height*, *angle*1, *angle*2], the angles must be specified in the effectively skewed coordinate system of the ellipse (for a circle, the angles and coordinate systems are identical). The relationship between these angles and angles expressed in the normal coordinate system of the screen (as measured with a protractor) is as follows:

$$\text{skewed-angle} = atan\left(\tan(\text{normal-angle}) * \frac{width}{height}\right) + adjust$$

The skewed-angle and normal-angle are expressed in radians (rather than in degrees scaled by 64) in the range $[0, 2\pi]$ and where atan returns a value in the range $[-\frac{\pi}{2}, \frac{\pi}{2}]$ and adjust is:

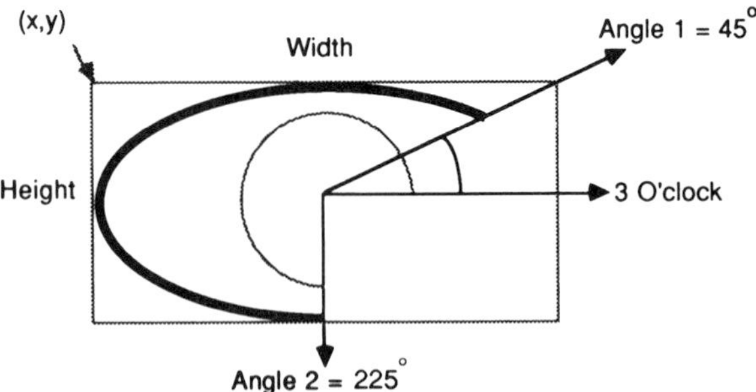

Figure 8.1. XDrawArc (DPY, W, GC, x, y, width, height, 45*64, 225*64)

0 for normal-angle in the range $[0, \frac{\pi}{2}]$

π for normal-angle in the range $[\frac{\pi}{2}, \frac{3\pi}{2}]$

2π for normal-angle in the range $[\frac{3\pi}{2}, 2\pi]$

For any given arc, `XDrawArc` and `XDrawArcs` do not draw a pixel more than once. If two arcs join correctly and if the line-width is greater than zero and the arcs intersect, `XDrawArc` and `XDrawArcs` do not draw a pixel more than once. Otherwise, the intersecting pixels of intersecting arcs are drawn multiple times. Specifying an arc with one endpoint and a clockwise extent draws the same pixels as specifying the other endpoint and an equivalent counterclockwise extent, except as it affects joins.

If the last point in one arc coincides with the first point in the following arc, the two arcs will join correctly. If the first point in the first arc coincides with the last point in the last arc, the two arcs will join correctly. By specifying one axis to be zero, a horizontal or vertical line can be drawn. Angles are computed based solely on the coordinate system and ignore the aspect ratio.

Both functions use these GC components: function, plane-mask, line-width, line-style, cap-style, join-style, fill-style, subwindow-mode, clip-x-origin, clip-y-origin, and clip-mask. They also use these GC mode-dependent components: foreground, background, tile, stipple, tile-stipple-x-origin, tile-stipple-y-origin, dash-offset, and dash-list.

`XDrawArc` and `XDrawArcs` can generate `BadDrawable`, `BadGC`, and `BadMatch` errors.

8.4 Filling Areas

Xlib provides functions that you can use to fill:

- A single rectangle or multiple rectangles
- A single polygon
- A single arc or multiple arcs

8.4.1 Filling Single and Multiple Rectangles

To fill a single rectangular area in a given drawable, use `XFillRectangle`.

XFillRectangle (*display*, *d*, *gc*, *x*, *y*, *width*, *height*)
    Display **display*;

```
    Drawable d;
    GC gc;
    int x, y;
    unsigned int width, height;
```

display Specifies the connection to the X server.
d Specifies the drawable.
gc Specifies the GC.
x
y Specify the x and y coordinates, which are relative to the origin of the drawable and specify the upper-left corner of the rectangle.
width
height Specify the width and height, which are the dimensions of the rectangle to be filled.

To fill multiple rectangular areas in a given drawable, use `XFillRectangles`.

```
XFillRectangles(display, d, gc, rectangles, nrectangles)
    Display *display;
    Drawable d;
    GC gc;
    XRectangle *rectangles;
    int nrectangles;
```

display Specifies the connection to the X server.
d Specifies the drawable.
gc Specifies the GC.
rectangles Specifies an array of rectangles.
nrectangles Specifies the number of rectangles in the array.

The `XFillRectangle` and `XFillRectangles` functions fill the specified rectangle or rectangles as if a four-point `FillPolygon` protocol request were specified for each rectangle:

[x,y] [x+width,y] [x+width,y+height] [x,y+height]

Each function uses the x and y coordinates, width and height dimensions, and GC you specify.

`XFillRectangles` fills the rectangles in the order listed in the array. For any given rectangle, `XFillRectangle` and `XFillRectangles` do not draw a pixel more than once. If rectangles intersect, the intersecting pixels are drawn multiple times.

Both functions use these GC components: function, plane-mask, fill-style, subwindow-mode, clip-x-origin, clip-y-origin, and clip-mask. They also use these GC mode-dependent components: foreground, background, tile, stipple, tile-stipple-x-origin, and tile-stipple-y-origin.

`XFillRectangle` and `XFillRectangles` can generate `BadDrawable`, `BadGC`, and `BadMatch` errors.

8.4.2 Filling a Single Polygon

To fill a polygon area in a given drawable, use `XFillPolygon`.

```
XFillPolygon ( display, d, gc, points, npoints, shape, mode)
    Display *display;
    Drawable d;
    GC gc;
    XPoint *points;
    int npoints;
    int shape;
    int mode;
```

display	Specifies the connection to the X server.
d	Specifies the drawable.
gc	Specifies the GC.
points	Specifies an array of points.
npoints	Specifies the number of points in the array.
shape	Specifies a shape that helps the server to improve performance. You can pass `Complex`, `Convex`, or `Nonconvex`.
mode	Specifies the coordinate mode. You can pass `CoordModeOrigin` or `CoordModePrevious`.

`XFillPolygon` fills the region closed by the specified path. The path is closed automatically if the last point in the list does not coincide with the first point. `XFillPolygon` does not draw a pixel of the region more than once. `CoordModeOrigin` treats all coordinates as relative to the origin, and `CoordModePrevious` treats all coordinates after the first as relative to the previous point.

Depending on the specified shape, the following occurs:

- If shape is `Complex`, the path may self-intersect. Note that contiguous coincident points in the path are not treated as self-intersection.
- If shape is `Convex`, for every pair of points inside the polygon, the line segment connecting them does not intersect the path. If known by the client, specifying `Convex` can

improve performance. If you specify `Convex` for a path that is not convex, the graphics results are undefined.

- If shape is `Nonconvex`, the path does not self-intersect, but the shape is not wholly convex. If known by the client, specifying `Nonconvex` instead of `Complex` may improve performance. If you specify `Nonconvex` for a self-intersecting path, the graphics results are undefined.

The fill-rule of the GC controls the filling behavior of self-intersecting polygons.

This function uses these GC components: function, plane-mask, fill-style, fill-rule, subwindow-mode, clip-x-origin, clip-y-origin, and clip-mask. It also uses these GC mode-dependent components: foreground, background, tile, stipple, tile-stipple-x-origin, and tile-stipple-y-origin.

`XFillPolygon` can generate `BadDrawable`, `BadGC`, `BadMatch`, and `BadValue` errors.

8.4.3 Filling Single and Multiple Arcs

To fill a single arc in a given drawable, use `XFillArc`.

XFillArc (*display, d, gc, x, y, width, height, angle1, angle2*)
  Display **display*;
  Drawable *d*;
  GC *gc*;
  int *x*, *y*;
  unsigned int *width*, *height*;
  int *angle1*, *angle2*;

display Specifies the connection to the X server.
d Specifies the drawable.
gc Specifies the GC.
x
y Specify the x and y coordinates, which are relative to the origin of the drawable and specify the upper-left corner of the bounding rectangle.
width
height Specify the width and height, which are the major and minor axes of the arc.
angle1 Specifies the start of the arc relative to the three-o'clock position from the center, in units of degrees * 64.
angle2 Specifies the path and extent of the arc relative to the start of the arc, in units of degrees * 64.

To fill multiple arcs in a given drawable, use `XFillArcs`.

```
XFillArcs ( display, d, gc, arcs, narcs)
    Display *display;
    Drawable d;
    GC gc;
    XArc *arcs;
    int narcs;
```

display	Specifies the connection to the X server.
d	Specifies the drawable.
gc	Specifies the GC.
arcs	Specifies an array of arcs.
narcs	Specifies the number of arcs in the array.

For each arc, `XFillArc` or `XFillArcs` fills the region closed by the infinitely thin path described by the specified arc and, depending on the arc-mode specified in the GC, one or two line segments. For `ArcChord`, the single line segment joining the endpoints of the arc is used. For `ArcPieSlice`, the two line segments joining the endpoints of the arc with the center point are used. `XFillArcs` fills the arcs in the order listed in the array. For any given arc, `XFillArc` and `XFillArcs` do not draw a pixel more than once. If regions intersect, the intersecting pixels are drawn multiple times.

Both functions use these GC components: function, plane-mask, fill-style, arc-mode, subwindow-mode, clip-x-origin, clip-y-origin, and clip-mask. They also use these GC mode-dependent components: foreground, background, tile, stipple, tile-stipple-x-origin, and tile-stipple-y-origin.

`XFillArc` and `XFillArcs` can generate `BadDrawable`, `BadGC`, and `BadMatch` errors.

8.5 Font Metrics

A font is a graphical description of a set of characters that are used to increase efficiency whenever a set of small, similar sized patterns are repeatedly used.

This section discusses how to:

- Load and free fonts
- Obtain and free font names
- Compute character string sizes

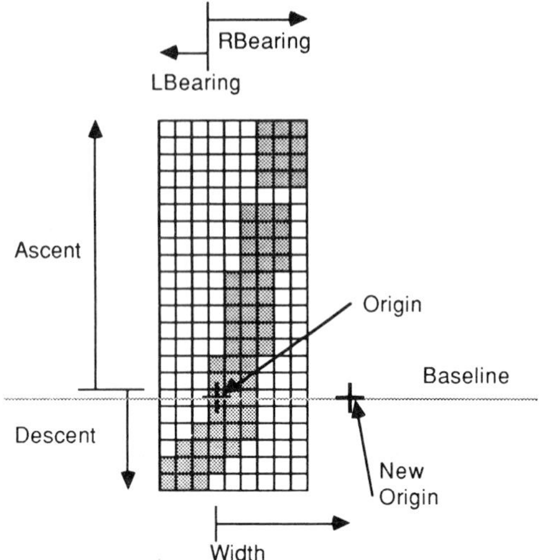

Figure 8.2. XCharStruct components

- Return logical extents
- Query character string sizes

The X server loads fonts whenever a program requests a new font. The server can cache fonts for quick lookup. Fonts are global across all screens in a server. Several levels are possible when dealing with fonts. Most applications simply use `XLoadQueryFont` to load a font and query the font metrics.

Characters in fonts are regarded as masks. Except for image text requests, the only pixels modified are those in which bits are set to 1 in the character. This means that it makes sense to draw text using stipples or tiles (for example, many menus gray-out unusable entries).

The `XFontStruct` structure contains all of the information for the font and consists of the font-specific information as well as a pointer to an array of `XCharStruct` structures for the characters contained in the font. The `XFontStruct`, `XFontProp`, and `XCharStruct` structures contain:

```
typedef struct {
    short lbearing;          /* origin to left edge of raster */
    short rbearing;          /* origin to right edge of raster */
    short width;             /* advance to next char's origin */
    short ascent;            /* baseline to top edge of raster */
```

```
    short descent;                   /* baseline to bottom edge of raster */
    unsigned short attributes;       /* per char flags (not predefined) */
} XCharStruct;

typedef struct {
    Atom name;
    unsigned long card32;
} XFontProp;

typedef struct {                     /* normal 16 bit characters are two bytes */
  unsigned char byte1;
  unsigned char byte2;
} XChar2b;

typedef struct {
    XExtData *ext_data;              /* hook for extension to hang data */
    Font fid;                        /* Font id for this font */
    unsigned direction;              /* hint about the direction font is painted */
    unsigned min_char_or_byte2;      /* first character */
    unsigned max_char_or_byte2;      /* last character */
    unsigned min_byte1;              /* first row that exists */
    unsigned max_byte1;              /* last row that exists */
    Bool all_chars_exist;            /* flag if all characters have nonzero size */
    unsigned default_char;           /* char to print for undefined character */
    int n_properties;                /* how many properties there are */
    XFontProp *properties;           /* pointer to array of additional properties */
    XCharStruct min_bounds;          /* minimum bounds over all existing char */
    XCharStruct max_bounds;          /* maximum bounds over all existing char */
    XCharStruct *per_char;           /* first_char to last_char information */
    int ascent;                      /* logical extent above baseline for spacing */
    int descent;                     /* logical decent below baseline for spacing */
} XFontStruct;
```

X supports single byte/character, two bytes/character matrix, and 16-bit character text operations. Note that any of these forms can be used with a font, but a single byte/character text request can only specify a single byte (that is, the first row of a 2-byte font). You should view 2-byte fonts as a two-dimensional matrix of defined characters: byte1 specifies the range of defined rows and byte2 defines the range of defined columns of the font. Single byte/character fonts have one row defined, and the byte2 range specified in the structure defines a range of characters.

The bounding box of a character is defined by the `XCharStruct` of that character. When characters are absent from a font, the default_char is used. When fonts have all characters of the same size, only the information in the `XFontStruct` min and max bounds are used.

The members of the `XFontStruct` have the following semantics:

- The direction member can be either `FontLeftToRight` or `FontRightToLeft`. It is just a hint as to whether most `XCharStruct` elements have a positive (`FontLeftToRight`) or a negative (`FontRightToLeft`) character width metric. The core protocol defines no support for vertical text.
- If the min_byte1 and max_byte1 members are both zero, min_char_or_byte2 specifies the linear character index corresponding to the first element of the per_char array, and max_char_or_byte2 specifies the linear character index of the last element.

  If either min_byte1 or max_byte1 are nonzero, both min_char_or_byte2 and max_char_or_byte2 are less than 256, and the 2-byte character index values corresponding to the per_char array element N (counting from 0) are:

  byte1 = N/D + min_byte1
  byte2 = N\D + min_char_or_byte2

  where:

  D = max_char_or_byte2 – min_char_or_byte2 + 1
  / = integer division
  \ = integer modulus

- If the per_char pointer is NULL, all glyphs between the first and last character indexes inclusive have the same information, as given by both min_bounds and max_bounds.
- If all_chars_exist is `True`, all characters in the per_char array have nonzero bounding boxes.
- The default_char member specifies the character that will be used when an undefined or nonexistent character is printed. The default_char is a 16-bit character (not a 2-byte character). For a font using 2-byte matrix format, the default_char has byte1 in the most-significant byte and byte2 in the least-significant byte. If the default_char itself specifies an undefined or nonexistent character, no printing is performed for an undefined or nonexistent character.
- The min_bounds and max_bounds members contain the most extreme values of each individual `XCharStruct` component over all elements of this array (and ignore nonexistent characters). The bounding box of the font (the smallest rectangle enclosing the shape obtained by superimposing all of the characters at the same origin [x,y]) has its upper-left coordinate at:

[x + min_bounds.lbearing, y – max_bounds.ascent]

Its width is:

max_bounds.rbearing – min_bounds.lbearing

Its height is:

max_bounds.ascent + max_bounds.descent

- The ascent member is the logical extent of the font above the baseline that is used for determining line spacing. Specific characters may extend beyond this.
- The descent member is the logical extent of the font at or below the baseline that is used for determining line spacing. Specific characters may extend beyond this.
- If the baseline is at Y-coordinate y, the logical extent of the font is inclusive between the Y-coordinate values (y – font.ascent) and (y + font.descent – 1). Typically, the minimum interline spacing between rows of text is given by ascent + descent.

For a character origin at [x,y], the bounding box of a character (that is, the smallest rectangle that encloses the character's shape) described in terms of `XCharStruct` components is a rectangle with its upper-left corner at:

[x + lbearing, y – ascent]

Its width is:

rbearing – lbearing

Its height is:

ascent + descent

The origin for the next character is defined to be:

[x + width, y]

The lbearing member defines the extent of the left edge of the character ink from the origin. The rbearing member defines the extent of the right edge of the character ink from the origin. The ascent member defines the extent of the top edge of the character ink from the origin. The descent member defines the extent of the bottom edge of the character ink from the origin. The width member defines the logical width of the character.

Note that the baseline (the y position of the character origin) is logically viewed as being the scanline just below nondescending characters. When descent is zero, only pixels with Y-coordinates less than y are drawn, and the origin is logically viewed as being coincident with the left edge of a nonkerned character. When lbearing is zero, no pixels with X-coordinate less than x are drawn. Any of the `XCharStruct` metric members could be negative. If the width is negative, the next character will be placed to the left of the current origin.

The X protocol does not define the interpretation of the attributes member in the `XCharStruct` structure. A nonexistent character is represented with all members of its `XCharStruct` set to zero.

A font is not guaranteed to have any properties. The interpretation of the property value (for example, long or unsigned long) must be derived from *a priori* knowledge of the property. A basic set of font properties is specified in part IV, "X Logical Font Description Conventions."

8.5.1 Loading and Freeing Fonts

Xlib provides functions that you can use to load fonts, get font information, unload fonts, and free font information. A few font functions use a `GContext` resource ID or a font ID interchangeably.

To load a given font, use `XLoadFont`.

```
Font XLoadFont(display, name)
    Display *display;
    char *name;
```

display Specifies the connection to the X server.

name Specifies the name of the font, which is a null-terminated string.

The `XLoadFont` function loads the specified font and returns its associated font ID. If the font name is not in the Host Portable Character Encoding, the result is implementation dependent. Use of uppercase or lowercase does not matter. The interpretation of characters "?" and "*" in the name is not defined by the core protocol but is reserved for future definition. A structured format for font names is specified in part IV, "X Logical Font Description Conventions." If `XLoadFont` was unsuccessful at loading the specified font, a `BadName` error results. Fonts are not associated with a particular screen and can be stored as a component of any GC. When the font is no longer needed, call `XUnloadFont`.

`XLoadFont` can generate `BadAlloc` and `BadName` errors.

To return information about an available font, use `XQueryFont`.

```
XFontStruct *XQueryFont(display, font_ID)
    Display *display;
    XID font_ID;
```

display Specifies the connection to the X server.

font_ID Specifies the font ID or the `GContext` ID.

The `XQueryFont` function returns a pointer to the `XFontStruct` structure, which contains information associated with the font. You can query a font or the font stored in a GC. The font ID stored in the `XFontStruct` structure will be the `GContext` ID, and you need to be careful when using this ID in other functions (see `XGContextFromGC`). If the font does not exist, `XQueryFont` returns NULL. To free this data, use `XFreeFontInfo`.

To perform a `XLoadFont` and `XQueryFont` in a single operation, use `XLoadQueryFont`.

```
XFontStruct *XLoadQueryFont(display, name)
    Display *display;
    char *name;
```

display Specifies the connection to the X server.

name Specifies the name of the font, which is a null-terminated string.

The `XLoadQueryFont` function provides the most common way for accessing a font. `XLoadQueryFont` both opens (loads) the specified font and returns a pointer to the appropriate `XFontStruct` structure. If the font name is not in the Host Portable Character Encoding, the result is implementation dependent. If the font does not exist, `XLoadQueryFont` returns NULL.

`XLoadQueryFont` can generate a `BadAlloc` error.

To unload the font and free the storage used by the font structure that was allocated by `XQueryFont` or `XLoadQueryFont`, use `XFreeFont`.

```
XFreeFont(display, font_struct)
    Display *display;
    XFontStruct *font_struct;
```

display Specifies the connection to the X server.

font_struct Specifies the storage associated with the font.

The `XFreeFont` function deletes the association between the font resource ID and the specified font and frees the `XFontStruct` structure. The font itself will be freed when no other resource references it. The data and the font should not be referenced again.

`XFreeFont` can generate a `BadFont` error.

To return a given font property, use `XGetFontProperty`.

```
Bool XGetFontProperty(font_struct, atom, value_return)
    XFontStruct *font_struct;
    Atom atom;
    unsigned long *value_return;
```

font_struct Specifies the storage associated with the font.

atom Specifies the atom for the property name you want returned.

value_return Returns the value of the font property.

Given the atom for that property, the `XGetFontProperty` function returns the value of the specified font property. `XGetFontProperty` also returns `False` if the property was not defined or `True` if it was defined. A set of predefined atoms exists for font properties, which can be found in `<X11/Xatom.h>`. This set contains the standard properties associated with a font. Although it is not guaranteed, it is likely that the predefined font properties will be present.

To unload a font that was loaded by `XLoadFont`, use `XUnloadFont`.

```
XUnloadFont(display, font)
    Display *display;
    Font font;
```

display Specifies the connection to the X server.

font Specifies the font.

The `XUnloadFont` function deletes the association between the font resource ID and the specified font. The font itself will be freed when no other resource references it. The font should not be referenced again.

`XUnloadFont` can generate a `BadFont` error.

8.5.2 Obtaining and Freeing Font Names and Information

You obtain font names and information by matching a wildcard specification when querying a font type for a list of available sizes and so on.

To return a list of the available font names, use `XListFonts`.

```
char **XListFonts(display, pattern, maxnames, actual_count_return)
    Display *display;
```

```
    char *pattern;
    int maxnames;
    int *actual_count_return;
```

display	Specifies the connection to the X server.
pattern	Specifies the null-terminated pattern string that can contain wildcard characters.
maxnames	Specifies the maximum number of names to be returned.
actual_count_return	Returns the actual number of font names.

The `XListFonts` function returns an array of available font names (as controlled by the font search path; see `XSetFontPath`) that match the string you passed to the pattern argument. The pattern string can contain any characters, but each asterisk (*) is a wildcard for any number of characters, and each question mark (?) is a wildcard for a single character. If the pattern string is not in the Host Portable Character Encoding, the result is implementation dependent. Use of uppercase or lowercase does not matter. Each returned string is null-terminated. If the data returned by the server is in the Latin Portable Character Encoding, then the returned strings are in the Host Portable Character Encoding. Otherwise, the result is implementation dependent. If there are no matching font names, `XListFonts` returns NULL. The client should call `XFreeFontNames` when finished with the result to free the memory.

To free a font name array, use `XFreeFontNames`.

```
XFreeFontNames (list)
    char *list[];
```

list Specifies the array of strings you want to free.

The `XFreeFontNames` function frees the array and strings returned by `XListFonts` or `XListFontsWithInfo`.

To obtain the names and information about available fonts, use `XListFontsWithInfo`.

```
char **XListFontsWithInfo (display, pattern, maxnames, count_return, info_return)
    Display *display;
    char *pattern;
    int maxnames;
```

int **count_return*;
XFontStruct ***info_return*;

display Specifies the connection to the X server.

pattern Specifies the null-terminated pattern string that can contain wildcard characters.

maxnames Specifies the maximum number of names to be returned.

count_return Returns the actual number of matched font names.

info_return Returns the font information.

The `XListFontsWithInfo` function returns a list of font names that match the specified pattern and their associated font information. The list of names is limited to size specified by maxnames. The information returned for each font is identical to what `XLoadQueryFont` would return except that the per-character metrics are not returned. The pattern string can contain any characters, but each asterisk (*) is a wildcard for any number of characters, and each question mark (?) is a wildcard for a single character. If the pattern string is not in the Host Portable Character Encoding, the result is implementation dependent. Use of uppercase or lowercase does not matter. Each returned string is null-terminated. If the data returned by the server is in the Latin Portable Character Encoding, then the returned strings are in the Host Portable Character Encoding. Otherwise, the result is implementation dependent. If there are no matching font names, `XListFontsWithInfo` returns NULL.

To free only the allocated name array, the client should call `XFreeFontNames`. To free both the name array and the font information array or to free just the font information array, the client should call `XFreeFontInfo`.

To free the font information array, use `XFreeFontInfo`.

XFreeFontInfo(*names*, *free_info*, *actual_count*)
char ***names*;
XFontStruct **free_info*;
int *actual_count*;

names Specifies the list of font names returned by `XListFontsWithInfo`.

free_info Specifies the font information returned by `XListFontsWithInfo`.

actual_count Specifies the actual number of matched font names returned by `XListFontsWithInfo`.

The `XFreeFontInfo` function frees the the font information array. To free an `XFontStruct` structure without closing the font, call `XFreeFontInfo` with the names argument specified as NULL.

8.5.3 Computing Character String Sizes

Xlib provides functions that you can use to compute the width, the logical extents, and the server information about 8-bit and 2-byte text strings. The width is computed by adding the character widths of all the characters. It does not matter if the font is an 8-bit or 2-byte font. These functions return the sum of the character metrics, in pixels.

To determine the width of an 8-bit character string, use `XTextWidth`.

int XTextWidth (*font_struct*, *string*, *count*)
  XFontStruct **font_struct*;
  char **string*;
  int *count*;

font_struct	Specifies the font used for the width computation.
string	Specifies the character string.
count	Specifies the character count in the specified string.

To determine the width of a 2-byte character string, use `XTextWidth16`.

int XTextWidth16 (*font_struct*, *string*, *count*)
  XFontStruct **font_struct*;
  XChar2b **string*;
  int *count*;

font_struct	Specifies the font used for the width computation.
string	Specifies the character string.
count	Specifies the character count in the specified string.

8.5.4 Computing Logical Extents

To compute the bounding box of an 8-bit character string in a given font, use `XTextExtents`.

XTextExtents (*font_struct*, *string*, *nchars*, *direction_return*, *font_ascent_return*,
    font_descent_return, *overall_return*)
  XFontStruct **font_struct*;
  char **string*;

```
    int nchars;
    int *direction_return;
    int *font_ascent_return, *font_descent_return;
    XCharStruct *overall_return;
```

font_struct	Specifies the `XFontStruct` structure.
string	Specifies the character string.
nchars	Specifies the number of characters in the character string.
direction_return	Returns the value of the direction hint (`FontLeftToRight` or `FontRightToLeft`).
font_ascent_return	Returns the font ascent.
font_descent_return	Returns the font descent.
overall_return	Returns the overall size in the specified `XCharStruct` structure.

To compute the bounding box of a 2-byte character string in a given font, use `XTextExtents16`.

```
XTextExtents16(font_struct, string, nchars, direction_return, font_ascent_return,
               font_descent_return, overall_return)
    XFontStruct *font_struct;
    XChar2b *string;
    int nchars;
    int *direction_return;
    int *font_ascent_return, *font_descent_return;
    XCharStruct *overall_return;
```

font_struct	Specifies the `XFontStruct` structure.
string	Specifies the character string.
nchars	Specifies the number of characters in the character string.
direction_return	Returns the value of the direction hint (`FontLeftToRight` or `FontRightToLeft`).
font_ascent_return	Returns the font ascent.
font_descent_return	Returns the font descent.
overall_return	Returns the overall size in the specified `XCharStruct` structure.

The `XTextExtents` and `XTextExtents16` functions perform the size computation locally and, thereby, avoid the round-trip overhead of `XQueryTextExtents` and `XQueryTextExtents16`. Both functions return an `XCharStruct` structure, whose members are set to the values as follows.

The ascent member is set to the maximum of the ascent metrics of all characters in the string. The descent member is set to the maximum of the descent metrics. The width member is set to the sum of the character-width metrics of all characters in the string. For each character in the string, let W be the sum of the character-width metrics of all characters preceding it in the string. Let L be the left-side-bearing metric of the character plus W. Let R be the right-side-bearing metric of the character plus W. The lbearing member is set to the minimum L of all characters in the string. The rbearing member is set to the maximum R.

For fonts defined with linear indexing rather than 2-byte matrix indexing, each `XChar2b` structure is interpreted as a 16-bit number with byte1 as the most-significant byte. If the font has no defined default character, undefined characters in the string are taken to have all zero metrics.

8.5.5 Querying Character String Sizes

To query the server for the bounding box of an 8-bit character string in a given font, use `XQueryTextExtents`.

XQueryTextExtents (*display, font_ID, string, nchars, direction_return, font_ascent_return, font_descent_return, overall_return*)
  Display **display*;
  XID *font_ID*;
  char **string*;
  int *nchars*;
  int **direction_return*;
  int **font_ascent_return*, **font_descent_return*;
  XCharStruct **overall_return*;

display	Specifies the connection to the X server.
font_ID	Specifies either the font ID or the `GContext` ID that contains the font.
string	Specifies the character string.
nchars	Specifies the number of characters in the character string.
direction_return	Returns the value of the direction hint (`FontLeftToRight` or `FontRightToLeft`).
font_ascent_return	Returns the font ascent.
font_descent_return	Returns the font descent.
overall_return	Returns the overall size in the specified `XCharStruct` structure.

To query the server for the bounding box of a 2-byte character string in a given font, use `XQueryTextExtents16`.

```
XQueryTextExtents16(display, font_ID, string, nchars, direction_return,
                    font_ascent_return, font_descent_return, overall_return)
    Display *display;
    XID font_ID;
    XChar2b *string;
    int nchars;
    int *direction_return;
    int *font_ascent_return, *font_descent_return;
    XCharStruct *overall_return;
```

display	Specifies the connection to the X server.
font_ID	Specifies either the font ID or the `GContext` ID that contains the font.
string	Specifies the character string.
nchars	Specifies the number of characters in the character string.
direction_return	Returns the value of the direction hint (`FontLeftToRight` or `FontRightToLeft`).
font_ascent_return	Returns the font ascent.
font_descent_return	Returns the font descent.
overall_return	Returns the overall size in the specified `XCharStruct` structure.

The `XQueryTextExtents` and `XQueryTextExtents16` functions return the bounding box of the specified 8-bit and 16-bit character string in the specified font or the font contained in the specified GC. These functions query the X server and, therefore, suffer the round-trip overhead that is avoided by `XTextExtents` and `XTextExtents16`. Both functions return a `XCharStruct` structure, whose members are set to the values as follows.

The ascent member is set to the maximum of the ascent metrics of all characters in the string. The descent member is set to the maximum of the descent metrics. The width member is set to the sum of the character-width metrics of all characters in the string. For each character in the string, let W be the sum of the character-width metrics of all characters preceding it in the string. Let L be the left-side-bearing metric of the character plus W. Let R be the right-side-bearing metric of the character plus W. The lbearing member is set to the minimum L of all characters in the string. The rbearing member is set to the maximum R.

For fonts defined with linear indexing rather than 2-byte matrix indexing, each `XChar2b` structure is interpreted as a 16-bit number with byte1 as the most-significant byte. If the font has no defined default character, undefined characters in the string are taken to have all zero metrics.

Characters with all zero metrics are ignored. If the font has no defined default_char, the undefined characters in the string are also ignored.

`XQueryTextExtents` and `XQueryTextExtents16` can generate `BadFont` and `BadGC` errors.

8.6 Drawing Text

This section discusses how to draw:

- Complex text
- Text characters
- Image text characters

The fundamental text functions `XDrawText` and `XDrawText16` use the following structures:

```
typedef struct {
    char *chars;        /* pointer to string */
    int nchars;         /* number of characters */
    int delta;          /* delta between strings */
    Font font;          /* Font to print it in, None don't change */
} XTextItem;

typedef struct {
    XChar2b *chars;     /* pointer to two-byte characters */
    int nchars;         /* number of characters */
    int delta;          /* delta between strings */
    Font font;          /* font to print it in, None don't change */
} XTextItem16;
```

If the font member is not `None`, the font is changed before printing and also is stored in the GC. If an error was generated during text drawing, the previous items may have been drawn. The baseline of the characters are drawn starting at the x and y coordinates that you pass in the text drawing functions.

For example, consider the background rectangle drawn by `XDrawImageString`. If you want the upper-left corner of the background rectangle to be at pixel coordinate (x,y), pass the (x,y + ascent) as the baseline origin coordinates to the text functions. The ascent is the font ascent, as given in the `XFontStruct` structure. If you want the lower-left corner of the background rectangle to be at pixel coordinate (x,y), pass the (x,y – descent + 1) as the baseline origin coordinates to the text functions. The descent is the font descent, as given in the `XFontStruct` structure.

8.6.1 Drawing Complex Text

To draw 8-bit characters in a given drawable, use `XDrawText`.

```
XDrawText(display, d, gc, x, y, items, nitems)
    Display *display;
    Drawable d;
    GC gc;
    int x, y;
    XTextItem *items;
    int nitems;
```

display Specifies the connection to the X server.

d Specifies the drawable.

gc Specifies the GC.

x

y Specify the x and y coordinates, which are relative to the origin of the specified drawable and define the origin of the first character.

items Specifies an array of text items.

nitems Specifies the number of text items in the array.

To draw 2-byte characters in a given drawable, use `XDrawText16`.

```
XDrawText16(display, d, gc, x, y, items, nitems)
    Display *display;
    Drawable d;
    GC gc;
    int x, y;
    XTextItem16 *items;
    int nitems;
```

display Specifies the connection to the X server.

d Specifies the drawable.

gc Specifies the GC.

x

y Specify the x and y coordinates, which are relative to the origin of the specified drawable and define the origin of the first character.

items Specifies an array of text items.

nitems Specifies the number of text items in the array.

The XDrawText16 function is similar to XDrawText except that it uses 2-byte or 16-bit characters. Both functions allow complex spacing and font shifts between counted strings.

Each text item is processed in turn. A font member other than None in an item causes the font to be stored in the GC and used for subsequent text. A text element delta specifies an additional change in the position along the x axis before the string is drawn. The delta is always added to the character origin and is not dependent on any characteristics of the font. Each character image, as defined by the font in the GC, is treated as an additional mask for a fill operation on the drawable. The drawable is modified only where the font character has a bit set to 1. If a text item generates a BadFont error, the previous text items may have been drawn.

For fonts defined with linear indexing rather than 2-byte matrix indexing, each XChar2b structure is interpreted as a 16-bit number with byte1 as the most-significant byte.

Both functions use these GC components: function, plane-mask, fill-style, font, subwindow-mode, clip-x-origin, clip-y-origin, and clip-mask. They also use these GC mode-dependent components: foreground, background, tile, stipple, tile-stipple-x-origin, and tile-stipple-y-origin.

XDrawText and XDrawText16 can generate BadDrawable, BadFont, BadGC, and BadMatch errors.

8.6.2 Drawing Text Characters

To draw 8-bit characters in a given drawable, use XDrawString.

```
XDrawString(display, d, gc, x, y, string, length)
    Display *display;
    Drawable d;
    GC gc;
    int x, y;
    char *string;
    int length;
```

display Specifies the connection to the X server.

d Specifies the drawable.

gc Specifies the GC.

x
y Specify the x and y coordinates, which are relative to the origin of the specified drawable and define the origin of the first character.
string Specifies the character string.
length Specifies the number of characters in the string argument.

To draw 2-byte characters in a given drawable, use `XDrawString16`.

```
XDrawString16(display, d, gc, x, y, string, length)
    Display *display;
    Drawable d;
    GC gc;
    int x, y;
    XChar2b *string;
    int length;
```

display Specifies the connection to the X server.
d Specifies the drawable.
gc Specifies the GC.
x
y Specify the x and y coordinates, which are relative to the origin of the specified drawable and define the origin of the first character.
string Specifies the character string.
length Specifies the number of characters in the string argument.

Each character image, as defined by the font in the GC, is treated as an additional mask for a fill operation on the drawable. The drawable is modified only where the font character has a bit set to 1. For fonts defined with 2-byte matrix indexing and used with `XDrawString16`, each byte is used as a byte2 with a byte1 of zero.

Both functions use these GC components: function, plane-mask, fill-style, font, subwindow-mode, clip-x-origin, clip-y-origin, and clip-mask. They also use these GC mode-dependent components: foreground, background, tile, stipple, tile-stipple-x-origin, and tile-stipple-y-origin.

`XDrawString` and `XDrawString16` can generate `BadDrawable`, `BadGC`, and `BadMatch` errors.

8.6.3 Drawing Image Text Characters

Some applications, in particular terminal emulators, need to print image text in which both the foreground and background bits of each character are painted. This prevents annoying flicker on many displays.

To draw 8-bit image text characters in a given drawable, use `XDrawImageString`.

```
XDrawImageString ( display, d, gc, x, y, string, length)
    Display *display;
    Drawable d;
    GC gc;
    int x, y;
    char *string;
    int length;
```

display Specifies the connection to the X server.

d Specifies the drawable.

gc Specifies the GC.

x

y Specify the x and y coordinates, which are relative to the origin of the specified drawable and define the origin of the first character.

string Specifies the character string.

length Specifies the number of characters in the string argument.

To draw 2-byte image text characters in a given drawable, use `XDrawImageString16`.

```
XDrawImageString16 ( display, d, gc, x, y, string, length)
    Display *display;
    Drawable d;
    GC gc;
    int x, y;
    XChar2b *string;
    int length;
```

display Specifies the connection to the X server.

d Specifies the drawable.

gc Specifies the GC.

x

y Specify the x and y coordinates, which are relative to the origin of the specified drawable and define the origin of the first character.

string Specifies the character string.

length Specifies the number of characters in the string argument.

The `XDrawImageString16` function is similar to `XDrawImageString` except that it uses 2-byte or 16-bit characters. Both functions also use both the foreground and background pixels of the GC in the destination.

The effect is first to fill a destination rectangle with the background pixel defined in the GC and then to paint the text with the foreground pixel. The upper-left corner of the filled rectangle is at:

[x, y – font-ascent]

The width is:

overall-width

The height is:

font-ascent + font-descent

The overall-width, font-ascent, and font-descent are as would be returned by `XQueryTextExtents` using gc and string. The function and fill-style defined in the GC are ignored for these functions. The effective function is `GXcopy`, and the effective fill-style is `FillSolid`.

For fonts defined with 2-byte matrix indexing and used with `XDrawImageString`, each byte is used as a byte2 with a byte1 of zero.

Both functions use these GC components: plane-mask, foreground, background, font, subwindow-mode, clip-x-origin, clip-y-origin, and clip-mask.

`XDrawImageString` and `XDrawImageString16` can generate `BadDrawable`, `BadGC`, and `BadMatch` errors.

8.7 Transferring Images between Client and Server

Xlib provides functions that you can use to transfer images between a client and the server. Because the server may require diverse data formats, Xlib provides an image object that fully describes the data in memory and that provides for basic operations on that data. You should reference the data through the image object rather than referencing the data directly. However, some implementations of the Xlib library may efficiently deal with frequently used data formats by replacing functions in the procedure vector with special case functions. Supported operations include destroying the image, getting a pixel, storing a pixel, extracting a subimage of an image, and adding a constant to an image (see section 16.8).

All the image manipulation functions discussed in this section make use of the `XImage` structure, which describes an image as it exists in the client's memory.

```
typedef struct _XImage {
    int width, height;              /* size of image */
    int xoffset;                    /* number of pixels offset in X direction */
    int format;                     /* XYBitmap, XYPixmap, ZPixmap */
    char *data;                     /* pointer to image data */
    int byte_order;                 /* data byte order, LSBFirst, MSBFirst */
    int bitmap_unit;                /* quant. of scanline 8, 16, 32 */
    int bitmap_bit_order;           /* LSBFirst, MSBFirst */
    int bitmap_pad;                 /* 8, 16, 32 either XY or ZPixmap */
    int depth;                      /* depth of image */
    int bytes_per_line;             /* accelerator to next scanline */
    int bits_per_pixel;             /* bits per pixel (ZPixmap) */
    unsigned long red_mask;         /* bits in z arrangement */
    unsigned long green_mask;
    unsigned long blue_mask;
    XPointer obdata;                /* hook for the object routines to hang on */
    struct funcs {                  /* image manipulation routines */
        struct _XImage *(*create_image)();
        int (*destroy_image)();
        unsigned long (*get_pixel)();
        int (*put_pixel)();
        struct _XImage *(*sub_image)();
        int (*add_pixel)();
        } f;
} XImage;
```

You may request that some of the members (for example, height, width, and xoffset) be changed when the image is sent to the server. That is, you may send a subset of the image. Other members (for example, byte_order, bitmap_unit, and so forth) are characteristics of both the image and the server. If these members differ between the image and the server, `XPutImage` makes the appropriate conversions. The first byte of the first scanline of plane n is located at the address (data + (n * height * bytes_per_line)).

To combine an image in memory with a rectangle of a drawable on the display, use `XPutImage`.

XPutImage (*display, d, gc, image, src_x, src_y, dest_x, dest_y, width, height*)
    Display **display*;
    Drawable *d*;

```
GC gc;
XImage *image;
int src_x, src_y;
int dest_x, dest_y;
unsigned int width, height;
```

display Specifies the connection to the X server.

d Specifies the drawable.

gc Specifies the GC.

image Specifies the image you want combined with the rectangle.

src_x Specifies the offset in X from the left edge of the image defined by the `XImage` structure.

src_y Specifies the offset in Y from the top edge of the image defined by the `XImage` structure.

dest_x
dest_y Specify the x and y coordinates, which are relative to the origin of the drawable and are the coordinates of the subimage.

width
height Specify the width and height of the subimage, which define the dimensions of the rectangle.

The `XPutImage` function combines an image in memory with a rectangle of the specified drawable. If `XYBitmap` format is used, the depth of the image must be one, or a `BadMatch` error results. The foreground pixel in the GC defines the source for the one bits in the image, and the background pixel defines the source for the zero bits. For `XYPixmap` and `ZPixmap`, the depth of the image must match the depth of the drawable, or a `BadMatch` error results. The section of the image defined by the src_x, src_y, width, and height arguments is drawn on the specified part of the drawable.

This function uses these GC components: function, plane-mask, subwindow-mode, clip-x-origin, clip-y-origin, and clip-mask. It also uses these GC mode-dependent components: foreground and background.

`XPutImage` can generate `BadDrawable`, `BadGC`, `BadMatch`, and `BadValue` errors.

To return the contents of a rectangle in a given drawable on the display, use `XGetImage`. This function specifically supports rudimentary screen dumps.

```
XImage *XGetImage (display, d, x, y, width, height, plane_mask, format)
    Display *display;
    Drawable d;
```

```
int x, y;
unsigned int width, height;
unsigned long plane_mask;
int format;
```

display Specifies the connection to the X server.

d Specifies the drawable.

x

y Specify the x and y coordinates, which are relative to the origin of the drawable and define the upper-left corner of the rectangle.

width

height Specify the width and height of the subimage, which define the dimensions of the rectangle.

plane_mask Specifies the plane mask.

format Specifies the format for the image. You can pass `XYPixmap` or `ZPixmap`.

The `XGetImage` function returns a pointer to an `XImage` structure. This structure provides you with the contents of the specified rectangle of the drawable in the format you specify. If the format argument is `XYPixmap`, the image contains only the bit planes you passed to the plane_mask argument. If the plane_mask argument only requests a subset of the planes of the display, the depth of the returned image will be the number of planes requested. If the format argument is `ZPixmap`, `XGetImage` returns as zero the bits in all planes not specified in the plane_mask argument. The function performs no range checking on the values in plane_mask and ignores extraneous bits.

`XGetImage` returns the depth of the image to the depth member of the `XImage` structure. The depth of the image is as specified when the drawable was created, except when getting a subset of the planes in `XYPixmap` format, when the depth is given by the number of bits set to 1 in plane_mask.

If the drawable is a pixmap, the given rectangle must be wholly contained within the pixmap, or a `BadMatch` error results. If the drawable is a window, the window must be viewable, and it must be the case that if there were no inferiors or overlapping windows, the specified rectangle of the window would be fully visible on the screen and wholly contained within the outside edges of the window, or a `BadMatch` error results. Note that the borders of the window can be included and read with this request. If the window has backing-store, the backing-store contents are returned for regions of the window that are obscured by noninferior windows. If the window does not have backing-store, the returned contents of such obscured regions are undefined. The returned contents of visible regions of inferiors of a different depth than the specified window's depth are also undefined. The pointer cursor image is not included in the returned contents. If a problem occurs, `XGetImage` returns NULL.

`XGetImage` can generate `BadDrawable`, `BadMatch`, and `BadValue` errors.

To copy the contents of a rectangle on the display to a location within a preexisting image structure, use `XGetSubImage`.

XImage *XGetSubImage (*display, d, x, y, width, height, plane_mask, format, dest_image, dest_x, dest_y*)
  Display **display*;
  Drawable *d*;
  int *x, y*;
  unsigned int *width, height*;
  unsigned long *plane_mask*;
  int *format*;
  XImage **dest_image*;
  int *dest_x, dest_y*;

display Specifies the connection to the X server.

d Specifies the drawable.

x
y Specify the x and y coordinates, which are relative to the origin of the drawable and define the upper-left corner of the rectangle.

width
height Specify the width and height of the subimage, which define the dimensions of the rectangle.

plane_mask Specifies the plane mask.

format Specifies the format for the image. You can pass `XYPixmap` or `ZPixmap`.

dest_image Specifies the destination image.

dest_x
dest_y Specify the x and y coordinates, which are relative to the origin of the destination rectangle, specify its upper-left corner, and determine where the subimage is placed in the destination image.

The `XGetSubImage` function updates dest_image with the specified subimage in the same manner as `XGetImage`. If the format argument is `XYPixmap`, the image contains only the bit planes you passed to the plane_mask argument. If the format argument is `ZPixmap`, `XGetSubImage` returns as zero the bits in all planes not specified in the plane_mask argument. The function performs no range checking on the values in plane_mask and ignores extraneous bits. As a convenience, XGetSubImage returns a pointer to the same XImage structure specified by dest_image.

The depth of the destination XImage structure must be the same as that of the drawable. If the specified subimage does not fit at the specified location on the destination image, the right and bottom edges are clipped. If the drawable is a pixmap, the given rectangle must be wholly contained within the pixmap, or a BadMatch error results. If the drawable is a window, the window must be viewable, and it must be the case that if there were no inferiors or overlapping windows, the specified rectangle of the window would be fully visible on the screen and wholly contained within the outside edges of the window, or a BadMatch error results. If the window has backing-store, then the backing-store contents are returned for regions of the window that are obscured by noninferior windows. If the window does not have backing-store, the returned contents of such obscured regions are undefined. The returned contents of visible regions of inferiors of a different depth than the specified window's depth are also undefined. If a problem occurs, XGetSubImage returns NULL.

XGetSubImage can generate BadDrawable, BadGC, BadMatch, and BadValue errors.

Chapter 9

Window and Session Manager Functions

Although it is difficult to categorize functions as exclusively for an application, a window manager, or a session manager, the functions in this chapter are most often used by window managers and session managers. It is not expected that these functions will be used by most application programs. Xlib provides management functions to:

- Change the parent of a window
- Control the lifetime of a window
- Manage installed colormaps
- Set and retrieve the font search path
- Grab the server
- Kill a client
- Control the screen saver
- Control host access

9.1 Changing the Parent of a Window

To change a window's parent to another window on the same screen, use `XReparentWindow`. There is no way to move a window between screens.

XReparentWindow (*display*, *w*, *parent*, *x*, *y*)
  Display **display*;

Window *w*;
Window *parent*;
int *x*, *y*;

display Specifies the connection to the X server.
w Specifies the window.
parent Specifies the parent window.
x
y Specify the x and y coordinates of the position in the new parent window.

If the specified window is mapped, `XReparentWindow` automatically performs an `UnmapWindow` request on it, removes it from its current position in the hierarchy, and inserts it as the child of the specified parent. The window is placed in the stacking order on top with respect to sibling windows.

After reparenting the specified window, `XReparentWindow` causes the X server to generate a `ReparentNotify` event. The override_redirect member returned in this event is set to the window's corresponding attribute. Window manager clients usually should ignore this window if this member is set to `True`. Finally, if the specified window was originally mapped, the X server automatically performs a `MapWindow` request on it.

The X server performs normal exposure processing on formerly obscured windows. The X server might not generate `Expose` events for regions from the initial `UnmapWindow` request that are immediately obscured by the final `MapWindow` request. A `BadMatch` error results if:

- The new parent window is not on the same screen as the old parent window.
- The new parent window is the specified window or an inferior of the specified window.
- The new parent is `InputOnly`, and the window is not.
- The specified window has a `ParentRelative` background, and the new parent window is not the same depth as the specified window.

`XReparentWindow` can generate `BadMatch` and `BadWindow` errors.

9.2 Controlling the Lifetime of a Window

The save-set of a client is a list of other clients' windows that, if they are inferiors of one of the client's windows at connection close, should not be destroyed and should be remapped if they are unmapped. For further information about close-connection processing, see section 2.6. To allow an application's window to survive when a window manager that has reparented a window fails, Xlib provides the save-set functions that you can use to control the longevity of subwindows that are normally destroyed when the parent is destroyed. For example, a window manager that wants to add decoration to a window by adding a frame might reparent an application's window. When the frame is destroyed, the application's window should not be destroyed but be returned to its previous place in the window hierarchy.

The X server automatically removes windows from the save-set when they are destroyed.

To add or remove a window from the client's save-set, use `XChangeSaveSet`.

```
XChangeSaveSet ( display, w, change_mode)
   Display *display;
   Window w;
   int change_mode;
```

display	Specifies the connection to the X server.
w	Specifies the window that you want to add to or delete from the client's save-set.
change_mode	Specifies the mode. You can pass `SetModeInsert` or `SetModeDelete`.

Depending on the specified mode, `XChangeSaveSet` either inserts or deletes the specified window from the client's save-set. The specified window must have been created by some other client, or a `BadMatch` error results.

`XChangeSaveSet` can generate `BadMatch`, `BadValue`, and `BadWindow` errors.

To add a window to the client's save-set, use `XAddToSaveSet`.

```
XAddToSaveSet ( display, w)
   Display *display;
   Window w;
```

display	Specifies the connection to the X server.
w	Specifies the window that you want to add to the client's save-set.

The `XAddToSaveSet` function adds the specified window to the client's save-set. The specified window must have been created by some other client, or a `BadMatch` error results.

`XAddToSaveSet` can generate `BadMatch` and `BadWindow` errors.

To remove a window from the client's save-set, use `XRemoveFromSaveSet`.

```
XRemoveFromSaveSet ( display, w)
    Display *display;
    Window w;
```

display Specifies the connection to the X server.

w Specifies the window that you want to delete from the client's save-set.

The `XRemoveFromSaveSet` function removes the specified window from the client's save-set. The specified window must have been created by some other client, or a `BadMatch` error results.

`XRemoveFromSaveSet` can generate `BadMatch` and `BadWindow` errors.

9.3 Managing Installed Colormaps

The X server maintains a list of installed colormaps. Windows using these colormaps are guaranteed to display with correct colors; windows using other colormaps may or may not display with correct colors. Xlib provides functions that you can use to install a colormap, uninstall a colormap, and obtain a list of installed colormaps.

At any time, there is a subset of the installed maps that is viewed as an ordered list and is called the required list. The length of the required list is at most M, where M is the minimum number of installed colormaps specified for the screen in the connection setup. The required list is maintained as follows. When a colormap is specified to `XInstallColormap`, it is added to the head of the list; the list is truncated at the tail, if necessary, to keep its length to at most M. When a colormap is specified to `XUninstallColormap` and it is in the required list, it is removed from the list. A colormap is not added to the required list when it is implicitly installed by the X server, and the X server cannot implicitly uninstall a colormap that is in the required list.

To install a colormap, use `XInstallColormap`.

```
XInstallColormap ( display, colormap)
    Display *display;
    Colormap colormap;
```

display Specifies the connection to the X server.

colormap Specifies the colormap.

The XInstallColormap function installs the specified colormap for its associated screen. All windows associated with this colormap immediately display with true colors. You associated the windows with this colormap when you created them by calling XCreateWindow, XCreateSimpleWindow, XChangeWindowAttributes, or XSetWindowColormap.

If the specified colormap is not already an installed colormap, the X server generates a ColormapNotify event on each window that has that colormap. In addition, for every other colormap that is installed as a result of a call to XInstallColormap, the X server generates a ColormapNotify event on each window that has that colormap.

XInstallColormap can generate a BadColor error.

To uninstall a colormap, use XUninstallColormap.

```
XUninstallColormap(display, colormap)
    Display *display;
    Colormap colormap;
```

display Specifies the connection to the X server.
colormap Specifies the colormap.

The XUninstallColormap function removes the specified colormap from the required list for its screen. As a result, the specified colormap might be uninstalled, and the X server might implicitly install or uninstall additional colormaps. Which colormaps get installed or uninstalled is server-dependent except that the required list must remain installed.

If the specified colormap becomes uninstalled, the X server generates a ColormapNotify event on each window that has that colormap. In addition, for every other colormap that is installed or uninstalled as a result of a call to XUninstallColormap, the X server generates a ColormapNotify event on each window that has that colormap.

XUninstallColormap can generate a BadColor error.

To obtain a list of the currently installed colormaps for a given screen, use XListInstalledColormaps.

```
Colormap *XListInstalledColormaps(display, w, num_return)
    Display *display;
    Window w;
    int *num_return;
```

display Specifies the connection to the X server.
w Specifies the window that determines the screen.
num_return Returns the number of currently installed colormaps.

The `XListInstalledColormaps` function returns a list of the currently installed colormaps for the screen of the specified window. The order of the colormaps in the list is not significant and is no explicit indication of the required list. When the allocated list is no longer needed, free it by using `XFree`.

`XListInstalledColormaps` can generate a `BadWindow` error.

9.4 Setting and Retrieving the Font Search Path

The set of fonts available from a server depends on a font search path. Xlib provides functions to set and retrieve the search path for a server.

To set the font search path, use `XSetFontPath`.

```
XSetFontPath ( display, directories, ndirs)
    Display *display;
    char **directories;
    int ndirs;
```

display Specifies the connection to the X server.
directories Specifies the directory path used to look for a font. Setting the path to the empty list restores the default path defined for the X server.
ndirs Specifies the number of directories in the path.

The `XSetFontPath` function defines the directory search path for font lookup. There is only one search path per X server, not one per client. The encoding and interpretation of the strings is implementation dependent, but typically they specify directories or font servers to be searched in the order listed. An X server is permitted to cache font information internally; for example, it might cache an entire font from a file and not check on subsequent opens of that font to see if the underlying font file has changed. However, when the font path is changed, the X server is guaranteed to flush all cached information about fonts for which there currently are no explicit resource IDs allocated. The meaning of an error from this request is implementation dependent.

`XSetFontPath` can generate a `BadValue` error.

To get the current font search path, use XGetFontPath.

```
char **XGetFontPath ( display, npaths_return)
    Display *display;
    int *npaths_return;
```

display Specifies the connection to the X server.

npaths_return Returns the number of strings in the font path array.

The XGetFontPath function allocates and returns an array of strings containing the search path. The contents of these strings are implementation dependent and are not intended to be interpreted by client applications. When it is no longer needed, the data in the font path should be freed by using XFreeFontPath.

To free data returned by XGetFontPath, use XFreeFontPath.

```
XFreeFontPath ( list)
    char **list;
```

list Specifies the array of strings you want to free.

The XFreeFontPath function frees the data allocated by XGetFontPath.

9.5 Server Grabbing

Xlib provides functions that you can use to grab and ungrab the server. These functions can be used to control processing of output on other connections by the window system server. While the server is grabbed, no processing of requests or close downs on any other connection will occur. A client closing its connection automatically ungrabs the server. Although grabbing the server is highly discouraged, it is sometimes necessary.

To grab the server, use XGrabServer.

```
XGrabServer ( display)
    Display *display;
```

display Specifies the connection to the X server.

The XGrabServer function disables processing of requests and close downs on all other connections than the one this request arrived on. You should not grab the X server any more than is absolutely necessary.

To ungrab the server, use `XUngrabServer`.

```
XUngrabServer(display)
    Display *display;
```

display Specifies the connection to the X server.

The `XUngrabServer` function restarts processing of requests and close downs on other connections. You should avoid grabbing the X server as much as possible.

9.6 Killing Clients

Xlib provides a function to cause the connection to a client to be closed and its resources to be destroyed. To destroy a client, use `XKillClient`.

```
XKillClient(display, resource)
    Display *display;
    XID resource;
```

display Specifies the connection to the X server.

resource Specifies any resource associated with the client that you want to destroy or `AllTemporary`.

The `XKillClient` function forces a close-down of the client that created the resource if a valid resource is specified. If the client has already terminated in either `RetainPermanent` or `RetainTemporary` mode, all of the client's resources are destroyed. If `AllTemporary` is specified, the resources of all clients that have terminated in `RetainTemporary` are destroyed (see section 2.5). This permits implementation of window manager facilities that aid debugging. A client can set its close-down mode to `RetainTemporary`. If the client then crashes, its windows would not be destroyed. The programmer can then inspect the application's window tree and use the window manager to destroy the zombie windows.

`XKillClient` can generate a `BadValue` error.

9.7 Screen Saver Control

Xlib provides functions that you can use to set or reset the mode of the screen saver, to force or activate the screen saver, or to obtain the current screen saver values.

To set the screen saver mode, use XSetScreenSaver.

```
XSetScreenSaver ( display, timeout, interval, prefer_blanking, allow_exposures)
   Display *display;
   int timeout, interval;
   int prefer_blanking;
   int allow_exposures;
```

display Specifies the connection to the X server.

timeout Specifies the timeout, in seconds, until the screen saver turns on.

interval Specifies the interval, in seconds, between screen saver alterations.

prefer_blanking Specifies how to enable screen blanking. You can pass DontPreferBlanking, PreferBlanking, or DefaultBlanking.

allow_exposures Specifies the screen save control values. You can pass DontAllowExposures, AllowExposures, or DefaultExposures.

Timeout and interval are specified in seconds. A timeout of 0 disables the screen saver (but an activated screen saver is not deactivated), and a timeout of −1 restores the default. Other negative values generate a BadValue error. If the timeout value is nonzero, XSetScreenSaver enables the screen saver. An interval of 0 disables the random-pattern motion. If no input from devices (keyboard, mouse, and so on) is generated for the specified number of timeout seconds once the screen saver is enabled, the screen saver is activated.

For each screen, if blanking is preferred and the hardware supports video blanking, the screen simply goes blank. Otherwise, if either exposures are allowed or the screen can be regenerated without sending Expose events to clients, the screen is tiled with the root window background tile randomly re-origined each interval seconds. Otherwise, the screens' state do not change, and the screen saver is not activated. The screen saver is deactivated, and all screen states are restored at the next keyboard or pointer input or at the next call to XForceScreenSaver with mode ScreenSaverReset.

If the server-dependent screen saver method supports periodic change, the interval argument serves as a hint about how long the change period should be, and zero hints that no periodic change should be made. Examples of ways to change the screen include scrambling the colormap periodically, moving an icon image around the screen periodically, or tiling the screen with the root window background tile, randomly re-origined periodically.

XSetScreenSaver can generate a BadValue error.

To force the screen saver on or off, use `XForceScreenSaver`.

```
XForceScreenSaver (display, mode)
    Display *display;
    int mode;
```

display Specifies the connection to the X server.

mode Specifies the mode that is to be applied. You can pass `ScreenSaverActive` or `ScreenSaverReset`.

If the specified mode is `ScreenSaverActive` and the screen saver currently is deactivated, `XForceScreenSaver` activates the screen saver even if the screen saver had been disabled with a timeout of zero. If the specified mode is `ScreenSaverReset` and the screen saver currently is enabled, `XForceScreenSaver` deactivates the screen saver if it was activated, and the activation timer is reset to its initial state (as if device input had been received).

`XForceScreenSaver` can generate a `BadValue` error.

To activate the screen saver, use `XActivateScreenSaver`.

```
XActivateScreenSaver (display)
    Display *display;
```

display Specifies the connection to the X server.

To reset the screen saver, use `XResetScreenSaver`.

```
XResetScreenSaver (display)
    Display *display;
```

display Specifies the connection to the X server.

To get the current screen saver values, use `XGetScreenSaver`.

```
XGetScreenSaver (display, timeout_return, interval_return, prefer_blanking_return,
                 allow_exposures_return)
    Display *display;
    int *timeout_return, *interval_return;
    int *prefer_blanking_return;
    int *allow_exposures_return;
```

display Specifies the connection to the X server.

timeout_return Returns the timeout, in seconds, until the screen saver turns on.

interval_return Returns the interval between screen saver invocations.

prefer_blanking_return Returns the current screen blanking preference (`DontPreferBlanking`, `PreferBlanking`, or `DefaultBlanking`).

allow_exposures_return Returns the current screen save control value (`DontAllowExposures`, `AllowExposures`, or `DefaultExposures`).

9.8 Controlling Host Access

This section discusses how to:

- Add, get, or remove hosts from the access control list
- Change, enable, or disable access

X does not provide any protection on a per-window basis. If you find out the resource ID of a resource, you can manipulate it. To provide some minimal level of protection, however, connections are permitted only from machines you trust. This is adequate on single-user workstations but obviously breaks down on timesharing machines. Although provisions exist in the X protocol for proper connection authentication, the lack of a standard authentication server leaves host-level access control as the only common mechanism.

The initial set of hosts allowed to open connections typically consists of:

- The host the window system is running on.
- On POSIX-conformant systems, each host listed in the `/etc/X?.hosts` file. The ? indicates the number of the display. This file should consist of host names separated by newlines. DECnet nodes must terminate in :: to distinguish them from Internet hosts.

If a host is not in the access control list when the access control mechanism is enabled and if the host attempts to establish a connection, the server refuses the connection. To change the access list, the client must reside on the same host as the server and/or must have been granted permission in the initial authorization at connection setup.

Servers also can implement other access control policies in addition to or in place of this host access facility. For further information about other access control implementations, see part II, "X Window System Protocol."

9.8.1 Adding, Getting, or Removing Hosts

Xlib provides functions that you can use to add, get, or remove hosts from the access control list. All the host access control functions use the `XHostAddress` structure, which contains:

```
typedef struct {
    int family;             /* for example FamilyInternet */
    int length;             /* length of address, in bytes */
    char *address;          /* pointer to where to find the address */
} XHostAddress;
```

The family member specifies which protocol address family to use (for example, TCP/IP or DECnet) and can be `FamilyInternet`, `FamilyDECnet`, or `FamilyChaos`. The length member specifies the length of the address in bytes. The address member specifies a pointer to the address.

For TCP/IP, the address should be in network byte order. For the DECnet family, the server performs no automatic swapping on the address bytes. A Phase IV address is two bytes long. The first byte contains the least-significant eight bits of the node number. The second byte contains the most-significant two bits of the node number in the least-significant two bits of the byte and the area in the most-significant six bits of the byte.

To add a single host, use `XAddHost`.

XAddHost (*display, host*)
  Display **display*;
  XHostAddress **host*;

display Specifies the connection to the X server.
host Specifies the host that is to be added.

The `XAddHost` function adds the specified host to the access control list for that display. The server must be on the same host as the client issuing the command, or a `BadAccess` error results.

`XAddHost` can generate `BadAccess` and `BadValue` errors.

To add multiple hosts at one time, use `XAddHosts`.

XAddHosts (*display, hosts, num_hosts*)
  Display **display*;

```
   XHostAddress *hosts;
   int num_hosts;
```

display Specifies the connection to the X server.
hosts Specifies each host that is to be added.
num_hosts Specifies the number of hosts.

The `XAddHosts` function adds each specified host to the access control list for that display. The server must be on the same host as the client issuing the command, or a `BadAccess` error results.

`XAddHosts` can generate `BadAccess` and `BadValue` errors.

To obtain a host list, use `XListHosts`.

```
XHostAddress *XListHosts(display, nhosts_return, state_return)
   Display *display;
   int *nhosts_return;
   Bool *state_return;
```

display Specifies the connection to the X server.
nhosts_return Returns the number of hosts currently in the access control list.
state_return Returns the state of the access control.

The `XListHosts` function returns the current access control list as well as whether the use of the list at connection setup was enabled or disabled. `XListHosts` allows a program to find out what machines can make connections. It also returns a pointer to a list of host structures that were allocated by the function. When no longer needed, this memory should be freed by calling `XFree`.

To remove a single host, use `XRemoveHost`.

```
XRemoveHost(display, host)
   Display *display;
   XHostAddress *host;
```

display Specifies the connection to the X server.
host Specifies the host that is to be removed.

The `XRemoveHost` function removes the specified host from the access control list for that display. The server must be on the same host as the client process, or a `BadAccess` error results. If you remove your machine from the access list, you can no longer connect to that server, and this operation cannot be reversed unless you reset the server.

XRemoveHost can generate BadAccess and BadValue errors.

To remove multiple hosts at one time, use XRemoveHosts.

```
XRemoveHosts ( display, hosts, num_hosts)
    Display *display;
    XHostAddress *hosts;
    int num_hosts;
```

display Specifies the connection to the X server.
hosts Specifies each host that is to be removed.
num_hosts Specifies the number of hosts.

The XRemoveHosts function removes each specified host from the access control list for that display. The X server must be on the same host as the client process, or a BadAccess error results. If you remove your machine from the access list, you can no longer connect to that server, and this operation cannot be reversed unless you reset the server.

XRemoveHosts can generate BadAccess and BadValue errors.

9.8.2 Changing, Enabling, or Disabling Access Control

Xlib provides functions that you can use to enable, disable, or change access control.

For these functions to execute successfully, the client application must reside on the same host as the X server and/or have been given permission in the initial authorization at connection setup.

To change access control, use XSetAccessControl.

```
XSetAccessControl ( display, mode)
    Display *display;
    int mode;
```

display Specifies the connection to the X server.
mode Specifies the mode. You can pass EnableAccess or DisableAccess.

The XSetAccessControl function either enables or disables the use of the access control list at each connection setup.

XSetAccessControl can generate BadAccess and BadValue errors.

To enable access control, use `XEnableAccessControl`.

```
XEnableAccessControl ( display)
    Display *display;
```

display Specifies the connection to the X server.

The `XEnableAccessControl` function enables the use of the access control list at each connection setup.

`XEnableAccessControl` can generate a `BadAccess` error.

To disable access control, use `XDisableAccessControl`.

```
XDisableAccessControl ( display)
    Display *display;
```

display Specifies the connection to the X server.

The `XDisableAccessControl` function disables the use of the access control list at each connection setup.

`XDisableAccessControl` can generate a `BadAccess` error.

Chapter 10

Events

A client application communicates with the X server through the connection you establish with the XOpenDisplay function. A client application sends requests to the X server over this connection. These requests are made by the Xlib functions that are called in the client application. Many Xlib functions cause the X server to generate events, and the user's typing or moving the pointer can generate events asynchronously. The X server returns events to the client on the same connection.

This chapter discusses the following topics associated with events:

- Event types
- Event structures
- Event mask
- Event processing

Functions for handling events are dealt with in the next chapter.

10.1 Event Types

An event is data generated asynchronously by the X server as a result of some device activity or as side effects of a request sent by an Xlib function. Device-related events propagate from the source window to ancestor windows until some client application has selected that event type or until the event is explicitly discarded. The X server generally sends an event to a client application only if the client has specifically asked to be informed of that event type, typically by setting the event-mask attribute of the window. The mask can also be set when you create a window or by changing the window's event-mask. You can also mask out events that would propagate to ancestor windows by manipulating the do-not-propagate mask of the window's attributes. However, `MappingNotify` events are always sent to all clients.

An event type describes a specific event generated by the X server. For each event type, a corresponding constant name is defined in `<X11/X.h>`, which is used when referring to an event type. The following table lists the event category and its associated event type or types. The processing associated with these events is discussed in section 10.5.

Event Category	*Event Type*
Keyboard events	`KeyPress`, `KeyRelease`
Pointer events	`ButtonPress`, `ButtonRelease`, `MotionNotify`
Window crossing events	`EnterNotify`, `LeaveNotify`
Input focus events	`FocusIn`, `FocusOut`
Keymap state notification event	`KeymapNotify`
Exposure events	`Expose`, `GraphicsExpose`, `NoExpose`
Structure control events	`CirculateRequest`, `ConfigureRequest`, `MapRequest`, `ResizeRequest`
Window state notification events	`CirculateNotify`, `ConfigureNotify`, `CreateNotify`, `DestroyNotify`, `GravityNotify`, `MapNotify`, `MappingNotify`, `ReparentNotify`, `UnmapNotify`, `VisibilityNotify`
Colormap state notification event	`ColormapNotify`
Client communication events	`ClientMessage`, `PropertyNotify`, `SelectionClear`, `SelectionNotify`, `SelectionRequest`

10.2 Event Structures

For each event type, a corresponding structure is declared in `<X11/Xlib.h>`. All the event structures have the following common members:

```
typedef struct {
    int type;
    unsigned long serial;          /* # of last request processed by server */
```

```
    Bool send_event;    /* true if this came from a SendEvent request */
    Display *display;   /* Display the event was read from */
    Window window;
} XAnyEvent;
```

The type member is set to the event type constant name that uniquely identifies it. For example, when the X server reports a `GraphicsExpose` event to a client application, it sends an `XGraphicsExposeEvent` structure with the type member set to `GraphicsExpose`. The display member is set to a pointer to the display the event was read on. The send_event member is set to `True` if the event came from a `SendEvent` protocol request. The serial member is set from the serial number reported in the protocol but expanded from the 16-bit least-significant bits to a full 32-bit value. The window member is set to the window that is most useful to toolkit dispatchers.

The X server can send events at any time in the input stream. Xlib stores any events received while waiting for a reply in an event queue for later use. Xlib also provides functions that allow you to check events in the event queue (see section 11.3).

In addition to the individual structures declared for each event type, the `XEvent` structure is a union of the individual structures declared for each event type. Depending on the type, you should access members of each event by using the `XEvent` union.

```
typedef union _XEvent {
    int type;                                   /* must not be changed */
    XAnyEvent xany;
    XKeyEvent xkey;
    XButtonEvent xbutton;
    XMotionEvent xmotion;
    XCrossingEvent xcrossing;
    XFocusChangeEvent xfocus;
    XExposeEvent xexpose;
    XGraphicsExposeEvent xgraphicsexpose;
    XNoExposeEvent xnoexpose;
    XVisibilityEvent xvisibility;
    XCreateWindowEvent xcreatewindow;
    XDestroyWindowEvent xdestroywindow;
    XUnmapEvent xunmap;
```

```
        XMapEvent xmap;
        XMapRequestEvent xmaprequest;
        XReparentEvent xreparent;
        XConfigureEvent xconfigure;
        XGravityEvent xgravity;
        XResizeRequestEvent xresizerequest;
        XConfigureRequestEvent xconfigurerequest;
        XCirculateEvent xcirculate;
        XCirculateRequestEvent xcirculaterequest;
        XPropertyEvent xproperty;
        XSelectionClearEvent xselectionclear;
        XSelectionRequestEvent xselectionrequest;
        XSelectionEvent xselection;
        XColormapEvent xcolormap;
        XClientMessageEvent xclient;
        XMappingEvent xmapping;
        XErrorEvent xerror;
        XKeymapEvent xkeymap;
        long pad[24];
} XEvent;
```

An XEvent structure's first entry always is the type member, which is set to the event type. The second member always is the serial number of the protocol request that generated the event. The third member always is send_event, which is a Bool that indicates if the event was sent by a different client. The fourth member always is a display, which is the display that the event was read from. Except for keymap events, the fifth member always is a window, which has been carefully selected to be useful to toolkit dispatchers. To avoid breaking toolkits, the order of these first five entries is not to change. Most events also contain a time member, which is the time at which an event occurred. In addition, a pointer to the generic event must be cast before it is used to access any other information in the structure.

10.3 Event Masks

Clients select event reporting of most events relative to a window. To do this, pass an event mask to an Xlib event-handling function that takes an event_mask argument. The bits of the event mask are defined in <X11/X.h>. Each bit in the event mask maps to an event mask name, which describes the event or events you want the X server to return to a client application.

Unless the client has specifically asked for them, most events are not reported to clients when they are generated. Unless the client suppresses them by setting graphics-exposures in the GC to False, GraphicsExpose and NoExpose are reported by default as a result of XCopyPlane and XCopyArea. SelectionClear, SelectionRequest, SelectionNotify, or ClientMessage cannot be masked. Selection related events are only sent to clients cooperating with selections (see section 4.5). When the keyboard or pointer mapping is changed, MappingNotify is always sent to clients.

The following table lists the event mask constants you can pass to the event_mask argument and the circumstances in which you would want to specify the event mask:

Event Mask	*Circumstances*
NoEventMask	No events wanted
KeyPressMask	Keyboard down events wanted
KeyReleaseMask	Keyboard up events wanted
ButtonPressMask	Pointer button down events wanted
ButtonReleaseMask	Pointer button up events wanted
EnterWindowMask	Pointer window entry events wanted
LeaveWindowMask	Pointer window leave events wanted
PointerMotionMask	Pointer motion events wanted
PointerMotionHintMask	Pointer motion hints wanted
Button1MotionMask	Pointer motion while button 1 down
Button2MotionMask	Pointer motion while button 2 down
Button3MotionMask	Pointer motion while button 3 down
Button4MotionMask	Pointer motion while button 4 down
Button5MotionMask	Pointer motion while button 5 down
ButtonMotionMask	Pointer motion while any button down
KeymapStateMask	Keyboard state wanted at window entry and focus in
ExposureMask	Any exposure wanted
VisibilityChangeMask	Any change in visibility wanted
StructureNotifyMask	Any change in window structure wanted
ResizeRedirectMask	Redirect resize of this window
SubstructureNotifyMask	Substructure notification wanted
SubstructureRedirectMask	Redirect structure requests on children
FocusChangeMask	Any change in input focus wanted

Event Mask	*Circumstances*
PropertyChangeMask	Any change in property wanted
ColormapChangeMask	Any change in colormap wanted
OwnerGrabButtonMask	Automatic grabs should activate with owner_events set to True

10.4 Event Processing Overview

The event reported to a client application during event processing depends on which event masks you provide as the event-mask attribute for a window. For some event masks, there is a one-to-one correspondence between the event mask constant and the event type constant. For example, if you pass the event mask ButtonPressMask, the X server sends back only ButtonPress events. Most events contain a time member, which is the time at which an event occurred.

In other cases, one event mask constant can map to several event type constants. For example, if you pass the event mask SubstructureNotifyMask, the X server can send back CirculateNotify, ConfigureNotify, CreateNotify, DestroyNotify, GravityNotify, MapNotify, ReparentNotify, or UnmapNotify events.

In another case, two event masks can map to one event type. For example, if you pass either PointerMotionMask or ButtonMotionMask, the X server sends back a MotionNotify event.

The table on pages 254–255 lists the event mask, its associated event type or types, and the structure name associated with the event type. Some of these structures actually are typedefs to a generic structure that is shared between two event types. Note that N.A. appears in columns for which the information is not applicable.

The sections that follow describe the processing that occurs when you select the different event masks. The sections are organized according to these processing categories:

- Keyboard and pointer events
- Window crossing events
- Input focus events

- Keymap state notification events
- Exposure events
- Window state notification events
- Structure control events
- Colormap state notification events
- Client communication events

10.5 Keyboard and Pointer Events

This section discusses:

- Pointer button events
- Keyboard and pointer events

10.5.1 Pointer Button Events

The following describes the event processing that occurs when a pointer button press is processed with the pointer in some window w and when no active pointer grab is in progress.

The X server searches the ancestors of w from the root down, looking for a passive grab to activate. If no matching passive grab on the button exists, the X server automatically starts an active grab for the client receiving the event and sets the last-pointer-grab time to the current server time. The effect is essentially equivalent to an `XGrabButton` with these client passed arguments:

Argument	*Value*
w	The event window
event_mask	The client's selected pointer events on the event window
pointer_mode	`GrabModeAsync`
keyboard_mode	`GrabModeAsync`
owner_events	`True`, if the client has selected `OwnerGrabButtonMask` on the event window, otherwise `False`
confine_to	`None`
cursor	`None`

The active grab is automatically terminated when the logical state of the pointer has all buttons released. Clients can modify the active grab by calling `XUngrabPointer` and `XChangeActivePointerGrab`.

Event Mask	*Event Type*	*Structure*	*Generic Structure*
ButtonMotionMask	MotionNotify	XPointerMovedEvent	XMotionEvent
Button1MotionMask			
Button2MotionMask			
Button3MotionMask			
Button4MotionMask			
Button5MotionMask			
ButtonPressMask	ButtonPress	XButtonPressedEvent	XButtonEvent
ButtonReleaseMask	ButtonRelease	XButtonReleasedEvent	XButtonEvent
ColormapChangeMask	ColormapNotify	XColormapEvent	
EnterWindowMask	EnterNotify	XEnterWindowEvent	XCrossingEvent
LeaveWindowMask	LeaveNotify	XLeaveWindowEvent	XCrossingEvent
ExposureMask	Expose	XExposeEvent	
GCGraphicsExposures in GC	GraphicsExpose	XGraphicsExposeEvent	
	NoExpose	XNoExposeEvent	
FocusChangeMask	FocusIn	XFocusInEvent	XFocusChangeEvent
	FocusOut	XFocusOutEvent	XFocusChangeEvent
KeymapStateMask	KeymapNotify	XKeymapEvent	
KeyPressMask	KeyPress	XKeyPressedEvent	XKeyEvent
KeyReleaseMask	KeyRelease	XKeyReleasedEvent	XKeyEvent
OwnerGrabButtonMask	N.A.	N.A.	
PointerMotionMask	MotionNotify	XPointerMovedEvent	XMotionEvent
PointerMotionHintMask	N.A.	N.A.	
PropertyChangeMask	PropertyNotify	XPropertyEvent	
ResizeRedirectMask	ResizeRequest	XResizeRequestEvent	
StructureNotifyMask	CirculateNotify	XCirculateEvent	
	ConfigureNotify	XConfigureEvent	
	DestroyNotify	XDestroyWindowEvent	

Event Mask	*Event Type*	*Structure*	*Generic Structure*
	GravityNotify	XGravityEvent	
	MapNotify	XMapEvent	
	ReparentNotify	XReparentEvent	
	UnmapNotify	XUnmapEvent	
SubstructureNotifyMask	CirculateNotify	XCirculateEvent	
	ConfigureNotify	XConfigureEvent	
	CreateNotify	XCreateWindowEvent	
	DestroyNotify	XDestroyWindowEvent	
	GravityNotify	XGravityEvent	
	MapNotify	XMapEvent	
	ReparentNotify	XReparentEvent	
	UnmapNotify	XUnmapEvent	
SubstructureRedirectMask	CirculateRequest	XCirculateRequestEvent	
	ConfigureRequest	XConfigureRequestEvent	
	MapRequest	XMapRequestEvent	
N.A.	ClientMessage	XClientMessageEvent	
N.A.	MappingNotify	XMappingEvent	
N.A.	SelectionClear	XSelectionClearEvent	
N.A.	SelectionNotify	XSelectionEvent	
N.A.	SelectionRequest	XSelectionRequestEvent	
VisibilityChangeMask	VisibilityNotify	XVisibilityEvent	

10.5.2 Keyboard and Pointer Events

This section discusses the processing that occurs for the keyboard events KeyPress and KeyRelease and the pointer events ButtonPress, ButtonRelease, and MotionNotify. For information about the keyboard event-handling utilities, see chapter 11.

The X server reports KeyPress or KeyRelease events to clients wanting information about keys that logically change state. Note that these events are generated for all keys, even those mapped to modifier bits. The X server reports ButtonPress or ButtonRelease events to clients wanting information about buttons that logically change state.

The X server reports MotionNotify events to clients wanting information about when the pointer logically moves. The X server generates this event whenever the pointer is moved and the pointer motion begins and ends in the window. The granularity of MotionNotify events is not guaranteed, but a client that selects this event type is guaranteed to receive at least one event when the pointer moves and then rests.

The generation of the logical changes lags the physical changes if device event processing is frozen.

To receive KeyPress, KeyRelease, ButtonPress, and ButtonRelease events, set KeyPressMask, KeyReleaseMask, ButtonPressMask, and ButtonReleaseMask bits in the event-mask attribute of the window.

To receive MotionNotify events, set one or more of the following event masks bits in the event-mask attribute of the window.

- Button1MotionMask – Button5MotionMask
  The client application receives MotionNotify events only when one or more of the specified buttons is pressed.
- ButtonMotionMask
  The client application receives MotionNotify events only when at least one button is pressed.
- PointerMotionMask
  The client application receives MotionNotify events independent of the state of the pointer buttons.
- PointerMotionHintMask
  If PointerMotionHintMask is selected in combination with one or more of the above masks, the X server is free to send only one MotionNotify event (with the is_hint member of the XPointerMovedEvent structure set to NotifyHint) to the client for the

event window, until either the key or button state changes, the pointer leaves the event window, or the client calls `XQueryPointer` or `XGetMotionEvents`. The server still may send `MotionNotify` events without is_hint set to `NotifyHint`.

The source of the event is the viewable window that the pointer is in. The window used by the X server to report these events depends on the window's position in the window hierarchy and whether any intervening window prohibits the generation of these events. Starting with the source window, the X server searches up the window hierarchy until it locates the first window specified by a client as having an interest in these events. If one of the intervening windows has its do-not-propagate-mask set to prohibit generation of the event type, the events of those types will be suppressed. Clients can modify the actual window used for reporting by performing active grabs and, in the case of keyboard events, by using the focus window.

The structures for these event types contain:

```
typedef struct {
    int type;                   /* ButtonPress or ButtonRelease */
    unsigned long serial;       /* # of last request processed by server */
    Bool send_event;            /* true if this came from a SendEvent request */
    Display *display;           /* Display the event was read from */
    Window window;              /* "event" window it is reported relative to */
    Window root;                /* root window that the event occurred on */
    Window subwindow;           /* child window */
    Time time;                  /* milliseconds */
    int x, y;                   /* pointer x, y coordinates in event window */
    int x_root, y_root;         /* coordinates relative to root */
    unsigned int state;         /* key or button mask */
    unsigned int button;        /* detail */
    Bool same_screen;           /* same screen flag */
} XButtonEvent;
typedef XButtonEvent XButtonPressedEvent;
typedef XButtonEvent XButtonReleasedEvent;

typedef struct {
    int type;                   /* KeyPress or KeyRelease */
    unsigned long serial;       /* # of last request processed by server */
    Bool send_event;            /* true if this came from a SendEvent request */
    Display *display;           /* Display the event was read from */
    Window window;              /* "event" window it is reported relative to */
```

```
    Window root;             /* root window that the event occurred on */
    Window subwindow;        /* child window */
    Time time;               /* milliseconds */
    int x, y;                /* pointer x, y coordinates in event window */
    int x_root, y_root;      /* coordinates relative to root */
    unsigned int state;      /* key or button mask */
    unsigned int keycode;    /* detail */
    Bool same_screen;        /* same screen flag */
} XKeyEvent;
typedef XKeyEvent XKeyPressedEvent;
typedef XKeyEvent XKeyReleasedEvent;

typedef struct {
    int type;                /* MotionNotify */
    unsigned long serial;    /* # of last request processed by server */
    Bool send_event;         /* true if this came from a SendEvent request */
    Display *display;        /* Display the event was read from */
    Window window;           /* ''event'' window reported relative to */
    Window root;             /* root window that the event occurred on */
    Window subwindow;        /* child window */
    Time time;               /* milliseconds */
    int x, y;                /* pointer x, y coordinates in event window */
    int x_root, y_root;      /* coordinates relative to root */
    unsigned int state;      /* key or button mask */
    char is_hint;            /* detail */
    Bool same_screen;        /* same screen flag */
} XMotionEvent;
typedef XMotionEvent XPointerMovedEvent;
```

These structures have the following common members: window, root, subwindow, time, x, y, x_root, y_root, state, and same_screen. The window member is set to the window on which the event was generated and is referred to as the event window. As long as the conditions previously discussed are met, this is the window used by the X server to report the event. The root member is set to the source window's root window. The x_root and y_root members are set to the pointer's coordinates relative to the root window's origin at the time of the event.

The same_screen member is set to indicate whether the event window is on the same screen as the root window and can be either `True` or `False`. If `True`, the event and root windows are on the same screen. If `False`, the event and root windows are not on the same screen.

If the source window is an inferior of the event window, the subwindow member of the structure is set to the child of the event window that is the source window or the child of the event window that is an ancestor of the source window. Otherwise, the X server sets the subwindow member to `None`. The time member is set to the time when the event was generated and is expressed in milliseconds.

If the event window is on the same screen as the root window, the x and y members are set to the coordinates relative to the event window's origin. Otherwise, these members are set to zero.

The state member is set to indicate the logical state of the pointer buttons and modifier keys just prior to the event, which is the bitwise inclusive OR of one or more of the button or modifier key masks: `Button1Mask`, `Button2Mask`, `Button3Mask`, `Button4Mask`, `Button5Mask`, `ShiftMask`, `LockMask`, `ControlMask`, `Mod1Mask`, `Mod2Mask`, `Mod3Mask`, `Mod4Mask`, and `Mod5Mask`.

Each of these structures also has a member that indicates the detail. For the `XKeyPressedEvent` and `XKeyReleasedEvent` structures, this member is called keycode. It is set to a number that represents a physical key on the keyboard. The keycode is an arbitrary representation for any key on the keyboard (see sections 12.7 and 16.1).

For the `XButtonPressedEvent` and `XButtonReleasedEvent` structures, this member is called button. It represents the pointer button that changed state and can be the `Button1`, `Button2`, `Button3`, `Button4`, or `Button5` value. For the `XPointerMovedEvent` structure, this member is called is_hint. It can be set to `NotifyNormal` or `NotifyHint`.

10.6 Window Entry/Exit Events

This section describes the processing that occurs for the window crossing events `EnterNotify` and `LeaveNotify`. If a pointer motion or a window hierarchy change causes the pointer to be in a different window than before, the X server reports `EnterNotify` or `LeaveNotify` events to clients who have selected for these events. All `EnterNotify` and `LeaveNotify` events caused by a hierarchy change are generated after any hierarchy event (`UnmapNotify`, `MapNotify`, `ConfigureNotify`, `GravityNotify`, `CirculateNotify`) caused by that change; however, the X protocol does not constrain the ordering of

EnterNotify and LeaveNotify events with respect to FocusOut, Visibility-Notify, and Expose events.

This contrasts with MotionNotify events, which are also generated when the pointer moves but only when the pointer motion begins and ends in a single window. An EnterNotify or LeaveNotify event also can be generated when some client application calls XGrabPointer and XUngrabPointer.

To receive EnterNotify or LeaveNotify events, set the EnterWindowMask or LeaveWindowMask bits of the event-mask attribute of the window.

The structure for these event types contains:

```
typedef struct {
    int type;                 /* EnterNotify or LeaveNotify */
    unsigned long serial;     /* # of last request processed by server */
    Bool send_event;          /* true if this came from a SendEvent request */
    Display *display;         /* Display the event was read from */
    Window window;            /* ''event'' window reported relative to */
    Window root;              /* root window that the event occurred on */
    Window subwindow;         /* child window */
    Time time;                /* milliseconds */
    int x, y;                 /* pointer x, y coordinates in event window */
    int x_root, y_root;       /* coordinates relative to root */
    int mode;                 /* NotifyNormal, NotifyGrab, NotifyUngrab */
    int detail;               /*
                               * NotifyAncestor, NotifyVirtual,
                               * NotifyInferior, NotifyNonlinear,
                               * NotifyNonlinearVirtual
                               */
    Bool same_screen;         /* same screen flag */
    Bool focus;               /* boolean focus */
    unsigned int state;       /* key or button mask */
} XCrossingEvent;
typedef XCrossingEvent XEnterWindowEvent;
typedef XCrossingEvent XLeaveWindowEvent;
```

The window member is set to the window on which the EnterNotify or LeaveNotify event was generated and is referred to as the event window. This is the window used by the X server to report the event, and is relative to the root window on which the event occurred. The root member is set to the root window of the screen on which the event occurred.

For a LeaveNotify event, if a child of the event window contains the initial position of the pointer, the subwindow component is set to that child. Otherwise, the X server sets the subwindow member to None. For an EnterNotify event, if a child of the event window contains the final pointer position, the subwindow component is set to that child or None.

The time member is set to the time when the event was generated and is expressed in milliseconds. The x and y members are set to the coordinates of the pointer position in the event window. This position is always the pointer's final position, not its initial position. If the event window is on the same screen as the root window, x and y are the pointer coordinates relative to the event window's origin. Otherwise, x and y are set to zero. The x_root and y_root members are set to the pointer's coordinates relative to the root window's origin at the time of the event.

The same_screen member is set to indicate whether the event window is on the same screen as the root window and can be either True or False. If True, the event and root windows are on the same screen. If False, the event and root windows are not on the same screen.

The focus member is set to indicate whether the event window is the focus window or an inferior of the focus window. The X server can set this member to either True or False. If True, the event window is the focus window or an inferior of the focus window. If False, the event window is not the focus window or an inferior of the focus window.

The state member is set to indicate the state of the pointer buttons and modifier keys just prior to the event. The X server can set this member to the bitwise inclusive OR of one or more of the button or modifier key masks: Button1Mask, Button2Mask, Button3Mask, Button4Mask, Button5Mask, ShiftMask, LockMask, ControlMask, Mod1Mask, Mod2Mask, Mod3Mask, Mod4Mask, Mod5Mask.

The mode member is set to indicate whether the events are normal events, pseudo-motion events when a grab activates, or pseudo-motion events when a grab deactivates. The X server can set this member to NotifyNormal, NotifyGrab, or NotifyUngrab.

The detail member is set to indicate the notify detail and can be NotifyAncestor, NotifyVirtual, NotifyInferior, NotifyNonlinear, or NotifyNonlinearVirtual.

10.6.1 Normal Entry/Exit Events

EnterNotify and LeaveNotify events are generated when the pointer moves from one window to another window. Normal events are identified by XEnterWindowEvent or XLeaveWindowEvent structures whose mode member is set to NotifyNormal.

- When the pointer moves from window A to window B and A is an inferior of B, the X server does the following:
  - — It generates a LeaveNotify event on window A, with the detail member of the XLeaveWindowEvent structure set to NotifyAncestor.
  - — It generates a LeaveNotify event on each window between window A and window B, exclusive, with the detail member of each XLeaveWindowEvent structure set to NotifyVirtual.
  - — It generates an EnterNotify event on window B, with the detail member of the XEnterWindowEvent structure set to NotifyInferior.
- When the pointer moves from window A to window B and B is an inferior of A, the X server does the following:
  - — It generates a LeaveNotify event on window A, with the detail member of the XLeaveWindowEvent structure set to NotifyInferior.
  - — It generates an EnterNotify event on each window between window A and window B, exclusive, with the detail member of each XEnterWindowEvent structure set to NotifyVirtual.
  - — It generates an EnterNotify event on window B, with the detail member of the XEnterWindowEvent structure set to NotifyAncestor.
- When the pointer moves from window A to window B and window C is their least common ancestor, the X server does the following:
  - — It generates a LeaveNotify event on window A, with the detail member of the XLeaveWindowEvent structure set to NotifyNonlinear.
  - — It generates a LeaveNotify event on each window between window A and window C, exclusive, with the detail member of each XLeaveWindowEvent structure set to NotifyNonlinearVirtual.
  - — It generates an EnterNotify event on each window between window C and window B, exclusive, with the detail member of each XEnterWindowEvent structure set to NotifyNonlinearVirtual.
  - — It generates an EnterNotify event on window B, with the detail member of the XEnterWindowEvent structure set to NotifyNonlinear.

- When the pointer moves from window A to window B on different screens, the X server does the following:
  - — It generates a LeaveNotify event on window A, with the detail member of the XLeaveWindowEvent structure set to NotifyNonlinear.
  - — If window A is not a root window, it generates a LeaveNotify event on each window above window A up to and including its root, with the detail member of each XLeaveWindowEvent structure set to NotifyNonlinearVirtual.
  - — If window B is not a root window, it generates an EnterNotify event on each window from window B's root down to but not including window B, with the detail member of each XEnterWindowEvent structure set to NotifyNonlinearVirtual.
  - — It generates an EnterNotify event on window B, with the detail member of the XEnterWindowEvent structure set to NotifyNonlinear.

10.6.2 Grab and Ungrab Entry/Exit Events

Pseudo-motion mode EnterNotify and LeaveNotify events are generated when a pointer grab activates or deactivates. Events in which the pointer grab activates are identified by XEnterWindowEvent or XLeaveWindowEvent structures whose mode member is set to NotifyGrab. Events in which the pointer grab deactivates are identified by XEnterWindowEvent or XLeaveWindowEvent structures whose mode member is set to NotifyUngrab (see XGrabPointer).

- When a pointer grab activates after any initial warp into a confine_to window and before generating any actual ButtonPress event that activates the grab, G is the grab_window for the grab, and P is the window the pointer is in, the X server does the following:
  - — It generates EnterNotify and LeaveNotify events (see section 10.6.1) with the mode members of the XEnterWindowEvent and XLeaveWindowEvent structures set to NotifyGrab. These events are generated as if the pointer were to suddenly warp from its current position in P to some position in G. However, the pointer does not warp, and the X server uses the pointer position as both the initial and final positions for the events.
- When a pointer grab deactivates after generating any actual ButtonRelease event that deactivates the grab, G is the grab_window for the grab, and P is the window the pointer is in, the X server does the following:
  - — It generates EnterNotify and LeaveNotify events (see section 10.6.1) with the mode members of the XEnterWindowEvent and XLeaveWindowEvent structures set to NotifyUngrab. These events are generated as if the pointer were to suddenly warp from some position in G to its current position in P. However, the pointer does not warp, and the X server uses the current pointer position as both the initial and final positions for the events.

10.7 Input Focus Events

This section describes the processing that occurs for the input focus events FocusIn and FocusOut. The X server can report FocusIn or FocusOut events to clients wanting information about when the input focus changes. The keyboard is always attached to some window (typically, the root window or a top-level window), which is called the focus window. The focus window and the position of the pointer determine the window that receives keyboard input. Clients may need to know when the input focus changes to control highlighting of areas on the screen.

To receive FocusIn or FocusOut events, set the FocusChangeMask bit in the event-mask attribute of the window.

The structure for these event types contains:

```
typedef struct {
    int type;                /* FocusIn or FocusOut */
    unsigned long serial;    /* # of last request processed by server */
    Bool send_event;         /* true if this came from a SendEvent request */
    Display *display;        /* Display the event was read from */
    Window window;           /* window of event */
    int mode;                /* NotifyNormal, NotifyGrab,
                              * NotifyUngrab */
    int detail;              /*
                              * NotifyAncestor, NotifyVirtual,
                              * NotifyInferior, NotifyNonlinear,
                              * NotifyNonlinearVirtual, NotifyPointer,
                              * NotifyPointerRoot, NotifyDetailNone
                             */
} XFocusChangeEvent;
typedef XFocusChangeEvent XFocusInEvent;
typedef XFocusChangeEvent XFocusOutEvent;
```

The window member is set to the window on which the FocusIn or FocusOut event was generated. This is the window used by the X server to report the event. The mode member is set to indicate whether the focus events are normal focus events, focus events while grabbed, focus events when a grab activates, or focus events when a grab deactivates. The X server can set the mode member to NotifyNormal, NotifyWhileGrabbed, NotifyGrab, or NotifyUngrab.

All `FocusOut` events caused by a window unmap are generated after any `UnmapNotify` event; however, the X protocol does not constrain the ordering of `FocusOut` events with respect to generated `EnterNotify`, `LeaveNotify`, `VisibilityNotify`, and `Expose` events.

Depending on the event mode, the detail member is set to indicate the notify detail and can be `NotifyAncestor`, `NotifyVirtual`, `NotifyInferior`, `NotifyNonlinear`, `NotifyNonlinearVirtual`, `NotifyPointer`, `NotifyPointerRoot`, or `NotifyDetailNone`.

10.7.1 Normal Focus Events and Focus Events While Grabbed

Normal focus events are identified by `XFocusInEvent` or `XFocusOutEvent` structures whose mode member is set to `NotifyNormal`. Focus events while grabbed are identified by `XFocusInEvent` or `XFocusOutEvent` structures whose mode member is set to `NotifyWhileGrabbed`. The X server processes normal focus and focus events while grabbed according to the following:

- When the focus moves from window A to window B, A is an inferior of B, and the pointer is in window P, the X server does the following:
  - It generates a `FocusOut` event on window A, with the detail member of the `XFocusOutEvent` structure set to `NotifyAncestor`.
  - It generates a `FocusOut` event on each window between window A and window B, exclusive, with the detail member of each `XFocusOutEvent` structure set to `NotifyVirtual`.
  - It generates a `FocusIn` event on window B, with the detail member of the `XFocusOutEvent` structure set to `NotifyInferior`.
  - If window P is an inferior of window B but window P is not window A or an inferior or ancestor of window A, it generates a `FocusIn` event on each window below window B, down to and including window P, with the detail member of each `XFocusInEvent` structure set to `NotifyPointer`.
- When the focus moves from window A to window B, B is an inferior of A, and the pointer is in window P, the X server does the following:
  - If window P is an inferior of window A but P is not an inferior of window B or an ancestor of B, it generates a `FocusOut` event on each window from window P up to but not including window A, with the detail member of each `XFocusOutEvent` structure set to `NotifyPointer`.
  - It generates a `FocusOut` event on window A, with the detail member of the `XFocusOutEvent` structure set to `NotifyInferior`.

— It generates a FocusIn event on each window between window A and window B, exclusive, with the detail member of each XFocusInEvent structure set to NotifyVirtual.

— It generates a FocusIn event on window B, with the detail member of the XFocusInEvent structure set to NotifyAncestor.

- When the focus moves from window A to window B, window C is their least common ancestor, and the pointer is in window P, the X server does the following:
  - — If window P is an inferior of window A, it generates a FocusOut event on each window from window P up to but not including window A, with the detail member of the XFocusOutEvent structure set to NotifyPointer.
  - — It generates a FocusOut event on window A, with the detail member of the XFocusOutEvent structure set to NotifyNonlinear.
  - — It generates a FocusOut event on each window between window A and window C, exclusive, with the detail member of each XFocusOutEvent structure set to NotifyNonlinearVirtual.
  - — It generates a FocusIn event on each window between C and B, exclusive, with the detail member of each XFocusInEvent structure set to NotifyNonlinearVirtual.
  - — It generates a FocusIn event on window B, with the detail member of the XFocusInEvent structure set to NotifyNonlinear.
  - — If window P is an inferior of window B, it generates a FocusIn event on each window below window B down to and including window P, with the detail member of the XFocusInEvent structure set to NotifyPointer.
- When the focus moves from window A to window B on different screens and the pointer is in window P, the X server does the following:
  - — If window P is an inferior of window A, it generates a FocusOut event on each window from window P up to but not including window A, with the detail member of each XFocusOutEvent structure set to NotifyPointer.
  - — It generates a FocusOut event on window A, with the detail member of the XFocusOutEvent structure set to NotifyNonlinear.
  - — If window A is not a root window, it generates a FocusOut event on each window above window A up to and including its root, with the detail member of each XFocusOutEvent structure set to NotifyNonlinearVirtual.
  - — If window B is not a root window, it generates a FocusIn event on each window from window B's root down to but not including window B, with the detail member of each XFocusInEvent structure set to NotifyNonlinearVirtual.
  - — It generates a FocusIn event on window B, with the detail member of each XFocusInEvent structure set to NotifyNonlinear.

— If window P is an inferior of window B, it generates a `FocusIn` event on each window below window B down to and including window P, with the detail member of each `XFocusInEvent` structure set to `NotifyPointer`.

- When the focus moves from window A to `PointerRoot` (events sent to the window under the pointer) or `None` (discard), and the pointer is in window P, the X server does the following:
  - — If window P is an inferior of window A, it generates a `FocusOut` event on each window from window P up to but not including window A, with the detail member of each `XFocusOutEvent` structure set to `NotifyPointer`.
  - — It generates a `FocusOut` event on window A, with the detail member of the `XFocusOutEvent` structure set to `NotifyNonlinear`.
  - — If window A is not a root window, it generates a `FocusOut` event on each window above window A up to and including its root, with the detail member of each `XFocusOutEvent` structure set to `NotifyNonlinearVirtual`.
  - — It generates a `FocusIn` event on the root window of all screens, with the detail member of each `XFocusInEvent` structure set to `NotifyPointerRoot` (or `NotifyDetailNone`).
  - — If the new focus is `PointerRoot`, it generates a `FocusIn` event on each window from window P's root down to and including window P, with the detail member of each `XFocusInEvent` structure set to `NotifyPointer`.
- When the focus moves from `PointerRoot` (events sent to the window under the pointer) or `None` to window A, and the pointer is in window P, the X server does the following:
  - — If the old focus is `PointerRoot`, it generates a `FocusOut` event on each window from window P up to and including window P's root, with the detail member of each `XFocusOutEvent` structure set to `NotifyPointer`.
  - — It generates a `FocusOut` event on all root windows, with the detail member of each `XFocusOutEvent` structure set to `NotifyPointerRoot` (or `NotifyDetailNone`).
  - — If window A is not a root window, it generates a `FocusIn` event on each window from window A's root down to but not including window A, with the detail member of each `XFocusInEvent` structure set to `NotifyNonlinearVirtual`.
  - — It generates a `FocusIn` event on window A, with the detail member of the `XFocusInEvent` structure set to `NotifyNonlinear`.
  - — If window P is an inferior of window A, it generates a `FocusIn` event on each window below window A down to and including window P, with the detail member of each `XFocusInEvent` structure set to `NotifyPointer`.
- When the focus moves from `PointerRoot` (events sent to the window under the pointer) to `None` (or vice versa), and the pointer is in window P, the X server does the following:

— If the old focus is PointerRoot, it generates a FocusOut event on each window from window P up to and including window P's root, with the detail member of each XFocusOutEvent structure set to NotifyPointer.

— It generates a FocusOut event on all root windows, with the detail member of each XFocusOutEvent structure set to either NotifyPointerRoot or NotifyDetailNone.

— It generates a FocusIn event on all root windows, with the detail member of each XFocusInEvent structure set to NotifyDetailNone or NotifyPointerRoot.

— If the new focus is PointerRoot, it generates a FocusIn event on each window from window P's root down to and including window P, with the detail member of each XFocusInEvent structure set to NotifyPointer.

10.7.2 Focus Events Generated by Grabs

Focus events in which the keyboard grab activates are identified by XFocusInEvent or XFocusOutEvent structures whose mode member is set to NotifyGrab. Focus events in which the keyboard grab deactivates are identified by XFocusInEvent or XFocusOutEvent structures whose mode member is set to NotifyUngrab (see XGrabKeyboard).

- When a keyboard grab activates before generating any actual KeyPress event that activates the grab, G is the grab_window, and F is the current focus, the X server does the following:
  — It generates FocusIn and FocusOut events, with the mode members of the XFocusInEvent and XFocusOutEvent structures set to NotifyGrab. These events are generated as if the focus were to change from F to G.
- When a keyboard grab deactivates after generating any actual KeyRelease event that deactivates the grab, G is the grab_window, and F is the current focus, the X server does the following:
  — It generates FocusIn and FocusOut events, with the mode members of the XFocusInEvent and XFocusOutEvent structures set to NotifyUngrab. These events are generated as if the focus were to change from G to F.

10.8 Key Map State Notification Events

The X server can report KeymapNotify events to clients that want information about changes in their keyboard state.

To receive KeymapNotify events, set the KeymapStateMask bit in the event-mask attribute of the window. The X server generates this event immediately after every EnterNotify and FocusIn event.

The structure for this event type contains:

```
/* generated on EnterWindow and FocusIn when KeymapState selected */
typedef struct {
    int type;                    /* KeymapNotify */
    unsigned long serial;        /* # of last request processed by server */
    Bool send_event;             /* true if this came from a SendEvent request */
    Display *display;            /* Display the event was read from */
    Window window;
    char key_vector[32];
} XKeymapEvent;
```

The window member is not used but is present to aid some toolkits. The key_vector member is set to the bit vector of the keyboard. Each bit set to 1 indicates that the corresponding key is currently pressed. The vector is represented as 32 bytes. Byte N (from 0) contains the bits for keys 8N to 8N + 7 with the least-significant bit in the byte representing key 8N.

10.9 Exposure Events

The X protocol does not guarantee to preserve the contents of window regions when the windows are obscured or reconfigured. Some implementations may preserve the contents of windows. Other implementations are free to destroy the contents of windows when exposed. X expects client applications to assume the responsibility for restoring the contents of an exposed window region. (An exposed window region describes a formerly obscured window whose region becomes visible.) Therefore, the X server sends `Expose` events describing the window and the region of the window that has been exposed. A naive client application usually redraws the entire window. A more sophisticated client application redraws only the exposed region.

10.9.1 Expose Events

The X server can report `Expose` events to clients wanting information about when the contents of window regions have been lost. The circumstances in which the X server generates `Expose` events are not as definite as those for other events. However, the X server never generates `Expose` events on windows whose class you specified as `InputOnly`. The X server can generate `Expose` events when no valid contents are available for regions of a window and either the regions are visible, the regions are viewable and the server is (perhaps newly) maintaining backing store on the window, or the window is not viewable but the server is (perhaps newly) honoring the window's backing-store attribute of Always or WhenMapped. The regions decompose into an (arbitrary) set of rectangles, and an Expose event is generated for each rectangle. For any given window, the X server guarantees to report contiguously all of the regions exposed by some action that causes Expose events, such as raising a window.

To receive Expose events, set the ExposureMask bit in the event-mask attribute of the window.

The structure for this event type contains:

```
typedef struct {
    int type;                    /* Expose */
    unsigned long serial;        /* # of last request processed by server */
    Bool send_event;             /* true if this came from a SendEvent request */
    Display *display;            /* Display the event was read from */
    Window window;
    int x, y;
    int width, height;
    int count;                   /* if nonzero, at least this many more */
} XExposeEvent;
```

The window member is set to the exposed (damaged) window. The x and y members are set to the coordinates relative to the window's origin and indicate the upper-left corner of the rectangle. The width and height members are set to the size (extent) of the rectangle. The count member is set to the number of Expose events that are to follow. If count is zero, no more Expose events follow for this window. However, if count is nonzero, at least that number of Expose events (and possibly more) follow for this window. Simple applications that do not want to optimize redisplay by distinguishing between subareas of its window can just ignore all Expose events with nonzero counts and perform full redisplays on events with zero counts.

10.9.2 GraphicsExpose and NoExpose Events

The X server can report GraphicsExpose events to clients wanting information about when a destination region could not be computed during certain graphics requests: XCopyArea or XCopyPlane. The X server generates this event whenever a destination region could not be computed due to an obscured or out-of-bounds source region. In addition, the X server guarantees to report contiguously all of the regions exposed by some graphics request (for example, copying an area of a drawable to a destination drawable).

The X server generates a `NoExpose` event whenever a graphics request that might produce a `GraphicsExpose` event does not produce any. In other words, the client is really asking for a `GraphicsExpose` event but instead receives a `NoExpose` event.

To receive `GraphicsExpose` or `NoExpose` events, you must first set the graphics-exposure attribute of the graphics context to `True`. You also can set the graphics-expose attribute when creating a graphics context using `XCreateGC` or by calling `XSetGraphicsExposures`.

The structures for these event types contain:

```
typedef struct {
    int type;                   /* GraphicsExpose */
    unsigned long serial;       /* # of last request processed by server */
    Bool send_event;            /* true if this came from a SendEvent request */
    Display *display;           /* Display the event was read from */
    Drawable drawable;
    int x, y;
    int width, height;
    int count;                  /* if nonzero, at least this many more */
    int major_code;             /* core is CopyArea or CopyPlane */
    int minor_code;             /* not defined in the core */
} XGraphicsExposeEvent;

typedef struct {
    int type;                   /* NoExpose */
    unsigned long serial;       /* # of last request processed by server */
    Bool send_event;            /* true if this came from a SendEvent request */
    Display *display;           /* Display the event was read from */
    Drawable drawable;
    int major_code;             /* core is CopyArea or CopyPlane */
    int minor_code;             /* not defined in the core */
} XNoExposeEvent;
```

Both structures have these common members: drawable major_code, and minor_code. The drawable member is set to the drawable of the destination region on which the graphics request was to be performed. The major_code member is set to the graphics request initiated by the client and can be either `X_CopyArea` or `X_CopyPlane`. If it is `X_CopyArea`, a call to `XCopyArea` initiated the request. If it is X_CopyPlane, a call to XCopyPlane initiated the request. These constants are defined in <X11/Xproto.h>. The minor_code member, like the major_code member, indicates which graphics request was initiated by the client. However, the minor_code member is not defined by the core X protocol and will be zero in these cases, although it may be used by an extension.

The XGraphicsExposeEvent structure has these additional members: x, y, width, height, and count. The x and y members are set to the coordinates relative to the drawable's origin and indicate the upper-left corner of the rectangle. The width and height members are set to the size (extent) of the rectangle. The count member is set to the number of GraphicsExpose events to follow. If count is zero, no more GraphicsExpose events follow for this window. However, if count is nonzero, at least that number of GraphicsExpose events (and possibly more) are to follow for this window.

10.10 Window State Change Events

The following sections discuss:

- CirculateNotify events
- ConfigureNotify events
- CreateNotify events
- DestroyNotify events
- GravityNotify events
- MapNotify events
- MappingNotify events
- ReparentNotify events
- UnmapNotify events
- VisibilityNotify events

10.10.1 CirculateNotify Events

The X server can report CirculateNotify events to clients wanting information about when a window changes its position in the stack. The X server generates this event type whenever a window is actually restacked as a result of a client application calling XCirculateSubwindows, XCirculateSubwindowsUp, or XCirculateSubwindowsDown.

To receive `CirculateNotify` events, set the `StructureNotifyMask` bit in the event-mask attribute of the window or the `SubstructureNotifyMask` bit in the event-mask attribute of the parent window (in which case, circulating any child generates an event).

The structure for this event type contains:

```
typedef struct {
    int type;                   /* CirculateNotify */
    unsigned long serial;       /* # of last request processed by server */
    Bool send_event;            /* true if this came from a SendEvent request */
    Display *display;           /* Display the event was read from */
    Window event;
    Window window;
    int place;                  /* PlaceOnTop, PlaceOnBottom */
} XCirculateEvent;
```

The event member is set either to the restacked window or to its parent, depending on whether `StructureNotify` or `SubstructureNotify` was selected. The window member is set to the window that was restacked. The place member is set to the window's position after the restack occurs and is either `PlaceOnTop` or `PlaceOnBottom`. If it is `PlaceOnTop`, the window is now on top of all siblings. If it is `PlaceOnBottom`, the window is now below all siblings.

10.10.2 ConfigureNotify Events

The X server can report `ConfigureNotify` events to clients wanting information about actual changes to a window's state, such as size, position, border, and stacking order. The X server generates this event type whenever one of the following configure window requests made by a client application actually completes:

- A window's size, position, border, and/or stacking order is reconfigured by calling `XConfigureWindow`.
- The window's position in the stacking order is changed by calling `XLowerWindow`, `XRaiseWindow`, or `XRestackWindows`.
- A window is moved by calling `XMoveWindow`.
- A window's size is changed by calling `XResizeWindow`.

- A window's size and location is changed by calling XMoveResizeWindow.
- A window is mapped and its position in the stacking order is changed by calling XMapRaised.
- A window's border width is changed by calling XSetWindowBorderWidth.

To receive ConfigureNotify events, set the StructureNotifyMask bit in the event-mask attribute of the window or the SubstructureNotifyMask bit in the event-mask attribute of the parent window (in which case, configuring any child generates an event).

The structure for this event type contains:

```
typedef struct {
    int type;                   /* ConfigureNotify */
    unsigned long serial;       /* # of last request processed by server */
    Bool send_event;            /* true if this came from a SendEvent request */
    Display *display;           /* Display the event was read from */
    Window event;
    Window window;
    int x, y;
    int width, height;
    int border_width;
    Window above;
    Bool override_redirect;
} XConfigureEvent;
```

The event member is set either to the reconfigured window or to its parent, depending on whether StructureNotify or SubstructureNotify was selected. The window member is set to the window whose size, position, border, and/or stacking order was changed.

The x and y members are set to the coordinates relative to the parent window's origin and indicate the position of the upper-left outside corner of the window. The width and height members are set to the inside size of the window, not including the border. The border_width member is set to the width of the window's border, in pixels.

The above member is set to the sibling window and is used for stacking operations. If the X server sets this member to None, the window whose state was changed is on the bottom of the stack with respect to sibling windows. However, if this member is set to a sibling window, the window whose state was changed is placed on top of this sibling window.

The override_redirect member is set to the override-redirect attribute of the window. Window manager clients normally should ignore this window if the override_redirect member is True.

10.10.3 CreateNotify Events

The X server can report CreateNotify events to clients wanting information about creation of windows. The X server generates this event whenever a client application creates a window by calling XCreateWindow or XCreateSimpleWindow.

To receive CreateNotify events, set the SubstructureNotifyMask bit in the event-mask attribute of the window. Creating any children then generates an event.

The structure for the event type contains:

```
typedef struct {
    int type;                   /* CreateNotify */
    unsigned long serial;       /* # of last request processed by server */
    Bool send_event;            /* true if this came from a SendEvent request */
    Display *display;           /* Display the event was read from */
    Window parent;              /* parent of the window */
    Window window;              /* window id of window created */
    int x, y;                   /* window location */
    int width, height;          /* size of window */
    int border_width;           /* border width */
    Bool override_redirect;     /* creation should be overridden */
} XCreateWindowEvent;
```

The parent member is set to the created window's parent. The window member specifies the created window. The x and y members are set to the created window's coordinates relative to the parent window's origin and indicate the position of the upper-left outside corner of the created window. The width and height members are set to the inside size of the created window (not including the border) and are always nonzero. The border_width member is set to the width of the created window's border, in pixels. The override_redirect member is set to the override-redirect attribute of the window. Window manager clients normally should ignore this window if the override_redirect member is True.

10.10.4 DestroyNotify Events

The X server can report DestroyNotify events to clients wanting information about which windows are destroyed. The X server generates this event whenever a client application destroys a window by calling XDestroyWindow or XDestroySubwindows.

The ordering of the DestroyNotify events is such that for any given window, DestroyNotify is generated on all inferiors of the window before being generated on the window itself. The X protocol does not constrain the ordering among siblings and across subhierarchies.

To receive DestroyNotify events, set the StructureNotifyMask bit in the event-mask attribute of the window or the SubstructureNotifyMask bit in the event-mask attribute of the parent window (in which case, destroying any child generates an event).

The structure for this event type contains:

```
typedef struct {
    int type;                /* DestroyNotify */
    unsigned long serial;    /* # of last request processed by server */
    Bool send_event;         /* true if this came from a SendEvent request */
    Display *display;        /* Display the event was read from */
    Window event;
    Window window;
} XDestroyWindowEvent;
```

The event member is set either to the destroyed window or to its parent, depending on whether StructureNotify or SubstructureNotify was selected. The window member is set to the window that is destroyed.

10.10.5 GravityNotify Events

The X server can report GravityNotify events to clients wanting information about when a window is moved because of a change in the size of its parent. The X server generates this event whenever a client application actually moves a child window as a result of resizing its parent by calling XConfigureWindow, XMoveResizeWindow, or XResizeWindow.

To receive GravityNotify events, set the StructureNotifyMask bit in the event-mask attribute of the window or the SubstructureNotifyMask bit in the event-mask attribute of the parent window (in which case, any child that is moved because its parent has been resized generates an event).

The structure for this event type contains:

```
typedef struct {
    int type;                     /* GravityNotify */
    unsigned long serial;         /* # of last request processed by server */
    Bool send_event;              /* true if this came from a SendEvent request */
    Display *display;             /* Display the event was read from */
    Window event;
    Window window;
    int x, y;
} XGravityEvent;
```

The event member is set either to the window that was moved or to its parent, depending on whether `StructureNotify` or `SubstructureNotify` was selected. The window member is set to the child window that was moved. The x and y members are set to the coordinates relative to the new parent window's origin and indicate the position of the upper-left outside corner of the window.

10.10.6 MapNotify Events

The X server can report `MapNotify` events to clients wanting information about which windows are mapped. The X server generates this event type whenever a client application changes the window's state from unmapped to mapped by calling `XMapWindow`, `XMapRaised`, `XMapSubwindows`, `XReparentWindow`, or as a result of save-set processing.

To receive `MapNotify` events, set the `StructureNotifyMask` bit in the event-mask attribute of the window or the `SubstructureNotifyMask` bit in the event-mask attribute of the parent window (in which case, mapping any child generates an event).

The structure for this event type contains:

```
typedef struct {
    int type;                     /* MapNotify */
    unsigned long serial;         /* # of last request processed by server */
    Bool send_event;              /* true if this came from a SendEvent request */
    Display *display;             /* Display the event was read from */
    Window event;
    Window window;
    Bool override_redirect;       /* boolean, is override set... */
} XMapEvent;
```

The event member is set either to the window that was mapped or to its parent, depending on whether StructureNotify or SubstructureNotify was selected. The window member is set to the window that was mapped. The override_redirect member is set to the override-redirect attribute of the window. Window manager clients normally should ignore this window if the override-redirect attribute is True, because these events usually are generated from pop-ups, which override structure control.

10.10.7 MappingNotify Events

The X server reports MappingNotify events to all clients. There is no mechanism to express disinterest in this event. The X server generates this event type whenever a client application successfully calls:

- XSetModifierMapping to indicate which KeyCodes are to be used as modifiers
- XChangeKeyboardMapping to change the keyboard mapping
- XSetPointerMapping to set the pointer mapping

The structure for this event type contains:

```
typedef struct {
    int type;                  /* MappingNotify */
    unsigned long serial;      /* # of last request processed by server */
    Bool send_event;           /* true if this came from a SendEvent request */
    Display *display;          /* Display the event was read from */
    Window window;             /* unused */
    int request;               /* one of MappingModifier, MappingKeyboard,
                                  MappingPointer */
    int first_keycode;         /* first keycode */
    int count;                 /* defines range of change w. first_keycode */
} XMappingEvent;
```

The request member is set to indicate the kind of mapping change that occurred and can be MappingModifier, MappingKeyboard, MappingPointer. If it is MappingModifier, the modifier mapping was changed. If it is MappingKeyboard, the keyboard mapping was changed. If it is MappingPointer, the pointer button mapping was changed. The first_keycode and count members are set only if the request member was set to MappingKeyboard. The number in first_keycode represents the first number in the range of the altered mapping, and count represents the number of keycodes altered.

To update the client application's knowledge of the keyboard, you should call XRefreshKeyboardMapping.

10.10.8 ReparentNotify Events

The X server can report ReparentNotify events to clients wanting information about changing a window's parent. The X server generates this event whenever a client application calls XReparentWindow and the window is actually reparented.

To receive ReparentNotify events, set the StructureNotifyMask bit in the event-mask attribute of the window or the SubstructureNotifyMask bit in the event-mask attribute of either the old or the new parent window (in which case, reparenting any child generates an event).

The structure for this event type contains:

```
typedef struct {
    int type;                   /* ReparentNotify */
    unsigned long serial;       /* # of last request processed by server */
    Bool send_event;            /* true if this came from a SendEvent request */
    Display *display;           /* Display the event was read from */
    Window event;
    Window window;
    Window parent;
    int x, y;
    Bool override_redirect;
} XReparentEvent;
```

The event member is set either to the reparented window or to the old or the new parent, depending on whether StructureNotify or Substructure-Notify was selected. The window member is set to the window that was reparented. The parent member is set to the new parent window. The x and y members are set to the reparented window's coordinates relative to the new parent window's origin and define the upper-left outer corner of the reparented window. The override_redirect member is set to the override-redirect attribute of the window specified by the window member. Window manager clients normally should ignore this window if the override_redirect member is True.

10.10.9 UnmapNotify Events

The X server can report UnmapNotify events to clients wanting information about which windows are unmapped. The X server generates this event type whenever a client application changes the window's state from mapped to unmapped.

To receive UnmapNotify events, set the StructureNotifyMask bit in the event-mask attribute of the window or the SubstructureNotifyMask bit in the event-mask attribute of the parent window (in which case, unmapping any child window generates an event).

The structure for this event type contains:

```
typedef struct {
    int type;                   /* UnmapNotify */
    unsigned long serial;       /* # of last request processed by server */
    Bool send_event;            /* true if this came from a SendEvent request */
    Display *display;           /* Display the event was read from */
    Window event;
    Window window;
    Bool from_configure;
} XUnmapEvent;
```

The event member is set either to the unmapped window or to its parent, depending on whether StructureNotify or SubstructureNotify was selected. This is the window used by the X server to report the event. The window member is set to the window that was unmapped. The from_configure member is set to True if the event was generated as a result of a resizing of the window's parent when the window itself had a win_gravity of UnmapGravity.

10.10.10 VisibilityNotify Events

The X server can report VisibilityNotify events to clients wanting any change in the visibility of the specified window. A region of a window is visible if someone looking at the screen can actually see it. The X server generates this event whenever the visibility changes state. However, this event is never generated for windows whose class is InputOnly.

All VisibilityNotify events caused by a hierarchy change are generated after any hierarchy event (UnmapNotify, MapNotify, ConfigureNotify,

GravityNotify, CirculateNotify) caused by that change. Any VisibilityNotify event on a given window is generated before any Expose events on that window, but it is not required that all VisibilityNotify events on all windows be generated before all Expose events on all windows. The X protocol does not constrain the ordering of VisibilityNotify events with respect to FocusOut, EnterNotify, and LeaveNotify events.

To receive VisibilityNotify events, set the VisibilityChangeMask bit in the event-mask attribute of the window.

The structure for this event type contains:

```
typedef struct {
    int type;                    /* VisibiltyNotify */
    unsigned long serial;        /* # of last request processed by server */
    Bool send_event;             /* true if this came from a SendEvent request */
    Display *display;            /* Display the event was read from */
    Window window;
    int state;
} XVisibilityEvent;
```

The window member is set to the window whose visibility state changes. The state member is set to the state of the window's visibility and can be VisibilityUnobscured, VisibilityPartiallyObscured, or Visibility-FullyObscured. The X server ignores all of a window's subwindows when determining the visibility state of the window and processes Visibility-Notify events according to the following:

- When the window changes state from partially obscured, fully obscured, or not viewable to viewable and completely unobscured, the X server generates the event with the state member of the XVisibilityEvent structure set to VisibilityUnobscured.
- When the window changes state from viewable and completely unobscured or not viewable to viewable and partially obscured, the X server generates the event with the state member of the XVisibilityEvent structure set to VisibilityPartiallyObscured.
- When the window changes state from viewable and completely unobscured, viewable and partially obscured, or not viewable to viewable and fully obscured, the X server generates the event with the state member of the XVisibilityEvent structure set to VisibilityFullyObscured.

10.11 Structure Control Events

This section discusses:

- CirculateRequest events
- ConfigureRequest events
- MapRequest events
- ResizeRequest events

10.11.1 CirculateRequest Events

The X server can report CirculateRequest events to clients wanting information about when another client initiates a circulate window request on a specified window. The X server generates this event type whenever a client initiates a circulate window request on a window and a subwindow actually needs to be restacked. The client initiates a circulate window request on the window by calling XCirculateSubwindows, XCirculateSubwindowsUp, or XCirculateSubwindowsDown.

To receive CirculateRequest events, set the SubstructureRedirectMask in the event-mask attribute of the window. Then, in the future, the circulate window request for the specified window is not executed, and thus, any subwindow's position in the stack is not changed. For example, suppose a client application calls XCirculateSubwindowsUp to raise a subwindow to the top of the stack. If you had selected SubstructureRedirectMask on the window, the X server reports to you a CirculateRequest event and does not raise the subwindow to the top of the stack.

The structure for this event type contains:

```
typedef struct {
    int type;                   /* CirculateRequest */
    unsigned long serial;       /* # of last request processed by server */
    Bool send_event;            /* true if this came from a SendEvent request */
    Display *display;           /* Display the event was read from */
    Window parent;
    Window window;
    int place;                  /* PlaceOnTop, PlaceOnBottom */
} XCirculateRequestEvent;
```

The parent member is set to the parent window. The window member is set to the subwindow to be restacked. The place member is set to what the new position in the stacking order should be and is either `PlaceOnTop` or `PlaceOnBottom`. If it is `PlaceOnTop`, the subwindow should be on top of all siblings. If it is `PlaceOnBottom`, the subwindow should be below all siblings.

10.11.2 ConfigureRequest Events

The X server can report `ConfigureRequest` events to clients wanting information about when a different client initiates a configure window request on any child of a specified window. The configure window request attempts to reconfigure a window's size, position, border, and stacking order. The X server generates this event whenever a different client initiates a configure window request on a window by calling `XConfigureWindow`, `XLowerWindow`, `XRaiseWindow`, `XMapRaised`, `XMoveResizeWindow`, `XMoveWindow`, `XResizeWindow`, `XRestackWindows`, or `XSetWindowBorderWidth`.

To receive `ConfigureRequest` events, set the `SubstructureRedirectMask` bit in the event-mask attribute of the window. `ConfigureRequest` events are generated when a `ConfigureWindow` protocol request is issued on a child window by another client. For example, suppose a client application calls `XLowerWindow` to lower a window. If you had selected `SubstructureRedirectMask` on the parent window and if the override-redirect attribute of the window is set to `False`, the X server reports a `ConfigureRequest` event to you and does not lower the specified window.

The structure for this event type contains:

```
typedef struct {
    int type;                   /* ConfigureRequest */
    unsigned long serial;       /* # of last request processed by server */
    Bool send_event;            /* true if this came from a SendEvent request */
    Display *display;           /* Display the event was read from */
    Window parent;
    Window window;
    int x, y;
    int width, height;
    int border_width;
    Window above;
    int detail;                 /* Above, Below, TopIf, BottomIf, Opposite */
    unsigned long value_mask;
} XConfigureRequestEvent;
```

The parent member is set to the parent window. The window member is set to the window whose size, position, border width, and/or stacking order is to be reconfigured. The value_mask member indicates which components were specified in the ConfigureWindow protocol request. The corresponding values are reported as given in the request. The remaining values are filled in from the current geometry of the window, except in the case of above (sibling) and detail (stack-mode), which are reported as Above and None, respectively, if they are not given in the request.

10.11.3 MapRequest Events

The X server can report MapRequest events to clients wanting information about a different client's desire to map windows. A window is considered mapped when a map window request completes. The X server generates this event whenever a different client initiates a map window request on an unmapped window whose override_redirect member is set to False. Clients initiate map window requests by calling XMapWindow, XMapRaised, or XMapSubwindows.

To receive MapRequest events, set the SubstructureRedirectMask bit in the event-mask attribute of the window. This means another client's attempts to map a child window by calling one of the map window request functions is intercepted, and you are sent a MapRequest instead. For example, suppose a client application calls XMapWindow to map a window. If you (usually a window manager) had selected SubstructureRedirectMask on the parent window and if the override-redirect attribute of the window is set to False, the X server reports a MapRequest event to you and does not map the specified window. Thus, this event gives your window manager client the ability to control the placement of subwindows.

The structure for this event type contains:

```
typedef struct {
    int type;                   /* MapRequest */
    unsigned long serial;       /* # of last request processed by server */
    Bool send_event;            /* true if this came from a SendEvent request */
    Display *display;           /* Display the event was read from */
    Window parent;
    Window window;
} XMapRequestEvent;
```

The parent member is set to the parent window. The window member is set to the window to be mapped.

10.11.4 ResizeRequest Events

The X server can report ResizeRequest events to clients wanting information about another client's attempts to change the size of a window. The X server generates this event whenever some other client attempts to change the size of the specified window by calling XConfigureWindow, XResizeWindow, or XMoveResizeWindow.

To receive ResizeRequest events, set the ResizeRedirect bit in the event-mask attribute of the window. Any attempts to change the size by other clients are then redirected.

The structure for this event type contains:

```
typedef struct {
    int type;                 /* ResizeRequest */
    unsigned long serial;     /* # of last request processed by server */
    Bool send_event;          /* true if this came from a SendEvent request */
    Display *display;         /* Display the event was read from */
    Window window;
    int width, height;
} XResizeRequestEvent;
```

The window member is set to the window whose size another client attempted to change. The width and height members are set to the inside size of the window, excluding the border.

10.12 Colormap State Change Events

The X server can report ColormapNotify events to clients wanting information about when the colormap changes and when a colormap is installed or uninstalled. The X server generates this event type whenever a client application:

- Changes the colormap member of the XSetWindowAttributes structure by calling XChangeWindowAttributes, XFreeColormap, or XSetWindowColormap
- Installs or uninstalls the colormap by calling XInstallColormap or XUninstall-Colormap

To receive ColormapNotify events, set the ColormapChangeMask bit in the event-mask attribute of the window.

The structure for this event type contains:

```
typedef struct {
    int type;                   /* ColormapNotify */
    unsigned long serial;       /* # of last request processed by server */
    Bool send_event;            /* true if this came from a SendEvent request */
    Display *display;           /* Display the event was read from */
    Window window;
    Colormap colormap;          /* colormap or None */
    Bool new;
    int state;                  /* ColormapInstalled, ColormapUninstalled */
} XColormapEvent;
```

The window member is set to the window whose associated colormap is changed, installed, or uninstalled. For a colormap that is changed, installed, or uninstalled, the colormap member is set to the colormap associated with the window. For a colormap that is changed by a call to XFreeColormap, the colormap member is set to None. The new member is set to indicate whether the colormap for the specified window was changed or installed or uninstalled and can be True or False. If it is True, the colormap was changed. If it is False, the colormap was installed or uninstalled. The state member is always set to indicate whether the colormap is installed or uninstalled and can be ColormapInstalled or ColormapUninstalled.

10.13 Client Communication Events

This section discusses:

- ClientMessage events
- PropertyNotify events
- SelectionClear events
- SelectionNotify events
- SelectionRequest events

10.13.1 ClientMessage Events

The X server generates ClientMessage events only when a client calls the function XSendEvent.

The structure for this event type contains:

```
typedef struct {
    int type;                   /* ClientMessage */
    unsigned long serial;       /* # of last request processed by server */
    Bool send_event;            /* true if this came from a SendEvent request */
    Display *display;           /* Display the event was read from */
    Window window;
    Atom message_type;
    int format;
    union {
        char b[20];
        short s[10];
        long l[5];
        } data;
} XClientMessageEvent;
```

The message_type member is set to an atom that indicates how the data should be interpreted by the receiving client. The format member is set to 8, 16, or 32 and specifies whether the data should be viewed as a list of bytes, shorts, or longs. The data member is a union that contains the members b, s, and l. The b, s, and l members represent data of 20 8-bit values, 10 16-bit values, and 5 32-bit values. Particular message types might not make use of all these values. The X server places no interpretation on the values in the window, message_type, or data members.

10.13.2 PropertyNotify Events

The X server can report `PropertyNotify` events to clients wanting information about property changes for a specified window.

To receive `PropertyNotify` events, set the `PropertyChangeMask` bit in the event-mask attribute of the window.

The structure for this event type contains:

```
typedef struct {
    int type;                   /* PropertyNotify */
    unsigned long serial;       /* # of last request processed by server */
    Bool send_event;            /* true if this came from a SendEvent request */
    Display *display;           /* Display the event was read from */
```

```
	Window window;
	Atom atom;
	Time time;
	int state;			/* PropertyNewValue or PropertyDelete */
} XPropertyEvent;
```

The window member is set to the window whose associated property was changed. The atom member is set to the property's atom and indicates which property was changed or desired. The time member is set to the server time when the property was changed. The state member is set to indicate whether the property was changed to a new value or deleted and can be PropertyNewValue or PropertyDelete. The state member is set to PropertyNewValue when a property of the window is changed using XChangeProperty or XRotateWindowProperties (even when adding zero-length data using XChangeProperty) and when replacing all or part of a property with identical data using XChangeProperty or XRotateWindowProperties. The state member is set to PropertyDelete when a property of the window is deleted using XDeleteProperty or, if the delete argument is True, XGetWindowProperty.

10.13.3 SelectionClear Events

The X server reports SelectionClear events to the client losing ownership of a selection. The X server generates this event type when another client asserts ownership of the selection by calling XSetSelectionOwner.

The structure for this event type contains:

```
typedef struct {
	int type;			/* SelectionClear */
	unsigned long serial;		/* # of last request processed by server */
	Bool send_event;		/* true if this came from a SendEvent request */
	Display *display;		/* Display the event was read from */
	Window window;
	Atom selection;
	Time time;
} XSelectionClearEvent;
```

The selection member is set to the selection atom. The time member is set to the last change time recorded for the selection. The window member is the window that was specified by the current owner (the owner losing the selection) in its `XSetSelectionOwner` call.

10.13.4 SelectionRequest Events

The X server reports `SelectionRequest` events to the owner of a selection. The X server generates this event whenever a client requests a selection conversion by calling `XConvertSelection` for the owned selection.

The structure for this event type contains:

```
typedef struct {
    int type;                   /* SelectionRequest */
    unsigned long serial;       /* # of last request processed by server */
    Bool send_event;            /* true if this came from a SendEvent request */
    Display *display;           /* Display the event was read from */
    Window owner;
    Window requestor;
    Atom selection;
    Atom target;
    Atom property;
    Time time;
} XSelectionRequestEvent;
```

The owner member is set to the window that was specified by the current owner in its `XSetSelectionOwner` call. The requestor member is set to the window requesting the selection. The selection member is set to the atom that names the selection. For example, PRIMARY is used to indicate the primary selection. The target member is set to the atom that indicates the type the selection is desired in. The property member can be a property name or `None`. The time member is set to the timestamp or `CurrentTime` value from the `ConvertSelection` request.

The owner should convert the selection based on the specified target type and send a `SelectionNotify` event back to the requestor. A complete specification for using selections is given in part III, "Inter-Client Communication Conventions Manual."

10.13.5 SelectionNotify Events

This event is generated by the X server in response to a `ConvertSelection` protocol request when there is no owner for the selection. When there is an owner, it should be generated by the owner of the selection by using `XSendEvent`. The owner of a selection should send this event to a requestor when a selection has been converted and stored as a property or when a selection conversion could not be performed (which is indicated by setting the property member to `None`).

If `None` is specified as the property in the `ConvertSelection` protocol request, the owner should choose a property name, store the result as that property on the requestor window, and then send a `SelectionNotify` giving that actual property name.

The structure for this event type contains:

```
typedef struct {
    int type;                  /* SelectionNotify */
    unsigned long serial;      /* # of last request processed by server */
    Bool send_event;           /* true if this came from a SendEvent request */
    Display *display;          /* Display the event was read from */
    Window requestor;
    Atom selection;
    Atom target;
    Atom property;             /* atom or None */
    Time time;
} XSelectionEvent;
```

The requestor member is set to the window associated with the requestor of the selection. The selection member is set to the atom that indicates the selection. For example, PRIMARY is used for the primary selection. The target member is set to the atom that indicates the converted type. For example, PIXMAP is used for a pixmap. The property member is set to the atom that indicates which property the result was stored on. If the conversion failed, the property member is set to `None`. The time member is set to the time the conversion took place and can be a timestamp or `CurrentTime`.

Chapter 11

Event Handling Functions

This chapter discusses the Xlib functions you can use to:

- Select events
- Handle the output buffer and the event queue
- Select events from the event queue
- Send and get events
- Handle protocol errors

Note Some toolkits use their own event-handling functions and do not allow you to interchange these event-handling functions with those in Xlib. For further information, see the documentation supplied with the toolkit.

Most applications simply are event loops: they wait for an event, decide what to do with it, execute some amount of code that results in changes to the display, and then wait for the next event.

11.1 Selecting Events

There are two ways to select the events you want reported to your client application. One way is to set the event_mask member of the `XSetWindowAttributes` structure when you call `XCreateWindow` and `XChangeWindowAttributes`. Another way is to use `XSelectInput`.

```
XSelectInput(display, w, event_mask)
    Display *display;
    Window w;
    long event_mask;
```

display Specifies the connection to the X server.

w Specifies the window whose events you are interested in.

event_mask Specifies the event mask.

The `XSelectInput` function requests that the X server report the events associated with the specified event mask. Initially, X will not report any of these events. Events are reported relative to a window. If a window is not interested in a device event, it usually propagates to the closest ancestor that is interested, unless the do_not_propagate mask prohibits it.

Setting the event-mask attribute of a window overrides any previous call for the same window but not for other clients. Multiple clients can select for the same events on the same window with the following restrictions:

- Multiple clients can select events on the same window because their event masks are disjoint. When the X server generates an event, it reports it to all interested clients.
- Only one client at a time can select `CirculateRequest`, `ConfigureRequest`, or `MapRequest` events, which are associated with the event mask `SubstructureRedirectMask`.
- Only one client at a time can select a `ResizeRequest` event, which is associated with the event mask `ResizeRedirectMask`.
- Only one client at a time can select a `ButtonPress` event, which is associated with the event mask `ButtonPressMask`.

The server reports the event to all interested clients.

`XSelectInput` can generate a `BadWindow` error.

11.2 Handling the Output Buffer

The output buffer is an area used by Xlib to store requests. The functions described in this section flush the output buffer if the function would block or not return an event. That is, all requests residing in the output buffer that have not yet been sent are transmitted to the X server. These functions differ in the additional tasks they might perform.

To flush the output buffer, use `XFlush`.

```
XFlush ( display)
   Display *display;
```

display Specifies the connection to the X server.

The `XFlush` function flushes the output buffer. Most client applications need not use this function because the output buffer is automatically flushed as needed by calls to `XPending`, `XNextEvent`, and `XWindowEvent`. Events generated by the server may be enqueued into the library's event queue.

To flush the output buffer and then wait until all requests have been processed, use `XSync`.

```
XSync ( display, discard)
   Display *display;
   Bool discard;
```

display Specifies the connection to the X server.

discard Specifies a Boolean value that indicates whether `XSync` discards all events on the event queue.

The `XSync` function flushes the output buffer and then waits until all requests have been received and processed by the X server. Any errors generated must be handled by the error handler. For each protocol error received by Xlib, `XSync` calls the client application's error handling routine (see section 11.8.2). Any events generated by the server are enqueued into the library's event queue.

Finally, if you passed `False`, `XSync` does not discard the events in the queue. If you passed `True`, `XSync` discards all events in the queue, including those events that were on the queue before `XSync` was called. Client applications seldom need to call `XSync`.

11.3 Event Queue Management

Xlib maintains an event queue. However, the operating system also may be buffering data in its network connection that is not yet read into the event queue.

To check the number of events in the event queue, use `XEventsQueued`.

```
int XEventsQueued(display, mode)
    Display *display;
    int mode;
```

display Specifies the connection to the X server.

mode Specifies the mode. You can pass `QueuedAlready`, `QueuedAfterFlush`, or `QueuedAfterReading`.

If mode is `QueuedAlready`, `XEventsQueued` returns the number of events already in the event queue (and never performs a system call). If mode is `QueuedAfterFlush`, `XEventsQueued` returns the number of events already in the queue if the number is nonzero. If there are no events in the queue, `XEventsQueued` flushes the output buffer, attempts to read more events out of the application's connection, and returns the number read. If mode is `QueuedAfterReading`, `XEventsQueued` returns the number of events already in the queue if the number is nonzero. If there are no events in the queue, `XEventsQueued` attempts to read more events out of the application's connection without flushing the output buffer and returns the number read.

`XEventsQueued` always returns immediately without I/O if there are events already in the queue. `XEventsQueued` with mode `QueuedAfterFlush` is identical in behavior to `XPending`. `XEventsQueued` with mode `QueuedAlready` is identical to the `XQLength` function.

To return the number of events that are pending, use `XPending`.

```
int XPending(display)
    Display *display;
```

display Specifies the connection to the X server.

The `XPending` function returns the number of events that have been received from the X server but have not been removed from the event queue. `XPending` is identical to `XEventsQueued` with the mode `QueuedAfterFlush` specified.

11.4 Manipulating the Event Queue

Xlib provides functions that let you manipulate the event queue. This section discusses how to:

- Obtain events, in order, and remove them from the queue
- Peek at events in the queue without removing them
- Obtain events that match the event mask or the arbitrary predicate procedures that you provide

11.4.1 Returning the Next Event

To get the next event and remove it from the queue, use `XNextEvent`.

XNextEvent (*display*, *event_return*)
  Display **display*;
  XEvent **event_return*;

display Specifies the connection to the X server.
event_return Returns the next event in the queue.

The `XNextEvent` function copies the first event from the event queue into the specified `XEvent` structure and then removes it from the queue. If the event queue is empty, `XNextEvent` flushes the output buffer and blocks until an event is received.

To peek at the event queue, use `XPeekEvent`.

XPeekEvent (*display*, *event_return*)
  Display **display*;
  XEvent **event_return*;

display Specifies the connection to the X server.
event_return Returns a copy of the matched event's associated structure.

The `XPeekEvent` function returns the first event from the event queue, but it does not remove the event from the queue. If the queue is empty, `XPeekEvent` flushes the output buffer and blocks until an event is received. It then copies the event into the client-supplied `XEvent` structure without removing it from the event queue.

11.4.2 Selecting Events Using a Predicate Procedure

Each of the functions discussed in this section requires you to pass a predicate procedure that determines if an event matches what you want. Your predicate procedure must decide only if the event is useful and must not call Xlib functions. In particular, a predicate is called from inside the event routine, which must lock data structures so that the event queue is consistent in a multi-threaded environment.

The predicate procedure and its associated arguments are:

```
Bool (*predicate) (display, event, arg)
    Display *display;
    XEvent *event;
    XPointer arg;
```

display	Specifies the connection to the X server.
event	Specifies the `XEvent` structure.
arg	Specifies the argument passed in from the `XIfEvent`, `XCheckIfEvent`, or `XPeekIfEvent` function.

The predicate procedure is called once for each event in the queue until it finds a match. After finding a match, the predicate procedure must return `True`. If it did not find a match, it must return `False`.

To check the event queue for a matching event and, if found, remove the event from the queue, use `XIfEvent`.

```
XIfEvent (display, event_return, predicate, arg)
    Display *display;
    XEvent *event_return;
    Bool (*predicate) ();
    XPointer arg;
```

display	Specifies the connection to the X server.
event_return	Returns the matched event's associated structure.
predicate	Specifies the procedure that is to be called to determine if the next event in the queue matches what you want.
arg	Specifies the user-supplied argument that will be passed to the predicate procedure.

The `XIfEvent` function completes only when the specified predicate procedure returns `True` for an event, which indicates an event in the queue matches. `XIfEvent` flushes the output buffer if it blocks waiting for additional events. `XIfEvent` removes the matching event from the queue and copies the structure into the client-supplied `XEvent` structure.

To check the event queue for a matching event without blocking, use `XCheckIfEvent`.

```
Bool XCheckIfEvent ( display, event_return, predicate, arg)
    Display *display;
    XEvent *event_return;
    Bool (*predicate) ();
    XPointer arg;
```

display	Specifies the connection to the X server.
event_return	Returns a copy of the matched event's associated structure.
predicate	Specifies the procedure that is to be called to determine if the next event in the queue matches what you want.
arg	Specifies the user-supplied argument that will be passed to the predicate procedure.

When the predicate procedure finds a match, `XCheckIfEvent` copies the matched event into the client-supplied `XEvent` structure and returns `True`. (This event is removed from the queue.) If the predicate procedure finds no match, `XCheckIfEvent` returns `False`, and the output buffer will have been flushed. All earlier events stored in the queue are not discarded.

To check the event queue for a matching event without removing the event from the queue, use `XPeekIfEvent`.

```
XPeekIfEvent ( display, event_return, predicate, arg)
    Display *display;
    XEvent *event_return;
    Bool (*predicate) ();
    XPointer arg;
```

display	Specifies the connection to the X server.
event_return	Returns a copy of the matched event's associated structure.
predicate	Specifies the procedure that is to be called to determine if the next event in the queue matches what you want.
arg	Specifies the user-supplied argument that will be passed to the predicate procedure.

The `XPeekIfEvent` function returns only when the specified predicate procedure returns `True` for an event. After the predicate procedure finds a match, `XPeekIfEvent` copies the matched event into the client-supplied `XEvent` structure without removing the event from the queue. `XPeekIfEvent` flushes the output buffer if it blocks waiting for additional events.

11.4.3 Selecting Events Using a Window or Event Mask

The functions discussed in this section let you select events by window or event types, allowing you to process events out of order.

To remove the next event that matches both a window and an event mask, use `XWindowEvent`.

```
XWindowEvent ( display, w, event_mask, event_return)
    Display *display;
    Window w;
    long event_mask;
    XEvent *event_return;
```

display	Specifies the connection to the X server.
w	Specifies the window whose events you are interested in.
event_mask	Specifies the event mask.
event_return	Returns the matched event's associated structure.

The `XWindowEvent` function searches the event queue for an event that matches both the specified window and event mask. When it finds a match, `XWindowEvent` removes that event from the queue and copies it into the specified `XEvent` structure. The other events stored in the queue are not discarded. If a matching event is not in the queue, `XWindowEvent` flushes the output buffer and blocks until one is received.

To remove the next event that matches both a window and an event mask (if any), use `XCheckWindowEvent`. This function is similar to `XWindowEvent` except that it never blocks and it returns a `Bool` indicating if the event was returned.

```
Bool XCheckWindowEvent ( display, w, event_mask, event_return)
    Display *display;
    Window w;
    long event_mask;
    XEvent *event_return;
```

display	Specifies the connection to the X server.
w	Specifies the window whose events you are interested in.
event_mask	Specifies the event mask.
event_return	Returns the matched event's associated structure.

The `XCheckWindowEvent` function searches the event queue and then the events available on the server connection for the first event that matches the specified window and event mask. If it finds a match, `XCheckWindowEvent` removes that event, copies it into the specified `XEvent` structure, and returns `True`. The other events stored in the queue are not discarded. If the event you requested is not available, `XCheckWindowEvent` returns `False`, and the output buffer will have been flushed.

To remove the next event that matches an event mask, use `XMaskEvent`.

XMaskEvent (*display*, *event_mask*, *event_return*)
Display **display*;
long *event_mask*;
XEvent **event_return*;

display	Specifies the connection to the X server.
event_mask	Specifies the event mask.
event_return	Returns the matched event's associated structure.

The `XMaskEvent` function searches the event queue for the events associated with the specified mask. When it finds a match, `XMaskEvent` removes that event and copies it into the specified `XEvent` structure. The other events stored in the queue are not discarded. If the event you requested is not in the queue, `XMaskEvent` flushes the output buffer and blocks until one is received.

To return and remove the next event that matches an event mask (if any), use `XCheckMaskEvent`. This function is similar to `XMaskEvent` except that it never blocks and it returns a `Bool` indicating if the event was returned.

Bool XCheckMaskEvent (*display*, *event_mask*, *event_return*)
Display **display*;
long *event_mask*;
XEvent **event_return*;

display	Specifies the connection to the X server.
event_mask	Specifies the event mask.
event_return	Returns the matched event's associated structure.

The `XCheckMaskEvent` function searches the event queue and then any events available on the server connection for the first event that matches the specified mask. If it finds a match, `XCheckMaskEvent` removes that event, copies it into the specified `XEvent` structure, and returns `True`. The other events stored in the queue are not discarded. If the event you requested is not available, `XCheckMaskEvent` returns `False`, and the output buffer will have been flushed.

To return and remove the next event in the queue that matches an event type, use `XCheckTypedEvent`.

```
Bool XCheckTypedEvent ( display, event_type, event_return)
    Display *display;
    int event_type;
    XEvent *event_return;
```

display	Specifies the connection to the X server.
event_type	Specifies the event type to be compared.
event_return	Returns the matched event's associated structure.

The `XCheckTypedEvent` function searches the event queue and then any events available on the server connection for the first event that matches the specified type. If it finds a match, `XCheckTypedEvent` removes that event, copies it into the specified `XEvent` structure, and returns `True`. The other events in the queue are not discarded. If the event is not available, `XCheckTypedEvent` returns `False`, and the output buffer will have been flushed.

To return and remove the next event in the queue that matches an event type and a window, use `XCheckTypedWindowEvent`.

```
Bool XCheckTypedWindowEvent ( display, w, event_type, event_return)
    Display *display;
    Window w;
    int event_type;
    XEvent *event_return;
```

display	Specifies the connection to the X server.
w	Specifies the window.
event_type	Specifies the event type to be compared.
event_return	Returns the matched event's associated structure.

The `XCheckTypedWindowEvent` function searches the event queue and then any events available on the server connection for the first event that matches the specified type and window. If it finds a match, `XCheckTypedWindowEvent` removes the event from the queue, copies it into the specified `XEvent` structure, and returns `True`. The other events in the queue are not discarded. If the event is not available, `XCheckTypedWindowEvent` returns `False`, and the output buffer will have been flushed.

11.5 Putting an Event Back into the Queue

To push an event back into the event queue, use `XPutBackEvent`.

```
XPutBackEvent(display, event)
    Display *display;
    XEvent *event;
```

display Specifies the connection to the X server.

event Specifies the event.

The `XPutBackEvent` function pushes an event back onto the head of the display's event queue by copying the event into the queue. This can be useful if you read an event and then decide that you would rather deal with it later. There is no limit to the number of times in succession that you can call `XPutBackEvent`.

11.6 Sending Events to Other Applications

To send an event to a specified window, use `XSendEvent`. This function is often used in selection processing. For example, the owner of a selection should use `XSendEvent` to send a `SelectionNotify` event to a requestor when a selection has been converted and stored as a property.

```
Status XSendEvent(display, w, propagate, event_mask, event_send)
    Display *display;
    Window w;
    Bool propagate;
    long event_mask;
    XEvent *event_send;
```

display Specifies the connection to the X server.

w Specifies the window the event is to be sent to, or `PointerWindow`, or `InputFocus`.

propagate Specifies a Boolean value.

event_mask Specifies the event mask.

event_send Specifies the event that is to be sent.

The XSendEvent function identifies the destination window, determines which clients should receive the specified events, and ignores any active grabs. This function requires you to pass an event mask. For a discussion of the valid event mask names, see section 10.3. This function uses the w argument to identify the destination window as follows:

- If w is PointerWindow, the destination window is the window that contains the pointer.
- If w is InputFocus and if the focus window contains the pointer, the destination window is the window that contains the pointer; otherwise, the destination window is the focus window.

To determine which clients should receive the specified events, XSendEvent uses the propagate argument as follows:

- If event_mask is the empty set, the event is sent to the client that created the destination window. If that client no longer exists, no event is sent.
- If propagate is False, the event is sent to every client selecting on destination any of the event types in the event_mask argument.
- If propagate is True and no clients have selected on destination any of the event types in event-mask, the destination is replaced with the closest ancestor of destination for which some client has selected a type in event-mask and for which no intervening window has that type in its do-not-propagate-mask. If no such window exists or if the window is an ancestor of the focus window and InputFocus was originally specified as the destination, the event is not sent to any clients. Otherwise, the event is reported to every client selecting on the final destination any of the types specified in event_mask.

The event in the XEvent structure must be one of the core events or one of the events defined by an extension (or a BadValue error results) so that the X server can correctly byte-swap the contents as necessary. The contents of the event are otherwise unaltered and unchecked by the X server except to force send_event to True in the forwarded event and to set the serial number in the event correctly.

XSendEvent returns zero if the conversion to wire protocol format failed and returns nonzero otherwise.

XSendEvent can generate BadValue and BadWindow errors.

11.7 Getting Pointer Motion History

Some X server implementations will maintain a more complete history of pointer motion than is reported by event notification. The pointer position at each pointer hardware interrupt may be stored in a buffer for later retrieval. This buffer is called the motion history buffer. For example, a few applications, such as paint programs, want to have a precise history of where the pointer traveled. However, this historical information is highly excessive for most applications.

To determine the approximate maximum number of elements in the motion buffer, use `XDisplayMotionBufferSize`.

```
unsigned long XDisplayMotionBufferSize(display)
    Display *display;
```

display Specifies the connection to the X server.

The server may retain the recent history of the pointer motion and do so to a finer granularity than is reported by `MotionNotify` events. The `XGetMotionEvents` function makes this history available.

To get the motion history for a specified window and time, use `XGetMotionEvents`.

```
XTimeCoord *XGetMotionEvents(display, w, start, stop, nevents_return)
    Display *display;
    Window w;
    Time start, stop;
    int *nevents_return;
```

display Specifies the connection to the X server.

w Specifies the window.

start

stop Specify the time interval in which the events are returned from the motion history buffer. You can pass a timestamp or `CurrentTime`.

nevents_return Returns the number of events from the motion history buffer.

The `XGetMotionEvents` function returns all events in the motion history buffer that fall between the specified start and stop times, inclusive, and that have coordinates that lie within the specified window (including its borders) at its present placement. If the server does not support motion history, if the start time is later than the stop time, or if the start time is in the future, no events are returned; `XGetMotionEvents` returns NULL. If the stop time is in the future, it is equivalent to specifying `CurrentTime`. The return type for this function is a structure defined as follows:

```
typedef struct {
    Time time;
    short x, y;
} XTimeCoord;
```

The time member is set to the time, in milliseconds. The x and y members are set to the coordinates of the pointer and are reported relative to the origin of the specified window. To free the data returned from this call, use XFree.

XGetMotionEvents can generate a BadWindow error.

11.8 Handling Protocol Errors

Xlib provides functions that you can use to enable or disable synchronization and to use the default error handlers.

11.8.1 Enabling or Disabling Synchronization

When debugging X applications, it often is very convenient to require Xlib to behave synchronously so that errors are reported as they occur. The following function lets you disable or enable synchronous behavior. Note that graphics may occur 30 or more times more slowly when synchronization is enabled. On POSIX-conformant systems, there is also a global variable _Xdebug that, if set to nonzero before starting a program under a debugger, will force synchronous library behavior.

After completing their work, all Xlib functions that generate protocol requests call what is known as an after function. XSetAfterFunction sets which function is to be called.

```
int (*XSetAfterFunction ( display, procedure)) ()
    Display *display;
    int (*procedure) ();
```

display Specifies the connection to the X server.

procedure Specifies the function to be called.

The specified procedure is called with only a display pointer. XSetAfterFunction returns the previous after function.

To enable or disable synchronization, use XSynchronize.

```
int (*XSynchronize ( display, onoff) ) ()
    Display *display;
```

```
   Bool onoff;
```

display Specifies the connection to the X server.

onoff Specifies a Boolean value that indicates whether to enable or disable synchronization.

The XSynchronize function returns the previous after function. If onoff is True, XSynchronize turns on synchronous behavior. If onoff is False, XSynchronize turns off synchronous behavior.

11.8.2 Using the Default Error Handlers

There are two default error handlers in Xlib: one to handle typically fatal conditions (for example, the connection to a display server dying because a machine crashed) and one to handle protocol errors from the X server. These error handlers can be changed to user-supplied routines if you prefer your own error handling and can be changed as often as you like. If either function is passed a NULL pointer, it will reinvoke the default handler. The action of the default handlers is to print an explanatory message and exit.

To set the error handler, use XSetErrorHandler.

```
int (*XSetErrorHandler ( handler) ) ( )
   int ( * handler) (Display *, XErrorEvent *)
```

handler Specifies the program's supplied error handler.

Xlib generally calls the program's supplied error handler whenever an error is received. It is not called on BadName errors from OpenFont, LookupColor, or AllocNamedColor protocol requests or on BadFont errors from a QueryFont protocol request. These errors generally are reflected back to the program through the procedural interface. Because this condition is not assumed to be fatal, it is acceptable for your error handler to return. However, the error handler should not call any functions (directly or indirectly) on the display that will generate protocol requests or that will look for input events. The previous error handler is returned.

The XErrorEvent structure contains:

```
typedef struct {
    int type;
    Display *display;                /* Display the event was read from */
```

```
    unsigned long serial;           /* serial number of failed request */
    unsigned char error_code;       /* error code of failed request */
    unsigned char request_code;     /* Major op-code of failed request */
    unsigned char minor_code;       /* Minor op-code of failed request */
    XID resourceid;                 /* resource id */
} XErrorEvent;
```

The serial member is the number of requests, starting from one, sent over the network connection since it was opened. It is the number that was the value of `NextRequest` immediately before the failing call was made. The request_code member is a protocol request of the procedure that failed, as defined in `<X11/Xproto.h>`. The following error codes can be returned by the functions described in this chapter:

Error Code	*Description*
`BadAccess`	A client attempts to grab a key/button combination already grabbed by another client. A client attempts to free a colormap entry that it had not already allocated or to free an entry in a colormap that was created with all entries writable. A client attempts to store into a read-only or unallocated colormap entry. A client attempts to modify the access control list from other than the local (or otherwise authorized) host. A client attempts to select an event type that another client has already selected.
`BadAlloc`	The server fails to allocate the requested resource. Note that the explicit listing of `BadAlloc` errors in requests only covers allocation errors at a very coarse level and is not intended to (nor can it in practice hope to) cover all cases of a server running out of allocation space in the middle of service. The semantics when a server runs out of allocation space are left unspecified, but a server may generate a `BadAlloc` error on any request for this reason, and clients should be prepared to receive such errors and handle or discard them.
`BadAtom`	A value for an atom argument does not name a defined atom.
`BadColor`	A value for a colormap argument does not name a defined colormap.

Error Code	*Description*
`BadCursor`	A value for a cursor argument does not name a defined cursor.
`BadDrawable`	A value for a drawable argument does not name a defined window or pixmap.
`BadFont`	A value for a font argument does not name a defined font (or, in some cases, `GContext`).
`BadGC`	A value for a `GContext` argument does not name a defined `GContext`.
`BadIDChoice`	The value chosen for a resource identifier either is not included in the range assigned to the client or is already in use. Under normal circumstances, this cannot occur and should be considered a server or Xlib error.
`BadImplementation`	The server does not implement some aspect of the request. A server that generates this error for a core request is deficient. As such, this error is not listed for any of the requests, but clients should be prepared to receive such errors and handle or discard them.
`BadLength`	The length of a request is shorter or longer than that required to contain the arguments. This is an internal Xlib or server error. The length of a request exceeds the maximum length accepted by the server.
`BadMatch`	In a graphics request, the root and depth of the graphics context does not match that of the drawable. An `InputOnly` window is used as a drawable. Some argument or pair of arguments has the correct type and range, but it fails to match in some other way required by the request. An `InputOnly` window lacks this attribute.
`BadName`	A font or color of the specified name does not exist.
`BadPixmap`	A value for a pixmap argument does not name a defined pixmap.
`BadRequest`	The major or minor opcode does not specify a valid request. This usually is an Xlib or server error.
`BadValue`	Some numeric value falls outside of the range of values accepted by the request. Unless a specific range is specified for an argument, the full range defined by the argument's type is accepted. Any argument defined as a set of alternatives typically can generate this error (due to the encoding).
`BadWindow`	A value for a window argument does not name a defined window.

Note The BadAtom, BadColor, BadCursor, BadDrawable, BadFont, BadGC, BadPixmap, and BadWindow errors are also used when the argument type is extended by a set of fixed alternatives.

To obtain textual descriptions of the specified error code, use XGetErrorText.

```
XGetErrorText(display, code, buffer_return, length)
    Display *display;
    int code;
    char *buffer_return;
    int length;
```

display	Specifies the connection to the X server.
code	Specifies the error code for which you want to obtain a description.
buffer_return	Returns the error description.
length	Specifies the size of the buffer.

The XGetErrorText function copies a null-terminated string describing the specified error code into the specified buffer. The returned text is in the encoding of the current locale. It is recommended that you use this function to obtain an error description because extensions to Xlib may define their own error codes and error strings.

To obtain error messages from the error database, use XGetErrorDatabaseText.

```
XGetErrorDatabaseText(display, name, message, default_string, buffer_return, length)
    Display *display;
    char *name, *message;
    char *default_string;
    char *buffer_return;
    int length;
```

display	Specifies the connection to the X server.
name	Specifies the name of the application.
message	Specifies the type of the error message.
default_string	Specifies the default error message if none is found in the database.
buffer_return	Returns the error description.
length	Specifies the size of the buffer.

The `XGetErrorDatabaseText` function returns a null-terminated message (or the default message) from the error message database. Xlib uses this function internally to look up its error messages. The text stored in the default_string argument is assumed to be in the encoding of the current locale, while the text stored in the buffer_return argument is in the encoding of the current locale.

The name argument should generally be the name of your application. The message argument should indicate which type of error message you want. If the name and message are not in the Host Portable Character Encoding, the result is implementation dependent. Xlib uses three predefined "application names" to report errors. In these names, uppercase and lowercase matter.

XProtoError	The protocol error number is used as a string for the message argument.
XlibMessage	These are the message strings that are used internally by the library.
XRequest	For a core protocol request, the major request protocol number is used for the message argument. For an extension request, the extension name (as given by `InitExtension`) followed by a period (.) and the minor request protocol number is used for the message argument. If no string is found in the error database, the default_string is returned to the buffer argument.

To report an error to the user when the requested display does not exist, use `XDisplayName`.

char *XDisplayName (*string*)
  char **string*;

string Specifies the character string.

The `XDisplayName` function returns the name of the display that `XOpenDisplay` would attempt to use. If a NULL string is specified, `XDisplayName` looks in the environment for the display and returns the display name that `XOpenDisplay` would attempt to use. This makes it easier to report to the user precisely which display the program attempted to open when the initial connection attempt failed.

To handle fatal I/O errors, use `XSetIOErrorHandler`.

```
int (*XSetIOErrorHandler(handler))()
    int (*handler)(Display *);
```

handler Specifies the program's supplied error handler.

The `XSetIOErrorHandler` sets the fatal I/O error handler. Xlib calls the program's supplied error handler if any sort of system call error occurs (for example, the connection to the server was lost). This is assumed to be a fatal condition, and the called routine should not return. If the I/O error handler does return, the client process exits.

Note that the previous error handler is returned.

Chapter 12

Input Device Functions

You can use the Xlib input device functions to:

- Grab the pointer and individual buttons on the pointer
- Grab the keyboard and individual keys on the keyboard
- Move the pointer
- Set the input focus
- Manipulate the keyboard and pointer settings
- Manipulate the keyboard encoding

12.1 Pointer Grabbing

Xlib provides functions that you can use to control input from the pointer, which usually is a mouse. Usually, as soon as keyboard and mouse events occur, the X server delivers them to the appropriate client, which is determined by the window and input focus. The X server provides sufficient control over event delivery to allow window managers to support mouse ahead and various other styles of user interface. Many of these user interfaces depend upon synchronous delivery of events. The delivery of pointer and keyboard events can be controlled independently.

When mouse buttons or keyboard keys are grabbed, events will be sent to the grabbing client rather than the normal client who would have received the event. If the keyboard or pointer is in asynchronous mode, further mouse and keyboard events will continue to be processed. If the keyboard or pointer is in synchronous mode, no further events are processed until the grabbing client allows them (see XAllowEvents). The keyboard or pointer is considered frozen during this interval. The event that triggered the grab can also be replayed.

Note that the logical state of a device (as seen by client applications) may lag the physical state if device event processing is frozen.

There are two kinds of grabs: active and passive. An active grab occurs when a single client grabs the keyboard and/or pointer explicitly (see XGrabPointer and XGrabKeyboard). A passive grab occurs when clients grab a particular keyboard key or pointer button in a window, and the grab will activate when the key or button is actually pressed. Passive grabs are convenient for implementing reliable pop-up menus. For example, you can guarantee that the pop-up is mapped before the up pointer button event occurs by grabbing a button requesting synchronous behavior. The down event will trigger the grab and freeze further processing of pointer events until you have the chance to map the pop-up window. You can then allow further event processing. The up event will then be correctly processed relative to the pop-up window.

For many operations, there are functions that take a time argument. The X server includes a timestamp in various events. One special time, called CurrentTime, represents the current server time. The X server maintains the time when the input focus was last changed, when the keyboard was last grabbed, when the pointer was last grabbed, or when a selection was last changed. Your application may be slow reacting to an event. You often need some way to specify that your request should not occur if another application has in the meanwhile taken control of the keyboard, pointer, or selection. By providing the timestamp from the event in the request, you can arrange that the operation not take effect if someone else has performed an operation in the meanwhile.

A timestamp is a time value, expressed in milliseconds. It typically is the time since the last server reset. Timestamp values wrap around (after about 49.7 days). The server, given its current time is represented by timestamp T, always interprets timestamps from clients by treating half of the timestamp space as being later in time than T. One timestamp value, named CurrentTime, is never generated by the server. This value is reserved for use in requests to represent the current server time.

For many functions in this section, you pass pointer event mask bits. The valid pointer event mask bits are: ButtonPressMask, ButtonReleaseMask, EnterWindowMask, LeaveWindowMask, PointerMotionMask, PointerMotionHintMask, Button1MotionMask, Button2MotionMask, Button3MotionMask, Button4MotionMask, Button5MotionMask, ButtonMotionMask, and KeyMapStateMask. For other functions in this section, you pass keymask bits. The valid keymask bits are: ShiftMask, LockMask, ControlMask, Mod1Mask, Mod2Mask, Mod3Mask, Mod4Mask, and Mod5Mask.

To grab the pointer, use XGrabPointer.

int XGrabPointer (*display*, *grab_window*, *owner_events*, *event_mask*, *pointer_mode*,
keyboard_mode, *confine_to*, *cursor*, *time*)
Display **display*;
Window *grab_window*;
Bool *owner_events*;
unsigned int *event_mask*;
int *pointer_mode*, *keyboard_mode*;
Window *confine_to*;
Cursor *cursor*;
Time *time*;

display	Specifies the connection to the X server.
grab_window	Specifies the grab window.
owner_events	Specifies a Boolean value that indicates whether the pointer events are to be reported as usual or reported with respect to the grab window if selected by the event mask.
event_mask	Specifies which pointer events are reported to the client. The mask is the bitwise inclusive OR of the valid pointer event mask bits.
pointer_mode	Specifies further processing of pointer events. You can pass GrabModeSync or GrabModeAsync.
keyboard_mode	Specifies further processing of keyboard events. You can pass GrabModeSync or GrabModeAsync.
confine_to	Specifies the window to confine the pointer in or None.
cursor	Specifies the cursor that is to be displayed during the grab or None.
time	Specifies the time. You can pass either a timestamp or CurrentTime.

The XGrabPointer function actively grabs control of the pointer and returns GrabSuccess if the grab was successful. Further pointer events are reported only to the grabbing client. XGrabPointer overrides any active pointer grab by this client. If owner_events is False, all generated pointer events are reported with respect to grab_window and are reported only if selected by event_mask. If owner_events is True and if a generated pointer event would normally be reported to this client, it is reported as usual. Otherwise, the event is reported with respect to the grab_window and is reported only if selected by event_mask. For either value of owner_events, unreported events are discarded.

If the pointer_mode is GrabModeAsync, pointer event processing continues as usual. If the pointer is currently frozen by this client, the processing of events for the pointer is resumed. If the pointer_mode is GrabModeSync, the state of the pointer, as seen by client applications, appears to freeze, and the X server generates no further pointer events until the grabbing client calls XAllowEvents or until the pointer grab is released. Actual pointer changes are not lost while the pointer is frozen; they are simply queued in the server for later processing.

If the keyboard_mode is GrabModeAsync, keyboard event processing is unaffected by activation of the grab. If the keyboard_mode is GrabModeSync, the state of the keyboard, as seen by client applications, appears to freeze, and the X server generates no further keyboard events until the grabbing client calls XAllowEvents or until the pointer grab is released. Actual keyboard changes are not lost while the pointer is frozen; they are simply queued in the server for later processing.

If a cursor is specified, it is displayed regardless of what window the pointer is in. If None is specified, the normal cursor for that window is displayed when the pointer is in grab_window or one of its subwindows; otherwise, the cursor for grab_window is displayed.

If a confine_to window is specified, the pointer is restricted to stay contained in that window. The confine_to window need have no relationship to the grab_window. If the pointer is not initially in the confine_to window, it is warped automatically to the closest edge just before the grab activates and enter/leave events are generated as usual. If the confine_to window is subsequently reconfigured, the pointer is warped automatically, as necessary, to keep it contained in the window.

The time argument allows you to avoid certain circumstances that come up if applications take a long time to respond or if there are long network delays. Consider a situation where you have two applications, both of which normally grab the pointer when clicked on. If both applications specify the timestamp from the event, the second application may wake up faster and successfully grab the pointer before the first application. The first application then will get an indication that the other application grabbed the pointer before its request was processed.

`XGrabPointer` generates `EnterNotify` and `LeaveNotify` events.

Either if grab_window or confine_to window is not viewable or if the confine_to window lies completely outside the boundaries of the root window, `XGrabPointer` fails and returns `GrabNotViewable`. If the pointer is actively grabbed by some other client, it fails and returns `AlreadyGrabbed`. If the pointer is frozen by an active grab of another client, it fails and returns `Grab-Frozen`. If the specified time is earlier than the last-pointer-grab time or later than the current X server time, it fails and returns `GrabInvalidTime`. Otherwise, the last-pointer-grab time is set to the specified time (`CurrentTime` is replaced by the current X server time).

`XGrabPointer` can generate `BadCursor`, `BadValue`, and `BadWindow` errors.

To ungrab the pointer, use `XUngrabPointer`.

```
XUngrabPointer ( display, time)
    Display *display;
    Time time;
```

display Specifies the connection to the X server.

time Specifies the time. You can pass either a timestamp or `CurrentTime`.

The `XUngrabPointer` function releases the pointer and any queued events if this client has actively grabbed the pointer from `XGrabPointer`, `XGrabButton`, or from a normal button press. `XUngrabPointer` does not release the pointer if the specified time is earlier than the last-pointer-grab time or is later than the current X server time. It also generates `EnterNotify` and `LeaveNotify` events. The X server performs an `UngrabPointer` request automatically if the event window or confine_to window for an active pointer grab becomes not viewable or if window reconfiguration causes the confine_to window to lie completely outside the boundaries of the root window.

To change an active pointer grab, use `XChangeActivePointerGrab`.

```
XChangeActivePointerGrab ( display, event_mask, cursor, time)
    Display *display;
    unsigned int event_mask;
```

```
   Cursor cursor;
   Time time;
```

display Specifies the connection to the X server.

event_mask Specifies which pointer events are reported to the client. The mask is the bitwise inclusive OR of the valid pointer event mask bits.

cursor Specifies the cursor that is to be displayed or `None`.

time Specifies the time. You can pass either a timestamp or `CurrentTime`.

The `XChangeActivePointerGrab` function changes the specified dynamic parameters if the pointer is actively grabbed by the client and if the specified time is no earlier than the last-pointer-grab time and no later than the current X server time. This function has no effect on the passive parameters of a `XGrabButton`. The interpretation of event_mask and cursor is the same as described in `XGrabPointer`.

`XChangeActivePointerGrab` can generate `BadCursor` and `BadValue` errors.

To grab a pointer button, use `XGrabButton`.

```
XGrabButton (display, button, modifiers, grab_window, owner_events, event_mask,
               pointer_mode, keyboard_mode, confine_to, cursor)
   Display *display;
   unsigned int button;
   unsigned int modifiers;
   Window grab_window;
   Bool owner_events;
   unsigned int event_mask;
   int pointer_mode, keyboard_mode;
   Window confine_to;
   Cursor cursor;
```

display Specifies the connection to the X server.

button Specifies the pointer button that is to be grabbed or `AnyButton`.

modifiers Specifies the set of keymasks or `AnyModifier`. The mask is the bitwise inclusive OR of the valid keymask bits.

grab_window Specifies the grab window.

owner_events Specifies a Boolean value that indicates whether the pointer events are to be reported as usual or reported with respect to the grab window if selected by the event mask.

event_mask Specifies which pointer events are reported to the client. The mask is the bitwise inclusive OR of the valid pointer event mask bits.

pointer_mode Specifies further processing of pointer events. You can pass `GrabModeSync` or `GrabModeAsync`.

keyboard_mode	Specifies further processing of keyboard events. You can pass GrabModeSync or GrabModeAsync.
confine_to	Specifies the window to confine the pointer in or None.
cursor	Specifies the cursor that is to be displayed or None.

The XGrabButton function establishes a passive grab. In the future, the pointer is actively grabbed (as for XGrabPointer), the last-pointer-grab time is set to the time at which the button was pressed (as transmitted in the ButtonPress event), and the ButtonPress event is reported if all of the following conditions are true:

- The pointer is not grabbed, and the specified button is logically pressed when the specified modifier keys are logically down, and no other buttons or modifier keys are logically down.
- The grab_window contains the pointer.
- The confine_to window (if any) is viewable.
- A passive grab on the same button/key combination does not exist on any ancestor of grab_window.

The interpretation of the remaining arguments is as for XGrabPointer. The active grab is terminated automatically when the logical state of the pointer has all buttons released (independent of the state of the logical modifier keys).

Note that the logical state of a device (as seen by client applications) may lag the physical state if device event processing is frozen.

This request overrides all previous grabs by the same client on the same button/key combinations on the same window. A modifiers of AnyModifier is equivalent to issuing the grab request for all possible modifier combinations (including the combination of no modifiers). It is not required that all modifiers specified have currently assigned KeyCodes. A button of AnyButton is equivalent to issuing the request for all possible buttons. Otherwise, it is not required that the specified button currently be assigned to a physical button.

If some other client has already issued a XGrabButton with the same button/key combination on the same window, a BadAccess error results. When using AnyModifier or AnyButton, the request fails completely, and a BadAccess error results (no grabs are established) if there is a conflicting grab for any combination. XGrabButton has no effect on an active grab.

XGrabButton can generate BadCursor, BadValue, and BadWindow errors.

To ungrab a pointer button, use `XUngrabButton`.

```
XUngrabButton ( display, button, modifiers, grab_window)
    Display *display;
    unsigned int button;
    unsigned int modifiers;
    Window grab_window;
```

display Specifies the connection to the X server.

button Specifies the pointer button that is to be released or `AnyButton`.

modifiers Specifies the set of keymasks or `AnyModifier`. The mask is the bitwise inclusive OR of the valid keymask bits.

grab_window Specifies the grab window.

The `XUngrabButton` function releases the passive button/key combination on the specified window if it was grabbed by this client. A modifiers of `AnyModifier` is equivalent to issuing the ungrab request for all possible modifier combinations, including the combination of no modifiers. A button of `AnyButton` is equivalent to issuing the request for all possible buttons. `XUngrabButton` has no effect on an active grab.

`XUngrabButton` can generate `BadValue` and `BadWindow` errors.

12.2 Keyboard Grabbing

Xlib provides functions that you can use to grab or ungrab the keyboard as well as allow events.

For many functions in this section, you pass keymask bits. The valid keymask bits are: `ShiftMask`, `LockMask`, `ControlMask`, `Mod1Mask`, `Mod2Mask`, `Mod3Mask`, `Mod4Mask`, and `Mod5Mask`.

To grab the keyboard, use `XGrabKeyboard`.

```
int XGrabKeyboard ( display, grab_window, owner_events, pointer_mode, keyboard_mode,
                    time)
    Display *display;
    Window grab_window;
    Bool owner_events;
    int pointer_mode, keyboard_mode;
    Time time;
```

display Specifies the connection to the X server.

grab_window Specifies the grab window.

owner_events	Specifies a Boolean value that indicates whether the keyboard events are to be reported as usual.
pointer_mode	Specifies further processing of pointer events. You can pass GrabModeSync or GrabModeAsync.
keyboard_mode	Specifies further processing of keyboard events. You can pass GrabModeSync or GrabModeAsync.
time	Specifies the time. You can pass either a timestamp or CurrentTime.

The XGrabKeyboard function actively grabs control of the keyboard and generates FocusIn and FocusOut events. Further key events are reported only to the grabbing client. XGrabKeyboard overrides any active keyboard grab by this client. If owner_events is False, all generated key events are reported with respect to grab_window. If owner_events is True and if a generated key event would normally be reported to this client, it is reported normally; otherwise, the event is reported with respect to the grab_window. Both KeyPress and KeyRelease events are always reported, independent of any event selection made by the client.

If the keyboard_mode argument is GrabModeAsync, keyboard event processing continues as usual. If the keyboard is currently frozen by this client, then processing of keyboard events is resumed. If the keyboard_mode argument is GrabModeSync, the state of the keyboard (as seen by client applications) appears to freeze, and the X server generates no further keyboard events until the grabbing client issues a releasing XAllowEvents call or until the keyboard grab is released. Actual keyboard changes are not lost while the keyboard is frozen; they are simply queued in the server for later processing.

If pointer_mode is GrabModeAsync, pointer event processing is unaffected by activation of the grab. If pointer_mode is GrabModeSync, the state of the pointer (as seen by client applications) appears to freeze, and the X server generates no further pointer events until the grabbing client issues a releasing XAllowEvents call or until the keyboard grab is released. Actual pointer changes are not lost while the pointer is frozen; they are simply queued in the server for later processing.

If the keyboard is actively grabbed by some other client, XGrabKeyboard fails and returns AlreadyGrabbed. If grab_window is not viewable, it fails and returns GrabNotViewable. If the keyboard is frozen by an active grab of another client, it fails and returns GrabFrozen. If the specified time is earlier than the last-keyboard-grab time or later than the current X server time, it fails and returns GrabInvalidTime. Otherwise, the last-keyboard-grab time is set to the specified time (CurrentTime is replaced by the current X server time).

XGrabKeyboard can generate BadValue and BadWindow errors.

To ungrab the keyboard, use XUngrabKeyboard.

```
XUngrabKeyboard(display, time)
    Display *display;
    Time time;
```

display Specifies the connection to the X server.

time Specifies the time. You can pass either a timestamp or CurrentTime.

The XUngrabKeyboard function releases the keyboard and any queued events if this client has it actively grabbed from either XGrabKeyboard or XGrabKey. XUngrabKeyboard does not release the keyboard and any queued events if the specified time is earlier than the last-keyboard-grab time or is later than the current X server time. It also generates FocusIn and FocusOut events. The X server automatically performs an UngrabKeyboard request if the event window for an active keyboard grab becomes not viewable.

To passively grab a single key of the keyboard, use XGrabKey.

```
XGrabKey(display, keycode, modifiers, grab_window, owner_events, pointer_mode,
        keyboard_mode)
    Display *display;
    int keycode;
    unsigned int modifiers;
    Window grab_window;
    Bool owner_events;
    int pointer_mode, keyboard_mode;
```

display Specifies the connection to the X server.

keycode Specifies the KeyCode or AnyKey.

modifiers Specifies the set of keymasks or AnyModifier. The mask is the bitwise inclusive OR of the valid keymask bits.

grab_window Specifies the grab window.

owner_events Specifies a Boolean value that indicates whether the keyboard events are to be reported as usual.

pointer_mode Specifies further processing of pointer events. You can pass `GrabModeSync` or `GrabModeAsync`.

keyboard_mode Specifies further processing of keyboard events. You can pass `GrabModeSync` or `GrabModeAsync`.

The `XGrabKey` function establishes a passive grab on the keyboard. In the future, the keyboard is actively grabbed (as for `XGrabKeyboard`), the last-keyboard-grab time is set to the time at which the key was pressed (as transmitted in the `KeyPress` event), and the `KeyPress` event is reported if all of the following conditions are true:

- The keyboard is not grabbed and the specified key (which can itself be a modifier key) is logically pressed when the specified modifier keys are logically down, and no other modifier keys are logically down.
- Either the grab_window is an ancestor of (or is) the focus window, or the grab_window is a descendant of the focus window and contains the pointer.
- A passive grab on the same key combination does not exist on any ancestor of grab_window.

The interpretation of the remaining arguments is as for `XGrabKeyboard`. The active grab is terminated automatically when the logical state of the keyboard has the specified key released (independent of the logical state of the modifier keys).

Note that the logical state of a device (as seen by client applications) may lag the physical state if device event processing is frozen.

A modifiers argument of `AnyModifier` is equivalent to issuing the request for all possible modifier combinations (including the combination of no modifiers). It is not required that all modifiers specified have currently assigned KeyCodes. A keycode argument of `AnyKey` is equivalent to issuing the request for all possible KeyCodes. Otherwise, the specified keycode must be in the range specified by min_keycode and max_keycode in the connection setup, or a `BadValue` error results.

If some other client has issued a `XGrabKey` with the same key combination on the same window, a `BadAccess` error results. When using `AnyModifier` or `AnyKey`, the request fails completely, and a `BadAccess` error results (no grabs are established) if there is a conflicting grab for any combination.

`XGrabKey` can generate `BadAccess`, `BadValue`, and `BadWindow` errors.

To ungrab a key, use XUngrabKey.

```
XUngrabKey ( display, keycode, modifiers, grab_window)
    Display *display;
    int keycode;
    unsigned int modifiers;
    Window grab_window;
```

display Specifies the connection to the X server.

keycode Specifies the KeyCode or AnyKey.

modifiers Specifies the set of keymasks or AnyModifier. The mask is the bitwise inclusive OR of the valid keymask bits.

grab_window Specifies the grab window.

The XUngrabKey function releases the key combination on the specified window if it was grabbed by this client. It has no effect on an active grab. A modifiers of AnyModifier is equivalent to issuing the request for all possible modifier combinations (including the combination of no modifiers). A keycode argument of AnyKey is equivalent to issuing the request for all possible key codes.

XUngrabKey can generate BadValue and BadWindow errors.

12.3 Resuming Event Processing

The previous sections discussed grab mechanisms with which processing of events by the server can be temporarily suspended. This section describes the mechanism for resuming event processing.

To allow further events to be processed when the device has been frozen, use XAllowEvents.

```
XAllowEvents ( display, event_mode, time)
    Display *display;
    int event_mode;
    Time time;
```

display Specifies the connection to the X server.

event_mode Specifies the event mode. You can pass AsyncPointer, SyncPointer, AsyncKeyboard, SyncKeyboard, ReplayPointer, ReplayKeyboard, AsyncBoth, or SyncBoth.

time Specifies the time. You can pass either a timestamp or CurrentTime.

The `XAllowEvents` function releases some queued events if the client has caused a device to freeze. It has no effect if the specified time is earlier than the last-grab time of the most recent active grab for the client or if the specified time is later than the current X server time. Depending on the event_mode argument, the following occurs:

`AsyncPointer`	If the pointer is frozen by the client, pointer event processing continues as usual. If the pointer is frozen twice by the client on behalf of two separate grabs, `AsyncPointer` thaws for both. `AsyncPointer` has no effect if the pointer is not frozen by the client, but the pointer need not be grabbed by the client.
`SyncPointer`	If the pointer is frozen and actively grabbed by the client, pointer event processing continues as usual until the next `ButtonPress` or `ButtonRelease` event is reported to the client. At this time, the pointer again appears to freeze. However, if the reported event causes the pointer grab to be released, the pointer does not freeze. `SyncPointer` has no effect if the pointer is not frozen by the client or if the pointer is not grabbed by the client.
`ReplayPointer`	If the pointer is actively grabbed by the client and is frozen as the result of an event having been sent to the client (either from the activation of a `XGrabButton` or from a previous `XAllowEvents` with mode `SyncPointer` but not from a `XGrabPointer`), the pointer grab is released and that event is completely reprocessed. This time, however, the function ignores any passive grabs at or above (towards the root of) the grab_window of the grab just released. The request has no effect if the pointer is not grabbed by the client or if the pointer is not frozen as the result of an event.
`AsyncKeyboard`	If the keyboard is frozen by the client, keyboard event processing continues as usual. If the keyboard is frozen twice by the client on behalf of two separate grabs, `AsyncKeyboard` thaws for both. `AsyncKeyboard` has no effect if the keyboard is not frozen by the client, but the keyboard need not be grabbed by the client.
`SyncKeyboard`	If the keyboard is frozen and actively grabbed by the client, keyboard event processing continues as usual until the next `KeyPress` or `KeyRelease` event is reported to the client. At this time, the keyboard again appears to freeze. However, if the reported event causes the keyboard grab to be released, the keyboard does not freeze. `SyncKeyboard` has no effect if the keyboard is not frozen by the client or if the keyboard is not grabbed by the client.

ReplayKeyboard	If the keyboard is actively grabbed by the client and is frozen as the result of an event having been sent to the client (either from the activation of a XGrabKey or from a previous XAllowEvents with mode SyncKeyboard but not from a XGrabKeyboard), the keyboard grab is released and that event is completely reprocessed. This time, however, the function ignores any passive grabs at or above (towards the root of) the grab_window of the grab just released. The request has no effect if the keyboard is not grabbed by the client or if the keyboard is not frozen as the result of an event.
SyncBoth	If both pointer and keyboard are frozen by the client, event processing for both devices continues as usual until the next ButtonPress, ButtonRelease, KeyPress, or KeyRelease event is reported to the client for a grabbed device (button event for the pointer, key event for the keyboard), at which time the devices again appear to freeze. However, if the reported event causes the grab to be released, then the devices do not freeze (but if the other device is still grabbed, then a subsequent event for it will still cause both devices to freeze). SyncBoth has no effect unless both pointer and keyboard are frozen by the client. If the pointer or keyboard is frozen twice by the client on behalf of two separate grabs, SyncBoth thaws for both (but a subsequent freeze for SyncBoth will only freeze each device once).
AsyncBoth	If the pointer and the keyboard are frozen by the client, event processing for both devices continues as usual. If a device is frozen twice by the client on behalf of two separate grabs, AsyncBoth thaws for both. AsyncBoth has no effect unless both pointer and keyboard are frozen by the client.

AsyncPointer, SyncPointer, and ReplayPointer have no effect on the processing of keyboard events. AsyncKeyboard, SyncKeyboard, and ReplayKeyboard have no effect on the processing of pointer events. It is possible for both a pointer grab and a keyboard grab (by the same or different clients) to be active simultaneously. If a device is frozen on behalf of either grab, no event processing is performed for the device. It is possible for a single device to be frozen because of both grabs. In this case, the freeze must be released on behalf of both grabs before events can again be processed. If a device is frozen twice by a single client, then a single AllowEvents releases both.

XAllowEvents can generate a BadValue error.

12.4 Moving the Pointer

Although movement of the pointer normally should be left to the control of the end user, sometimes it is necessary to move the pointer to a new position under program control.

To move the pointer to an arbitrary point in a window, use `XWarpPointer`.

```
XWarpPointer ( display, src_w, dest_w, src_x, src_y, src_width, src_height, dest_x, dest_y)
    Display *display;
    Window src_w, dest_w;
    int src_x, src_y;
    unsigned int src_width, src_height;
    int dest_x, dest_y;
```

display Specifies the connection to the X server.
src_w Specifies the source window or `None`.
dest_w Specifies the destination window or `None`.
src_x
src_y
src_width
src_height Specify a rectangle in the source window.
dest_x
dest_y Specify the x and y coordinates within the destination window.

If dest_w is `None`, `XWarpPointer` moves the pointer by the offsets (dest_x, dest_y) relative to the current position of the pointer. If dest_w is a window, `XWarpPointer` moves the pointer to the offsets (dest_x, dest_y) relative to the origin of dest_w. However, if src_w is a window, the move only takes place if the window src_w contains the pointer and if the specified rectangle of src_w contains the pointer.

The src_x and src_y coordinates are relative to the origin of src_w. If src_height is zero, it is replaced with the current height of src_w minus src_y. If src_width is zero, it is replaced with the current width of src_w minus src_x.

There is seldom any reason for calling this function. The pointer should normally be left to the user. If you do use this function, however, it generates events just as if the user had instantaneously moved the pointer from one position to another. Note that you cannot use `XWarpPointer` to move the pointer outside the confine_to window of an active pointer grab. An attempt to do so will only move the pointer as far as the closest edge of the confine_to window.

`XWarpPointer` can generate a `BadWindow` error.

12.5 Controlling Input Focus

Xlib provides functions that you can use to set and get the input focus. The input focus is a shared resource, and cooperation among clients is required for correct interaction. See part III, "Inter-Client Communication Conventions Manual," for input focus policy.

To set the input focus, use `XSetInputFocus`.

```
XSetInputFocus ( display, focus, revert_to, time)
    Display *display;
    Window focus;
    int revert_to;
    Time time;
```

display Specifies the connection to the X server.

focus Specifies the window, `PointerRoot`, or `None`.

revert_to Specifies where the input focus reverts to if the window becomes not viewable. You can pass `RevertToParent`, `RevertToPointerRoot`, or `RevertToNone`.

time Specifies the time. You can pass either a timestamp or `CurrentTime`.

The `XSetInputFocus` function changes the input focus and the last-focus-change time. It has no effect if the specified time is earlier than the current last-focus-change time or is later than the current X server time. Otherwise, the last-focus-change time is set to the specified time (`CurrentTime` is replaced by the current X server time). `XSetInputFocus` causes the X server to generate `FocusIn` and `FocusOut` events.

Depending on the focus argument, the following occurs:

- If focus is `None`, all keyboard events are discarded until a new focus window is set, and the revert_to argument is ignored.
- If focus is a window, it becomes the keyboard's focus window. If a generated keyboard event would normally be reported to this window or one of its inferiors, the event is reported as usual. Otherwise, the event is reported relative to the focus window.
- If focus is `PointerRoot`, the focus window is dynamically taken to be the root window of whatever screen the pointer is on at each keyboard event. In this case, the revert_to argument is ignored.

The specified focus window must be viewable at the time `XSetInputFocus` is called, or a `BadMatch` error results. If the focus window later becomes not viewable, the X server evaluates the revert_to argument to determine the new focus window as follows:

- If revert_to is `RevertToParent`, the focus reverts to the parent (or the closest viewable ancestor), and the new revert_to value is taken to be `RevertToNone`.
- If revert_to is `RevertToPointerRoot` or `RevertToNone`, the focus reverts to `PointerRoot` or `None`, respectively. When the focus reverts, the X server generates `FocusIn` and `FocusOut` events, but the last-focus-change time is not affected.

`XSetInputFocus` can generate `BadMatch`, `BadValue`, and `BadWindow` errors.

To obtain the current input focus, use `XGetInputFocus`.

XGetInputFocus (*display*, *focus_return*, *revert_to_return*)
  Display **display*;
  Window **focus_return*;
  int **revert_to_return*;

display	Specifies the connection to the X server.
focus_return	Returns the focus window, `PointerRoot`, or `None`.
revert_to_return	Returns the current focus state (`RevertToParent`, `RevertToPointerRoot`, or `RevertToNone`).

The `XGetInputFocus` function returns the focus window and the current focus state.

12.6 Keyboard and Pointer Settings

Xlib provides functions that you can use to change the keyboard control, obtain a list of the auto-repeat keys, turn keyboard auto-repeat on or off, ring the bell, set or obtain the pointer button or keyboard mapping, and obtain a bit vector for the keyboard.

This section discusses the user-preference options of bell, key click, pointer behavior, and so on. The default values for many of these functions are determined by command line arguments to the X server. Not all implementations will actually be able to control all of these parameters.

The `XChangeKeyboardControl` function changes control of a keyboard and operates on a `XKeyboardControl` structure:

```
/* Mask bits for ChangeKeyboardControl */
#define KBKeyClickPercent        (1L<<0)
#define KBBellPercent            (1L<<1)
#define KBBellPitch              (1L<<2)
#define KBBellDuration           (1L<<3)
#define KBLed                    (1L<<4)
#define KBLedMode                (1L<<5)
#define KBKey                    (1L<<6)
#define KBAutoRepeatMode         (1L<<7)
/* Values */
typedef struct {
    int key_click_percent;
    int bell_percent;
    int bell_pitch;
    int bell_duration;
    int led;
    int led_mode;                /* LedModeOn, LedModeOff */
    int key;
    int auto_repeat_mode;        /* AutoRepeatModeOff, AutoRepeatModeOn,
                                    AutoRepeatModeDefault */
} XKeyboardControl;
```

The key_click_percent member sets the volume for key clicks between 0 (off) and 100 (loud) inclusive, if possible. A setting of −1 restores the default. Other negative values generate a BadValue error.

The bell_percent sets the base volume for the bell between 0 (off) and 100 (loud) inclusive, if possible. A setting of −1 restores the default. Other negative values generate a BadValue error. The bell_pitch member sets the pitch (specified in Hz) of the bell, if possible. A setting of −1 restores the default. Other negative values generate a BadValue error. The bell_duration member sets the duration of the bell specified in milliseconds, if possible. A setting of −1 restores the default. Other negative values generate a BadValue error.

If both the led_mode and led members are specified, the state of that LED is changed, if possible. The led_mode member can be set to LedModeOn or LedModeOff. If only led_mode is specified, the state of all LEDs are changed, if possible. At most 32 LEDs numbered from one are supported. No standard interpretation of LEDs is defined. If led is specified without led_mode, a BadMatch error results.

If both the auto_repeat_mode and key members are specified, the auto_repeat_mode of that key is changed (according to AutoRepeatModeOn, AutoRepeatModeOff, or AutoRepeatModeDefault), if possible. If only auto_repeat_mode is specified, the global auto_repeat_mode for the entire keyboard is changed, if possible, and does not affect the per key settings. If a key is specified without an auto_repeat_mode, a BadMatch error results. Each key has an individual mode of whether or not it should auto-repeat and a default setting for the mode. In addition, there is a global mode of whether auto-repeat should be enabled or not and a default setting for that mode. When global mode is AutoRepeatModeOn, keys should obey their individual auto-repeat modes. When global mode is AutoRepeatModeOff, no keys should auto-repeat. An auto-repeating key generates alternating KeyPress and KeyRelease events. When a key is used as a modifier, it is desirable for the key not to auto-repeat, regardless of its auto-repeat setting.

A bell generator connected with the console but not directly on a keyboard is treated as if it were part of the keyboard. The order in which controls are verified and altered is server-dependent. If an error is generated, a subset of the controls may have been altered.

XChangeKeyboardControl (*display*, *value_mask*, *values*)
  Display **display*;
  unsigned long *value_mask*;
  XKeyboardControl **values*;

display	Specifies the connection to the X server.
value_mask	Specifies which controls to change. This mask is the bitwise inclusive OR of the valid control mask bits.
values	Specifies one value for each bit set to 1 in the mask.

The XChangeKeyboardControl function controls the keyboard characteristics defined by the XKeyboardControl structure. The value_mask argument specifies which values are to be changed.

XChangeKeyboardControl can generate BadMatch and BadValue errors.

To obtain the current control values for the keyboard, use XGetKeyboard-Control.

XGetKeyboardControl (*display*, *values_return*)
  Display **display*;
  XKeyboardState **values_return*;

display Specifies the connection to the X server.
values_return Returns the current keyboard controls in the specified `XKeyboardState` structure.

The `XGetKeyboardControl` function returns the current control values for the keyboard to the `XKeyboardState` structure.

```
typedef struct {
    int key_click_percent;
    int bell_percent;
    unsigned int bell_pitch, bell_duration;
    unsigned long led_mask;
    int global_auto_repeat;
    char auto_repeats[32];
} XKeyboardState;
```

For the LEDs, the least-significant bit of led_mask corresponds to LED one, and each bit set to 1 in led_mask indicates an LED that is lit. The global_auto_repeat member can be set to `AutoRepeatModeOn` or `AutoRepeatModeOff`. The auto_repeats member is a bit vector. Each bit set to 1 indicates that auto-repeat is enabled for the corresponding key. The vector is represented as 32 bytes. Byte N (from 0) contains the bits for keys 8N to 8N + 7 with the least-significant bit in the byte representing key 8N.

To turn on keyboard auto-repeat, use `XAutoRepeatOn`.

```
XAutoRepeatOn ( display )
  Display *display;
```

display Specifies the connection to the X server.

The `XAutoRepeatOn` function turns on auto-repeat for the keyboard on the specified display.

To turn off keyboard auto-repeat, use `XAutoRepeatOff`.

```
XAutoRepeatOff ( display )
  Display *display;
```

display Specifies the connection to the X server.

The `XAutoRepeatOff` function turns off auto-repeat for the keyboard on the specified display.

To ring the bell, use `XBell`.

```
XBell ( display, percent)
    Display *display;
    int percent;
```

display Specifies the connection to the X server.

percent Specifies the volume for the bell, which can range from –100 to 100 inclusive.

The `XBell` function rings the bell on the keyboard on the specified display, if possible. The specified volume is relative to the base volume for the keyboard. If the value for the percent argument is not in the range –100 to 100 inclusive, a `BadValue` error results. The volume at which the bell rings when the percent argument is nonnegative is:

$$\text{base} - [(\text{base} * \text{percent}) / 100] + \text{percent}$$

The volume at which the bell rings when the percent argument is negative is:

$$\text{base} + [(\text{base} * \text{percent}) / 100]$$

To change the base volume of the bell, use `XChangeKeyboardControl`.

`XBell` can generate a `BadValue` error.

To obtain a bit vector that describes the state of the keyboard, use `XQueryKeymap`.

```
XQueryKeymap ( display, keys_return)
    Display *display;
    char keys_return[32];
```

display Specifies the connection to the X server.

keys_return Returns an array of bytes that identifies which keys are pressed down. Each bit represents one key of the keyboard.

The `XQueryKeymap` function returns a bit vector for the logical state of the keyboard, where each bit set to 1 indicates that the corresponding key is currently pressed down. The vector is represented as 32 bytes. Byte N (from 0) contains the bits for keys 8N to 8N + 7 with the least-significant bit in the byte representing key 8N.

Note that the logical state of a device (as seen by client applications) may lag the physical state if device event processing is frozen.

To set the mapping of the pointer buttons, use XSetPointerMapping.

```
int XSetPointerMapping ( display, map, nmap)
    Display *display;
    unsigned char map[];
    int nmap;
```

display Specifies the connection to the X server.
map Specifies the mapping list.
nmap Specifies the number of items in the mapping list.

The XSetPointerMapping function sets the mapping of the pointer. If it succeeds, the X server generates a MappingNotify event, and XSetPointerMapping returns MappingSuccess. Element map[i] defines the logical button number for the physical button i+1. The length of the list must be the same as XGetPointerMapping would return, or a BadValue error results. A zero element disables a button, and elements are not restricted in value by the number of physical buttons. However, no two elements can have the same nonzero value, or a BadValue error results. If any of the buttons to be altered are logically in the down state, XSetPointerMapping returns MappingBusy, and the mapping is not changed.

XSetPointerMapping can generate a BadValue error.

To get the pointer mapping, use XGetPointerMapping.

```
int XGetPointerMapping ( display, map_return, nmap)
    Display *display;
    unsigned char map_return[];
    int nmap;
```

display Specifies the connection to the X server.
map_return Returns the mapping list.
nmap Specifies the number of items in the mapping list.

The XGetPointerMapping function returns the current mapping of the pointer. Pointer buttons are numbered starting from one. XGetPointerMapping returns the number of physical buttons actually on the pointer. The nominal mapping for a pointer is map[i]=i+1. The nmap argument specifies the length of the array where the pointer mapping is returned, and only the first nmap elements are returned in map_return.

To control the pointer's interactive feel, use `XChangePointerControl`.

```
XChangePointerControl(display, do_accel, do_threshold, accel_numerator,
                      accel_denominator, threshold)
    Display *display;
    Bool do_accel, do_threshold;
    int accel_numerator, accel_denominator;
    int threshold;
```

display	Specifies the connection to the X server.
do_accel	Specifies a Boolean value that controls whether the values for the accel_numerator or accel_denominator are used.
do_threshold	Specifies a Boolean value that controls whether the value for the threshold is used.
accel_numerator	Specifies the numerator for the acceleration multiplier.
accel_denominator	Specifies the denominator for the acceleration multiplier.
threshold	Specifies the acceleration threshold.

The `XChangePointerControl` function defines how the pointing device moves. The acceleration, expressed as a fraction, is a multiplier for movement. For example, specifying 3/1 means the pointer moves three times as fast as normal. The fraction may be rounded arbitrarily by the X server. Acceleration only takes effect if the pointer moves more than threshold pixels at once and only applies to the amount beyond the value in the threshold argument. Setting a value to −1 restores the default. The values of the do_accel and do_threshold arguments must be `True` for the pointer values to be set, or the parameters are unchanged. Negative values (other than −1) generate a `BadValue` error, as does a zero value for the accel_denominator argument.

`XChangePointerControl` can generate a `BadValue` error.

To get the current pointer parameters, use `XGetPointerControl`.

```
XGetPointerControl(display, accel_numerator_return, accel_denominator_return,
                   threshold_return)
    Display *display;
    int *accel_numerator_return, *accel_denominator_return;
    int *threshold_return;
```

display	Specifies the connection to the X server.
accel_numerator_return	Returns the numerator for the acceleration multiplier.
accel_denominator_return	Returns the denominator for the acceleration multiplier.
threshold_return	Returns the acceleration threshold.

The `XGetPointerControl` function returns the pointer's current acceleration multiplier and acceleration threshold.

12.7 Keyboard Encoding

A KeyCode represents a physical (or logical) key. KeyCodes lie in the inclusive range [8,255]. A KeyCode value carries no intrinsic information, although server implementors may attempt to encode geometry (for example, matrix) information in some fashion so that it can be interpreted in a server-dependent fashion. The mapping between keys and KeyCodes cannot be changed.

A KeySym is an encoding of a symbol on the cap of a key. The set of defined KeySyms includes the ISO Latin character sets (1–4), Katakana, Arabic, Cyrillic, Greek, Technical, Special, Publishing, APL, Hebrew, and a special miscellany of keys found on keyboards (Return, Help, Tab, and so on). To the extent possible, these sets are derived from international standards. In areas where no standards exist, some of these sets are derived from Digital Equipment Corporation standards. The list of defined symbols can be found in `<X11/keysymdef.h>`. Unfortunately, some C preprocessors have limits on the number of defined symbols. If you must use KeySyms not in the Latin 1–4, Greek, and miscellaneous classes, you may have to define a symbol for those sets. Most applications usually only include `<X11/keysym.h>`, which defines symbols for ISO Latin 1–4, Greek, and miscellaneous.

A list of KeySyms is associated with each KeyCode. The list is intended to convey the set of symbols on the corresponding key. If the list (ignoring trailing `NoSymbol` entries) is a single KeySym "*K*", then the list is treated as if it were the list "*K* NoSymbol *K* NoSymbol". If the list (ignoring trailing `NoSymbol` entries) is a pair of KeySyms "*K1 K2*", then the list is treated as if it were the list "*K1 K2 K1 K2*". If the list (ignoring trailing `NoSymbol` entries) is a triple of KeySyms "*K1 K2 K3*", then the list is treated as if it were the list "*K1 K2 K3* NoSymbol". When an explicit "void" element is desired in the list, the value `VoidSymbol` can be used.

The first four elements of the list are split into two groups of KeySyms. Group 1 contains the first and second KeySyms; Group 2 contains the third and fourth KeySyms. Within each group, if the second element of the group is `NoSymbol`, then the group should be treated as if the second element were the same as the first element, except when the first element is an alphabetic

KeySym "*K*" for which both lowercase and uppercase forms are defined. In that case, the group should be treated as if the first element were the lowercase form of "*K*" and the second element were the uppercase form of "*K*".

The standard rules for obtaining a KeySym from a `KeyPress` event make use of only the Group 1 and Group 2 KeySyms; no interpretation of other KeySyms in the list is given. Which group to use is determined by the modifier state. Switching between groups is controlled by the KeySym named MODE SWITCH, by attaching that KeySym to some KeyCode and attaching that KeyCode to any one of the modifiers `Mod1` through `Mod5`. This modifier is called the *group modifier*. For any KeyCode, Group 1 is used when the group modifier is off, and Group 2 is used when the group modifier is on.

Within a group, the modifier state also determines which KeySym to use. The first KeySym is used when the `Shift` and `Lock` modifiers are off. The second KeySym is used when the `Shift` modifier is on, when the `Lock` modifier is on and the second KeySym is uppercase alphabetic, or when the `Lock` modifier is on and is interpreted as ShiftLock. Otherwise, when the `Lock` modifier is on and is interpreted as CapsLock, the state of the `Shift` modifier is applied first to select a KeySym; but if that KeySym is lowercase alphabetic, then the corresponding uppercase KeySym is used instead.

No spatial geometry of the symbols on the key is defined by their order in the KeySym list, although a geometry might be defined on a vendor-specific basis. The X server does not use the mapping between KeyCodes and KeySyms. Rather, it stores it merely for reading and writing by clients.

The KeyMask modifier named `Lock` is intended to be mapped to either a CapsLock or a ShiftLock key, but which one is left as application-specific and/or user-specific. However, it is suggested that the determination be made according to the associated KeySym(s) of the corresponding KeyCode.

To obtain the legal KeyCodes for a display, use `XDisplayKeycodes`.

XDisplayKeycodes (*display*, *min_keycodes_return*, *max_keycodes_return*)
    Display * *display*;
    int * *min_keycodes_return*, * *max_keycodes_return*;

display	Specifies the connection to the X server.
min_keycodes_return	Returns the minimum number of KeyCodes.
max_keycodes_return	Returns the maximum number of KeyCodes.

The XDisplayKeycodes function returns the min-keycodes and max-keycodes supported by the specified display. The minimum number of KeyCodes returned is never less than 8, and the maximum number of KeyCodes returned is never greater than 255. Not all KeyCodes in this range are required to have corresponding keys.

To obtain the symbols for the specified KeyCodes, use XGetKeyboardMapping.

```
KeySym *XGetKeyboardMapping(display, first_keycode, keycode_count,
                            keysyms_per_keycode_return)
   Display *display;
   KeyCode first_keycode;
   int keycode_count;
   int *keysyms_per_keycode_return;
```

display	Specifies the connection to the X server.
first_keycode	Specifies the first KeyCode that is to be returned.
keycode_count	Specifies the number of KeyCodes that are to be returned.
keysyms_per_keycode_return	Returns the number of KeySyms per KeyCode.

The XGetKeyboardMapping function returns the symbols for the specified number of KeyCodes starting with first_keycode. The value specified in first_keycode must be greater than or equal to min_keycode as returned by XDisplayKeycodes, or a BadValue error results. In addition, the following expression must be less than or equal to max_keycode as returned by XDisplayKeycodes:

first_keycode + keycode_count – 1

If this is not the case, a BadValue error results. The number of elements in the KeySyms list is:

keycode_count * keysyms_per_keycode_return

KeySym number N, counting from zero, for KeyCode K has the following index in the list, counting from zero:

(K – first_code) * keysyms_per_code_return + N

The X server arbitrarily chooses the keysyms_per_keycode_return value to be large enough to report all requested symbols. A special KeySym value of `NoSymbol` is used to fill in unused elements for individual KeyCodes. To free the storage returned by `XGetKeyboardMapping`, use `XFree`.

`XGetKeyboardMapping` can generate a `BadValue` error.

To change the keyboard mapping, use `XChangeKeyboardMapping`.

XChangeKeyboardMapping(*display, first_keycode, keysyms_per_keycode, keysyms, num_codes*)
  Display **display*;
  int *first_keycode*;
  int *keysyms_per_keycode*;
  KeySym **keysyms*;
  int *num_codes*;

display	Specifies the connection to the X server.
first_keycode	Specifies the first KeyCode that is to be changed.
keysyms_per_keycode	Specifies the number of KeySyms per KeyCode.
keysyms	Specifies an array of KeySyms.
num_codes	Specifies the number of KeyCodes that are to be changed.

The `XChangeKeyboardMapping` function defines the symbols for the specified number of KeyCodes starting with first_keycode. The symbols for KeyCodes outside this range remain unchanged. The number of elements in keysyms must be:

num_codes * keysyms_per_keycode

The specified first_keycode must be greater than or equal to min_keycode returned by `XDisplayKeycodes`, or a `BadValue` error results. In addition, the following expression must be less than or equal to max_keycode as returned by `XDisplayKeycodes`, or a `BadValue` error results:

first_keycode + num_codes – 1

KeySym number N, counting from zero, for KeyCode K has the following index in keysyms, counting from zero:

(K – first_keycode) * keysyms_per_keycode + N

The specified keysyms_per_keycode can be chosen arbitrarily by the client to be large enough to hold all desired symbols. A special KeySym value of `NoSymbol` should be used to fill in unused elements for individual KeyCodes. It is legal for NoSymbol to appear in nontrailing positions of the effective list for a KeyCode. XChangeKeyboardMapping generates a MappingNotify event.

There is no requirement that the X server interpret this mapping. It is merely stored for reading and writing by clients.

XChangeKeyboardMapping can generate BadAlloc and BadValue errors.

The next five functions make use of the XModifierKeymap data structure, which contains:

```
typedef struct {
    int max_keypermod;          /* This server's max number of keys per modifier */
    KeyCode *modifiermap;       /* An 8 by max_keypermod array of the modifiers */
} XModifierKeymap;
```

To create an XModifierKeymap structure, use XNewModifiermap.

XModifierKeymap *XNewModifiermap(*max_keys_per_mod*)
    int *max_keys_per_mod*;

max_keys_per_mod Specifies the number of KeyCode entries preallocated to the modifiers in the map.

The XNewModifiermap function returns a pointer to XModifierKeymap structure for later use.

To add a new entry to an XModifierKeymap structure, use XInsert-ModifiermapEntry.

XModifierKeymap *XInsertModifiermapEntry (*modmap*, *keycode_entry*, *modifier*)
    XModifierKeymap **modmap*;
    KeyCode *keycode_entry*;
    int *modifier*;

modmap Specifies the XModifierKeymap structure.

keycode_entry Specifies the KeyCode.

modifier Specifies the modifier.

The XInsertModifiermapEntry function adds the specified KeyCode to the set that controls the specified modifier and returns the resulting XModifierKeymap structure (expanded as needed).

To delete an entry from an XModifierKeymap structure, use XDelete-ModifiermapEntry.

```
XModifierKeymap *XDeleteModifiermapEntry(modmap, keycode_entry, modifier)
    XModifierKeymap *modmap;
    KeyCode keycode_entry;
    int modifier;
```

modmap Specifies the XModifierKeymap structure.

keycode_entry Specifies the KeyCode.

modifier Specifies the modifier.

The XDeleteModifiermapEntry function deletes the specified KeyCode from the set that controls the specified modifier and returns a pointer to the resulting XModifierKeymap structure.

To destroy an XModifierKeymap structure, use XFreeModifiermap.

```
XFreeModifiermap(modmap)
    XModifierKeymap *modmap;
```

modmap Specifies the XModifierKeymap structure.

The XFreeModifiermap function frees the specified XModifierKeymap structure.

To set the KeyCodes to be used as modifiers, use XSetModifierMapping.

```
int XSetModifierMapping(display, modmap)
    Display *display;
    XModifierKeymap *modmap;
```

display Specifies the connection to the X server.

modmap Specifies the XModifierKeymap structure.

The XSetModifierMapping function specifies the KeyCodes of the keys (if any) that are to be used as modifiers. If it succeeds, the X server generates a MappingNotify event, and XSetModifierMapping returns MappingSuccess. X permits at most eight modifier keys. If more than eight are specified in the XModifierKeymap structure, a BadLength error results.

The modifiermap member of the XModifierKeymap structure contains eight sets of max_keypermod KeyCodes, one for each modifier in the order Shift, Lock, Control, Mod1, Mod2, Mod3, Mod4, and Mod5. Only nonzero KeyCodes have meaning in each set, and zero KeyCodes are ignored. In addition, all of the nonzero KeyCodes must be in the range specified by min_keycode and max_keycode in the `Display` structure, or a `BadValue` error results.

An X server can impose restrictions on how modifiers can be changed, for example, if certain keys do not generate up transitions in hardware, if auto-repeat cannot be disabled on certain keys, or if multiple modifier keys are not supported. If some such restriction is violated, the status reply is `MappingFailed`, and none of the modifiers are changed. If the new KeyCodes specified for a modifier differ from those currently defined and any (current or new) keys for that modifier are in the logically down state, `XSetModifierMapping` returns `MappingBusy`, and none of the modifiers is changed.

`XSetModifierMapping` can generate `BadAlloc` and `BadValue` errors.

To obtain the KeyCodes used as modifiers, use `XGetModifierMapping`.

```
XModifierKeymap *XGetModifierMapping(display)
    Display *display;
```

display Specifies the connection to the X server.

The `XGetModifierMapping` function returns a pointer to a newly created `XModifierKeymap` structure that contains the keys being used as modifiers. The structure should be freed after use by calling `XFreeModifiermap`. If only zero values appear in the set for any modifier, that modifier is disabled.

Chapter 13

Locales and Internationalized Text Functions

An internationalized application is one that is adaptable to the requirements of different native languages, local customs, and character string encodings. The process of adapting the operation to a particular native language, local custom, or string encoding is called localizaton. A goal of internationalization is to permit localization without program source modifications or recompilation.

Internationalization in X is based on the concept of a *locale*. A locale defines the localized behavior of a program at run time. Locales affect Xlib in its:

- Encoding and processing of input method text
- Encoding of resource files and values
- Encoding and imaging of text strings
- Encoding and decoding for inter-client text communication

Characters from various languages are represented in a computer using an encoding. Different languages have different encodings, and there are even different encodings for the same characters in the same language.

This chapter defines support for localized text imaging and text input and describes the locale mechanism that controls all locale-dependent Xlib functions. Sets of functions are provided for multibyte (char *) text as well as wide character (wchar_t) text in the form supported by the host C language environment. The multibyte and wide character functions are equivalent except for the form of the text argument.

The Xlib internationalization functions are not meant to provide support for multilingual applications (mixing multiple languages within a single piece of text), but they make it possible to implement applications that work in limited fashion with more than one language in independent contexts.

13.1 X Locale Management

X supports one or more of the locales defined by the host environment. On implementations that conform to the ANSI C library, the locale announcement method is `setlocale`. This function configures the locale operation of both the host C library and Xlib. The operation of Xlib is governed by the LC_CTYPE category; this is called the *current locale.* An implementation is permitted to provide implementation dependent mechanisms for announcing the locale in addition to `setlocale`.

On implementations that do not conform to the ANSI C library, the locale announcement method is Xlib implementation dependent.

The mechanism by which the semantic operation of Xlib is defined for a specific locale is implementation dependent.

X is not required to support all the locales supported by the host. To determine if the current locale is supported by X, use `XSupportsLocale`.

```
Bool XSupportsLocale ( )
```

The `XSupportsLocale` function returns `True` if Xlib functions are capable of operating under the current locale. If it returns `False`, Xlib locale-dependent functions for which the `XLocaleNotSupported` return status is defined will return `XLocaleNotSupported`. Other Xlib locale-dependent routines will operate in the "C" locale.

The client is responsible for selecting its locale and X modifiers. Clients should provide a means for the user to override the clients' locale selection at client invocation. Most single-display X clients operate in a single locale for both X and the host processing environment. They will configure the locale by calling three functions: the host locale configuration function, `XSupportsLocale`, and `XSetLocaleModifiers`.

The semantics of certain categories of X internationalization capabilities can be configured by setting modifiers. Modifiers are named by implementation dependent and locale-specific strings. The only standard use for this capability at present is selecting one of several styles of keyboard input method.

To configure Xlib locale modifiers for the current locale, use `XSetLocaleModifiers`.

```
char *XSetLocaleModifiers(modifier_list)
   char *modifier_list;
```

modifier_list Specifies the modifiers.

The `XSetLocaleModifiers` function sets the X modifiers for the current locale setting. The modifier_list argument is a null-terminated string of the form "{@*category*=*value*}", that is, having zero or more concatenated "@*category*=*value*" entries where *category* is a category name and *value* is the (possibly empty) setting for that category. The values are encoded in the current locale. Category names are restricted to the POSIX Portable Filename Character Set.

The local host X locale modifiers announcer (on POSIX-compliant systems, the XMODIFIERS environment variable) is appended to the modifier_list to provide default values on the local host. If a given category appears more than once in the list, the first setting in the list is used. If a given category is not included in the full modifier list, the category is set to an implementation dependent default for the current locale. An empty value for a category explicitly specifies the implementation dependent default.

If the function is successful, it returns a pointer to a string. The contents of the string are such that a subsequent call with that string (in the same locale) will restore the modifiers to the same settings. If modifier_list is a NULL pointer, `XSetLocaleModifiers` also returns a pointer to such a string, and the current locale modifiers are not changed.

If invalid values are given for one or more modifier categories supported by the locale, a NULL pointer is returned, and none of the current modifiers are changed.

At program startup, the modifiers that are in effect are unspecified until the first successful call to set them. Whenever the locale is changed, the modifiers that are in effect become unspecified until the next successful call to set them.

Clients should always call `XSetLocaleModifiers` with a non-NULL modifier_list after setting the locale before they call any locale-dependent Xlib routine.

The only standard modifier category currently defined is "im", which identifies the desired input method. The values for input method are not standardized. A single locale may use multiple input methods, switching input method under user control. The modifier may specify the initial input method in effect or an ordered list of input methods. Multiple input methods may be specified in a single im value string in an implementation dependent manner.

The returned modifiers string is owned by Xlib and should not be modified or freed by the client. It may be freed by Xlib after the current locale or modifiers are changed. Until freed, it will not be modified by Xlib.

The recommended procedure for clients initializing their locale and modifiers is to obtain locale and modifier announcers separately from one of the following prioritized sources:

- A command line option
- A resource
- The empty string ("")

The first of these that is defined should be used. Note that when a locale command line option or locale resource is defined, the effect should be to set all categories to the specified locale, overriding any category-specific settings in the local host environment.

13.2 Locale and Modifier Dependencies

The internationalized Xlib functions operate in the current locale configured by the host environment and X locale modifiers set by `XSetLocaleModifiers`, or in the locale and modifiers configured at the time some object supplied to the function was created. For each locale-dependent function, the following table describes the locale (and modifiers) dependency:

Locale from	*Affects the Function*	*In*
	Locale Query/Configuration:	
`setlocale`	`XSupportsLocale`	Locale queried
	`XSetLocaleModifiers`	Locale modified

Locale from	*Affects the Function*	*In*
	Resources:	
setlocale	XrmGetFileDatabase	Locale of XrmDatabase
	XrmGetStringDatabase	
XrmDatabase	XrmPutFileDatabase	Locale of XrmDatabase
	XrmLocaleOfDatabase	
	Setting Standard Properties:	
setlocale	XmbSetWMProperties	Encoding of supplied/returned text (some WM_ property text in environment locale)
setlocale	XmbTextPropertyToTextList	Encoding of supplied/returned text
	XwcTextPropertyToTextList	
	XmbTextListToTextProperty	
	XwcTextListToTextProperty	
	Text Input:	
setlocale	XOpenIM	XIM input method selection
XIM	XCreateIC	XIC input method configuration
	XLocaleOfIM, and so on	Queried locale
XIC	XmbLookupText	Keyboard layout
	XwcLookupText	Encoding of returned text
	Text Drawing:	
setlocale	XCreateFontSet	Charsets of fonts in XFontSet
XFontSet	XmbDrawText,	Locale of supplied text
	XwcDrawText, and so on	Locale of supplied text
	XExtentsOfFontSet, and so on	Locale-dependent metrics
	XmbTextExtents,	
	XwcTextExtents, and so on	
	Xlib Errors:	
setlocale	XGetErrorDatabaseText	Locale of error message
	XGetErrorText	

Clients may assume that a locale-encoded text string returned by an X function can be passed to a C library routine, or vice-versa, if the locale is the same at the two calls.

All text strings processed by internationalized Xlib functions are assumed to begin in the initial state of the encoding of the locale, if the encoding is state-dependent.

All Xlib functions behave as if they do not change the current locale or X modifier setting. (This means that if they do change locale or call `XSetLocaleModifiers` with a non-NULL argument, they must save and restore the current state on entry and exit.) Also, Xlib functions on implementations that conform to the ANSI C library do not alter the global state associated with the ANSI C functions `mblen`, `mbtowc`, `wctomb`, and `strtok`.

13.3 Creating and Freeing a Font Set

Xlib international text drawing is done using a set of one or more fonts, as needed for the locale of the text. Fonts are loaded according to a list of base font names supplied by the client and the charsets required by the locale. The `XFontSet` is an opaque type.

To create an international text drawing font set, use `XCreateFontSet`.

XFontSet XCreateFontSet (*display*, *base_font_name_list*, *missing_charset_list_return*, *missing_charset_count_return*, *def_string_return*)
  Display **display*;
  char **base_font_name_list*;
  char ****missing_charset_list_return*;
  int **missing_charset_count_return*;
  char ***def_string_return*;

display	Specifies the connection to the X server.
base_font_name_list	Specifies the base font names.
missing_charset_list_return	Returns the missing charsets.
missing_charset_count_return	Returns the number of missing charsets.
def_string_return	Returns the string drawn for missing charsets.

The `XCreateFontSet` function creates a font set for the specified display. The font set is bound to the current locale when `XCreateFontSet` is called. The font set may be used in subsequent calls to obtain font and character information and to image text in the locale of the font set.

The base_font_name_list argument is a list of base font names that Xlib uses to load the fonts needed for the locale. The base font names are a comma-separated list. The string is null-terminated and is assumed to be in the Host Portable Character Encoding; otherwise, the result is implementation dependent. White space immediately on either side of a separating comma is ignored.

Use of XLFD font names permits Xlib to obtain the fonts needed for a variety of locales from a single locale-independent base font name. The single base font name should name a family of fonts whose members are encoded in the various charsets needed by the locales of interest.

An XLFD base font name can explicitly name a charset needed for the locale. This allows the user to specify an exact font for use with a charset required by a locale, fully controlling the font selection.

If a base font name is not an XLFD name, Xlib will attempt to obtain an XLFD name from the font properties for the font. If this action is successful in obtaining an XLFD name, the `XBaseFontNameListOfFontSet` function will return this XLFD name instead of the client-supplied name.

Xlib uses the following algorithm to select the fonts that will be used to display text with the `XFontSet`. For each font charset required by the locale, the base font name list is searched for the first appearance of one of the following cases that names a set of fonts that exist at the server:

1. The first XLFD-conforming base font name that specifies the required charset or a superset of the required charset in its `CharSetRegistry` and `CharSetEncoding` fields. The implementation may use a base font name whose specified charset is a superset of the required charset, for example, an ISO8859-1 font for an ASCII charset.
2. The first set of one or more XLFD-conforming base font names that specify one or more charsets that can be remapped to support the required charset. The Xlib implementation may recognize various mappings from a required charset to one or more other charsets and use the fonts for those charsets. For example, JIS Roman is ASCII with tilde and backslash replaced by yen and overbar; Xlib may load an ISO8859-1 font to support this character set if a JIS Roman font is not available.
3. The first XLFD-conforming font name or the first non-XLFD font name for which an XLFD font name can be obtained, combined with the required charset (replacing the `CharSetRegistry` and `CharSetEncoding` fields in the XLFD font name). As in case 1, the implementation may use a charset that is a superset of the required charset.
4. The first font name that can be mapped in some implementation dependent manner to one or more fonts that support imaging text in the charset.

For example, assume a locale required the charsets:

ISO8859-1
JISX0208.1983
JISX0201.1976
GB2312-1980.0

The user could supply a base_font_name_list that explicitly specifies the charsets, insuring that specific fonts get used if they exist. For example:

"-JIS-Fixed-Medium-R-Normal–26-180-100-100-C-240-JISX0208.1983-0,\
-JIS-Fixed-Medium-R-Normal–26-180-100-100-C-120-JISX0201.1976-0,\
-GB-Fixed-Medium-R-Normal–26-180-100-100-C-240-GB2312-1980.0,\
-Adobe-Courier-Bold-R-Normal–25-180-75-75-M-150-ISO8859-1"

Alternatively, the user could supply a base_font_name_list that omits the charsets, letting Xlib select font charsets required for the locale. For example:

"-JIS-Fixed-Medium-R-Normal–26-180-100-100-C-240,\
-JIS-Fixed-Medium-R-Normal–26-180-100-100-C-120,\
-GB-Fixed-Medium-R-Normal–26-180-100-100-C-240,\
-Adobe-Courier-Bold-R-Normal–25-180-100-100-M-150"

Alternatively, the user could simply supply a single base font name that allows Xlib to select from all available fonts that meet certain minimum XLFD property requirements. For example:

"-*-*-*-R-Normal–*-180-100-100-*-*"

If `XCreateFontSet` is unable to create the font set, either because there is insufficient memory or because the current locale is not supported, `XCreateFontSet` returns NULL, missing_charset_list_return is set to NULL, and missing_charset_count_return is set to zero. If fonts exist for all of the charsets required by the current locale, `XCreateFontSet` returns a valid `XFontSet`, missing_charset_list_return is set to NULL, and missing_charset_count_return is set to zero.

If no font exists for one or more of the required charsets, `XCreateFontSet` sets missing_charset_list_return to a list of one or more null-terminated charset names for which no font exists and sets missing_charset_count_return to the number of missing fonts. The charsets are from the list of the required charsets for the encoding of the locale and do not include any charsets to which Xlib may be able to remap a required charset.

If no font exists for any of the required charsets or if the locale definition in Xlib requires that a font exist for a particular charset and a font is not found for that charset, `XCreateFontSet` returns NULL. Otherwise, `XCreateFontSet` returns a valid `XFontSet` to font_set.

When an Xmb/wc drawing or measuring function is called with an `XFontSet` that has missing charsets, some characters in the locale will not be drawable. If def_string_return is non-NULL, `XCreateFontSet` returns a pointer to a string that represents the glyphs that are drawn with this `XFontSet` when the charsets of the available fonts do not include all font glyphs required to draw a codepoint. The string does not necessarily consist of valid characters in the current locale and is not necessarily drawn with the fonts loaded for the font set, but the client can draw and measure the default glyphs by including this string in a string being drawn or measured with the `XFontSet`.

If the string returned to def_string_return is the empty string (""), no glyphs are drawn, and the escapement is zero. The returned string is null-terminated. It is owned by Xlib and should not be modified or freed by the client. It will be freed by a call to `XFreeFontSet` with the associated `XFontSet`. Until freed, its contents will not be modified by Xlib.

The client is responsible for constructing an error message from the missing charset and default string information and may choose to continue operation in the case that some fonts did not exist.

The returned `XFontSet` and missing charset list should be freed with `XFreeFontSet` and `XFreeStringList`, respectively. The client-supplied base_font_name_list may be freed by the client after calling `XCreateFontSet`.

To obtain a list of `XFontStruct` structures and full font names given an `XFontSet`, use `XFontsOfFontSet`.

int XFontsOfFontSet (*font_set*, *font_struct_list_return*, *font_name_list_return*)
    XFontSet *font_set*;
    XFontStruct ****font_struct_list_return*;
    char ****font_name_list_return*;

font_set	Specifies the font set.
font_struct_list_return	Returns the list of font structs.
font_name_list_return	Returns the list of font names.

The `XFontsOfFontSet` function returns a list of one or more `XFontStructs` and font names for the fonts used by the Xmb and Xwc layers, for the given font set. A list of pointers to the `XFontStruct` structures is returned to font_struct_list_return. A list of pointers to null-terminated, fully specified font name strings in the locale of the font set is returned to font_name_list_return. The font_name_list order corresponds to the font_struct_list order. The number of XFontStruct structures and font names is returned as the value of the function.

Because it is not guaranteed that a given character will be imaged using a single font glyph, there is no provision for mapping a character or default string to the font properties, font ID, or direction hint for the font for the character. The client may access the XFontStruct list to obtain these values for all the fonts currently in use.

Xlib does not require that fonts be loaded from the server at the creation of an XFontSet. Xlib may choose to cache font data, loading it only as needed to draw text or compute text dimensions. Therefore, existence of the per_char metrics in the XFontStruct structures in the XFontStructSet is undefined. Also, note that all properties in the XFontStruct structures are in the STRING encoding.

The XFontStruct and font name lists are owned by Xlib and should not be modified or freed by the client. They will be freed by a call to XFreeFontSet with the associated XFontSet. Until freed, their contents will not be modified by Xlib.

To obtain the base font name list and the selected font name list given an XFontSet, use XBaseFontNameListOfFontSet.

```
char *XBaseFontNameListOfFontSet (font_set)
    XFontSet font_set;
```

font_set Specifies the font set.

The XBaseFontNameListOfFontSet function returns the original base font name list supplied by the client when the XFontSet was created. A null-terminated string containing a list of comma-separated font names is returned as the value of the function. White space may appear immediately on either side of separating commas.

If XCreateFontSet obtained an XLFD name from the font properties for the font specified by a non-XLFD base name, the XBaseFontNameListOfFontSet function will return the XLFD name instead of the non-XLFD base name.

The base font name list is owned by Xlib and should not be modified or freed by the client. It will be freed by a call to `XFreeFontSet` with the associated `XFontSet`. Until freed, its contents will not be modified by Xlib.

To obtain the locale name given an `XFontSet`, use `XLocaleOfFontSet`.

```
char *XLocaleOfFontSet (font_set)
    XFontSet font_set;
```

font_set Specifies the font set.

The `XLocaleOfFontSet` function returns the name of the locale bound to the specified `XFontSet`, as a null-terminated string.

The returned locale name string is owned by Xlib and should not be modified or freed by the client. It may be freed by a call to `XFreeFontSet` with the associated `XFontSet`. Until freed, it will not be modified by Xlib.

To free a font set, use `XFreeFontSet`.

```
void XFreeFontSet ( display, font_set)
    Display *display;
    XFontSet font_set;
```

display Specifies the connection to the X server.

font_set Specifies the font set.

The `XFreeFontSet` function frees the specified font set. The associated base font name list, font name list, `XFontStruct` list, and `XFontSetExtents`, if any, are freed.

13.4 Obtaining Font Set Metrics

Metrics for the internationalized text drawing functions are defined in terms of a primary draw direction, which is the default direction in which the character origin advances for each succeeding character in the string. The Xlib interface is currently defined to support only a left-to-right primary draw direction. The drawing origin is the position passed to the drawing function when the text is drawn. The baseline is a line drawn through the drawing origin parallel to the primary draw direction. Character ink is the pixels painted in the foreground color and does not include interline or intercharacter spacing or image text background pixels.

The drawing functions are allowed to implement implicit text directionality control, reversing the order in which characters are rendered along the primary draw direction in response to locale-specific lexical analysis of the string.

Regardless of the character rendering order, the origins of all characters are on the primary draw direction side of the drawing origin. The screen location of a particular character image may be determined with `XmbTextPerCharExtents` or `XwcTextPerCharExtents`.

The drawing functions are allowed to implement context-dependent rendering, where the glyphs drawn for a string are not simply a concatenation of the glyphs that represent each individual character. A string of two characters drawn with `XmbDrawString` may render differently than if the two characters were drawn with separate calls to `XmbDrawString`. If the client appends or inserts a character in a previously drawn string, the client may need to redraw some adjacent characters to obtain proper rendering.

To find out about context-dependent rendering, use `XContextDependentDrawing`.

```
Bool XContextDependentDrawing (font_set)
    XFontSet font_set;
```

font_set Specifies the font set.

The `XContextDependentDrawing` function returns `True` if text drawn with the font_set might include context-dependent drawing.

The drawing functions do not interpret newline, tab, or other control characters. The behavior when nonprinting characters other than space are drawn is implementation dependent. It is the client's responsibility to interpret control characters in a text stream.

The maximum character extents for the fonts that are used by the text drawing layers can be accessed by the `XFontSetExtents` structure:

```
typedef struct {
    XRectangle max_ink_extent;        /* over all drawable characters */
    XRectangle max_logical_extent;    /* over all drawable characters */
} XFontSetExtents;
```

The `XRectangles` function used to return font set metrics are the usual Xlib screen-oriented `XRectangles`, with x, y giving the upper-left corner and width and height always positive.

The max_ink_extent member gives the maximum extent, over all drawable characters, of the rectangles that bound the character glyph image drawn in the foreground color, relative to a constant origin. See `XmbTextExtents` and `XwcTextExtents` for detailed semantics.

The max_logical_extent member gives the maximum extent, over all drawable characters, of the rectangles that specify minimum spacing to other graphical features, relative to a constant origin. Other graphical features drawn by the client, for example, a border surrounding the text, should not intersect this rectangle. The max_logical_extent member should be used to compute minimum interline spacing and the minimum area that must be allowed in a text field to draw a given number of arbitrary characters.

Due to context-dependent rendering, appending a given character to a string may increase the string's extent by an amount that exceeds the font's max extent:

max possible added extent = (max_extent * <total # chars>) – prev_string_extent

The rectangles for a given character in a string can be obtained from `XmbPerCharExtents` or `XwcPerCharExtents`.

To obtain the maximum extents structure given an `XFontSet`, use `XExtentsOfFontSet`.

XFontSetExtents *XExtentsOfFontSet (*font_set*)
    XFontSet *font_set*;

font_set Specifies the font set.

The `XExtentsOfFontSet` function returns an `XFontSetExtents` structure for the fonts used by the Xmb and Xwc layers, for the given font set.

The `XFontSetExtents` structure is owned by Xlib and should not be modified or freed by the client. It will be freed by a call to `XFreeFontSet` with the associated `XFontSet`. Until freed, its contents will not be modified by Xlib.

To obtain the escapement in pixels of the specified text as a value, use `XmbTextEscapement` or `XwcTextEscapement`.

int XmbTextEscapement (*font_set*, *string*, *num_bytes*)
    XFontSet *font_set*;
    char **string*;
    int *num_bytes*;

```
int XwcTextEscapement (font_set, string, num_wchars)
    XFontSet font_set;
    wchar_t *string;
    int num_wchars;
```

font_set	Specifies the font set.
string	Specifies the character string.
num_bytes	Specifies the number of bytes in the string argument.
num_wchars	Specifies the number of characters in the string argument.

The `XmbTextEscapement` and `XwcTextEscapement` functions return the escapement in pixels of the specified string as a value, using the fonts loaded for the specified font set. The escapement is the distance in pixels in the primary draw direction from the drawing origin to the origin of the next character to be drawn, assuming that the rendering of the next character is not dependent on the supplied string.

Regardless of the character rendering order, the escapement is always positive.

To obtain the overall_ink_return and overall_logical_return arguments, the overall bounding box of the string's image, and a logical bounding box, use `XmbTextExtents` or `XwcTextExtents`.

```
int XmbTextExtents (font_set, string, num_bytes, overall_return)
    XFontSet font_set;
    char *string;
    int num_bytes;
    XRectangle *overall_ink_return;
    XRectangle *overall_logical_return;

int XwcTextExtents (font_set, string, num_wchars, overall_return)
    XFontSet font_set;
    wchar_t *string;
    int num_wchars;
    XRectangle *overall_ink_return;
    XRectangle *overall_logical_return;
```

font_set	Specifies the font set.
string	Specifies the character string.
num_bytes	Specifies the number of bytes in the string argument.
num_wchars	Specifies the number of characters in the string argument.
overall_ink_return	Returns the overall ink dimensions.
overall_logical_return	Returns the overall logical dimensions.

The `XmbTextExtents` and `XwcTextExtents` functions set the components of the specified overall_ink_return and overall_logical_return arguments to the overall bounding box of the string's image and a logical bounding box for spacing purposes, respectively. They return the value returned by `XmbTextEscapement` or `XwcTextEscapement`. These metrics are relative to the drawing origin of the string, using the fonts loaded for the specified font set.

If the overall_ink_return argument is non-NULL, it is set to the bounding box of the string's character ink. The overall_ink_return for a nondescending, horizontally drawn Latin character is conventionally entirely above the baseline; that is, overall_ink_return.height ≤ –overall_ink_return.y. The overall_ink_return for a nonkerned character is entirely at, and to the right of, the origin; that is, overall_ink_return.x ≥ 0. A character consisting of a single pixel at the origin would set overall_ink_return fields y = 0, x = 0, width = 1, and height = 1.

If the overall_logical_return argument is non-NULL, it is set to the bounding box that provides minimum spacing to other graphical features for the string. Other graphical features, for example, a border surrounding the text, should not intersect this rectangle.

When the `XFontSet` has missing charsets, metrics for each unavailable character are taken from the default string returned by `XCreateFontSet` so that the metrics represent the text as it will actually be drawn. The behavior for an invalid codepoint is undefined.

To determine the effective drawing origin for a character in a drawn string, the client should call `XmbTextPerCharExtents` on the entire string, then on the character, and subtract the x values of the returned `XRectangles` for the character. This is useful to redraw portions of a line of text or to justify words, but for context-dependent rendering, the client should not assume that it can redraw the character by itself and get the same rendering.

To obtain per-character information for a text string, use `XmbTextPerCharExtents` or `XwcTextPerCharExtents`.

Status XmbTextPerCharExtents (*font_set, string, num_bytes, ink_array_return,*
logical_array_return, array_size, num_chars_return,
overall_return)

XFontSet *font_set*;
char **string*;

```
    int num_bytes;
    XRectangle *ink_array_return;
    XRectangle *logical_array_return;
    int array_size;
    int *num_chars_return;
    XRectangle *overall_ink_return;
    XRectangle *overall_logical_return;

Status XwcTextPerCharExtents (font_set, string, num_wchars, ink_array_return,
                              logical_array_return, array_size, num_chars_return,
                              overall_return)
    XFontSet font_set;
    wchar_t *string;
    int num_wchars;
    XRectangle *ink_array_return;
    XRectangle *logical_array_return;
    int array_size;
    int *num_chars_return;
    XRectangle *overall_ink_return;
    XRectangle *overall_logical_return;
```

font_set	Specifies the font set.
string	Specifies the character string.
num_bytes	Specifies the number of bytes in the string argument.
num_wchars	Specifies the number of characters in the string argument.
ink_array_return	Returns the ink dimensions for each character.
logical_array_return	Returns the logical dimensions for each character.
array_size	Specifies the size of ink_array_return and logical_array_return. The caller must pass in arrays of this size.
num_chars_return	Returns the number of characters in the string argument.
overall_ink_return	Returns the overall ink extents of the entire string.
overall_logical_return	Returns the overall logical extents of the entire string.

The `XmbTextPerCharExtents` and `XwcTextPerCharExtents` functions return the text dimensions of each character of the specified text, using the fonts loaded for the specified font set. Each successive element of ink_array_return and logical_array_return is set to the successive character's drawn metrics, relative to the drawing origin of the string and one `XRectangle` for each character in the supplied text string. The number of elements of ink_array_return and logical_array_return that have been set is returned to num_chars_return.

Each element of ink_array_return is set to the bounding box of the corresponding character's drawn foreground color. Each element of logical_array_return is set to the bounding box that provides minimum spacing to other graphical features for the corresponding character. Other graphical features should not intersect any of the logical_array_return rectangles.

Note that an `XRectangle` represents the effective drawing dimensions of the character, regardless of the number of font glyphs that are used to draw the character or the direction in which the character is drawn. If multiple characters map to a single character glyph, the dimensions of all the `XRectangles` of those characters are the same.

When the `XFontSet` has missing charsets, metrics for each unavailable character are taken from the default string returned by `XCreateFontSet` so that the metrics represent the text as it will actually be drawn. The behavior for an invalid codepoint is undefined.

If the array_size is too small for the number of characters in the supplied text, the functions return zero and num_chars_return is set to the number of rectangles required. Otherwise, the functions return a nonzero value.

If the overall_ink_return or overall_logical_return argument is non-NULL, `XmbTextPerCharExtents` and `XwcTextPerCharExtents` return the maximum extent of the string's metrics to overall_ink_return or overall_logical_return, as returned by `XmbTextExtents` or `XwcTextExtents`.

13.5 Drawing Text Using Font Sets

The functions defined in this section draw text at a specified location in a drawable. They are similar to the functions `XDrawText`, `XDrawString`, and `XDrawImageString` except that they work with font sets instead of single fonts and interpret the text based on the locale of the font set instead of treating the bytes of the string as direct font indexes. See section 8.6 for details of the use of GCs and possible protocol errors. If a `BadFont` error is generated, characters prior to the offending character may have been drawn.

The text is drawn using the fonts loaded for the specified font set; the font in the GC is ignored and may be modified by the functions. No validation that all fonts conform to some width rule is performed.

The text functions `XmbDrawText` and `XwcDrawText` use the following structures:

```
typedef struct {
      char *chars;              /* pointer to string */
      int nchars;               /* number of bytes */
      int delta;                /* pixel delta between strings */
      XFontSet font_set;        /* fonts, None means don't change */
} XmbTextItem;

typedef struct {
      wchar_t *chars;           /* pointer to wide char string */
      int nchars;               /* number of wide characters */
      int delta;                /* pixel delta between strings */
      XFontSet font_set;        /* fonts, None means don't change */
} XwcTextItem;
```

To draw text using multiple font sets in a given drawable, use `XmbDrawText` or `XwcDrawText`.

```
void XmbDrawText(display, d, gc, x, y, items, nitems)
   Display *display;
   Drawable d;
   GC gc;
   int x, y;
   XmbTextItem *items;
   int nitems;

void XwcDrawText(display, d, gc, x, y, items, nitems)
   Display *display;
   Drawable d;
   GC gc;
   int x, y;
   XwcTextItem *items;
   int nitems;
```

display Specifies the connection to the X server.
d Specifies the drawable.
gc Specifies the GC.
x
y Specify the x and y coordinates.
items Specifies an array of text items.
nitems Specifies the number of text items in the array.

The `XmbDrawText` and `XwcDrawText` functions allow complex spacing and font set shifts between text strings. Each text item is processed in turn, with the origin of a text element advanced in the primary draw direction by the escapement of the previous text item. A text item delta specifies an additional escapement of the text item drawing origin in the primary draw direction. A font_set member other than `None` in an item causes the font set to be used for this and subsequent text items in the text_items list. Leading text items with a font_set member set to `None` will not be drawn.

`XmbDrawText` and `XwcDrawText` do not perform any context-dependent rendering between text segments. Clients may compute the drawing metrics by passing each text segment to `XmbTextExtents` and `XwcTextExtents` or `XmbTextPerCharExtents` and `XwcTextPerCharExtents`. When the `XFontSet` has missing charsets, each unavailable character is drawn with the default string returned by `XCreateFontSet`. The behavior for an invalid codepoint is undefined.

To draw text using a single font set in a given drawable, use `XmbDrawString` or `XwcDrawString`.

```
void XmbDrawString ( display, d, font_set, gc, x, y, string, num_bytes)
    Display *display;
    Drawable d;
    XFontSet font_set;
    GC gc;
    int x, y;
    char *string;
    int num_bytes;

void XwcDrawString ( display, d, font_set, gc, x, y, string, num_wchars)
    Display *display;
    Drawable d;
    XFontSet font_set;
    GC gc;
    int x, y;
    wchar_t *string;
    int num_wchars;
```

display	Specifies the connection to the X server.
d	Specifies the drawable.
font_set	Specifies the font set.

gc	Specifies the GC.
x	
y	Specify the x and y coordinates.
string	Specifies the character string.
num_bytes	Specifies the number of bytes in the string argument.
num_wchars	Specifies the number of characters in the string argument.

The `XmbDrawString` and `XwcDrawString` functions draw the specified text with the foreground pixel. When the `XFontSet` has missing charsets, each unavailable character is drawn with the default string returned by `XCreateFontSet`. The behavior for an invalid codepoint is undefined.

To draw image text using a single font set in a given drawable, use `XmbDrawImageString` or `XwcDrawImageString`.

```
void XmbDrawImageString ( display, d, font_set, gc, x, y, string, num_bytes)
    Display *display;
    Drawable d;
    XFontSet font_set;
    GC gc;
    int x, y;
    char *string;
    int num_bytes;

void XwcDrawImageString ( display, d, font_set, gc, x, y, string, num_wchars)
    Display *display;
    Drawable d;
    XFontSet font_set;
    GC gc;
    int x, y;
    wchar_t *string;
    int num_wchars;
```

display	Specifies the connection to the X server.
d	Specifies the drawable.
font_set	Specifies the font set.
gc	Specifies the GC.
x	
y	Specify the x and y coordinates.
string	Specifies the character string.
num_bytes	Specifies the number of bytes in the string argument.
num_wchars	Specifies the number of characters in the string argument.

The `XmbDrawImageString` and `XwcDrawImageString` functions fill a destination rectangle with the background pixel defined in the GC and then paint the text with the foreground pixel. The filled rectangle is the rectangle returned to overall_logical_return by `XmbTextExtents` or `XwcTextExtents` for the same text and `XFontSet`.

When the `XFontSet` has missing charsets, each unavailable character is drawn with the default string returned by `XCreateFontSet`. The behavior for an invalid codepoint is undefined.

13.6 Input Method Overview

This section provides definitions for terms and concepts used for internationalized text input and a brief overview of the intended use of the mechanisms provided by Xlib.

A large number of languages in the world use alphabets consisting of a small set of symbols (letters) to form words. To enter text into a computer in an alphabetic language, a user usually has a keyboard on which there exists key symbols corresponding to the alphabet. Sometimes, a few characters of an alphabetic language are missing on the keyboard. Many computer users, who speak a Latin-alphabet-based language only have an English-based keyboard. They need to hit a combination of keystrokes to enter a character that does not exist directly on the keyboard. A number of algorithms have been developed for entering such characters. These are known as European input methods, the compose input method, or the dead-keys input method.

Japanese is an example of a language with a phonetic symbol set, where each symbol represents a specific sound. There are two phonetic symbol sets in Japanese: Katakana and Hiragana. In general, Katakana is used for words that are of foreign origin, and Hiragana is used for writing native Japanese words. Collectively, the two systems are called Kana. Each set consists of 48 characters.

Korean also has a phonetic symbol set, called Hangul. Each of the 24 basic phonetic symbols (14 consonants and 10 vowels) represents a specific sound. A syllable is composed of two or three parts: the initial consonants, the vowels, and the optional last consonants. With Hangul, syllables can be treated as the basic units on which text processing is done. For example, a delete operation may work on a phonetic symbol or a syllable. Korean code sets include several thousands of these syllables. A user types the phonetic symbols that make up the syllables of the words to be entered. The display may change as each phonetic symbol is entered. For example, when the second phonetic symbol of a syllable is entered, the first phonetic symbol may change its shape and size. Likewise, when the third phonetic symbol is entered, the first two phonetic symbols may change their shape and size.

Not all languages rely solely on alphabetic or phonetic systems. Some languages, including Japanese and Korean, employ an ideographic writing system. In an ideographic system, rather than taking a small set of symbols and combining them in different ways to create words, each word consists of one unique symbol (or, occasionally, several symbols). The number of symbols can be very large: approximately 50,000 have been identified in Hanzi, the Chinese ideographic system.

There are two major aspects of ideographic systems that impact their use with computers. First, the standard computer character sets in Japan, China, and Korea include roughly 8,000 characters, while sets in Taiwan have between 15,000 and 30,000 characters. This makes it necessary to use more than one byte to represent a character. Second, it obviously is impractical to have a keyboard that includes all of a given language's ideographic symbols. Therefore, a mechanism is required for entering characters so that a keyboard with a reasonable number of keys can be used. Those input methods are usually based on phonetics, but there also exist methods based on the graphical properties of characters.

In Japan, both Kana and the ideographic system Kanji are used. In Korea, Hangul and sometimes the ideographic system Hanja are used. Now consider entering ideographs in Japan, Korea, China, and Taiwan.

In Japan, either Kana or English characters are typed and then a region is selected (sometimes automatically) for conversion to Kanji. Several Kanji characters may have the same phonetic representation. If that is the case with the string entered, a menu of characters is presented and the user must choose the appropriate one. If no choice is necessary or a preference has been established, the input method does the substitution directly. When Latin characters are converted to Kana or Kanji, it is called a romaji conversion.

In Korea, it is usually acceptable to keep Korean text in Hangul form, but some people may choose to write Hanja-originated words in Hanja rather than in Hangul. To change Hangul to Hanja, the user selects a region for conversion and then follows the same basic method as that described for Japanese.

Probably because there are well-accepted phonetic writing systems for Japanese and Korean, computer input methods in these countries for entering ideographs are fairly standard. Keyboard keys have both English characters and phonetic symbols engraved on them, and the user can switch between the two sets.

The situation is different for Chinese. While there is a phonetic system called Pinyin promoted by authorities, there is no consensus for entering Chinese text. Some vendors use a phonetic decomposition (Pinyin or another), others use ideographic decomposition of Chinese words, with various implementations and keyboard layouts. There are about 16 known methods, none of which is a clear standard.

Also, there are actually two ideographic sets used: Traditional Chinese (the original written Chinese) and Simplified Chinese. Several years ago, the People's Republic of China launched a campaign to simplify some ideographic characters and eliminate redundancies altogether. Under the plan, characters would be streamlined every five years. Characters have been revised several times now, resulting in the smaller, simpler set that makes up Simplified Chinese.

13.6.1 Input Method Architecture

As shown in the previous section, there are many different input methods in use today, each varying with language, culture, and history. A common feature of many input methods is that the user may type multiple keystrokes to compose a single character (or set of characters). The process of composing characters from keystrokes is called *preediting*. It may require complex algorithms and large dictionaries involving substantial computer resources.

Input methods may require one or more areas in which to show the feedback of the actual keystrokes, to propose disambiguation to the user, to list dictionaries, and so on. The input method areas of concern are as follows:

- The *status* area is a logical extension of the LEDs that exist on the physical keyboard. It is a window that is intended to present the internal state of the input method that is critical to the user. The status area may consist of text data and bitmaps or some combination.
- The *preedit* area displays the intermediate text for those languages that are composing prior to the client handling the data.

- The *auxiliary* area is used for pop-up menus and customizing dialogs that may be required for an input method. There may be multiple auxiliary areas for any input method. Auxiliary areas are managed by the input method independent of the client. Auxiliary areas are assumed to be a separate dialog, which is maintained by the input method.

There are various user interaction styles used for preediting. The ones supported by Xlib are as follows:

- For *on-the-spot* input methods, preediting data will be displayed directly in the application window. Application data is moved to allow preedit data to appear at the point of insertion.
- *Over-the-spot* preediting means that the data is displayed in a preedit window that is placed over the point of insertion.
- *Off-the-spot* preediting means that the preedit window is inside the application window but not at the point of insertion. Often, this type of window is placed at the bottom of the application window.
- *Root-window* preediting refers to input methods that use a preedit window that is the child of `RootWindow`.

It would require a lot of computing resources if portable applications had to include input methods for all the languages in the world. To avoid this, a goal of the Xlib design is to allow an application to communicate with an input method placed in a separate process. Such a process is called an *input server*. The server to which the application should connect is dependent on the environment when the application is started up, that is, the user language and the actual encoding to be used for it. The input method connection is said to be *locale-dependent*. It is also user-dependent. For a given language, the user can choose, to some extent, the user interface style of input method (if choice is possible among several).

Using an input server implies communication overhead, but applications can be migrated without relinking. Input methods can be implemented either as a stub communicating to an input server or as a local library.

An input method may be based on a *front-end* or *back-end* architecture. In front-end architecture, there are two separate connections to the X server: keystrokes go directly from the X server to the input method on one connection and other events go to the regular client connection. The input method is then acting as a filter and sends composed strings to the client. Front-end architecture requires synchronization between the two connections to avoid lost key events or locking issues.

In back-end architecture, a single X server connection is used. A dispatching mechanism must decide on this channel to delegate appropriate keystrokes to the input method. For instance, it may retain a Help keystroke for its own purpose. In the case where the input method is a separate process (that is, a server), there must be a special communication protocol between the back-end client and the input server.

Front-end architecture introduces synchronization issues and filtering mechanism for noncharacter keystrokes (Functions, Help, and so on). Back-end architecture sometimes implies more communication overhead and more process switching. If all three processes are running on a single workstation (for example, an X server, input server, or client), there are two process switches for each keystroke in back-end architecture, but there is only one in front-end architecture.

The abstraction used by a client to communicate with an input method is an opaque data structure represented by the `XIM` data type. This data structure is returned by the `XOpenIM` function, which opens an input method on a given display. Subsequent operations on this data structure encapsulate all communication between client and input method. There is no need for an X client to use any networking library or natural language package to use an input method.

A single input server may be used for one or more languages, supporting one or more encoding schemes. But the strings returned from an input method will always be encoded in the (single) locale associated with `XIM` object.

13.6.2 Input Contexts

Xlib provides the ability to manage a multithreaded state for text input. A client may be using multiple windows, each window with multiple text entry areas, and the user possibly switching among them at any time. The abstraction for representing the state of a particular input thread is called an *input context*. The Xlib representation of an input context is an `XIC`.

An input context is the abstraction retaining the state, properties, and semantics of communication between a client and an input method. An input context is a combination of an input method, a locale specifying the encoding of the character strings to be returned, a client window, internal state information, and various layout or appearance characteristics. The input context concept somewhat matches for input the graphics context abstraction defined for graphics output.

One input context belongs to exactly one input method. Different input contexts may be associated with the same input method, possibly with the same client window. An `XIC` is created with the `XCreateIC` function, providing an `XIM` argument and affiliating the input context to the input method for its lifetime. When an input method is closed with `XCloseIM`, all of its affiliated input contexts should not be used any more (and should preferably be destroyed before closing the input method).

Considering the example of a client window with multiple text entry areas, the application programmer could, for example, choose to implement as follows:

- As many input contexts are created as text entry areas, and the client will get the input accumulated on each context each time it looks up that context.
- A single context is created for a top-level window in the application. If such a window contains several text entry areas, each time the user moves to another text entry area, the client has to indicate changes in the context.

A range of choices can be made by application designers to use either a single or multiple input contexts, according to the needs of their application.

13.6.3 Getting Keyboard Input

To obtain characters from an input method, a client must call the function `XmbLookupString` or `XwcLookupString` with an input context created from that input method. Both a locale and display are bound to an input method when it is opened, and an input context inherits this locale and display. Any strings returned by `XmbLookupString` or `XwcLookupString` will be encoded in that locale.

13.6.4 Focus Management

For each text entry area in which the `XmbLookupString` or `XwcLookupString` routines are used, there will be an associated input context.

When the application focus moves to a text entry area, the application must set the input context focus to the input context associated with that area. The input context focus is set by calling `XSetICFocus` with the appropriate input context.

Also, when the application focus moves out of a text entry area, the application should unset the focus for the associated input context by calling `XUnsetICFocus`. As an optimization, if `XSetICFocus` is called successively on two different input contexts, setting the focus on the second will automatically unset the focus on the first.

To set and unset the input context focus correctly, it will be necessary to track application-level focus changes. Such focus changes do not necessarily correspond to X server focus changes.

If a single input context is being used to do input for multiple text entry areas, it will also be necessary to set the focus window of the input context whenever the focus window changes (see section 13.10.3).

13.6.5 Geometry Management

In most input method architectures (on-the-spot being the notable exception), the input method will perform the display of its own data. To provide better visual locality, it is often desirable to have the input method areas embedded within a client. To do this, the client may need to allocate space for an input method. Xlib provides support that allows the size and position of input method areas to be provided by a client. The input method areas that are supported for geometry management are the status area and the preedit area.

The fundamental concept on which geometry management for input method windows is based is the proper division of responsibilities between the client (or toolkit) and the input method. The division of responsibilities is as follows:

- The client is responsible for the geometry of the input method window.
- The input method is responsible for the contents of the input method window.

An input method is able to suggest a size to the client, but it cannot suggest a placement. Also the input method can only suggest a size. It does not determine the size, and it must accept the size it is given.

Before a client provides geometry management for an input method, it must determine if geometry management is needed. The input method indicates the need for geometry management by setting `XIMPreeditArea` or `XIMStatusArea` in its `XIMStyles` value returned by `XGetIMValues`. When a client has decided that it will provide geometry management for an input method, it indicates that decision by setting the `XNInputStyle` value in the `XIC`.

After a client has established with the input method that it will do geometry management, the client must negotiate the geometry with the input method. The geometry is negotiated by the following steps:

- The client suggests an area to the input method by setting the `XNAreaNeeded` value for that area. If the client has no constraints for the input method, it either will not suggest an area or will set the width and height to zero. Otherwise, it will set one of the values.
- The client will get the XIC value `XNAreaNeeded`. The input method will return its suggested size in this value. The input method should pay attention to any constraints suggested by the client.
- The client sets the XIC value `XNArea` to inform the input method of the geometry of its window. The client should try to honor the geometry requested by the input method. The input method must accept this geometry.

Clients doing geometry management must be aware that setting other IC values may affect the geometry desired by an input method. For example, `XNFontSet` and `XNLineSpacing` may change the geometry desired by the input method.

The table of XIC values (see section 13.10) indicates the values that can cause the desired geometry to change when they are set. It is the responsibility of the client to renegotiate the geometry of the input method window when it is needed.

In addition, a geometry management callback is provided by which an input method can initiate a geometry change.

13.6.6 Event Filtering

A filtering mechanism is provided to allow input methods to capture X events transparently to clients. It is expected that toolkits (or clients) using `XmbLookupString` or `XwcLookupString` will call this filter at some point in the event processing mechanism to make sure that events needed by an input method can be filtered by that input method.

If there were no filter, a client could receive and discard events that are necessary for the proper functioning of an input method. The following provides a few examples of such events:

- Expose events on preedit window in local mode.
- Events may be used by an input method to communicate with an input server. Such input server protocol related events have to be intercepted if one does not want to disturb client code.
- Key events can be sent to a filter before they are bound to translations such as the X Toolkit Intrinsics library provides.

Clients are expected to get the XIC value `XNFilterEvents` and augment the event mask for the client window with that event mask. This mask may be zero.

13.6.7 Callbacks

When an on-the-spot input method is implemented, only the client can insert or delete preedit data in place and possibly scroll existing text. This means the echo of the keystrokes has to be achieved by the client itself, tightly coupled with the input method logic.

When the user enters a keystroke, the client calls `XmbLookupString` or `XwcLookupString`. At this point, in the on-the-spot case, the echo of the keystroke in the preedit has not yet been done. Before returning to the client logic that handles the input characters, the look-up function must call the echoing logic for inserting the new keystroke. If the keystrokes entered so far make up a character, the keystrokes entered need to be deleted, and the composed character will be returned. Hence, what happens is that, while being called by client code, input method logic has to call back to the client before it returns. The client code, that is, a callback routine, is called from the input method logic.

There are a number of cases where the input method logic has to call back the client. Each of those cases is associated with a well-defined callback action. It is possible for the client to specify, for each input context, what callback is to be called for each action.

There are also callbacks provided for feedback of status information and a callback to initiate a geometry request for an input method.

13.7 Variable Argument Lists

Several input method functions have arguments that conform to the ANSI C variable argument list calling convention. Each function denoted with an argument in the form "..." takes a variable length list of name and value pairs, where each name is a string and each value is of type `XPointer`. A name argument containing NULL identifies the end of the list.

A variable length argument list may contain a nested list. If the name `XVaNestedList` is specified in place of an argument name, then the following value is interpreted as a `XVaNestedList` value, which specifies a list of values logically inserted into the original list at the point of declaration. A NULL identifies the end of a nested list.

To allocate a nested variable argument list dynamically, use `XVaCreateNestedList`.

```
typedef void * XVaNestedList;

XVaNestedList XVaCreateNestedList ( dummy, ...)
    int dummy;
```

dummy Specifies an unused argument (required by ANSI C).

... Specifies the variable length argument list.

The `XVaCreateNestedList` function allocates memory and copies its arguments into a single list pointer, which may be used as a value for arguments requiring a list value. Any entries are copied as specified. Data passed by reference is not copied; the caller must ensure data remains valid for the lifetime of the nested list. The list should be freed using `XFree` when it is no longer needed.

13.8 Input Method Functions

To open a connection, use `XOpenIM`.

```
XIM XOpenIM ( display, db, res_name, res_class)
    Display *display;
    XrmDataBase db;
    char *res_name;
    char *res_class;
```

display Specifies the connection to the X server.
db Specifies a pointer to the resource database.
res_name Specifies the full resource name of the application.
res_class Specifies the full class name of the application.

The `XOpenIM` function opens an input method, matching the current locale and modifiers specification. Current locale and modifiers are bound to the input method at opening time. The locale associated with an input method cannot be changed dynamically. This implies the strings returned by `XmbLookupString` or `XwcLookupString`, for any input context affiliated with a given input method, will be encoded in the locale current at the time the input method is opened.

The specific input method to which this call will be routed is identified on the basis of the current locale. `XOpenIM` will identify a default input method corresponding to the current locale. That default can be modified using `XSetLocaleModifiers` for the input method modifier.

The db argument is the resource database to be used by the input method for looking up resources that are private to the input method. It is not intended that this database be used to look up values that can be set as IC values in an input context. If db is NULL, no database is passed to the input method.

The res_name and res_class arguments specify the resource name and class of the application. They are intended to be used as prefixes by the input method when looking up resources that are common to all input contexts that may be created for this input method. The characters used for resource names and classes must be in the X Portable Character Set. The resources looked up are not fully specified if res_name or res_class is NULL.

The res_name and res_class arguments are not assumed to exist beyond the call to `XOpenIM`. The specified resource database is assumed to exist for the lifetime of the input method.

`XOpenIM` returns NULL if no input method could be opened.

To close a connection, use `XCloseIM`.

Status XCloseIM (*im*)
XIM *im*;

im Specifies the input method.

⌋ `XCloseIM` function closes the specified input method.

To query an input method, use XGetIMValues.

```
char * XGetIMValues ( im, ...)
   XIM im;
```

im Specifies the input method.

... Specifies the variable length argument list to get XIM values.

The XGetIMValues function presents a variable argument list programming interface for querying properties or features of the specified input method. This function returns NULL if it succeeds; otherwise, it returns the name of the first argument that could not be obtained.

Only one standard argument is defined by Xlib: XNQueryInputStyle, which must be used to query about input styles supported by the input method.

A client should always query the input method to determine which styles are supported. The client should then find an input style it is capable of supporting.

If the client cannot find an input style that it can support, it should negotiate with the user the continuation of the program (exit, choose another input method, and so on).

The argument value must be a pointer to a location where the returned value will be stored. The returned value is a pointer to a structure of type XIMStyles. Clients are responsible for freeing the XIMStyles structure. To do so, use XFree.

The XIMStyles structure is defined as follows:

```
typedef unsigned long XIMStyle;

#define XIMPreeditArea          0x0001L
#define XIMPreeditCallbacks     0x0002L
#define XIMPreeditPosition      0x0004L
#define XIMPreeditNothing       0x0008L
#define XIMPreeditNone          0x0010L

#define XIMStatusArea           0x0100L
#define XIMStatusCallbacks      0x0200L
#define XIMStatusNothing        0x0400L
#define XIMStatusNone           0x0800L
```

```
typedef struct {
    unsigned short count_styles;
    XIMStyle * supported_styles;
} XIMStyles;
```

An `XIMStyles` structure contains the number of input styles supported in its count_styles field. This is also the size of the array in the supported_styles field.

The supported styles is a list of bitmask combinations, which indicate the combination of styles for each of the areas supported. These areas are described below. Each element in the list should select one of the bitmask values for each area. The list describes the complete set of combinations supported. Only these combinations are supported by the input method.

The preedit category defines what type of support is provided by the input method for preedit information.

`XIMPreeditArea`	If chosen, the input method would require the client to provide some area values for it to do its preediting. Refer to XIC values `XNArea` and `XNAreaNeeded`.
`XIMPreeditPosition`	If chosen, the input method would require the client to provide positional values. Refer to XIC values `XNSpotLocation` and `XNFocusWindow`.
`XIMPreeditCallbacks`	If chosen, the input method would require the client to define the set of preedit callbacks. Refer to XIC values `XNPreeditStartCallback`, `XNPreeditDoneCallback`, `XNPreeditDrawCallback`, and `XNPreeditCaretCallback`.
`XIMPreeditNothing`	If chosen, the input method can function without any preedit values.
`XIMPreeditNone`	The input method does not provide any preedit feedback. Any preedit value is ignored. This style is mutually exclusive with the other preedit styles.

The status category defines what type of support is provided by the input method for status information.

`XIMStatusArea`	The input method requires the client to provide some area values for it to do its status feedback. See `XNArea` and `XNAreaNeeded`.
`XIMStatusCallbacks`	The input method requires the client to define the set of status callbacks, `XNStatusStartCallback`, `XNStatusDoneCallback`, and `XNStatusDrawCallback`.

`XIMStatusNothing`	The input method can function without any status values.
`XIMStatusNone`	The input method does not provide any status feedback. If chosen, any status value is ignored. This style is mutually exclusive with the other status styles.

To obtain the display associated with an input method, use `XDisplayOfIM`.

```
Display * XDisplayOfIM ( im)
    XIM im;
```

im Specifies the input method.

The `XDisplayOfIM` function returns the display associated with the specified input method.

To get the locale associated with an input method, use `XLocaleOfIM`.

```
char * XLocaleOfIM ( im)
    XIM im;
```

im Specifies the input method.

The `XLocaleOfIM` function returns the locale associated with the specified input method.

13.9 Input Context Functions

An input context is an abstraction that is used to contain both the data required (if any) by an input method and the information required to display that data. There may be multiple input contexts for one input method. The programming interfaces for creating, reading, or modifying an input context use a variable argument list. The name elements of the argument lists are referred to as XIC values. It is intended that input methods be controlled by these XIC values. As new XIC values are created, they should be registered with the X Consortium.

To create an input context, use `XCreateIC`.

```
XIC XCreateIC ( im, ...)
    XIM im;
```

im Specifies the input method.

... Specifies the variable length argument list to set XIC values.

The `XCreateIC` function creates a context within the specified input method.

Some of the arguments are mandatory at creation time, and the input context will not be created if those arguments are not provided. The mandatory arguments are the input style and the set of text callbacks (if the input style selected requires callbacks). All other input context values can be set later.

`XCreateIC` returns a NULL value if no input context could be created. A NULL value could be returned for any of the following reasons:

- A required argument was not set.
- A read-only argument was set (for example, `XNFilterEvents`).
- The argument name is not recognized.
- The input method encountered an input method implementation dependent error.

`XCreateIC` can generate `BadAtom`, `BadColor`, `BadPixmap`, and `BadWindow` errors.

To destroy an input context, use `XDestroyIC`.

```
void XDestroyIC ( ic)
   XIC ic;
```

ic Specifies the input context.

`XDestroyIC` destroys the specified input context.

To communicate to and synchronize with input method for any changes in keyboard focus from the client side, use `XSetICFocus` and `XUnsetICFocus`.

```
void XSetICFocus ( ic)
   XIC ic;
```

ic Specifies the input context.

The `XSetICFocus` function allows a client to notify an input method that the focus window attached to the specified input context has received keyboard focus. The input method should take action to provide appropriate feedback. Complete feedback specification is a matter of user interface policy.

```
void XUnsetICFocus ( ic)
   XIC ic;
```

ic Specifies the input context.

The XUnsetICFocus function allows a client to notify an input method that the specified input context has lost the keyboard focus and that no more input is expected on the focus window attached to that input context. The input method should take action to provide appropriate feedback. Complete feedback specification is a matter of user interface policy.

To reset the state of an input context to its initial state, use XmbResetIC or XwcResetIC.

```
char * XmbResetIC ( ic)
    XIC ic;

wchar_t * XwcResetIC ( ic)
    XIC ic;
```

ic Specifies the input context.

The XmbResetIC and XwcResetIC functions reset an input context to its initial state. Any input pending on that context is deleted. The input method is required to clear the preedit area, if any, and update the status accordingly. Calling XmbResetIC or XwcResetIC does not change the focus.

The return value of XmbResetIC is its current preedit string as a multibyte string. The return value of XwcResetIC is its current preedit string as a wide character string. It is input method implementation dependent whether these routines return a non-NULL string or NULL.

The client should free the returned string by calling XFree.

To get the input method associated with an input context, use XIMOfIC.

```
XIM XIMOfIC ( ic)
    XIC ic;
```

ic Specifies the input context.

The XIMOfIC function returns the input method associated with the specified input context.

Xlib provides two functions for setting and reading XIC values, respectively, XSetICValues and XGetICValues. Both functions have a variable length argument list. In that argument list, any XIC value's name must be denoted with a character string using the X Portable Character Set.

To set XIC values, use `XSetICValues`.

```
char * XSetICValues ( ic, ...)
    XIC ic;
```

ic Specifies the input context.

... Specifies the variable length argument list to set XIC values.

The `XSetICValues` function returns NULL if no error occurred; otherwise, it returns the name of the first argument that could not be set. An argument could not be set for any of the following reasons:

- A read-only argument was set (for example, `XNFilterEvents`).
- The argument name is not recognized.
- The input method encountered an input method implementation dependent error.

Each value to be set must be an appropriate datum, matching the data type imposed by the semantics of the argument.

`XSetICValues` can generate `BadAtom`, `BadColor`, `BadCursor`, `BadPixmap`, and `BadWindow` errors.

To obtain XIC values, use `XGetICValues`.

```
char * XGetICValues ( ic, ...)
    XIC ic;
```

ic Specifies the input context.

... Specifies the variable length argument list to get XIC values.

The `XGetICValues` function returns NULL if no error occurred; otherwise, it returns the name of the first argument that could not be obtained. An argument could not be obtained for any of the following reasons:

- The argument name is not recognized.
- The input method encountered an implementation dependent error.

Each IC attribute value argument (following a name) must point to a location where the IC value is to be stored. That is, if the IC value is of type T, the argument must be of type T*. If T itself is a pointer, then `XGetICValues` allocates memory to store the actual data, and the client is responsible for freeing this data by calling `XFree` with the returned pointer. The exception to this rule is for an IC value of type `XVaNestedList` (for preedit and status attributes). In this case, the argument must also be of type `XVaNestedList`. Then, the rule of changing type T to T* and freeing the allocated data applies to each element of the nested list.

13.10 XIC Value Arguments

The following tables describe how XIC values are interpreted by an input method depending on the input style chosen by the user.

The first column lists the XIC values. The second column indicates which values are involved in affecting, negotiating, and setting the geometry of the input method windows. The subentries under the third column indicate the different input styles that are supported. Each of these columns indicates how each of the XIC values are treated by that input style.

The following keys apply to these tables.

Keys	*Explanation*
C	This value must be set with `XCreateIC`.
D	This value may be set using `XCreateIC`. If it is not set, a default is provided.
G	This value may be read using `XGetICValues`.
GN	This value may cause geometry negotiation when its value is set by means of `XCreateIC` or `XSetICValues`.
GR	This value will be the response of the input method when any GN value is changed.
GS	This value will cause the geometry of the input method window to be set.
O	This value must be set once and only once. It need not be set at create time.
S	This value may be set with `XSetICValues`.
Ignored	This value is ignored by the input method for the given input style.

		Input Style				
XIC Value	*Geometry Management*	*Preedit Callback*	*Preedit Position*	*Preedit Area*	*Preedit Nothing*	*Preedit None*
Input Style		C-G	C-G	C-G	C-G	C-G
Client Window		O-G	O-G	O-G	O-G	Ignored
Focus Window	GN	D-S-G	D-S-G	D-S-G	D-S-G	Ignored
Resource Name		Ignored	D-S-G	D-S-G	D-S-G	Ignored
Resource Class		Ignored	D-S-G	D-S-G	D-S-G	Ignored
Geometry Callback		Ignored	Ignored	D-S-G	Ignored	Ignored
Filter Events		G	G	G	G	Ignored
Preedit						
Area	GS	Ignored	D-S-G	D-S-G	Ignored	Ignored
Area Needed	GN-GR	Ignored	Ignored	S-G	Ignored	Ignored

XIC Value	*Geometry Management*	*Input Style*				
		Preedit Callback	*Preedit Position*	*Preedit Area*	*Preedit Nothing*	*Preedit None*
Spot Location		Ignored	S-G	Ignored	Ignored	Ignored
Colormap		Ignored	D-S-G	D-S-G	D-S-G	Ignored
Foreground		Ignored	D-S-G	D-S-G	D-S-G	Ignored
Background		Ignored	D-S-G	D-S-G	D-S-G	Ignored
Background Pixmap		Ignored	D-S-G	D-S-G	D-S-G	Ignored
Font Set	GN	Ignored	S-G	C-S-G	D-S-G	Ignored
Line Spacing	GN	Ignored	D-S-G	D-S-G	D-S-G	Ignored
Cursor		Ignored	D-S-G	D-S-G	D-S-G	Ignored
Preedit Callbacks		C-S-G	Ignored	Ignored	Ignored	Ignored

XIC Value	*Geometry Management*	*Input Style*			
		Status Callback	*Status Area*	*Status Nothing*	*Status None*
Input Style		C-G	C-G	C-G	C-G
Client Window		O-G	O-G	O-G	Ignored
Focus Window	GN	D-S-G	D-S-G	D-S-G	Ignored
Resource Name		Ignored	D-S-G	D-S-G	Ignored
Resource Class		Ignored	D-S-G	D-S-G	Ignored
Geometry Callback		Ignored	D-S-G	Ignored	Ignored
Filter Events		G	G	G	G
Status					
Area	GS	Ignored	D-S-G	Ignored	Ignored
Area Needed	GN-GR	Ignored	S-G	Ignored	Ignored
Colormap		Ignored	D-S-G	D-S-G	Ignored
Foreground		Ignored	D-S-G	D-S-G	Ignored
Background		Ignored	D-S-G	D-S-G	Ignored
Background Pixmap		Ignored	D-S-G	D-S-G	Ignored
Font Set	GN	Ignored	C-S-G	D-S-G	Ignored
Line Spacing	GN	Ignored	D-S-G	D-S-G	Ignored
Cursor		Ignored	D-S-G	D-S-G	Ignored
Status Callbacks		C-S-G	Ignored	Ignored	Ignored

13.10.1 Input Style

The `XNInputStyle` argument specifies the input style to be used. The value of this argument must be one of the values returned by the `XGetIMValues` function with the XNQueryInputStyle argument specified in the supported_styles list.

Note that this argument must be set at creation time and cannot be changed.

13.10.2 Client Window

The XNClientWindow argument specifies to the input method the client window in which the input method can display data or create subwindows. Geometry values for input method areas are given with respect to the client window. Dynamic change of client window is not supported. This argument may be set only once and should be set before any input is done using this input context. If it is not set, the input method may not operate correctly.

If an attempt is made to set this value a second time with XSetICValues, the string XNClientWindow will be returned by XSetICValues, and the client window will not be changed.

If the client window is not a valid window ID on the display attached to the input method, a BadWindow error can be generated when this value is used by the input method.

13.10.3 Focus Window

The XNFocusWindow argument specifies the focus window. The primary purpose of the XNFocusWindow is to identify the window that will receive the key event when input is composed. In addition, the input method may possibly affect the focus window as follows:

- Select events on it
- Send events to it
- Modify its properties
- Grab the keyboard within that window

The value associated to the argument must be of type Window. If the focus window is not a valid window ID on the display attached to the input method, a BadWindow error can be generated when this value is used by the input method.

When this XIC value is left unspecified, the input method will use the client window as the default focus window.

13.10.4 Resource Name and Class

The `XNResourceName` and `XNResourceClass` arguments are strings that specify the full name and class used by the client to obtain resources for the client window. These values should be used as prefixes for name and class when looking up resources that may vary according to the input context. If these values are not set, the resources will not be fully specified.

It is not intended that values that can be set as XIC values be set as resources.

13.10.5 Geometry Callback

The `XNGeometryCallback` argument is a structure of type `XIMCallback` (see section 13.10.7.10).

The `XNGeometryCallback` argument specifies the geometry callback that a client can set. This callback is not required for correct operation of either an input method or a client. It can be set for a client whose user interface policy permits an input method to request the dynamic change of that input method's window. An input method that does dynamic change will need to filter any events that it uses to initiate the change.

13.10.6 Filter Events

The `XNFilterEvents` argument returns the event mask that an input method needs to have selected for. The client is expected to augment its own event mask for the client window with this one.

This argument is read-only, is set by the input method at create time, and is never changed.

The type of this argument is `unsigned long`. Setting this value will cause an error.

13.10.7 Preedit and Status Attributes

The `XNPreeditAttributes` and `XNStatusAttributes` arguments specify to an input method the attributes to be used for the preedit and status areas, if any. Those attributes are passed to `XSetICValues` or `XGetICValues` as a nested variable length list. The names to be used in these lists are described in the following sections.

13.10.7.1 Area

The value of the XNArea argument must be a pointer to a structure of type XRectangle. The interpretation of the XNArea argument is dependent on the input method style that has been set.

If the input method style is XIMPreeditPosition, XNArea specifies the clipping region within which preediting will take place. If the focus window has been set, the coordinates are assumed to be relative to the focus window. Otherwise, the coordinates are assumed to be relative to the client window. If neither has been set, the results are undefined. If XNArea is not specified, the input method will default the clipping region to the geometry of the XNFocusWindow. If the area specified is NULL or invalid, the results are undefined.

If the input style is XIMPreeditArea or XIMStatusArea, XNArea specifies the geometry provided by the client to the input method. The input method may use this area to display its data, either preedit or status depending on the area designated. The input method may create a window as a child of the client window with dimensions that fit the XNArea. The coordinates are relative to the client window. If the client window has not been set yet, the input method should save these values and apply them when the client window is set. If XNArea is not specified, is set to NULL, or is invalid, the results are undefined.

13.10.7.2 Area Needed

When set, the XNAreaNeeded argument specifies the geometry suggested by the client for this area (preedit or status). The value associated with the argument must be a pointer to a structure of type XRectangle. Note that the x, y values are not used and that nonzero values for width or height are the constraints that the client wishes the input method to respect.

When read, the XNAreaNeeded argument specifies the preferred geometry desired by the input method for the area.

This argument is only valid if the input style is XIMPreeditArea or XIMStatusArea. It is used for geometry negotiation between the client and the input method and has no other effect upon the input method (see section 13.6.5).

13.10.7.3 Spot Location

The XNSpotLocation argument specifies to the input method the coordinates of the spot to be used by an input method executing with XNInputStyle set to

`XIMPreeditPosition`. When specified to any input method other than `XIMPreeditPosition`, this XIC value is ignored.

The x coordinate specifies the position where the next character would be inserted. The y coordinate is the position of the baseline used by the current text line in the focus window. The x and y coordinates are relative to the focus window, if it has been set; otherwise, they are relative to the client window. If neither the focus window nor the client window has been set, the results are undefined.

The value of the argument is a pointer to a structure of type `XPoint`.

13.10.7.4 Colormap

Two different arguments can be used to indicate what colormap the input method should use to allocate colors, a colormap ID, or a standard colormap name.

The `XNColormap` argument is used to specify a colormap ID. The argument value is of type `Colormap`. An invalid argument may generate a `BadColor` error when it is used by the input method.

The `XNStdColormap` argument is used to indicate the name of the standard colormap in which the input method should allocate colors. The argument value is an `Atom` that should be a valid atom for calling `XGetRGBColormaps`. An invalid argument may generate a `BadAtom` error when it is used by the input method.

If the colormap is left unspecified, the client window colormap becomes the default.

13.10.7.5 Foreground and Background

The `XNForeground` and `XNBackground` arguments specify the foreground and background pixel, respectively. The argument value is of type `unsigned long`. It must be a valid pixel in the input method colormap.

If these values are left unspecified, the default is determined by the input method.

13.10.7.6 Background Pixmap

The `XNBackgroundPixmap` argument specifies a background pixmap to be used as the background of the window. The value must be of type `Pixmap`. An invalid argument may generate a `BadPixmap` error when it is used by the input method.

If this value is left unspecified, the default is determined by the input method.

13.10.7.7 Font Set

The `XNFontSet` argument specifies to the input method what font set is to be used. The argument value is of type `XFontSet`.

If this value is left unspecified, the default is determined by the input method.

13.10.7.8 Line Spacing

The `XNLineSpace` argument specifies to the input method what line spacing is to be used in the preedit window if more than one line is to be used. This argument is of type `int`.

If this value is left unspecified, the default is determined by the input method.

13.10.7.9 Cursor

The `XNCursor` argument specifies to the input method what cursor is to be used in the specified window. This argument is of type `Cursor`.

An invalid argument may generate a `BadCursor` error when it is used by the input method. If this value is left unspecified, the default is determined by the input method.

13.10.7.10 Preedit and Status Callbacks

A client that wants to support the input style `XIMPreeditCallbacks` must provide a set of preedit callbacks to the input method. The set of preedit callbacks are as follows:

`XNPreeditStartCallback`	This is called when the input method starts preedit.
`XNPreeditDoneCallback`	This is called when the input method stops preedit.
`XNPreeditDrawCallback`	This is called when a number of preedit keystrokes should be echoed.
`XNPreeditCaretCallback`	This is called to move the text insertion point within the preedit string.

A client that wants to support the input style `XIMStatusCallbacks` must provide a set of status callbacks to the input method. The set of status callbacks are as follows:

`XNStatusStartCallback`	This is called when the input method initializes the status area.
`XNStatusDoneCallback`	This is called when the input method no longer needs the status area.
`XNStatusDrawCallback`	This is called when updating of the status area is required.

The value of any status or preedit argument is a pointer to a structure of type `XIMCallback`.

```
typedef void (*XIMProc) ();
typedef struct {
    XPointer client_data;
    XIMProc callback;
} XIMCallback;
```

Each callback has some particular semantics and will carry the data that expresses the environment necessary to the client into a specific data structure. This paragraph only describes the arguments to be used to set the callback. For a complete description of the semantics, see section 13.11.

Setting any of these values while doing preedit may cause unexpected results.

13.11 Callback Semantics

Callbacks are functions defined by clients or text drawing packages that are to be called from the input method when selected events occur. Most clients will use a text editing package or a toolkit and, hence, will not need to define such callbacks. This section defines the callback semantics, when they are triggered, and what their arguments are. This information is mostly useful for X toolkit implementors.

Callbacks are mostly provided so that clients (or text editing packages) can implement on-the-spot preediting in their own window. In that case, the input method needs to communicate and synchronize with the client. The input method needs to communicate changes in the preedit window when it is under control of the client. Those callbacks allow the client to initialize the preedit area, display a new preedit string, move the text insertion point inside during preedit, terminate preedit, or update the status area.

All callback functions follow the generic prototype:

```
void CallbackPrototype ( ic, client_data, call_data)
   XIC ic;
   XPointer client_data;
   SomeType call_data;
```

ic Specifies the input context.

client_data Specifies the additional client data.

call_data Specifies data specific to the callback.

The call_data argument is a structure that expresses the arguments needed to achieve the semantics; that is, it is a specific data structure appropriate to the callback. In cases where no data is needed in the callback, this call_data argument is NULL. The client_data argument is a closure that has been initially specified by the client when specifying the callback and passed back. It may serve, for example, to inherit application context in the callback.

The following paragraphs describe the programming semantics and specific data structure associated with the different reasons.

13.11.1 Geometry Callback

The geometry callback is triggered by the input method to indicate that it wants the client to negotiate geometry. The generic prototype is as follows:

```
void GeometryCallback ( ic, client_data, call_data)
   XIC ic;
   XPointer client_data;
   XPointer call_data;
```

ic Specifies the input context.

client_data Specifies the additional client data.

call_data Not used for this callback and always passed as NULL.

A GeometryCallback is called with a NULL call_data argument.

13.11.2 Preedit State Callbacks

When the input method turns input conversion on or off, a PreeditStart-Callback or PreeditDoneCallback callback is triggered to let the toolkit do the setup or the cleanup for the preedit region.

```
int PreeditStartCallback ( ic, client_data, call_data)
    XIC ic;
    XPointer client_data;
    XPointer call_data;
```

ic	Specifies the input context.
client_data	Specifies the additional client data.
call_data	Not used for this callback and always passed as NULL.

When preedit starts on the specified input context, the callback is called with a NULL call_data argument. PreeditStartCallback will return the maximum size of the preedit string. A positive number indicates the maximum number of bytes allowed in the preedit string, and a value of −1 indicates there is no limit.

```
void PreeditDoneCallback ( ic, client_data, call_data)
    XIC ic;
    XPointer client_data;
    XPointer call_data;
```

ic	Specifies the input context.
client_data	Specifies the additional client data.
call_data	Not used for this callback and always passed as NULL.

When preedit stops on the specified input context, the callback is called with a NULL call_data argument. The client can release the data allocated by PreeditStartCallback.

PreeditStartCallback should initialize appropriate data needed for displaying preedit information and for handling further PreeditDrawCallback calls. Once PreeditStartCallback is called, it will not be called again before PreeditDoneCallback has been called.

13.11.3 Preedit Draw Callback

This callback is triggered to draw and insert, delete or replace, preedit text in the preedit region. The preedit text may include unconverted input text such as Japanese Kana, converted text such as Japanese Kanji characters, or characters of both kinds. That string is either a multibyte or wide character string, whose encoding matches the locale bound to the input context. The callback prototype is as follows:

```
void PreeditDrawCallback (ic, client_data, call_data)
    XIC ic;
    XPointer client_data;
    XIMPreeditDrawCallbackStruct *call_data;
```

ic	Specifies the input context.
client_data	Specifies the additional client data.
call_data	Specifies the preedit drawing information.

The callback is passed a `XIMPreeditDrawCallbackStruct` structure in the call_data argument. The text member of this structure contains the text to be drawn. After the string has been drawn, the caret should be moved to the specified location.

The `XIMPreeditDrawCallbackStruct` structure is defined as follows:

```
typedef struct _XIMPreeditDrawCallbackStruct {
    int caret;              /* Cursor offset within preedit string */
    int chg_first;          /* Starting change position */
    int chg_length;         /* Length of the change in character count */
    XIMText *text;
} XIMPreeditDrawCallbackStruct;
```

The client must keep updating a buffer of the preedit text and the callback arguments referring to indexes in that buffer. The call_data fields have specific meanings according to the operation, as follows:

- To indicate text deletion, the call_data specifies a NULL text field. The text to be deleted is then the current text in the buffer from position chg_first (starting at zero) on a character length of chg_length.
- When text is non-NULL, it indicates insertion or replacement of text in the buffer.

  A positive chg_length indicates that the characters starting from chg_first to ch_first+chg_length must be deleted and must be replaced by text, whose length is specified in the `XIMText` structure.

  A chg_length value of zero indicates that text must be inserted right at the position specified by chg_first. A value of zero for chg_first specifies the first character in the buffer.
- The caret member is an index in the preedit text buffer that specifies the character after which the cursor should move after text has been drawn or deleted.

```
typedef struct _XIMText {
    unsigned short length;
    XIMFeedback * feedback;
    Bool encoding_is_wchar;
    union {
        char * multi_byte;
        wchar_t * wide_char;
        } string;
} XIMText;
```

The text string passed is actually a structure specifying the following:

- The length member is the text length in characters.
- The encoding_is_wchar member is a value that indicates if the text string is encoded in wide character or multibyte format. This value should be set by the client when it sets the callback.
- The string member is the text string.
- The feedback member indicates rendering type.

The feedback member expresses the types of rendering feedback the callback should apply when drawing text. Rendering of the text to be drawn is specified either in generic ways (for example, primary, secondary) or in specific ways (reverse, underline). When generic indications are given, the client is free to choose the rendering style. It is necessary, however, that primary and secondary are mapped to two distinct rendering styles.

The feedback member also specifies how the rendering of the text argument should be achieved. If feedback is NULL, then rendering is assumed to be the same as rendering of other characters in the text entry. Otherwise, it specifies an array defining the rendering of each character of the string (hence, the length of the array is length).

If an input method wants to indicate that it is only updating the feedback of the preedit text without changing the content of it, the `XIMText` structure should contain a NULL value for the string field, the number of characters affected in the length field, and the feedback field should point to an array of `XIMFeedback`.

Each element in the array is a bitmask represented by a value of type `XIMFeedback`. The valid masks names are as follows:

```
typedef unsigned long XIMFeedback;

#define XIMReverse          1L
#define XIMUnderline        (1L<<1)
#define XIMHighlight        (1L<<2)
#define XIMPrimary          (1L<<3)
#define XIMSecondary        (1L<<4)
#define XIMTertiary         (1L<<5)
```

13.11.4 Preedit Caret Callback

An input method may have its own navigation keys to allow the user to move the text insertion point in the preedit area (for example, to move backward or forward). Consequently, input method needs to indicate to the client that it should move the text insertion point. It then calls the PreeditCaretCallback.

void PreeditCaretCallback (*ic*, *client_data*, *call_data*)
  XIC *ic*;
  XPointer *client_data*;
  XIMPreeditCaretCallbackStruct **call_data*;

ic	Specifies the input context.
client_data	Specifies the additional client data.
call_data	Specifies the preedit caret information.

The input method will trigger PreeditCaretCallback to move the text insertion point during preedit. The call_data argument contains a pointer to an `XIMPreeditCaretCallbackStruct` structure, which indicates where the caret should be moved. The callback must move the insertion point to its new location and return, in field position, the new offset value from the initial position.

The `XIMPreeditCaretCallbackStruct` structure is defined as follows:

```
typedef struct _XIMPreeditCaretCallbackStruct {
    int position;                    /* Caret offset within preedit string */
    XIMCaretDirection direction;     /* Caret moves direction */
    XIMCaretStyle style;             /* Feedback of the caret */
} XIMPreeditCaretCallbackStruct;
```

The `XIMCaretStyle` structure is defined as follows:

```
typedef enum {
    XIMIsInvisible,        /* Disable caret feedback */
    XIMIsPrimary,          /* UI defined caret feedback */
    XIMIsSecondary,        /* UI defined caret feedback */
} XIMCaretStyle;
```

The `XIMCaretDirection` structure is defined as follows:

```
typedef enum {
    XIMForwardChar, XIMBackwardChar,
    XIMForwardWord, XIMBackwardWord,
    XIMCaretUp, XIMCaretDown,
    XIMNextLine, XIMPreviousLine,
    XIMLineStart, XIMLineEnd,
    XIMAbsolutePosition,
    XIMDontChange,
} XIMCaretDirection;
```

These values are defined as follows:

`XIMForwardChar`	Move the caret forward one character position.
`XIMBackwardChar`	Move the caret backward one character position.
`XIMForwardWord`	Move the caret forward one word position.
`XIMBackwardWord`	Move the caret backward one word position.
`XIMCaretUp`	Move the caret up one line keeping the current offset.
`XIMCaretDown`	Move the caret down one line keeping the current offset.
`XIMPreviousLine`	Move the caret up one line.
`XIMNextLine`	Move the caret down one line.
`XIMLineStart`	Move the caret to the beginning of the current display line that contains the caret.
`XIMLineEnd`	Move the caret to the end of the current display line that contains the caret.
`XIMAbsolutePosition`	The callback must move to the location specified by the position field of the callback data, indicated in characters, starting from the beginning of the preedit text. Hence, a value of zero means move back to the beginning of the preedit text.
`XIMDontChange`	The caret position does not change.

13.11.5 Status Callbacks

An input method may communicate changes in the status of an input context (for example, created, destroyed, or focus changes) with three status callbacks: StatusStartCallback, StatusDoneCallback, and StatusDrawCallback.

When the input context is created or gains focus, the input method calls the StatusStartCallback callback.

void StatusStartCallback (*ic*, *client_data*, *call_data*)
  XIC *ic*;
  XPointer *client_data*;
  XPointer *call_data*;

ic	Specifies the input context.
client_data	Specifies the additional client data.
call_data	Not used for this callback and always passed as NULL.

The callback should initialize appropriate data for displaying status and be prepared to further StatusDrawCallback calls. Once StatusStartCallback is called, it will not be called again before StatusDoneCallback has been called.

When an input context is destroyed or when it loses focus, the input method calls StatusDoneCallback.

void StatusDoneCallback (*ic*, *client_data*, *call_data*)
  XIC *ic*;
  XPointer *client_data*;
  XPointer *call_data*;

ic	Specifies the input context.
client_data	Specifies the additional client data.
call_data	Not used for this callback and always passed as NULL.

The callback may release any data allocated on `StatusStart`.

When an input context status has to be updated, the input method calls StatusDrawCallback.

void StatusDrawCallback (*ic*, *client_data*, *call_data*)
  XIC *ic*;
  XPointer *client_data*;
  XIMStatusDrawCallbackStruct * *call_data*;

ic	Specifies the input context.
client_data	Specifies the additional client data.
call_data	Specifies the status drawing information.

The callback should update the status area by either drawing a string or imaging a bitmap in the status area.

The `XIMStatusDataType` and `XIMStatusDrawCallbackStruct` structures are defined as follows:

```
typedef enum {
     XIMTextType,
     XIMBitmapType,
} XIMStatusDataType;

typedef struct _XIMStatusDrawCallbackStruct {
     XIMStatusDataType type;
     union {
             XIMText *text;
             Pixmap  bitmap;
     } data;
} XIMStatusDrawCallbackStruct;
```

13.12 Event Filtering

Xlib provides the ability for an input method to register a filter internal to Xlib. This filter is called by a client (or toolkit) by calling `XFilterEvent` after calling `XNextEvent`. Any client that uses the `XIM` interface should call `XFilterEvent` to allow input methods to process their events without knowledge of the client's dispatching mechanism. A client's user interface policy may determine the priority of event filters with respect to other event handling mechanisms (for example, modal grabs).

Clients may not know how many filters there are, if any, and what they do. They may only know if an event has been filtered on return of `XFilterEvent`. Clients should discard filtered events.

To filter an event, use `XFilterEvent`.

```
Bool XFilterEvent (event, w)
   XEvent *event;
   Window w;
```

event Specifies the event to filter.

w Specifies the window for which the filter is to be applied.

If the window argument is `None`, `XFilterEvent` applies the filter to the window specified in the `XEvent` structure. The window argument is provided so that layers above Xlib that do event redirection can indicate to which window an event has been redirected.

If `XFilterEvent` returns `True`, then some input method has filtered the event, and the client should discard the event. If `XFilterEvent` returns `False`, then the client should continue processing the event.

If a grab has occurred in the client and `XFilterEvent` returns `True`, the client should ungrab the keyboard.

13.13 Getting Keyboard Input

To get composed input from an input method, use `XmbLookupString` or `XwcLookupString`.

```
int XmbLookupString(ic, event, buffer_return, bytes_buffer, keysym_return, status_return)
    XIC ic;
    XKeyPressedEvent *event;
    char *buffer_return;
    int bytes_buffer;
    KeySym *keysym_return;
    Status *status_return;
```

```
int XwcLookupString(ic, event, buffer_return, bytes_buffer, keysym_return, status_return)
    XIC ic;
    XKeyPressedEvent *event;
    wchar_t *buffer_return;
    int wchars_buffer;
    KeySym *keysym_return;
    Status *status_return;
```

ic Specifies the input context.

event Specifies the key event to be used.

buffer_return Returns a multibyte string or wide character string (if any) from the input method.

bytes_buffer

wchars_buffer Specifies space available in the return buffer.

keysym_return Returns the KeySym computed from the event if this argument is not NULL.

status_return Returns a value indicating what kind of data is returned.

The `XmbLookupString` and `XwcLookupString` functions return the string from the input method specified in the buffer_return argument. If no string is returned, the buffer_return argument is unchanged.

The KeySym into which the KeyCode from the event was mapped is returned in the keysym_return argument if it is non-NULL and the status_return argument indicates that a KeySym was returned. If both a string and a KeySym are returned, the KeySym value does not necessarily correspond to the string returned.

`XmbLookupString` returns the length of the string in bytes, and `XwcLookupString` returns the length of the string in characters. Both `XmbLookupString` and `XwcLookupString` return text in the encoding of the locale bound to the input method of the specified input context.

Each string returned by `XmbLookupString` and `XwcLookupString` begins in the initial state of the encoding of the locale (if the encoding of the locale is state-dependent).

Note To insure proper input processing, it is essential that the client pass only `KeyPress` events to `XmbLookupString` and `XwcLookupString`. Their behavior when a client passes a `KeyRelease` event is undefined.

Clients should check the status_return argument before using the other returned values. These two functions both return a value to status_return that indicates what has been returned in the other arguments. The possible values returned are:

`XBufferOverflow`	The input string to be returned is too large for the supplied buffer_return. The required size (`XmbLookupString` in bytes; `XwcLookupString` in characters) is returned as the value of the function, and the contents of buffer_return and keysym_return are not modified. The client should recall the function with the same event and a buffer of adequate size to obtain the string.
`XLookupNone`	No consistent input has been composed so far. The contents of buffer_return and keysym_return are not modified, and the function returns zero.

XLookupChars	Some input characters have been composed. They are placed in the buffer_return argument, and the string length is returned as the value of the function. The string is encoded in the locale bound to the input context. The content of the keysym_return argument is not modified.
XLookupKeySym	A KeySym has been returned instead of a string and is returned in keysym_return. The content of the buffer_return argument is not modified, and the function returns zero.
XLookupBoth	Both a KeySym and a string are returned; XLookupChars and XLookupKeySym occur simultaneously.

It does not make any difference if the input context passed as an argument to XmbLookupString and XwcLookupString is the one currently in possession of the focus or not. Input may have been composed within an input context before it lost the focus, and that input may be returned on subsequent calls to XmbLookupString or XwcLookupString even though it does not have any more keyboard focus.

13.14 Input Method Conventions

The input method architecture is transparent to the client. However, clients should respect a number of conventions in order to work properly. Clients must also be aware of possible effects of synchronization between input method and library in the case of a remote input server.

13.14.1 Client Conventions

A well-behaved client (or toolkit) should first query the input method style. If the client cannot satisfy the requirements of the supported styles (in terms of geometry management or callbacks), it should negotiate with the user continuation of the program or raise an exception or error of some sort.

13.14.2 Synchronization Conventions

A KeyPress event with a KeyCode of zero is used exclusively as a signal that an input method has composed input that can be returned by XmbLookupString or XwcLookupString. No other use is made of a KeyPress event with KeyCode of zero.

Such an event may be generated by either a front-end or a back-end input method in an implementation dependent manner. Some possible ways to generate this event include:

- A synthetic event sent by an input method server
- An artificial event created by a input method filter and pushed onto a client's event queue
- A `KeyPress` event whose KeyCode value is modified by an input method filter

When callback support is specified by client, input methods will not take action unless they explicitly called back the client and obtained no response (the callback is not specified or returned invalid data).

13.15 String Constants

The following symbols for string constants are defined in `<X11/Xlib.h>`. Although they are shown here with particular macro definitions, they may be implemented as macros, as global symbols, or as a mixture of the two. The string pointer value itself is not significant; clients must not assume that inequality of two values implies inequality of the actual string data.

```
#define XNVaNestedList            "XNVaNestedList"
#define XNQueryInputStyle         "queryInputStyle"
#define XNClientWindow            "clientWindow"
#define XNInputStyle              "inputStyle"
#define XNFocusWindow             "focusWindow"
#define XNResourceName            "resourceName"
#define XNResourceClass           "resourceClass"
#define XNGeometryCallback        "geometryCallback"
#define XNFilterEvents            "filterEvents"
#define XNPreeditStartCallback    "preeditStartCallback"
#define XNPreeditDoneCallback     "preeditDoneCallback"
#define XNPreeditDrawCallback     "preeditDrawCallback"
#define XNPreeditCaretCallback    "preeditCaretCallback"
#define XNPreeditAttributes       "preeditAttributes"
#define XNStatusStartCallback     "statusStartCallback"
#define XNStatusDoneCallback      "statusDoneCallback"
#define XNStatusDrawCallback      "statusDrawCallback"
#define XNStatusAttributes        "statusAttributes"
```

```
#define XNArea                     "area"
#define XNAreaNeeded               "areaNeeded"
#define XNSpotLocation             "spotLocation"
#define XNColormap                 "colorMap"
#define XNStdColormap              "stdColorMap"
#define XNForeground               "foreground"
#define XNBackground               "background"
#define XNBackgroundPixmap         "backgroundPixmap"
#define XNFontSet                  "fontSet"
#define XNLineSpace                "lineSpace"
#define XNCursor                   "cursor"
```

Chapter 14

Inter-Client Communication Functions

Part III, "Inter-Client Communication Conventions Manual," hereafter referred to as the ICCCM, details the X Consortium approved conventions that govern inter-client communications. These conventions ensure peer-to-peer client cooperation in the use of selections, cut buffers, and shared resources as well as client cooperation with window and session managers. For further information, see part III.

Xlib provides a number of standard properties and programming interfaces that are ICCCM compliant. The predefined atoms for some of these properties are defined in the `<X11/Xatom.h>` header file, where to avoid name conflicts with user symbols their `#define` name has an XA_ prefix. For further information about atoms and properties, see section 4.3.

Xlib's selection and cut buffer mechanisms provide the primary programming interfaces by which peer client applications communicate with each other (see sections 4.5 and 16.6). The functions discussed in this chapter provide the primary programming interfaces by which client applications communicate with their window and session managers as well as share standard colormaps.

The standard properties that are of special interest for communicating with window and session managers are:

Name	*Type*	*Format*	*Description*
WM_CLASS	STRING	8	Set by application programs to allow window and session managers to obtain the application's resources from the resource database.
WM_CLIENT_MACHINE	TEXT		The string name of the machine on which the client application is running.
WM_COLORMAP_WINDOWS	WINDOW	32	The list of window IDs that may need a different colormap than that of their top-level window.
WM_COMMAND	TEXT		The command and arguments, null-separated, used to invoke the application.
WM_HINTS	WM_HINTS	32	Additional hints set by the client for use by the window manager. The C type of this property is `XWMHints`.
WM_ICON_NAME	TEXT		The name to be used in an icon.
WM_ICON_SIZE	WM_ICON_SIZE	32	The window manager may set this property on the root window to specify the icon sizes it supports. The C type of this property is `XIconSize`.
WM_NAME	TEXT		The name of the application.
WM_NORMAL_HINTS	WM_SIZE_HINTS	32	Size hints for a window in its normal state. The C type of this property is `XSizeHints`.
WM_PROTOCOLS	ATOM	32	List of atoms that identify the communications protocols between the client and window manager in which the client is willing to participate.

Name	*Type*	*Format*	*Description*
WM_STATE	WM_STATE	32	Intended for communication between window and session managers only.
WM_TRANSIENT_FOR	WINDOW	32	Set by application programs to indicate to the window manager that a transient top-level window, such as a dialog box.

The remainder of this chapter discusses:

- Client-to-window-manager communication
- Client-to-session-manager communication
- Standard colormaps

14.1 Client to Window Manager Communication

This section discusses how to:

- Manipulate top-level windows
- Convert string lists
- Set and read text properties
- Set and read the WM_NAME property
- Set and read the WM_ICON_NAME property
- Set and read the WM_HINTS property
- Set and read the WM_NORMAL_HINTS property
- Set and read the WM_CLASS property
- Set and read the WM_TRANSIENT_FOR property
- Set and read the WM_PROTOCOLS property
- Set and read the WM_COLORMAP_WINDOWS property
- Set and read the WM_ICON_SIZE property
- Use window manager convenience functions

14.1.1 Manipulating Top-Level Windows

Xlib provides functions that you can use to change the visibility or size of top-level windows (that is, those that were created as children of the root window). Note that the subwindows that you create are ignored by window managers. Therefore, you should use the basic window functions described in chapter 3 to manipulate your application's subwindows.

To request that a top-level window be iconified, use `XIconifyWindow`.

```
Status XIconifyWindow( display, w, screen_number)
    Display *display;
    Window w;
    int screen_number;
```

display	Specifies the connection to the X server.
w	Specifies the window.
screen_number	Specifies the appropriate screen number on the host server.

The `XIconifyWindow` function sends a WM_CHANGE_STATE `ClientMessage` event with a format of 32 and a first data element of `IconicState` (as described in section 4.1.4 of part III, "Inter-Client Communication Conventions Manual") and a window of w to the root window of the specified screen with an event mask set to `SubstructureNotifyMask|SubstructureRedirectMask`. Window managers may elect to receive this message and if the window is in its normal state, may treat it as a request to change the window's state from normal to iconic. If the WM_CHANGE_STATE property cannot be interned, `XIconifyWindow` does not send a message and returns a zero status. It returns a nonzero status if the client message is sent successfully; otherwise, it returns a zero status.

To request that a top-level window be withdrawn, use `XWithdrawWindow`.

```
Status XWithdrawWindow( display, w, screen_number)
    Display *display;
    Window w;
    int screen_number;
```

display	Specifies the connection to the X server.
w	Specifies the window.
screen_number	Specifies the appropriate screen number on the host server.

The `XWithdrawWindow` function unmaps the specified window and sends a synthetic `UnmapNotify` event to the root window of the specified screen. Window managers may elect to receive this message and may treat it as a request to change the window's state to withdrawn. When a window is in the withdrawn state, neither its normal nor its iconic representations is visible. It returns a nonzero status if the `UnmapNotify` event is successfully sent; otherwise, it returns a zero status.

`XWithdrawWindow` can generate a `BadWindow` error.

To request that a top-level window be reconfigured, use `XReconfigureWMWindow`.

Status XReconfigureWMWindow (*display, w, screen_number, value_mask, values*)
  Display **display*;
  Window *w*;
  int *screen_number*;
  unsigned int *value_mask*;
  XWindowChanges **values*;

display	Specifies the connection to the X server.
w	Specifies the window.
screen_number	Specifies the appropriate screen number on the host server.
value_mask	Specifies which values are to be set using information in the values structure. This mask is the bitwise inclusive OR of the valid configure window values bits.
values	Specifies the `XWindowChanges` structure.

The `XReconfigureWMWindow` function issues a `ConfigureWindow` request on the specified top-level window. If the stacking mode is changed and the request fails with a `BadMatch` error, the error is trapped by Xlib and a synthetic `ConfigureRequestEvent` containing the same configuration parameters is sent to the root of the specified window. Window managers may elect to receive this event and treat it as a request to reconfigure the indicated window. It returns a nonzero status if the request or event is successfully sent; otherwise, it returns a zero status.

`XReconfigureWMWindow` can generate `BadValue` and `BadWindow` errors.

14.1.2 Converting String Lists

Many of the text properties allow a variety of types and formats. Because the data stored in these properties are not simple null-terminated strings, a

XTextProperty structure is used to describe the encoding, type, and length of the text as well as its value. The XTextProperty structure contains:

```
typedef struct {
    unsigned char *value;       /* property data */
    Atom encoding;              /* type of property */
    int format;                 /* 8, 16, or 32 */
    unsigned long nitems;       /* number of items in value */
} XTextProperty;
```

Xlib provides functions to convert localized text to or from encodings that support the inter-client communication conventions for text. In addition, functions are provided for converting between lists of pointers to character strings and text properties in the STRING encoding.

The functions for localized text return a signed integer error status that encodes Success as zero, specific error conditions as negative numbers, and partial conversion as a count of unconvertible characters.

```
#define XNoMemory               -1
#define XLocaleNotSupported     -2
#define XConverterNotFound      -3

typedef enum {
    XStringStyle,           /* STRING */
    XCompoundTextStyle,     /* COMPOUND_TEXT */
    XTextStyle,             /* text in owner's encoding (current locale) */
    XStdICCTextStyle        /* STRING, else COMPOUND_TEXT */
} XICCEncodingStyle;
```

To convert a list of text strings to an XTextProperty structure, use XmbTextListToTextProperty or XwcTextListToTextProperty.

```
int XmbTextListToTextProperty ( display, list, count, style, text_prop_return)
    Display *display;
    char **list;
    int count;
    XICCEncodingStyle style;
    XTextProperty *text_prop_return;

int XwcTextListToTextProperty ( display, list, count, style, text_prop_return)
    Display *display;
```

```
wchar_t **list;
int count;
XICCEncodingStyle style;
XTextProperty *text_prop_return;
```

display	Specifies the connection to the X server.
list	Specifies a list of null-terminated character strings.
count	Specifies the number of strings specified.
style	Specifies the manner in which the property is encoded.
text_prop_return	Returns the `XTextProperty` structure.

The `XmbTextListToTextProperty` and `XwcTextListToTextProperty` functions set the specified `XTextProperty` value to a set of null-separated elements representing the concatenation of the specified list of null-terminated text strings. A final terminating null is stored at the end of the value field of text_prop_return but is not included in the nitems member.

The functions set the encoding field of text_prop_return to an `Atom` for the specified display naming the encoding determined by the specified style and convert the specified text list to this encoding for storage in the text_prop_return value field. If the style `XStringStyle` or `XCompoundTextStyle` is specified, this encoding is "STRING" or "COMPOUND_TEXT", respectively. If the style `XTextStyle` is specified, this encoding is the encoding of the current locale. If the style `XStdICCTextStyle` is specified, this encoding is "STRING" if the text is fully convertible to STRING, else "COMPOUND_TEXT".

If insufficient memory is available for the new value string, the functions return `XNoMemory`. If the current locale is not supported, the functions return `XLocaleNotSupported`. In both of these error cases, the functions do not set text_prop_return.

To determine if the functions are guaranteed not to return `XLocaleNotSupported`, use `XSupportsLocale`.

If the supplied text is not fully convertible to the specified encoding, the functions return the number of unconvertible characters. Each unconvertible character is converted to an implementation-defined and encoding-specific default string. Otherwise, the functions return `Success`. Note that full convertibility to all styles except `XStringStyle` is guaranteed.

To free the storage for the value field, use `XFree`.

To obtain a list of text strings from an `XTextProperty` structure, use `XmbTextPropertyToTextList` or `XwcTextPropertyToTextList`.

```
int XmbTextPropertyToTextList ( display, text_prop, list_return, count_return)
    Display *display;
    XTextProperty *text_prop;
    char ***list_return;
    int *count_return;

int XwcTextPropertyToTextList ( display, text_prop, list_return, count_return)
    Display *display;
    XTextProperty *text_prop;
    wchar_t ***list_return;
    int *count_return;
```

display	Specifies the connection to the X server.
text_prop	Specifies the `XTextProperty` structure to be used.
list_return	Returns a list of null-terminated character strings.
count_return	Returns the number of strings.

The `XmbTextPropertyToTextList` and `XwcTextPropertyToTextList` functions return a list of text strings in the current locale representing the null-separated elements of the specified `XTextProperty` structure. The data in text_prop must be format 8.

Multiple elements of the property (for example, the strings in a disjoint text selection) are separated by a null byte. The contents of the property are not required to be null-terminated; any terminating null should not be included in text_prop.nitems.

If insufficient memory is available for the list and its elements, `XmbTextPropertyToTextList` and `XwcTextPropertyToTextList` return `XNoMemory`. If the current locale is not supported, the functions return `XLocaleNotSupported`. Otherwise, if the encoding field of text_prop is not convertible to the encoding of the current locale, the functions return `XConverterNotFound`. For supported locales, the existence of a converter from COMPOUND_TEXT, STRING or the encoding of the current locale is guaranteed if `XSupportsLocale` returns `True` for the current locale (but the actual text may contain unconvertible characters). Conversion of other encodings is implementation dependent. In all of these error cases, the functions do not set any return values.

Otherwise, XmbTextPropertyToTextList and XwcTextPropertyToTextList return the list of null-terminated text strings to list_return and the number of text strings to count_return.

If the value field of text_prop is not fully convertible to the encoding of the current locale, the functions return the number of unconvertible characters. Each unconvertible character is converted to a string in the current locale that is specific to the current locale. To obtain the value of this string, use XDefaultString. Otherwise, XmbTextPropertyToTextList and XwcTextPropertyToTextList return Success.

To free the storage for the list and its contents returned by XmbTextPropertyToTextList, use XFreeStringList. To free the storage for the list and its contents returned by XwcTextPropertyToTextList, use XwcFreeStringList.

To free the in-memory data associated with the specified wide character string list, use XwcFreeStringList.

void XwcFreeStringList (*list*)
    wchar_t ***list*;

list Specifies the list of strings to be freed.

The XwcFreeStringList function frees memory allocated by XwcTextPropertyToTextList.

To obtain the default string for text conversion in the current locale, use XDefaultString.

char *XDefaultString ( )

The XDefaultString function returns the default string used by Xlib for text conversion (for example, in XmbTextPropertyToTextList). The default string is the string in the current locale that is output when an unconvertible character is found during text conversion. If the string returned by XDefaultString is the empty string (""), no character is output in the converted text. XDefaultString does not return NULL.

The string returned by `XDefaultString` is independent of the default string for text drawing; see `XCreateFontSet` to obtain the default string for an `XFontSet`.

The behavior when an invalid codepoint is supplied to any Xlib function is undefined.

The returned string is null-terminated. It is owned by Xlib and should not be modified or freed by the client. It may be freed after the current locale is changed. Until freed, it will not be modified by Xlib.

To set the specified list of strings in the STRING encoding to a `XTextProperty` structure, use `XStringListToTextProperty`.

Status XStringListToTextProperty (*list, count, text_prop_return*)
  char ***list*;
  int *count*;
  XTextProperty **text_prop_return*;

list	Specifies a list of null-terminated character strings.
count	Specifies the number of strings.
text_prop_return	Returns the `XTextProperty` structure.

The `XStringListToTextProperty` function sets the specified `XTextProperty` to be of type STRING (format 8) with a value representing the concatenation of the specified list of null-separated character strings. An extra null byte (which is not included in the nitems member) is stored at the end of the value field of text_prop_return. The strings are assumed (without verification) to be in the STRING encoding. If insufficient memory is available for the new value string, `XStringListToTextProperty` does not set any fields in the `XTextProperty` structure and returns a zero status. Otherwise, it returns a nonzero status. To free the storage for the value field, use `XFree`.

To obtain a list of strings from a specified `XTextProperty` structure in the STRING encoding, use `XTextPropertyToStringList`.

Status XTextPropertyToStringList (*text_prop, list_return, count_return*)
  XTextProperty **text_prop*;
  char ****list_return*;
  int **count_return*;

text_prop	Specifies the `XTextProperty` structure to be used.
list_return	Returns a list of null-terminated character strings.
count_return	Returns the number of strings.

The `XTextPropertyToStringList` function returns a list of strings representing the null-separated elements of the specified `XTextProperty` structure. The data in text_prop must be of type STRING and format 8. Multiple elements of the property (for example, the strings in a disjoint text selection) are separated by NULL (encoding 0). The contents of the property are not null-terminated. If insufficient memory is available for the list and its elements, `XTextPropertyToStringList` sets no return values and returns a zero status. Otherwise, it returns a nonzero status. To free the storage for the list and its contents, use `XFreeStringList`.

To free the in-memory data associated with the specified string list, use `XFreeStringList`.

```
void XFreeStringList ( list)
    char **list;
```

list Specifies the list of strings to be freed.

The `XFreeStringList` function releases memory allocated by `XmbTextPropertyToTextList` and `XTextPropertyToStringList` and the missing charset list allocated by `XCreateFontSet`.

14.1.3 Setting and Reading Text Properties

Xlib provides two functions that you can use to set and read the text properties for a given window. You can use these functions to set and read those properties of type TEXT (WM_NAME, WM_ICON_NAME, WM_COMMAND, and WM_CLIENT_MACHINE). In addition, Xlib provides separate convenience functions that you can use to set each of these properties. For further information about these convenience functions, see sections 14.1.4, 14.1.5, 14.2.1, and 14.2.2, respectively.

To set one of a window's text properties, use `XSetTextProperty`.

```
void XSetTextProperty ( display, w, text_prop, property)
    Display *display;
    Window w;
    XTextProperty *text_prop;
    Atom property;
```

display	Specifies the connection to the X server.
w	Specifies the window.
text_prop	Specifies the XTextProperty structure to be used.
property	Specifies the property name.

The XSetTextProperty function replaces the existing specified property for the named window with the data, type, format, and number of items determined by the value field, the encoding field, the format field, and the nitems field, respectively, of the specified XTextProperty structure. If the property does not already exist, XSetTextProperty sets it for the specified window.

XSetTextProperty can generate BadAlloc, BadAtom, BadValue, and BadWindow errors.

To read one of a window's text properties, use XGetTextProperty.

```
Status XGetTextProperty (display, w, text_prop_return, property)
    Display *display;
    Window w;
    XTextProperty *text_prop_return;
    Atom property;
```

display	Specifies the connection to the X server.
w	Specifies the window.
text_prop_return	Returns the XTextProperty structure.
property	Specifies the property name.

The XGetTextProperty function reads the specified property from the window and stores the data in the returned XTextProperty structure. It stores the data in the value field, the type of the data in the encoding field, the format of the data in the format field, and the number of items of data in the nitems field. An extra byte containing null (which is not included in the nitems member) is stored at the end of the value field of text_prop_return. The particular interpretation of the property's encoding and data as text is left to the calling application. If the specified property does not exist on the window, XGetTextProperty sets the value field to NULL, the encoding field to None, the format field to zero, and the nitems field to zero.

If it was able to read and store the data in the XTextProperty structure, XGetTextProperty returns a nonzero status; otherwise, it returns a zero status.

XGetTextProperty can generate BadAtom and BadWindow errors.

14.1.4 Setting and Reading the WM_NAME Property

Xlib provides convenience functions that you can use to set and read the WM_NAME property for a given window.

To set a window's WM_NAME property with the supplied convenience function, use `XSetWMName`.

```
void XSetWMName ( display, w, text_prop)
    Display *display;
    Window w;
    XTextProperty *text_prop;
```

display	Specifies the connection to the X server.
w	Specifies the window.
text_prop	Specifies the `XTextProperty` structure to be used.

The `XSetWMName` convenience function calls `XSetTextProperty` to set the WM_NAME property.

To read a window's WM_NAME property with the supplied convenience function, use `XGetWMName`.

```
Status XGetWMName ( display, w, text_prop_return)
    Display *display;
    Window w;
    XTextProperty *text_prop_return;
```

display	Specifies the connection to the X server.
w	Specifies the window.
text_prop_return	Returns the `XTextProperty` structure.

The `XGetWMName` convenience function calls `XGetTextProperty` to obtain the WM_NAME property. It returns nonzero status on success; otherwise, it returns a zero status.

The following two functions have been superseded by `XSetWMName` and `XGetWMName`, respectively. You can use these additional convenience functions for window names that are encoded as STRING properties.

To assign a name to a window, use `XStoreName`.

```
XStoreName ( display, w, window_name)
    Display *display;
```

```
   Window w;
   char *window_name;
```

display Specifies the connection to the X server.

w Specifies the window.

window_name Specifies the window name, which should be a null-terminated string.

The XStoreName function assigns the name passed to window_name to the specified window. A window manager can display the window name in some prominent place, such as the title bar, to allow users to identify windows easily. Some window managers may display a window's name in the window's icon, although they are encouraged to use the window's icon name if one is provided by the application. If the string is not in the Host Portable Character Encoding, the result is implementation dependent.

XStoreName can generate BadAlloc and BadWindow errors.

To get the name of a window, use XFetchName.

```
Status XFetchName(display, w, window_name_return)
   Display *display;
   Window w;
   char **window_name_return;
```

display Specifies the connection to the X server.

w Specifies the window.

window_name_return Returns the window name, which is a null-terminated string.

The XFetchName function returns the name of the specified window. If it succeeds, it returns nonzero; otherwise, no name has been set for the window, and it returns zero. If the WM_NAME property has not been set for this window, XFetchName sets window_name_return to NULL. If the data returned by the server is in the Latin Portable Character Encoding, then the returned string is in the Host Portable Character Encoding. Otherwise, the result is implementation dependent. When finished with it, a client must free the window name string using XFree.

XFetchName can generate a BadWindow error.

14.1.5 Setting and Reading the WM_ICON_NAME Property

Xlib provides convenience functions that you can use to set and read the WM_ICON_NAME property for a given window.

To set a window's WM_ICON_NAME property, use `XSetWMIconName`.

```
void XSetWMIconName ( display, w, text_prop)
    Display *display;
    Window w;
    XTextProperty *text_prop;
```

display	Specifies the connection to the X server.
w	Specifies the window.
text_prop	Specifies the `XTextProperty` structure to be used.

The `XSetWMIconName` convenience function calls `XSetTextProperty` to set the WM_ICON_NAME property.

To read a window's WM_ICON_NAME property, use `XGetWMIconName`.

```
Status XGetWMIconName ( display, w, text_prop_return)
    Display *display;
    Window w;
    XTextProperty *text_prop_return;
```

display	Specifies the connection to the X server.
w	Specifies the window.
text_prop_return	Returns the `XTextProperty` structure.

The `XGetWMIconName` convenience function calls `XGetTextProperty` to obtain the WM_ICON_NAME property. It returns a nonzero status if successful; otherwise, it returns a zero status.

The next two functions have been superseded by `XSetWMIconName` and `XGetWMIconName`, respectively. You can use these additional convenience functions for window names that are encoded as STRING properties.

To set the name to be displayed in a window's icon, use `XSetIconName`.

```
XSetIconName ( display, w, icon_name)
    Display *display;
    Window w;
    char *icon_name;
```

display	Specifies the connection to the X server.
w	Specifies the window.
icon_name	Specifies the icon name, which should be a null-terminated string.

If the string is not in the Host Portable Character Encoding, the result is implementation dependent. `XSetIconName` can generate `BadAlloc` and `BadWindow` errors.

To get the name a window wants displayed in its icon, use `XGetIconName`.

```
Status XGetIconName ( display, w, icon_name_return)
    Display *display;
    Window w;
    char **icon_name_return;
```

display Specifies the connection to the X server.

w Specifies the window.

icon_name_return Returns the window's icon name, which is a null-terminated string.

The `XGetIconName` function returns the name to be displayed in the specified window's icon. If it succeeds, it returns nonzero; otherwise, if no icon name has been set for the window, it returns zero. If you never assigned a name to the window, `XGetIconName` sets icon_name_return to NULL. If the data returned by the server is in the Latin Portable Character Encoding, then the returned string is in the Host Portable Character Encoding. Otherwise, the result is implementation dependent. When finished with it, a client must free the icon name string using `XFree`.

`XGetIconName` can generate a `BadWindow` error.

14.1.6 Setting and Reading the WM_HINTS Property

Xlib provides functions that you can use to set and read the WM_HINTS property for a given window. These functions use the flags and the `XWMHints` structure, as defined in the `<X11/Xutil.h>` header file.

To allocate an `XWMHints` structure, use `XAllocWMHints`.

```
XWMHints *XAllocWMHints ( )
```

The `XAllocWMHints` function allocates and returns a pointer to a `XWMHints` structure. Note that all fields in the `XWMHints` structure are initially set to zero. If insufficient memory is available, `XAllocWMHints` returns NULL. To free the memory allocated to this structure, use `XFree`.

The `XWMHints` structure contains:

```
/* Window manager hints mask bits */
#define InputHint           (1L << 0)
#define StateHint           (1L << 1)
#define IconPixmapHint      (1L << 2)
#define IconWindowHint      (1L << 3)
#define IconPositionHint    (1L << 4)
#define IconMaskHint        (1L << 5)
#define WindowGroupHint     (1L << 6)
#define AllHints            (InputHint|StateHint|IconPixmapHint|
                             IconWindowHint|IconPositionHint|
                             IconMaskHint|WindowGroupHint)

Values /*
typedef struct {
    long flags;               /* marks which fields in this structure are defined */
    Bool input;               /* does this application rely on the window manager to
                                 get keyboard input? */
    int initial_state;        /* see below */
    Pixmap icon_pixmap;       /* pixmap to be used as icon */
    Window icon_window;       /* window to be used as icon */
    int icon_x, icon_y;       /* initial position of icon */
    Pixmap icon_mask;         /* pixmap to be used as mask for icon_pixmap */
    XID window_group;         /* id of related window group */
                              /* this structure may be extended in the future */
} XWMHints;
```

The input member is used to communicate to the window manager the input focus model used by the application. Applications that expect input but never explicitly set focus to any of their subwindows (that is, use the push model of focus management), such as X Version 10 style applications that use real-estate driven focus, should set this member to `True`. Similarly, applications that set input focus to their subwindows only when it is given to their top-level window by a window manager should also set this member to `True`. Applications that manage their own input focus by explicitly setting focus to one of their subwindows whenever they want keyboard input (that is, use the pull model of focus management) should set this member to `False`. Applications that never expect any keyboard input also should set this member to `False`.

Pull model window managers should make it possible for push model applications to get input by setting input focus to the top-level windows of applications whose input member is `True`. Push model window managers should make sure that pull model applications do not break them by resetting input focus to `PointerRoot` when it is appropriate (for example, whenever an application whose input member is `False` sets input focus to one of its subwindows).

The definitions for the initial_state flag are:

```
#define WithdrawnState    0
#define NormalState       1    /* most applications start this way */
#define IconicState       3    /* application wants to start as an icon */
```

The icon_mask specifies which pixels of the icon_pixmap should be used as the icon. This allows for nonrectangular icons. Both icon_pixmap and icon_mask must be bitmaps. The icon_window lets an application provide a window for use as an icon for window managers that support such use. The window_group lets you specify that this window belongs to a group of other windows. For example, if a single application manipulates multiple top-level windows, this allows you to provide enough information that a window manager can iconify all of the windows rather than just the one window.

To set a window's WM_HINTS property, use `XSetWMHints`.

```
XSetWMHints(display, w, wmhints)
    Display *display;
    Window w;
    XWMHints *wmhints;
```

display Specifies the connection to the X server.

w Specifies the window.

wmhints Specifies the `XWMHints` structure to be used.

The `XSetWMHints` function sets the window manager hints that include icon information and location, the initial state of the window, and whether the application relies on the window manager to get keyboard input.

`XSetWMHints` can generate `BadAlloc` and `BadWindow` errors.

To read a window's WM_HINTS property, use `XGetWMHints`.

```
XWMHints *XGetWMHints(display, w)
    Display *display;
```

```
    Window w;
display  Specifies the connection to the X server.
w        Specifies the window.
```

The `XGetWMHints` function reads the window manager hints and returns NULL if no WM_HINTS property was set on the window or returns a pointer to a `XWMHints` structure if it succeeds. When finished with the data, free the space used for it by calling `XFree`.

`XGetWMHints` can generate a `BadWindow` error.

14.1.7 Setting and Reading the WM_NORMAL_HINTS Property

Xlib provides functions that you can use to set or read the WM_NORMAL_HINTS property for a given window. The functions use the flags and the `XSizeHints` structure, as defined in the `<X11/Xutil.h>` header file.

To allocate an `XSizeHints` structure, use `XAllocSizeHints`.

```
XSizeHints *XAllocSizeHints( )
```

The `XAllocSizeHints` function allocates and returns a pointer to a `XSizeHints` structure. Note that all fields in the `XSizeHints` structure are initially set to zero. If insufficient memory is available, `XAllocSizeHints` returns NULL. To free the memory allocated to this structure, use `XFree`.

The `XSizeHints` structure contains:

```
/* Size hints mask bits */
#define USPosition   (1L << 0)   /* user specified x, y */
#define USSize       (1L << 1)   /* user specified width, height */
#define PPosition    (1L << 2)   /* program specified position */
#define PSize        (1L << 3)   /* program specified size */
#define PMinSize     (1L << 4)   /* program specified minimum size */
#define PMaxSize     (1L << 5)   /* program specified maximum size */
#define PResizeInc   (1L << 6)   /* program specified resize increments */
#define PAspect      (1L << 7)   /* program specified min and max aspect
                                    ratios */
#define PBaseSize    (1L << 8)
```

```
#define PWinGravity    (1L<<9)
#define PAllHints      (PPosition|PSize|PMinSize|PMaxSize|
                        PResizeInc|PAspect)

/* Values */
typedef struct {
    long flags;                    /* marks which fields in this structure are defined */
    int x, y;                      /* Obsolete */
    int width, height;             /* Obsolete */
    int min_width, min_height;
    int max_width, max_height;
    int width_inc, height_inc;
    struct {
        int x;                     /* numerator */
        int y;                     /* denominator */
    } min_aspect, max_aspect;
    int base_width, base_height;
    int win_gravity;
} XSizeHints;
```

The x, y, width, and height members are now obsolete and are left solely for compatibility reasons. The min_width and min_height members specify the minimum window size that still allows the application to be useful. The max_width and max_height members specify the maximum window size. The width_inc and height_inc members define an arithmetic progression of sizes (minimum to maximum) into which the window prefers to be resized. The min_aspect and max_aspect members are expressed as ratios of x and y, and they allow an application to specify the range of aspect ratios it prefers. The base_width and base_height members define the desired size of the window. The window manager will interpret the position of the window and its border width to position the point of the outer rectangle of the overall window specified by the win_gravity member. The outer rectangle of the window includes any borders or decorations supplied by the window manager. In other words, if the window manager decides to place the window where the client asked, the position on the parent window's border named by the win_gravity will be placed where the client window would have been placed in the absence of a window manager.

Note that use of the PAllHints macro is highly discouraged.

To set a window's WM_NORMAL_HINTS property, use `XSetWMNormalHints`.

```
void XSetWMNormalHints ( display, w, hints)
    Display *display;
    Window w;
    XSizeHints *hints;
```

display	Specifies the connection to the X server.
w	Specifies the window.
hints	Specifies the size hints for the window in its normal state.

The `XSetWMNormalHints` function replaces the size hints for the WM_NORMAL_HINTS property on the specified window. If the property does not already exist, `XSetWMNormalHints` sets the size hints for the WM_NORMAL_HINTS property on the specified window. The property is stored with a type of WM_SIZE_HINTS and a format of 32.

`XSetWMNormalHints` can generate `BadAlloc` and `BadWindow` errors.

To read a window's WM_NORMAL_HINTS property, use `XGetWMNormalHints`.

```
Status XGetWMNormalHints ( display, w, hints_return, supplied_return)
    Display *display;
    Window w;
    XSizeHints *hints_return;
    long *supplied_return;
```

display	Specifies the connection to the X server.
w	Specifies the window.
hints_return	Returns the size hints for the window in its normal state.
supplied_return	Returns the hints that were supplied by the user.

The `XGetWMNormalHints` function returns the size hints stored in the WM_NORMAL_HINTS property on the specified window. If the property is of type WM_SIZE_HINTS, is of format 32, and is long enough to contain either an old (pre-ICCCM) or new size hints structure, `XGetWMNormalHints` sets the various fields of the `XSizeHints` structure, sets the supplied_return argument to the list of fields that were supplied by the user (whether or not they contained defined values), and returns a nonzero status. Otherwise, it returns a zero status.

If `XGetWMNormalHints` returns successfully and a pre-ICCCM size hints property is read, the supplied_return argument will contain the following bits:

```
(USPosition|USSize|PPosition|PSize|PMinSize|
 PMaxSize|PResizeInc|PAspect)
```

If the property is large enough to contain the base size and window gravity fields as well, the supplied_return argument will also contain the following bits:

```
PBaseSize|PWinGravity
```

`XGetWMNormalHints` can generate a `BadWindow` error.

To set a window's WM_SIZE_HINTS property, use `XSetWMSizeHints`.

void XSetWMSizeHints (*display, w, hints, property*)
Display **display*;
Window *w*;
XSizeHints **hints*;
Atom *property*;

display	Specifies the connection to the X server.
w	Specifies the window.
hints	Specifies the `XSizeHints` structure to be used.
property	Specifies the property name.

The `XSetWMSizeHints` function replaces the size hints for the specified property on the named window. If the specified property does not already exist, `XSetWMSizeHints` sets the size hints for the specified property on the named window. The property is stored with a type of WM_SIZE_HINTS and a format of 32. To set a window's normal size hints, you can use the `XSetWMNormalHints` function.

`XSetWMSizeHints` can generate `BadAlloc`, `BadAtom`, and `BadWindow` errors.

To read a window's WM_SIZE_HINTS property, use `XGetWMSizeHints`.

Status XGetWMSizeHints (*display, w, hints_return, supplied_return, property*)
Display **display*;
Window *w*;
XSizeHints **hints_return*;
long **supplied_return*;
Atom *property*;

display	Specifies the connection to the X server.
w	Specifies the window.
hints_return	Returns the XSizeHints structure.
supplied_return	Returns the hints that were supplied by the user.
property	Specifies the property name.

The XGetWMSizeHints function returns the size hints stored in the specified property on the named window. If the property is of type WM_SIZE_HINTS, is of format 32, and is long enough to contain either an old (pre-ICCCM) or new size hints structure, XGetWMSizeHints sets the various fields of the XSizeHints structure, sets the supplied_return argument to the list of fields that were supplied by the user (whether or not they contained defined values), and returns a nonzero status. Otherwise, it returns a zero status. To get a window's normal size hints, you can use the XGetWMNormalHints function.

If XGetWMSizeHints returns successfully and a pre-ICCCM size hints property is read, the supplied_return argument will contain the following bits:

```
(USPosition|USSize|PPosition|PSize|PMinSize|
 PMaxSize|PResizeInc|PAspect)
```

If the property is large enough to contain the base size and window gravity fields as well, the supplied_return argument will also contain the following bits:

```
PBaseSize|PWinGravity
```

XGetWMSizeHints can generate BadAtom and BadWindow errors.

14.1.8 Setting and Reading the WM_CLASS Property

Xlib provides functions that you can use to set and get the WM_CLASS property for a given window. These functions use the XClassHint structure, which is defined in the <X11/Xutil.h> header file.

To allocate an XClassHint structure, use XAllocClassHint.

```
XClassHint *XAllocClassHint( )
```

The XAllocClassHint function allocates and returns a pointer to a XClassHint structure. Note that the pointer fields in the XClassHint structure are initially set to NULL. If insufficient memory is available, `XAllocClassHint` returns NULL. To free the memory allocated to this structure, use `XFree`.

The `XClassHint` contains:

```
typedef struct {
    char *res_name;
    char *res_class;
} XClassHint;
```

The res_name member contains the application name, and the res_class member contains the application class. Note that the name set in this property may differ from the name set as WM_NAME. That is, WM_NAME specifies what should be displayed in the title bar and, therefore, can contain temporal information (for example, the name of a file currently in an editor's buffer). On the other hand, the name specified as part of WM_CLASS is the formal name of the application that should be used when retrieving the application's resources from the resource database.

To set a window's WM_CLASS property, use `XSetClassHint`.

```
XSetClassHint(display, w, class_hints)
    Display *display;
    Window w;
    XClassHint *class_hints;
```

display Specifies the connection to the X server.

w Specifies the window.

class_hints Specifies the `XClassHint` structure that is to be used.

The `XSetClassHint` function sets the class hint for the specified window. If the strings are not in the Host Portable Character Encoding, the result is implementation dependent.

`XSetClassHint` can generate `BadAlloc` and `BadWindow` errors.

To read a window's WM_CLASS property, use `XGetClassHint`.

```
Status XGetClassHint(display, w, class_hints_return)
    Display *display;
    Window w;
    XClassHint *class_hints_return;
```

display	Specifies the connection to the X server.
w	Specifies the window.
class_hints_return	Returns the XClassHint structure.

The XGetClassHint function returns the class hint of the specified window to the members of the supplied structure. If the data returned by the server is in the Latin Portable Character Encoding, then the returned strings are in the Host Portable Character Encoding. Otherwise, the result is implementation dependent. It returns a nonzero status if successful; otherwise, it returns a zero status. To free res_name and res_class when finished with the strings, use XFree on each individually.

XGetClassHint can generate a BadWindow error.

14.1.9 Setting and Reading the WM_TRANSIENT_FOR Property

Xlib provides functions that you can use to set and read the WM_TRANSIENT_FOR property for a given window.

To set a window's WM_TRANSIENT_FOR property, use XSetTransient-ForHint.

```
XSetTransientForHint(display, w, prop_window)
    Display *display;
    Window w;
    Window prop_window;
```

display	Specifies the connection to the X server.
w	Specifies the window.
prop_window	Specifies the window that the WM_TRANSIENT_FOR property is to be set to.

The XSetTransientForHint function sets the WM_TRANSIENT_FOR property of the specified window to the specified prop_window.

XSetTransientForHint can generate BadAlloc and BadWindow errors.

To read a window's WM_TRANSIENT_FOR property, use XGetTransient-ForHint.

```
Status XGetTransientForHint(display, w, prop_window_return)
    Display *display;
    Window w;
    Window *prop_window_return;
```

display	Specifies the connection to the X server.
w	Specifies the window.
prop_window_return	Returns the WM_TRANSIENT_FOR property of the specified window.

The `XGetTransientForHint` function returns the WM_TRANSIENT_FOR property for the specified window. It returns a nonzero status if successful; otherwise, it returns a zero status.

`XGetTransientForHint` can generate a `BadWindow` error.

14.1.10 Setting and Reading the WM_PROTOCOLS Property

Xlib provides functions that you can use to set and read the WM_PROTOCOLS property for a given window.

To set a window's WM_PROTOCOLS property, use `XSetWMProtocols`.

```
Status XSetWMProtocols ( display, w, protocols, count)
    Display *display;
    Window w;
    Atom *protocols;
    int count;
```

display	Specifies the connection to the X server.
w	Specifies the window.
protocols	Specifies the list of protocols.
count	Specifies the number of protocols in the list.

The `XSetWMProtocols` function replaces the WM_PROTOCOLS property on the specified window with the list of atoms specified by the protocols argument. If the property does not already exist, `XSetWMProtocols` sets the WM_PROTOCOLS property on the specified window to the list of atoms specified by the protocols argument. The property is stored with a type of ATOM and a format of 32. If it cannot intern the WM_PROTOCOLS atom, `XSetWMProtocols` returns a zero status. Otherwise, it returns a nonzero status.

`XSetWMProtocols` can generate `BadAlloc` and `BadWindow` errors.

To read a window's WM_PROTOCOLS property, use `XGetWMProtocols`.

```
Status XGetWMProtocols ( display, w, protocols_return, count_return)
    Display *display;
    Window w;
```

```
   Atom **protocols_return;
   int *count_return;
```

display	Specifies the connection to the X server.
w	Specifies the window.
protocols_return	Returns the list of protocols.
count_return	Returns the number of protocols in the list.

The `XGetWMProtocols` function returns the list of atoms stored in the WM_PROTOCOLS property on the specified window. These atoms describe window manager protocols in which the owner of this window is willing to participate. If the property exists, is of type ATOM, is of format 32, and the atom WM_PROTOCOLS can be interned, `XGetWMProtocols` sets the protocols_return argument to a list of atoms, sets the count_return argument to the number of elements in the list, and returns a nonzero status. Otherwise, it sets neither of the return arguments and returns a zero status. To release the list of atoms, use `XFree`.

`XGetWMProtocols` can generate a `BadWindow` error.

14.1.11 Setting and Reading the WM_COLORMAP_WINDOWS Property

Xlib provides functions that you can use to set and read the WM_COLORMAP_WINDOWS property for a given window.

To set a window's WM_COLORMAP_WINDOWS property, use `XSetWMColormapWindows`.

```
Status XSetWMColormapWindows(display, w, colormap_windows, count)
   Display *display;
   Window w;
   Window *colormap_windows;
   int count;
```

display	Specifies the connection to the X server.
w	Specifies the window.
colormap_windows	Specifies the list of windows.
count	Specifies the number of windows in the list.

The `XSetWMColormapWindows` function replaces the WM_COLORMAP_WINDOWS property on the specified window with the list of windows specified by the colormap_windows argument. It the property does not already exist, XSetWMColormapWindows sets the WM_COLORMAP_WINDOWS property on the specified window to the list of windows specified by the colormap_windows argument. The property is stored with a type of WINDOW and a format of 32. If it cannot intern the WM_COLORMAP_WINDOWS atom, XSetWMColormapWindows returns a zero status. Otherwise, it returns a nonzero status.

XSetWMColormapWindows can generate BadAlloc and BadWindow errors.

To read a window's WM_COLORMAP_WINDOWS property, use XGetWMColormapWindows.

```
Status XGetWMColormapWindows(display, w, colormap_windows_return, count_return)
    Display *display;
    Window w;
    Window **colormap_windows_return;
    int *count_return;
```

display	Specifies the connection to the X server.
w	Specifies the window.
colormap_windows_return	Returns the list of windows.
count_return	Returns the number of windows in the list.

The XGetWMColormapWindows function returns the list of window identifiers stored in the WM_COLORMAP_WINDOWS property on the specified window. These identifiers indicate the colormaps that the window manager may need to install for this window. If the property exists, is of type WINDOW, is of format 32, and the atom WM_COLORMAP_WINDOWS can be interned, XGetWMColormapWindows sets the windows_return argument to a list of window identifiers, sets the count_return argument to the number of elements in the list, and returns a nonzero status. Otherwise, it sets neither of the return arguments and returns a zero status. To release the list of window identifiers, use XFree.

XGetWMColormapWindows can generate a BadWindow error.

14.1.12 Setting and Reading the WM_ICON_SIZE Property

Xlib provides functions that you can use to set and read the WM_ICON_SIZE property for a given window. These functions use the XIconSize structure, which is defined in the <X11/Xutil.h> header file.

To allocate an XIconSize structure, use XAllocIconSize.

```
XIconSize *XAllocIconSize ( )
```

The XAllocIconSize function allocates and returns a pointer to a XIconSize structure. Note that all fields in the XIconSize structure are initially set to zero. If insufficient memory is available, XAllocIconSize returns NULL. To free the memory allocated to this structure, use XFree.

The XIconSize structure contains:

```
typedef struct {
     int min_width, min_height;
     int max_width, max_height;
     int width_inc, height_inc;
} XIconSize;
```

The width_inc and height_inc members define an arithmetic progression of sizes (minimum to maximum) that represent the supported icon sizes.

To set a window's WM_ICON_SIZE property, use XSetIconSizes.

```
XSetIconSizes ( display, w, size_list, count)
   Display *display;
   Window w;
   XIconSize *size_list;
   int count;
```

display Specifies the connection to the X server.
w Specifies the window.
size_list Specifies the size list.
count Specifies the number of items in the size list.

The XSetIconSizes function is used only by window managers to set the supported icon sizes.

XSetIconSizes can generate BadAlloc and BadWindow errors.

To read a window's WM_ICON_SIZE property, use XGetIconSizes.

```
Status XGetIconSizes ( display, w, size_list_return, count_return)
   Display *display;
```

```
Window w;
XIconSize **size_list_return;
int *count_return;
```

display Specifies the connection to the X server.
w Specifies the window.
size_list_return Returns the size list.
count_return Returns the number of items in the size list.

The `XGetIconSizes` function returns zero if a window manager has not set icon sizes; otherwise, it return nonzero. `XGetIconSizes` should be called by an application that wants to find out what icon sizes would be most appreciated by the window manager under which the application is running. The application should then use `XSetWMHints` to supply the window manager with an icon pixmap or window in one of the supported sizes. To free the data allocated in size_list_return, use `XFree`.

`XGetIconSizes` can generate a `BadWindow` error.

14.1.13 Using Window Manager Convenience Functions

The `XmbSetWMProperties` function stores the standard set of window manager properties, with text properties in standard encodings for internationalized text communication. The standard window manager properties for a given window are WM_NAME, WM_ICON_NAME, WM_HINTS, WM_NORMAL_HINTS, WM_CLASS, WM_COMMAND, WM_CLIENT_MACHINE, and WM_LOCALE_NAME.

```
void XmbSetWMProperties(display, w, window_name, icon_name, argv, argc,
                        normal_hints, wm_hints, class_hints)
    Display *display;
    Window w;
    char *window_name;
    char *icon_name;
    char *argv[];
    int argc;
    XSizeHints *normal_hints;
    XWMHints *wm_hints;
    XClassHint *class_hints;
```

display Specifies the connection to the X server.
w Specifies the window.
window_name Specifies the window name, which should be a null-terminated string.

icon_name	Specifies the icon name, which should be a null-terminated string.
argv	Specifies the application's argument list.
argc	Specifies the number of arguments.
hints	Specifies the size hints for the window in its normal state.
wm_hints	Specifies the `XWMHints` structure to be used.
class_hints	Specifies the `XClassHint` structure to be used.

The `XmbSetWMProperties` convenience function provides a simple programming interface for setting those essential window properties that are used for communicating with other clients (particularly window and session managers).

If the window_name argument is non-NULL, `XmbSetWMProperties` sets the WM_NAME property. If the icon_name argument is non-NULL, `XmbSetWMProperties` sets the WM_ICON_NAME property. The window_name and icon_name arguments are null-terminated strings in the encoding of the current locale. If the arguments can be fully converted to the STRING encoding, the properties are created with type "STRING"; otherwise, the arguments are converted to Compound Text, and the properties are created with type "COMPOUND_TEXT".

If the normal_hints argument is non-NULL, `XmbSetWMProperties` calls `XSetWMNormalHints`, which sets the WM_NORMAL_HINTS property (see section 14.1.7). If the wm_hints argument is non-NULL, `XmbSetWMProperties` calls `XSetWMHints`, which sets the WM_HINTS property (see section 14.1.6).

If the argv argument is non-NULL, `XmbSetWMProperties` sets the WM_COMMAND property from argv and argc. An argc of zero indicates a zero-length command.

The hostname of the machine is stored using `XSetWMClientMachine` (see section 14.2.2).

If the class_hints argument is non-NULL, `XmbSetWMProperties` sets the WM_CLASS property. If the res_name member in the `XClassHint` structure is set to the NULL pointer and the RESOURCE_NAME environment variable is set, the value of the environment variable is substituted for res_name. If the res_name member is NULL, the environment variable is not set, and argv and argv[0] are set, then the value of argv[0], stripped of any directory prefixes, is substituted for res_name.

It is assumed that the supplied class_hints.res_name and argv, the RESOURCE_NAME environment variable, and the hostname of the machine are in the encoding of the locale announced for the LC_CTYPE category (on POSIX-compliant systems, the LC_CTYPE, else LANG environment variable). The corresponding WM_CLASS, WM_COMMAND, and WM_CLIENT_MACHINE properties are typed according to the local host locale announcer. No encoding conversion is performed prior to storage in the properties.

For clients that need to process the property text in a locale, `XmbSetWMProperties` sets the WM_LOCALE_NAME property to be the name of the current locale. The name is assumed to be in the Host Portable Character Encoding and is converted to STRING for storage in the property.

`XmbSetWMProperties` can generate `BadAlloc` and `BadWindow` errors.

To set a window's standard window manager properties with strings in the STRING encoding, use `XSetWMProperties`. The standard window manager properties for a given window are WM_NAME, WM_ICON_NAME, WM_HINTS, WM_NORMAL_HINTS, WM_CLASS, WM_COMMAND, and WM_CLIENT_MACHINE.

```
void XSetWMProperties ( display, w, window_name, icon_name, argv, argc, normal_hints,
                        wm_hints, class_hints)
    Display *display;
    Window w;
    XTextProperty *window_name;
    XTextProperty *icon_name;
    char **argv;
    int argc;
    XSizeHints *normal_hints;
    XWMHints *wm_hints;
    XClassHint *class_hints;
```

display	Specifies the connection to the X server.
w	Specifies the window.
window_name	Specifies the window name, which should be a null-terminated string.
icon_name	Specifies the icon name, which should be a null-terminated string.
argv	Specifies the application's argument list.
argc	Specifies the number of arguments.
normal_hints	Specifies the size hints for the window in its normal state.
wm_hints	Specifies the `XWMHints` structure to be used.
class_hints	Specifies the `XClassHint` structure to be used.

The XSetWMProperties convenience function provides a single programming interface for setting those essential window properties that are used for communicating with other clients (particularly window and session managers).

If the window_name argument is non-NULL, XSetWMProperties calls XSetWMName, which in turn sets the WM_NAME property (see section 14.1.4). If the icon_name argument is non-NULL, XSetWMProperties calls XSetWMIconName, which sets the WM_ICON_NAME property (see section 14.1.5). If the argv argument is non-NULL, XSetWMProperties calls XSetCommand, which sets the WM_COMMAND property (see section 14.2.1). Note that an argc of zero is allowed to indicate a zero-length command. Note also that the hostname of this machine is stored using XSetWMClientMachine (see section 14.2.2).

If the normal_hints argument is non-NULL, XSetWMProperties calls XSetWMNormalHints, which sets the WM_NORMAL_HINTS property (see section 14.1.7). If the wm_hints argument is non-NULL, XSetWMProperties calls XSetWMHints, which sets the WM_HINTS property (see section 14.1.6).

If the class_hints argument is non-NULL, XSetWMProperties calls XSetClassHint, which sets the WM_CLASS property (see section 14.1.8). If the res_name member in the XClassHint structure is set to the NULL pointer and the RESOURCE_NAME environment variable is set, then the value of the environment variable is substituted for res_name. If the res_name member is NULL, the environment variable is not set, and argv and argv[0] are set, then the value of argv[0], stripped of any directory prefixes, is substituted for res_name.

XSetWMProperties can generate BadAlloc and BadWindow errors.

14.2 Client to Session Manager Communication

This section discusses how to:

- Set and read the WM_COMMAND property
- Set and read the WM_CLIENT_MACHINE property

14.2.1 Setting and Reading the WM_COMMAND Property

Xlib provides functions that you can use to set and read the WM_COMMAND property for a given window.

To set a window's WM_COMMAND property, use `XSetCommand`.

```
XSetCommand ( display, w, argv, argc)
   Display *display;
   Window w;
   char **argv;
   int argc;
```

display Specifies the connection to the X server.
w Specifies the window.
argv Specifies the application's argument list.
argc Specifies the number of arguments.

The `XSetCommand` function sets the command and arguments used to invoke the application. (Typically, argv is the argv array of your main program.) If the strings are not in the Host Portable Character Encoding, the result is implementation dependent.

`XSetCommand` can generate `BadAlloc` and `BadWindow` errors.

To read a window's WM_COMMAND property, use `XGetCommand`.

```
Status XGetCommand ( display, w, argv_return, argc_return)
   Display *display;
   Window w;
   char ***argv_return;
   int *argc_return;
```

display Specifies the connection to the X server.
w Specifies the window.
argv_return Returns the application's argument list.
argc_return Returns the number of arguments returned.

The `XGetCommand` function reads the WM_COMMAND property from the specified window and returns a string list. If the WM_COMMAND property exists, it is of type STRING and format 8. If sufficient memory can be allocated to contain the string list, `XGetCommand` fills in the argv_return and argc_return arguments and returns a nonzero status. Otherwise, it returns a zero status. If the data returned by the server is in the Latin Portable Character Encoding, then the returned strings are in the Host Portable Character Encoding. Otherwise, the result is implementation dependent. To free the memory allocated to the string list, use `XFreeStringList`.

14.2.2 Setting and Reading the WM_CLIENT_MACHINE Property

Xlib provides functions that you can use to set and read the WM_CLIENT_MACHINE property for a given window.

To set a window's WM_CLIENT_MACHINE property, use `XSetWMClientMachine`.

```
void XSetWMClientMachine ( display, w, text_prop)
    Display *display;
    Window w;
    XTextProperty *text_prop;
```

display Specifies the connection to the X server.

w Specifies the window.

text_prop Specifies the `XTextProperty` structure to be used.

The `XSetWMClientMachine` convenience function calls `XSetTextProperty` to set the WM_CLIENT_MACHINE property.

To read a window's WM_CLIENT_MACHINE property, use `XGetWMClientMachine`.

```
Status XGetWMClientMachine ( display, w, text_prop_return)
    Display *display;
    Window w;
    XTextProperty *text_prop_return;
```

display Specifies the connection to the X server.

w Specifies the window.

text_prop_return Returns the `XTextProperty` structure.

The `XGetWMClientMachine` convenience function performs an `XGetTextProperty` on the WM_CLIENT_MACHINE property. It returns a nonzero status if successful; otherwise, it returns a zero status.

14.3 Standard Colormaps

Applications with color palettes, smooth-shaded drawings, or digitized images demand large numbers of colors. In addition, these applications often require an efficient mapping from color triples to pixel values that display the appropriate colors.

As an example, consider a three-dimensional display program that wants to draw a smoothly shaded sphere. At each pixel in the image of the sphere, the program computes the intensity and color of light reflected back to the viewer. The result of each computation is a triple of RGB coefficients in the range 0.0 to 1.0. To draw the sphere, the program needs a colormap that provides a large range of uniformly distributed colors. The colormap should be arranged so that the program can convert its RGB triples into pixel values very quickly, because drawing the entire sphere requires many such conversions.

On many current workstations, the display is limited to 256 or fewer colors. Applications must allocate colors carefully, not only to make sure they cover the entire range they need but also to make use of as many of the available colors as possible. On a typical X display, many applications are active at once. Most workstations have only one hardware look-up table for colors, so only one application colormap can be installed at a given time. The application using the installed colormap is displayed correctly, and the other applications go technicolor and are displayed with false colors.

As another example, consider a user who is running an image processing program to display earth-resources data. The image processing program needs a colormap set up with 8 reds, 8 greens, and 4 blues, for a total of 256 colors. Because some colors are already in use in the default colormap, the image processing program allocates and installs a new colormap.

The user decides to alter some of the colors in the image by invoking a color palette program to mix and choose colors. The color palette program also needs a colormap with eight reds, eight greens, and four blues, so just like the image processing program, it must allocate and install a new colormap.

Because only one colormap can be installed at a time, the color palette may be displayed incorrectly whenever the image processing program is active. Conversely, whenever the palette program is active, the image may be displayed incorrectly. The user can never match or compare colors in the palette and image. Contention for colormap resources can be reduced if applications with similar color needs share colormaps.

The image processing program and the color palette program could share the same colormap if there existed a convention that described how the colormap was set up. Whenever either program was active, both would be displayed correctly.

The standard colormap properties define a set of commonly used colormaps. Applications that share these colormaps and conventions display true colors more often and provide a better interface to the user.

Standard colormaps allow applications to share commonly used color resources. This allows many applications to be displayed in true colors simultaneously, even when each application needs an entirely filled colormap.

Several standard colormaps are described in this section. Usually, a window manager creates these colormaps. Applications should use the standard colormaps if they already exist.

To allocate an `XStandardColormap` structure, use `XAllocStandardColormap`.

```
XStandardColormap *XAllocStandardColormap ( )
```

The `XAllocStandardColormap` function allocates and returns a pointer to a `XStandardColormap` structure. Note that all fields in the `XStandardColormap` structure are initially set to zero. If insufficient memory is available, `XAllocStandardColormap` returns NULL. To free the memory allocated to this structure, use `XFree`.

The `XStandardColormap` structure contains:

```
/* Hints */
#define ReleaseByFreeingColormap    ( (XID) 1L)
/* Values */
typedef struct {
    Colormap colormap;
    unsigned long red_max;
    unsigned long red_mult;
    unsigned long green_max;
    unsigned long green_mult;
    unsigned long blue_max;
    unsigned long blue_mult;
    unsigned long base_pixel;
    VisualID visualid;
    XID killid;
} XStandardColormap;
```

The colormap member is the colormap created by the XCreateColormap function. The red_max, green_max, and blue_max members give the maximum red, green, and blue values, respectively. Each color coefficient ranges from zero to its max, inclusive. For example, a common colormap allocation is 3/3/2 (3 planes for red, 3 planes for green, and 2 planes for blue). This colormap would have red_max = 7, green_max = 7, and blue_max = 3. An alternate allocation that uses only 216 colors is red_max = 5, green_max = 5, and blue_max = 5.

The red_mult, green_mult, and blue_mult members give the scale factors used to compose a full pixel value. (See the discussion of the base_pixel members for further information.) For a 3/3/2 allocation, red_mult might be 32, green_mult might be 4, and blue_mult might be 1. For a 6-colors-each allocation, red_mult might be 36, green_mult might be 6, and blue_mult might be 1.

The base_pixel member gives the base pixel value used to compose a full pixel value. Usually, the base_pixel is obtained from a call to the XAllocColorPlanes function. Given integer red, green, and blue coefficients in their appropriate ranges, one then can compute a corresponding pixel value by using the following expression:

(r * red_mult + g * green_mult + b * blue_mult + base_pixel) & 0xFFFFFFFF

For GrayScale colormaps, only the colormap, red_max, red_mult, and base_pixel members are defined. The other members are ignored. To compute a GrayScale pixel value, use the following expression:

(gray * red_mult + base_pixel) & 0xFFFFFFFF

Negative multipliers can be represented by converting the 2's complement representation of the multiplier into an unsigned long and storing the result in the appropriate _mult field. The step of masking by 0xFFFFFFFF effectively converts the resulting positive multiplier into a negative one. The masking step will take place automatically on many machine architectures, depending on the size of the integer type used to do the computation,

The visualid member gives the ID number of the visual from which the colormap was created. The killid member gives a resource ID that indicates whether the cells held by this standard colormap are to be released by freeing the colormap ID or by calling the `XKillClient` function on the indicated resource. (Note that this method is necessary for allocating out of an existing colormap.)

The properties containing the `XStandardColormap` information have the type RGB_COLOR_MAP.

The remainder of this section discusses standard colormap properties and atoms as well as how to manipulate standard colormaps.

14.3.1 Standard Colormap Properties and Atoms

Several standard colormaps are available. Each standard colormap is defined by a property, and each such property is identified by an atom. The following list names the atoms and describes the colormap associated with each one. The `<X11/Xatom.h>` header file contains the definitions for each of the following atoms, which are prefixed with XA_.

RGB_DEFAULT_MAP
This atom names a property. The value of the property is an array of `XStandardColormap` structures. Each entry in the array describes an RGB subset of the default color map for the Visual specified by visual_id.

Some applications only need a few RGB colors and may be able to allocate them from the system default colormap. This is the ideal situation because the fewer colormaps that are active in the system the more applications are displayed with correct colors at all times.

A typical allocation for the RGB_DEFAULT_MAP on 8-plane displays is 6 reds, 6 greens, and 6 blues. This gives 216 uniformly distributed colors (6 intensities of 36 different hues) and still leaves 40 elements of a 256-element colormap available for special-purpose colors for text, borders, and so on.

RGB_BEST_MAP
This atom names a property. The value of the property is an `XStandardColormap`.

The property defines the best RGB colormap available on the screen. (Of course, this is a subjective evaluation.) Many image processing and three-dimensional applications need to use all available colormap cells and to distribute as many perceptually distinct colors as possible over those cells. This implies that there may be more green values available than red, as well as more green or red than blue.

For an 8-plane `PseudoColor` visual, RGB_BEST_MAP is likely to be a 3/3/2 allocation. For a 24-plane `DirectColor` visual, RGB_BEST_MAP is normally an 8/8/8 allocation.

RGB_RED_MAP
RGB_GREEN_MAP
RGB_BLUE_MAP
These atoms name properties. The value of each property is an `XStandardColormap`.

The properties define all-red, all-green, and all-blue colormaps, respectively. These maps are used by applications that want to make color-separated images. For example, a user might generate a full-color image on an 8-plane display both by rendering an image three times (once with high color resolution in red, once with green, and once with blue) and by multiply-exposing a single frame in a camera.

RGB_GRAY_MAP
This atom names a property. The value of the property is an `XStandardColormap`.

The property describes the best `GrayScale` colormap available on the screen. As previously mentioned, only the colormap, red_max, red_mult, and base_pixel members of the `XStandardColormap` structure are used for `GrayScale` colormaps.

14.3.2 Setting and Obtaining Standard Colormaps

Xlib provides functions that you can use to set and obtain an `XStandardColormap` structure.

To set an `XStandardColormap` structure, use `XSetRGBColormaps`.

```
void XSetRGBColormaps ( display, w, std_colormap, count, property)
    Display *display;
    Window w;
    XStandardColormap *std_colormap;
    int count;
    Atom property;
```

display	Specifies the connection to the X server.
w	Specifies the window.
std_colormap	Specifies the `XStandardColormap` structure to be used.
count	Specifies the number of colormaps.
property	Specifies the property name.

The `XSetRGBColormaps` function replaces the RGB colormap definition in the specified property on the named window. If the property does not already exist, `XSetRGBColormaps` sets the RGB colormap definition in the specified property on the named window. The property is stored with a type of RGB_COLOR_MAP and a format of 32. Note that it is the caller's responsibility to honor the ICCCM restriction that only RGB_DEFAULT_MAP contain more than one definition.

The `XSetRGBColormaps` function usually is only used by window or session managers. To create a standard colormap, follow this procedure:

1. Open a new connection to the same server.
2. Grab the server.
3. See if the property is on the property list of the root window for the screen.
4. If the desired property is not present:

- Create a colormap (unless you are using the default colormap of the screen).
- Determine the color characteristics of the visual.
- Call `XAllocColorPlanes` or `XAllocColorCells` to allocate cells in the colormap.
- Call `XStoreColors` to store appropriate color values in the colormap.
- Fill in the descriptive members in the `XStandardColormap` structure.
- Attach the property to the root window.
- Use `XSetCloseDownMode` to make the resource permanent.

5. Ungrab the server.

`XSetRGBColormaps` can generate `BadAlloc`, `BadAtom`, and `BadWindow` errors.

To obtain the `XStandardColormap` structure associated with the specified property, use `XGetRGBColormaps`.

```
Status XGetRGBColormaps(display, w, std_colormap_return, count_return, property)
    Display *display;
    Window w;
    XStandardColormap **std_colormap_return;
    int *count_return;
    Atom property;
```

display	Specifies the connection to the X server.
w	Specifies the window.
std_colormap_return	Returns the XStandardColormap structure.
count_return	Returns the number of colormaps.
property	Specifies the property name.

The XGetRGBColormaps function returns the RGB colormap definitions stored in the specified property on the named window. If the property exists, is of type RGB_COLOR_MAP, is of format 32, and is long enough to contain a colormap definition, XGetRGBColormaps allocates and fills in space for the returned colormaps and returns a nonzero status. If the visualid is not present, XGetRGBColormaps assumes the default visual for the screen on which the window is located; if the killid is not present, None is assumed, which indicates that the resources cannot be released. Otherwise, none of the fields are set, and XGetRGBColormaps returns a zero status. Note that it is the caller's responsibility to honor the ICCCM restriction that only RGB_DEFAULT_MAP contain more than one definition.

XGetRGBColormaps can generate BadAtom and BadWindow errors.

Chapter 15

Resource Manager Functions

A program often needs a variety of options in the X environment (for example, fonts, colors, icons, and cursors). Specifying all of these options on the command line is awkward because users may want to customize many aspects of the program and need a convenient way to establish these customizations as the default settings. The resource manager is provided for this purpose. Resource specifications are usually stored in human-readable files and in server properties.

The resource manager is a database manager with a twist. In most database systems, you perform a query using an imprecise specification, and you get back a set of records. The resource manager, however, allows you to specify a large set of values with an imprecise specification, to query the database with a precise specification, and to get back only a single value. This should be used by applications that need to know what the user prefers for colors, fonts, and other resources. It is this use as a database for dealing with X resources that inspired the name "Resource Manager," although the resource manager can be and is used in other ways.

For example, a user of your application may want to specify that all windows should have a blue background but that all mail-reading windows should have a red background. With well-engineered and coordinated applications, a user can define this information using only two lines of specifications.

As an example of how the resource manager works, consider a mail-reading application called xmh. Assume that it is designed so that it uses a complex window hierarchy all the way down to individual command buttons, which may be actual small subwindows in some toolkits. These are often called objects or widgets. In such toolkit systems, each user interface object can be composed of other objects and can be assigned a name and a class. Fully qualified names or classes can have arbitrary numbers of component names, but a fully qualified name always has the same number of component names as a fully qualified class. This generally reflects the structure of the application as composed of these objects, starting with the application itself.

For example, the xmh mail program has a name "xmh" and is one of a class of "Mail" programs. By convention, the first character of class components is capitalized, and the first letter of name components is in lowercase. Each name and class finally has an attribute (for example "foreground" or "font"). If each window is properly assigned a name and class, it is easy for the user to specify attributes of any portion of the application.

At the top level, the application might consist of a paned window (that is, a window divided into several sections) named "toc". One pane of the paned window is a button box window named "buttons" and is filled with command buttons. One of these command buttons is used to incorporate new mail and has the name "incorporate". This window has a fully qualified name, "xmh.toc.buttons.incorporate", and a fully qualified class, "Xmh.Paned.Box.Command". Its fully qualified name is the name of its parent, "xmh.toc.buttons", followed by its name, "incorporate". Its class is the class of its parent, "Xmh.Paned.Box", followed by its particular class, "Command". The fully qualified name of a resource is the attribute's name appended to the object's fully qualified name, and the fully qualified class is its class appended to the object's class.

The incorporate button might need the following resources: Title string, Font, Foreground color for its inactive state, Background color for its inactive state, Foreground color for its active state, and Background color for its active state. Each resource is considered to be an attribute of the button and, as such, has a name and a class. For example, the foreground color for the button in its active state might be named "activeForeground", and its class might be "Foreground".

When an application looks up a resource (for example, a color), it passes the complete name and complete class of the resource to a look-up routine. The resource manager compares this complete specification against the incomplete specifications of entries in the resource database, finds the best match, and returns the corresponding value for that entry.

The definitions for the resource manager are contained in <X11/Xresource.h>.

15.1 Resource File Syntax

The syntax of a resource file is a sequence of resource lines terminated by newline characters or the end of the file. The syntax of an individual resource line is:

```
 ResourceLine  =  Comment | IncludeFile | ResourceSpec | <empty line>
      Comment  =  "!" {<any character except null or newline>}
  IncludeFile  =  "#" WhiteSpace "include" WhiteSpace FileName WhiteSpace
     FileName  =  <valid filename for operating system>
 ResourceSpec  =  WhiteSpace ResourceName WhiteSpace ":" WhiteSpace Value
 ResourceName  =  [Binding] {Component Binding} ComponentName
      Binding  =  "." | "*"
   WhiteSpace  =  {<space> | <horizontal tab>}
    Component  =  "?" | ComponentName
ComponentName  =  NameChar {NameChar}
     NameChar  =  "a"–"z" | "A"–"Z" | "0"–"9" | "_" | "-"
        Value  =  {<any character except null or unescaped newline>}
```

Elements separated by vertical bar (|) are alternatives. Curly braces ({...}) indicate zero or more repetitions of the enclosed elements. Square brackets ([...]) indicate that the enclosed element is optional. Quotes (“...”) are used around literal characters.

IncludeFile lines are interpreted by replacing the line with the contents of the specified file. The word “include” must be in lowercase. The file name is interpreted relative to the directory of the file in which the line occurs (for example, if the file name contains no directory or contains a relative directory specification).

If a ResourceName contains a contiguous sequence of two or more Binding characters, the sequence will be replaced with single “.” character if the sequence contains only “.” characters; otherwise, the sequence will be replaced with a single “*” character.

A resource database never contains more than one entry for a given ResourceName. If a resource file contains multiple lines with the same ResourceName, the last line in the file is used.

Any white space character before or after the name or colon in a ResourceSpec are ignored. To allow a Value to begin with white space, the two-character sequence "*space*" (backslash followed by space) is recognized and replaced by a space character, and the two-character sequence "*tab*" (backslash followed by horizontal tab) is recognized and replaced by a horizontal tab character. To allow a Value to contain embedded newline characters, the two-character sequence "\n" is recognized and replaced by a newline character. To allow a Value to be broken across multiple lines in a text file, the two-character sequence "*newline*" (backslash followed by newline) is recognized and removed from the value. To allow a Value to contain arbitrary character codes, the four-character sequence "*nnn*", where each *n* is a digit character in the range of "0"–"7", is recognized and replaced with a single byte that contains the octal value specified by the sequence. Finally, the two-character sequence "\\" is recognized and replaced with a single backslash.

As an example of these sequences, the following resource line contains a value consisting of four characters: a backslash, a null, a "z", and a newline:

```
magic.values: \\\000\
z\n
```

15.2 Resource Manager Matching Rules

The algorithm for determining which resource database entry matches a given query is the heart of the resource manager. All queries must fully specify the name and class of the desired resource (use of the characters "*" and "?" are not permitted). The library supports up to 100 components in a full name or class. Resources are stored in the database with only partially specified names and classes, using pattern matching constructs. An asterisk (*) is a loose binding and is used to represent any number of intervening components, including none. A period (.) is a tight binding and is used to separate immediately adjacent components. A question mark (?) is used to match any single component name or class. A database entry cannot end in a loose binding; the final component (which cannot be the character "?") must be specified. The lookup algorithm searches the database for the entry that most closely matches (is most specific for) the full name and class being queried. When more than one database entry matches the full name and class, precedence rules are used to select just one.

The full name and class are scanned from left to right (from highest level in the hierarchy to lowest), one component at a time. At each level, the corresponding component and/or binding of each matching entry is determined, and these matching components and bindings are compared according to precedence rules. Each of the rules is applied at each level before moving to the next level, until a rule selects a single entry over all others. The rules, in order of precedence, are:

1. An entry that contains a matching component (whether name, class, or the character "?") takes precedence over entries that elide the level (that is, entries that match the level in a loose binding).
2. An entry with a matching name takes precedence over both entries with a matching class and entries that match using the character "?". An entry with a matching class takes precedence over entries that match using the character "?".
3. An entry preceded by a tight binding takes precedence over entries preceded by a loose binding.

To illustrate these rules, consider the following resource database entries:

```
xmh*Paned*activeForeground:               red      (entry A)
*incorporate.Foreground:                  blue     (entry B)
xmh.toc*Command*activeForeground:         green    (entry C)
xmh.toc*?.Foreground:                     white    (entry D)
xmh.toc*Command.activeForeground:         black    (entry E)
```

Consider a query for the resource:

```
xmh.toc.messagefunctions.incorporate.activeForeground   (name)
Xmh.Paned.Box.Command.Foreground                        (class)
```

At the first level (xmh, Xmh), rule 1 eliminates entry B. At the second level (toc, Paned), rule 2 eliminates entry A. At the third level (messagefunctions, Box), no entries are eliminated. At the fourth level (incorporate, Command), rule 2 eliminates entry D. At the fifth level (activeForeground, Foreground), rule 3 eliminates entry C.

15.3 Quarks

Most uses of the resource manager involve defining names, classes, and representation types as string constants. However, always referring to strings in the resource manager can be slow, because it is so heavily used in some toolkits. To solve this problem, a shorthand for a string is used in place of the string in many of the resource manager functions. Simple comparisons can be performed rather than string comparisons. The shorthand name for a string is called a quark and is the type `XrmQuark`. On some occasions, you may want to allocate a quark that has no string equivalent.

A quark is to a string what an atom is to a string in the server, but its use is entirely local to your application.

To allocate a new quark, use `XrmUniqueQuark`.

```
XrmQuark XrmUniqueQuark ( )
```

The `XrmUniqueQuark` function allocates a quark that is guaranteed not to represent any string that is known to the resource manager.

Each name, class, and representation type is typedef'd as an `XrmQuark`.

```
typedef int XrmQuark, *XrmQuarkList;
typedef XrmQuark XrmName;
typedef XrmQuark XrmClass;
typedef XrmQuark XrmRepresentation;
#define NULLQUARK ((XrmQuark) 0)
```

Lists are represented as null-terminated arrays of quarks. The size of the array must be large enough for the number of components used.

```
typedef XrmQuarkList XrmNameList;
typedef XrmQuarkList XrmClassList;
```

To convert a string to a quark, use `XrmStringToQuark` or `XrmPermStringToQuark`.

```
#define XrmStringToName(string) XrmStringToQuark(string)
#define XrmStringToClass(string) XrmStringToQuark(string)
#define XrmStringToRepresentation(string) XrmStringToQuark(string)
```

XrmQuark XrmStringToQuark (*string*)
    char **string*;

XrmQuark XrmPermStringToQuark (*string*)
    char **string*;

string Specifies the string for which a quark is to be allocated.

These functions can be used to convert from string to quark representation. If the string is not in the Host Portable Character Encoding, the conversion is implementation dependent. The string argument to `XrmStringToQuark` need not be permanently allocated storage. `XrmPermStringToQuark` is just like `XrmStringToQuark`, except that Xlib is permitted to assume the string argument is permanently allocated, and, hence, that it can be used as the value to be returned by `XrmQuarkToString`.

For any given quark, if `XrmStringToQuark` returns a non-NULL value, all future calls will return the same value (identical address).

To convert a quark to a string, use `XrmQuarkToString`.

#define XrmNameToString(name) XrmQuarkToString(name)
#define XrmClassToString(class) XrmQuarkToString(class)
#define XrmRepresentationToString(type) XrmQuarkToString(type)

char *XrmQuarkToString (*quark*)
    XrmQuark *quark*;

quark Specifies the quark for which the equivalent string is desired.

These functions can be used to convert from quark representation to string. The string pointed to by the return value must not be modified or freed. The returned string is byte-for-byte equal to the original string passed to one of the string-to-quark routines. If no string exists for that quark, `XrmQuarkToString` returns NULL. For any given quark, if `XrmQuarkToString` returns a non-NULL value, all future calls will return the same value (identical address).

To convert a string with one or more components to a quark list, use `XrmStringToQuarkList`.

#define XrmStringToNameList(str, name) XrmStringToQuarkList((str), (name))
#define XrmStringToClassList(str,class) XrmStringToQuarkList((str), (class))

```
void XrmStringToQuarkList(string, quarks_return)
    char *string;
    XrmQuarkList quarks_return;
```

string Specifies the string for which a quark list is to be allocated.

quarks_return Returns the list of quarks.

The `XrmStringToQuarkList` function converts the null-terminated string (generally a fully qualified name) to a list of quarks. Note that the string must be in the valid ResourceName format (see section 15.1). If the string is not in the Host Portable Character Encoding, the conversion is implementation dependent.

A binding list is a list of type `XrmBindingList` and indicates if components of name or class lists are bound tightly or loosely (that is, if wildcarding of intermediate components is specified).

```
typedef enum {XrmBindTightly, XrmBindLoosely} XrmBinding, *XrmBindingList;
```

`XrmBindTightly` indicates that a period separates the components, and `XrmBindLoosely` indicates that an asterisk separates the components.

To convert a string with one or more components to a binding list and a quark list, use `XrmStringToBindingQuarkList`.

```
XrmStringToBindingQuarkList(string, bindings_return, quarks_return)
    char *string;
    XrmBindingList bindings_return;
    XrmQuarkList quarks_return;
```

string Specifies the string for which a quark list is to be allocated.

bindings_return Returns the binding list. The caller must allocate sufficient space for the binding list before calling `XrmStringToBindingQuarkList`.

quarks_return Returns the list of quarks. The caller must allocate sufficient space for the quarks list before calling `XrmStringToBindingQuarkList`.

Component names in the list are separated by a period or an asterisk character. The string must be in the format of a valid ResourceName (see section 15.1). If the string does not start with a period or an asterisk, a tight binding is assumed. For example, the string "*a.b*c" becomes:

quarks:	a	b	c
bindings:	loose	tight	loose

15.4 Creating and Storing Databases

A resource database is an opaque type, `XrmDatabase`. Each database value is stored in an `XrmValue` structure. This structure consists of a size, an address, and a representation type. The size is specified in bytes. The representation type is a way for you to store data tagged by some application-defined type (for example, the strings "font" or "color"). It has nothing to do with the C data type or with its class. The `XrmValue` structure is defined as:

```
typedef struct {
    unsigned int size;
    XPointer addr;
} XrmValue, *XrmValuePtr;
```

To initialize the resource manager, use `XrmInitialize`.

```
void XrmInitialize ( );
```

To retrieve a database from disk, use `XrmGetFileDatabase`.

XrmDatabase XrmGetFileDatabase (*filename*)
  char **filename*;

filename Specifies the resource database file name.

The `XrmGetFileDatabase` function opens the specified file, creates a new resource database, and loads it with the specifications read in from the specified file. The specified file must contain a sequence of entries in valid ResourceLine format (see section 15.1). The file is parsed in the current locale, and the database is created in the current locale. If it cannot open the specified file, `XrmGetFileDatabase` returns NULL.

To store a copy of a database to disk, use `XrmPutFileDatabase`.

void XrmPutFileDatabase (*database, stored_db*)
  XrmDatabase *database*;
  char **stored_db*;

database Specifies the database that is to be used.

stored_db Specifies the file name for the stored database.

The `XrmPutFileDatabase` function stores a copy of the specified database in the specified file. Text is written to the file as a sequence of entries in valid ResourceLine format (see section 15.1). The file is written in the locale of the database. Entries containing resource names that are not in the Host Portable Character Encoding or containing values that are not in the encoding of the database locale, are written in an implementation dependent manner. The order in which entries are written is implementation dependent. Entries with representation types other than "String" are ignored.

To obtain a pointer to the screen independent resources of a display, use `XResourceManagerString`.

char *XResourceManagerString (*display*)
Display **display*;

display Specifies the connection to the X server.

The `XResourceManagerString` function returns the RESOURCE_MANAGER property from the server's root window of screen zero, which was returned when the connection was opened using `XOpenDisplay`. The property is converted from type STRING to the current locale. The conversion is identical to that produced by `XmbTextPropertyToTextList` for a single element STRING property. The returned string is owned by Xlib and should not be freed by the client. The property value must be in a format that is acceptable to `XrmGetStringDatabase`. If no property exists, NULL is returned.

To obtain a pointer to the screen-specific resources of a screen, use `XScreenResourceString`.

char *XScreenResourceString (*screen*)
Screen **screen*;

screen Specifies the screen.

The `XScreenResourceString` function returns the SCREEN_RESOURCES property from the root window of the specified screen. The property is converted from type STRING to the current locale. The conversion is identical to that produced by `XmbTextPropertyToTextList` for a single element STRING property. The property value must be in a format that is acceptable to `XrmGetStringDatabase`. If no property exists, NULL is returned. The caller is responsible for freeing the returned string by using `XFree`.

To create a database from a string, use `XrmGetStringDatabase`.

```
XrmDatabase XrmGetStringDatabase (data)
    char *data;
```

data Specifies the database contents using a string.

The `XrmGetStringDatabase` function creates a new database and stores the resources specified in the specified null-terminated string. `XrmGetStringDatabase` is similar to `XrmGetFileDatabase` except that it reads the information out of a string instead of out of a file. The string must contain a sequence of entries in valid ResourceLine format (see section 15.1). The string is parsed in the current locale, and the database is created in the current locale.

To obtain locale name of a database, use `XrmLocaleOfDatabase`.

```
char *XrmLocaleOfDatabase (database)
    XrmDatabase database;
```

database Specifies the resource database.

The `XrmLocaleOfDatabase` function returns the name of the locale bound to the specified database, as a null-terminated string. The returned locale name string is owned by Xlib and should not be modified or freed by the client. Xlib is not permitted to free the string until the database is destroyed. Until the string is freed, it will not be modified by Xlib.

To destroy a resource database and free its allocated memory, use `XrmDestroyDatabase`.

```
void XrmDestroyDatabase (database)
    XrmDatabase database;
```

database Specifies the resource database.

If database is NULL, `XrmDestroyDatabase` returns immediately.

To associate a resource database with a display, use `XrmSetDatabase`.

```
void XrmSetDatabase (display, database)
    Display *display;
    XrmDatabase database;
```

display Specifies the connection to the X server.

database Specifies the resource database.

The `XrmSetDatabase` function associates the specified resource database (or NULL) with the specified display. The database previously associated with the display (if any) is not destroyed. A client or toolkit may find this function convenient for retaining a database once it is constructed.

To get the resource database associated with a display, use `XrmGetDatabase`.

XrmDatabase XrmGetDatabase (*display*)
   Display **display*;

display Specifies the connection to the X server.

The `XrmGetDatabase` function returns the database associated with the specified display. It returns NULL if a database has not yet been set.

15.5 Merging Resource Databases

To merge the contents of a resource file into a database, use `XrmCombineFileDatabase`.

void XrmCombineFileDatabase (*filename*, *target_db*, *override*)
   char **filename*;
   XrmDatabase **target_db*;
   Bool *override*;

filename Specifies the resource database file name.

target_db Specifies the resource database into which the source database is to be merged.

The `XrmCombineFileDatabase` function merges the contents of a resource file into a database. If the same specifier is used for an entry in both the file and the database, the entry in the file will replace the entry in the database if override is `True`; otherwise, the entry in the file is discarded. The file is parsed in the current locale. If the file cannot be read, a zero status is returned; otherwise, a nonzero status is returned. If target_db contains NULL, `XrmCombineFileDatabase` creates and returns a new database to it. Otherwise, the database pointed to by target_db is not destroyed by the merge. The database entries are merged without changing values or types, regardless of the locale of the database. The locale of the target database is not modified.

To merge the contents of one database into another database, use `XrmCombineDatabase`.

```
void XrmCombineDatabase(source_db, target_db, override)
    XrmDatabase source_db, *target_db;
    Bool override;
```

source_db Specifies the resource database that is to be merged into the target database.

target_db Specifies the resource database into which the source database is to be merged.

override Specifies whether source entries override target ones.

The `XrmCombineDatabase` function merges the contents of one database into another. If the same specifier is used for an entry in both databases, the entry in the source_db will replace the entry in the target_db if override is `True`; otherwise, the entry in source_db is discarded. If target_db contains NULL, `XrmCombineDatabase` simply stores source_db in it. Otherwise, source_db is destroyed by the merge, but the database pointed to by target_db is not destroyed. The database entries are merged without changing values or types, regardless of the locales of the databases. The locale of the target database is not modified.

To merge the contents of one database into another database with override semantics, use `XrmMergeDatabases`.

```
void XrmMergeDatabases(source_db, target_db)
    XrmDatabase source_db, *target_db;
```

source_db Specifies the resource database that is to be merged into the target database.

target_db Specifies the resource database into which the source database is to be merged.

The `XrmMergeDatabases` function merges the contents of one database into another. If the same specifier is used for an entry in both databases, the entry in the source_db will replace the entry in the target_db (that is, it overrides target_db). If target_db contains NULL, `XrmMergeDatabases` simply stores source_db in it. Otherwise, source_db is destroyed by the merge, but the database pointed to by target_db is not destroyed. The database entries are merged without changing values or types, regardless of the locales of the databases. The locale of the target database is not modified.

15.6 Looking Up Resources

To retrieve a resource from a resource database, use `XrmGetResource`, `XrmQGetResource`, or `XrmQGetSearchResource`.

```
Bool XrmGetResource ( database, str_name, str_class, str_type_return, value_return)
   XrmDatabase database;
   char *str_name;
   char *str_class;
   char **str_type_return;
   XrmValue *value_return;
```

database	Specifies the database that is to be used.
str_name	Specifies the fully qualified name of the value being retrieved (as a string).
str_class	Specifies the fully qualified class of the value being retrieved (as a string).
str_type_return	Returns the representation type of the destination (as a string).
value_return	Returns the value in the database.

```
Bool XrmQGetResource ( database, quark_name, quark_class, quark_type_return,
                       value_return)
   XrmDatabase database;
   XrmNameList quark_name;
   XrmClassList quark_class;
   XrmRepresentation *quark_type_return;
   XrmValue *value_return;
```

database	Specifies the database that is to be used.
quark_name	Specifies the fully qualified name of the value being retrieved (as a quark).
quark_class	Specifies the fully qualified class of the value being retrieved (as a quark).
quark_type_return	Returns the representation type of the destination (as a quark).
value_return	Returns the value in the database.

The `XrmGetResource` and `XrmQGetResource` functions retrieve a resource from the specified database. Both take a fully qualified name/class pair, a destination resource representation, and the address of a value (size/address pair). The value and returned type point into database memory; therefore, you must not modify the data.

The database only frees or overwrites entries on `XrmPutResource`, `XrmQPutResource`, or `XrmMergeDatabases`. A client that is not storing new values into the database or is not merging the database should be safe using the address passed back at any time until it exits. If a resource was found, both `XrmGetResource` and `XrmQGetResource` return `True`; otherwise, they return `False`.

Most applications and toolkits do not make random probes into a resource database to fetch resources. The X toolkit access pattern for a resource database is quite stylized. A series of from 1 to 20 probes are made with only the last name/class differing in each probe. The `XrmGetResource` function is at worst a 2^n algorithm, where n is the length of the name/class list. This can be improved upon by the application programmer by prefetching a list of database levels that might match the first part of a name/class list.

To obtain a list of database levels, use `XrmQGetSearchList`.

typedef XrmHashTable *XrmSearchList;

Bool XrmQGetSearchList (*database, names, classes, list_return, list_length*)
  XrmDatabase *database*;
  XrmNameList *names*;
  XrmClassList *classes*;
  XrmSearchList *list_return*;
  int *list_length*;

database	Specifies the database that is to be used.
names	Specifies a list of resource names.
classes	Specifies a list of resource classes.
list_return	Returns a search list for further use. The caller must allocate sufficient space for the list before calling `XrmQGetSearchList`.
list_length	Specifies the number of entries (not the byte size) allocated for list_return.

The `XrmQGetSearchList` function takes a list of names and classes and returns a list of database levels where a match might occur. The returned list is in best-to-worst order and uses the same algorithm as `XrmGetResource` for determining precedence. If list_return was large enough for the search list, `XrmQGetSearchList` returns `True`; otherwise, it returns `False`.

The size of the search list that the caller must allocate is dependent upon the number of levels and wildcards in the resource specifiers that are stored in the database. The worst case length is 3^n, where n is the number of name or class components in names or classes.

When using XrmQGetSearchList followed by multiple probes for resources with a common name and class prefix, only the common prefix should be specified in the name and class list to XrmQGetSearchList.

To search resource database levels for a given resource, use XrmQGetSearch-Resource.

```
Bool XrmQGetSearchResource (list, name, class, type_return, value_return)
    XrmSearchList list;
    XrmName name;
    XrmClass class;
    XrmRepresentation *type_return;
    XrmValue *value_return;
```

list	Specifies the search list returned by XrmQGetSearchList.
name	Specifies the resource name.
class	Specifies the resource class.
type_return	Returns data representation type.
value_return	Returns the value in the database.

The XrmQGetSearchResource function searches the specified database levels for the resource that is fully identified by the specified name and class. The search stops with the first match. XrmQGetSearchResource returns True if the resource was found; otherwise, it returns False.

A call to XrmQGetSearchList with a name and class list containing all but the last component of a resource name followed by a call to XrmQGetSearch-Resource with the last component name and class returns the same database entry as XrmGetResource and XrmQGetResource with the fully qualified name and class.

15.7 Storing Into a Resource Database

To store resources into the database, use XrmPutResource or XrmQPut-Resource. Both functions take a partial resource specification, a representation type, and a value. This value is copied into the specified database.

```
void XrmPutResource ( database, specifier, type, value)
    XrmDatabase *database;
    char *specifier;
    char *type;
    XrmValue *value;
```

database Specifies the resource database.
specifier Specifies a complete or partial specification of the resource.
type Specifies the type of the resource.
value Specifies the value of the resource, which is specified as a string.

If database contains NULL, `XrmPutResource` creates a new database and returns a pointer to it. `XrmPutResource` is a convenience function that calls `XrmStringToBindingQuarkList` followed by:

```
XrmQPutResource(database, bindings, quarks, XrmStringToQuark(type), value)
```

If the specifier and type are not in the Host Portable Character Encoding, the result is implementation dependent. The value is stored in the database without modification.

```
void XrmQPutResource ( database, bindings, quarks, type, value)
    XrmDatabase *database;
    XrmBindingList bindings;
    XrmQuarkList quarks;
    XrmRepresentation type;
    XrmValue *value;
```

database Specifies the resource database.
bindings Specifies a list of bindings.
quarks Specifies the complete or partial name or the class list of the resource.
type Specifies the type of the resource.
value Specifies the value of the resource, which is specified as a string.

If database contains NULL, `XrmQPutResource` creates a new database and returns a pointer to it. If a resource entry with the identical bindings and quarks already exists in the database, the previous value is replaced by the new specified value. The value is stored in the database without modification.

To add a resource that is specified as a string, use `XrmPutStringResource`.

```
void XrmPutStringResource ( database, specifier, value)
    XrmDatabase *database;
```

```
   char *specifier;
   char *value;
```

database Specifies the resource database.

specifier Specifies a complete or partial specification of the resource.

value Specifies the value of the resource, which is specified as a string.

If database contains NULL, `XrmPutStringResource` creates a new database and returns a pointer to it. `XrmPutStringResource` adds a resource with the specified value to the specified database. `XrmPutStringResource` is a convenience function that first calls `XrmStringToBindingQuarkList` on the specifier and then calls `XrmQPutResource`, using a "String" representation type. If the specifier is not in the Host Portable Character Encoding, the result is implementation dependent. The value is stored in the database without modification.

To add a string resource using quarks as a specification, use `XrmQPutStringResource`.

```
void XrmQPutStringResource ( database, bindings, quarks, value)
   XrmDatabase *database;
   XrmBindingList bindings;
   XrmQuarkList quarks;
   char *value;
```

database Specifies the resource database.

bindings Specifies a list of bindings.

quarks Specifies the complete or partial name or the class list of the resource.

value Specifies the value of the resource, which is specified as a string.

If database contains NULL, `XrmQPutStringResource` creates a new database and returns a pointer to it. `XrmQPutStringResource` is a convenience routine that constructs an `XrmValue` for the value string (by calling `strlen` to compute the size) and then calls `XrmQPutResource`, using a "String" representation type. The value is stored in the database without modification.

To add a single resource entry that is specified as a string that contains both a name and a value, use `XrmPutLineResource`.

```
void XrmPutLineResource ( database, line)
   XrmDatabase *database;
   char *line;
```

database Specifies the resource database.
line Specifies the resource name and value pair as a single string.

If database contains NULL, `XrmPutLineResource` creates a new database and returns a pointer to it. `XrmPutLineResource` adds a single resource entry to the specified database. The line must be in valid ResourceLine format (see section 15.1). The string is parsed in the locale of the database. If the `ResourceName` is not in the Host Portable Character Encoding, the result is implementation dependent. Note that comment lines are not stored.

15.8 Enumerating Database Entries

To enumerate the entries of a database, use `XrmEnumerateDatabase`.

```
#define XrmEnumAllLevels   0
#define XrmEnumOneLevel    1
```

```
Bool XrmEnumerateDatabase ( database, name_prefix, class_prefix, mode, proc, arg)
    XrmDatabase database;
    XrmNameList name_prefix;
    XrmClassList class_prefix;
    int mode;
    Bool (*proc) ();
    XPointer arg;
```

database Specifies the resource database.
name_prefix Specifies the resource name prefix.
class_prefix Specifies the resource class prefix.
mode Specifies the number of levels to enumerate.
proc Specifies the procedure that is to be called for each matching entry.
arg Specifies the user-supplied argument that will be passed to the procedure.

The `XrmEnumerateDatabase` function calls the specified procedure for each resource in the database that would match some completion of the given name/class resource prefix. The order in which resources are found is implementation dependent. If mode is `XrmEnumOneLevel`, a resource must match the given name/class prefix with just a single name and class appended. If mode is `XrmEnumAllLevels`, the resource must match the given name/class prefix with one or more names and classes appended. If the procedure returns `True`, the enumeration terminates and the function returns `True`. If the procedure always returns `False`, all matching resources are enumerated and the function returns `False`.

The procedure is called with the following arguments:

```
(*proc) ( database, bindings, quarks, type, value, arg)
    XrmDatabase *database;
    XrmBindingList bindings;
    XrmQuarkList quarks;
    XrmRepresentation *type;
    XrmValue *value;
    XPointer closure;
```

The bindings and quarks lists are terminated by `NULLQUARK`. Note that pointers to the database and type are passed, but these values should not be modified.

15.9 Parsing Command Line Options

The `XrmParseCommand` function can be used to parse the command line arguments to a program and modify a resource database with selected entries from the command line.

```
typedef enum {
    XrmoptionNoArg,        /* Value is specified in XrmOptionDescRec.value */
    XrmoptionIsArg,        /* Value is the option string itself */
    XrmoptionStickyArg,    /* Value is characters immediately following option */
    XrmoptionSepArg,       /* Value is next argument in argv */
    XrmoptionResArg,       /* Resource and value in next argument in argv */
    XrmoptionSkipArg,      /* Ignore this option and the next argument in argv */
    XrmoptionSkipLine,     /* Ignore this option and the rest of argv */
    XrmoptionSkipNArgs     /* Ignore this option and the next
                              XrmOptionDescRec.value arguments in argv */
} XrmOptionKind;
```

Note that `XrmoptionSkipArg` is equivalent to `XrmoptionSkipNArgs` with the `XrmOptionDescRec.value` field containing the value one. Note also that the value zero for `XrmoptionSkipNArgs` indicates that only the option itself is to be skipped.

```
typedef struct {
    char *option;              /* Option specification string in argv */
    char *specifier;           /* Binding and resource name (sans application name) */
    XrmOptionKind argKind;/* Which style of option it is */
    XPointer value;            /* Value to provide if XrmoptionNoArg or
                                  XrmoptionSkipNArgs */
} XrmOptionDescRec, *XrmOptionDescList;
```

To load a resource database from a C command line, use `XrmParseCommand`.

```
void XrmParseCommand (database, table, table_count, name, argc_in_out, argv_in_out)
    XrmDatabase *database;
    XrmOptionDescList table;
    int table_count;
    char *name;
    int *argc_in_out;
    char **argv_in_out;
```

database	Specifies the resource database.
table	Specifies the table of command line arguments to be parsed.
table_count	Specifies the number of entries in the table.
name	Specifies the application name.
argc_in_out	Specifies the number of arguments and returns the number of remaining arguments.
argv_in_out	Specifies the command line arguments and returns the remaining arguments.

The `XrmParseCommand` function parses an (argc, argv) pair according to the specified option table, loads recognized options into the specified database with type "String," and modifies the (argc, argv) pair to remove all recognized options. If database contains NULL, `XrmParseCommand` creates a new database and returns a pointer to it. Otherwise, entries are added to the database specified. If a database is created, it is created in the current locale.

The specified table is used to parse the command line. Recognized options in the table are removed from argv, and entries are added to the specified resource database. The table entries contain information on the option string, the option name, the style of option, and a value to provide if the option kind is `XrmoptionNoArg`. The option names are compared byte-for-byte to arguments in argv, independent of any locale. The resource values given in the table are stored in the resource database without modification. All resource database entries are created using a "String" representation type. The argc argument specifies the number of arguments in argv and is set on return to the remaining number of arguments that were not parsed. The name argument should be the name of your application for use in building the database entry. The name argument is prefixed to the resourceName in the option table before storing a database entry. No separating (binding) character is inserted, so the table must contain either a period (.) or an asterisk (*) as the first character in each resourceName entry. To specify a more completely qualified resource name, the resourceName entry can contain multiple components. If the name argument and the resourceNames are not in the Host Portable Character Encoding, the result is implementation dependent.

The following provides a sample option table:

```
static XrmOptionDescRec opTable[] = {
{"-background",   "*background",                  XrmoptionSepArg,   (XPointer) NULL},
{"-bd",           "*borderColor",                 XrmoptionSepArg,   (XPointer) NULL},
{"-bg",           "*background",                  XrmoptionSepArg,   (XPointer) NULL},
{"-borderwidth",  "*TopLevelShell.borderWidth",   XrmoptionSepArg,   (XPointer) NULL},
{"-bordercolor",  "*borderColor",                 XrmoptionSepArg,   (XPointer) NULL},
{"-bw",           "*TopLevelShell.borderWidth",   XrmoptionSepArg,   (XPointer) NULL},
{"-display",      ".display",                     XrmoptionSepArg,   (XPointer) NULL},
{"-fg",           "*foreground",                  XrmoptionSepArg,   (XPointer) NULL},
{"-fn",           "*font",                        XrmoptionSepArg,   (XPointer) NULL},
{"-font",         "*font",                        XrmoptionSepArg,   (XPointer) NULL},
{"-foreground",   "*foreground",                  XrmoptionSepArg,   (XPointer) NULL},
{"-geometry",     ".TopLevelShell.geometry",      XrmoptionSepArg,   (XPointer) NULL},
{"-iconic",       ".TopLevelShell.iconic",        XrmoptionNoArg,    (XPointer) "on"},
{"-name",         ".name",                        XrmoptionSepArg,   (XPointer) NULL},
{"-reverse",      "*reverseVideo",                XrmoptionNoArg,    (XPointer) "on"},
{"-rv",           "*reverseVideo",                XrmoptionNoArg,    (XPointer) "on"},
{"-synchronous",  "*synchronous",                 XrmoptionNoArg,    (XPointer) "on"},
{"-title",        ".TopLevelShell.title",         XrmoptionSepArg,   (XPointer) NULL},
{"-xrm",          NULL,                           XrmoptionResArg,   (XPointer) NULL},
};
```

In this table, if the –background (or –bg) option is used to set background colors, the stored resource specifier matches all resources of attribute background. If the –borderwidth option is used, the stored resource specifier applies only to border width attributes of class TopLevelShell (that is, outermost windows, including pop-up windows). If the –title option is used to set a window name, only the topmost application windows receive the resource.

When parsing the command line, any unique unambiguous abbreviation for an option name in the table is considered a match for the option. Note that uppercase and lowercase matter.

Chapter 16

Application Utility Functions

Once you have initialized the X system, you can use the Xlib utility functions to:

- Obtain and classify KeySyms
- Allocate permanent storage
- Parse window geometry strings
- Manipulate regions
- Use cut buffers
- Determine the appropriate visual
- Manipulate images
- Manipulate bitmaps
- Use the context manager

As a group, the functions discussed in this chapter provide the functionality that is frequently needed and that spans toolkits. Many of these functions do not generate actual protocol requests to the server.

16.1 Keyboard Utility Functions

This section discusses mapping between KeyCodes and KeySyms, names for KeySyms, and KeySym classification macros. The functions in this section operate on a cached copy of the server keyboard mapping. The first four

KeySyms for each KeyCode are modified according to the rules given in section 12.7. If you want the untransformed KeySyms defined for a key, you should only use the functions described in section 12.7.

To obtain a KeySym for the KeyCode of an event, use `XLookupKeysym`.

```
KeySym XLookupKeysym(key_event, index)
    XKeyEvent *key_event;
    int index;
```

key_event Specifies the `KeyPress` or `KeyRelease` event.

index Specifies the index into the KeySyms list for the event's KeyCode.

The `XLookupKeysym` function uses a given keyboard event and the index you specified to return the KeySym from the list that corresponds to the KeyCode member in the `XKeyPressedEvent` or `XKeyReleasedEvent` structure. If no KeySym is defined for the KeyCode of the event, `XLookupKeysym` returns `NoSymbol`.

To obtain a KeySym for a specific KeyCode, use `XKeycodeToKeysym`.

```
KeySym XKeycodeToKeysym (display, keycode, index)
    Display *display;
    KeyCode keycode;
    int index;
```

display Specifies the connection to the X server.

keycode Specifies the KeyCode.

index Specifies the element of KeyCode vector.

The `XKeycodeToKeysym` function uses internal Xlib tables and returns the KeySym defined for the specified KeyCode and the element of the KeyCode vector. If no symbol is defined, `XKeycodeToKeysym` returns `NoSymbol`.

To obtain a KeyCode for a key having a specific KeySym, use `XKeysymToKeycode`.

```
KeyCode XKeysymToKeycode (display, keysym)
    Display *display;
    KeySym keysym;
```

display Specifies the connection to the X server.

keysym Specifies the KeySym that is to be searched for.

If the specified KeySym is not defined for any KeyCode, `XKeysymToKeycode` returns zero.

The mapping between KeyCodes and KeySyms is cached internal to Xlib. When this information is changed at the server, an Xlib function must be called to refresh the cache. To refresh the stored modifier and keymap information, use `XRefreshKeyboardMapping`.

```
XRefreshKeyboardMapping(event_map)
    XMappingEvent *event_map;
```

event_map Specifies the mapping event that is to be used.

The `XRefreshKeyboardMapping` function refreshes the stored modifier and keymap information. You usually call this function when a `MappingNotify` event with a request member of `MappingKeyboard` or `MappingModifier` occurs. The result is to update Xlib's knowledge of the keyboard.

KeySyms have string names as well as numeric codes. To convert the name of the KeySym to the KeySym code, use `XStringToKeysym`.

```
KeySym XStringToKeysym(string)
    char *string;
```

string Specifies the name of the KeySym that is to be converted.

Standard KeySym names are obtained from `<X11/keysymdef.h>` by removing the XK_ prefix from each name. KeySyms that are not part of the Xlib standard also may be obtained with this function. The set of KeySyms that are available in this manner and the mechanisms by which Xlib obtains them is implementation dependent.

If the KeySym name is not in the Host Portable Character Encoding, the result is implementation dependent. If the specified string does not match a valid KeySym, `XStringToKeysym` returns `NoSymbol`.

To convert a KeySym code to the name of the KeySym, use `XKeysymToString`.

```
char *XKeysymToString(keysym)
    KeySym keysym;
```

keysym Specifies the KeySym that is to be converted.

The returned string is in a static area and must not be modified. The returned string is in the Host Portable Character Encoding. If the specified KeySym is not defined, `XKeysymToString` returns a NULL.

16.1.1 KeySym Classification Macros

You may want to test if a KeySym is, for example, on the keypad or on one of the function keys. You can use the KeySym macros to perform the following tests.

IsCursorKey (*keysym*)

keysym Specifies the KeySym that is to be tested.

Returns `True` if the specified KeySym is a cursor key.

IsFunctionKey (*keysym*)

keysym Specifies the KeySym that is to be tested.

Returns `True` if the specified KeySym is a function key.

IsKeypadKey (*keysym*)

keysym Specifies the KeySym that is to be tested.

Returns `True` if the specified KeySym is a keypad key.

IsMiscFunctionKey (*keysym*)

keysym Specifies the KeySym that is to be tested.

Returns `True` if the specified KeySym is a miscellaneous function key.

IsModifierKey (*keysym*)

keysym Specifies the KeySym that is to be tested.

Returns `True` if the specified KeySym is a modifier key.

IsPFKey (*keysym*)

keysym Specifies the KeySym that is to be tested.

Returns `True` if the specified KeySym is a PF key.

16.2 Latin-1 Keyboard Event Functions

Chapter 13 describes internationalized text input facilities, but sometimes it is expedient to write an application that only deals with Latin-1 characters and ASCII controls, so Xlib provides a simple function for that purpose. `XLookupString` handles the standard modifier semantics described in section 12.7. This function does not use any of the input method facilities described in chapter 13 and does not depend on the current locale.

To map a key event to an ISO Latin-1 string, use `XLookupString`.

int XLookupString(*event_struct, buffer_return, bytes_buffer, keysym_return, status_in_out*)
  XKeyEvent **event_struct*;
  char **buffer_return*;
  int *bytes_buffer*;
  KeySym **keysym_return*;
  XComposeStatus **status_in_out*;

event_struct Specifies the key event structure to be used. You can pass `XKeyPressedEvent` or `XKeyReleasedEvent`.

buffer_return Returns the translated characters.

bytes_buffer Specifies the length of the buffer. No more than bytes_buffer of translation are returned.

keysym_return Returns the KeySym computed from the event if this argument is not NULL.

status_in_out Specifies or returns the `XComposeStatus` structure or NULL.

The `XLookupString` function translates a key event to a KeySym and a string. The KeySym is obtained by using the standard interpretation of the `Shift`, `Lock`, and group modifiers as defined in the X Protocol specification. If the KeySym has been rebound (see `XRebindKeysym`), the bound string will be stored in the buffer. Otherwise, the KeySym is mapped, if possible, to an ISO Latin-1 character or (if the Control modifier is on) to an ASCII control character, and that character is stored in the buffer. `XLookupString` returns the number of characters that are stored in the buffer.

If present (non-NULL), the `XComposeStatus` structure records the state, which is private to Xlib, that needs preservation across calls to `XLookupString` to implement compose processing. The creation of `XComposeStatus` structures is implementation dependent; a portable program must pass NULL for this argument.

XLookupString depends on the cached keyboard information mentioned in the previous section, so it is necessary to use XRefreshKeyboardMapping to keep this information up-to-date.

To rebind the meaning of a KeySym for XLookupString, use XRebind-Keysym.

```
XRebindKeysym( display, keysym, list, mod_count, string, num_bytes)
    Display *display;
    KeySym keysym;
    KeySym list[ ];
    int mod_count;
    unsigned char *string;
    int num_bytes;
```

display	Specifies the connection to the X server.
keysym	Specifies the KeySym that is to be rebound.
list	Specifies the KeySyms to be used as modifiers.
mod_count	Specifies the number of modifiers in the modifier list.
string	Specifies the string that is copied and will be returned by XLookupString.
num_bytes	Specifies the number of bytes in the string argument.

The XRebindKeysym function can be used to rebind the meaning of a KeySym for the client. It does not redefine any key in the X server but merely provides an easy way for long strings to be attached to keys. XLookupString returns this string when the appropriate set of modifier keys are pressed and when the KeySym would have been used for the translation. No text conversions are performed; the client is responsible for supplying appropriately encoded strings. Note that you can rebind a KeySym that may not exist.

16.3 Allocating Permanent Storage

To allocate some memory you will never give back, use Xpermalloc.

```
char *Xpermalloc ( size)
    unsigned int size;
```

The Xpermalloc function allocates storage that can never be freed for the life of the program. The memory is allocated with alignment for the C type double. This function may provide some performance and space savings over the standard operating system memory allocator.

16.4 Parsing the Window Geometry

To parse standard window geometry strings, use `XParseGeometry`.

```
int XParseGeometry (parsestring, x_return, y_return, width_return, height_return)
    char *parsestring;
    int *x_return, *y_return;
    unsigned int *width_return, *height_return;
```

parsestring Specifies the string you want to parse.

x_return

y_return Return the x and y offsets.

width_return

height_return Return the width and height determined.

By convention, X applications use a standard string to indicate window size and placement. `XParseGeometry` makes it easier to conform to this standard because it allows you to parse the standard window geometry. Specifically, this function lets you parse strings of the form:

[=] [<*width*>{xX}<*height*>] [{+-}<*xoffset*>{+-}<*yoffset*>]

The fields map into the arguments associated with this function. (Items enclosed in <> are integers, items in [] are optional, and items enclosed in {} indicate "choose one of." Note that the brackets should not appear in the actual string.) If the string is not in the Host Portable Character Encoding, the result is implementation dependent.

The `XParseGeometry` function returns a bitmask that indicates which of the four values (width, height, xoffset, and yoffset) were actually found in the string and whether the x and y values are negative. By convention, –0 is not equal to +0, because the user needs to be able to say "position the window relative to the right or bottom edge." For each value found, the corresponding argument is updated. For each value not found, the argument is left unchanged. The bits are represented by `XValue`, `YValue`, `WidthValue`, `HeightValue`, `XNegative`, or `YNegative` and are defined in <`X11/Xutil.h`>. They will be set whenever one of the values is defined or one of the signs is set.

If the function returns either the `XValue` or `YValue` flag, you should place the window at the requested position.

To construct a window's geometry information, use `XWMGeometry`.

```
int XWMGeometry(display, screen, user_geom, def_geom, bwidth, hints, x_return, y_return,
                width_return, height_return, gravity_return)
    Display *display;
    int screen;
    char *user_geom;
    char *def_geom;
    unsigned int bwidth;
    XSizeHints *hints;
    int *x_return, *y_return;
    int *width_return;
    int *height_return;
    int *gravity_return;
```

display	Specifies the connection to the X server.
screen	Specifies the screen.
user_geom	Specifies the user-specified geometry or NULL.
def_geom	Specifies the application's default geometry or NULL.
bwidth	Specifies the border width.
hints	Specifies the size hints for the window in its normal state.
x_return *y_return*	Return the x and y offsets.
width_return *height_return*	Return the width and height determined.
gravity_return	Returns the window gravity.

The `XWMGeometry` function combines any geometry information (given in the format used by `XParseGeometry`) specified by the user and by the calling program with size hints (usually the ones to be stored in WM_NORMAL_HINTS) and returns the position, size, and gravity (`NorthWestGravity`, `NorthEastGravity`, `SouthEastGravity`, or `SouthWestGravity`) that describe the window. If the base size is not set in the `XSizeHints` structure, the minimum size is used if set. Otherwise, a base size of zero is assumed. If no minimum size is set in the hints structure, the base size is used. A mask (in the form returned by `XParseGeometry`) that describes which values came from the user specification and whether or not the position coordinates are relative to the right and bottom edges is returned. Note that these coordinates will have already been accounted for in the x_return and y_return values.

Note that invalid geometry specifications can cause a width or height of zero to be returned. The caller may pass the address of the hints win_gravity field as gravity_return to update the hints directly.

16.5 Manipulating Regions

Regions are arbitrary sets of pixel locations. Xlib provides functions for manipulating regions. The opaque type `Region` is defined in `<X11/Xutil.h>`. Xlib provides functions that you can use to manipulate regions. This section discusses how to:

- Create, copy, or destroy regions
- Move or shrink regions
- Compute with regions
- Determine if regions are empty or equal
- Locate a point or rectangle in a region

16.5.1 Creating, Copying, or Destroying Regions

To create a new empty region, use `XCreateRegion`.

Region XCreateRegion ()

To generate a region from a polygon, use `XPolygonRegion`.

Region XPolygonRegion (*points*, *n*, *fill_rule*)
  XPoint *points[]*;
  int *n*;
  int *fill_rule*;

points Specifies an array of points.
n Specifies the number of points in the polygon.
fill_rule Specifies the fill-rule you want to set for the specified GC. You can pass `EvenOddRule` or `WindingRule`.

The `XPolygonRegion` function returns a region for the polygon defined by the points array. For an explanation of fill_rule, see `XCreateGC`.

To set the clip-mask of a GC to a region, use `XSetRegion`.

```
XSetRegion ( display, gc, r)
    Display *display;
    GC gc;
    Region r;
```

display Specifies the connection to the X server.
gc Specifies the GC.
r Specifies the region.

The `XSetRegion` function sets the clip-mask in the GC to the specified region. Once it is set in the GC, the region can be destroyed.

To deallocate the storage associated with a specified region, use `XDestroyRegion`.

```
XDestroyRegion ( r)
    Region r;
```

r Specifies the region.

16.5.2 Moving or Shrinking Regions

To move a region by a specified amount, use `XOffsetRegion`.

```
XOffsetRegion ( r, dx, dy)
    Region r;
    int dx, dy;
```

r Specifies the region.
dx
dy Specify the x and y coordinates, which define the amount you want to move the specified region.

To reduce a region by a specified amount, use `XShrinkRegion`.

```
XShrinkRegion ( r, dx, dy)
    Region r;
    int dx, dy;
```

r Specifies the region.
dx
dy Specify the x and y coordinates, which define the amount you want to shrink the specified region.

Positive values shrink the size of the region, and negative values expand the region.

16.5.3 Computing with Regions

To generate the smallest rectangle enclosing a region, use `XClipBox`.

```
XClipBox (r, rect_return)
    Region r;
    XRectangle *rect_return;
```

r Specifies the region.
rect_return Returns the smallest enclosing rectangle.

The `XClipBox` function returns the smallest rectangle enclosing the specified region.

To compute the intersection of two regions, use `XIntersectRegion`.

```
XIntersectRegion (sra, srb, dr_return)
    Region sra, srb, dr_return;
```

sra
srb Specify the two regions with which you want to perform the computation.
dr_return Returns the result of the computation.

To compute the union of two regions, use `XUnionRegion`.

```
XUnionRegion (sra, srb, dr_return)
    Region sra, srb, dr_return;
```

sra
srb Specify the two regions with which you want to perform the computation.
dr_return Returns the result of the computation.

To create a union of a source region and a rectangle, use `XUnionRectWithRegion`.

```
XUnionRectWithRegion (rectangle, src_region, dest_region_return)
    XRectangle *rectangle;
    Region src_region;
    Region dest_region_return;
```

rectangle Specifies the rectangle.
src_region Specifies the source region to be used.
dest_region_return Returns the destination region.

The `XUnionRectWithRegion` function updates the destination region from a union of the specified rectangle and the specified source region.

To subtract two regions, use `XSubtractRegion`.

```
XSubtractRegion ( sra, srb, dr_return)
   Region sra, srb, dr_return;
```

sra
srb Specify the two regions with which you want to perform the computation.
dr_return Returns the result of the computation.

The `XSubtractRegion` function subtracts srb from sra and stores the results in dr_return.

To calculate the difference between the union and intersection of two regions, use `XXorRegion`.

```
XXorRegion ( sra, srb, dr_return)
   Region sra, srb, dr_return;
```

sra
srb Specify the two regions with which you want to perform the computation.
dr_return Returns the result of the computation.

16.5.4 Determining if Regions Are Empty or Equal

To determine if the specified region is empty, use `XEmptyRegion`.

```
Bool XEmptyRegion ( r)
   Region r;
```

r Specifies the region.

The `XEmptyRegion` function returns `True` if the region is empty.

To determine if two regions have the same offset, size, and shape, use `XEqualRegion`.

```
Bool XEqualRegion ( r1, r2)
   Region r1, r2;
```

r1
r2 Specify the two regions.

The `XEqualRegion` function returns `True` if the two regions have the same offset, size, and shape.

16.5.5 Locating a Point or a Rectangle in a Region

To determine if a specified point resides in a specified region, use `XPointInRegion`.

```
Bool XPointInRegion (r, x, y)
    Region r;
    int x, y;
```

r Specifies the region.

x

y Specify the x and y coordinates, which define the point.

The `XPointInRegion` function returns `True` if the point (x, y) is contained in the region r.

To determine if a specified rectangle is inside a region, use `XRectInRegion`.

```
int XRectInRegion (r, x, y, width, height)
    Region r;
    int x, y;
    unsigned int width, height;
```

r Specifies the region.

x

y Specify the x and y coordinates, which define the coordinates of the upper-left corner of the rectangle.

width

height Specify the width and height, which define the rectangle .

The `XRectInRegion` function returns `RectangleIn` if the rectangle is entirely in the specified region, `RectangleOut` if the rectangle is entirely out of the specified region, and `RectanglePart` if the rectangle is partially in the specified region.

16.6 Using Cut Buffers

Xlib provides functions to manipulate cut buffers, a very simple form of cut and paste inter-client communication. Selections are a much more powerful and useful mechanism for interchanging data between clients (see section 4.5), and generally should be used instead of cut buffers.

Cut buffers are implemented as properties on the first root window of the display. The buffers can only contain text, in the STRING encoding. The text encoding is not changed by Xlib when fetching or storing. Eight buffers are provided and can be accessed as a ring or as explicit buffers (numbered 0 through 7).

To store data in cut buffer 0, use `XStoreBytes`.

```
XStoreBytes ( display, bytes, nbytes)
    Display *display;
    char *bytes;
    int nbytes;
```

display Specifies the connection to the X server.
bytes Specifies the bytes, which are not necessarily ASCII or null-terminated.
nbytes Specifies the number of bytes to be stored.

Note that the data can have embedded null characters and need not be null-terminated. The cut buffer's contents can be retrieved later by any client calling `XFetchBytes`.

`XStoreBytes` can generate a `BadAlloc` error.

To store data in a specified cut buffer, use `XStoreBuffer`.

```
XStoreBuffer ( display, bytes, nbytes, buffer)
    Display *display;
    char *bytes;
    int nbytes;
    int buffer;
```

display Specifies the connection to the X server.
bytes Specifies the bytes, which are not necessarily ASCII or null-terminated.
nbytes Specifies the number of bytes to be stored.
buffer Specifies the buffer in which you want to store the bytes.

If an invalid buffer is specified, the call has no effect. Note that the data can have embedded null characters and need not be null-terminated.

`XStoreBuffer` can generate a `BadAlloc` error.

To return data from cut buffer 0, use `XFetchBytes`.

```
char *XFetchBytes(display, nbytes_return)
    Display *display;
    int *nbytes_return;
```

display Specifies the connection to the X server.

nbytes_return Returns the number of bytes in the buffer.

The `XFetchBytes` function returns the number of bytes in the nbytes_return argument, if the buffer contains data. Otherwise, the function returns NULL and sets nbytes to 0. The appropriate amount of storage is allocated and the pointer returned. The client must free this storage when finished with it by calling `XFree`.

To return data from a specified cut buffer, use `XFetchBuffer`.

```
char *XFetchBuffer(display, nbytes_return, buffer)
    Display *display;
    int *nbytes_return;
    int buffer;
```

display Specifies the connection to the X server.

nbytes_return Returns the number of bytes in the buffer.

buffer Specifies the buffer from which you want the stored data returned.

The `XFetchBuffer` function returns zero to the nbytes_return argument if there is no data in the buffer or if an invalid buffer is specified.

To rotate the cut buffers, use `XRotateBuffers`.

```
XRotateBuffers(display, rotate)
    Display *display;
    int rotate;
```

display Specifies the connection to the X server.

rotate Specifies how much to rotate the cut buffers.

The `XRotateBuffers` function rotates the cut buffers, such that buffer 0 becomes buffer n, buffer 1 becomes n + 1 mod 8, and so on. This cut buffer numbering is global to the display. Note that `XRotateBuffers` generates `BadMatch` errors if any of the eight buffers have not been created.

16.7 Determining the Appropriate Visual Type

A single display can support multiple screens. Each screen can have several different visual types supported at different depths. You can use the functions described in this section to determine which visual to use for your application.

The functions in this section use the visual information masks and the XVisualInfo structure, which is defined in <X11/Xutil.h> and contains:

```
/* Visual information mask bits */
#define VisualNoMask              0x0
#define VisualIDMask              0x1
#define VisualScreenMask          0x2
#define VisualDepthMask           0x4
#define VisualClassMask           0x8
#define VisualRedMaskMask         0x10
#define VisualGreenMaskMask       0x20
#define VisualBlueMaskMask        0x40
#define VisualColormapSizeMask    0x80
#define VisualBitsPerRGBMask      0x100
#define VisualAllMask             0x1FF
/* Values */
typedef struct {
    Visual *visual;
    VisualID visualid;
    int screen;
    unsigned int depth;
    int class;
    unsigned long red_mask;
    unsigned long green_mask;
    unsigned long blue_mask;
    int colormap_size;
    int bits_per_rgb;
} XVisualInfo;
```

To obtain a list of visual information structures that match a specified template, use XGetVisualInfo.

```
XVisualInfo *XGetVisualInfo ( display, vinfo_mask, vinfo_template, nitems_return)
   Display *display;
   long vinfo_mask;
   XVisualInfo *vinfo_template;
   int *nitems_return;
```

display	Specifies the connection to the X server.
vinfo_mask	Specifies the visual mask value.
vinfo_template	Specifies the visual attributes that are to be used in matching the visual structures.
nitems_return	Returns the number of matching visual structures.

The `XGetVisualInfo` function returns a list of visual structures that have attributes equal to the attributes specified by vinfo_template. If no visual structures match the template using the specified vinfo_mask, `XGetVisualInfo` returns a NULL. To free the data returned by this function, use `XFree`.

To obtain the visual information that matches the specified depth and class of the screen, use `XMatchVisualInfo`.

```
Status XMatchVisualInfo ( display, screen, depth, class, vinfo_return)
    Display *display;
    int screen;
    int depth;
    int class;
    XVisualInfo *vinfo_return;
```

display	Specifies the connection to the X server.
screen	Specifies the screen.
depth	Specifies the depth of the screen.
class	Specifies the class of the screen.
vinfo_return	Returns the matched visual information.

The `XMatchVisualInfo` function returns the visual information for a visual that matches the specified depth and class for a screen. Because multiple visuals that match the specified depth and class can exist, the exact visual chosen is undefined. If a visual is found, `XMatchVisualInfo` returns nonzero and the information on the visual to vinfo_return. Otherwise, when a visual is not found, `XMatchVisualInfo` returns zero.

16.8 Manipulating Images

Xlib provides several functions that perform basic operations on images. All operations on images are defined using an `XImage` structure, as defined in `<X11/Xlib.h>`. Because the number of different types of image formats can be very large, this hides details of image storage properly from applications.

This section describes the functions for generic operations on images. Manufacturers can provide very fast implementations of these for the formats frequently encountered on their hardware. These functions are neither sufficient nor desirable to use for general image processing. Rather, they are here to provide minimal functions on screen format images. The basic operations for getting and putting images are `XGetImage` and `XPutImage`.

Note that no functions have been defined, as yet, to read and write images to and from disk files.

The `XImage` structure describes an image as it exists in the client's memory. The user can request that some of the members such as height, width, and xoffset be changed when the image is sent to the server. Note that bytes_per_line in concert with offset can be used to extract a subset of the image. Other members (for example, byte order, bitmap_unit, and so forth) are characteristics of both the image and the server. If these members differ between the image and the server, `XPutImage` makes the appropriate conversions. The first byte of the first line of plane n must be located at the address (data + (n * height * bytes_per_line)). For a description of the `XImage` structure, see section 8.7.

To allocate sufficient memory for an `XImage` structure, use `XCreateImage`.

XImage *XCreateImage (*display, visual, depth, format, offset, data, width, height, bitmap_pad, bytes_per_line*)
  Display **display*;
  Visual **visual*;
  unsigned int *depth*;
  int *format*;
  int *offset*;
  char **data*;
  unsigned int *width*;
  unsigned int *height*;
  int *bitmap_pad*;
  int *bytes_per_line*;

display Specifies the connection to the X server.

visual Specifies the `Visual` structure.

depth Specifies the depth of the image.

format Specifies the format for the image. You can pass `XYBitmap`, `XYPixmap`, or `ZPixmap`.

offset Specifies the number of pixels to ignore at the beginning of the scanline.
data Specifies the image data.
width Specifies the width of the image, in pixels.
height Specifies the height of the image, in pixels.
bitmap_pad Specifies the quantum of a scanline (8, 16, or 32). In other words, the start of one scanline is separated in client memory from the start of the next scanline by an integer multiple of this many bits.
bytes_per_line Specifies the number of bytes in the client image between the start of one scanline and the start of the next.

The `XCreateImage` function allocates the memory needed for an `XImage` structure for the specified display but does not allocate space for the image itself. Rather, it initializes the structure byte-order, bit-order, and bitmap-unit values from the display and returns a pointer to the `XImage` structure. The red, green, and blue mask values are defined for Z format images only and are derived from the `Visual` structure passed in. Other values also are passed in. The offset permits the rapid displaying of the image without requiring each scanline to be shifted into position. If you pass a zero value in bytes_per_line, Xlib assumes that the scanlines are contiguous in memory and calculates the value of bytes_per_line itself.

Note that when the image is created using `XCreateImage`, `XGetImage`, or `XSubImage`, the destroy procedure that the `XDestroyImage` function calls frees both the image structure and the data pointed to by the image structure.

The basic functions used to get a pixel, set a pixel, create a subimage, and add a constant value to an image are defined in the image object. The functions in this section are really macro invocations of the functions in the image object and are defined in `<X11/Xutil.h>`.

To obtain a pixel value in an image, use `XGetPixel`.

```
unsigned long XGetPixel ( ximage, x, y)
    XImage *ximage;
    int x;
    int y;
```

ximage Specifies the image.
x
y Specify the x and y coordinates.

The XGetPixel function returns the specified pixel from the named image. The pixel value is returned in normalized format (that is, the least-significant byte of the long is the least-significant byte of the pixel). The image must contain the x and y coordinates.

To set a pixel value in an image, use XPutPixel.

XPutPixel (*ximage*, *x*, *y*, *pixel*)
  XImage **ximage*;
  int *x*;
  int *y*;
  unsigned long *pixel*;

ximage Specifies the image.
x
y Specify the x and y coordinates.
pixel Specifies the new pixel value.

The XPutPixel function overwrites the pixel in the named image with the specified pixel value. The input pixel value must be in normalized format (that is, the least-significant byte of the long is the least-significant byte of the pixel). The image must contain the x and y coordinates.

To create a subimage, use XSubImage.

XImage *XSubImage (*ximage*, *x*, *y*, *subimage_width*, *subimage_height*)
  XImage **ximage*;
  int *x*;
  int *y*;
  unsigned int *subimage_width*;
  unsigned int *subimage_height*;

ximage Specifies the image.
x
y Specify the x and y coordinates.
subimage_width Specifies the width of the new subimage, in pixels.
subimage_height Specifies the height of the new subimage, in pixels.

The XSubImage function creates a new image that is a subsection of an existing one. It allocates the memory necessary for the new XImage structure and returns a pointer to the new image. The data is copied from the source image, and the image must contain the rectangle defined by x, y, subimage_width, and subimage_height.

To increment each pixel in an image by a constant value, use `XAddPixel`.

```
XAddPixel ( ximage, value)
   XImage *ximage;
   long value;
```

ximage Specifies the image.

value Specifies the constant value that is to be added.

The `XAddPixel` function adds a constant value to every pixel in an image. It is useful when you have a base pixel value from allocating color resources and need to manipulate the image to that form.

To deallocate the memory allocated in a previous call to `XCreateImage`, use `XDestroyImage`.

```
XDestroyImage ( ximage)
    XImage *ximage;
```

ximage Specifies the image.

The `XDestroyImage` function deallocates the memory associated with the `XImage` structure.

Note that when the image is created using `XCreateImage`, `XGetImage`, or `XSubImage`, the destroy procedure that this macro calls frees both the image structure and the data pointed to by the image structure.

16.9 Manipulating Bitmaps

Xlib provides functions that you can use to read a bitmap from a file, save a bitmap to a file, or create a bitmap. This section describes those functions that transfer bitmaps to and from the client's file system, thus allowing their reuse in a later connection (for example, from an entirely different client or to a different display or server).

The X version 11 bitmap file format is:

```
#define name_width width
#define name_height height
#define name_x_hot x
#define name_y_hot y
static unsigned char name_bits[] = { 0xNN,... }
```

The lines for the variables ending with _x_hot and _y_hot suffixes are optional because they are present only if a hotspot has been defined for this bitmap. The lines for the other variables are required. The word "unsigned" is optional; that is, the type of the _bits array can be "char" or "unsigned char". The _bits array must be large enough to contain the size bitmap. The bitmap unit is eight. The name is derived from the name of the file that you specified on the original command line by deleting the directory path and extension.

To read a bitmap from a file, use `XReadBitmapFile`.

int XReadBitmapFile(*display*, *d*, *filename*, *width_return*, *height_return*, *bitmap_return*, *x_hot_return*, *y_hot_return*)
  Display **display*;
  Drawable *d*;
  char **filename*;
  unsigned int **width_return*, **height_return*;
  Pixmap **bitmap_return*;
  int **x_hot_return*, **y_hot_return*;

display	Specifies the connection to the X server.
d	Specifies the drawable that indicates the screen.
filename	Specifies the file name to use. The format of the file name is operating-system dependent.
width_return	
height_return	Return the width and height values of the read in bitmap file.
bitmap_return	Returns the bitmap that is created.
x_hot_return	
y_hot_return	Return the hotspot coordinates.

The `XReadBitmapFile` function reads in a file containing a bitmap. The file is parsed in the encoding of the current locale. The ability to read other than the standard format is implementation dependent. If the file cannot be opened, `XReadBitmapFile` returns `BitmapOpenFailed`. If the file can be opened but does not contain valid bitmap data, it returns `BitmapFileInvalid`. If insufficient working storage is allocated, it returns `BitmapNoMemory`. If the file is readable and valid, it returns `BitmapSuccess`.

`XReadBitmapFile` returns the bitmap's height and width, as read from the file, to width_return and height_return. It then creates a pixmap of the appropriate size, reads the bitmap data from the file into the pixmap, and assigns the pixmap to the caller's variable bitmap. The caller must free the bitmap using `XFreePixmap` when finished. If *name*_x_hot and *name*_y_hot exist, `XReadBitmapFile` returns them to x_hot_return and y_hot_return; otherwise, it returns −1,−1.

`XReadBitmapFile` can generate `BadAlloc` and `BadDrawable` errors.

To write out a bitmap to a file, use `XWriteBitmapFile`.

int XWriteBitmapFile(*display*, *filename*, *bitmap*, *width*, *height*, *x_hot*, *y_hot*)
  Display **display*;
  char **filename*;
  Pixmap *bitmap*;
  unsigned int *width*, *height*;
  int *x_hot*, *y_hot*;

display Specifies the connection to the X server.

filename Specifies the file name to use. The format of the file name is operating-system dependent.

bitmap Specifies the bitmap.

width
height Specify the width and height.

x_hot
y_hot Specify where to place the hotspot coordinates (or −1,−1 if none are present) in the file.

The `XWriteBitmapFile` function writes a bitmap out to a file in the X version 11 format. The file is written in the encoding of the current locale. If the file cannot be opened for writing, it returns `BitmapOpenFailed`. If insufficient memory is allocated, `XWriteBitmapFile` returns `BitmapNoMemory`; otherwise, on no error, it returns `BitmapSuccess`. If x_hot and y_hot are not −1, −1, `XWriteBitmapFile` writes them out as the hotspot coordinates for the bitmap.

`XWriteBitmapFile` can generate `BadDrawable` and `BadMatch` errors.

To create a pixmap and then store bitmap-format data into it, use `XCreatePixmapFromBitmapData`.

Pixmap XCreatePixmapFromBitmapData (*display*, *d*, *data*, *width*, *height*, *fg*, *bg*, *depth*)
  Display **display*;
  Drawable *d*;
  char **data*;

```
   unsigned int width, height;
   unsigned long fg, bg;
   unsigned int depth;
```

display Specifies the connection to the X server.

d Specifies the drawable that indicates the screen.

data Specifies the data in bitmap format.

width
height Specify the width and height.

fg
bg Specify the foreground and background pixel values to use.

depth Specifies the depth of the pixmap.

The `XCreatePixmapFromBitmapData` function creates a pixmap of the given depth and then does a bitmap-format `XPutImage` of the data into it. The depth must be supported by the screen of the specified drawable, or a `BadMatch` error results.

`XCreatePixmapFromBitmapData` can generate `BadAlloc` and `BadMatch` errors.

To include a bitmap written out by `XWriteBitmapFile` in a program directly, as opposed to reading it in every time at run time, use `XCreateBitmapFromData`.

```
Pixmap XCreateBitmapFromData( display, d, data, width, height)
   Display *display;
   Drawable d;
   char *data;
   unsigned int width, height;
```

display Specifies the connection to the X server.

d Specifies the drawable that indicates the screen.

data Specifies the location of the bitmap data.

width
height Specify the width and height.

The `XCreateBitmapFromData` function allows you to include in your C program (using `#include`) a bitmap file that was written out by `XWriteBitmapFile` (X version 11 format only) without reading in the bitmap file. The following example creates a gray bitmap:

```
#include "gray.bitmap"

Pixmap bitmap;
bitmap = XCreateBitmapFromData(display, window, gray_bits, gray_width,
        gray_height);
```

If insufficient working storage was allocated, `XCreateBitmapFromData` returns `None`. It is your responsibility to free the bitmap using `XFreePixmap` when finished.

`XCreateBitmapFromData` can generate a `BadAlloc` error.

16.10 Using the Context Manager

The context manager provides a way of associating data with an X resource ID (mostly typically a window) in your program. Note that this is local to your program; the data is not stored in the server on a property list. Any amount of data in any number of pieces can be associated with a resource ID, and each piece of data has a type associated with it. The context manager requires knowledge of the resource ID and type to store or retrieve data.

Essentially, the context manager can be viewed as a two-dimensional, sparse array: one dimension is subscripted by the X resource ID and the other by a context type field. Each entry in the array contains a pointer to the data. Xlib provides context management functions with which you can save data values, get data values, delete entries, and create a unique context type. The symbols used are in `<X11/Xutil.h>`.

To save a data value that corresponds to a resource ID and context type, use `XSaveContext`.

```
int XSaveContext(display, rid, context, data)
    Display *display;
    XID rid;
    XContext context;
    XPointer data;
```

display Specifies the connection to the X server.
rid Specifies the resource ID with which the data is associated.
context Specifies the context type to which the data belongs.
data Specifies the data to be associated with the window and type.

If an entry with the specified resource ID and type already exists, `XSaveContext` overrides it with the specified context. The `XSaveContext` function returns a nonzero error code if an error has occurred and zero otherwise. Possible errors are `XCNOMEM` (out of memory).

To get the data associated with a resource ID and type, use `XFindContext`.

int XFindContext(*display, rid, context, data_return*)
Display **display*;
XID *rid*;
XContext *context*;
XPointer **data_return*;

display	Specifies the connection to the X server.
rid	Specifies the resource ID with which the data is associated.
context	Specifies the context type to which the data belongs.
data_return	Returns the data.

Because it is a return value, the data is a pointer. The `XFindContext` function returns a nonzero error code if an error has occurred and zero otherwise. Possible errors are `XCNOENT` (context-not-found).

To delete an entry for a given resource ID and type, use `XDeleteContext`.

int XDeleteContext(*display, rid, context*)
Display **display*;
XID *rid*;
XContext *context*;

display	Specifies the connection to the X server.
rid	Specifies the resource ID with which the data is associated.
context	Specifies the context type to which the data belongs.

The `XDeleteContext` function deletes the entry for the given resource ID and type from the data structure. This function returns the same error codes that `XFindContext` returns if called with the same arguments. `XDeleteContext` does not free the data whose address was saved.

To create a unique context type that may be used in subsequent calls to `XSaveContext` and `XFindContext`, use `XUniqueContext`.

XContext XUniqueContext()

Part II. X Window System Protocol

SECTION 1. PROTOCOL FORMATS

Request Format

Every request contains an 8-bit major opcode and a 16-bit length field expressed in units of four bytes. Every request consists of four bytes of a header (containing the major opcode, the length field, and a data byte) followed by zero or more additional bytes of data. The length field defines the total length of the request, including the header. The length field in a request must equal the minimum length required to contain the request. If the specified length is smaller or larger than the required length, an error is generated. Unused bytes in a request are not required to be zero. Major opcodes 128 through 255 are reserved for extensions. Extensions are intended to contain multiple requests, so extension requests typically have an additional minor opcode encoded in the second data byte in the request header. However, the placement and interpretation of this minor opcode and of all other fields in extension requests are not defined by the core protocol. Every request on a given connection is implicitly assigned a sequence number, starting with one, that is used in replies, errors, and events.

Reply Format

Every reply contains a 32-bit length field expressed in units of four bytes. Every reply consists of 32 bytes followed by zero or more additional bytes of data, as specified in the length field. Unused bytes within a reply are not guaranteed to be zero. Every reply also contains the least-significant 16 bits of the sequence number of the corresponding request.

Error Format

Error reports are 32 bytes long. Every error includes an 8-bit error code. Error codes 128 through 255 are reserved for extensions. Every error also includes the major and minor opcodes of the failed request and the least-significant 16 bits of the sequence number of the request. For the following errors (see section 4), the failing resource ID is also returned: `Colormap`, `Cursor`, `Drawable`, `Font`, `GContext`, `IDChoice`, `Pixmap`, and `Window`. For `Atom` errors, the failing atom is returned. For `Value` errors, the failing value is returned. Other core errors return no additional data. Unused bytes within an error are not guaranteed to be zero.

Event Format

Events are 32 bytes long. Unused bytes within an event are not guaranteed to be zero. Every event contains an 8-bit type code. The most-significant bit in this code is set if the event was generated from a `SendEvent` request. Event codes 64 through 127 are reserved for extensions, although the core protocol does not define a mechanism for selecting interest in such events. Every core event (with the exception of `KeymapNotify`) also contains the least-significant 16 bits of the sequence number of the last request issued by the client that was (or is currently being) processed by the server.

SECTION 2. SYNTACTIC CONVENTIONS

The rest of this document uses the following syntactic conventions.

- The syntax { . . .} encloses a set of alternatives.
- The syntax [. . .] encloses a set of structure components.
- In general, TYPEs are in uppercase and `AlternativeValues` are capitalized.
- Requests in section 9 are described in the following format:

RequestName

arg1: type1

. . .

argN: typeN

→

result1: type1

. . .

resultM: typeM

Errors: kind1, . . . , kindK

Description.

If no → is present in the description, then the request has no reply (it is asynchronous), although errors may still be reported. If →+ is used, then one or more replies can be generated for a single request.

- Events in section 11 are described in the following format:

EventName

value1: type1

. . .

valueN: typeN

Description.

SECTION 3. COMMON TYPES

Name	*Value*
LISTofFOO	A type name of the form LISTofFOO means a counted list of elements of type FOO. The size of the length field may vary (it is not necessarily the same size as a FOO), and in some cases, it may be implicit. It is fully specified in appendix F. Except where explicitly noted, zero-length lists are legal.
BITMASK	The types BITMASK and LISTofVALUE are somewhat special. Various requests contain arguments of the form: *value-mask*: BITMASK *value-list*: LISTofVALUE These are used to allow the client to specify a subset of a heterogeneous collection of optional arguments. The value-mask specifies which arguments are to be provided; each such argument is assigned a unique bit position. The representation of the BITMASK will typically contain more bits than there are defined arguments. The unused bits in the value-mask must be zero (or the server generates a `Value` error). The value-list contains one value for each bit set to 1 in the mask, from least-significant to most-significant bit in the mask. Each value is represented with four bytes, but the actual value occupies only the least-significant bytes as required. The values of the unused bytes do not matter.

Name	*Value*
OR	A type of the form "T1 or . . . or Tn" means the union of the indicated types. A single-element type is given as the element without enclosing braces.
WINDOW	32-bit value (top three bits guaranteed to be zero)
PIXMAP	32-bit value (top three bits guaranteed to be zero)
CURSOR	32-bit value (top three bits guaranteed to be zero)
FONT	32-bit value (top three bits guaranteed to be zero)
GCONTEXT	32-bit value (top three bits guaranteed to be zero)
COLORMAP	32-bit value (top three bits guaranteed to be zero)
DRAWABLE	WINDOW or PIXMAP
FONTABLE	FONT or GCONTEXT
ATOM	32-bit value (top three bits guaranteed to be zero)
VISUALID	32-bit value (top three bits guaranteed to be zero)
VALUE	32-bit quantity (used only in LISTofVALUE)
BYTE	8-bit value
INT8	8-bit signed integer
INT16	16-bit signed integer
INT32	32-bit signed integer
CARD8	8-bit unsigned integer
CARD16	16-bit unsigned integer
CARD32	32-bit unsigned integer
TIMESTAMP	CARD32
BITGRAVITY	{Forget, Static, NorthWest, North, NorthEast, West, Center, East, SouthWest, South, SouthEast}
WINGRAVITY	{Unmap, Static, NorthWest, North, NorthEast, West, Center, East, SouthWest, South, SouthEast}
BOOL	{True, False}
EVENT	{KeyPress, KeyRelease, OwnerGrabButton, ButtonPress, ButtonRelease, EnterWindow, LeaveWindow, PointerMotion, PointerMotionHint, Button1Motion, Button2Motion, Button3Motion, Button4Motion, Button5Motion, ButtonMotion, Exposure, VisibilityChange, StructureNotify, ResizeRedirect, SubstructureNotify, SubstructureRedirect, FocusChange, PropertyChange, ColormapChange, KeymapState}
POINTEREVENT	{ButtonPress, ButtonRelease, EnterWindow, LeaveWindow, PointerMotion, PointerMotionHint, Button1Motion, Button2Motion, Button3Motion, Button4Motion, Button5Motion, ButtonMotion, KeymapState}

Name	*Value*
DEVICEEVENT	{KeyPress, KeyRelease, ButtonPress, ButtonRelease, PointerMotion, Button1Motion, Button2Motion, Button3Motion, Button4Motion, Button5Motion, ButtonMotion}
KEYSYM	32-bit value (top three bits guaranteed to be zero)
KEYCODE	CARD8
BUTTON	CARD8
KEYMASK	{Shift, Lock, Control, Mod1, Mod2, Mod3, Mod4, Mod5}
BUTMASK	{Button1, Button2, Button3, Button4, Button5}
KEYBUTMASK	KEYMASK or BUTMASK
STRING8	LISTofCARD8
STRING16	LISTofCHAR2B
CHAR2B	[byte1, byte2: CARD8]
POINT	[x, y: INT16]
RECTANGLE	[x, y: INT16, width, height: CARD16]
ARC	[x, y: INT16, width, height: CARD16, angle1, angle2: INT16]
HOST	[family: { Internet, DECnet, Chaos} address: LISTofBYTE]

The [x,y] coordinates of a RECTANGLE specify the upper-left corner.

The primary interpretation of large characters in a STRING16 is that they are composed of two bytes used to index a two-dimensional matrix; hence, the use of CHAR2B rather than CARD16. This corresponds to the JIS/ISO method of indexing 2-byte characters. It is expected that most large fonts will be defined with 2-byte matrix indexing. For large fonts constructed with linear indexing, a CHAR2B can be interpreted as a 16-bit number by treating byte1 as the most-significant byte. This means that clients should always transmit such 16-bit character values most-significant byte first, as the server will never byte-swap CHAR2B quantities.

The length, format, and interpretation of a HOST address are specific to the family (see ChangeHosts request).

SECTION 4. ERRORS

In general, when a request terminates with an error, the request has no side effects (that is, there is no partial execution). The only requests for which this is not true are ChangeWindowAttributes, ChangeGC, PolyText8, PolyText16, FreeColors, StoreColors, and ChangeKeyboardControl.

The following error codes result from various requests as follows:

Error	*Description*
Access	An attempt is made to grab a key/button combination already grabbed by another client. An attempt is made to free a colormap entry not allocated by the client or to free an entry in a colormap that was created with all entries writable. An attempt is made to store into a read-only or an unallocated colormap entry. An attempt is made to modify the access control list from other than the local host (or otherwise authorized client). An attempt is made to select an event type that only one client can select at a time when another client has already selected it.
Alloc	The server failed to allocate the requested resource. Note that the explicit listing of Alloc errors in request only covers allocation errors at a very coarse level and is not intended to cover all cases of a server running out of allocation space in the middle of service. The semantics when a server runs out of allocation space are left unspecified, but a server may generate an Alloc error on any request for this reason, and clients should be prepared to receive such errors and handle or discard them.
Atom	A value for an ATOM argument does not name a defined ATOM.
Colormap	A value for a COLORMAP argument does not name a defined COLORMAP.
Cursor	A value for a CURSOR argument does not name a defined CURSOR.
Drawable	A value for a DRAWABLE argument does not name a defined WINDOW or PIXMAP.
Font	A value for a FONT argument does not name a defined FONT. A value for a FONTABLE argument does not name a defined FONT or a defined GCONTEXT.
GContext	A value for a GCONTEXT argument does not name a defined GCONTEXT.
IDChoice	The value chosen for a resource identifier either is not included in the range assigned to the client or is already in use.
Implementation	The server does not implement some aspect of the request. A server that generates this error for a core request is deficient. As

Error	*Description*
	such, this error is not listed for any of the requests, but clients should be prepared to receive such errors and handle or discard them.
`Length`	The length of a request is shorter or longer than that required to minimally contain the arguments. The length of a request exceeds the maximum length accepted by the server.
`Match`	An `InputOnly` window is used as a DRAWABLE. In a graphics request, the GCONTEXT argument does not have the same root and depth as the destination DRAWABLE argument. Some argument (or pair of arguments) has the correct type and range, but it fails to match in some other way required by the request.
`Name`	A font or color of the specified name does not exist.
`Pixmap`	A value for a PIXMAP argument does not name a defined PIXMAP.
`Request`	The major or minor opcode does not specify a valid request.
`Value`	Some numeric value falls outside the range of values accepted by the request. Unless a specific range is specified for an argument, the full range defined by the argument's type is accepted. Any argument defined as a set of alternatives typically can generate this error (due to the encoding).
`Window`	A value for a WINDOW argument does not name a defined WINDOW.

Note The `Atom`, `Colormap`, `Cursor`, `Drawable`, `Font`, `GContext`, `Pixmap`, and `Window` errors are also used when the argument type is extended by union with a set of fixed alternatives, for example, <WINDOW or `PointerRoot` or `None`>.

SECTION 5. KEYBOARDS

A KEYCODE represents a physical (or logical) key. Keycodes lie in the inclusive range [8,255]. A keycode value carries no intrinsic information, although server implementors may attempt to encode geometry information (for example, matrix) to be interpreted in a server-dependent fashion. The mapping between keys and keycodes cannot be changed using the protocol.

A KEYSYM is an encoding of a symbol on the cap of a key. The set of defined KEYSYMs include the character sets Latin-1, Latin-2, Latin-3, Latin-4, Kana, Arabic, Cyrillic, Greek, Tech, Special, Publish, APL, and Hebrew as well as a set of symbols common on keyboards (Return, Help, Tab, and so on). KEYSYMs with the most-significant bit (of the 29 bits) set are reserved as vendor-specific.

A list of KEYSYMs is associated with each KEYCODE. The list is intended to convey the set of symbols on the corresponding key. If the list (ignoring trailing `NoSymbol` entries) is a single KEYSYM "*K*", then the list is treated as if it were the list "*K* NoSymbol *K* NoSymbol". If the list (ignoring trailing `NoSymbol` entries) is a pair of KEYSYMs "*K1 K2*", then the list is treated as if it were the list "*K1 K2 K1 K2*". If the list (ignoring trailing `NoSymbol` entries) is a triple of KEYSYMs "*K1 K2 K3*", then the list is treated as if it were the list "*K1 K2 K3* NoSymbol". When an explicit "void" element is desired in the list, the value `VoidSymbol` can be used.

The first four elements of the list are split into two groups of KEYSYMs. Group 1 contains the first and second KEYSYMs, Group 2 contains the third and fourth KEYSYMs. Within each group, if the second element of the group is `NoSymbol`, then the group should be treated as if the second element were the same as the first element, except when the first element is an alphabetic KEYSYM "*K*" for which both lowercase and uppercase forms are defined. In that case, the group should be treated as if the first element were the lowercase form of "*K*" and the second element were the uppercase form of "*K*".

The standard rules for obtaining a KEYSYM from a `KeyPress` event make use of only the Group 1 and Group 2 KEYSYMs; no interpretation of other KEYSYMs in the list is defined. The modifier state determines which group to use. Switching between groups is controlled by the KEYSYM named MODE SWITCH, by attaching that KEYSYM to some KEYCODE and attaching that KEYCODE to any one of the modifiers `Mod1` through `Mod5`. This modifier is called the *group modifier*. For any KEYCODE, Group 1 is used when the group modifier is off, and Group 2 is used when the group modifier is on.

Within a group, the modifier state determines which KEYSYM to use. The first KEYSYM is used when the `Shift` and `Lock` modifiers are off. The second KEYSYM is used when the `Shift` modifier is on, or when the `Lock` modifier is on and the second KEYSYM is uppercase alphabetic, or when the `Lock` modifier is on and is interpreted as ShiftLock. Otherwise, when the `Lock` modifier is on and is interpreted as CapsLock, the state of the `Shift` modifier is applied first to select a KEYSYM; but if that KEYSYM is lowercase alphabetic, then the corresponding uppercase KEYSYM is used instead.

The mapping between KEYCODEs and KEYSYMs is not used directly by the server; it is merely stored for reading and writing by clients.

The KEYMASK modifier named `Lock` is intended to be mapped to either a CapsLock or a ShiftLock key, but which one is left as application-specific and/or user-specific. However, it is suggested that the determination be made according to the associated KEYSYM(s) of the corresponding KEYCODE.

SECTION 6. POINTERS

Buttons are always numbered starting with one.

SECTION 7. PREDEFINED ATOMS

Predefined atoms are not strictly necessary and may not be useful in all environments, but they will eliminate many `InternAtom` requests in most applications. Note that they are predefined only in the sense of having numeric values, not in the sense of having required semantics. The core protocol imposes no semantics on these names, but semantics are specified in other X Consortium standards. See part III, "Inter-Client Communication Conventions Manual," and part IV, "X Logical Font Description Conventions."

The following names have predefined atom values. Note that uppercase and lowercase matter.

ARC	ITALIC_ANGLE	STRING
ATOM	MAX_SPACE	SUBSCRIPT_X
BITMAP	MIN_SPACE	SUBSCRIPT_Y
CAP_HEIGHT	NORM_SPACE	SUPERSCRIPT_X
CARDINAL	NOTICE	SUPERSCRIPT_Y
COLORMAP	PIXMAP	UNDERLINE_POSITION
COPYRIGHT	POINT	UNDERLINE_THICKNESS
CURSOR	POINT_SIZE	VISUALID
CUT_BUFFER0	PRIMARY	WEIGHT
CUT_BUFFER1	QUAD_WIDTH	WINDOW
CUT_BUFFER2	RECTANGLE	WM_CLASS
CUT_BUFFER3	RESOLUTION	WM_CLIENT_MACHINE
CUT_BUFFER4	RESOURCE_MANAGER	WM_COMMAND

CUT_BUFFER5
CUT_BUFFER6
CUT_BUFFER7
DRAWABLE
END_SPACE
FAMILY_NAME
FONT
FONT_NAME
FULL_NAME
INTEGER
RGB_BEST_MAP
RGB_BLUE_MAP
RGB_COLOR_MAP
RGB_DEFAULT_MAP
RGB_GRAY_MAP
RGB_GREEN_MAP
RGB_RED_MAP
SECONDARY
STRIKEOUT_ASCENT
WM_HINTS
WM_ICON_NAME
WM_ICON_SIZE
WM_NAME
WM_NORMAL_HINTS
WM_SIZE_HINTS
WM_TRANSIENT_FOR
WM_ZOOM_HINTS
X_HEIGHT
STRIKEOUT_DESCENT

To avoid conflicts with possible future names for which semantics might be imposed (either at the protocol level or in terms of higher level user interface models), names beginning with an underscore should be used for atoms that are private to a particular vendor or organization. To guarantee no conflicts between vendors and organizations, additional prefixes need to be used. However, the protocol does not define the mechanism for choosing such prefixes. For names private to a single application or end user but stored in globally accessible locations, it is suggested that two leading underscores be used to avoid conflicts with other names.

SECTION 8. CONNECTION SETUP

For remote clients, the X protocol can be built on top of any reliable byte stream.

Connection Initiation

The client must send an initial byte of data to identify the byte order to be employed. The value of the byte must be octal 102 or 154. The value 102 (ASCII uppercase B) means values are transmitted most-significant byte first, and value 154 (ASCII lowercase l) means values are transmitted least-significant byte first. Except where explicitly noted in the protocol, all 16-bit and 32-bit quantities sent by the client must be transmitted with this byte order, and all 16-bit and 32-bit quantities returned by the server will be transmitted with this byte order.

Following the byte-order byte, the client sends the following information at connection setup:

protocol-major-version: CARD16
protocol-minor-version: CARD16
authorization-protocol-name: STRING8
authorization-protocol-data: STRING8

The version numbers indicate what version of the protocol the client expects the server to implement.

The authorization name indicates what authorization protocol the client expects the server to use, and the data is specific to that protocol. Specification of valid authorization mechanisms is not part of the core X protocol. It is hoped that eventually one authorization protocol will be agreed upon. In the meantime, a server that implements a different protocol than the client expects or that only implements the host-based mechanism may simply ignore this information. If both name and data strings are empty, this is to be interpreted as "no explicit authorization."

Server Response

The client receives the following information at connection setup:

success: BOOL
protocol-major-version: CARD16
protocol-minor-version: CARD16
length: CARD16

Length is the amount of additional data to follow, in units of four bytes. The version numbers are an escape hatch in case future revisions of the protocol are necessary. In general, the major version would increment for incompatible changes, and the minor version would increment for small upward compatible changes. Barring changes, the major version will be 11, and the minor version will be 0. The protocol version numbers returned indicate the protocol the server actually supports. This might not equal the version sent by the client. The server can (but need not) refuse connections from clients that offer a different version than the server supports. A server can (but need not) support more than one version simultaneously.

The client receives the following additional data if authorization fails:

reason: STRING8

The client receives the following additional data if authorization is accepted:

vendor: STRING8
release-number: CARD32
resource-id-base, resource-id-mask: CARD32
image-byte-order: {LSBFirst,MSBFirst}
bitmap-scanline-unit: {8, 16, 32}
bitmap-scanline-pad: {8, 16, 32}
bitmap-bit-order: {LeastSignificant,MostSignificant}
pixmap-formats: LISTofFORMAT
roots: LISTofSCREEN
motion-buffer-size: CARD32
maximum-request-length: CARD16
min-keycode, max-keycode: KEYCODE

where:

FORMAT: [depth: CARD8,
bits-per-pixel: {1, 4, 8, 16, 24, 32}
scanline-pad: {8, 16, 32}]

SCREEN: [root: WINDOW
width-in-pixels, height-in-pixels: CARD16
width-in-millimeters, height-in-millimeters: CARD16
allowed-depths: LISTofDEPTH
root-depth: CARD8
root-visual: VISUALID
default-colormap: COLORMAP
white-pixel, black-pixel: CARD32
min-installed-maps, max-installed-maps: CARD16
backing-stores: {Never,WhenMapped,Always}
save-unders: BOOL
current-input-masks: SETofEVENT]

DEPTH: [depth: CARD8
visuals: LISTofVISUALTYPE]

VISUALTYPE: [visual-id: VISUALID
class: {StaticGray,StaticColor,TrueColor,GrayScale,
PseudoColor,DirectColor}
red-mask, green-mask, blue-mask: CARD32
bits-per-rgb-value: CARD8
colormap-entries: CARD16]

Server Information

The information that is global to the server is:

The vendor string gives some identification of the owner of the server implementation. The vendor controls the semantics of the release number.

The resource-id-mask contains a single contiguous set of bits (at least 18). The client allocates resource IDs for types WINDOW, PIXMAP, CURSOR, FONT, GCONTEXT, and COLORMAP by choosing a value with only some subset of these bits set and ORing it with resource-id-base. Only values constructed in this way can be used to name newly created resources over this connection. Resource IDs never have the top three bits set. The client is not restricted to linear or contiguous allocation of resource IDs. Once an ID has been freed, it can be reused, but this should not be necessary. An ID must be unique with respect to the IDs of all other resources, not just other resources of the same type. However, note that the value spaces of resource identifiers, atoms, visualids, and keysyms are distinguished by context, and as such, are not required to be disjoint; for example, a given numeric value might be both a valid window ID, a valid atom, and a valid keysym.

Although the server is in general responsible for byte-swapping data to match the client, images are always transmitted and received in formats (including byte order) specified by the server. The byte order for images is given by image-byte-order and applies to each scanline unit in XY format (bitmap format) and to each pixel value in Z format.

A bitmap is represented in scanline order. Each scanline is padded to a multiple of bits as given by bitmap-scanline-pad. The pad bits are of arbitrary value. The scanline is quantized in multiples of bits as given by bitmap-scanline-unit. The bitmap-scanline-unit is always less than or equal to the bitmap-scanline-pad. Within each unit, the leftmost bit in the bitmap is either the least-significant or most-significant bit in the unit, as given by bitmap-bit-order. If a pixmap is represented in XY format, each plane is represented as a bitmap, and the planes appear from most-significant to least-significant in bit order with no padding between planes.

Pixmap-formats contains one entry for each depth value. The entry describes the Z format used to represent images of that depth. An entry for a depth is included if any screen supports that depth, and all screens supporting that depth must support only that Z format for that depth. In Z format, the pixels are in scanline order, left to right within a scanline. The number of bits used to hold each pixel is given by bits-per-pixel. Bits-per-pixel may be larger than strictly required by the depth, in which case the least-significant bits are used to hold the pixmap data, and the values of the unused high-order bits are undefined. When the bits-per-pixel is 4, the order of nibbles in the byte is the same as the image byte-order. When the bits-per-pixel is 1, the format is identical for bitmap format. Each scanline is padded to a multiple of bits as given by scanline-pad. When bits-per-pixel is 1, this will be identical to bitmap-scanline-pad.

How a pointing device roams the screens is up to the server implementation and is transparent to the protocol. No geometry is defined among screens.

The server may retain the recent history of pointer motion and do so to a finer granularity than is reported by `MotionNotify` events. The `GetMotionEvents` request makes such history available. The motion-buffer-size gives the approximate maximum number of elements in the history buffer.

Maximum-request-length specifies the maximum length of a request accepted by the server, in 4-byte units. That is, length is the maximum value that can appear in the length field of a request. Requests larger than this maximum generate a `Length` error, and the server will read and simply discard the entire request. Maximum-request-length will always be at least 4096 (that is, requests of length up to and including 16384 bytes will be accepted by all servers).

Min-keycode and max-keycode specify the smallest and largest keycode values transmitted by the server. Min-keycode is never less than 8, and max-keycode is never greater than 255. Not all keycodes in this range are required to have corresponding keys.

Screen Information

The information that applies per screen is:

The allowed-depths specifies what pixmap and window depths are supported. Pixmaps are supported for each depth listed, and windows of that depth are supported if at least one visual type is listed for the depth. A pixmap depth of one is always supported and listed, but windows of depth one might not be supported. A depth of zero is never listed, but zero-depth `InputOnly` windows are always supported.

Root-depth and root-visual specify the depth and visual type of the root window. Width-in-pixels and height-in-pixels specify the size of the root window (which cannot be changed). The class of the root window is always `InputOutput`. Width-in-millimeters and height-in-millimeters can be used to determine the physical size and the aspect ratio.

The default-colormap is the one initially associated with the root window. Clients with minimal color requirements creating windows of the same depth as the root may want to allocate from this map by default.

Black-pixel and white-pixel can be used in implementing a monochrome application. These pixel values are for permanently allocated entries in the default-colormap. The actual RGB values may be settable on some screens and, in any case, may not actually be black and white. The names are intended to convey the expected relative intensity of the colors.

The border of the root window is initially a pixmap filled with the black-pixel. The initial background of the root window is a pixmap filled with some unspecified two-color pattern using black-pixel and white-pixel.

Min-installed-maps specifies the number of maps that can be guaranteed to be installed simultaneously (with `InstallColormap`), regardless of the number of entries allocated in each map. Max-installed-maps specifies the maximum number of maps that might possibly be installed simultaneously, depending on their allocations. Multiple static-visual colormaps with identical contents but differing in resource ID should be considered as a single map for the purposes of this number. For the typical case of a single hardware colormap, both values will be 1.

Backing-stores indicates when the server supports backing stores for this screen, although it may be storage limited in the number of windows it can support at once. If save-unders is `True`, the server can support the save-under mode in `CreateWindow` and `ChangeWindowAttributes`, although again it may be storage limited.

The current-input-events is what `GetWindowAttributes` would return for the all-event-masks for the root window.

Visual Information

The information that applies per visual-type is:

A given visual type might be listed for more than one depth or for more than one screen.

For `PseudoColor`, a pixel value indexes a colormap to produce independent RGB values; the RGB values can be changed dynamically. `GrayScale` is treated in the same way as `PseudoColor` except which primary drives the screen is undefined; thus, the client should always store the same value for red, green, and blue in colormaps. For `DirectColor`, a pixel value is decomposed into separate RGB subfields, and each subfield separately indexes the colormap for the corresponding value. The RGB values can be changed dynamically. `TrueColor` is treated in the same way as `DirectColor` except the colormap has predefined read-only RGB values. These values are server-dependent but provide linear or near-linear increasing ramps in each primary. `StaticColor` is treated in the same way as `PseudoColor` except the colormap has predefined read-only RGB values, which are server-dependent. `StaticGray` is treated in the same way as `StaticColor` except the red, green, and blue values are equal for any single pixel value, resulting in shades of gray. `StaticGray` with a two-entry colormap can be thought of as monochrome.

The red-mask, green-mask, and blue-mask are only defined for `DirectColor` and `TrueColor`. Each has one contiguous set of bits set to 1 with no intersections. Usually each mask has the same number of bits set to 1.

The bits-per-rgb-value specifies the log base 2 of the number of distinct color intensity values (individually) of red, green, and blue. This number need not bear any relation to the number of colormap entries. Actual RGB values are always passed in the protocol within a 16-bit spectrum, with 0 being minimum intensity and 65535 being the maximum intensity. On hardware that provides a linear zero-based intensity ramp, the following relationship exists:

hw-intensity = protocol-intensity / (65536 / total-hw-intensities)

Colormap entries are indexed from 0. The colormap-entries defines the number of available colormap entries in a newly created colormap. For `DirectColor` and `TrueColor`, this will usually be 2 to the power of the maximum number of bits set to 1 in red-mask, green-mask, and blue-mask.

SECTION 9. REQUESTS

CreateWindow

wid, parent: WINDOW
class: `{InputOutput,InputOnly,CopyFromParent}`

depth: CARD8
visual: VISUALID or CopyFromParent
x, y: INT16
width, height, border-width: CARD16
value-mask: BITMASK
value-list: LISTofVALUE

Errors: Alloc, Colormap, Cursor, IDChoice, Match, Pixmap, Value, Window

This request creates an unmapped window and assigns the identifier wid to it.

A class of CopyFromParent means the class is taken from the parent. A depth of zero for class InputOutput or CopyFromParent means the depth is taken from the parent. A visual of CopyFromParent means the visual type is taken from the parent. For class InputOutput, the visual type and depth must be a combination supported for the screen (or a Match error results). The depth need not be the same as the parent, but the parent must not be of class InputOnly (or a Match error results). For class InputOnly, the depth must be zero (or a Match error results), and the visual must be one supported for the screen (or a Match error results). However, the parent can have any depth and class.

The server essentially acts as if InputOnly windows do not exist for the purposes of graphics requests, exposure processing, and VisibilityNotify events. An InputOnly window cannot be used as a drawable (as a source or destination for graphics requests). InputOnly and InputOutput windows act identically in other respects–properties, grabs, input control, and so on.

The coordinate system has the X axis horizontal and the Y axis vertical with the origin [0, 0] at the upper-left corner. Coordinates are integral, in terms of pixels, and coincide with pixel centers. Each window and pixmap has its own coordinate system. For a window, the origin is inside the border at the inside, upper-left corner.

The x and y coordinates for the window are relative to the parent's origin and specify the position of the upper-left outer corner of the window (not the origin). The width and height specify the inside size (not including the border) and must be nonzero (or a Value error results). The border-width for an InputOnly window must be zero (or a Match error results).

The window is placed on top in the stacking order with respect to siblings.

The value-mask and value-list specify attributes of the window that are to be explicitly initialized. The possible values are:

Attribute	*Type*
background-pixmap	PIXMAP or None or ParentRelative
background-pixel	CARD32
border-pixmap	PIXMAP or CopyFromParent
border-pixel	CARD32
bit-gravity	BITGRAVITY
win-gravity	WINGRAVITY
backing-store	{NotUseful,WhenMapped,Always}
backing-planes	CARD32
backing-pixel	CARD32
save-under	BOOL
event-mask	SETofEVENT
do-not-propagate-mask	SETofDEVICEEVENT
override-redirect	BOOL
colormap	COLORMAP or CopyFromParent
cursor	CURSOR or None

The default values when attributes are not explicitly initialized are:

Attribute	*Default*
background-pixmap	None
border-pixmap	CopyFromParent
bit-gravity	Forget
win-gravity	NorthWest
backing-store	NotUseful
backing-planes	all ones
backing-pixel	zero
save-under	False
event-mask	{} (empty set)
do-not-propagate-mask	{} (empty set)
override-redirect	False
colormap	CopyFromParent
cursor	None

Only the following attributes are defined for InputOnly windows:

- win-gravity
- event-mask
- do-not-propagate-mask

- override-redirect
- cursor

It is a `Match` error to specify any other attributes for `InputOnly` windows.

If background-pixmap is given, it overrides the default background-pixmap. The background pixmap and the window must have the same root and the same depth (or a `Match` error results). Any size pixmap can be used, although some sizes may be faster than others. If background `None` is specified, the window has no defined background. If background `ParentRelative` is specified, the parent's background is used, but the window must have the same depth as the parent (or a `Match` error results). If the parent has background `None`, then the window will also have background `None`. A copy of the parent's background is not made. The parent's background is reexamined each time the window background is required. If background-pixel is given, it overrides the default background-pixmap and any background-pixmap given explicitly, and a pixmap of undefined size filled with background-pixel is used for the background. Range checking is not performed on the background-pixel value; it is simply truncated to the appropriate number of bits. For a `ParentRelative` background, the background tile origin always aligns with the parent's background tile origin. Otherwise, the background tile origin is always the window origin.

When no valid contents are available for regions of a window and the regions are either visible or the server is maintaining backing store, the server automatically tiles the regions with the window's background unless the window has a background of `None`. If the background is `None`, the previous screen contents from other windows of the same depth as the window are simply left in place if the contents come from the parent of the window or an inferior of the parent; otherwise, the initial contents of the exposed regions are undefined. Exposure events are then generated for the regions, even if the background is `None`.

The border tile origin is always the same as the background tile origin. If border-pixmap is given, it overrides the default border-pixmap. The border pixmap and the window must have the same root and the same depth (or a `Match` error results). Any size pixmap can be used, although some sizes may be faster than others. If `CopyFromParent` is given, the parent's border pixmap is copied (subsequent changes to the parent's border attribute do not affect the child), but the window must have the same depth as the parent (or a `Match` error results). The pixmap might be copied by sharing the same pixmap object between the child and parent or by making a complete copy of the pixmap contents. If border-pixel is given, it overrides the default border-pixmap and any border-pixmap given explicitly, and a pixmap of undefined size filled with border-pixel is used for the border. Range checking is not performed on the border-pixel value; it is simply truncated to the appropriate number of bits.

Output to a window is always clipped to the inside of the window, so that the border is never affected.

The bit-gravity defines which region of the window should be retained if the window is resized, and win-gravity defines how the window should be repositioned if the parent is resized (see `ConfigureWindow` request).

A backing-store of `WhenMapped` advises the server that maintaining contents of obscured regions when the window is mapped would be beneficial. A backing-store of `Always` advises the server that maintaining contents even when the window is unmapped would be beneficial. In this case, the server may generate an exposure event when the window is created. A value of `NotUseful` advises the server that maintaining contents is unnecessary, although a server may still choose to maintain contents while the window is mapped. Note that if the server maintains contents, then the server should maintain complete contents not just the region within the parent boundaries, even if the window is larger than its parent. While the server maintains contents, exposure events will not normally be generated, but the server may stop maintaining contents at any time.

If save-under is `True`, the server is advised that when this window is mapped, saving the contents of windows it obscures would be beneficial.

When the contents of obscured regions of a window are being maintained, regions obscured by noninferior windows are included in the destination (and source, when the window is the source) of graphics requests, but regions obscured by inferior windows are not included.

The backing-planes indicates (with bits set to 1) which bit planes of the window hold dynamic data that must be preserved in backing-stores and during save-unders. The backing-pixel specifies what value to use in planes not covered by backing-planes. The server is free to save only the specified bit planes in the backing-store or save-under and regenerate the remaining planes with the specified pixel value. Any bits beyond the specified depth of the window in these values are simply ignored.

The event-mask defines which events the client is interested in for this window (or for some event types, inferiors of the window). The do-not-propagate-mask defines which events should not be propagated to ancestor windows when no client has the event type selected in this window.

The override-redirect specifies whether map and configure requests on this window should override a `SubstructureRedirect` on the parent, typically to inform a window manager not to tamper with the window.

The colormap specifies the colormap that best reflects the true colors of the window. Servers capable of supporting multiple hardware colormaps may use this information, and window managers may use it for `InstallColormap` requests. The colormap must have the same visual type and root as the window (or a `Match` error results). If `CopyFromParent` is specified, the parent's colormap is copied (subsequent changes to the parent's colormap attribute do not affect the child). However, the window must have the same visual type as the parent (or a `Match` error results), and the parent must not have a colormap of `None` (or a `Match` error results). For an explanation of `None`, see `FreeColormap` request. The colormap is copied by sharing the colormap object between the child and the parent, not by making a complete copy of the colormap contents.

If a cursor is specified, it will be used whenever the pointer is in the window. If `None` is specified, the parent's cursor will be used when the pointer is in the window, and any change in the parent's cursor will cause an immediate change in the displayed cursor.

This request generates a `CreateNotify` event.

The background and border pixmaps and the cursor may be freed immediately if no further explicit references to them are to be made.

Subsequent drawing into the background or border pixmap has an undefined effect on the window state. The server might or might not make a copy of the pixmap.

ChangeWindowAttributes

window: WINDOW
value-mask: BITMASK
value-list: LISTofVALUE

Errors: `Access`, `Colormap`, `Cursor`, `Match`, `Pixmap`, `Value`, `Window`

The value-mask and value-list specify which attributes are to be changed. The values and restrictions are the same as for `CreateWindow`.

Setting a new background, whether by background-pixmap or background-pixel, overrides any previous background. Setting a new border, whether by border-pixel or border-pixmap, overrides any previous border.

Changing the background does not cause the window contents to be changed. Setting the border or changing the background such that the border tile origin changes causes the border to be repainted. Changing the background of a root window to `None` or `ParentRelative` restores the default background pixmap. Changing the border of a root window to `CopyFromParent` restores the default border pixmap.

Changing the win-gravity does not affect the current position of the window.

Changing the backing-store of an obscured window to `WhenMapped` or `Always` or changing the backing-planes, backing-pixel, or save-under of a mapped window may have no immediate effect.

Multiple clients can select input on the same window; their event-masks are disjoint. When an event is generated, it will be reported to all interested clients. However, only one client at a time can select for `SubstructureRedirect`, only one client at a time can select for `ResizeRedirect`, and only one client at a time can select for `ButtonPress`. An attempt to violate these restrictions results in an `Access` error.

There is only one do-not-propagate-mask for a window, not one per client.

Changing the colormap of a window (by defining a new map, not by changing the contents of the existing map) generates a `ColormapNotify` event. Changing the colormap of a visible window might have no immediate effect on the screen (see `InstallColormap` request).

Changing the cursor of a root window to `None` restores the default cursor.

The order in which attributes are verified and altered is server-dependent. If an error is generated, a subset of the attributes may have been altered.

GetWindowAttributes

window: WINDOW

→

visual: VISUALID
class: {`InputOutput`,`InputOnly`}
bit-gravity: BITGRAVITY
win-gravity: WINGRAVITY
backing-store: {`NotUseful`,`WhenMapped`,`Always`}

backing-planes: CARD32
backing-pixel: CARD32
save-under: BOOL
colormap: COLORMAP or `None`
map-is-installed: BOOL
map-state: {`Unmapped`, `Unviewable`, `Viewable`}
all-event-masks, your-event-mask: SETofEVENT
do-not-propagate-mask: SETofDEVICEEVENT
override-redirect: BOOL

Errors: `Window`

This request returns the current attributes of the window. A window is `Unviewable` if it is mapped but some ancestor is unmapped. All-event-masks is the inclusive-OR of all event masks selected on the window by clients. Your-event-mask is the event mask selected by the querying client.

DestroyWindow

window: WINDOW

Errors: `Window`

If the argument window is mapped, an `UnmapWindow` request is performed automatically. The window and all inferiors are then destroyed, and a `DestroyNotify` event is generated for each window. The ordering of the `DestroyNotify` events is such that for any given window, `DestroyNotify` is generated on all inferiors of the window before being generated on the window itself. The ordering among siblings and across subhierarchies is not otherwise constrained.

Normal exposure processing on formerly obscured windows is performed.

If the window is a root window, this request has no effect.

DestroySubwindows

window: WINDOW

Errors: `Window`

This request performs a `DestroyWindow` request on all children of the window, in bottom-to-top stacking order.

ChangeSaveSet

window: WINDOW
mode: {Insert,Delete}

Errors: Match, Value, Window

This request adds or removes the specified window from the client's save-set. The window must have been created by some other client (or a Match error results). For further information about the use of the save-set, see section 10.

When windows are destroyed, the server automatically removes them from the save-set.

ReparentWindow

window, parent: WINDOW
x, y: INT16

Errors: Match, Window

If the window is mapped, an UnmapWindow request is performed automatically first. The window is then removed from its current position in the hierarchy and is inserted as a child of the specified parent. The x and y coordinates are relative to the parent's origin and specify the new position of the upper-left outer corner of the window. The window is placed on top in the stacking order with respect to siblings. A ReparentNotify event is then generated. The override-redirect attribute of the window is passed on in this event; a value of True indicates that a window manager should not tamper with this window. Finally, if the window was originally mapped, a MapWindow request is performed automatically.

Normal exposure processing on formerly obscured windows is performed. The server might not generate exposure events for regions from the initial unmap that are immediately obscured by the final map.

A Match error is generated if:

- The new parent is not on the same screen as the old parent.
- The new parent is the window itself or an inferior of the window.
- The new parent is InputOnly, and the window is not.
- The window has a ParentRelative background, and the new parent is not the same depth as the window.

MapWindow

window: WINDOW

Errors: `Window`

If the window is already mapped, this request has no effect.

If the override-redirect attribute of the window is `False` and some other client has selected `SubstructureRedirect` on the parent, then a `MapRequest` event is generated, but the window remains unmapped. Otherwise, the window is mapped, and a `MapNotify` event is generated.

If the window is now viewable and its contents have been discarded, the window is tiled with its background (if no background is defined, the existing screen contents are not altered), and zero or more exposure events are generated. If a backing-store has been maintained while the window was unmapped, no exposure events are generated. If a backing-store will now be maintained, a full-window exposure is always generated. Otherwise, only visible regions may be reported. Similar tiling and exposure take place for any newly viewable inferiors.

MapSubwindows

window: WINDOW

Errors: `Window`

This request performs a `MapWindow` request on all unmapped children of the window, in top-to-bottom stacking order.

UnmapWindow

window: WINDOW

Errors: `Window`

If the window is already unmapped, this request has no effect. Otherwise, the window is unmapped, and an `UnmapNotify` event is generated. Normal exposure processing on formerly obscured windows is performed.

UnmapSubwindows

window: WINDOW

Errors: Window

This request performs an UnmapWindow request on all mapped children of the window, in bottom-to-top stacking order.

ConfigureWindow

window: WINDOW
value-mask: BITMASK
value-list: LISTofVALUE

Errors: Match, Value, Window

This request changes the configuration of the window. The value-mask and value-list specify which values are to be given. The possible values are:

Attribute	*Type*
x	INT16
y	INT16
width	CARD16
height	CARD16
border-width	CARD16
sibling	WINDOW
stack-mode	{Above, Below, TopIf, BottomIf, Opposite}

The x and y coordinates are relative to the parent's origin and specify the position of the upper-left outer corner of the window. The width and height specify the inside size, not including the border, and must be nonzero (or a Value error results). Those values not specified are taken from the existing geometry of the window. Note that changing just the border-width leaves the outer-left corner of the window in a fixed position but moves the absolute position of the window's origin. It is a Match error to attempt to make the border-width of an InputOnly window nonzero.

If the override-redirect attribute of the window is False and some other client has selected SubstructureRedirect on the parent, a ConfigureRequest event is generated, and no further processing is performed. Otherwise, the following is performed:

If some other client has selected `ResizeRedirect` on the window and the inside width or height of the window is being changed, a `ResizeRequest` event is generated, and the current inside width and height are used instead. Note that the override-redirect attribute of the window has no effect on `ResizeRedirect` and that `SubstructureRedirect` on the parent has precedence over `ResizeRedirect` on the window.

The geometry of the window is changed as specified, the window is restacked among siblings, and a `ConfigureNotify` event is generated if the state of the window actually changes. If the inside width or height of the window has actually changed, then children of the window are affected, according to their win-gravity. Exposure processing is performed on formerly obscured windows (including the window itself and its inferiors if regions of them were obscured but now are not). Exposure processing is also performed on any new regions of the window (as a result of increasing the width or height) and on any regions where window contents are lost.

If the inside width or height of a window is not changed but the window is moved or its border is changed, then the contents of the window are not lost but move with the window. Changing the inside width or height of the window causes its contents to be moved or lost, depending on the bit-gravity of the window. It also causes children to be reconfigured, depending on their win-gravity. For a change of width and height of W and H, we define the [x, y] pairs as:

Direction	*Deltas*
`NorthWest`	[0, 0]
`North`	[W/2, 0]
`NorthEast`	[W, 0]
`West`	[0, H/2]
`Center`	[W/2, H/2]
`East`	[W, H/2]
`SouthWest`	[0, H]
`South`	[W/2, H]
`SouthEast`	[W, H]

When a window with one of these bit-gravities is resized, the corresponding pair defines the change in position of each pixel in the window. When a window with one of these win-gravities has its parent window resized, the corresponding pair defines the change in position of the window within the parent. This repositioning generates a `GravityNotify` event. `GravityNotify` events are generated after the `ConfigureNotify` event is generated.

A gravity of `Static` indicates that the contents or origin should not move relative to the origin of the root window. If the change in size of the window is coupled with a change in position of [X, Y], then for bit-gravity the change in position of each pixel is [–X, –Y] and for win-gravity the change in position of a child when its parent is so resized is [–X, –Y]. Note that `Static` gravity still only takes effect when the width or height of the window is changed, not when the window is simply moved.

A bit-gravity of `Forget` indicates that the window contents are always discarded after a size change, even if backing-store or save-under has been requested. The window is tiled with its background (except, if no background is defined, the existing screen contents are not altered) and zero or more exposure events are generated.

The contents and borders of inferiors are not affected by their parent's bit-gravity. A server is permitted to ignore the specified bit-gravity and use `Forget` instead.

A win-gravity of `Unmap` is like `NorthWest`, but the child is also unmapped when the parent is resized, and an `UnmapNotify` event is generated. `UnmapNotify` events are generated after the `ConfigureNotify` event is generated.

If a sibling and a stack-mode are specified, the window is restacked as follows:

`Above`	The window is placed just above the sibling.
`Below`	The window is placed just below the sibling.
`TopIf`	If the sibling occludes the window, then the window is placed at the top of the stack.
`BottomIf`	If the window occludes the sibling, then the window is placed at the bottom of the stack.
`Opposite`	If the sibling occludes the window, then the window is placed at the top of the stack. Otherwise, if the window occludes the sibling, then the window is placed at the bottom of the stack.

If a stack-mode is specified but no sibling is specified, the window is restacked as follows:

`Above`	The window is placed at the top of the stack.
`Below`	The window is placed at the bottom of the stack.
`TopIf`	If any sibling occludes the window, then the window is placed at the top of the stack.
`BottomIf`	If the window occludes any sibling, then the window is placed at the bottom of the stack.
`Opposite`	If any sibling occludes the window, then the window is placed at the top of the stack. Otherwise, if the window occludes any sibling, then the window is placed at the bottom of the stack.

It is a `Match` error if a sibling is specified without a stack-mode or if the window is not actually a sibling.

Note that the computations for `BottomIf`, `TopIf`, and `Opposite` are performed with respect to the window's final geometry (as controlled by the other arguments to the request), not to its initial geometry.

Attempts to configure a root window have no effect.

CirculateWindow

window: WINDOW
direction: {`RaiseLowest`, `LowerHighest`}

Errors: `Value`, `Window`

If some other client has selected `SubstructureRedirect` on the window, then a `CirculateRequest` event is generated, and no further processing is performed. Otherwise, the following is performed, and then a `CirculateNotify` event is generated if the window is actually restacked.

For `RaiseLowest`, `CirculateWindow` raises the lowest mapped child (if any) that is occluded by another child to the top of the stack. For `LowerHighest`, `CirculateWindow` lowers the highest mapped child (if any) that occludes another child to the bottom of the stack. Exposure processing is performed on formerly obscured windows.

GetGeometry

drawable: DRAWABLE
→
root: WINDOW

depth: CARD8
x, y: INT16
width, height, border-width: CARD16

Errors: Drawable

This request returns the root and current geometry of the drawable. The depth is the number of bits per pixel for the object. The x, y, and border-width will always be zero for pixmaps. For a window, the x and y coordinates specify the upper-left outer corner of the window relative to its parent's origin, and the width and height specify the inside size, not including the border.

It is legal to pass an InputOnly window as a drawable to this request.

QueryTree

window: WINDOW
→
root: WINDOW
parent: WINDOW or None
children: LISTofWINDOW

Errors: Window

This request returns the root, the parent, and the children of the window. The children are listed in bottom-to-top stacking order.

InternAtom

name: STRING8
only-if-exists: BOOL
→
atom: ATOM or None

Errors: Alloc, Value

This request returns the atom for the given name. If only-if-exists is False, then the atom is created if it does not exist. The string should use the ISO Latin-1 encoding. Uppercase and lowercase matter.

The lifetime of an atom is not tied to the interning client. Atoms remain defined until server reset (see section 10).

GetAtomName

atom: ATOM
→
name: STRING8

Errors: `Atom`

This request returns the name for the given atom.

ChangeProperty

window: WINDOW
property, type: ATOM
format: {8, 16, 32}
mode: {`Replace`, `Prepend`, `Append`}
data: LISTofINT8 or LISTofINT16 or LISTofINT32

Errors: `Alloc`, `Atom`, `Match`, `Value`, `Window`

This request alters the property for the specified window. The type is uninterpreted by the server. The format specifies whether the data should be viewed as a list of 8-bit, 16-bit, or 32-bit quantities so that the server can correctly byte-swap as necessary.

If the mode is `Replace`, the previous property value is discarded. If the mode is `Prepend` or `Append`, then the type and format must match the existing property value (or a `Match` error results). If the property is undefined, it is treated as defined with the correct type and format with zero-length data. For `Prepend`, the data is tacked on to the beginning of the existing data, and for `Append`, it is tacked on to the end of the existing data.

This request generates a `PropertyNotify` event on the window.

The lifetime of a property is not tied to the storing client. Properties remain until explicitly deleted, until the window is destroyed, or until server reset (see section 10).

The maximum size of a property is server-dependent and may vary dynamically.

DeleteProperty

window: WINDOW
property: ATOM

Errors: `Atom`, `Window`

This request deletes the property from the specified window if the property exists and generates a PropertyNotify event on the window unless the property does not exist.

GetProperty

window: WINDOW
property: ATOM
type: ATOM or AnyPropertyType
long-offset, long-length: CARD32
delete: BOOL

→

type: ATOM or None
format: {0, 8, 16, 32}
bytes-after: CARD32
value: LISTofINT8 or LISTofINT16 or LISTofINT32

Errors: Atom, Value, Window

If the specified property does not exist for the specified window, then the return type is None, the format and bytes-after are zero, and the value is empty. The delete argument is ignored in this case. If the specified property exists but its type does not match the specified type, then the return type is the actual type of the property, the format is the actual format of the property (never zero), the bytes-after is the length of the property in bytes (even if the format is 16 or 32), and the value is empty. The delete argument is ignored in this case. If the specified property exists and either AnyPropertyType is specified or the specified type matches the actual type of the property, then the return type is the actual type of the property, the format is the actual format of the property (never zero), and the bytes-after and value are as follows, given:

N = actual length of the stored property in bytes
(even if the format is 16 or 32)
I = 4 * long-offset
T = N − I
L = MINIMUM(T, 4 * long-length)
A = N − (I + L)

The returned value starts at byte index I in the property (indexing from 0), and its length in bytes is L. However, it is a Value error if long-offset is given such that L is negative. The value of bytes-after is A, giving the number of trailing unread bytes in the stored property. If delete is True and the bytes-after is zero, the property is also deleted from the window, and a PropertyNotify event is generated on the window.

RotateProperties

window: WINDOW
delta: INT16
properties: LISTofATOM

Errors: Atom, Match, Window

If the property names in the list are viewed as being numbered starting from zero, and there are N property names in the list, then the value associated with property name I becomes the value associated with property name (I + delta) mod N, for all I from zero to N – 1. The effect is to rotate the states by delta places around the virtual ring of property names (right for positive delta, left for negative delta).

If delta mod N is nonzero, a PropertyNotify event is generated for each property in the order listed.

If an atom occurs more than once in the list or no property with that name is defined for the window, a Match error is generated. If an Atom or Match error is generated, no properties are changed.

ListProperties

window: WINDOW
→
atoms: LISTofATOM

Errors: Window

This request returns the atoms of properties currently defined on the window.

SetSelectionOwner

selection: ATOM
owner: WINDOW or None
time: TIMESTAMP or CurrentTime

Errors: Atom, Window

This request changes the owner, owner window, and last-change time of the specified selection. This request has no effect if the specified time is earlier than the current last-change time of the specified selection or is later than the current server time. Otherwise, the last-change time is set to the specified time with `CurrentTime` replaced by the current server time. If the owner window is specified as `None`, then the owner of the selection becomes `None` (that is, no owner). Otherwise, the owner of the selection becomes the client executing the request. If the new owner (whether a client or `None`) is not the same as the current owner and the current owner is not `None`, then the current owner is sent a `SelectionClear` event.

If the client that is the owner of a selection is later terminated (that is, its connection is closed) or if the owner window it has specified in the request is later destroyed, then the owner of the selection automatically reverts to `None`, but the last-change time is not affected.

The selection atom is uninterpreted by the server. The owner window is returned by the `GetSelectionOwner` request and is reported in `SelectionRequest` and `SelectionClear` events.

Selections are global to the server.

GetSelectionOwner

selection: ATOM

→

owner: WINDOW or `None`

Errors: `Atom`

This request returns the current owner window of the specified selection, if any. If `None` is returned, then there is no owner for the selection.

ConvertSelection

selection, *target*: ATOM
property: ATOM or `None`
requestor: WINDOW
time: TIMESTAMP or `CurrentTime`

Errors: `Atom`, `Window`

If the specified selection has an owner, the server sends a SelectionRequest event to that owner. If no owner for the specified selection exists, the server generates a SelectionNotify event to the requestor with property None. The arguments are passed on unchanged in either of the events.

SendEvent

destination: WINDOW or PointerWindow or InputFocus
propagate: BOOL
event-mask: SETofEVENT
event: <normal-event-format>

Errors: Value, Window

If PointerWindow is specified, destination is replaced with the window that the pointer is in. If InputFocus is specified and the focus window contains the pointer, destination is replaced with the window that the pointer is in. Otherwise, destination is replaced with the focus window.

If the event-mask is the empty set, then the event is sent to the client that created the destination window. If that client no longer exists, no event is sent.

If propagate is False, then the event is sent to every client selecting on destination any of the event types in event-mask.

If propagate is True and no clients have selected on destination any of the event types in event-mask, then destination is replaced with the closest ancestor of destination for which some client has selected a type in event-mask and no intervening window has that type in its do-not-propagate-mask. If no such window exists or if the window is an ancestor of the focus window and InputFocus was originally specified as the destination, then the event is not sent to any clients. Otherwise, the event is reported to every client selecting on the final destination any of the types specified in event-mask.

The event code must be one of the core events or one of the events defined by an extension (or a Value error results) so that the server can correctly byte-swap the contents as necessary. The contents of the event are otherwise unaltered and unchecked by the server except to force on the most-significant bit of the event code and to set the sequence number in the event correctly.

Active grabs are ignored for this request.

GrabPointer

grab-window: WINDOW
owner-events: BOOL
event-mask: SETofPOINTEREVENT
pointer-mode, keyboard-mode: {Synchronous, Asynchronous}
confine-to: WINDOW or None
cursor: CURSOR or None
time: TIMESTAMP or CurrentTime
→
status: {Success, AlreadyGrabbed, Frozen, InvalidTime, NotViewable}

Errors: Cursor, Value, Window

This request actively grabs control of the pointer. Further pointer events are only reported to the grabbing client. The request overrides any active pointer grab by this client.

If owner-events is False, all generated pointer events are reported with respect to grab-window and are only reported if selected by event-mask. If owner-events is True and a generated pointer event would normally be reported to this client, it is reported normally. Otherwise, the event is reported with respect to the grab-window and is only reported if selected by event-mask. For either value of owner-events, unreported events are simply discarded.

If pointer-mode is Asynchronous, pointer event processing continues normally. If the pointer is currently frozen by this client, then processing of pointer events is resumed. If pointer-mode is Synchronous, the state of the pointer (as seen by means of the protocol) appears to freeze, and no further pointer events are generated by the server until the grabbing client issues a releasing AllowEvents request or until the pointer grab is released. Actual pointer changes are not lost while the pointer is frozen. They are simply queued for later processing.

If keyboard-mode is Asynchronous, keyboard event processing is unaffected by activation of the grab. If keyboard-mode is Synchronous, the state of the keyboard (as seen by means of the protocol) appears to freeze, and no further keyboard events are generated by the server until the grabbing client issues a releasing AllowEvents request or until the pointer grab is released. Actual keyboard changes are not lost while the keyboard is frozen. They are simply queued for later processing.

If a cursor is specified, then it is displayed regardless of what window the pointer is in. If no cursor is specified, then when the pointer is in grab-window or one of its subwindows, the normal cursor for that window is displayed. Otherwise, the cursor for grab-window is displayed.

If a confine-to window is specified, then the pointer will be restricted to stay contained in that window. The confine-to window need have no relationship to the grab-window. If the pointer is not initially in the confine-to window, then it is warped automatically to the closest edge (and enter/leave events are generated normally) just before the grab activates. If the confine-to window is subsequently reconfigured, the pointer will be warped automatically as necessary to keep it contained in the window.

This request generates `EnterNotify` and `LeaveNotify` events.

The request fails with status `AlreadyGrabbed` if the pointer is actively grabbed by some other client. The request fails with status `Frozen` if the pointer is frozen by an active grab of another client. The request fails with status `NotViewable` if grab-window or confine-to window is not viewable or if the confine-to window lies completely outside the boundaries of the root window. The request fails with status `InvalidTime` if the specified time is earlier than the last-pointer-grab time or later than the current server time. Otherwise, the last-pointer-grab time is set to the specified time, with `CurrentTime` replaced by the current server time.

UngrabPointer

time: TIMESTAMP or `CurrentTime`

This request releases the pointer if this client has it actively grabbed (from either `GrabPointer` or `GrabButton` or from a normal button press) and releases any queued events. The request has no effect if the specified time is earlier than the last-pointer-grab time or is later than the current server time.

This request generates `EnterNotify` and `LeaveNotify` events.

An `UngrabPointer` request is performed automatically if the event window or confine-to window for an active pointer grab becomes not viewable or if window reconfiguration causes the confine-to window to lie completely outside the boundaries of the root window.

GrabButton

modifiers: SETofKEYMASK or AnyModifier
button: BUTTON or AnyButton
grab-window: WINDOW
owner-events: BOOL
event-mask: SETofPOINTEREVENT
pointer-mode, keyboard-mode: {Synchronous,Asynchronous}
confine-to: WINDOW or None
cursor: CURSOR or None

Errors: Access, Cursor, Value, Window

This request establishes a passive grab. In the future, the pointer is actively grabbed as described in GrabPointer, the last-pointer-grab time is set to the time at which the button was pressed (as transmitted in the ButtonPress event), and the ButtonPress event is reported if all of the following conditions are true:

- The pointer is not grabbed and the specified button is logically pressed when the specified modifier keys are logically down, and no other buttons or modifier keys are logically down.
- The grab-window contains the pointer.
- The confine-to window (if any) is viewable.
- A passive grab on the same button/key combination does not exist on any ancestor of grab-window.

The interpretation of the remaining arguments is the same as for GrabPointer. The active grab is terminated automatically when the logical state of the pointer has all buttons released, independent of the logical state of modifier keys. Note that the logical state of a device (as seen by means of the protocol) may lag the physical state if device event processing is frozen.

This request overrides all previous passive grabs by the same client on the same button/key combinations on the same window. A modifier of AnyModifier is equivalent to issuing the request for all possible modifier combinations (including the combination of no modifiers). It is not required that all specified modifiers have currently assigned keycodes. A button of AnyButton is equivalent to issuing the request for all possible buttons. Otherwise, it is not required that the button specified currently be assigned to a physical button.

An Access error is generated if some other client has already issued a GrabButton request with the same button/key combination on the same window. When using AnyModifier or AnyButton, the request fails completely (no grabs are established), and an Access error is generated if there is a conflicting grab for any combination. The request has no effect on an active grab.

UngrabButton

modifiers: SETofKEYMASK or AnyModifier
button: BUTTON or AnyButton
grab-window: WINDOW

Errors: Value, Window

This request releases the passive button/key combination on the specified window if it was grabbed by this client. A modifiers argument of AnyModifier is equivalent to issuing the request for all possible modifier combinations (including the combination of no modifiers). A button of AnyButton is equivalent to issuing the request for all possible buttons. The request has no effect on an active grab.

ChangeActivePointerGrab

event-mask: SETofPOINTEREVENT
cursor: CURSOR or None
time: TIMESTAMP or CurrentTime

Errors: Cursor, Value

This request changes the specified dynamic parameters if the pointer is actively grabbed by the client and the specified time is no earlier than the last-pointer-grab time and no later than the current server time. The interpretation of event-mask and cursor are the same as in GrabPointer. This request has no effect on the parameters of any passive grabs established with GrabButton.

GrabKeyboard

grab-window: WINDOW
owner-events: BOOL
pointer-mode, keyboard-mode: {Synchronous, Asynchronous}

time: TIMESTAMP or CurrentTime

→

status: {Success, AlreadyGrabbed, Frozen, InvalidTime, NotViewable}

Errors: Value, Window

This request actively grabs control of the keyboard. Further key events are reported only to the grabbing client. This request overrides any active keyboard grab by this client.

If owner-events is False, all generated key events are reported with respect to grab-window. If owner-events is True and if a generated key event would normally be reported to this client, it is reported normally. Otherwise, the event is reported with respect to the grab-window. Both KeyPress and KeyRelease events are always reported, independent of any event selection made by the client.

If keyboard-mode is Asynchronous, keyboard event processing continues normally. If the keyboard is currently frozen by this client, then processing of keyboard events is resumed. If keyboard-mode is Synchronous, the state of the keyboard (as seen by means of the protocol) appears to freeze. No further keyboard events are generated by the server until the grabbing client issues a releasing AllowEvents request or until the keyboard grab is released. Actual keyboard changes are not lost while the keyboard is frozen. They are simply queued for later processing.

If pointer-mode is Asynchronous, pointer event processing is unaffected by activation of the grab. If pointer-mode is Synchronous, the state of the pointer (as seen by means of the protocol) appears to freeze. No further pointer events are generated by the server until the grabbing client issues a releasing AllowEvents request or until the keyboard grab is released. Actual pointer changes are not lost while the pointer is frozen. They are simply queued for later processing.

This request generates FocusIn and FocusOut events.

The request fails with status AlreadyGrabbed if the keyboard is actively grabbed by some other client. The request fails with status Frozen if the keyboard is frozen by an active grab of another client. The request fails with status NotViewable if grab-window is not viewable. The request fails with status InvalidTime if the specified time is earlier than the last-keyboard-grab time or later than the current server time. Otherwise, the last-keyboard-grab time is set to the specified time with `CurrentTime` replaced by the current server time.

UngrabKeyboard

time: TIMESTAMP or `CurrentTime`

This request releases the keyboard if this client has it actively grabbed (as a result of either `GrabKeyboard` or `GrabKey`) and releases any queued events. The request has no effect if the specified time is earlier than the last-keyboard-grab time or is later than the current server time.

This request generates `FocusIn` and `FocusOut` events.

An `UngrabKeyboard` is performed automatically if the event window for an active keyboard grab becomes not viewable.

GrabKey

key: KEYCODE or `AnyKey`
modifiers: SETofKEYMASK or `AnyModifier`
grab-window: WINDOW
owner-events: BOOL
pointer-mode, keyboard-mode: `{Synchronous, Asynchronous}`

Errors: `Access, Value, Window`

This request establishes a passive grab on the keyboard. In the future, the keyboard is actively grabbed as described in `GrabKeyboard`, the last-keyboard-grab time is set to the time at which the key was pressed (as transmitted in the `KeyPress` event), and the `KeyPress` event is reported if all of the following conditions are true:

- The keyboard is not grabbed and the specified key (which can itself be a modifier key) is logically pressed when the specified modifier keys are logically down, and no other modifier keys are logically down.
- Either the grab-window is an ancestor of (or is) the focus window, or the grab-window is a descendent of the focus window and contains the pointer.
- A passive grab on the same key combination does not exist on any ancestor of grab-window.

The interpretation of the remaining arguments is the same as for GrabKeyboard. The active grab is terminated automatically when the logical state of the keyboard has the specified key released, independent of the logical state of modifier keys. Note that the logical state of a device (as seen by means of the protocol) may lag the physical state if device event processing is frozen.

This request overrides all previous passive grabs by the same client on the same key combinations on the same window. A modifier of AnyModifier is equivalent to issuing the request for all possible modifier combinations (including the combination of no modifiers). It is not required that all modifiers specified have currently assigned keycodes. A key of AnyKey is equivalent to issuing the request for all possible keycodes. Otherwise, the key must be in the range specified by min-keycode and max-keycode in the connection setup (or a Value error results).

An Access error is generated if some other client has issued a GrabKey with the same key combination on the same window. When using AnyModifier or AnyKey, the request fails completely (no grabs are established), and an Access error is generated if there is a conflicting grab for any combination.

UngrabKey

key: KEYCODE or AnyKey
modifiers: SETofKEYMASK or AnyModifier
grab-window: WINDOW

Errors: Value, Window

This request releases the key combination on the specified window if it was grabbed by this client. A modifiers argument of AnyModifier is equivalent to issuing the request for all possible modifier combinations (including the combination of no modifiers). A key of AnyKey is equivalent to issuing the request for all possible keycodes. This request has no effect on an active grab.

AllowEvents

mode: {AsyncPointer, SyncPointer, ReplayPointer, AsyncKeyboard, SyncKeyboard, ReplayKeyboard, AsyncBoth, SyncBoth}
time: TIMESTAMP or CurrentTime

Errors: Value

This request releases some queued events if the client has caused a device to freeze. The request has no effect if the specified time is earlier than the last-grab time of the most recent active grab for the client or if the specified time is later than the current server time.

For `AsyncPointer`, if the pointer is frozen by the client, pointer event processing continues normally. If the pointer is frozen twice by the client on behalf of two separate grabs, `AsyncPointer` thaws for both. `AsyncPointer` has no effect if the pointer is not frozen by the client, but the pointer need not be grabbed by the client.

For `SyncPointer`, if the pointer is frozen and actively grabbed by the client, pointer event processing continues normally until the next `ButtonPress` or `ButtonRelease` event is reported to the client, at which time the pointer again appears to freeze. However, if the reported event causes the pointer grab to be released, then the pointer does not freeze. `SyncPointer` has no effect if the pointer is not frozen by the client or if the pointer is not grabbed by the client.

For `ReplayPointer`, if the pointer is actively grabbed by the client and is frozen as the result of an event having been sent to the client (either from the activation of a `GrabButton` or from a previous `AllowEvents` with mode `SyncPointer` but not from a `GrabPointer`), then the pointer grab is released and that event is completely reprocessed, this time ignoring any passive grabs at or above (towards the root) the grab-window of the grab just released. The request has no effect if the pointer is not grabbed by the client or if the pointer is not frozen as the result of an event.

For `AsyncKeyboard`, if the keyboard is frozen by the client, keyboard event processing continues normally. If the keyboard is frozen twice by the client on behalf of two separate grabs, `AsyncKeyboard` thaws for both. `AsyncKeyboard` has no effect if the keyboard is not frozen by the client, but the keyboard need not be grabbed by the client.

For `SyncKeyboard`, if the keyboard is frozen and actively grabbed by the client, keyboard event processing continues normally until the next `KeyPress` or `KeyRelease` event is reported to the client, at which time the keyboard again appears to freeze. However, if the reported event causes the keyboard grab to be released, then the keyboard does not freeze. `SyncKeyboard` has no effect if the keyboard is not frozen by the client or if the keyboard is not grabbed by the client.

For `ReplayKeyboard`, if the keyboard is actively grabbed by the client and is frozen as the result of an event having been sent to the client (either from the activation of a GrabKey or from a previous AllowEvents with mode SyncKeyboard but not from a GrabKeyboard), then the keyboard grab is released and that event is completely reprocessed, this time ignoring any passive grabs at or above (towards the root) the grab-window of the grab just released. The request has no effect if the keyboard is not grabbed by the client or if the keyboard is not frozen as the result of an event.

For SyncBoth, if both pointer and keyboard are frozen by the client, event processing (for both devices) continues normally until the next ButtonPress, ButtonRelease, KeyPress, or KeyRelease event is reported to the client for a grabbed device (button event for the pointer, key event for the keyboard), at which time the devices again appear to freeze. However, if the reported event causes the grab to be released, then the devices do not freeze (but if the other device is still grabbed, then a subsequent event for it will still cause both devices to freeze). SyncBoth has no effect unless both pointer and keyboard are frozen by the client. If the pointer or keyboard is frozen twice by the client on behalf of two separate grabs, SyncBoth thaws for both (but a subsequent freeze for SyncBoth will only freeze each device once).

For AsyncBoth, if the pointer and the keyboard are frozen by the client, event processing for both devices continues normally. If a device is frozen twice by the client on behalf of two separate grabs, AsyncBoth thaws for both. AsyncBoth has no effect unless both pointer and keyboard are frozen by the client.

AsyncPointer, SyncPointer, and ReplayPointer have no effect on processing of keyboard events. AsyncKeyboard, SyncKeyboard, and ReplayKeyboard have no effect on processing of pointer events.

It is possible for both a pointer grab and a keyboard grab to be active simultaneously (by the same or different clients). When a device is frozen on behalf of either grab, no event processing is performed for the device. It is possible for a single device to be frozen because of both grabs. In this case, the freeze must be released on behalf of both grabs before events can again be processed. If a device is frozen twice by a single client, then a single AllowEvents releases both.

GrabServer

This request disables processing of requests and close-downs on all connections other than the one this request arrived on.

UngrabServer

This request restarts processing of requests and close-downs on other connections.

QueryPointer

window: WINDOW

→

root: WINDOW
child: WINDOW or `None`
same-screen: BOOL
root-x, root-y, win-x, win-y: INT16
mask: SETofKEYBUTMASK

Errors: `Window`

The root window the pointer is logically on and the pointer coordinates relative to the root's origin are returned. If same-screen is `False`, then the pointer is not on the same screen as the argument window, child is `None`, and win-x and win-y are zero. If same-screen is `True`, then win-x and win-y are the pointer coordinates relative to the argument window's origin, and child is the child containing the pointer, if any. The current logical state of the modifier keys and the buttons are also returned. Note that the logical state of a device (as seen by means of the protocol) may lag the physical state if device event processing is frozen.

GetMotionEvents

start, stop: TIMESTAMP or `CurrentTime`
window: WINDOW

→

events: LISTofTIMECOORD

where:

TIMECOORD: [x, y: INT16
time: TIMESTAMP]

Errors: `Window`

This request returns all events in the motion history buffer that fall between the specified start and stop times (inclusive) and that have coordinates that lie within (including borders) the specified window at its present placement. The x and y coordinates are reported relative to the origin of the window.

If the start time is later than the stop time or if the start time is in the future, no events are returned. If the stop time is in the future, it is equivalent to specifying `CurrentTime`.

TranslateCoordinates

src-window, dst-window: WINDOW
src-x, src-y: INT16
→
same-screen: BOOL
child: WINDOW or `None`
dst-x, dst-y: INT16

Errors: `Window`

The src-x and src-y coordinates are taken relative to src-window's origin and are returned as dst-x and dst-y coordinates relative to dst-window's origin. If same-screen is `False`, then src-window and dst-window are on different screens, and dst-x and dst-y are zero. If the coordinates are contained in a mapped child of dst-window, then that child is returned.

WarpPointer

src-window: WINDOW or `None`
dst-window: WINDOW or `None`
src-x, src-y: INT16
src-width, src-height: CARD16
dst-x, dst-y: INT16

Errors: `Window`

If dst-window is `None`, this request moves the pointer by offsets [dst-x, dst-y] relative to the current position of the pointer. If dst-window is a window, this request moves the pointer to [dst-x, dst-y] relative to dst-window's origin. However, if src-window is not `None`, the move only takes place if src-window contains the pointer and the pointer is contained in the specified rectangle of src-window.

The src-x and src-y coordinates are relative to src-window's origin. If src-height is zero, it is replaced with the current height of src-window minus src-y. If src-width is zero, it is replaced with the current width of src-window minus src-x.

This request cannot be used to move the pointer outside the confine-to window of an active pointer grab. An attempt will only move the pointer as far as the closest edge of the confine-to window.

This request will generate events just as if the user had instantaneously moved the pointer.

SetInputFocus

focus: WINDOW or `PointerRoot` or `None`
revert-to: `{Parent, PointerRoot, None}`
time: TIMESTAMP or `CurrentTime`

Errors: `Match, Value, Window`

This request changes the input focus and the last-focus-change time. The request has no effect if the specified time is earlier than the current last-focus-change time or is later than the current server time. Otherwise, the last-focus-change time is set to the specified time with `CurrentTime` replaced by the current server time.

If `None` is specified as the focus, all keyboard events are discarded until a new focus window is set. In this case, the revert-to argument is ignored.

If a window is specified as the focus, it becomes the keyboard's focus window. If a generated keyboard event would normally be reported to this window or one of its inferiors, the event is reported normally. Otherwise, the event is reported with respect to the focus window.

If `PointerRoot` is specified as the focus, the focus window is dynamically taken to be the root window of whatever screen the pointer is on at each keyboard event. In this case, the revert-to argument is ignored.

This request generates `FocusIn` and `FocusOut` events.

The specified focus window must be viewable at the time of the request (or a Match error results). If the focus window later becomes not viewable, the new focus window depends on the revert-to argument. If revert-to is Parent, the focus reverts to the parent (or the closest viewable ancestor) and the new revert-to value is taken to be None. If revert-to is PointerRoot or None, the focus reverts to that value. When the focus reverts, FocusIn and FocusOut events are generated, but the last-focus-change time is not affected.

GetInputFocus

→
focus: WINDOW or PointerRoot or None
revert-to: {Parent, PointerRoot, None}

This request returns the current focus state.

QueryKeymap

→
keys: LISTofCARD8

This request returns a bit vector for the logical state of the keyboard. Each bit set to 1 indicates that the corresponding key is currently pressed. The vector is represented as 32 bytes. Byte N (from 0) contains the bits for keys 8N to 8N + 7 with the least-significant bit in the byte representing key 8N. Note that the logical state of a device (as seen by means of the protocol) may lag the physical state if device event processing is frozen.

OpenFont

fid: FONT
name: STRING8

Errors: Alloc, IDChoice, Name

This request loads the specified font, if necessary, and associates identifier fid with it. The font name should use the ISO Latin-1 encoding, and uppercase and lowercase do not matter. The interpretation of characters "?" (octal value 77) and "*" (octal value 52) in the name is not defined by the core protocol, but is reserved for future definition. A structured format for font names is specified in part IV, "X Logical Font Description Conventions."

Fonts are not associated with a particular screen and can be stored as a component of any graphics context.

CloseFont

font: FONT

Errors: `Font`

This request deletes the association between the resource ID and the font. The font itself will be freed when no other resource references it.

QueryFont

font: FONTABLE

→

font-info: FONTINFO
char-infos: LISTofCHARINFO

where:

FONTINFO: [draw-direction: {`LeftToRight`, `RightToLeft`}
min-char-or-byte2, max-char-or-byte2: CARD16
min-byte1, max-byte1: CARD8
all-chars-exist: BOOL
default-char: CARD16
min-bounds: CHARINFO
max-bounds: CHARINFO
font-ascent: INT16
font-descent: INT16
properties: LISTofFONTPROP]
FONTPROP: [name: ATOM
value: <32-bit-value>]
CHARINFO: [left-side-bearing: INT16
right-side-bearing: INT16
character-width: INT16
ascent: INT16
descent: INT16
attributes: CARD16]

Errors: `Font`

This request returns logical information about a font. If a gcontext is given for font, the currently contained font is used.

The draw-direction is just a hint and indicates whether most char-infos have a positive, `LeftToRight`, or a negative, `RightToLeft`, character-width metric. The core protocol defines no support for vertical text.

If min-byte1 and max-byte1 are both zero, then min-char-or-byte2 specifies the linear character index corresponding to the first element of char-infos, and max-char-or-byte2 specifies the linear character index of the last element. If either min-byte1 or max-byte1 are nonzero, then both min-char-or-byte2 and max-char-or-byte2 will be less than 256, and the 2-byte character index values corresponding to char-infos element N (counting from 0) are:

$$\text{byte1} = N/D + \text{min-byte1}$$
$$\text{byte2} = N\backslash D + \text{min-char-or-byte2}$$

where:

$$D = \text{max-char-or-byte2} - \text{min-char-or-byte2} + 1$$
$$/ = \text{integer division}$$
$$\backslash = \text{integer modulus}$$

If char-infos has length zero, then min-bounds and max-bounds will be identical, and the effective char-infos is one filled with this char-info, of length:

$$L = D * (\text{max-byte1} - \text{min-byte1} + 1)$$

That is, all glyphs in the specified linear or matrix range have the same information, as given by min-bounds (and max-bounds). If all-chars-exist is `True`, then all characters in char-infos have nonzero bounding boxes.

The default-char specifies the character that will be used when an undefined or nonexistent character is used. Note that default-char is a CARD16, not CHAR2B. For a font using 2-byte matrix format, the default-char has byte1 in the most-significant byte and byte2 in the least-significant byte. If the default-char itself specifies an undefined or nonexistent character, then no printing is performed for an undefined or nonexistent character.

The min-bounds and max-bounds contain the minimum and maximum values of each individual CHARINFO component over all char-infos (ignoring nonexistent characters). The bounding box of the font (that is, the smallest rectangle enclosing the shape obtained by superimposing all characters at the same origin [x,y]) has its upper-left coordinate at:

[x + min-bounds.left-side-bearing, y – max-bounds.ascent]

with a width of:

max-bounds.right-side-bearing – min-bounds.left-side-bearing

and a height of:

max-bounds.ascent + max-bounds.descent

The font-ascent is the logical extent of the font above the baseline and is used for determining line spacing. Specific characters may extend beyond this. The font-descent is the logical extent of the font at or below the baseline and is used for determining line spacing. Specific characters may extend beyond this. If the baseline is at Y-coordinate y, then the logical extent of the font is inclusive between the Y-coordinate values (y – font-ascent) and (y + font-descent – 1).

A font is not guaranteed to have any properties. The interpretation of the property value (for example, INT32, CARD32) must be derived from *a priori* knowledge of the property. A basic set of font properties is specified in part IV, "X Logical Font Description Conventions."

For a character origin at [x,y], the bounding box of a character (that is, the smallest rectangle enclosing the character's shape), described in terms of CHARINFO components, is a rectangle with its upper-left corner at:

[x + left-side-bearing, y – ascent]

with a width of:

right-side-bearing – left-side-bearing

and a height of:

ascent + descent

and the origin for the next character is defined to be:

[x + character-width, y]

Note that the baseline is logically viewed as being just below nondescending characters (when descent is zero, only pixels with Y-coordinates less than y are drawn) and that the origin is logically viewed as being coincident with the left edge of a nonkerned character (when left-side-bearing is zero, no pixels with X-coordinate less than x are drawn).

Note that CHARINFO metric values can be negative.

A nonexistent character is represented with all CHARINFO components zero.

The interpretation of the per-character attributes field is server-dependent.

QueryTextExtents

font: FONTABLE
string: STRING16

→

draw-direction: {LeftToRight,RightToLeft}
font-ascent: INT16
font-descent: INT16
overall-ascent: INT16
overall-descent: INT16
overall-width: INT32
overall-left: INT32
overall-right: INT32

Errors: Font

This request returns the logical extents of the specified string of characters in the specified font. If a gcontext is given for font, the currently contained font is used. The draw-direction, font-ascent, and font-descent are the same as described in QueryFont. The overall-ascent is the maximum of the ascent metrics of all characters in the string, and the overall-descent is the maximum of the descent metrics. The overall-width is the sum of the character-width metrics of all characters in the string. For each character in the string, let W be the sum of the character-width metrics of all characters preceding it in the string, let L be the left-side-bearing metric of the character plus W, and let R be the right-side-bearing metric of the character plus W. The overall-left is the minimum L of all characters in the string, and the overall-right is the maximum R.

For fonts defined with linear indexing rather than 2-byte matrix indexing, the server will interpret each CHAR2B as a 16-bit number that has been transmitted most-significant byte first (that is, byte1 of the CHAR2B is taken as the most-significant byte).

Characters with all zero metrics are ignored. If the font has no defined default-char, then undefined characters in the string are also ignored.

ListFonts

pattern: STRING8
max-names: CARD16
→
names: LISTofSTRING8

This request returns a list of available font names (as controlled by the font search path; see `SetFontPath` request) that match the pattern. At most, max-names names will be returned. The pattern should use the ISO Latin-1 encoding, and uppercase and lowercase do not matter. In the pattern, the "?" character (octal value 77) will match any single character, and the "*" character (octal value 52) will match any number of characters. The returned names are in lowercase.

ListFontsWithInfo

pattern: STRING8
max-names: CARD16
→+
name: STRING8
info: FONTINFO
replies-hint: CARD32

where:

FONTINFO: <same type definition as in `QueryFont`>

This request is similar to `ListFonts`, but it also returns information about each font. The information returned for each font is identical to what `QueryFont` would return except that the per-character metrics are not returned. Note that this request can generate multiple replies. With each reply, replies-hint may provide an indication of how many more fonts will be returned. This number is a hint only and may be larger or smaller than the number of fonts actually returned. A zero value does not guarantee that no more fonts will be returned. After the font replies, a reply with a zero-length name is sent to indicate the end of the reply sequence.

SetFontPath

path: LISTofSTRING8

Errors: `Value`

This request defines the search path for font lookup. There is only one search path per server, not one per client. The interpretation of the strings is operating-system-dependent, but the strings are intended to specify directories to be searched in the order listed.

Setting the path to the empty list restores the default path defined for the server.

As a side effect of executing this request, the server is guaranteed to flush all cached information about fonts for which there currently are no explicit resource IDs allocated.

The meaning of an error from this request is system specific.

GetFontPath

→

path: LISTofSTRING8

This request returns the current search path for fonts.

CreatePixmap

pid: PIXMAP
drawable: DRAWABLE
depth: CARD8
width, height: CARD16

Errors: `Alloc`, `Drawable`, `IDChoice`, `Value`

This request creates a pixmap and assigns the identifier pid to it. The width and height must be nonzero (or a `Value` error results). The depth must be one of the depths supported by the root of the specified drawable (or a `Value` error results). The initial contents of the pixmap are undefined.

It is legal to pass an `InputOnly` window as a drawable to this request.

FreePixmap

pixmap: PIXMAP

Errors: `Pixmap`

This request deletes the association between the resource ID and the pixmap. The pixmap storage will be freed when no other resource references it.

CreateGC

cid: GCONTEXT
drawable: DRAWABLE
value-mask: BITMASK
value-list: LISTofVALUE

Errors: `Alloc`, `Drawable`, `Font`, `IDChoice`, `Match`, `Pixmap`, `Value`

This request creates a graphics context and assigns the identifier cid to it. The gcontext can be used with any destination drawable having the same root and depth as the specified drawable; use with other drawables results in a `Match` error.

The value-mask and value-list specify which components are to be explicitly initialized. The context components are:

Component	*Type*
function	`{Clear,And,AndReverse,Copy,AndInverted,NoOp, Xor,Or,Nor,Equiv,Invert,OrReverse, CopyInverted,OrInverted,Nand,Set}`
plane-mask	CARD32
foreground	CARD32
background	CARD32
line-width	CARD16
line-style	`{Solid,OnOffDash,DoubleDash}`
cap-style	`{NotLast,Butt,Round,Projecting}`
join-style	`{Miter,Round,Bevel}`
fill-style	`{Solid,Tiled,OpaqueStippled,Stippled}`
fill-rule	`{EvenOdd,Winding}`
arc-mode	`{Chord,PieSlice}`
tile	PIXMAP
stipple	PIXMAP

Component	*Type*
tile-stipple-x-origin	INT16
tile-stipple-y-origin	INT16
font	FONT
subwindow-mode	{ClipByChildren, IncludeInferiors}
graphics-exposures	BOOL
clip-x-origin	INT16
clip-y-origin	INT16
clip-mask	PIXMAP or None
dash-offset	CARD16
dashes	CARD8

In graphics operations, given a source and destination pixel, the result is computed bitwise on corresponding bits of the pixels; that is, a Boolean operation is performed in each bit plane. The plane-mask restricts the operation to a subset of planes, so the result is:

((src FUNC dst) AND plane-mask) OR (dst AND (NOT plane-mask))

Range checking is not performed on the values for foreground, background, or plane-mask. They are simply truncated to the appropriate number of bits.

The meanings of the functions are:

Function	*Operation*
Clear	0
And	src AND dst
AndReverse	src AND (NOT dst)
Copy	src
AndInverted	(NOT src) AND dst
NoOp	dst
Xor	src XOR dst
Or	src OR dst
Nor	(NOT src) AND (NOT dst)
Equiv	(NOT src) XOR dst
Invert	NOT dst
OrReverse	src OR (NOT dst)
CopyInverted	NOT src
OrInverted	(NOT src) OR dst
Nand	(NOT src) OR (NOT dst)
Set	1

The line-width is measured in pixels and can be greater than or equal to one, a wide line, or the special value zero, a thin line.

Wide lines are drawn centered on the path described by the graphics request. Unless otherwise specified by the join or cap style, the bounding box of a wide line with endpoints [x1, y1], [x2, y2] and width w is a rectangle with vertices at the following real coordinates:

[x1 – (w*sn/2), y1 + (w*cs/2)], [x1 + (w*sn/2), y1 – (w*cs/2)],
[x2 – (w*sn/2), y2 + (w*cs/2)], [x2 + (w*sn/2), y2 – (w*cs/2)]

The sn is the sine of the angle of the line and cs is the cosine of the angle of the line. A pixel is part of the line (and hence drawn) if the center of the pixel is fully inside the bounding box, which is viewed as having infinitely thin edges. If the center of the pixel is exactly on the bounding box, it is part of the line if and only if the interior is immediately to its right (x increasing direction). Pixels with centers on a horizontal edge are a special case and are part of the line if and only if the interior or the boundary is immediately below (y increasing direction) and if the interior or the boundary is immediately to the right (x increasing direction). Note that this description is a mathematical model describing the pixels that are drawn for a wide line and does not imply that trigonometry is required to implement such a model. Real or fixed point arithmetic is recommended for computing the corners of the line endpoints for lines greater than one pixel in width.

Thin lines (zero line-width) are nominally one pixel wide lines drawn using an unspecified, device-dependent algorithm. There are only two constraints on this algorithm. First, if a line is drawn unclipped from [x1,y1] to [x2,y2] and another line is drawn unclipped from [x1+dx,y1+dy] to [x2+dx,y2+dy], then a point [x,y] is touched by drawing the first line if and only if the point [x+dx,y+dy] is touched by drawing the second line. Second, the effective set of points comprising a line cannot be affected by clipping. Thus, a point is touched in a clipped line if and only if the point lies inside the clipping region and the point would be touched by the line when drawn unclipped.

Note that a wide line drawn from [x1,y1] to [x2,y2] always draws the same pixels as a wide line drawn from [x2,y2] to [x1,y1], not counting cap-style and join-style. Implementors are encouraged to make this property true for thin lines, but it is not required. A line-width of zero may differ from a line-width of one in which pixels are drawn. In general, drawing a thin line will be faster than drawing a wide line of width one, but thin lines may not mix well aesthetically with wide lines because of the different drawing algorithms. If it is desirable to obtain precise and uniform results across all displays, a client should always use a line-width of one, rather than a line-width of zero.

The line-style defines which sections of a line are drawn:

`Solid`	The full path of the line is drawn.
`DoubleDash`	The full path of the line is drawn, but the even dashes are filled differently than the odd dashes (see fill-style), with `Butt` cap-style used where even and odd dashes meet.
`OnOffDash`	Only the even dashes are drawn, and cap-style applies to all internal ends of the individual dashes (except `NotLast` is treated as `Butt`).

The cap-style defines how the endpoints of a path are drawn:

`NotLast`	The result is equivalent to `Butt`, except that for a line-width of zero the final endpoint is not drawn.
`Butt`	The result is square at the endpoint (perpendicular to the slope of the line) with no projection beyond.
`Round`	The result is a circular arc with its diameter equal to the line-width, centered on the endpoint; it is equivalent to `Butt` for line-width zero.
`Projecting`	The result is square at the end, but the path continues beyond the endpoint for a distance equal to half the line-width; it is equivalent to `Butt` for line-width zero.

The join-style defines how corners are drawn for wide lines:

`Miter`	The outer edges of the two lines extend to meet at an angle. However, if the angle is less than 11 degrees, a `Bevel` join-style is used instead.
`Round`	The result is a circular arc with a diameter equal to the line-width, centered on the joinpoint.
`Bevel`	The result is `Butt` endpoint styles, and then the triangular notch is filled.

For a line with coincident endpoints (x1 = x2, y1 = y2), when the cap-style is applied to both endpoints, the semantics depends on the line-width and the cap-style:

NotLast	thin	This is device-dependent, but the desired effect is that nothing is drawn.
Butt	thin	This is device-dependent, but the desired effect is that a single pixel is drawn.
Round	thin	This is the same as Butt/thin.
Projecting	thin	This is the same as Butt/thin.
Butt	wide	Nothing is drawn.
Round	wide	The closed path is a circle, centered at the endpoint and with a diameter equal to the line-width.
Projecting	wide	The closed path is a square, aligned with the coordinate axes, centered at the endpoint and with sides equal to the line-width.

For a line with coincident endpoints (x1=x2, y1=y2), when the join-style is applied at one or both endpoints, the effect is as if the line was removed from the overall path. However, if the total path consists of (or is reduced to) a single point joined with itself, the effect is the same as when the cap-style is applied at both endpoints.

The tile/stipple represents an infinite two-dimensional plane with the tile/stipple replicated in all dimensions. When that plane is superimposed on the drawable for use in a graphics operation, the upper-left corner of some instance of the tile/stipple is at the coordinates within the drawable specified by the tile/stipple origin. The tile/stipple and clip origins are interpreted relative to the origin of whatever destination drawable is specified in a graphics request.

The tile pixmap must have the same root and depth as the gcontext (or a Match error results). The stipple pixmap must have depth one and must have the same root as the gcontext (or a Match error results). For fill-style Stippled (but not fill-style OpaqueStippled), the stipple pattern is tiled in a single plane and acts as an additional clip mask to be ANDed with the clip-mask. Any size pixmap can be used for tiling or stippling, although some sizes may be faster to use than others.

The fill-style defines the contents of the source for line, text, and fill requests. For all text and fill requests (for example, PolyText8, PolyText16, PolyFillRectangle, FillPoly, and PolyFillArc) as well as for line requests with line-style Solid, (for example, PolyLine, PolySegment, PolyRectangle, PolyArc) and for the even dashes for line requests with line-style OnOffDash or DoubleDash:

`Solid`	Foreground
`Tiled`	Tile
`OpaqueStippled`	A tile with the same width and height as stipple but with background everywhere stipple has a zero and with foreground everywhere stipple has a one
`Stippled`	Foreground masked by stipple

For the odd dashes for line requests with line-style `DoubleDash`:

`Solid`	Background
`Tiled`	Same as for even dashes
`OpaqueStippled`	Same as for even dashes
`Stippled`	Background masked by stipple

The dashes value allowed here is actually a simplified form of the more general patterns that can be set with `SetDashes`. Specifying a value of N here is equivalent to specifying the two element list [N, N] in `SetDashes`. The value must be nonzero (or a `Value` error results). The meaning of dash-offset and dashes are explained in the `SetDashes` request.

The clip-mask restricts writes to the destination drawable. Only pixels where the clip-mask has bits set to 1 are drawn. Pixels are not drawn outside the area covered by the clip-mask or where the clip-mask has bits set to 0. The clip-mask affects all graphics requests, but it does not clip sources. The clip-mask origin is interpreted relative to the origin of whatever destination drawable is specified in a graphics request. If a pixmap is specified as the clip-mask, it must have depth 1 and have the same root as the gcontext (or a `Match` error results). If clip-mask is `None`, then pixels are always drawn, regardless of the clip origin. The clip-mask can also be set with the `SetClipRectangles` request.

For `ClipByChildren`, both source and destination windows are additionally clipped by all viewable `InputOutput` children. For `IncludeInferiors`, neither source nor destination window is clipped by inferiors. This will result in including subwindow contents in the source and drawing through subwindow boundaries of the destination. The use of `IncludeInferiors` with a source or destination window of one depth with mapped inferiors of differing depth is not illegal, but the semantics is undefined by the core protocol.

The fill-rule defines what pixels are inside (that is, are drawn) for paths given in `FillPoly` requests. `EvenOdd` means a point is inside if an infinite ray with the point as origin crosses the path an odd number of times. For `Winding`, a point is inside if an infinite ray with the point as origin crosses an unequal number of clockwise and counterclockwise directed path segments. A clockwise directed path segment is one that crosses the ray from left to right as observed from the point. A counter-clockwise segment is one that crosses the ray from right to left as observed from the point. The case where a directed line segment is coincident with the ray is uninteresting because one can simply choose a different ray that is not coincident with a segment.

For both fill rules, a point is infinitely small and the path is an infinitely thin line. A pixel is inside if the center point of the pixel is inside and the center point is not on the boundary. If the center point is on the boundary, the pixel is inside if and only if the polygon interior is immediately to its right (x increasing direction). Pixels with centers along a horizontal edge are a special case and are inside if and only if the polygon interior is immediately below (y increasing direction).

The arc-mode controls filling in the `PolyFillArc` request.

The graphics-exposures flag controls `GraphicsExposure` event generation for `CopyArea` and `CopyPlane` requests (and any similar requests defined by extensions).

The default component values are:

Component	*Default*
function	`Copy`
plane-mask	all ones
foreground	0
background	1
line-width	0
line-style	`Solid`
cap-style	`Butt`
join-style	`Miter`
fill-style	`Solid`
fill-rule	`EvenOdd`
arc-mode	`PieSlice`
tile	Pixmap of unspecified size filled with foreground pixel (that is, client specified pixel if any, else 0) (subsequent changes to foreground do not affect this pixmap)
stipple	Pixmap of unspecified size filled with ones
tile-stipple-x-origin	0
tile-stipple-y-origin	0
font	<server-dependent-font>

Component	*Default*
subwindow-mode	ClipByChildren
graphics-exposures	True
clip-x-origin	0
clip-y-origin	0
clip-mask	None
dash-offset	0
dashes	4 (that is, the list [4, 4])

Storing a pixmap in a gcontext might or might not result in a copy being made. If the pixmap is later used as the destination for a graphics request, the change might or might not be reflected in the gcontext. If the pixmap is used simultaneously in a graphics request as both a destination and as a tile or stipple, the results are not defined.

It is quite likely that some amount of gcontext information will be cached in display hardware and that such hardware can only cache a small number of gcontexts. Given the number and complexity of components, clients should view switching between gcontexts with nearly identical state as significantly more expensive than making minor changes to a single gcontext.

ChangeGC

gc: GCONTEXT
value-mask: BITMASK
value-list: LISTofVALUE

Errors: Alloc, Font, GContext, Match, Pixmap, Value

This request changes components in gc. The value-mask and value-list specify which components are to be changed. The values and restrictions are the same as for CreateGC.

Changing the clip-mask also overrides any previous SetClipRectangles request on the context. Changing dash-offset or dashes overrides any previous SetDashes request on the context.

The order in which components are verified and altered is server-dependent. If an error is generated, a subset of the components may have been altered.

CopyGC

src-gc, dst-gc: GCONTEXT
value-mask: BITMASK

Errors: Alloc, GContext, Match, Value

This request copies components from src-gc to dst-gc. The value-mask specifies which components to copy, as for CreateGC. The two gcontexts must have the same root and the same depth (or a Match error results).

SetDashes

gc: GCONTEXT
dash-offset: CARD16
dashes: LISTofCARD8

Errors: Alloc, GContext, Value

This request sets dash-offset and dashes in gc for dashed line styles. Dashes cannot be empty (or a Value error results). Specifying an odd-length list is equivalent to specifying the same list concatenated with itself to produce an even-length list. The initial and alternating elements of dashes are the even dashes; the others are the odd dashes. Each element specifies a dash length in pixels. All of the elements must be nonzero (or a Value error results). The dash-offset defines the phase of the pattern, specifying how many pixels into dashes the pattern should actually begin in any single graphics request. Dashing is continuous through path elements combined with a join-style but is reset to the dash-offset between each sequence of joined lines.

The unit of measure for dashes is the same as in the ordinary coordinate system. Ideally, a dash length is measured along the slope of the line, but implementations are only required to match this ideal for horizontal and vertical lines. Failing the ideal semantics, it is suggested that the length be measured along the major axis of the line. The major axis is defined as the x axis for lines drawn at an angle of between –45 and +45 degrees or between 135 and 225 degrees from the x axis. For all other lines, the major axis is the y axis.

SetClipRectangles

gc: GCONTEXT
clip-x-origin, clip-y-origin: INT16

rectangles: LISTofRECTANGLE
ordering: {UnSorted,YSorted,YXSorted,YXBanded}

Errors: Alloc, GContext, Match, Value

This request changes clip-mask in gc to the specified list of rectangles and sets the clip origin. Output will be clipped to remain contained within the rectangles. The clip origin is interpreted relative to the origin of whatever destination drawable is specified in a graphics request. The rectangle coordinates are interpreted relative to the clip origin. The rectangles should be nonintersecting, or graphics results will be undefined. Note that the list of rectangles can be empty, which effectively disables output. This is the opposite of passing None as the clip-mask in CreateGC and ChangeGC.

If known by the client, ordering relations on the rectangles can be specified with the ordering argument. This may provide faster operation by the server. If an incorrect ordering is specified, the server may generate a Match error, but it is not required to do so. If no error is generated, the graphics results are undefined. UnSorted means that the rectangles are in arbitrary order. YSorted means that the rectangles are nondecreasing in their Y origin. YXSorted additionally constrains YSorted order in that all rectangles with an equal Y origin are nondecreasing in their X origin. YXBanded additionally constrains YXSorted by requiring that, for every possible Y scanline, all rectangles that include that scanline have identical Y origins and Y extents.

FreeGC

gc: GCONTEXT

Errors: GContext

This request deletes the association between the resource ID and the gcontext and destroys the gcontext.

ClearArea

window: WINDOW
x, y: INT16
width, height: CARD16
exposures: BOOL

Errors: Match, Value, Window

The x and y coordinates are relative to the window's origin and specify the upper-left corner of the rectangle. If width is zero, it is replaced with the current width of the window minus x. If height is zero, it is replaced with the current height of the window minus y. If the window has a defined background tile, the rectangle is tiled with a plane-mask of all ones and function of `Copy` and a subwindow-mode of `ClipByChildren`. If the window has background `None`, the contents of the window are not changed. In either case, if exposures is `True`, then one or more exposure events are generated for regions of the rectangle that are either visible or are being retained in a backing store.

It is a `Match` error to use an `InputOnly` window in this request.

CopyArea

src-drawable, dst-drawable: DRAWABLE
gc: GCONTEXT
src-x, src-y: INT16
width, height: CARD16
dst-x, dst-y: INT16

Errors: `Drawable`, `GContext`, `Match`

This request combines the specified rectangle of src-drawable with the specified rectangle of dst-drawable. The src-x and src-y coordinates are relative to src-drawable's origin. The dst-x and dst-y are relative to dst-drawable's origin, each pair specifying the upper-left corner of the rectangle. The src-drawable must have the same root and the same depth as dst-drawable (or a `Match` error results).

If regions of the source rectangle are obscured and have not been retained in backing store or if regions outside the boundaries of the source drawable are specified, then those regions are not copied, but the following occurs on all corresponding destination regions that are either visible or are retained in backing-store. If the dst-drawable is a window with a background other than `None`, these corresponding destination regions are tiled (with plane-mask of all ones and function `Copy`) with that background. Regardless of tiling and whether the destination is a window or a pixmap, if graphics-exposures in gc is `True`, then `GraphicsExposure` events for all corresponding destination regions are generated.

If graphics-exposures is `True` but no `GraphicsExposure` events are generated, then a `NoExposure` event is generated.

GC components: function, plane-mask, subwindow-mode, graphics-exposures, clip-x-origin, clip-y-origin, clip-mask

CopyPlane

src-drawable, dst-drawable: DRAWABLE
gc: GCONTEXT
src-x, src-y: INT16
width, height: CARD16
dst-x, dst-y: INT16
bit-plane: CARD32

Errors: `Drawable`, `GContext`, `Match`, `Value`

The src-drawable must have the same root as dst-drawable (or a `Match` error results), but it need not have the same depth. The bit-plane must have exactly one bit set to 1 and the value of bit-plane must be less than 2^n where n is the depth of src-drawable (or a `Value` error results). Effectively, a pixmap of the same depth as dst-drawable and with size specified by the source region is formed using the foreground/background pixels in gc (foreground everywhere the bit-plane in src-drawable contains a bit set to 1, background everywhere the bit-plane contains a bit set to 0), and the equivalent of a `CopyArea` is performed, with all the same exposure semantics. This can also be thought of as using the specified region of the source bit-plane as a stipple with a fill-style of `OpaqueStippled` for filling a rectangular area of the destination.

GC components: function, plane-mask, foreground, background, subwindow-mode, graphics-exposures, clip-x-origin, clip-y-origin, clip-mask

PolyPoint

drawable: DRAWABLE
gc: GCONTEXT
coordinate-mode: {`Origin`, `Previous`}
points: LISTofPOINT

Errors: `Drawable`, `GContext`, `Match`, `Value`

This request combines the foreground pixel in gc with the pixel at each point in the drawable. The points are drawn in the order listed.

The first point is always relative to the drawable's origin. The rest are relative either to that origin or the previous point, depending on the coordinate-mode.

GC components: function, plane-mask, foreground, subwindow-mode, clip-x-origin, clip-y-origin, clip-mask

PolyLine

drawable: DRAWABLE
gc: GCONTEXT
coordinate-mode: {Origin,Previous}
points: LISTofPOINT

Errors: Drawable, GContext, Match, Value

This request draws lines between each pair of points (point[i], point[i+1]). The lines are drawn in the order listed. The lines join correctly at all intermediate points, and if the first and last points coincide, the first and last lines also join correctly.

For any given line, no pixel is drawn more than once. If thin (zero line-width) lines intersect, the intersecting pixels are drawn multiple times. If wide lines intersect, the intersecting pixels are drawn only once, as though the entire PolyLine were a single filled shape.

The first point is always relative to the drawable's origin. The rest are relative either to that origin or the previous point, depending on the coordinate-mode.

GC components: function, plane-mask, line-width, line-style, cap-style, join-style, fill-style, subwindow-mode, clip-x-origin, clip-y-origin, clip-mask

GC mode-dependent components: foreground, background, tile, stipple, tile-stipple-x-origin, tile-stipple-y-origin, dash-offset, dashes

PolySegment

drawable: DRAWABLE
gc: GCONTEXT
segments: LISTofSEGMENT

where:

SEGMENT: [x1, y1, x2, y2: INT16]

Errors: Drawable, GContext, Match

For each segment, this request draws a line between [x1, y1] and [x2, y2]. The lines are drawn in the order listed. No joining is performed at coincident endpoints. For any given line, no pixel is drawn more than once. If lines intersect, the intersecting pixels are drawn multiple times.

GC components: function, plane-mask, line-width, line-style, cap-style, fill-style, subwindow-mode, clip-x-origin, clip-y-origin, clip-mask

GC mode-dependent components: foreground, background, tile, stipple, tile-stipple-x-origin, tile-stipple-y-origin, dash-offset, dashes

PolyRectangle

drawable: DRAWABLE
gc: GCONTEXT
rectangles: LISTofRECTANGLE

Errors: `Drawable`, `GContext`, `Match`

This request draws the outlines of the specified rectangles, as if a five-point `PolyLine` were specified for each rectangle:

[x,y] [x+width,y] [x+width,y+height] [x,y+height] [x,y]

The x and y coordinates of each rectangle are relative to the drawable's origin and define the upper-left corner of the rectangle.

The rectangles are drawn in the order listed. For any given rectangle, no pixel is drawn more than once. If rectangles intersect, the intersecting pixels are drawn multiple times.

GC components: function, plane-mask, line-width, line-style, cap-style, join-style, fill-style, subwindow-mode, clip-x-origin, clip-y-origin, clip-mask

GC mode-dependent components: foreground, background, tile, stipple, tile-stipple-x-origin, tile-stipple-y-origin, dash-offset, dashes

PolyArc

drawable: DRAWABLE
gc: GCONTEXT
arcs: LISTofARC

Errors: `Drawable`, `GContext`, `Match`

This request draws circular or elliptical arcs. Each arc is specified by a rectangle and two angles. The angles are signed integers in degrees scaled by 64, with positive indicating counterclockwise motion and negative indicating clockwise motion. The start of the arc is specified by angle1 relative to the three-o'clock position from the center of the rectangle, and the path and extent of the arc is specified by angle2 relative to the start of the arc. If the magnitude of angle2 is greater than 360 degrees, it is truncated to 360 degrees. The x and y coordinates of the rectangle are relative to the origin of the drawable. For an arc specified as [x,y,w,h,a1,a2], the origin of the major and minor axes is at [x+(w/2),y+(h/2)], and the infinitely thin path describing the entire circle/ellipse intersects the horizontal axis at [x,y+(h/2)] and [x+w,y+(h/2)] and intersects the vertical axis at [x+(w/2),y] and [x+(w/2),y+h]. These coordinates can be fractional; that is, they are not truncated to discrete coordinates. The path should be defined by the ideal mathematical path. For a wide line with line-width lw, the bounding outlines for filling are given by the two infinitely thin paths consisting of all points whose perpendicular distance from the path of the circle/ellipse is equal to lw/2 (which may be a fractional value). The cap-style and join-style are applied the same as for a line corresponding to the tangent of the circle/ellipse at the endpoint.

For an arc specified as [x,y,w,h,a1,a2], the angles must be specified in the effectively skewed coordinate system of the ellipse (for a circle, the angles and coordinate systems are identical). The relationship between these angles and angles expressed in the normal coordinate system of the screen (as measured with a protractor) is as follows:

skewed-angle = atan(tan(normal-angle) * w/h) + adjust

The skewed-angle and normal-angle are expressed in radians (rather than in degrees scaled by 64) in the range [0,2*PI). The atan returns a value in the range [–PI/2,PI/2]. The adjust is:

0	for normal-angle in the range [0,PI/2)
PI	for normal-angle in the range [PI/2,(3*PI)/2)
2*PI	for normal-angle in the range [(3*PI)/2,2*PI)

The arcs are drawn in the order listed. If the last point in one arc coincides with the first point in the following arc, the two arcs will join correctly. If the first point in the first arc coincides with the last point in the last arc, the two arcs will join correctly. For any given arc, no pixel is drawn more than once. If two arcs join correctly and the line-width is greater than zero and the arcs intersect, no pixel is drawn more than once. Otherwise, the intersecting pixels of intersecting arcs are drawn multiple times. Specifying an arc with one endpoint and a clockwise extent draws the same pixels as specifying the other endpoint and an equivalent counterclockwise extent, except as it affects joins.

By specifying one axis to be zero, a horizontal or vertical line can be drawn.

Angles are computed based solely on the coordinate system, ignoring the aspect ratio.

GC components: function, plane-mask, line-width, line-style, cap-style, join-style, fill-style, subwindow-mode, clip-x-origin, clip-y-origin, clip-mask

GC mode-dependent components: foreground, background, tile, stipple, tile-stipple-x-origin, tile-stipple-y-origin, dash-offset, dashes

FillPoly

drawable: DRAWABLE
gc: GCONTEXT
shape: {`Complex`,`Nonconvex`,`Convex`}
coordinate-mode: {`Origin`,`Previous`}
points: LISTofPOINT

Errors: `Drawable`,`GContext`,`Match`,`Value`

This request fills the region closed by the specified path. The path is closed automatically if the last point in the list does not coincide with the first point. No pixel of the region is drawn more than once.

The first point is always relative to the drawable's origin. The rest are relative either to that origin or the previous point, depending on the coordinate-mode.

The shape parameter may be used by the server to improve performance. `Complex` means the path may self-intersect. Contiguous coincident points in the path are not treated as self-intersection.

`Nonconvex` means the path does not self-intersect, but the shape is not wholly convex. If known by the client, specifying `Nonconvex` over `Complex` may improve performance. If `Nonconvex` is specified for a self-intersecting path, the graphics results are undefined.

Convex means that for every pair of points inside the polygon, the line segment connecting them does not intersect the path. If known by the client, specifying Convex can improve performance. If Convex is specified for a path that is not convex, the graphics results are undefined.

GC components: function, plane-mask, fill-style, fill-rule, subwindow-mode, clip-x-origin, clip-y-origin, clip-mask

GC mode-dependent components: foreground, background, tile, stipple, tile-stipple-x-origin, tile-stipple-y-origin

PolyFillRectangle

drawable: DRAWABLE
gc: GCONTEXT
rectangles: LISTofRECTANGLE

Errors: Drawable, GContext, Match

This request fills the specified rectangles, as if a four-point FillPoly were specified for each rectangle:

[x,y] [x+width,y] [x+width,y+height] [x,y+height]

The x and y coordinates of each rectangle are relative to the drawable's origin and define the upper-left corner of the rectangle.

The rectangles are drawn in the order listed. For any given rectangle, no pixel is drawn more than once. If rectangles intersect, the intersecting pixels are drawn multiple times.

GC components: function, plane-mask, fill-style, subwindow-mode, clip-x-origin, clip-y-origin, clip-mask

GC mode-dependent components: foreground, background, tile, stipple, tile-stipple-x-origin, tile-stipple-y-origin

PolyFillArc

drawable: DRAWABLE
gc: GCONTEXT
arcs: LISTofARC

Errors: Drawable, GContext, Match

For each arc, this request fills the region closed by the infinitely thin path described by the specified arc and one or two line segments, depending on the arc-mode. For Chord, the single line segment joining the endpoints of the arc is used. For PieSlice, the two line segments joining the endpoints of the arc with the center point are used. The arcs are as specified in the PolyArc request.

The arcs are filled in the order listed. For any given arc, no pixel is drawn more than once. If regions intersect, the intersecting pixels are drawn multiple times.

GC components: function, plane-mask, fill-style, arc-mode, subwindow-mode, clip-x-origin, clip-y-origin, clip-mask

GC mode-dependent components: foreground, background, tile, stipple, tile-stipple-x-origin, tile-stipple-y-origin

PutImage

drawable: DRAWABLE
gc: GCONTEXT
depth: CARD8
width, height: CARD16
dst-x, dst-y: INT16
left-pad: CARD8
format: {Bitmap,XYPixmap,ZPixmap}
data: LISTofBYTE

Errors: Drawable,GContext,Match,Value

This request combines an image with a rectangle of the drawable. The dst-x and dst-y coordinates are relative to the drawable's origin.

If Bitmap format is used, then depth must be one (or a Match error results), and the image must be in XY format. The foreground pixel in gc defines the source for bits set to 1 in the image, and the background pixel defines the source for the bits set to 0.

For XYPixmap and ZPixmap, the depth must match the depth of the drawable (or a Match error results). For XYPixmap, the image must be sent in XY format. For ZPixmap, the image must be sent in the Z format defined for the given depth.

The left-pad must be zero for ZPixmap format (or a Match error results). For Bitmap and XYPixmap format, left-pad must be less than bitmap-scanline-pad as given in the server connection setup information (or a `Match` error results). The first left-pad bits in every scanline are to be ignored by the server. The actual image begins that many bits into the data. The width argument defines the width of the actual image and does not include left-pad.

GC components: function, plane-mask, subwindow-mode, clip-x-origin, clip-y-origin, clip-mask

GC mode-dependent components: foreground, background

GetImage

drawable: DRAWABLE
x, y: INT16
width, height: CARD16
plane-mask: CARD32
format: {`XYPixmap`, `ZPixmap`}
→
depth: CARD8
visual: VISUALID or `None`
data: LISTofBYTE

Errors: `Drawable`, `Match`, `Value`

This request returns the contents of the given rectangle of the drawable in the given format. The x and y coordinates are relative to the drawable's origin and define the upper-left corner of the rectangle. If `XYPixmap` is specified, only the bit planes specified in plane-mask are transmitted, with the planes appearing from most-significant to least-significant in bit order. If `ZPixmap` is specified, then bits in all planes not specified in plane-mask are transmitted as zero. Range checking is not performed on plane-mask; extraneous bits are simply ignored. The returned depth is as specified when the drawable was created and is the same as a depth component in a FORMAT structure (in the connection setup), not a bits-per-pixel component. If the drawable is a window, its visual type is returned. If the drawable is a pixmap, the visual is `None`.

If the drawable is a pixmap, then the given rectangle must be wholly contained within the pixmap (or a `Match` error results). If the drawable is a window, the window must be viewable, and it must be the case that, if there were no inferiors or overlapping windows, the specified rectangle of the window would be fully visible on the screen and wholly contained within the outside edges of the window (or a Match error results). Note that the borders of the window can be included and read with this request. If the window has a backing store, then the backing-store contents are returned for regions of the window that are obscured by noninferior windows; otherwise, the returned contents of such obscured regions are undefined. Also undefined are the returned contents of visible regions of inferiors of different depth than the specified window. The pointer cursor image is not included in the contents returned.

This request is not general-purpose in the same sense as other graphics-related requests. It is intended specifically for rudimentary hardcopy support.

PolyText8

drawable: DRAWABLE
gc: GCONTEXT
x, y: INT16
items: LISTofTEXTITEM8

where:

TEXTITEM8: TEXTELT8 or FONT
TEXTELT8: [delta: INT8
string: STRING8]

Errors: Drawable, Font, GContext, Match

The x and y coordinates are relative to the drawable's origin and specify the baseline starting position (the initial character origin). Each text item is processed in turn. A font item causes the font to be stored in gc and to be used for subsequent text. Switching among fonts does not affect the next character origin. A text element delta specifies an additional change in the position along the x axis before the string is drawn; the delta is always added to the character origin. Each character image, as defined by the font in gc, is treated as an additional mask for a fill operation on the drawable.

All contained FONTs are always transmitted most-significant byte first.

If a Font error is generated for an item, the previous items may have been drawn.

For fonts defined with 2-byte matrix indexing, each STRING8 byte is interpreted as a byte2 value of a CHAR2B with a byte1 value of zero.

GC components: function, plane-mask, fill-style, font, subwindow-mode, clip-x-origin, clip-y-origin, clip-mask

GC mode-dependent components: foreground, background, tile, stipple, tile-stipple-x-origin, tile-stipple-y-origin

PolyText16

drawable: DRAWABLE
gc: GCONTEXT
x, y: INT16
items: LISTofTEXTITEM16

where:

TEXTITEM16: TEXTELT16 or FONT
TEXTELT16: [delta: INT8
string: STRING16]

Errors: `Drawable`, `Font`, `GContext`, `Match`

This request is similar to `PolyText8`, except 2-byte (or 16-bit) characters are used. For fonts defined with linear indexing rather than 2-byte matrix indexing, the server will interpret each CHAR2B as a 16-bit number that has been transmitted most-significant byte first (that is, byte1 of the CHAR2B is taken as the most-significant byte).

ImageText8

drawable: DRAWABLE
gc: GCONTEXT
x, y: INT16
string: STRING8

Errors: `Drawable`, `GContext`, `Match`

The x and y coordinates are relative to the drawable's origin and specify the baseline starting position (the initial character origin). The effect is first to fill a destination rectangle with the background pixel defined in gc and then to paint the text with the foreground pixel. The upper-left corner of the filled rectangle is at:

[x, y – font-ascent]

the width is:

overall-width

and the height is:

font-ascent + font-descent

The overall-width, font-ascent, and font-descent are as they would be returned by a `QueryTextExtents` call using gc and string.

The function and fill-style defined in gc are ignored for this request. The effective function is `Copy`, and the effective fill-style `Solid`.

For fonts defined with 2-byte matrix indexing, each STRING8 byte is interpreted as a byte2 value of a CHAR2B with a byte1 value of zero.

GC components: plane-mask, foreground, background, font, subwindow-mode, clip-x-origin, clip-y-origin, clip-mask

ImageText16

drawable: DRAWABLE
gc: GCONTEXT
x, *y*: INT16
string: STRING16

Errors: `Drawable`, `GContext`, `Match`

This request is similar to `ImageText8`, except 2-byte (or 16-bit) characters are used. For fonts defined with linear indexing rather than 2-byte matrix indexing, the server will interpret each CHAR2B as a 16-bit number that has been transmitted most-significant byte first (that is, byte1 of the CHAR2B is taken as the most-significant byte).

CreateColormap

mid: COLORMAP
visual: VISUALID
window: WINDOW
alloc: {`None`, `All`}

Errors: `Alloc`, `IDChoice`, `Match`, `Value`, `Window`

This request creates a colormap of the specified visual type for the screen on which the window resides and associates the identifier mid with it. The visual type must be one supported by the screen (or a `Match` error results). The initial values of the colormap entries are undefined for classes `GrayScale`, `PseudoColor`, and `DirectColor`. For `StaticGray`, `StaticColor`, and `TrueColor`, the entries will have defined values, but those values are specific to the visual and are not defined by the core protocol. For `StaticGray`, `StaticColor`, and `TrueColor`, alloc must be specified as `None` (or a `Match` error results). For the other classes, if alloc is `None`, the colormap initially has no allocated entries, and clients can allocate entries.

If alloc is `All`, then the entire colormap is allocated writable. The initial values of all allocated entries are undefined. For `GrayScale` and `PseudoColor`, the effect is as if an `AllocColorCells` request returned all pixel values from zero to N – 1, where N is the colormap-entries value in the specified visual. For `DirectColor`, the effect is as if an `AllocColorPlanes` request returned a pixel value of zero and red-mask, green-mask, and blue-mask values containing the same bits as the corresponding masks in the specified visual. However, in all cases, none of these entries can be freed with `FreeColors`.

FreeColormap

cmap: COLORMAP

Errors: `Colormap`

This request deletes the association between the resource ID and the colormap and frees the colormap storage. If the colormap is an installed map for a screen, it is uninstalled (see `UninstallColormap` request). If the colormap is defined as the colormap for a window (by means of `CreateWindow` or `ChangeWindowAttributes`), the colormap for the window is changed to `None`, and a `ColormapNotify` event is generated. The protocol does not define the colors displayed for a window with a colormap of `None`.

This request has no effect on a default colormap for a screen.

CopyColormapAndFree

mid, src-cmap: COLORMAP

Errors: `Alloc`, `Colormap`, `IDChoice`

This request creates a colormap of the same visual type and for the same screen as src-cmap, and it associates identifier mid with it. It also moves all of the client's existing allocations from src-cmap to the new colormap with their color values intact and their read-only or writable characteristics intact, and it frees those entries in src-cmap. Color values in other entries in the new colormap are undefined. If src-cmap was created by the client with alloc `All` (see `CreateColormap` request), then the new colormap is also created with alloc `All`, all color values for all entries are copied from src-cmap, and then all entries in src-cmap are freed. If src-cmap was not created by the client with alloc `All`, then the allocations to be moved are all those pixels and planes that have been allocated by the client using either `AllocColor`, `AllocNamedColor`, `AllocColorCells`, or `AllocColorPlanes` and that have not been freed since they were allocated.

InstallColormap

cmap: COLORMAP

Errors: `Colormap`

This request makes this colormap an installed map for its screen. All windows associated with this colormap immediately display with true colors. As a side effect, additional colormaps might be implicitly installed or uninstalled by the server. Which other colormaps get installed or uninstalled is server-dependent except that the required list must remain installed.

If cmap is not already an installed map, a `ColormapNotify` event is generated on every window having cmap as an attribute. In addition, for every other colormap that is installed or uninstalled as a result of the request, a `ColormapNotify` event is generated on every window having that colormap as an attribute.

At any time, there is a subset of the installed maps that are viewed as an ordered list and are called the required list. The length of the required list is at most M, where M is the min-installed-maps specified for the screen in the connection setup. The required list is maintained as follows. When a colormap is an explicit argument to `InstallColormap`, it is added to the head of the list; the list is truncated at the tail, if necessary, to keep the length of the list to at most M. When a colormap is an explicit argument to `UninstallColormap` and it is in the required list, it is removed from the list. A colormap is not added to the required list when it is installed implicitly by the server, and the server cannot implicitly uninstall a colormap that is in the required list.

Initially the default colormap for a screen is installed (but is not in the required list).

UninstallColormap

cmap: COLORMAP

Errors: `Colormap`

If cmap is on the required list for its screen (see `InstallColormap` request), it is removed from the list. As a side effect, cmap might be uninstalled, and additional colormaps might be implicitly installed or uninstalled. Which colormaps get installed or uninstalled is server-dependent except that the required list must remain installed.

If cmap becomes uninstalled, a `ColormapNotify` event is generated on every window having cmap as an attribute. In addition, for every other colormap that is installed or uninstalled as a result of the request, a `ColormapNotify` event is generated on every window having that colormap as an attribute.

ListInstalledColormaps

window: WINDOW

→

cmaps: LISTofCOLORMAP

Errors: `Window`

This request returns a list of the currently installed colormaps for the screen of the specified window. The order of colormaps is not significant, and there is no explicit indication of the required list (see `InstallColormap` request).

AllocColor

cmap: COLORMAP
red, green, blue: CARD16

→
pixel: CARD32
red, green, blue: CARD16

Errors: `Alloc`, `Colormap`

This request allocates a read-only colormap entry corresponding to the closest RGB values provided by the hardware. It also returns the pixel and the RGB values actually used. Multiple clients requesting the same effective RGB values can be assigned the same read-only entry, allowing entries to be shared.

AllocNamedColor

cmap: COLORMAP
name: STRING8
→
pixel: CARD32
exact-red, exact-green, exact-blue: CARD16
visual-red, visual-green, visual-blue: CARD16

Errors: `Alloc`, `Colormap`, `Name`

This request looks up the named color with respect to the screen associated with the colormap. Then, it does an `AllocColor` on cmap. The name should use the ISO Latin-1 encoding, and uppercase and lowercase do not matter. The exact RGB values specify the true values for the color, and the visual values specify the values actually used in the colormap.

AllocColorCells

cmap: COLORMAP
colors, planes: CARD16
contiguous: BOOL
→
pixels, masks: LISTofCARD32

Errors: `Alloc`, `Colormap`, `Value`

The number of colors must be positive, and the number of planes must be nonnegative (or a `Value` error results). If C colors and P planes are requested, then C pixels and P masks are returned. No mask will have any bits in common with any other mask or with any of the pixels. By ORing together masks and pixels, $C*2^P$ distinct pixels can be produced; all of these are allocated writable by the request. For `GrayScale` or `PseudoColor`, each mask will have exactly one bit set to 1; for `DirectColor`, each will have exactly three bits set to 1. If contiguous is `True` and if all masks are ORed together, a single contiguous set of bits will be formed for `GrayScale` or `PseudoColor`, and three contiguous sets of bits (one within each pixel subfield) for `DirectColor`. The RGB values of the allocated entries are undefined.

AllocColorPlanes

cmap: COLORMAP
colors, reds, greens, blues: CARD16
contiguous: BOOL
→
pixels: LISTofCARD32
red-mask, green-mask, blue-mask: CARD32

Errors: `Alloc`, `Colormap`, `Value`

The number of colors must be positive, and the reds, greens, and blues must be nonnegative (or a `Value` error results). If C colors, R reds, G greens, and B blues are requested, then C pixels are returned, and the masks have R, G, and B bits set, respectively. If contiguous is `True`, then each mask will have a contiguous set of bits. No mask will have any bits in common with any other mask or with any of the pixels. For `DirectColor`, each mask will lie within the corresponding pixel subfield. By ORing together subsets of masks with pixels, $C*2^{R+G+B}$ distinct pixels can be produced; all of these are allocated writable by the request. The initial RGB values of the allocated entries are undefined. In the colormap, there are only $C*2^{R}$ independent red entries, $C*2^{G}$ independent green entries, and $C*2^{B}$ independent blue entries. This is true even for `PseudoColor`. When the colormap entry for a pixel value is changed using `StoreColors` or `StoreNamedColor`, the pixel is decomposed according to the masks and the corresponding independent entries are updated.

FreeColors

cmap: COLORMAP
pixels: LISTofCARD32
plane-mask: CARD32

Errors: `Access`, `Colormap`, `Value`

The plane-mask should not have any bits in common with any of the pixels. The set of all pixels is produced by ORing together subsets of plane-mask with the pixels. The request frees all of these pixels that were allocated by the client (using `AllocColor`, `AllocNamedColor`, `AllocColorCells`, and `AllocColorPlanes`). Note that freeing an individual pixel obtained from `AllocColorPlanes` may not actually allow it to be reused until all of its related pixels are also freed. Similarly, a read-only entry is not actually freed until it has been freed by all clients, and if a client allocates the same read-only entry multiple times, it must free the entry that many times before the entry is actually freed.

All specified pixels that are allocated by the client in cmap are freed, even if one or more pixels produce an error. A `Value` error is generated if a specified pixel is not a valid index into cmap. An `Access` error is generated if a specified pixel is not allocated by the client (that is, is unallocated or is only allocated by another client) or if the colormap was created with all entries writable (using an alloc value of `All` in `CreateColormap`). If more than one pixel is in error, it is arbitrary as to which pixel is reported.

StoreColors

cmap: COLORMAP
items: LISTofCOLORITEM

where:

COLORITEM: [pixel: CARD32
do-red, do-green, do-blue: BOOL
red, green, blue: CARD16]

Errors: `Access`, `Colormap`, `Value`

This request changes the colormap entries of the specified pixels. The do-red, do-green, and do-blue fields indicate which components should actually be changed. If the colormap is an installed map for its screen, the changes are visible immediately.

All specified pixels that are allocated writable in cmap (by any client) are changed, even if one or more pixels produce an error. A `Value` error is generated if a specified pixel is not a valid index into cmap, and an `Access` error is generated if a specified pixel is unallocated or is allocated read-only. If more than one pixel is in error, it is arbitrary as to which pixel is reported.

StoreNamedColor

cmap: COLORMAP
pixel: CARD32
name: STRING8
do-red, do-green, do-blue: BOOL

Errors: `Access`, `Colormap`, `Name`, `Value`

This request looks up the named color with respect to the screen associated with cmap and then does a `StoreColors` in cmap. The name should use the ISO Latin-1 encoding, and uppercase and lowercase do not matter. The `Access` and `Value` errors are the same as in `StoreColors`.

QueryColors

cmap: COLORMAP
pixels: LISTofCARD32
→
colors: LISTofRGB

where:

RGB: [red, green, blue: CARD16]

Errors: `Colormap`, `Value`

This request returns the hardware-specific color values stored in cmap for the specified pixels. The values returned for an unallocated entry are undefined. A `Value` error is generated if a pixel is not a valid index into cmap. If more than one pixel is in error, it is arbitrary as to which pixel is reported.

LookupColor

cmap: COLORMAP
name: STRING8
→
exact-red, exact-green, exact-blue: CARD16
visual-red, visual-green, visual-blue: CARD16

Errors: `Colormap`, `Name`

This request looks up the string name of a color with respect to the screen associated with cmap and returns both the exact color values and the closest values provided by the hardware with respect to the visual type of cmap. The name should use the ISO Latin-1 encoding, and uppercase and lowercase do not matter.

CreateCursor

cid: CURSOR
source: PIXMAP
mask: PIXMAP or `None`
fore-red, fore-green, fore-blue: CARD16
back-red, back-green, back-blue: CARD16
x, y: CARD16

Errors: `Alloc`, `IDChoice`, `Match`, `Pixmap`

This request creates a cursor and associates identifier cid with it. The foreground and background RGB values must be specified, even if the server only has a `StaticGray` or `GrayScale` screen. The foreground is used for the bits set to 1 in the source, and the background is used for the bits set to 0. Both source and mask (if specified) must have depth one (or a `Match` error results), but they can have any root. The mask pixmap defines the shape of the cursor. That is, the bits set to 1 in the mask define which source pixels will be displayed, and where the mask has bits set to 0, the corresponding bits of the source pixmap are ignored. If no mask is given, all pixels of the source are displayed. The mask, if present, must be the same size as the source (or a `Match` error results). The x and y coordinates define the hotspot relative to the source's origin and must be a point within the source (or a `Match` error results).

The components of the cursor may be transformed arbitrarily to meet display limitations.

The pixmaps can be freed immediately if no further explicit references to them are to be made.

Subsequent drawing in the source or mask pixmap has an undefined effect on the cursor. The server might or might not make a copy of the pixmap.

CreateGlyphCursor

cid: CURSOR
source-font: FONT

mask-font: FONT or `None`
source-char, mask-char: CARD16
fore-red, fore-green, fore-blue: CARD16
back-red, back-green, back-blue: CARD16

Errors: `Alloc`, `Font`, `IDChoice`, `Value`

This request is similar to `CreateCursor`, except the source and mask bitmaps are obtained from the specified font glyphs. The source-char must be a defined glyph in source-font, and if mask-font is given, mask-char must be a defined glyph in mask-font (or a `Value` error results). The mask font and character are optional. The origins of the source and mask (if it is defined) glyphs are positioned coincidently and define the hotspot. The source and mask need not have the same bounding box metrics, and there is no restriction on the placement of the hotspot relative to the bounding boxes. If no mask is given, all pixels of the source are displayed. Note that source-char and mask-char are CARD16, not CHAR2B. For 2-byte matrix fonts, the 16-bit value should be formed with byte1 in the most-significant byte and byte2 in the least-significant byte.

The components of the cursor may be transformed arbitrarily to meet display limitations.

The fonts can be freed immediately if no further explicit references to them are to be made.

FreeCursor

cursor: CURSOR

Errors: `Cursor`

This request deletes the association between the resource ID and the cursor. The cursor storage will be freed when no other resource references it.

RecolorCursor

cursor: CURSOR
fore-red, fore-green, fore-blue: CARD16
back-red, back-green, back-blue: CARD16

Errors: `Cursor`

This request changes the color of a cursor. If the cursor is being displayed on a screen, the change is visible immediately.

QueryBestSize

class: {Cursor,Tile,Stipple}
drawable: DRAWABLE
width, height: CARD16
→
width, height: CARD16

Errors: Drawable, Match, Value

This request returns the best size that is closest to the argument size. For Cursor, this is the largest size that can be fully displayed. For Tile, this is the size that can be tiled fastest. For Stipple, this is the size that can be stippled fastest.

For Cursor, the drawable indicates the desired screen. For Tile and Stipple, the drawable indicates the screen and also possibly the window class and depth. An InputOnly window cannot be used as the drawable for Tile or Stipple (or a Match error results).

QueryExtension

name: STRING8
→
present: BOOL
major-opcode: CARD8
first-event: CARD8
first-error: CARD8

This request determines if the named extension is present. If so, the major opcode for the extension is returned, if it has one. Otherwise, zero is returned. Any minor opcode and the request formats are specific to the extension. If the extension involves additional event types, the base event type code is returned. Otherwise, zero is returned. The format of the events is specific to the extension. If the extension involves additional error codes, the base error code is returned. Otherwise, zero is returned. The format of additional data in the errors is specific to the extension.

The extension name should use the ISO Latin-1 encoding, and uppercase and lowercase matter.

ListExtensions

→
  names: LISTofSTRING8

This request returns a list of all extensions supported by the server.

SetModifierMapping

keycodes-per-modifier: CARD8
keycodes: LISTofKEYCODE
→
  status: {`Success`, `Busy`, `Failed`}

Errors: `Alloc`, `Value`

This request specifies the keycodes (if any) of the keys to be used as modifiers. The number of keycodes in the list must be 8*keycodes-per-modifier (or a `Length` error results). The keycodes are divided into eight sets, with each set containing keycodes-per-modifier elements. The sets are assigned to the modifiers `Shift`, `Lock`, `Control`, `Mod1`, `Mod2`, `Mod3`, `Mod4`, and `Mod5`, in order. Only nonzero keycode values are used within each set; zero values are ignored. All of the nonzero keycodes must be in the range specified by min-keycode and max-keycode in the connection setup (or a `Value` error results). The order of keycodes within a set does not matter. If no nonzero values are specified in a set, the use of the corresponding modifier is disabled, and the modifier bit will always be zero. Otherwise, the modifier bit will be one whenever at least one of the keys in the corresponding set is in the down position.

A server can impose restrictions on how modifiers can be changed (for example, if certain keys do not generate up transitions in hardware, if autorepeat cannot be disabled on certain keys, or if multiple keys per modifier are not supported). The status reply is `Failed` if some such restriction is violated, and none of the modifiers is changed.

If the new nonzero keycodes specified for a modifier differ from those currently defined and any (current or new) keys for that modifier are logically in the down state, then the status reply is `Busy`, and none of the modifiers is changed.

This request generates a `MappingNotify` event on a `Success` status.

GetModifierMapping

→
keycodes-per-modifier: CARD8
keycodes: LISTofKEYCODE

This request returns the keycodes of the keys being used as modifiers. The number of keycodes in the list is 8*keycodes-per-modifier. The keycodes are divided into eight sets, with each set containing keycodes-per-modifier elements. The sets are assigned to the modifiers `Shift`, `Lock`, `Control`, `Mod1`, `Mod2`, `Mod3`, `Mod4`, and `Mod5`, in order. The keycodes-per-modifier value is chosen arbitrarily by the server; zeroes are used to fill in unused elements within each set. If only zero values are given in a set, the use of the corresponding modifier has been disabled. The order of keycodes within each set is chosen arbitrarily by the server.

ChangeKeyboardMapping

first-keycode: KEYCODE
keysyms-per-keycode: CARD8
keysyms: LISTofKEYSYM

Errors: `Alloc`, `Value`

This request defines the symbols for the specified number of keycodes, starting with the specified keycode. The symbols for keycodes outside this range remained unchanged. The number of elements in the keysyms list must be a multiple of keysyms-per-keycode (or a `Length` error results). The first-keycode must be greater than or equal to min-keycode as returned in the connection setup (or a `Value` error results) and:

first-keycode + (keysyms-length / keysyms-per-keycode) – 1

must be less than or equal to max-keycode as returned in the connection setup (or a `Value` error results). KEYSYM number N (counting from zero) for keycode K has an index (counting from zero) of:

(K – first-keycode) * keysyms-per-keycode + N

in keysyms. The keysyms-per-keycode can be chosen arbitrarily by the client to be large enough to hold all desired symbols. A special KEYSYM value of `NoSymbol` should be used to fill in unused elements for individual keycodes. It is legal for `NoSymbol` to appear in nontrailing positions of the effective list for a keycode.

This request generates a `MappingNotify` event.

There is no requirement that the server interpret this mapping; it is merely stored for reading and writing by clients (see section 5).

GetKeyboardMapping

first-keycode: KEYCODE
count: CARD8
→
keysyms-per-keycode: CARD8
keysyms: LISTofKEYSYM

Errors: `Value`

This request returns the symbols for the specified number of keycodes, starting with the specified keycode. The first-keycode must be greater than or equal to min-keycode as returned in the connection setup (or a `Value` error results), and:

first-keycode + count – 1

must be less than or equal to max-keycode as returned in the connection setup (or a `Value` error results). The number of elements in the keysyms list is:

count * keysyms-per-keycode

and KEYSYM number N (counting from zero) for keycode K has an index (counting from zero) of:

(K – first-keycode) * keysyms-per-keycode + N

in keysyms. The keysyms-per-keycode value is chosen arbitrarily by the server to be large enough to report all requested symbols. A special KEYSYM value of `NoSymbol` is used to fill in unused elements for individual keycodes.

ChangeKeyboardControl

value-mask: BITMASK
value-list: LISTofVALUE

Errors: Match, Value

This request controls various aspects of the keyboard. The value-mask and value-list specify which controls are to be changed. The possible values are:

Control	*Type*
key-click-percent	INT8
bell-percent	INT8
bell-pitch	INT16
bell-duration	INT16
led	CARD8
led-mode	{On, Off}
key	KEYCODE
auto-repeat-mode	{On, Off, Default}

The key-click-percent sets the volume for key clicks between 0 (off) and 100 (loud) inclusive, if possible. Setting to −1 restores the default. Other negative values generate a Value error.

The bell-percent sets the base volume for the bell between 0 (off) and 100 (loud) inclusive, if possible. Setting to −1 restores the default. Other negative values generate a Value error.

The bell-pitch sets the pitch (specified in Hz) of the bell, if possible. Setting to −1 restores the default. Other negative values generate a Value error.

The bell-duration sets the duration of the bell (specified in milliseconds), if possible. Setting to −1 restores the default. Other negative values generate a Value error.

If both led-mode and led are specified, then the state of that LED is changed, if possible. If only led-mode is specified, then the state of all LEDs are changed, if possible. At most 32 LEDs, numbered from one, are supported. No standard interpretation of LEDs is defined. It is a Match error if an led is specified without an led-mode.

If both auto-repeat-mode and key are specified, then the auto-repeat mode of that key is changed, if possible. If only auto-repeat-mode is specified, then the global auto-repeat mode for the entire keyboard is changed, if possible, without affecting the per-key settings. It is a `Match` error if a key is specified without an auto-repeat-mode. Each key has an individual mode of whether or not it should auto-repeat and a default setting for that mode. In addition, there is a global mode of whether auto-repeat should be enabled or not and a default setting for that mode. When the global mode is `On`, keys should obey their individual auto-repeat modes. When the global mode is `Off`, no keys should auto-repeat. An auto-repeating key generates alternating `KeyPress` and `KeyRelease` events. When a key is used as a modifier, it is desirable for the key not to auto-repeat, regardless of the auto-repeat setting for that key.

A bell generator connected with the console but not directly on the keyboard is treated as if it were part of the keyboard.

The order in which controls are verified and altered is server-dependent. If an error is generated, a subset of the controls may have been altered.

GetKeyboardControl

→
key-click-percent: CARD8
bell-percent: CARD8
bell-pitch: CARD16
bell-duration: CARD16
led-mask: CARD32
global-auto-repeat: {`On`,`Off`}
auto-repeats: LISTofCARD8

This request returns the current control values for the keyboard. For the LEDs, the least-significant bit of led-mask corresponds to LED one, and each one bit in led-mask indicates an LED that is lit. The auto-repeats is a bit vector; each one bit indicates that auto-repeat is enabled for the corresponding key. The vector is represented as 32 bytes. Byte N (from 0) contains the bits for keys 8N to 8N + 7, with the least-significant bit in the byte representing key 8N.

Bell

percent: INT8

Errors: `Value`

This request rings the bell on the keyboard at a volume relative to the base volume for the keyboard, if possible. Percent can range from −100 to 100 inclusive (or a Value error results). The volume at which the bell is rung when percent is nonnegative is:

base − [(base * percent) / 100] + percent

When percent is negative, it is:

base + [(base * percent) / 100]

SetPointerMapping

map: LISTofCARD8
→
status: {Success, Busy}

Errors: Value

This request sets the mapping of the pointer. Elements of the list are indexed starting from one. The length of the list must be the same as GetPointerMapping would return (or a Value error results). The index is a core button number, and the element of the list defines the effective number.

A zero element disables a button. Elements are not restricted in value by the number of physical buttons, but no two elements can have the same nonzero value (or a Value error results).

If any of the buttons to be altered are logically in the down state, the status reply is Busy, and the mapping is not changed.

This request generates a MappingNotify event on a Success status.

GetPointerMapping

→
map: LISTofCARD8

This request returns the current mapping of the pointer. Elements of the list are indexed starting from one. The length of the list indicates the number of physical buttons.

The nominal mapping for a pointer is the identity mapping: map[i] = i.

ChangePointerControl

do-acceleration, do-threshold: BOOL
acceleration-numerator, acceleration-denominator: INT16
threshold: INT16

Errors: `Value`

This request defines how the pointer moves. The acceleration is a multiplier for movement expressed as a fraction. For example, specifying 3/1 means the pointer moves three times as fast as normal. The fraction can be rounded arbitrarily by the server. Acceleration only takes effect if the pointer moves more than threshold number of pixels at once and only applies to the amount beyond the threshold. Setting a value to −1 restores the default. Other negative values generate a `Value` error, as does a zero value for acceleration-denominator.

GetPointerControl

→
acceleration-numerator, acceleration-denominator: CARD16
threshold: CARD16

This request returns the current acceleration and threshold for the pointer.

SetScreenSaver

timeout, interval: INT16
prefer-blanking: `{Yes,No,Default}`
allow-exposures: `{Yes,No,Default}`

Errors: `Value`

The timeout and interval are specified in seconds; setting a value to −1 restores the default. Other negative values generate a `Value` error. If the timeout value is zero, screen-saver is disabled (but an activated screen-saver is not deactivated). If the timeout value is nonzero, screen-saver is enabled. Once screen-saver is enabled, if no input from the keyboard or pointer is generated for timeout seconds, screen-saver is activated. For each screen, if blanking is preferred and the hardware supports video blanking, the screen will simply go blank. Otherwise, if either exposures are allowed or the screen can be regenerated without sending exposure events to clients, the screen is changed in a server-dependent fashion to avoid phosphor burn. Otherwise, the state of the screens does not change, and screen-saver is not activated. At the next keyboard or pointer input or at the next ForceScreenSaver with mode Reset, screen-saver is deactivated, and all screen states are restored.

If the server-dependent screen-saver method is amenable to periodic change, interval serves as a hint about how long the change period should be, with zero hinting that no periodic change should be made. Examples of ways to change the screen include scrambling the color map periodically, moving an icon image about the screen periodically, or tiling the screen with the root window background tile, randomly reorigined periodically.

GetScreenSaver

→
timeout, interval: CARD16
prefer-blanking: {Yes, No}
allow-exposures: {Yes, No}

This request returns the current screen-saver control values.

ForceScreenSaver

mode: {Activate, Reset}

Errors: Value

If the mode is Activate and screen-saver is currently deactivated, then screen-saver is activated (even if screen-saver has been disabled with a timeout value of zero). If the mode is Reset and screen-saver is currently enabled, then screen-saver is deactivated (if it was activated), and the activation timer is reset to its initial state as if device input had just been received.

ChangeHosts

mode: {Insert, Delete}
host: HOST

Errors: Access, Value

This request adds or removes the specified host from the access control list. When the access control mechanism is enabled and a host attempts to establish a connection to the server, the host must be in this list, or the server will refuse the connection.

The client must reside on the same host as the server and/or have been granted permission by a server-dependent method to execute this request (or an `Access` error results).

An initial access control list can usually be specified, typically by naming a file that the server reads at startup and reset.

The following address families are defined. A server is not required to support these families and may support families not listed here. Use of an unsupported family, an improper address format, or an improper address length within a supported family results in a `Value` error.

For the Internet family, the address must be four bytes long. The address bytes are in standard IP order; the server performs no automatic swapping on the address bytes. For a Class A address, the network number is the first byte in the address, and the host number is the remaining three bytes, most-significant byte first. For a Class B address, the network number is the first two bytes and the host number is the last two bytes, each most-significant byte first. For a Class C address, the network number is the first three bytes, most-significant byte first, and the last byte is the host number.

For the DECnet family, the server performs no automatic swapping on the address bytes. A Phase IV address is two bytes long: the first byte contains the least-significant eight bits of the node number, and the second byte contains the most-significant two bits of the node number in the least-significant two bits of the byte and the area in the most significant six bits of the byte.

For the Chaos family, the address must be two bytes long. The host number is always the first byte in the address, and the subnet number is always the second byte. The server performs no automatic swapping on the address bytes.

ListHosts

→

mode: `{Enabled,Disabled}`
hosts: LISTofHOST

This request returns the hosts on the access control list and whether use of the list at connection setup is currently enabled or disabled.

Each HOST is padded to a multiple of four bytes.

SetAccessControl

mode: {Enable, Disable}

Errors: Access, Value

This request enables or disables the use of the access control list at connection setups.

The client must reside on the same host as the server and/or have been granted permission by a server-dependent method to execute this request (or an Access error results).

SetCloseDownMode

mode: {Destroy, RetainPermanent, RetainTemporary}

Errors: Value

This request defines what will happen to the client's resources at connection close. A connection starts in Destroy mode. The meaning of the close-down mode is described in section 10.

KillClient

resource: CARD32 or AllTemporary

Errors: Value

If a valid resource is specified, KillClient forces a close-down of the client that created the resource. If the client has already terminated in either RetainPermanent or RetainTemporary mode, all of the client's resources are destroyed (see section 10). If AllTemporary is specified, then the resources of all clients that have terminated in RetainTemporary are destroyed.

NoOperation

This request has no arguments and no results, but the request length field can be nonzero, which allows the request to be any multiple of four bytes in length. The bytes contained in the request are uninterpreted by the server.

This request can be used in its minimum four byte form as padding where necessary by client libraries that find it convenient to force requests to begin on 64-bit boundaries.

SECTION 10. CONNECTION CLOSE

At connection close, all event selections made by the client are discarded. If the client has the pointer actively grabbed, an UngrabPointer is performed. If the client has the keyboard actively grabbed, an UngrabKeyboard is performed. All passive grabs by the client are released. If the client has the server grabbed, an UngrabServer is performed. All selections (see SetSelectionOwner request) owned by the client are disowned. If close-down mode (see SetCloseDownMode request) is RetainPermanent or RetainTemporary, then all resources (including colormap entries) allocated by the client are marked as permanent or temporary, respectively (but this does not prevent other clients from explicitly destroying them). If the mode is Destroy, all of the client's resources are destroyed.

When a client's resources are destroyed, for each window in the client's save-set, if the window is an inferior of a window created by the client, the save-set window is reparented to the closest ancestor such that the save-set window is not an inferior of a window created by the client. If the save-set window is unmapped, a MapWindow request is performed on it (even if it was not an inferior of a window created by the client). The reparenting leaves unchanged the absolute coordinates (with respect to the root window) of the upper-left outer corner of the save-set window. After save-set processing, all windows created by the client are destroyed. For each nonwindow resource created by the client, the appropriate Free request is performed. All colors and colormap entries allocated by the client are freed.

A server goes through a cycle of having no connections and having some connections. At every transition to the state of having no connections as a result of a connection closing with a Destroy close-down mode, the server resets its state as if it had just been started. This starts by destroying all lingering resources from clients that have terminated in RetainPermanent or RetainTemporary mode. It additionally includes deleting all but the predefined atom identifiers, deleting all properties on all root windows, resetting all device maps and attributes (key click, bell volume, acceleration), resetting the access control list, restoring the standard root tiles and cursors, restoring the default font path, and restoring the input focus to state `PointerRoot`.

Note that closing a connection with a close-down mode of `RetainPermanent` or `RetainTemporary` will not cause the server to reset.

SECTION 11. EVENTS

When a button press is processed with the pointer in some window W and no active pointer grab is in progress, the ancestors of W are searched from the root down, looking for a passive grab to activate. If no matching passive grab on the button exists, then an active grab is started automatically for the client receiving the event, and the last-pointer-grab time is set to the current server time. The effect is essentially equivalent to a `GrabButton` with arguments:

Argument	*Value*
event-window	Event window
event-mask	Client's selected pointer events on the event window
pointer-mode and keyboard-mode	`Asynchronous`
owner-events	`True` if the client has `OwnerGrabButton` selected on the event window, otherwise `False`
confine-to	`None`
cursor	`None`

The grab is terminated automatically when the logical state of the pointer has all buttons released. `UngrabPointer` and `ChangeActivePointerGrab` can both be used to modify the active grab.

KeyPress
KeyRelease
ButtonPress
ButtonRelease
MotionNotify

root, event: WINDOW
child: WINDOW or `None`
same-screen: BOOL

root-x, root-y, event-x, event-y: INT16
detail: <see below>
state: SETofKEYBUTMASK
time: TIMESTAMP

These events are generated either when a key or button logically changes state or when the pointer logically moves. The generation of these logical changes may lag the physical changes if device event processing is frozen. Note that `KeyPress` and `KeyRelease` are generated for all keys, even those mapped to modifier bits. The source of the event is the window the pointer is in. The window the event is reported with respect to is called the event window. The event window is found by starting with the source window and looking up the hierarchy for the first window on which any client has selected interest in the event (provided no intervening window prohibits event generation by including the event type in its do-not-propagate-mask). The actual window used for reporting can be modified by active grabs and, in the case of keyboard events, can be modified by the focus window.

The root is the root window of the source window, and root-x and root-y are the pointer coordinates relative to root's origin at the time of the event. Event is the event window. If the event window is on the same screen as root, then event-x and event-y are the pointer coordinates relative to the event window's origin. Otherwise, event-x and event-y are zero. If the source window is an inferior of the event window, then child is set to the child of the event window that is an ancestor of (or is) the source window. Otherwise, it is set to `None`. The state component gives the logical state of the buttons and modifier keys just before the event. The detail component type varies with the event type:

Event	*Component*
`KeyPress,KeyRelease`	KEYCODE
`ButtonPress,ButtonRelease`	BUTTON
`MotionNotifyl`	`{Normal,Hint}`

`MotionNotify` events are only generated when the motion begins and ends in the window. The granularity of motion events is not guaranteed, but a client selecting for motion events is guaranteed to get at least one event when the pointer moves and comes to rest. Selecting `PointerMotion` receives events independent of the state of the pointer buttons. By selecting some subset of Button[1-5]Motion instead, MotionNotify events will only be received when one or more of the specified buttons are pressed. By selecting ButtonMotion, MotionNotify events will be received only when at least one button is pressed. The events are always of type MotionNotify, independent of the selection. If PointerMotionHint is selected, the server is free to send only one MotionNotify event (with detail Hint) to the client for the event window until either the key or button state changes, the pointer leaves the event window, or the client issues a QueryPointer or GetMotionEvents request.

EnterNotify
LeaveNotify

root, event: WINDOW
child: WINDOW or None
same-screen: BOOL
root-x, root-y, event-x, event-y: INT16
mode: {Normal, Grab, Ungrab}
detail: {Ancestor, Virtual, Inferior, Nonlinear, NonlinearVirtual}
focus: BOOL
state: SETofKEYBUTMASK
time: TIMESTAMP

If pointer motion or window hierarchy change causes the pointer to be in a different window than before, EnterNotify and LeaveNotify events are generated instead of a MotionNotify event. Only clients selecting EnterWindow on a window receive EnterNotify events, and only clients selecting LeaveWindow receive LeaveNotify events. The pointer position reported in the event is always the final position, not the initial position of the pointer. The root is the root window for this position, and root-x and root-y are the pointer coordinates relative to root's origin at the time of the event. Event is the event window. If the event window is on the same screen as root, then event-x and event-y are the pointer coordinates relative to the event window's origin. Otherwise, event-x and event-y are zero. In a LeaveNotify event, if a child of the event window contains the initial position of the pointer, then the child component is set to that child. Otherwise, it is None. For an EnterNotify event, if a child of the event window contains the final pointer position, then the child component is set to that child. Otherwise, it is None. If the event window is the focus window or an inferior of the focus window, then focus is True. Otherwise, focus is False.

Normal pointer motion events have mode Normal. Pseudo-motion events when a grab activates have mode Grab, and pseudo-motion events when a grab deactivates have mode Ungrab.

All EnterNotify and LeaveNotify events caused by a hierarchy change are generated after any hierarchy event caused by that change (that is, UnmapNotify, MapNotify, ConfigureNotify, GravityNotify, CirculateNotify), but the ordering of EnterNotify and LeaveNotify events with respect to FocusOut, VisibilityNotify, and Expose events is not constrained.

Normal events are generated as follows:

When the pointer moves from window A to window B and A is an inferior of B:

- LeaveNotify with detail Ancestor is generated on A.
- LeaveNotify with detail Virtual is generated on each window between A and B exclusive (in that order).
- EnterNotify with detail Inferior is generated on B.

When the pointer moves from window A to window B and B is an inferior of A:

- LeaveNotify with detail Inferior is generated on A.
- EnterNotify with detail Virtual is generated on each window between A and B exclusive (in that order).
- EnterNotify with detail Ancestor is generated on B.

When the pointer moves from window A to window B and window C is their least common ancestor:

- LeaveNotify with detail Nonlinear is generated on A.
- LeaveNotify with detail NonlinearVirtual is generated on each window between A and C exclusive (in that order).
- EnterNotify with detail NonlinearVirtual is generated on each window between C and B exclusive (in that order).
- EnterNotify with detail Nonlinear is generated on B.

When the pointer moves from window A to window B on different screens:

- LeaveNotify with detail Nonlinear is generated on A.
- If A is not a root window, LeaveNotify with detail NonlinearVirtual is generated on each window above A up to and including its root (in order).
- If B is not a root window, EnterNotify with detail NonlinearVirtual is generated on each window from B's root down to but not including B (in order).
- EnterNotify with detail Nonlinear is generated on B.

When a pointer grab activates (but after any initial warp into a confine-to window and before generating any actual ButtonPress event that activates the grab), G is the grab-window for the grab, and P is the window the pointer is in:

- EnterNotify and LeaveNotify events with mode Grab are generated (as for Normal above) as if the pointer were to suddenly warp from its current position in P to some position in G. However, the pointer does not warp, and the pointer position is used as both the initial and final positions for the events.

When a pointer grab deactivates (but after generating any actual ButtonRelease event that deactivates the grab), G is the grab-window for the grab, and P is the window the pointer is in:

- EnterNotify and LeaveNotify events with mode Ungrab are generated (as for Normal above) as if the pointer were to suddenly warp from some position in G to its current position in P. However, the pointer does not warp, and the current pointer position is used as both the initial and final positions for the events.

FocusIn
FocusOut

event: WINDOW
mode: {Normal,WhileGrabbed,Grab,Ungrab}
detail: {Ancestor,Virtual,Inferior,Nonlinear,NonlinearVirtual,Pointer,
PointerRoot,None}

These events are generated when the input focus changes and are reported to clients selecting FocusChange on the window. Events generated by SetInputFocus when the keyboard is not grabbed have mode Normal. Events generated by SetInputFocus when the keyboard is grabbed have mode WhileGrabbed.

Events generated when a keyboard grab activates have mode `Grab`, and events generated when a keyboard grab deactivates have mode `Ungrab`.

All `FocusOut` events caused by a window unmap are generated after any `UnmapNotify` event, but the ordering of `FocusOut` with respect to generated `EnterNotify`, `LeaveNotify`, `VisibilityNotify`, and `Expose` events is not constrained.

`Normal` and `WhileGrabbed` events are generated as follows:

When the focus moves from window A to window B, A is an inferior of B, and the pointer is in window P:

- `FocusOut` with detail `Ancestor` is generated on A.
- `FocusOut` with detail `Virtual` is generated on each window between A and B exclusive (in order).
- `FocusIn` with detail `Inferior` is generated on B.
- If P is an inferior of B but P is not A or an inferior of A or an ancestor of A, `FocusIn` with detail `Pointer` is generated on each window below B down to and including P (in order).

When the focus moves from window A to window B, B is an inferior of A, and the pointer is in window P:

- If P is an inferior of A but P is not an inferior of B or an ancestor of B, `FocusOut` with detail `Pointer` is generated on each window from P up to but not including A (in order).
- `FocusOut` with detail `Inferior` is generated on A.
- `FocusIn` with detail `Virtual` is generated on each window between A and B exclusive (in order).
- `FocusIn` with detail `Ancestor` is generated on B.

When the focus moves from window A to window B, window C is their least common ancestor, and the pointer is in window P:

- If P is an inferior of A, `FocusOut` with detail `Pointer` is generated on each window from P up to but not including A (in order).
- `FocusOut` with detail `Nonlinear` is generated on A.
- `FocusOut` with detail `NonlinearVirtual` is generated on each window between A and C exclusive (in order).
- `FocusIn` with detail `NonlinearVirtual` is generated on each window between C and B exclusive (in order).

- `FocusIn` with detail `Nonlinear` is generated on B.
- If P is an inferior of B, `FocusIn` with detail `Pointer` is generated on each window below B down to and including P (in order).

When the focus moves from window A to window B on different screens and the pointer is in window P:

- If P is an inferior of A, `FocusOut` with detail `Pointer` is generated on each window from P up to but not including A (in order).
- `FocusOut` with detail `Nonlinear` is generated on A.
- If A is not a root window, `FocusOut` with detail `NonlinearVirtual` is generated on each window above A up to and including its root (in order).
- If B is not a root window, `FocusIn` with detail `NonlinearVirtual` is generated on each window from B's root down to but not including B (in order).
- `FocusIn` with detail `Nonlinear` is generated on B.
- If P is an inferior of B, `FocusIn` with detail `Pointer` is generated on each window below B down to and including P (in order).

When the focus moves from window A to `PointerRoot` (or `None`) and the pointer is in window P:

- If P is an inferior of A, `FocusOut` with detail `Pointer` is generated on each window from P up to but not including A (in order).
- `FocusOut` with detail `Nonlinear` is generated on A.
- If A is not a root window, `FocusOut` with detail `NonlinearVirtual` is generated on each window above A up to and including its root (in order).
- `FocusIn` with detail `PointerRoot` (or `None`) is generated on all root windows.
- If the new focus is `PointerRoot`, `FocusIn` with detail `Pointer` is generated on each window from P's root down to and including P (in order).

When the focus moves from `PointerRoot` (or `None`) to window A and the pointer is in window P:

- If the old focus is `PointerRoot`, `FocusOut` with detail `Pointer` is generated on each window from P up to and including P's root (in order).
- `FocusOut` with detail `PointerRoot` (or `None`) is generated on all root windows.
- If A is not a root window, `FocusIn` with detail `NonlinearVirtual` is generated on each window from A's root down to but not including A (in order).

- FocusIn with detail Nonlinear is generated on A.
- If P is an inferior of A, FocusIn with detail Pointer is generated on each window below A down to and including P (in order).

When the focus moves from PointerRoot to None (or vice versa) and the pointer is in window P:

- If the old focus is PointerRoot, FocusOut with detail Pointer is generated on each window from P up to and including P's root (in order).
- FocusOut with detail PointerRoot (or None) is generated on all root windows.
- FocusIn with detail None (or PointerRoot) is generated on all root windows.
- If the new focus is PointerRoot, FocusIn with detail Pointer is generated on each window from P's root down to and including P (in order).

When a keyboard grab activates (but before generating any actual KeyPress event that activates the grab), G is the grab-window for the grab, and F is the current focus:

- FocusIn and FocusOut events with mode Grab are generated (as for Normal above) as if the focus were to change from F to G.

When a keyboard grab deactivates (but after generating any actual KeyRelease event that deactivates the grab), G is the grab-window for the grab, and F is the current focus:

- FocusIn and FocusOut events with mode Ungrab are generated (as for Normal above) as if the focus were to change from G to F.

KeymapNotify

keys: LISTofCARD8

The value is a bit vector as described in QueryKeymap. This event is reported to clients selecting KeymapState on a window and is generated immediately after every EnterNotify and FocusIn.

Expose

window: WINDOW
x, y, width, height: CARD16
count: CARD16

This event is reported to clients selecting Exposure on the window. It is generated when no valid contents are available for regions of a window, and either the regions are visible, the regions are viewable and the server is (perhaps newly) maintaining backing store on the window, or the window is not viewable but the server is (perhaps newly) honoring window's backing-store attribute of Always or WhenMapped. The regions are decomposed into an arbitrary set of rectangles, and an Expose event is generated for each rectangle.

For a given action causing exposure events, the set of events for a given window are guaranteed to be reported contiguously. If count is zero, then no more Expose events for this window follow. If count is nonzero, then at least that many more Expose events for this window follow (and possibly more).

The x and y coordinates are relative to window's origin and specify the upper-left corner of a rectangle. The width and height specify the extent of the rectangle.

Expose events are never generated on InputOnly windows.

All Expose events caused by a hierarchy change are generated after any hierarchy event caused by that change (for example, UnmapNotify, MapNotify, ConfigureNotify, GravityNotify, CirculateNotify). All Expose events on a given window are generated after any VisibilityNotify event on that window, but it is not required that all Expose events on all windows be generated after all Visibilitity events on all windows. The ordering of Expose events with respect to FocusOut, EnterNotify, and LeaveNotify events is not constrained.

GraphicsExposure

drawable: DRAWABLE
x, y, width, height: CARD16
count: CARD16
major-opcode: CARD8
minor-opcode: CARD16

This event is reported to clients selecting graphics-exposures in a graphics context and is generated when a destination region could not be computed due to an obscured or out-of-bounds source region. All of the regions exposed by a given graphics request are guaranteed to be reported contiguously. If count is zero then no more GraphicsExposure events for this window follow. If count is nonzero, then at least that many more GraphicsExposure events for this window follow (and possibly more).

The x and y coordinates are relative to drawable's origin and specify the upper-left corner of a rectangle. The width and height specify the extent of the rectangle.

The major and minor opcodes identify the graphics request used. For the core protocol, major-opcode is always CopyArea or CopyPlane, and minor-opcode is always zero.

NoExposure

drawable: DRAWABLE
major-opcode: CARD8
minor-opcode: CARD16

This event is reported to clients selecting graphics-exposures in a graphics context and is generated when a graphics request that might produce Graphics-Exposure events does not produce any. The drawable specifies the destination used for the graphics request.

The major and minor opcodes identify the graphics request used. For the core protocol, major-opcode is always CopyArea or CopyPlane, and the minor-opcode is always zero.

VisibilityNotify

window: WINDOW
state: {Unobscured,PartiallyObscured,FullyObscured}

This event is reported to clients selecting VisibilityChange on the window. In the following, the state of the window is calculated ignoring all of the window's subwindows. When a window changes state from partially or fully obscured or not viewable to viewable and completely unobscured, an event with Unobscured is generated. When a window changes state from viewable and completely unobscured or not viewable, to viewable and partially obscured, an event with PartiallyObscured is generated. When a window changes state from viewable and completely unobscured, from viewable and partially obscured, or from not viewable to viewable and fully obscured, an event with FullyObscured is generated.

VisibilityNotify events are never generated on InputOnly windows.

All VisibilityNotify events caused by a hierarchy change are generated after any hierarchy event caused by that change (for example, UnmapNotify, MapNotify, ConfigureNotify, GravityNotify, CirculateNotify). Any VisibilityNotify event on a given window is generated before any Expose events on that window, but it is not required that all VisibilityNotify events on all windows be generated before all Expose events on all windows. The ordering of VisibilityNotify events with respect to FocusOut, EnterNotify, and LeaveNotify events is not constrained.

CreateNotify

parent, window: WINDOW
x, y: INT16
width, height, border-width: CARD16
override-redirect: BOOL

This event is reported to clients selecting SubstructureNotify on the parent and is generated when the window is created. The arguments are as in the CreateWindow request.

DestroyNotify

event, window: WINDOW

This event is reported to clients selecting StructureNotify on the window and to clients selecting SubstructureNotify on the parent. It is generated when the window is destroyed. The event is the window on which the event was generated, and the window is the window that is destroyed.

The ordering of the DestroyNotify events is such that for any given window, DestroyNotify is generated on all inferiors of the window before being generated on the window itself. The ordering among siblings and across subhierarchies is not otherwise constrained.

UnmapNotify

event, window: WINDOW
from-configure: BOOL

This event is reported to clients selecting StructureNotify on the window and to clients selecting SubstructureNotify on the parent. It is generated when the window changes state from mapped to unmapped. The event is the window on which the event was generated, and the window is the window that is unmapped. The from-configure flag is `True` if the event was generated as a result of the window's parent being resized when the window itself had a win-gravity of `Unmap`.

MapNotify

event, window: WINDOW
override-redirect: BOOL

This event is reported to clients selecting `StructureNotify` on the window and to clients selecting `SubstructureNotify` on the parent. It is generated when the window changes state from unmapped to mapped. The event is the window on which the event was generated, and the window is the window that is mapped. The override-redirect flag is from the window's attribute.

MapRequest

parent, window: WINDOW

This event is reported to the client selecting `SubstructureRedirect` on the parent and is generated when a `MapWindow` request is issued on an unmapped window with an override-redirect attribute of `False`.

ReparentNotify

event, window, parent: WINDOW
x, y: INT16
override-redirect: BOOL

This event is reported to clients selecting `SubstructureNotify` on either the old or the new parent and to clients selecting `StructureNotify` on the window. It is generated when the window is reparented. The event is the window on which the event was generated. The window is the window that has been rerooted. The parent specifies the new parent. The x and y coordinates are relative to the new parent's origin and specify the position of the upper-left outer corner of the window. The override-redirect flag is from the window's attribute.

ConfigureNotify

event, window: WINDOW
x, y: INT16

width, height, border-width: CARD16
above-sibling: WINDOW or `None`
override-redirect: BOOL

This event is reported to clients selecting `StructureNotify` on the window and to clients selecting `SubstructureNotify` on the parent. It is generated when a `ConfigureWindow` request actually changes the state of the window. The event is the window on which the event was generated, and the window is the window that is changed. The x and y coordinates are relative to the new parent's origin and specify the position of the upper-left outer corner of the window. The width and height specify the inside size, not including the border. If above-sibling is `None`, then the window is on the bottom of the stack with respect to siblings. Otherwise, the window is immediately on top of the specified sibling. The override-redirect flag is from the window's attribute.

GravityNotify

event, window: WINDOW
x, y: INT16

This event is reported to clients selecting `SubstructureNotify` on the parent and to clients selecting `StructureNotify` on the window. It is generated when a window is moved because of a change in size of the parent. The event is the window on which the event was generated, and the window is the window that is moved. The x and y coordinates are relative to the new parent's origin and specify the position of the upper-left outer corner of the window.

ResizeRequest

window: WINDOW
width, height: CARD16

This event is reported to the client selecting `ResizeRedirect` on the window and is generated when a `ConfigureWindow` request by some other client on the window attempts to change the size of the window. The width and height are the inside size, not including the border.

ConfigureRequest

parent, window: WINDOW
x, y: INT16
width, height, border-width: CARD16

sibling: WINDOW or None
stack-mode: {Above, Below, TopIf, BottomIf, Opposite}
value-mask: BITMASK

This event is reported to the client selecting SubstructureRedirect on the parent and is generated when a ConfigureWindow request is issued on the window by some other client. The value-mask indicates which components were specified in the request. The value-mask and the corresponding values are reported as given in the request. The remaining values are filled in from the current geometry of the window, except in the case of sibling and stack-mode, which are reported as None and Above (respectively) if not given in the request.

CirculateNotify

event, window: WINDOW
place: {Top, Bottom}

This event is reported to clients selecting StructureNotify on the window and to clients selecting SubstructureNotify on the parent. It is generated when the window is actually restacked from a CirculateWindow request. The event is the window on which the event was generated, and the window is the window that is restacked. If place is Top, the window is now on top of all siblings. Otherwise, it is below all siblings.

CirculateRequest

parent, window: WINDOW
place: {Top, Bottom}

This event is reported to the client selecting SubstructureRedirect on the parent and is generated when a CirculateWindow request is issued on the parent and a window actually needs to be restacked. The window specifies the window to be restacked, and the place specifies what the new position in the stacking order should be.

PropertyNotify

window: WINDOW
atom: ATOM
state: {NewValue, Deleted}
time: TIMESTAMP

This event is reported to clients selecting PropertyChange on the window and is generated with state NewValue when a property of the window is changed using ChangeProperty or RotateProperties, even when adding zero-length data using ChangeProperty and when replacing all or part of a property with identical data using ChangeProperty or RotateProperties. It is generated with state Deleted when a property of the window is deleted using request DeleteProperty or GetProperty. The timestamp indicates the server time when the property was changed.

SelectionClear

owner: WINDOW
selection: ATOM
time: TIMESTAMP

This event is reported to the current owner of a selection and is generated when a new owner is being defined by means of SetSelectionOwner. The timestamp is the last-change time recorded for the selection. The owner argument is the window that was specified by the current owner in its SetSelectionOwner request.

SelectionRequest

owner: WINDOW
selection: ATOM
target: ATOM
property: ATOM or None
requestor: WINDOW
time: TIMESTAMP or CurrentTime

This event is reported to the owner of a selection and is generated when a client issues a ConvertSelection request. The owner argument is the window that was specified in the SetSelectionOwner request. The remaining arguments are as in the ConvertSelection request.

The owner should convert the selection based on the specified target type and send a SelectionNotify back to the requestor. A complete specification for using selections is given in part III, "Inter-Client Communication Conventions Manual."

SelectionNotify

requestor: WINDOW
selection, target: ATOM
property: ATOM or None
time: TIMESTAMP or CurrentTime

This event is generated by the server in response to a ConvertSelection request when there is no owner for the selection. When there is an owner, it should be generated by the owner using SendEvent. The owner of a selection should send this event to a requestor either when a selection has been converted and stored as a property or when a selection conversion could not be performed (indicated with property None).

ColormapNotify

window: WINDOW
colormap: COLORMAP or None
new: BOOL
state: {Installed,Uninstalled}

This event is reported to clients selecting ColormapChange on the window. It is generated with value True for new when the colormap attribute of the window is changed and is generated with value False for new when the colormap of a window is installed or uninstalled. In either case, the state indicates whether the colormap is currently installed.

MappingNotify

request: {Modifier,Keyboard,Pointer}
first-keycode, count: CARD8

This event is sent to all clients. There is no mechanism to express disinterest in this event. The detail indicates the kind of change that occurred: Modifiers for a successful SetModifierMapping, Keyboard for a successful ChangeKeyboard-Mapping, and Pointer for a successful SetPointerMapping. If the detail is Keyboard, then first-keycode and count indicate the range of altered keycodes.

ClientMessage

window: WINDOW
type: ATOM

format: {8, 16, 32}
data: LISTofINT8 or LISTofINT16 or LISTofINT32

This event is only generated by clients using `SendEvent`. The type specifies how the data is to be interpreted by the receiving client; the server places no interpretation on the type or the data. The format specifies whether the data should be viewed as a list of 8-bit, 16-bit, or 32-bit quantities, so that the server can correctly byte-swap, as necessary. The data always consists of either 20 8-bit values or 10 16-bit values or 5 32-bit values, although particular message types might not make use of all of these values.

SECTION 12. FLOW CONTROL AND CONCURRENCY

Whenever the server is writing to a given connection, it is permissible for the server to stop reading from that connection (but if the writing would block, it must continue to service other connections). The server is not required to buffer more than a single request per connection at one time. For a given connection to the server, a client can block while reading from the connection but should undertake to read (events and errors) when writing would block. Failure on the part of a client to obey this rule could result in a deadlocked connection, although deadlock is probably unlikely unless either the transport layer has very little buffering or the client attempts to send large numbers of requests without ever reading replies or checking for errors and events.

Whether or not a server is implemented with internal concurrency, the overall effect must be as if individual requests are executed to completion in some serial order, and requests from a given connection must be executed in delivery order (that is, the total execution order is a shuffle of the individual streams). The execution of a request includes validating all arguments, collecting all data for any reply, and generating and queueing all required events. However, it does not include the actual transmission of the reply and the events. In addition, the effect of any other cause that can generate multiple events (for example, activation of a grab or pointer motion) must effectively generate and queue all required events indivisibly with respect to all other causes and requests. For a request from a given client, any events destined for that client that are caused by executing the request must be sent to the client before any reply or error is sent.

Part III. Inter-Client Communication Conventions Manual

Version 1.1

SECTION 1. INTRODUCTION

It was an explicit design goal of X Version 11 to specify mechanism, not policy. As a result, a client that converses with the server using the protocol defined in part II, "X Window System Protocol," may operate correctly in isolation but may not coexist properly with others sharing the same server.

Being a good citizen in the X Version 11 world involves adhering to conventions that govern inter-client communications in the following areas:

- Selection mechanism
- Cut buffers
- Window manager
- Session manager
- Manipulation of shared resources
- Device color characterization

This part of the book proposes suitable conventions without attempting to enforce any particular user interface. To permit clients written in different languages to communicate, these conventions are expressed solely in terms of protocol operations, not in terms of their associated Xlib interfaces, which are probably more familiar. The binding of these operations to the Xlib interface for C and to the equivalent interfaces for other languages is the subject of other documents.

1.1 Evolution of the Conventions

In the interests of timely acceptance, the "Inter-Client Communication Conventions Manual" (ICCCM) covers only a minimal set of required conventions. These conventions will be added to and updated as appropriate, based on the experiences of the X Consortium.

As far as possible, these conventions are upwardly compatible with those in the February 25, 1988, draft that was distributed with the X Version 11, Release 2 of the software. In some areas, semantic problems were discovered with those conventions, and, thus, complete upward compatibility could not be assured.

In the course of developing these conventions, a number of minor changes to the protocol were identified as desirable. They also are identified in the text and are offered as input to a future protocol revision process. If and when a protocol revision incorporating these changes is undertaken, it is anticipated that the ICCCM will need to be revised. Because it is difficult to ensure that clients and servers are upgraded simultaneously, clients using the revised conventions should examine the minor protocol revision number and be prepared to use the older conventions when communicating with an older server.

It is expected that these revisions will ensure that clients using the conventions appropriate to protocol minor revision *n* will interoperate correctly with those that use the conventions appropriate to protocol minor revision *n*+1 if the server supports both.

1.2 Atoms

Many of the conventions use atoms. To assist the reader, the following sections attempt to amplify the description of atoms that is provided in part II, "X Window System Protocol."

1.2.1 What Are Atoms?

At the conceptual level, atoms are unique names that clients can use to communicate information to each other. They can be thought of as a bundle of octets, like a string but without an encoding being specified. The elements are not necessarily ASCII characters, and no case folding happens.[1]

The protocol designers felt that passing these sequences of bytes back and forth across the wire would be too costly. Further, they thought it important

[1] The comment in the protocol specification for `InternAtom` that ISO Latin-1 encoding should be used is in the nature of a convention; the server treats the string as a byte sequence.

that events as they appear on the wire have a fixed size (in fact, 32 bytes) and that because some events contain atoms, a fixed-size representation for them was needed.

To allow a fixed-size representation, a protocol request (`InternAtom`) was provided to register a byte sequence with the server, which returns a 32-bit value (with the top three bits zero) that maps to the byte sequence. The inverse operator is also available (`GetAtomName`).

1.2.2 Predefined Atoms

The protocol specifies a number of atoms as being predefined:

> Predefined atoms are not strictly necessary and may not be useful in all environments, but they will eliminate many `InternAtom` requests in most applications. Note that they are predefined only in the sense of having numeric values, not in the sense of having required semantics.

Predefined atoms are an implementation trick to avoid the cost of interning many of the atoms that are expected to be used during the startup phase of all applications. The results of the `InternAtom` requests, which require a handshake, can be assumed *a priori.*

Language interfaces should probably cache the atom-name mappings and get them only when required. The CLX interface, for instance, makes no distinction between predefined atoms and other atoms; all atoms are viewed as symbols at the interface. However, a CLX implementation will typically keep a symbol or atom cache and will typically initialize this cache with the predefined atoms.

1.2.3 Naming Conventions

The built-in atoms are composed of uppercase ASCII characters with the logical words separated by an underscore character (_), for example, WM_ICON_NAME. The protocol specification recommends that atoms used for private vendor-specific reasons should begin with an underscore. To prevent conflicts among organizations, additional prefixes should be chosen (for example, _DEC_WM_DECORATION_GEOMETRY).

The names were chosen in this fashion to make it easy to use them in a natural way within LISP. Keyword constructors allow the programmer to specify the atoms as LISP atoms. If the atoms were not all uppercase, special quoting conventions would have to be used.

1.2.4 Semantics

The core protocol imposes no semantics on atoms except as they are used in FONTPROP structures. For further information on FONTPROP semantics, see part IV, "X Logical Font Description Conventions."

1.2.5 Name Spaces

The protocol defines six distinct spaces in which atoms are interpreted. Any particular atom may or may not have some valid interpretation with respect to each of these name spaces.

Space	*Briefly*	*Examples*
Property name	Name	(WM_HINTS, WM_NAME, RGB_BEST_MAP, and so on)
Property type	Type	(WM_HINTS, CURSOR, RGB_COLOR_MAP, and so on)
Selection name	Selection	(PRIMARY, SECONDARY, CLIPBOARD)
Selection target	Target	(FILE_NAME, POSTSCRIPT, PIXMAP, and so on)
Font property		(QUAD_WIDTH, POINT_SIZE, and so on)
`ClientMessage` type		(WM_SAVE_YOURSELF, _DEC_SAVE_EDITS, and so on)

SECTION 2. PEER-TO-PEER COMMUNICATION BY MEANS OF SELECTIONS

Selections are the primary mechanism that X Version 11 defines for the exchange of information between clients, for example, by cutting and pasting between windows. Note that there can be an arbitrary number of selections (each named by an atom) and that they are global to the server. Section 2.6 discusses the choice of an atom. Each selection is owned by a client and is attached to a window.

Selections communicate between an owner and a requestor. The owner has the data representing the value of its selection, and the requestor receives it. A requestor wishing to obtain the value of a selection provides the following:

- The name of the selection
- The name of a property
- A window
- The atom representing the data type required

If the selection is currently owned, the owner receives an event and is expected to do the following:

- Convert the contents of the selection to the requested data type
- Place this data in the named property on the named window
- Send the requestor an event to let it know the property is available

Clients are strongly encouraged to use this mechanism. In particular, displaying text in a permanent window without providing the ability to select and convert it into a string is definitely considered antisocial.

Note that all data transferred between an owner and a requestor must usually go by means of the server in an X Version 11 environment. A client cannot assume that another client can open the same files or even communicate directly. The other client may be talking to the server by means of a completely different networking mechanism (for example, one client might be DECnet and the other TCP/IP). Thus, passing indirect references to data (such as file names, host names and port numbers, and so on) is permitted only if both clients specifically agree.

2.1 Acquiring Selection Ownership

A client wishing to acquire ownership of a particular selection should call `SetSelectionOwner`, which is defined as follows:

SetSelectionOwner

selection: ATOM
owner: WINDOW or `None`
time: TIMESTAMP or `CurrentTime`

The client should set the specified selection to the atom that represents the selection, set the specified owner to some window that the client created, and set the specified time to some time between the current last-change time of the selection concerned and the current server time. This time value usually will be obtained from the timestamp of the event that triggers the acquisition of the selection. Clients should not set the time value to `CurrentTime`, because if they do so, they have no way of finding when they gained ownership of the selection. Clients must use a window they created so that requestors can route events to the owner of the selection.[2]

Convention

Clients attempting to acquire a selection must set the time value of the `SetSelectionOwner` request to the timestamp of the event triggering the acquisition attempt, not to `CurrentTime`. A zero-length append to a property is a way to obtain a timestamp for this purpose; the timestamp is in the corresponding `PropertyNotify` event.

If the time in the `SetSelectionOwner` request is in the future relative to the server's current time or is in the past relative to the last time the specified selection changed hands, the `SetSelectionOwner` request appears to the client to succeed, but ownership is not actually transferred.

Because clients cannot name other clients directly, the specified owner window is used to refer to the owning client in the replies to `GetSelectionOwner`, in `SelectionRequest` and `SelectionClear` events, and possibly as a place to put properties describing the selection in question. To discover the owner of a particular selection, a client should invoke `GetSelectionOwner`, which is defined as follows:

GetSelectionOwner

selection: ATOM

→

owner: WINDOW or `None`

Convention

Clients are expected to provide some visible confirmation of selection ownership. To make this feedback reliable, a client must perform a sequence like the following:

```
SetSelectionOwner(selection=PRIMARY, owner=Window, time=timestamp)
owner = GetSelectionOwner(selection=PRIMARY)
if (owner != Window) Failure
```

[2] At present, no part of the protocol requires requestors to send events to the owner of a selection. This restriction is imposed to prepare for possible future extensions.

If the SetSelectionOwner request succeeds (not merely appears to succeed), the client that issues it is recorded by the server as being the owner of the selection for the time period starting at the specified time.

Problem

There is no way for anyone to find out the last-change time of a selection. At the next protocol revision, GetSelectionOwner should be changed to return the last-change time as well as the owner.

2.2 Responsibilities of the Selection Owner

When a requestor wants the value of a selection, the owner receives a SelectionRequest event, which is defined as follows:

SelectionRequest

owner: WINDOW
selection: ATOM
target: ATOM
property: ATOM or None
requestor: WINDOW
time: TIMESTAMP or CurrentTime

The specified owner and selection will be the values that were specified in the SetSelectionOwner request. The owner should compare the timestamp with the period it has owned the selection and, if the time is outside, refuse the SelectionRequest by sending the requestor window a SelectionNotify event with the property set to None (by means of a SendEvent request with an empty event mask).

More advanced selection owners are free to maintain a history of the value of the selection and to respond to requests for the value of the selection during periods they owned it even though they do not own it now.

If the specified property is None, the requestor is an obsolete client. Owners are encouraged to support these clients by using the specified target atom as the property name to be used for the reply.

Otherwise, the owner should use the target to decide the form into which the selection should be converted. If the selection cannot be converted into that form, however, the owner should refuse the SelectionRequest, as previously described.

If the specified property is not None, the owner should place the data resulting from converting the selection into the specified property on the requestor window and should set the property's type to some appropriate value, which need not be the same as the specified target.

Convention

All properties used to reply to SelectionRequest events must be placed on the requestor window.

In either case, if the data comprising the selection cannot be stored on the requestor window (for example, because the server cannot provide sufficient memory), the owner must refuse the SelectionRequest, as previously described. See also section 2.5.

If the property is successfully stored, the owner should acknowledge the successful conversion by sending the requestor window a SelectionNotify event (by means of a SendEvent request with an empty mask). SelectionNotify is defined as follows:

SelectionNotify

requestor: WINDOW
selection, target: ATOM
property: ATOM or None
time: TIMESTAMP or CurrentTime

The owner should set the specified selection, target, time, and property arguments to the values received in the SelectionRequest event. (Note that setting the property argument to None indicates that the conversion requested could not be made.)

Convention

The selection, target, time, and property arguments in the SelectionNotify event should be set to the values received in the SelectionRequest event.

The data stored in the property must eventually be deleted. A convention is needed to assign the responsibility for doing so.

Convention

Selection requestors are responsible for deleting properties whose names they receive in SelectionNotify events (see section 2.4) or in properties with type MULTIPLE.

A selection owner will often need confirmation that the data comprising the selection has actually been transferred. (For example, if the operation has side effects on the owner's internal data structures, these should not take place until the requestor has indicated that it has successfully received the data.) Owners should express interest in `PropertyNotify` events for the specified requestor window and wait until the property in the `SelectionNotify` event has been deleted before assuming that the selection data has been transferred.

When some other client acquires a selection, the previous owner receives a `SelectionClear` event, which is defined as follows:

SelectionClear

owner: WINDOW
selection: ATOM
time: TIMESTAMP

The timestamp argument is the time at which the ownership changed hands, and the owner argument is the window the previous owner specified in its `SetSelectionOwner` request.

If an owner loses ownership while it has a transfer in progress (that is, before it receives notification that the requestor has received all the data), it must continue to service the ongoing transfer until it is complete.

2.3 Giving Up Selection Ownership

Clients may either give up selection ownership voluntarily or lose it forcibly as the result of some other client's actions.

2.3.1 Voluntarily Giving Up Selection Ownership

To relinquish ownership of a selection voluntarily, a client should execute a `SetSelectionOwner` request for that selection atom, with owner specified as `None` and the time specified as the timestamp that was used to acquire the selection.

Alternatively, the client may destroy the window used as the owner value of the `SetSelectionOwner` request, or the client may terminate. In both cases, the ownership of the selection involved will revert to `None`.

2.3.2 Forcibly Giving Up Selection Ownership

If a client gives up ownership of a selection or if some other client executes a `SetSelectionOwner` for it and thus reassigns it forcibly, the previous owner will receive a `SelectionClear` event. For the definition of a `SelectionClear` event, see section 2.2.

The timestamp is the time the selection changed hands. The specified owner is the window that was specified by the previous owner in its `SetSelectionOwner` request.

2.4 Requesting a Selection

A client that wishes to obtain the value of a selection in a particular form (the requestor) issues a `ConvertSelection` request, which is defined as follows:

ConvertSelection

selection, target: ATOM
property: ATOM or `None`
requestor: WINDOW
time: TIMESTAMP or `CurrentTime`

The selection argument specifies the particular selection involved, and the target argument specifies the required form of the information. For information about the choice of suitable atoms to use, see section 2.6. The requestor should set the requestor argument to a window that it created; the owner will place the reply property there. The requestor should set the time argument to the timestamp on the event that triggered the request for the selection value. Note that clients should not specify `CurrentTime`.

Convention

Clients should not use `CurrentTime` for the time argument of a `ConvertSelection` request. Instead, they should use the timestamp of the event that caused the request to be made.

The requestor should set the property argument to the name of a property that the owner can use to report the value of the selection. Note that the requestor of a selection need not know the client that owns the selection or the window it is attached to.

The protocol allows the property field to be set to `None`, in which case the owner is supposed to choose a property name. However, it is difficult for the owner to make this choice safely.

Conventions

1. Requestors should not use `None` for the property argument of a `ConvertSelection` request.
2. Owners receiving `ConvertSelection` requests with a property argument of `None` are talking to an obsolete client. They should choose the target atom as the property name to be used for the reply.

The result of the `ConvertSelection` request is that a `SelectionNotify` event will be received. For the definition of a `SelectionNotify` event, see section 2.2.

The requestor, selection, time, and target arguments will be the same as those on the `ConvertSelection` request.

If the property argument is `None`, the conversion has been refused. This can mean either that there is no owner for the selection, that the owner does not support the conversion implied by the target, or that the server did not have sufficient space to accommodate the data.

If the property argument is not `None`, then that property will exist on the requestor window. The value of the selection can be retrieved from this property by using the `GetProperty` request, which is defined as follows:

GetProperty

window: WINDOW
property: ATOM
type: ATOM or `AnyPropertyType`
long-offset, long-length: CARD32
delete: BOOL

→

type: ATOM or `None`
format: {0, 8, 16, 32}
bytes-after: CARD32
value: LISTofINT8 or LISTofINT16 or LISTofINT32

When using `GetProperty` to retrieve the value of a selection, the property argument should be set to the corresponding value in the `SelectionNotify` event. Because the requestor has no way of knowing beforehand what type the selection owner will use, the type argument should be set to `AnyPropertyType`. Several `GetProperty` requests may be needed to retrieve all the data in the selection; each should set the long-offset argument to the amount of data received so far, and the size argument to some reasonable buffer size (see section 2.5). If the returned value of bytes-after is zero, the whole property has been transferred.

Once all the data in the selection has been retrieved (which may require getting the values of several properties–see section 2.7), the requestor should delete the property in the `SelectionNotify` request by using a `GetProperty` request with the delete argument set to `True`. As previously discussed, the owner has no way of knowing when the data has been transferred to the requestor unless the property is removed.

Convention

The requestor must delete the property named in the `SelectionNotify` once all the data has been retrieved. The requestor should invoke either `DeleteProperty` or `GetProperty`(delete==True) after it has successfully retrieved all the data in the selection. For further information, see section 2.5.

2.5 Large Data Transfers

Selections can get large, which poses two problems:

- Transferring large amounts of data to the server is expensive.
- All servers will have limits on the amount of data that can be stored in properties. Exceeding this limit will result in an `Alloc` error on the `ChangeProperty` request that the selection owner uses to store the data.

The problem of limited server resources is addressed by the following conventions:

Conventions

1. Selection owners should transfer the data describing a large selection (relative to the maximum-request-size they received in the connection handshake) using the INCR property mechanism (see section 2.7.2).
2. Any client using `SetSelectionOwner` to acquire selection ownership should arrange to process `Alloc` errors in property change requests. For clients using

Xlib, this involves using the XSetErrorHandler function to override the default handler.

3. A selection owner must confirm that no Alloc error occurred while storing the properties for a selection before replying with a confirming SelectionNotify event.
4. When storing large amounts of data (relative to maximum-request-size), clients should use a sequence of ChangeProperty(mode==Append) requests for reasonable quantities of data. This avoids locking servers up and limits the waste of data an Alloc error would cause.
5. If an Alloc error occurs during the storing of the selection data, all properties stored for this selection should be deleted and the ConvertSelection request should be refused (see section 2.2).
6. To avoid locking servers up for inordinate lengths of time, requestors retrieving large quantities of data from a property should perform a series of GetProperty requests, each asking for a reasonable amount of data.

Problem

Single-threaded servers should be changed to avoid locking up during large data transfers.

2.6 Use of Selection Atoms

Defining a new atom consumes resources in the server that are not released until the server reinitializes. Thus, reducing the need for newly minted atoms is an important goal for the use of the selection atoms.

2.6.1 Selection Atoms

There can be an arbitrary number of selections, each named by an atom. To conform with the inter-client conventions, however, clients need deal with only these three selections:

- PRIMARY
- SECONDARY
- CLIPBOARD

Other selections may be used freely for private communication among related groups of clients.

Problem

How does a client find out which selection atoms are valid?

2.6.1.1 The PRIMARY Selection

The selection named by the atom PRIMARY is used for all commands that take only a single argument and is the principal means of communication between clients that use the selection mechanism.

2.6.1.2 The SECONDARY Selection

The selection named by the atom SECONDARY is used:

- As the second argument to commands taking two arguments (for example, "exchange primary and secondary selections")
- As a means of obtaining data when there is a primary selection and the user does not want to disturb it

2.6.1.3 The CLIPBOARD Selection

The selection named by the atom CLIPBOARD is used to hold data that is being transferred between clients, that is, data that usually is being cut or copied, and then pasted. Whenever a client wants to transfer data to the clipboard:

- It should assert ownership of the CLIPBOARD.
- If it succeeds in acquiring ownership, it should be prepared to respond to a request for the contents of the CLIPBOARD in the usual way (retaining the data to be able to return it). The request may be generated by the clipboard client described below.
- If it fails to acquire ownership, a cutting client should not actually perform the cut or provide feedback that would suggest that it has actually transferred data to the clipboard.

The owner should repeat this process whenever the data to be transferred would change.

Clients wanting to paste data from the clipboard should request the contents of the CLIPBOARD selection in the usual way.

Except while a client is actually deleting or copying data, the owner of the CLIPBOARD selection may be a single, special client implemented for the purpose. This client maintains the content of the clipboard up-to-date and responds to requests for data from the clipboard as follows:

- It should assert ownership of the CLIPBOARD selection and reassert it any time the clipboard data changes.
- If it loses the selection (because another client has some new data for the clipboard), it should:
  - — Obtain the contents of the selection from the new owner by using the timestamp in the `SelectionClear` event.
  - — Attempt to reassert ownership of the CLIPBOARD selection by using the same timestamp.
  - — Restart the process using a newly acquired timestamp if this attempt fails. This timestamp should be obtained by asking the current owner of the CLIPBOARD selection to convert it to a TIMESTAMP. If this conversion is refused or if the same timestamp is received twice, the clipboard client should acquire a fresh timestamp in the usual way (for example by a zero-length append to a property).
- It should respond to requests for the CLIPBOARD contents in the usual way.

A special CLIPBOARD client is not necessary. The protocol used by the cutting client and the pasting client is the same whether the CLIPBOARD client is running or not. The reasons for running the special client include:

- Stability—If the cutting client were to crash or terminate, the clipboard value would still be available.
- Feedback—The clipboard client can display the contents of the clipboard.
- Simplicity—A client deleting data does not have to retain it for so long, thus reducing the chance of race conditions causing problems.

The reasons not to run the clipboard client include:

- Performance—Data is only transferred if it is actually required (that is, when some client actually wants the data).
- Flexibility—The clipboard data may be available as more than one target.

2.6.2 Target Atoms

The atom that a requestor supplies as the target of a `ConvertSelection` request determines the form of the data supplied. The set of such atoms is extensible, but a generally accepted base set of target atoms is needed. As a starting point for this, the following table contains those that have been suggested so far.

Atom	*Type*	*Data Received*
TARGETS	ATOM	A list of valid target atoms
MULTIPLE	ATOM_PAIR	(see the discussion that follows)
TIMESTAMP	INTEGER	The timestamp used to acquire the selection
STRING	STRING	ISO Latin-1 (+TAB+NEWLINE) text
COMPOUND_TEXT	COMPOUND_TEXT	Compound Text
TEXT	TEXT	The text in the owner's choice of encoding
LIST_LENGTH	INTEGER	The number of disjoint parts of the selection
PIXMAP	DRAWABLE	A list of pixmap IDs
DRAWABLE	DRAWABLE	A list of drawable IDs
BITMAP	BITMAP	A list of bitmap IDs
FOREGROUND	PIXEL	A list of pixmap values
BACKGROUND	PIXEL	A list of pixel values
COLORMAP	COLORMAP	A list of colormap IDs
ODIF	TEXT	ISO Office Document Interchange Format
OWNER_OS	TEXT	The operating system of the owner client
FILE_NAME	TEXT	The full path name of a file
HOST_NAME	TEXT	(see section 5.1.1.2)
CHARACTER_POSITION	SPAN	The start and end of the selection in bytes
LINE_NUMBER	SPAN	The start and end line numbers
COLUMN_NUMBER	SPAN	The start and end column numbers
LENGTH	INTEGER	The number of bytes in the selection
USER	TEXT	The name of the user running the owner
PROCEDURE	TEXT	The name of the selected procedure
MODULE	TEXT	The name of the selected procedure
PROCESS	INTEGER, TEXT	The process ID of the owner
TASK	INTEGER, TEXT	The task ID of the owner
CLASS	TEXT	(see section 4.1.2.5)
NAME	TEXT	(see section 4.1.2.1)
CLIENT_WINDOW	WINDOW	A top-level window of the owner
DELETE	NULL	(see section 2.6.3.1)
INSERT_SELECTION	NULL	(see section 2.6.3.2)
INSERT_PROPERTY	NULL	(see section 2.6.3.3)

It is expected that this table will grow over time.

Selection owners are required to support the following targets. All other targets are optional.

- TARGETS—The owner should return a list of atoms that represent the targets for which an attempt to convert the current selection will succeed (barring unforseeable problems such as `Alloc` errors). This list should include all the required atoms.
- MULTIPLE—The MULTIPLE target atom is valid only when a property is specified on the `ConvertSelection` request. If the property argument in the `SelectionRequest` event is `None` and the target is MULTIPLE, it should be refused.

  When a selection owner receives a `SelectionRequest`(target==MULTIPLE) request, the contents of the property named in the request will be a list of atom pairs: the first atom naming a target and the second naming a property (`None` is not valid here). The effect should be as if the owner had received a sequence of `SelectionRequest` events (one for each atom pair) except that:

  — The owner should reply with a `SelectionNotify` only when all the requested conversions have been performed.

  — If the owner fails to convert the target used by an atom in the MULTIPLE property, it should replace that atom in the property with `None`.

  Convention

  The entries in a MULTIPLE property must be processed in the order they appear in the property. For further information, see section 2.6.3.

- TIMESTAMP – To avoid some race conditions, it is important that requestors be able to discover the timestamp the owner used to acquire ownership. Until and unless the protocol is changed so that a `GetSelectionOwner` request returns the timestamp used to acquire ownership, selection owners must support conversion to TIMESTAMP, returning the timestamp they used to obtain the selection.

  Problem

  The protocol should be changed to return in response to a `GetSelectionOwner` request the timestamp used to acquire the selection.

2.6.3 Selection Targets with Side Effects

Some targets (for example, DELETE) have side effects. To render these targets unambiguous, the entries in a MULTIPLE property must be processed in the order that they appear in the property.

In general, targets with side effects will return no information; that is, they will return a zero-length property of type NULL. (Type NULL means the result of `InternAtom` on the string "NULL", not the value zero.) In all cases, the requested side effect must be performed before the conversion is accepted. If the requested side effect cannot be performed, the corresponding conversion request must be refused.

Conventions

1. Targets with side effects should return no information (that is, they should have a zero-length property of type NULL).
2. The side effect of a target must be performed before the conversion is accepted.
3. If the side effect of a target cannot be performed, the corresponding conversion request must be refused.

Problem

The need to delay responding to the `ConvertSelection` request until a further conversion has succeeded poses problems for the Intrinsics interface that need to be addressed.

These side effect targets are used to implement operations such as "exchange PRIMARY and SECONDARY selections."

2.6.3.1 DELETE

When the owner of a selection receives a request to convert it to DELETE, it should delete the corresponding selection (whatever doing so means for its internal data structures) and return a zero-length property of type NULL if the deletion was successful.

2.6.3.2 INSERT_SELECTION

When the owner of a selection receives a request to convert it to INSERT_SELECTION, the property named will be of type ATOM_PAIR. The first atom will name a selection, and the second will name a target. The owner should use the selection mechanism to convert the named selection into the named target and should insert it at the location of the selection for which it got the INSERT_SELECTION request (whatever doing so means for its internal data structures).

2.6.3.3 INSERT_PROPERTY

When the owner of a selection receives a request to convert it to INSERT_PROPERTY, it should insert the property named in the request at the location of the selection for which it got the INSERT_SELECTION request (whatever doing so means for its internal data structures).

2.7 Use of Selection Properties

The names of the properties used in selection data transfer are chosen by the requestor. The use of `None` property fields in `ConvertSelection` requests (which request the selection owner to choose a name) is not permitted by these conventions.

The selection owner always chooses the type of the property in the selection data transfer. Some types have special semantics assigned by convention, and these are reviewed in the following sections.

In all cases, a request for conversion to a target should return either a property of one of the types listed in the previous table for that property or a property of type INCR and then a property of one of the listed types.

The selection owner will return a list of zero or more items of the type indicated by the property type. In general, the number of items in the list will correspond to the number of disjoint parts of the selection. Some targets (for example, side-effect targets) will be of length zero irrespective of the number of disjoint selection parts. In the case of fixed-size items, the requestor may determine the number of items by the property size. For variable-length items such as text, the separators are listed in the following table:

Type Atom	*Format*	*Separator*
STRING	8	Null
COMPOUND_TEXT	8	Null
ATOM	32	Fixed-size
ATOM_PAIR	32	Fixed-size
BITMAP	32	Fixed-size
PIXMAP	32	Fixed-size
DRAWABLE	32	Fixed-size
SPAN	32	Fixed-size
INTEGER	32	Fixed-size
WINDOW	32	Fixed-size
INCR	32	Fixed-size

It is expected that this table will grow over time.

2.7.1 TEXT Properties

In general, the encoding for the characters in a text string property is specified by its type. It is highly desirable for there to be a simple, invertible mapping between string property types and any character set names embedded within font names in any font naming standard adopted by the Consortium.

The atom TEXT is a polymorphic target. Requesting conversion into TEXT will convert into whatever encoding is convenient for the owner. The encoding chosen will be indicated by the type of the property returned. TEXT is not defined as a type; it will never be the returned type from a selection conversion request.

If the requestor wants the owner to return the contents of the selection in a specific encoding, it should request conversion into the name of that encoding.

In the table in section 2.6.2, the word TEXT (in the Type column) is used to indicate one of the registered encoding names. The type would not actually be TEXT; it would be STRING or some other ATOM naming the encoding chosen by the owner.

STRING as a type or a target specifies the ISO Latin-1 character set plus the control characters TAB (octal 11) and NEWLINE (octal 12). The spacing interpretation of TAB is context dependent. Other ASCII control characters are explicitly not included in STRING at the present time.

COMPOUND_TEXT as a type or a target specifies the Compound Text interchange format; see appendix I, "Compound Text Encoding."

Type STRING and COMPOUND_TEXT properties will consist of a list of elements separated by null characters; other encodings will need to specify an appropriate list format.

2.7.2 INCR Properties

Requestors may receive a property of type INCR[3] in response to any target that results in selection data. This indicates that the owner will send the actual data incrementally. The contents of the INCR property will be an integer, which represents a lower bound on the number of bytes of data in the selection. The requestor and the selection owner transfer the data in the selection in the following manner.

[3] These properties were called INCREMENTAL in an earlier draft. The protocol for using them has changed, and so the name has changed to avoid confusion.

The selection requestor starts the transfer process by deleting the (type==INCR) property forming the reply to the selection.

The selection owner then:

- Appends the data in suitable-size chunks to the same property on the same window as the selection reply with a type corresponding to the actual type of the converted selection. The size should be less than the maximum-request-size in the connection handshake.
- Waits between each append for a `PropertyNotify`(state==Deleted) event that shows that the requestor has read the data. The reason for doing this is to limit the consumption of space in the server.
- Waits (after the entire data has been transferred to the server) until a `PropertyNotify`(state==Deleted) event that shows that the data has been read by the requestor and then writes zero-length data to the property.

The selection requestor:

- Waits for the `SelectionNotify` event.
- Loops:
  — Retrieving data using `GetProperty` with the delete argument `True`.
  — Waiting for a `PropertyNotify` with the state argument `NewValue`.
- Waits until the property named by the `PropertyNotify` event is zero-length.
- Deletes the zero-length property.

The type of the converted selection is the type of the first partial property. The remaining partial properties must have the same type.

2.7.3 DRAWABLE Properties

Requestors may receive properties of type PIXMAP, BITMAP, DRAWABLE, or WINDOW, which contain an appropriate ID. While information about these drawables is available from the server by means of the `GetGeometry` request, the following items are not:

- Foreground pixel
- Background pixel
- Colormap ID

In general, requestors converting into targets whose returned type in the table in section 2.6.2 is one of the DRAWABLE types should expect to convert also into the following targets (using the MULTIPLE mechanism):

- FOREGROUND returns a PIXEL value.
- BACKGROUND returns a PIXEL value.
- COLORMAP returns a colormap ID.

2.7.4 SPAN Properties

Properties with type SPAN contain a list of cardinal-pairs with the length of the cardinals determined by the format. The first specifies the starting position, and the second specifies the ending position plus one. The base is zero. If they are the same, the span is zero-length and is before the specified position. The units are implied by the target atom, such as LINE_NUMBER or CHARACTER_POSITION.

SECTION 3. PEER-TO-PEER COMMUNICATION BY MEANS OF CUT BUFFERS

The cut buffer mechanism is much simpler but much less powerful than the selection mechanism. The selection mechanism is active in that it provides a link between the owner and requestor clients. The cut buffer mechanism is passive; an owner places data in a cut buffer from which a requestor retrieves the data at some later time.

The cut buffers consist of eight properties on the root of screen zero, named by the predefined atoms CUT_BUFFER0 to CUT_BUFFER7. These properties must, at present, have type STRING and format 8. A client that uses the cut buffer mechanism must initially ensure that all eight properties exist by using `ChangeProperty` requests to append zero-length data to each.

A client that stores data in the cut buffers (an owner) first must rotate the ring of buffers by plus 1 by using `RotateProperties` requests to rename each buffer; that is, CUT_BUFFER0 to CUT_BUFFER1, CUT_BUFFER1 to CUT_BUFFER2, . . . , and CUT_BUFFER7 to CUT_BUFFER0. It then must store the data into CUT_BUFFER0 by using a `ChangeProperty` request in mode `Replace`.

A client that obtains data from the cut buffers should use a `GetProperty` request to retrieve the contents of CUT_BUFFER0.

In response to a specific user request, a client may rotate the cut buffers by minus 1 by using `RotateProperties` requests to rename each buffer; that is, CUT_BUFFER7 to CUT_BUFFER6, CUT_BUFFER6 to CUT_BUFFER5, . . . , and CUT_BUFFER0 to CUT_BUFFER7.

Data should be stored to the cut buffers and the ring rotated only when requested by explicit user action. Users depend on their mental model of cut buffer operation and need to be able to identify operations that transfer data to and fro.

SECTION 4. CLIENT TO WINDOW MANAGER COMMUNICATION

To permit window managers to perform their role of mediating the competing demands for resources such as screen space, the clients being managed must adhere to certain conventions and must expect the window managers to do likewise. These conventions are covered here from the client's point of view and again from the window manager's point of view in the forthcoming *Window and Session Manager Conventions Manual.*

In general, these conventions are somewhat complex and will undoubtedly change as new window management paradigms are developed. Thus, there is a strong bias toward defining only those conventions that are essential and that apply generally to all window management paradigms. Clients designed to run with a particular window manager can easily define private protocols to add to these conventions, but they must be aware that their users may decide to run some other window manager no matter how much the designers of the private protocol are convinced that they have seen the "one true light" of user interfaces.

It is a principle of these conventions that a general client should neither know nor care which window manager is running or, indeed, if one is running at all. The conventions do not support all client functions without a window manager running; for example, the concept of Iconic is not directly supported by clients. If no window manager is running, the concept of Iconic does not apply. A goal of the conventions is to make it possible to kill and restart window managers without loss of functionality.

Each window manager will implement a particular window management policy; the choice of an appropriate window management policy for the user's circumstances is not one for an individual client to make but will be made by the user or the user's system administrator. This does not exclude the possibility of writing clients that use a private protocol to restrict themselves to operating only under a specific window manager. Rather, it merely ensures that no claim of general utility is made for such programs.

For example, the claim is often made: "The client I'm writing is important, and it needs to be on top." Perhaps it is important when it is being run in earnest, and it should then be run under the control of a window manager that recognizes important windows through some private protocol and ensures that they are on top. However, imagine, for example, that the important client is being debugged. Then, ensuring that it is always on top is no longer the appropriate window management policy, and it should be run under a window manager that allows other windows (for example, the debugger) to appear on top.

4.1 Client's Actions

In general, the object of the X Version 11 design is that clients should, as far as possible, do exactly what they would do in the absence of a window manager, except for the following:

- Hinting to the window manager about the resources they would like to obtain
- Cooperating with the window manager by accepting the resources they are allocated even if they are not those requested
- Being prepared for resource allocations to change at any time

4.1.1 Creating a Top-Level Window

A client usually would expect to create its top-level windows as children of one or more of the root windows by using some boilerplate like the following:

```
win = XCreateSimpleWindow(dpy, DefaultRootWindow(dpy), xsh.x, xsh.y,
                          xsh.width, xsh.height, bw, bd, bg);
```

If a particular one of the root windows was required, however, it could use something like the following:

```
win = XCreateSimpleWindow(dpy, RootWindow(dpy, screen), xsh.x, xsh.y,
                          xsh.width, xsh.height, bw, bd, bg);
```

Ideally, it should be possible to override the choice of a root window and allow clients (including window managers) to treat a nonroot window as a pseudo-root. This would allow, for example, the testing of window managers and the use of application-specific window managers to control the subwindows owned by the members of a related suite of clients. Doing so properly requires an extension, the design of which is under study.

From the client's point of view, the window manager will regard its top-level window as being in one of three states:

- Normal
- Iconic
- Withdrawn

Newly created windows start in the Withdrawn state. Transitions between states happen when the top-level window is mapped and unmapped and when the window manager receives certain messages. For further details, see sections 4.1.2.4 and 4.1.4.

4.1.2 Client Properties

Once the client has one or more top-level windows, it should place properties on those windows to inform the window manager of the behavior that the client desires. Window managers will assume values they find convenient for any of these properties that are not supplied; clients that depend on particular values must explicitly supply them. The window manager will not change properties written by the client.

The window manager will examine the contents of these properties when the window makes the transition from the Withdrawn state and will monitor some properties for changes while the window is in the Iconic or Normal state. When the client changes one of these properties, it must use `Replace` mode to overwrite the entire property with new data; the window manager will retain no memory of the old value of the property. All fields of the property must be set to suitable values in a single `Replace` mode `ChangeProperty` request. This ensures that the full contents of the property will be available to a new window manager if the existing one crashes, if it is shut down and restarted, or if the session needs to be shut down and restarted by the session manager.

Convention

Clients writing or rewriting window manager properties must ensure that the entire content of each property remains valid at all times.

If these properties are longer than expected, clients should ignore the remainder of the property. Extending these properties is reserved to the X Consortium; private extensions to them are forbidden. Private additional communication between clients and window managers should take place using separate properties.

The next sections describe each of the properties the clients need to set, in turn. They are summarized in the table in section 4.3.

4.1.2.1 WM_NAME Property

The WM_NAME property is an uninterpreted string that the client wants the window manager to display in association with the window (for example, in a window headline bar).

The encoding used for this string (and all other uninterpreted string properties) is implied by the type of the property. The type atoms to be used for this purpose are described in section 2.7.1.

Window managers are expected to make an effort to display this information. Simply ignoring WM_NAME is not acceptable behavior. Clients can assume that at least the first part of this string is visible to the user and that if the information is not visible to the user, it is because the user has taken an explicit action to make it invisible.

On the other hand, there is no guarantee that the user can see the WM_NAME string even if the window manager supports window headlines. The user may have placed the headline off-screen or have covered it by other windows. WM_NAME should not be used for application-critical information or to announce asynchronous changes of an application's state that require timely user response. The expected uses are to permit the user to identify one of a number of instances of the same client and to provide the user with non-critical state information.

Even window managers that support headline bars will place some limit on the length of the WM_NAME string that can be visible; brevity here will pay dividends.

4.1.2.2 WM_ICON_NAME Property

The WM_ICON_NAME property is an uninterpreted string that the client wants to be displayed in association with the window when it is iconified (for example, in an icon label). In other respects, including the type, it is similar to WM_NAME. For obvious geometric reasons, fewer characters will normally be visible in WM_ICON_NAME than WM_NAME.

Clients should not attempt to display this string in their icon pixmaps or windows; rather, they should rely on the window manager to do so.

4.1.2.3 WM_NORMAL_HINTS Property

The type of the WM_NORMAL_HINTS property is WM_SIZE_HINTS. Its contents are as follows:

Field	*Type*	*Comments*
flags	CARD32	(see the next table)
pad	4*CARD32	For backwards compatibility
min_width	INT32	If missing, assume base_width
min_height	INT32	If missing, assume base_height
max_width	INT32	
max_height	INT32	
width_inc	INT32	
height_inc	INT32	
min_aspect	(INT32,INT32)	
max_aspect	(INT32,INT32)	
base_width	INT32	If missing, assume min-width
base_height	INT32	If missing, assume min_height
win_gravity	INT32	If missing, assume `NorthWest`

The WM_SIZE_HINTS.flags bit definitions are as follows:

Name	*Value*	*Field*
`USPosition`	1	User-specified x, y
`USSize`	2	User-specified width, height
`PPosition`	4	Program-specified position
`PSize`	8	Program-specified size

Name	*Value*	*Field*
`PMinSize`	16	Program-specified minimum size
`PMaxSize`	32	Program-specified maximum size
`PResizeInc`	64	Program-specified resize increments
`PAspect`	128	Program-specified min and max aspect ratios
`PBaseSize`	256	Program-specified base size
`PWinGravity`	512	Program-specified window gravity

To indicate that the size and position of the window (when mapped from the Withdrawn state) was specified by the user, the client should set the `USPosition` and `USSize` flags, which allow a window manager to know that the user specifically asked where the window should be placed or how the window should be sized and that further interaction is superfluous. To indicate that it was specified by the client without any user involvement, the client should set `PPosition` and `PSize`.

The size specifiers refer to the width and height of the client's window excluding borders. The window manager will interpret the position of the window and its border width to position the point of the outer rectangle of the overall window specified by the win_gravity in the size hints. The outer rectangle of the window includes any borders or decorations supplied by the window manager. In other words, if the window manager decides to place the window where the client asked, the position on the parent window's border named by the win_gravity will be placed where the client window would have been placed in the absence of a window manager.

The defined values for win_gravity are those specified for WINGRAVITY in the core X protocol with the exception of `Unmap` and `Static`: `NorthWest` (1), `North` (2), `NorthEast` (3), `West` (4), `Center` (5), `East` (6), `SouthWest` (7), `South` (8), and `SouthEast` (9).

The min_width and min_height elements specify the minimum size that the window can be for the client to be useful. The max_width and max_height elements specify the maximum size. The base_width and base_height elements in conjunction with width_inc and height_inc define an arithmetic progression of preferred window widths and heights for nonnegative integers *i* and *j*:

width = base_width + (i * width_inc)
height = base_height + (j * height_inc)

Window managers are encouraged to use *i* and *j* instead of width and height in reporting window sizes to users. If a base size is not provided, the minimum size is to be used in its place and vice versa.

The min_aspect and max_aspect fields are fractions with the numerator first and the denominator second, and they allow a client to specify the range of aspect ratios it prefers.

4.1.2.4 WM_HINTS Property

The WM_HINTS property (whose type is WM_HINTS) is used to communicate to the window manager. It conveys the information the window manager needs other than the window geometry, which is available from the window itself; the constraints on that geometry, which is available from the WM_NORMAL_HINTS structure; and various strings, which need separate properties, such as WM_NAME. The contents of the properties are as follows:

Field	*Type*	*Comments*
flags	CARD32	(see the next table)
input	CARD32	The client's input model
initial_state	CARD32	The state when first mapped
icon_pixmap	PIXMAP	The pixmap for the icon image
icon_window	WINDOW	The window for the icon image
icon_x	INT32	The icon location
icon_y	INT32	
icon_mask	PIXMAP	The mask for the icon shape
window_group	WINDOW	The ID of the group leader window

The WM_HINTS.flags bit definitions are as follows:

Name	*Value*	*Field*
`InputHint`	1	input
`StateHint`	2	initial_state
`IconPixmapHint`	4	icon_pixmap
`IconWindowHint`	8	icon_window
`IconPositionHint`	16	icon_x & icon_y

Name	*Value*	*Field*
`IconMaskHint`	32	icon_mask
`WindowGroupHint`	64	window_group
`MessageHint`	128	This bit is obsolete

Window managers are free to assume convenient values for all fields of the WM_HINTS property if a window is mapped without one.

The input field is used to communicate to the window manager the input focus model used by the client (see section 4.1.7).

Clients with the Globally Active and No Input models should set the input flag to `False`. Clients with the Passive and Locally Active models should set the input flag to `True`.

From the client's point of view, the window manager will regard the client's top-level window as being in one of three states:

- Normal
- Iconic
- Withdrawn

The semantics of these states are described in section 4.1.4. Newly created windows start in the Withdrawn state. Transitions between states happen when a non-override-redirect top-level window is mapped and unmapped and when the window manager receives certain messages.

The value of the initial_state field determines the state the client wishes to be in at the time the top-level window is mapped from the Withdrawn state, as shown in the following table:

State	*Value*	*Comments*
`NormalState`	1	The window is visible
`IconicState`	3	The icon is visible

The icon_pixmap field may specify a pixmap to be used as an icon. This pixmap should be:

- One of the sizes specified in the WM_ICON_SIZE property on the root if it exists (see section 4.1.3.2).

- 1-bit deep. The window manager will select, through the defaults database, suitable background (for the 0 bits) and foreground (for the 1 bits) colors. These defaults can, of course, specify different colors for the icons of different clients.

The icon_mask specifies which pixels of the icon_pixmap should be used as the icon, allowing for icons to appear nonrectangular.

The icon_window field is the ID of a window the client wants used as its icon. Most, but not all, window managers will support icon windows. Those that do not are likely to have a user interface in which small windows that behave like icons are completely inappropriate. Clients should not attempt to remedy the omission by working around it.

Clients that need more capabilities from the icons than a simple two-color bitmap should use icon windows. Rules for clients that do are set out in section 4.1.9.

The (icon_x,icon_y) coordinate is a hint to the window manager as to where it should position the icon. The policies of the window manager control the positioning of icons, so clients should not depend on attention being paid to this hint.

The window_group field lets the client specify that this window belongs to a group of windows. An example is a single client manipulating multiple children of the root window.

Conventions

1. The window_group field should be set to the ID of the group leader. The window group leader may be a window that exists only for that purpose; a placeholder group leader of this kind would never be mapped either by the client or by the window manager.
2. The properties of the window group leader are those for the group as a whole (for example, the icon to be shown when the entire group is iconified).

Window managers may provide facilities for manipulating the group as a whole. Clients, at present, have no way to operate on the group as a whole.

The messages bit, if set in the flags field, indicates that the client is using an obsolete window manager communication protocol,[4] rather than the WM_PROTOCOLS mechanism of section 4.1.2.7.

[4] This obsolete protocol was described in the July 27, 1988 draft of the ICCCM. Windows using it can also be detected because their WM_HINTS properties are four bytes longer than expected. Window managers are free to support clients using the obsolete protocol in a backwards compatibility mode.

4.1.2.5 WM_CLASS Property

The WM_CLASS property (of type STRING without control characters) contains two consecutive null-terminated strings. These specify the Instance and Class names to be used by both the client and the window manager for looking up resources for the application or as identifying information. This property must be present when the window leaves the Withdrawn state and may be changed only while the window is in the Withdrawn state. Window managers may examine the property only when they start up and when the window leaves the Withdrawn state, but there should be no need for a client to change its state dynamically.

The two strings, respectively, are:

- A string that names the particular instance of the application to which the client that owns this window belongs. Resources that are specified by instance name override any resources that are specified by class name. Instance names can be specified by the user in an operating-system specific manner. On POSIX-conformant systems, the following conventions are used:
  — If "–name NAME" is given on the command line, NAME is used as the instance name.
  — Otherwise, if the environment variable RESOURCE_NAME is set, its value will be used as the instance name.
  — Otherwise, the trailing part of the name used to invoke the program (argv[0] stripped of any directory names) is used as the instance name.
- A string that names the general class of applications to which the client that owns this window belongs. Resources that are specified by class apply to all applications that have the same class name. Class names are specified by the application writer. Examples of commonly used class names include: "Emacs", "XTerm", "XClock", "XLoad", and so on.

Note that WM_CLASS strings are null-terminated and, thus, differ from the general conventions that STRING properties are null-separated. This inconsistency is necessary for backwards compatibility.

4.1.2.6 WM_TRANSIENT_FOR Property

The WM_TRANSIENT_FOR property (of type WINDOW) contains the ID of another top-level window. The implication is that this window is a pop-up on behalf of the named window, and window managers may decide not to decorate transient windows or may treat them differently in other ways. In particular, window managers should present newly mapped WM_TRANSIENT_FOR windows without requiring any user interaction, even if mapping top-level windows normally does require interaction. Dialogue boxes, for example, are an example of windows that should have WM_TRANSIENT_FOR set.

It is important not to confuse WM_TRANSIENT_FOR with override-redirect. WM_TRANSIENT_FOR should be used in those cases where the pointer is not grabbed while the window is mapped (in other words, if other windows are allowed to be active while the transient is up). If other windows must be prevented from processing input (for example, when implementing pop-up menus), use override-redirect and grab the pointer while the window is mapped.

4.1.2.7 WM_PROTOCOLS Property

The WM_PROTOCOLS property (of type ATOM) is a list of atoms. Each atom identifies a communication protocol between the client and the window manager in which the client is willing to participate. Atoms can identify both standard protocols and private protocols specific to individual window managers.

All the protocols in which a client can volunteer to take part involve the window manager sending the client a `ClientMessage` event and the client taking appropriate action. For details of the contents of the event, see section 4.2.8. In each case, the protocol transactions are initiated by the window manager.

The WM_PROTOCOLS property is not required. If it is not present, the client does not want to participate in any window manager protocols.

The X Consortium will maintain a registry of protocols to avoid collisions in the name space. The following table lists the protocols that have been defined to date.

Protocol	*Section*	*Purpose*
WM_TAKE_FOCUS	4.1.7	Assignment of input focus
WM_SAVE_YOURSELF	5.2.1	Save client state warning
WM_DELETE_WINDOW	5.2.2	Request to delete top-level window

It is expected that this table will grow over time.

4.1.2.8 WM_COLORMAP_WINDOWS Property

The WM_COLORMAP_WINDOWS property (of type WINDOW) on a top-level window is a list of the IDs of windows that may need colormaps installed that differ from the colormap of the top-level window. The window manager will watch this list of windows for changes in their colormap attributes. The top-level window is always (implicitly or explicitly) on the watch list. For the details of this mechanism, see section 4.1.8.

4.1.3 Window Manager Properties

The properties that were described in the previous section are those that the client is responsible for maintaining on its top-level windows. This section describes the properties that the window manager places on client's top-level windows and on the root.

4.1.3.1 WM_STATE Property

The window manager will place a WM_STATE property (of type WM_STATE) on each top-level client window. In general, clients should not need to examine the contents of this property; it is intended for communication between window and session managers. See section 5.1.1.3 for more details.

4.1.3.2 WM_ICON_SIZE Property

A window manager that wishes to place constraints on the sizes of icon pixmaps and/or windows should place a property called WM_ICON_SIZE on the root. The contents of this property are listed in the following table.

Field	*Type*	*Comments*
min_width	CARD32	The data for the icon size series
min_height	CARD32	
max_width	CARD32	
max_height	CARD32	
width_inc	CARD32	
height_inc	CARD32	

For more details see section 14.1.12 in part I, "Xlib — C Language X Interface."

4.1.4 Changing Window State

From the client's point of view, the window manager will regard each of the client's top-level nonoverride-redirect windows as being in one of three states, whose semantics are as follows:

- `NormalState` —The client's top-level window is visible.
- `IconicState` —The client's top-level window is iconic (whatever that means for this window manager). The client can assume that its icon_window (if any) will be visible and, failing that, its icon_pixmap (if any) or its WM_ICON_NAME will be visible.
- `WithdrawnState` —Neither the client's top-level window nor its icon are visible.

In fact, the window manager may implement states with semantics other than those described above. For example, a window manager might implement a concept of InactiveState in which an infrequently used client's window would be represented as a string in a menu. But this state is invisible to the client, which would see itself merely as being in IconicState.

Newly created top-level windows are in the Withdrawn state. Once the window has been provided with suitable properties, the client is free to change its state as follows:[5]

- Withdrawn → Normal—The client should map the window with WM_HINTS.initial_state being `NormalState`.
- Withdrawn → Iconic—The client should map the window with WM_HINTS.initial_state being `IconicState`.
- Normal → Iconic—The client should send a client message event as described later in this section.
- Normal → Withdrawn—The client should unmap the window and follow it with a synthetic `UnmapNotify` event as described later in this section.[6]
- Iconic → Normal – The client should map the window. The contents of WM_HINTS.initial_state are irrelevant in this case.
- Iconic → Withdrawn – The client should unmap the window and follow it with a synthetic `UnmapNotify` event as described below.

[5] The conventions described in earlier drafts of the ICCCM had some serious semantic problems. These new conventions are designed to be compatible with clients using earlier conventions, except in areas where the earlier conventions would not actually have worked.

[6] For compatibility with obsolete clients, window managers should trigger the transition on the real `UnmapNotify` rather than wait for the synthetic one. They should also trigger the transition if they receive a synthetic `UnmapNotify` on a window for which they have not yet received a real `UnmapNotify`.

Once a client's nonoverride-redirect top-level window has left the Withdrawn state, the client will know that the window is in the Normal state if it is mapped and that the window is in the Iconic state if it is not mapped. It may select for `StructureNotify` events on the top-level window, and it will receive an `UnmapNotify` event when it moves to the Iconic state and a `MapNotify` event when it moves to the Normal state. This implies that a reparenting window manager will unmap the top-level window as well as the parent window when changing to the Iconic state.

Convention

Reparenting window managers must unmap the client's top-level window whenever they unmap the window to which they have reparented it.

If the transition is to the Withdrawn state, a synthetic `UnmapNotify` event, in addition to unmapping the window itself, must be sent by using a `SendEvent` request with the following arguments:

Argument	*Value*
destination:	The root
propagate:	`False`
event-mask:	`(SubstructureRedirect|SubstructureNotify)`
event: an `UnmapNotify` with:	
event:	The root
window:	The window itself
from-configure:	`False`

The reason for doing this is to ensure that the window manager gets some notification of the desire to change state, even though the window may already be unmapped when the desire is expressed.

If the transition is from the Normal to the Iconic state, the client should send a `ClientMessage` event to the root with:

- Window == the window to be iconified
- Type == the atom WM_CHANGE_STATE[7]
- Format == 32
- Data[0] == IconicState[8]

[7] The type field of the `ClientMessage` event (called the message_type field by Xlib) should not be confused with the code field of the event itself, which will have the value 33 (`ClientMessage`).

[8] We use the notation data[n] to indicate the nth element of the LISTofINT8, LISTofINT16, or LISTofINT32 in the data field of the `ClientMessage`, according to the format field. The list is indexed from zero.

Other values of data[0] are reserved for future extensions to these conventions.[9] The parameters of the SendEvent event should be those described for the synthetic UnmapNotify event.

Clients can also select for VisibilityChange events on their top-level or icon windows. They will then receive a VisibilityNotify(state==FullyObscured) event when the window concerned becomes completely obscured even though mapped (and thus, perhaps a waste of time to update) and a VisibilityNotify(state!=FullyObscured) event when it becomes even partly viewable.

4.1.5 Configuring the Window

Clients can resize and reposition their top-level windows by using the ConfigureWindow request. The attributes of the window that can be altered with this request are as follows:

- The [x,y] location of the window's upper left-outer corner
- The [width,height] of the inner region of the window (excluding borders)
- The border width of the window
- The window's position in the stack

The coordinate system in which the location is expressed is that of the root (irrespective of any reparenting that may have occurred). The border width to be used and win_gravity position hint to be used are those most recently requested by the client. Client configure requests are interpreted by the window manager in the same manner as the initial window geometry mapped from the Withdrawn state, as described in section 4.1.2.3. Clients must be aware that there is no guarantee that the window manager will allocate them the requested size or location and must be prepared to deal with any size and location. If the window manager decides to respond to a ConfigureRequest request by:

- Not changing the size or location of the window at all
  A client will receive a synthetic ConfigureNotify event that describes the (unchanged) state of the window. The (x,y) coordinates will be in the root coordinate system and

[9] The format of this ClientMessage event does not match the format of ClientMessages in section 4.2.8. This is because they are sent by the window manager to clients, and this is sent by clients to the window manager.

adjusted for the border width the client requested, irrespective of any reparenting that has taken place. The border_width will be the border width the client requested. The client will not receive a real ConfigureNotify event because no change has actually taken place.

- Moving the window without resizing it
  A client will receive a synthetic ConfigureNotify event following the move that describes the new state of the window, whose (x,y) coordinates will be in the root coordinate system adjusted for the border width the client requested. The border_width will be the border width the client requested. The client may not receive a real ConfigureNotify event that describes this change because the window manager may have reparented the top-level window. If the client does receive a real event, the synthetic event will follow the real one.
- Resizing the window (whether or not it is moved)
  A client that has selected for StructureNotify events will receive a ConfigureNotify event. Note that the coordinates in this event are relative to the parent, which may not be the root if the window has been reparented. The coordinates will reflect the actual border width of the window (which the window manager may have changed). The TranslateCoordinates request can be used to convert the coordinates if required.

The general rule is that coordinates in real ConfigureNotify events are in the parent's space; in synthetic events, they are in the root space.

Clients should be aware that their borders may not be visible. Window managers are free to use reparenting techniques to decorate client's top-level windows with borders containing titles, controls, and other details to maintain a consistent look-and-feel. If they do, they are likely to override the client's attempts to set the border width and set it to zero. Clients, therefore, should not depend on the top-level window's border being visible or use it to display any critical information. Other window managers will allow the top-level windows border to be visible.

Convention

Clients should set the desired value of the border-width attribute on all ConfigureWindow requests to avoid a race condition.

Clients that change their position in the stack must be aware that they may have been reparented, which means that windows that used to be siblings no longer are. Using a nonsibling as the sibling parameter on a ConfigureWindow request will cause an error.

Convention

Clients that use a `ConfigureWindow` request to request a change in their position in the stack should do so using `None` in the sibling field.

Clients that must position themselves in the stack relative to some window that was originally a sibling must do the `ConfigureWindow` request (in case they are running under a nonreparenting window manager), be prepared to deal with a resulting error, and then follow with a synthetic `ConfigureRequest` event by invoking a `SendEvent` request with the following arguments:

Argument	*Value*
destination:	The root
propagate:	`False`
event-mask:	`(SubstructureRedirect|SubstructureNotify)`
event: a `ConfigureRequest` with:	
event:	The root
window:	The window itself
....	Other parameters from the `ConfigureWindow`

Doing this is deprecated, and window managers are in any case free to position windows in the stack as they see fit. Clients should ignore the above field of both real and synthetic `ConfigureNotify` events that they receive on their nonoverride-redirect top-level windows because they cannot be guaranteed to contain useful information.

4.1.6 Changing Window Attributes

The attributes that may be supplied when a window is created may be changed by using the `ChangeWindowAttributes` request. The window attributes are listed in the following table.

Attribute	*Private to Client*
Background pixmap	Yes
Background pixel	Yes
Border pixmap	Yes
Border pixel	Yes
Bit gravity	Yes

Attribute	*Private to Client*
Window gravity	No
Backing-store hint	Yes
Save-under hint	No
Event mask	No
Do-not-propagate mask	Yes
Override-redirect flag	No
Colormap	Yes
Cursor	Yes

Most attributes are private to the client and will never be interfered with by the window manager. For the attributes that are not private to the client:

- The window manager is free to override the window gravity; a reparenting window manager may want to set the top-level window's window gravity for its own purposes.
- Clients are free to set the save-under hint on their top-level windows, but they must be aware that the hint may be overridden by the window manager.
- Windows, in effect, have per-client event masks, and so, clients may select for whatever events are convenient irrespective of any events the window manager is selecting for. There are some events for which only one client at a time may select, but the window manager should not select for them on any of the client's windows.
- Clients can set override-redirect on top-level windows but are encouraged not to do so except as described in sections 4.1.10 and 4.2.9.

4.1.7 Input Focus

There are four models of input handling:

- No Input—The client never expects keyboard input. An example would be `xload` or another output-only client.
- Passive Input—The client expects keyboard input but never explicitly sets the input focus. An example would be a simple client with no subwindows, which will accept input in `PointerRoot` mode or when the window manager sets the input focus to its top-level window (in click-to-type mode).
- Locally Active Input—The client expects keyboard input and explicitly sets the input focus, but it only does so when one of its windows already has the focus. An example would be a client with subwindows defining various data entry fields that uses Next and Prev keys to move the input focus between the fields. It does so when its top-level window has acquired the focus in `PointerRoot` mode or when the window manager sets the input focus to its top-level window (in click-to-type mode).

- Globally Active Input – The client expects keyboard input and explicitly sets the input focus, even when it is in windows the client does not own. An example would be a client with a scroll bar that wants to allow users to scroll the window without disturbing the input focus even if it is in some other window. It wants to acquire the input focus when the user clicks in the scrolled region but not when the user clicks in the scroll bar itself. Thus, it wants to prevent the window manager from setting the input focus to any of its windows.

The four input models and the corresponding values of the input field and the presence or absence of the WM_TAKE_FOCUS atom in the WM_PROTOCOLS property are listed in the following table:

Input Model	*Input Field*	*WM_TAKE_FOCUS*
No Input	`False`	Absent
Passive	`True`	Absent
Locally Active	`True`	Present
Globally Active	`False`	Present

Passive and Locally Active clients set the input field of WM_HINTS to `True`, which indicates that they require window manager assistance in acquiring the input focus. No Input and Globally Active clients set the input field to `False`, which requests that the window manager not set the input focus to their top-level window.

Clients that use a `SetInputFocus` request must set the time field to the timestamp of the event that caused them to make the attempt. This cannot be a `FocusIn` event because they do not have timestamps. Clients may also acquire the focus without a corresponding `EnterNotify`. Note that clients must not use `CurrentTime` in the time field.

Clients using the Globally Active model can only use a `SetInputFocus` request to acquire the input focus when they do not already have it on receipt of one of the following events:

- `ButtonPress`
- `ButtonRelease`
- Passive-grabbed `KeyPress`
- Passive-grabbed `KeyRelease`

In general, clients should avoid using passive-grabbed key events for this purpose, except when they are unavoidable (as, for example, a selection tool that establishes a passive grab on the keys that cut, copy, or paste).

The method by which the user commands the window manager to set the focus to a window is up to the window manager. For example, clients cannot determine whether they will see the click that transfers the focus.

Windows with the atom WM_TAKE_FOCUS in their WM_PROTOCOLS property may receive a `ClientMessage` event from the window manager (as described in section 4.2.8) with WM_TAKE_FOCUS in their data[0] field. If they want the focus, they should respond with a `SetInputFocus` request with its window field set to the window of theirs that last had the input focus or to their default input window, and the time field set to the timestamp in the message. For further information, see section 4.2.7.

A client could receive WM_TAKE_FOCUS when opening from an icon or when the user has clicked outside the top-level window in an area that indicates to the window manager that it should assign the focus (for example, clicking in the headline bar can be used to assign the focus).

The goal is to support window managers that want to assign the input focus to a top-level window in such a way that the top-level window either can assign it to one of its subwindows or can decline the offer of the focus. For example, a clock or a text editor with no currently open frames might not want to take focus even though the window manager generally believes that clients should take the input focus after being deiconified or raised.

Problem

There would be no need for WM_TAKE_FOCUS if the `FocusIn` event contained a timestamp and a previous-focus field. This could avoid the potential race condition. There is space in the event for this information; it should be added at the next protocol revision.

Clients that set the input focus need to decide a value for the revert-to field of the `SetInputFocus` request. This determines the behavior of the input focus if the window the focus has been set to becomes not viewable. The value can be any of the following:

- `Parent`—In general, clients should use this value when assigning focus to one of their subwindows. Unmapping the subwindow will cause focus to revert to the parent, which is probably what you want.

- `PointerRoot` —Using this value with a click-to-type focus management policy leads to race conditions because the window becoming unviewable may coincide with the window manager deciding to move the focus elsewhere.
- `None` —Using this value causes problems if the window manager reparents the window, as most window managers will, and then crashes. The input focus will be `None`, and there will probably be no way to change it.

Note that neither `PointerRoot` nor `None` is really safe to use.

Convention

Clients that invoke a `SetInputFocus` request should set the revert-to argument to `Parent`.

A convention is also required for clients that want to give up the input focus. There is no safe value set for them to set the input focus to; therefore, they should ignore input material.

Convention

Clients should not give up the input focus of their own volition. They should ignore input that they receive instead.

4.1.8 Colormaps

The window manager is responsible for installing and uninstalling colormaps.[10] Clients provide the window manager with hints as to which colormaps to install and uninstall, but clients must not install or uninstall colormaps themselves. When a client's top-level window gets the colormap focus (as a result of whatever colormap focus policy is implemented by the window manager), the window manager will insure that one or more of the client's colormaps are installed. The reason for this convention is that there is no safe way for multiple clients to install and uninstall colormaps.

Convention

Clients must not use `InstallColormap` or `UninstallColormap` requests.

There are two possible ways in which clients could hint to the window manager about the colormaps they want installed. Using a property, they could tell the window manager one of the following:

[10] The conventions described in earlier drafts by which clients and window managers shared responsibility for installing colormaps suffered from semantic problems.

- A priority ordered list of the colormaps they want installed
- A priority ordered list of the windows whose colormaps they want installed

The second of these alternatives has been selected because:

- It allows window managers to know the visuals for the colormaps, thus, permitting visual-dependent colormap installation policies.
- It allows window managers to select for `VisibilityChange` events on the windows concerned and ensure that maps are only installed if the windows that need them are visible.

Clients whose top-level windows and subwindows all use the same colormap should set its ID in the colormap field of the window's attributes. They should not set a WM_COLORMAP_WINDOWS property on the top-level window. If they want to change the colormap, they should change the window attribute. The window manager will install the colormap for them.

Clients that create windows can use the value `CopyFromParent` to inherit their parent's colormap. Window managers will ensure that the root window's colormap field contains a colormap that is suitable for clients to inherit. In particular, the colormap will provide distinguishable colors for `BlackPixel` and `WhitePixel`.

Top-level windows that have subwindows or override-redirect pop-up windows whose colormap requirements differ from the top-level window should have a WM_COLORMAP_WINDOWS property. This property contains a list of IDs for windows whose colormaps the window manager should attempt to have installed when, in the course of its individual colormap focus policy, it assigns the colormap focus to the top-level window (see section 4.1.2.8). The list is ordered by the importance to the client of having the colormaps installed. If this order changes, the property should be updated. The window manager will track changes to this property and will track changes to the colormap attribute of the windows in the property.

WM_TRANSIENT_FOR windows either can have their own WM_COLORMAP_WINDOWS property or can appear in the property of the window they are transient for, as appropriate.

Clients should be aware of the min-installed-maps and max-installed-maps fields of the connection startup information, and the effect that the minimum value has on the so-called "required list:"

> At any time, there is a subset of the installed maps, viewed as an ordered list, called the required list. The length of the required list is at most M, where M is the min-installed-maps specified for the screen in the connection setup. The required list is maintained as follows. When a colormap is an explicit argument to `InstallColormap`, it is added to the head of the list, and the list is truncated at the tail if necessary to keep the length of the list to at most M. When a colormap is an explicit argument to `UninstallColormap` and it is in the required list, it is removed from the list. A colormap is not added to the required list when it is installed implicitly by the server, and the server cannot implicitly uninstall a colormap that is in the required list.

In less precise words, the min-installed-maps most recently installed maps are guaranteed to be installed. Min-installed-maps will often be one; clients needing multiple colormaps should beware.

The window manager will identify and track changes to the colormap attribute of the windows identified by the WM_COLORMAP_WINDOWS property and the top-level window if it does not appear in the list. If the top-level window does not appear in the list, it will be assumed to be higher priority than any window in the list. It will also track changes in the contents of the WM_COLORMAP_WINDOWS property, in case the set of windows or their relative priority changes. The window manager will define some colormap focus policy and, whenever the top-level window has the colormap focus, will attempt to maximize the number of colormaps from the head of the WM_COLORMAP_WINDOWS list that is installed.

4.1.9 Icons

A client can hint to the window manager about the desired appearance of its icon by setting:

- A string in WM_ICON_NAME
  All clients should do this because it provides a fallback for window managers whose ideas about icons differ widely from those of the client.
- A `Pixmap` into the icon_pixmap field of the WM_HINTS property and possibly another into the icon_mask field
  The window manager is expected to display the pixmap masked by the mask. The pixmap should be one of the sizes found in the WM_ICON_SIZE property on the root. If this property is not found, the window manager is unlikely to display icon pixmaps. Window managers usually will clip or tile pixmaps that do not match WM_ICON_SIZE.

- A window into the icon_window field of the WM_HINTS property
  The window manager is expected to map that window whenever the client is in the Iconic state. In general, the size of the icon window should be one of those specified in WM_ICON_SIZE on the root, if it exists. Window managers are free to resize icon windows.

In the Iconic state, the window manager usually will ensure that:

- If the window's WM_HINTS.icon_window is set, the window it names is visible.
- If the window's WM_HINTS.icon_window is not set but the window's WM_HINTS.icon_pixmap is set, the pixmap it names is visible.
- Otherwise, the window's WM_ICON_NAME string is visible.

Clients should observe the following conventions about their icon windows:

Conventions

1. The icon window should be an `InputOutput` child of the root.
2. The icon window should be one of the sizes specified in the WM_ICON_SIZE property on the root.
3. The icon window should use the root visual and default colormap for the screen in question.
4. Clients should not map their icon windows.
5. Clients should not unmap their icon windows.
6. Clients should not configure their icon windows.
7. Clients should not set override-redirect on their icon windows or select for `ResizeRedirect` events on them.
8. Clients must not depend on being able to receive input events by means of their icon windows.
9. Clients must not manipulate the borders of their icon windows.
10. Clients must select for `Exposure` events on their icon window and repaint it when requested.

Window managers will differ as to whether they support input events to client's icon windows; most will allow the client to receive some subset of the keys and buttons.

Window managers will ignore any WM_NAME, WM_ICON_NAME, WM_NORMAL_HINTS, WM_HINTS, WM_CLASS, WM_TRANSIENT_FOR, WM_PROTOCOLS, or WM_COLORMAP_WINDOWS properties they find on icon windows. Session managers will ignore any WM_COMMAND or WM_CLIENT_MACHINE properties they find on icon windows.

4.1.10 Pop-up Windows

Clients that wish to pop up a window can do one of three things:

1. They can create and map another normal top-level window, which will get decorated and managed as normal by the window manager. See the discussion of window groups that follows.
2. If the window will be visible for a relatively short time and deserves a somewhat lighter treatment, they can set the WM_TRANSIENT_FOR property. They can expect less decoration but can set all the normal window manager properties on the window. An example would be a dialog box.
3. If the window will be visible for a very short time and should not be decorated at all, the client can set override-redirect on the window. In general, this should be done only if the pointer is grabbed while the window is mapped. The window manager will never interfere with these windows, which should be used with caution. An example of an appropriate use is a pop-up menu.

Window managers are free to decide if WM_TRANSIENT_FOR windows should be iconified when the window they are transient for is. Clients displaying WM_TRANSIENT_FOR windows that have (or request to have) the window they are transient for iconified do not need to request that the same operation be performed on the WM_TRANSIENT_FOR window; the window manager will change its state if that is the policy it wishes to enforce.

4.1.11 Window Groups

A set of top-level windows that should be treated from the user's point of view as related (even though they may belong to a number of clients) should be linked together using the window_group field of the WM_HINTS structure.

One of the windows (that is, the one the others point to) will be the group leader and will carry the group as opposed to the individual properties. Window managers may treat the group leader differently from other windows in the group. For example, group leaders may have the full set of decorations, and other group members may have a restricted set.

It is not necessary that the client ever map the group leader; it may be a window that exists solely as a placeholder.

It is up to the window manager to determine the policy for treating the windows in a group. At present, there is no way for a client to request a group, as opposed to an individual, operation.

4.2 Client Responses to Window Manager Actions

The window manager performs a number of operations on client resources, primarily on their top-level windows. Clients must not try to fight this but may elect to receive notification of the window manager's operations.

4.2.1 Reparenting

Clients must be aware that some window managers will reparent their nonoverride-redirect top-level windows so that a window that was created as a child of the root will be displayed as a child of some window belonging to the window manager. The effects that this reparenting will have on the client are as follows:

- The parent value returned by a `QueryTree` request will no longer be the value supplied to the `CreateWindow` request that created the reparented window. There should be no need for the client to be aware of the identity of the window to which the top-level window has been reparented. In particular, a client that wishes to create further top-level windows should continue to use the root as the parent for these new windows.
- The server will interpret the (x,y) coordinates in a `ConfigureWindow` request in the new parent's coordinate space. In fact, they usually will not be interpreted by the server because a reparenting window manager usually will have intercepted these operations (see section 4.2.2). Clients should use the root coordinate space for these requests (see section 4.1.5).
- `ConfigureWindow` requests that name a specific sibling window may fail because the window named, which used to be a sibling, no longer is after the reparenting operation (see section 4.1.5).
- The (x,y) coordinates returned by a `GetGeometry` request are in the parent's coordinate space and are thus not directly useful after a reparent operation.
- A background of `ParentRelative` will have unpredictable results.
- A cursor of `None` will have unpredictable results.

Clients that want to be notified when they are reparented can select for `StructureNotify` events on their top-level window. They will receive a `ReparentNotify` event if and when reparenting takes place.

If the window manager reparents a client's window, the reparented window will be placed in the save-set of the parent window. This means that the reparented window will not be destroyed if the window manager terminates and will be remapped if it was unmapped. Note that this applies to all client windows the window manager reparents, including transient windows and client icon windows.

When the window manager gives up control over a client's top-level window, it will reparent it (and any associated windows, for example, WM_TRANSIENT_FOR windows) back to the root.

There is a potential race condition here. A client might want to reuse the top-level window, reparenting it somewhere else.

Convention

Clients that want to reparent their top-level windows should do so only when they have their original parents. They may select for `StructureNotify` events on their top-level windows and will receive `ReparentNotify` events informing them when this is true.

4.2.2 Redirection of Operations

Clients must be aware that some window managers will arrange for some client requests to be intercepted and redirected. Redirected requests are not executed; they result instead in events being sent to the window manager, which may decide to do nothing, to alter the arguments, or to perform the request on behalf of the client.

The possibility that a request may be redirected means that a client cannot assume that any redirectable request is actually performed when the request is issued or is actually performed at all. For example, the following is incorrect because the `MapWindow` request may be intercepted and the `PolyLine` output made to an unmapped window:

```
MapWindow A
PolyLine A GC <point> <point>....
```

The client must wait for an `Expose` event before drawing in the window.[11]

This next example incorrectly assumes that the `ConfigureWindow` request is actually executed with the arguments supplied:

```
ConfigureWindow width=N height=M
<output assuming window is N by M>
```

[11]This is true even if the client set the backing-store attribute to `Always`. The backing-store attribute is only a hint, and the server may stop maintaining backing-store contents at any time.

The requests that may be redirected are:

- `MapWindow`
- `ConfigureWindow`
- `CirculateWindow`

A window with the override-redirect bit set is immune from redirection, but the bit should be set on top-level windows only in cases where other windows should be prevented from processing input while the override-redirect window is mapped (see section 4.1.10) and while responding to `ResizeRequest` events (see section 4.2.9).

Clients that have no non-Withdrawn top-level windows and that map an override-redirect top-level window are taking over total responsibility for the state of the system. It is their responsibility to:

- Prevent any preexisting window manager from interfering with their activities
- Restore the status quo exactly after they unmap the window so that any preexisting window manager does not get confused

In effect, clients of this kind are acting as temporary window managers. Doing so is strongly discouraged because these clients will be unaware of the user interface policies the window manager is trying to maintain and because their user interface behavior is likely to conflict with that of less demanding clients.

4.2.3 Window Move

If the window manager moves a top-level window without changing its size, the client will receive a synthetic `ConfigureNotify` event following the move that describes the new location in terms of the root coordinate space. Clients must not respond to being moved by attempting to move themselves to a better location.

Any real `ConfigureNotify` event on a top-level window implies that the window's position on the root may have changed, even though the event reports that the window's position in its parent is unchanged because the window may have been reparented. Note that the coordinates in the event will not, in this case, be directly useful.

The window manager will send these events by using a `SendEvent` request with the following arguments:

Argument	*Value*
destination:	The client's window
propagate:	`False`
event-mask:	`StructureNotify`

4.2.4 Window Resize

The client can elect to receive notification of being resized by selecting for `StructureNotify` events on its top-level windows. It will receive a `ConfigureNotify` event. The size information in the event will be correct, but the location will be in the parent window (which may not be the root).

The response of the client to being resized should be to accept the size it has been given and to do its best with it. Clients must not respond to being resized by attempting to resize themselves to a better size. If the size is impossible to work with, clients are free to request to change to the Iconic state.

4.2.5 Iconify and Deiconify

A nonoverride-redirect window that is not Withdrawn will be in the Normal state if it is mapped and in the Iconic state if it is unmapped. This will be true even if the window has been reparented; the window manager will unmap the window as well as its parent when switching to the Iconic state.

The client can elect to be notified of these state changes by selecting for `StructureNotify` events on the top-level window. It will receive a `UnmapNotify` event when it goes Iconic and a `MapNotify` event when it goes Normal.

4.2.6 Colormap Change

Clients that wish to be notified of their colormaps being installed or uninstalled should select for `ColormapNotify` events on their top-level windows and on any windows they have named in WM_COLORMAP_WINDOWS properties on their top-level windows. They will receive `ColormapNotify` events with the new field FALSE when the colormap for that window is installed or uninstalled.

Problem

There is an inadequacy in the protocol. At the next revision, the `InstallColormap` request should be changed to include a timestamp to avoid the possibility of race conditions if more than one client attempts to install and uninstall colormaps. These conventions attempt to avoid the problem by restricting use of these requests to the window manager.

4.2.7 Input Focus

Clients can request notification that they have the input focus by selecting for `FocusChange` events on their top-level windows; they will receive `FocusIn` and `FocusOut` events. Clients that need to set the input focus to one of their subwindows should not do so unless they have set WM_TAKE_FOCUS in their WM_PROTOCOLS property and have done one of the following:

- Set the input field of WM_HINTS to `True` and actually have the input focus in one of their top-level windows
- Set the input field of WM_HINTS to `False` and have received a suitable event as described in section 4.1.7
- Have received a WM_TAKE_FOCUS message as described in section 4.1.7

Clients should not warp the pointer in an attempt to transfer the focus; they should set the focus and leave the pointer alone. For further information, see section 6.2.

Once a client satisfies these conditions, it may transfer the focus to another of its windows by using the `SetInputFocus` request, which is defined as follows:

SetInputFocus

focus: WINDOW or `PointerRoot` or `None`
revert-to: `{Parent, PointerRoot, None}`
time: TIMESTAMP or `CurrentTime`

Conventions

1. Clients that use a `SetInputFocus` request must set the time argument to the timestamp of the event that caused them to make the attempt. This cannot be a `FocusIn` event because they do not have timestamps. Clients may also acquire the focus without a corresponding `EnterNotify` event. Clients must not use `CurrentTime` for the time argument.
2. Clients that use a `SetInputFocus` request to set the focus to one of their windows must set the revert-to field to `Parent`.

4.2.8 ClientMessage Events

There is no way for clients to prevent themselves being sent `ClientMessage` events.

Top-level windows with a WM_PROTOCOLS property may be sent `ClientMessage` events specific to the protocols named by the atoms in the property (see section 4.1.2.7). For all protocols, the `ClientMessage` events have the following:

- WM_PROTOCOLS as the type field
- Format 32
- The atom that names their protocol in the data[0] field
- A timestamp in their data[1] field

The remaining fields of the event, including the window field, are determined by the protocol.

These events will be sent by using a `SendEvent` request with the following arguments:

Argument	*Value*
destination:	The client's window
propagate:	`False`
event-mask:	() empty
event:	As specified by the protocol

4.2.9 Redirecting Requests

Normal clients can use the redirection mechanism just as window managers do by selecting for `SubstructureRedirect` events on a parent window or `ResizeRedirect` events on a window itself. However, at most, one client per window can select for these events, and a convention is needed to avoid clashes.

Convention

Clients (including window managers) should select for `SubstructureRedirect` and `ResizeRedirect` events only on windows that they own.

In particular, clients that need to take some special action if they are resized can select for `ResizeRedirect` events on their top-level windows. They will receive a `ResizeRequest` event if the window manager resizes their window, and the resize will not actually take place. Clients are free to make what use they like of the information that the window manager wants to change their size, but they must configure the window to the width and height specified in the event in a timely fashion. To ensure that the resize will actually happen at this stage instead of being intercepted and executed by the window manager (and thus restarting the process), the client needs temporarily to set override-redirect on the window.

Convention

Clients receiving `ResizeRequest` events must respond by doing the following:

- Setting override-redirect on the window specified in the event
- Configuring the window specified in the event to the width and height specified in the event as soon as possible and before making any other geometry requests
- Clearing override-redirect on the window specified in the event

If a window manager detects that a client is not obeying this convention, it is free to take whatever measures it deems appropriate to deal with the client.

4.3 Summary of Window Manager Property Types

The window manager properties are summarized in the following table (see also section 14.1 of part I, "Xlib — C Language X Interface").

Name	*Type*	*Format*	*See Section*
WM_CLASS	STRING	8	4.1.2.5
WM_COLORMAP_WINDOWS	WINDOW	32	4.1.2.8
WM_HINTS	WM_HINTS	32	4.1.2.4
WM_ICON_NAME	TEXT		4.1.2.2
WM_ICON_SIZE	WM_ICON_SIZE	32	4.1.3.2
WM_NAME	TEXT		4.1.2.1
WM_NORMAL_HINTS	WM_SIZE_HINTS	32	4.1.2.3
WM_PROTOCOLS	ATOM	32	4.1.2.7
WM_STATE	WM_STATE	32	4.1.3.1
WM_TRANSIENT_FOR	WINDOW	32	4.1.2.6

SECTION 5. CLIENT TO SESSION MANAGER COMMUNICATION

The session manager's role is to manage a collection of clients. It should be capable of:

- Starting a collection of clients as a group
- Remembering the state of a collection of clients so that they can be restarted in the same state
- Stopping a collection of clients in a controlled way

It may also provide a user interface to these capabilities.

5.1 Client Actions

There are two ways in which clients should cooperate with the session manager:

1. Stateful clients should cooperate with the session manager by providing it with information it can use to restart them if that should become necessary.
2. Clients, typically those with more than one top-level window, whose server connection needs to survive the deletion of their top-level window should take part in the WM_DELETE_WINDOW protocol (see section 5.2.2).

5.1.1 Properties

The client communicates with the session manager by placing two properties (WM_COMMAND and WM_CLIENT_MACHINE) on its top-level window. If the client has a group of top-level windows, these properties should be placed on the group leader window.

The window manager is responsible for placing a WM_STATE property on each top-level client window for use by session managers and other clients that need to be able to identify top-level client windows and their state.

5.1.1.1 WM_COMMAND Property

The WM_COMMAND property represents the command used to start or restart the client. By updating this property, clients should ensure that it always reflects a command that will restart them in their current state. The content and type of the property depends on the operating system of the machine running the client. On POSIX-conformant systems using ISO Latin-1 characters for their command lines, the property should:

- Be of type STRING
- Contain a list of null-terminated strings
- Be initialized from argv

Other systems will need to set appropriate conventions for the type and contents of WM_COMMAND properties. Window and session managers should not assume that STRING is the type of WM_COMMAND or that they will be able to understand or display its contents.

Note that WM_COMMAND strings are null-terminated and differ from the general conventions that STRING properties are null-separated. This inconsistency is necessary for backwards-compatibility.

A client with multiple top-level windows should ensure that exactly one of them has a WM_COMMAND with nonzero length. Zero-length WM_COMMAND properties can be used to reply to WM_SAVE_YOURSELF messages on other top-level windows but will otherwise be ignored (see section 5.2.1).

5.1.1.2 WM_CLIENT_MACHINE Property

The client should set the WM_CLIENT_MACHINE property (of one of the TEXT types) to a string that forms the name of the machine running the client as seen from the machine running the server.

5.1.1.3 WM_STATE Property

The window manager will place a WM_STATE property (of type WM_STATE) on each top-level client window.

Programs like `xprop` that want to operate on client's top-level windows can use this property to identify them. A client's top-level window is one that has override-redirect set to `False` and a WM_STATE property or that is a mapped child of the root that has no descendant with a WM_STATE property.

Recursion is necessary to cover all window manager reparenting possibilities. Note that clients other than window and session managers should not need to examine the contents of WM_STATE properties, which are not formally defined by the ICCCM. The presence or absence of the property is all they need to know.

Suggested contents of the WM_STATE property are listed in the following table:

Field	*Type*	*Comments*
state	CARD32	(see the next table)
icon	WINDOW	ID of icon window

The following table lists the WM_STATE.state values:

State	*Value*
`WithdrawnState`	0
`NormalState`	1
`IconicState`	3

Adding other fields to this property is reserved to the X Consortium.

The icon field should either contain the window ID of the window that the window manager uses as the icon window for the window on which this property is set if one exists or `None` if one does not. Note that this window is not necessarily the same as the icon window that the client may have specified. It can be one of the following:

- The client's icon window
- A window that the window manager supplied and that contains the client's icon pixmap
- The least ancestor of the client's icon window (or of the window that contains the client's icon pixmap), which contains no other icons

The state field describes the window manager's idea of the state the window is in, which may not match the client's idea as expressed in the initial_state field of the WM_HINTS property (for example, if the user has asked the window manager to iconify the window). If it is `NormalState`, the window manager believes the client should be animating its window. If it is `IconicState`, the client should animate its icon window. In either state, clients should be prepared to handle exposure events from either window.

The contents of WM_STATE properties and other aspects of the communication between window and session managers will be specified in the forthcoming *Window and Session Manager Conventions Manual.*

5.1.2 Termination

Because they communicate by means of unreliable network connections, clients must be prepared for their connection to the server to be terminated at any time without warning. They cannot depend on getting notification that termination is imminent or on being able to use the server to negotiate with the user about their fate. For example, clients cannot depend on being able to put up a dialog box.

Similarly, clients may terminate at any time without notice to the session manager. When a client terminates itself rather than being terminated by the session manager, it is viewed as having resigned from the session in question, and it will not be revived if the session is revived.

5.2 Client Responses to Session Manager Actions

Clients may need to respond to session manager actions in two ways:

- Saving their internal state
- Deleting a window

5.2.1 Saving Client State

Clients that want to be warned when the session manager feels that they should save their internal state (for example, when termination impends) should include the atom WM_SAVE_YOURSELF in the WM_PROTOCOLS property on their top-level windows to participate in the WM_SAVE_YOURSELF protocol. They will receive a `ClientMessage` event as described in section 4.2.8 with the atom WM_SAVE_YOURSELF in its data[0] field.

Clients that receive WM_SAVE_YOURSELF should place themselves in a state from which they can be restarted and should update WM_COMMAND to be a command that will restart them in this state. The session manager will be waiting for a `PropertyNotify` event on WM_COMMAND as a confirmation that the client has saved its state. Therefore, WM_COMMAND should be updated (perhaps with a zero-length append) even if its contents are correct. No interactions with the user are permitted during this process.

Once it has received this confirmation, the session manager will feel free to terminate the client if that is what the user asked for. Otherwise, if the user asked for the session to be put to sleep, the session manager will ensure that the client does not receive any mouse or keyboard events.

After receiving a WM_SAVE_YOURSELF, saving its state, and updating WM_COMMAND, the client should not change its state (in the sense of doing anything that would require a change to WM_COMMAND) until it receives a mouse or keyboard event. Once it does so, it can assume that the danger is over. The session manager will ensure that these events do not reach clients until the danger is over or until the clients have been killed.

Irrespective of how they are arranged in window groups, clients with multiple top-level windows should ensure the following:

- Only one of their top-level windows has a nonzero-length WM_COMMAND property.
- They respond to a WM_SAVE_YOURSELF message by:
  — First, updating the nonzero-length WM_COMMAND property, if necessary
  — Second, updating the WM_COMMAND property on the window for which they received the WM_SAVE_YOURSELF message if it was not updated in the first step

Receiving WM_SAVE_YOURSELF on a window is, conceptually, a command to save the entire client state.[12]

5.2.2 Window Deletion

Clients, usually those with multiple top-level windows, whose server connection must survive the deletion of some of their top-level windows should include the atom WM_DELETE_WINDOW in the WM_PROTOCOLS property on each such window. They will receive a `ClientMessage` event as described in section 4.2.8 whose data[0] field is WM_DELETE_WINDOW.

Clients receiving a WM_DELETE_WINDOW message should behave as if the user selected the "delete window" entry from a hypothetical menu. They should perform any confirmation dialog with the user and, if they decide to complete the deletion, should do the following:

- Either change the window's state to Withdrawn (as described in section 4.1.4) or destroy the window
- Destroy any internal state associated with the window

[12] This convention has changed since earlier drafts because of the introduction of the protocol in the next section. In the public review draft, there was ambiguity as to whether WM_SAVE_YOURSELF was a checkpoint or a shutdown facility. It is now unambiguously a checkpoint facility; if a shutdown facility is judged to be necessary, a separate WM_PROTOCOLS protocol will be developed and registered with the X Consortium.

If the user aborts the deletion during the confirmation dialog, the client should ignore the message.

Clients are permitted to interact with the user and ask, for example, whether a file associated with the window to be deleted should be saved or the window deletion should be cancelled. Clients are not required to destroy the window itself; the resource may be reused, but all associated state (for example, backing store) should be released.

If the client aborts a destroy and the user then selects DELETE WINDOW again, the window manager should start the WM_DELETE_WINDOW protocol again. Window managers should not use `DestroyWindow` requests on a window that has WM_DELETE_WINDOW in its WM_PROTOCOLS property.

Clients that choose not to include WM_DELETE_WINDOW in the WM_PROTOCOLS property may be disconnected from the server if the user asks for one of the client's top-level windows to be deleted.

Note that the WM_SAVE_YOURSELF and WM_DELETE_WINDOW protocols are orthogonal to each other and may be selected independently.

5.3 Summary of Session Manager Property Types

The session manager properties are listed in the following table:

Name	*Type*	*Format*	*See Section*
WM_CLIENT_MACHINE	TEXT		5.1.1.2
WM_COMMAND	TEXT		5.1.1.1
WM_STATE	WM_STATE	32	5.1.1.3

SECTION 6. MANIPULATION OF SHARED RESOURCES

X Version 11 permits clients to manipulate a number of shared resources, for example, the input focus, the pointer, and colormaps. Conventions are required so that clients share resources in an orderly fashion.

6.1 The Input Focus

Clients that explicitly set the input focus must observe one of two modes:

- Locally active mode
- Globally active mode

Conventions

1. Locally active clients should set the input focus to one of their windows only when it is already in one of their windows or when they receive a WM_TAKE_FOCUS message. They should set the input field of the WM_HINTS structure to `True`.
2. Globally active clients should set the input focus to one of their windows only when they receive a button event and a passive-grabbed key event, or when they receive a WM_TAKE_FOCUS message. They should set the input field of the WM_HINTS structure to `False`.
3. In addition, clients should use the timestamp of the event that caused them to attempt to set the input focus as the time field on the `SetInputFocus` request, not `CurrentTime`.

6.2 The Pointer

In general, clients should not warp the pointer. Window managers, however, may do so (for example, to maintain the invariant that the pointer is always in the window with the input focus). Other window managers may want to preserve the illusion that the user is in sole control of the pointer.

Conventions

1. Clients should not warp the pointer.
2. Clients that insist on warping the pointer should do so only with the src-window argument of the `WarpPointer` request set to one of their windows.

6.3 Grabs

A client's attempt to establish a button or a key grab on a window will fail if some other client has already established a conflicting grab on the same window. The grabs, therefore, are shared resources, and their use requires conventions.

In conformance with the principle that clients should behave, as far as possible, when a window manager is running as they would when it is not, a client that has the input focus may assume that it can receive all the available keys and buttons.

Convention

Window managers should ensure that they provide some mechanism for their clients to receive events from all keys and all buttons, except for events involving keys whose KeySyms are registered as being for window management functions (for example, a hypothetical WINDOW KeySym).

In other words, window managers must provide some mechanism by which a client can receive events from every key and button (regardless of modifiers) unless and until the X Consortium registers some KeySyms as being reserved for window management functions. Currently, no KeySyms are registered for window management functions.

Even so, clients are advised to allow the key and button combinations used to elicit program actions to be modified, because some window managers may choose not to observe this convention or may not provide a convenient method for the user to transmit events from some keys.

Convention

Clients should establish button and key grabs only on windows that they own.

In particular, this convention means that a window manager that wishes to establish a grab over the client's top-level window should either establish the grab on the root, or reparent the window and establish the grab on a proper ancestor. In some cases, a window manager may want to consume the event received, placing the window in a state where a subsequent such event will go to the client. Examples are:

- Clicking in a window to set focus with the click not being offered to the client
- Clicking in a buried window to raise it, again, with the click not offered to the client

More typically, a window manager should add to rather than replace the client's semantics for key+button combinations by allowing the event to be used by the client after the window manager is done with it. To ensure this, the window manager should establish the grab on the parent by using the following:

pointer/keyboard-mode == Synchronous

Then, the window manager should release the grab by using an `AllowEvents` request with the following specified:

mode == ReplayPointer/Keyboard

In this way, the client will receive the events as if they had not been intercepted.

Obviously, these conventions place some constraints on possible user interface policies. There is a trade-off here between freedom for window managers to implement their user interface policies and freedom for clients to implement theirs. The dilemma is resolved by:

- Allowing window managers to decide if and when a client will receive an event from any given key or button
- Placing a requirement on the window manager to provide some mechanism, perhaps a "Quote" key, by which the user can send an event from any key or button to the client.

6.4 Colormaps

Section 4.1.8 prescribes the following:

Conventions

1. If a client has a top-level window that has subwindows or override-redirect pop-up windows whose colormap requirements differ from the top-level window, it should set a WM_COLORMAP_WINDOWS property on the top-level window. The WM_COLORMAP_WINDOWS property contains a list of the window IDs of windows that the window manager should track for colormap changes.
2. When a client's colormap requirements change, the client should change the colormap window attribute of a top-level window or one of the windows indicated by a WM_COLORMAP_WINDOWS property.
3. Clients must not use `InstallColormap` or `UninstallColormap` requests.

If your clients are `DirectColor` type applications, you should consult section 14.3 of part I, "Xlib — C Language X Interface," for conventions connected with sharing standard colormaps. They should look for and create the properties described there on the root window of the appropriate screen.

The contents of the RGB_COLOR_MAP type property are as follows:

Field	*Type*	*Comments*
colormap	COLORMAP	ID of the colormap described
red_max	CARD32	Values for pixel calculations
red_mult	CARD32	
green_max	CARD32	
green_mult	CARD32	
blue_max	CARD32	
blue_mult	CARD32	
base_pixel	CARD32	
visual_id	VISUALID	Visual to which colormap belongs
kill_id	CARD32	ID for destroying the resources

When deleting or replacing an RGB_COLOR_MAP, it is not sufficient to delete the property; it is important to free the associated colormap resources as well. If kill_id is greater than one, the resources should be freed by issuing a `KillClient` request with kill_id as the argument. If kill_id is one, the resources should be freed by issuing a `FreeColormap` request with colormap as the colormap argument. If kill_id is zero, no attempt should be made to free the resources. A client that creates an RGB_COLOR_MAP for which the colormap resource is created specifically for this purpose should set kill_id to one (and can create more than one such standard colormap using a single connection). A client that creates an RGB_COLOR_MAP for which the colormap resource is shared in some way (for example, is the default colormap for the root window) should create an arbitrary resource and use its resource ID for kill_id (and should create no other standard colormaps on the connection).

Convention

If an RGB_COLOR_MAP property is too short to contain the visual_id field, it can be assumed that the visual_id is the root visual of the appropriate screen. If an RGB_COLOR_MAP property is too short to contain the kill_id field, a value of zero can be assumed.

During the connection handshake, the server informs the client of the default colormap for each screen. This is a colormap for the root visual, and clients can use it to improve the extent of colormap sharing if they use the root visual.

6.5 The Keyboard Mapping

The X server contains a table (which is read by `GetKeyboardMapping` requests) that describes the set of symbols appearing on the corresponding key for each keycode generated by the server. This table does not affect the server's operations in any way; it is simply a database used by clients that attempt to understand the keycodes they receive. Nevertheless, it is a shared resource and requires conventions.

It is possible for clients to modify this table by using a `ChangeKeyboardMapping` request. In general, clients should not do this. In particular, this is not the way in which clients should implement key bindings or key remapping. The conversion between a sequence of keycodes received from the server and a string in a particular encoding is a private matter for each client (as it must be in a world where applications may be using different encodings to support different languages and fonts). See part I, "Xlib — C Language Reference," for converting keyboard events to text.

The only valid reason for using a `ChangeKeyboardMapping` request is when the symbols written on the keys have changed as, for example, when a Dvorak key conversion kit or a set of APL keycaps has been installed. Of course, a client may have to take the change to the keycap on trust.

The following illustrates a permissible interaction between a client and a user:

Client: "You just started me on a server without a Pause key. Please choose a key to be the Pause key and press it now."

User: Presses the Scroll Lock key

Client: "Adding Pause to the symbols on the Scroll Lock key: Confirm or Abort."

User: Confirms

Client: Uses a `ChangeKeyboardMapping` request to add Pause to the keycode that already contains Scroll Lock and issues this request, "Please paint Pause on the Scroll Lock key."

Convention

Clients should not use `ChangeKeyboardMapping` requests.

If a client succeeds in changing the keyboard mapping table, all clients will receive `MappingNotify`(request==Keyboard) events. There is no mechanism to avoid receiving these events.

Convention

Clients receiving `MappingNotify`(request==Keyboard) events should update any internal keycode translation tables they are using.

6.6 The Modifier Mapping

X Version 11 supports eight modifier bits of which three are preassigned to Shift, Lock, and Control. Each modifier bit is controlled by the state of a set of keys, and these sets are specified in a table accessed by `GetModifierMapping` and `SetModifierMapping` requests. This table is a shared resource and requires conventions.

A client that needs to use one of the preassigned modifiers should assume that the modifier table has been set up correctly to control these modifiers. The Lock modifier should be interpreted as Caps Lock or Shift Lock according as the keycodes in its controlling set include XK_Caps_Lock or XK_Shift_Lock.

Convention

Clients should determine the meaning of a modifier bit from the KeySyms being used to control it.

A client that needs to use an extra modifier (for example, META) should do the following:

- Scan the existing modifier mappings. If it finds a modifier that contains a keycode whose set of KeySyms includes XK_Meta_L or XK_Meta_R, it should use that modifier bit.
- If there is no existing modifier controlled by XK_Meta_L or XK_Meta_R, it should select an unused modifier bit (one with an empty controlling set) and do the following:
  — If there is a keycode with XL_Meta_L in its set of KeySyms, add that keycode to the set for the chosen modifier.
  — If there is a keycode with XL_Meta_R in its set of KeySyms, add that keycode to the set for the chosen modifier.
  — If the controlling set is still empty, interact with the user to select one or more keys to be META.
- If there are no unused modifier bits, ask the user to take corrective action.

Conventions

1. Clients needing a modifier not currently in use should assign keycodes carrying suitable KeySyms to an unused modifier bit.
2. Clients assigning their own modifier bits should ask the user politely to remove his or her hands from the key in question if their `SetModifierMapping` request returns a `Busy` status.

There is no good solution to the problem of reclaiming assignments to the five nonpreassigned modifiers when they are no longer being used.

Convention

The user has to use `xmodmap` or some other utility to deassign obsolete modifier mappings by hand.

Problem

This is unpleasantly low-tech.

When a client succeeds in performing a `SetModifierMapping` request, all clients will receive `MappingNotify`(request==Modifier) events. There is no mechanism for preventing these events from being received. A client that uses one of the nonpreassigned modifiers that receives one of these events should do a `GetModifierMapping` request to discover the new mapping, and if the modifier it is using has been cleared, it should reinstall the modifier.

Note that a `GrabServer` request must be used to make the `GetModifierMapping` and `SetModifierMapping` pair in these transactions atomic.

SECTION 7. DEVICE COLOR CHARACTERIZATION

The X protocol provides explicit RGB values, which are used to directly drive a monitor, and color names. RGB values provide a mechanism for accessing the full capabilities of the display device, but at the expense of having the color perceived by the user remain unknowable through the protocol. Color names were originally designed to provide access to a device-independent color database by having the server vendor tune the definitions of the colors in that textual database. Unfortunately, this still does not provide the client any way of using an existing device-independent color, nor for the client to get device-independent color information back about colors that it has selected.

Furthermore, the client must be able to discover which set of colors are displayable by the device (the device gamut), both to allow colors to be intelligently modified to fit within the device capabilities (gamut compression) and to enable the user interface to display a representation of the reachable color space to the user (gamut display).

Therefore, a system is needed that will provide full access to device-independent color spaces for X clients. This system should use a standard mechanism for naming the colors, be able to provide names for existing colors, and provide means by which unreachable colors can be modified to fall within the device gamut.

We are fortunate in this area to have a seminal work, the 1931 CIE color standard, which is nearly universally agreed upon as adequate for describing colors on CRT devices. This standard uses a tristimulus model called CIE XYZ in which each perceivable color is specified as a triplet of numbers. Other appropriate device-independent color models do exist, but most of them are directly traceable back to this original work.

X device color characterization provides device-independent color spaces to X clients. It does this by providing the barest possible amount of information to the client that allows the client to construct a mapping between CIE XYZ and the regular X RGB color descriptions.

Device color characterization is defined by the name and contents of two window properties that, together, permit converting between CIE XYZ space and linear RGB device space (such as standard CRTs). Linear RGB devices require just two pieces of information to completely characterize them:

- A 3x3 matrix M (and its inverse, M^{-1}), which convert between XYZ and RGB intensity ($RGB_{intensity}$):

$$RGB_{intensity} = M \times XYZ$$
$$XYZ = M^{-1} \times RGB_{intensity}$$

- A way of mapping between RGB intensity and RGB protocol value. XDCCC supports three mechanisms, which will be outlined below.

If other device types are eventually necessary, additional properties will be required to describe them.

7.1 XYZ $\leftrightarrow$ RGB Conversion Matrices

Because of the limited dynamic range of both XYZ and RGB intensity, these matrices will be encoded using a fixed-point representation of a 32-bit 2s complement number scaled by 2^{27}, giving a range of -16 to $16-\varepsilon$, where $\varepsilon = 2^{-37}$.

These matrices will be packed into an 18-element list of 32-bit values, XYZ $\rightarrow$ RGB matrix first, in row major order and stored in the XDCCC_LINEAR_RGB_MATRICES properties (format = 32) on the root window of each screen, using values appropriate for that screen.

This will be encoded as shown in the following table:

XDCCC_LINEAR_RGB_MATRICES Property Contents

Field	*Type*	*Comments*
$M_{0,0}$	INT32	Interpreted as a fixed point number $-16 \le x < 16$
$M_{0,1}$	INT32	
...		
$M_{3,3}$	INT32	

Field	*Type*	*Comments*
$M^{-1}{}_{0,0}$	INT32	
$M^{-1}{}_{0,1}$	INT32	
...		
$M^{-1}{}_{3,3}$	INT32	

7.2 Intensity ↔ RGB Value Conversion

XDCCC provides two representations for describing the conversion between RGB intensity and the actual X protocol RGB values:

0 RGB value/RGB intensity level pairs
1 RGB intensity ramp

In both cases, the relevant data will be stored in the XDCCC_LINEAR_RGB_CORRECTION properties on the root window of each screen, using values appropriate for that screen, in whatever format provides adequate resolution. Each property can consist of multiple entries concatenated together, if different visuals for the screen require different conversion data. An entry with a VisualID of 0 specifies data for all visuals of the screen that are not otherwise explicitly listed.

The first representation is an array of RGB value/intensity level pairs, with the RGB values in strictly increasing order. When converting, the client must linearly interpolate between adjacent entries in the table to compute the desired value. This allows the server to perform gamma correction itself and encode that fact in a short two-element correction table. The intensity will be encoded as an unsigned number to be interpreted as a value between 0 and 1 (inclusive). The precision of this value will depend on the format of the property in which it is stored (8, 16, or 32 bits). For 16- and 32-bit formats, the RGB value will simply be the value stored in the property. When stored in 8-bit format, the RGB value can be computed from the value in the property by:

$$RGB_{value} = \frac{Property\ Value \times 65535}{255}$$

Because the three electron guns in the device may not be exactly alike in response characteristics, it is necessary to allow for three separate tables, one each for red, green, and blue. Therefore, each table will be preceded by the number of entries in that table, and the set of tables will be preceded by the number of tables. When three tables are provided, they will be in red, green, blue order.

This will be encoded as shown in the following table:

XDCCC_LINEAR_RGB_CORRECTION Property Contents for Type 0 Correction

Field	*Type*	*Comments*
VisualID0	CARD	Most-significant portion of VisualID
VisualID1	CARD	Exists if and only if property format is 8
VisualID2	CARD	Exists if and only if property format is 8
VisualID3	CARD	Least-significant, exists if and only if property format is 8 or 16
type	CARD	0 for this type of correction
count	CARD	Number of tables following (either 1 or 3)
length	CARD	Number of pairs – 1 following in this table
value	CARD	X Protocol RGB value
intensity	CARD	Interpret as a number 0 ≤ intensity ≤ 1
...	...	Total of *length+1* pairs of value/intensity values
lengthg	CARD	Number of pairs – 1 following in this table (if and only if *count* is 3)
value	CARD	X Protocol RGB value
intensity	CARD	Interpret as a number 0 ≤ intensity ≤ 1
...	...	Total of *lengthg+1* pairs of value/intensity values
lengthb	CARD	Number of pairs – 1 following in this table (if and only if *count* is 3)
value	CARD	X Protocol RGB value
intensity	CARD	Interpret as a number 0 ≤ intensity ≤ 1
...	...	Total of *lengthb+1* pairs of value/intensity values

The VisualID is stored in 4, 2, or 1 pieces, depending on whether the property format is 8, 16, or 32, respectively. The VisualID is always stored most-significant piece first. Note that the length fields are stored as one less than the actual length, so 256 entries can be stored in format 8.

The second representation is a simple array of intensities for a linear subset of RGB values. The expected size of this table is the bits-per-RGB-value of the screen, but it can be any length. This is similar to the first mechanism, except that the RGB value numbers are implicitly defined by the index in the array (indices start at 0):

$$RGB_{value} = \frac{Array\ Index \times 65535}{Array\ Size - 1}$$

When converting, the client may linearly interpolate between entries in this table. The intensity values will be encoded just as in the first representation.

This will be encoded as shown in the following table:

XDCCC_LINEAR_RGB_CORRECTION Property Contents for Type 1 Correction

Field	*Type*	*Comments*
VisualID0	CARD	Most-significant portion of VisualID
VisualID1	CARD	Exists if and only if property format is 8
VisualID2	CARD	Exists if and only if property format is 8
VisualID3	CARD	Least-significant, exists if and only if property format is 8 or 16
type	CARD	1 for this type of correction
count	CARD	Number of tables following (either 1 or 3)
length	CARD	Number of elements – 1 following in this table
intensity	CARD	Interpret as a number 0 ≤ intensity ≤ 1
...	...	Total of *length+1* intensity elements
lengthg	CARD	Number of elements – 1 following in this table (if and only if *count* is 3)
intensity	CARD	Interpret as a number 0 ≤ intensity ≤ 1
...	...	Total of *lengthg+1* intensity elements
lengthb	CARD	Number of elements – 1 following in this table (if and only if *count* is 3)
intensity	CARD	Interpret as a number 0 ≤ intensity ≤ 1
...	...	Total of *lengthb+1* intensity elements

SECTION 8. CONCLUSION

This part of the book provides the protocol-level specification of the minimal conventions needed to ensure that X Version 11 clients can interoperate properly. A further document is required, specifically a *Window and Session Manager Conventions Manual* to cover these conventions from the opposite point of view and to add extra conventions of interest to window and session manager implementors.

Part IV. X Logical Font Descriptions

Version 1.4

SECTION 1. INTRODUCTION

It is a requirement that X client applications must be portable across server implementations, with very different file systems, naming conventions, and font libraries. However, font access requests, as defined by part II, "X Window System Protocol," neither specify server-independent conventions for font names nor provide adequate font properties for logically describing typographic fonts.

X clients must be able to dynamically determine the fonts available on any given server so that understandable information can be presented to the user or that intelligent font fallbacks can be chosen. It is desirable for the most common queries to be accomplished without the overhead of opening each font and inspecting font properties, by means of simple `ListFonts` requests. For example, if a user selected a Helvetica typeface family, a client application should be able to query the server for all Helvetica fonts and present only those setwidths, weights, slants, point sizes, and character sets available for that family.

This part of the book gives a standard logical font description (hereafter referred to as XLFD) and the conventions to be used in the core protocol so that clients can query and access screen type libraries in a consistent manner across all X servers. In addition to completely specifying a given font by means of its `FontName`, the XLFD also provides for a standard set of key `FontProperties` that describe the font in more detail.

The XLFD provides an adequate set of typographic font properties, such as CAP_HEIGHT, X_HEIGHT, RELATIVE_SETWIDTH, for publishing and other applications to do intelligent font matching or substitution when handling documents created on some foreign server that use potentially unknown fonts.

In addition, this information is required by certain clients to position subscripts automatically and determine small capital heights, recommended leading, word-space values, and so on.

SECTION 2. REQUIREMENTS AND GOALS

The XLFD meets the short and long-term goals to have a standard logical font description that:

- Provides unique, descriptive font names that support simple pattern matching
- Supports multiple font vendors, arbitrary character sets, and encodings
- Supports naming and instancing of scalable fonts
- Is independent of X server and operating or file system implementations
- Supports arbitrarily complex font matching or substitution
- Is extensible

2.1 Provide Unique and Descriptive Font Names

It should be possible to have font names that are long enough and descriptive enough to have a reasonable probability of being unique without inventing a new registration organization. Resolution and size-dependent font masters, multivendor font libraries, and so on must be anticipated and handled by the font name alone.

The name itself should be structured to be amenable to simple pattern matching and parsing, thus, allowing X clients to restrict font queries to some subset of all possible fonts in the server.

2.2 Support Multiple Font Vendors and Character Sets

The font name and properties should distinguish between fonts that were supplied by different font vendors but that possibly share the same name. We anticipate a highly competitive font market where users will be able to buy fonts from many sources according to their particular requirements.

A number of font vendors deliver each font with all glyphs designed for that font, where charset mappings are defined by encoding vectors. Some server implementations may force these mappings to proprietary or standard charsets statically in the font data. Others may desire to perform the mapping dynamically in the server. Provisions must be made in the font name that allows a font request to specify or identify specific charset mappings in server environments where multiple charsets are supported.

2.3 Support Scalable Fonts

If a font source can be scaled to an arbitrary size, it should be possible for an application to determine that fact from the font name, and the application should be able to construct a font name for any specific size.

2.4 Be Independent of X Server and Operating or File System Implementations

X client applications that require a particular font should be able to use the descriptive name without knowledge of the file system or other repository in use by the server. However, it should be possible for servers to translate a given font name into a file name syntax that it knows how to deal with, without compromising the uniqueness of the font name. This algorithm should be reversible (exactly how this translation is done is implementation dependent).

2.5 Support Arbitrarily Complex Font Matching and Substitution

In addition to the font name, the XLFD should define a standard list of descriptive font properties, with agreed upon fallbacks for all fonts. This allows client applications to derive font-specific formatting or display data and to perform font matching or substitution when asked to handle potentially unknown fonts, as required.

2.6 Be Extensible

The XLFD must be extensible so that new and/or private descriptive font properties can be added to conforming fonts without making existing X client or server implementations obsolete.

SECTION 3. X Logical Font Description

XLFD is divided into two basic components: the `FontName`, which gives all font information needed to uniquely identify a font in X protocol requests (for example, `OpenFont`, `ListFonts`, and so on) and a variable list of optional `FontProperties`, which describe a font in more detail.

The `FontName` is used in font queries and is returned as data in certain X protocol requests. It is also specified as the data value for the `FONT` item in the

X Consortium Character Bitmap Distribution Format Standard (BDF V2.1—see appendix H).

The `FontProperties` are supplied on a font-by-font basis and are returned as data in certain X protocol requests as part of the `XFontStruct` data structure. The names and associated data values for each of the `FontProperties` may also appear as items of the STARTPROPERTIES. . .ENDPROPERTIES list in the BDF V2.1 specification.

3.1 FontName

Each `FontName` is logically composed of two strings: a `FontNameRegistry` prefix that is followed by a `FontNameSuffix`. The `FontNameRegistry` is an x-registered-name (a name that has been registered with the X Consortium) that identifies the registration authority that owns the specified `FontNameSuffix` syntax and semantics.

All font names that conform to this specification are to use a `FontNameRegistry` prefix, which is defined to be the string "–" (that is, ISO 8859-1 HYPHEN - Column/Row 02/13). All `FontNameRegistry` prefixes of the form: *+version–*, where the specified version indicates some future XLFD specification, are reserved by the X Consortium for future extensions to XLFD font names. If required, extensions to the current XLFD font name shall be constructed by appending new fields to the current structure, each delimited by the existing field delimiter. The availability of other `FontNameRegistry` prefixes or fonts that support other registries is server implementation dependent.

In the X protocol specification, the `FontName` is required to be a string; hence, numeric field values are represented in the name as string equivalents. All `FontNameSuffix` fields are also defined as `FontProperties`; numeric property values are represented as signed or unsigned integers, as appropriate.

3.1.1 FontName Syntax

The `FontName` is a structured, parsable string (of type STRING8) whose Backus-Naur Form syntax description is as follows:

FontName ::=	XFontNameRegistry XFontNameSuffix | PrivFontNameRegistry PrivFontNameSuffix
XFontNameRegistry ::=	XFNDelim | XFNExtPrefix Version XFNDelim

XFontNameSuffix ::=	FOUNDRY XFNDelim FAMILY_NAME XFNDelim WEIGHT_NAME XFNDelim SLANT XFNDelim SETWIDTH_NAME XFNDelim ADD_ STYLE_NAME XFNDelim PIXEL_SIZE XFNDelim POINT_SIZE XFNDelim RESOLUTION_X XFNDelim RESOLUTION_Y XFNDelim SPACING XFNDelim AVERAGE_WIDTH XFNDelim CHARSET_REGISTRY XFNDelim CHARSET_ENCODING
Version ::=	STRING8 – the XLFD version that defines an extension to the font name syntax (for example, "1.4")
XFNExtPrefix ::=	OCTET – the value of ISO8859-1 PLUS (Column/Row 02/11)
XFNDelim ::=	OCTET – the value of ISO8859-1 HYPHEN (Column/Row 02/13)
PrivFontNameRegistry ::=	STRING8 – other than those strings reserved by XLFD
PrivFontNameSuffix ::=	STRING8

Field values are constructed as strings of ISO8859-1 graphic characters, excluding the following:

- HYPHEN (02/13), the XLFD font name delimiter character
- QUESTION MARK (03/15) and ASTERISK (02/10), the X protocol fontname wildcard characters

Alphabetic case distinctions are allowed but are for human readability concerns only. Conforming X servers will perform matching on font name query or open requests independent of case. The entire font name string must have no more than 255 characters. It is recommended that clients construct font name query patterns by explicitly including all field delimiters to avoid unexpected results. Note that SPACE is a valid character of a `FontName` field; for example, the string "ITC Avant Garde Gothic" might be a FAMILY_NAME.

3.1.2 FontName Field Definitions

This section discusses the `FontName`:

- FOUNDRY field
- FAMILY_NAME field
- WEIGHT_NAME field
- SLANT field
- SETWIDTH_NAME field

- ADD_STYLE_NAME field
- PIXEL_SIZE field
- POINT_SIZE field
- RESOLUTION_X and RESOLUTION_Y fields
- SPACING field
- AVERAGE_WIDTH field
- CHARSET_REGISTRY and CHARSET_ENCODING fields

3.1.2.1 FOUNDRY Field

FOUNDRY is an x-registered-name, the name or identifier of the digital type foundry that digitized and supplied the font data, or if different, the identifier of the organization that last modified the font shape or metric information.

The reason this distinction is necessary is that a given font design may be licensed from one source (for example, ITC) but digitized and sold by any number of different type suppliers. Each digital version of the original design, in general, will be somewhat different in metrics and shape from the idealized original font data, because each font foundry, for better or for worse, has its own standards and practices for tweaking a typeface for a particular generation of output technologies or has its own perception of market needs.

It is up to the type supplier to register with the X Consortium a suitable name for this `FontName` field according to the registration procedures defined by the Consortium.

The X Consortium shall define procedures for registering foundry and other names and shall maintain and publish, as part of its public distribution, a registry of such registered names for use in XLFD font names and properties.

3.1.2.2 FAMILY_NAME Field

FAMILY_NAME is a string that identifies the range or family of typeface designs that are all variations of one basic typographic style. This must be spelled out in full, with words separated by spaces, as required. This name must be human-understandable and suitable for presentation to a font user to identify the typeface family.

It is up to the type supplier to supply and maintain a suitable string for this field and font property, to secure the proper legal title to a given name, and to guard against the infringement of other's copyrights or trademarks. By convention, FAMILY_NAME is not translated. FAMILY_NAME may include an indication of design ownership if considered a valid part of the typeface family name.

The following are examples of FAMILY_NAME:

- Helvetica
- ITC Avant Garde Gothic
- Times
- Times Roman
- Bitstream Amerigo
- Stone

3.1.2.3 WEIGHT_NAME Field

WEIGHT_NAME is a string that identifies the font's typographic weight, that is, the nominal blackness of the font, according to the FOUNDRY's judgment. This name must be human-understandable and suitable for presentation to a font user.

The interpretation of this field is somewhat problematic because the typographic judgment of weight has traditionally depended on the overall design of the typeface family in question; that is, it is possible that the DemiBold weight of one font could be almost equivalent in typographic feel to a Bold font from another family.

WEIGHT_NAME is captured as an arbitrary string because it is an important part of a font's complete human-understandable name. However, it should not be used for font matching or substitution. For this purpose, X client applications should use the weight-related font properties (RELATIVE_WEIGHT and WEIGHT) that give the coded relative weight and the calculated weight, respectively.

3.1.2.4 SLANT Field

SLANT is a code-string that indicates the overall posture of the typeface design used in the font. The encoding is as follows:

Code	*English Translation*	*Description*
"R"	Roman	Upright design
"I"	Italic	Italic design, slanted clockwise from the vertical
"O"	Oblique	Obliqued upright design, slanted clockwise from the vertical
"RI"	Reverse Italic	Italic design, slanted counterclockwise from the vertical
"RO"	Reverse Oblique	Obliqued upright design, slanted counterclockwise from the vertical
"OT"	Other	Other

The SLANT codes are for programming convenience only and usually are converted into their equivalent human-understandable form before being presented to a user.

3.1.2.5 SETWIDTH_NAME Field

SETWIDTH_NAME is a string that gives the font's typographic proportionate width, that is, the nominal width per horizontal unit of the font, according to the FOUNDRY's judgment.

As with WEIGHT_NAME, the interpretation of this field or font property is somewhat problematic, because the designer's judgment of setwidth has traditionally depended on the overall design of the typeface family in question. For purposes of font matching or substitution, X client applications should either use the RELATIVE_SETWIDTH font property that gives the relative coded proportionate width or calculate the proportionate width.

The following are examples of SETWIDTH_NAME:

- Normal
- Condensed
- Narrow
- Double Wide

3.1.2.6 ADD_STYLE_NAME Field

ADD_STYLE_NAME is a string that identifies additional typographic style information that is not captured by other fields but is needed to identify the particular font.

ADD_STYLE_NAME is not a typeface classification field and is only used for uniqueness. Its use, as such, is not limited to typographic style distinctions.

The following are examples of ADD_STYLE_NAME:

- Serif
- Sans Serif
- Informal
- Decorated

3.1.2.7 PIXEL_SIZE Field

PIXEL_SIZE is an unsigned integer-string typographic metric in device pixels that gives the body size of the font at a particular POINT_SIZE and RESOLUTION_Y. PIXEL_SIZE usually incorporates additional vertical spacing that is considered part of the font design. (Note, however, that this value is not necessarily equivalent to the height of the font bounding box.) PIXEL_SIZE is in the range zero to a very large number. Zero is used to indicate a scalable font; see section 4.

PIXEL_SIZE usually is used by X client applications that need to query fonts according to device-dependent size, regardless of the point size or vertical resolution for which the font was designed.

3.1.2.8 POINT_SIZE Field

POINT_SIZE is an unsigned integer-string typographic metric in device-independent units that gives the body size for which the font was designed. This field usually incorporates additional vertical spacing that is considered part of the font design. (Note, however, that POINT_SIZE is not necessarily equivalent to the height of the font bounding box.) POINT_SIZE is expressed in decipoints (where points are as defined in the X protocol or 72.27 points equal 1 inch) in the range zero to a very large number. Zero is used to indicate a scalable font; see section 4.

POINT_SIZE and RESOLUTION_Y are used by X clients to query fonts according to device-independent size to maintain constant text size on the display regardless of the PIXEL_SIZE used for the font.

3.1.2.9 RESOLUTION_X and RESOLUTION_Y Fields

RESOLUTION_X and RESOLUTION_Y are unsigned integer-strings that give the horizontal and vertical resolution, measured in pixels or dots per inch (dpi), for which the font was designed. Horizontal and vertical values are required because a separate bitmap font must be designed for displays with very different aspect ratios (for example, 1:1, 4:3, 2:1, and so on).

The separation of pixel or point size and resolution is necessary because X allows for servers with very different video characteristics (for example, horizontal and vertical resolution, screen and pixel size, pixel shape, and so on) to potentially access the same font library. The font name, for example, must differentiate between a 14 point font designed for 75 dpi (body size of about 14 pixels) or a 14 point font designed for 150 dpi (body size of about 28 pixels). Further, in servers that implement some or all fonts as continuously scaled and scan-converted outlines, POINT_SIZE and RESOLUTION_Y will help the server to differentiate between potentially separate font masters for text, title, and display sizes or for other typographic considerations.

3.1.2.10 SPACING Field

SPACING is a code-string that indicates the escapement class of the font, that is, monospace (fixed pitch), proportional (variable pitch), or charcell (a special monospaced font that conforms to the traditional data processing character cell font model). The encoding is as follows:

Code	*English Translation*	*Description*
"P"	Proportional	A font whose logical character widths vary for each glyph. Note that no other restrictions are placed on the metrics of a proportional font.
"M"	Monospaced	A font whose logical character widths are constant (that is, every glyph in the font has the same logical width). No other restrictions are placed on the metrics of a monospaced font.
"C"	CharCell	A monospaced font that follows the standard typewriter character cell model (that is, the glyphs of the font can be modeled by X clients as "boxes" of the same width and height that are imaged side-by-side to form text strings or top-to-bottom to form text lines. By definition, all glyphs have the same logical character width, and no glyphs have "ink" outside of the character cell. There is no kerning (that is, on a per character basis with positive metrics: 0 ≤ left-bearing ≤ right-bearing ≤ width; with negative metrics: width

Code	*English Translation*	*Description*
		≤ left-bearing ≤ right-bearing ≤ zero). Also, the vertical extents of the font do not exceed the vertical spacing (that is, on a per character basis: ascent ≤ font-ascent and descent ≤ font-descent). The cell height = font-descent + font-ascent, and the width = AVERAGE_WIDTH.

3.1.2.11 AVERAGE_WIDTH Field

AVERAGE_WIDTH is an unsigned integer-string typographic metric value that gives the unweighted arithmetic mean width of all glyphs in the font (measured in tenths of pixels). For monospaced and character cell fonts, this is the width of all glyphs in the font. AVERAGE_WIDTH has a range from zero to a very large number. Zero is used to indicate a scalable font; see section 4.

3.1.2.12 CHARSET_REGISTRY and CHARSET_ENCODING Fields

The character set used to encode the glyphs of the font (and implicitly the font's glyph repertoire), as maintained by the X Consortium character set registry. CHARSET_REGISTRY is an x-registered-name that identifies the registration authority that owns the specified encoding. CHARSET_ENCODING is a registered-name that identifies the coded character set as defined by that registration authority.

Although the X protocol does not explicitly have any knowledge about character set encodings, it is expected that server implementers will prefer to embed knowledge of certain proprietary or standard charsets into their font library for reasons of performance and convenience. The CHARSET_REGISTRY and CHARSET_ENCODING fields or properties allow an X client font request to specify a specific charset mapping in server environments where multiple charsets are supported. The availability of any particular character set is font and server implementation dependent.

To prevent collisions when defining character set names, it is recommended that CHARSET_REGISTRY and CHARSET_ENCODING name pairs be constructed according to the following conventions:

CharsetRegistry ::=	StdCharsetRegistryName | PrivCharsetRegistry-Name

CharsetEncoding ::=	StdCharsetEncodingName | PrivCharsetEncoding-Name
StdCharsetRegistryName ::=	StdOrganizationId StdNumber | StdOrganizationId StdNumber Dot Year
PrivCharsetRegistryName ::=	OrganizationId STRING8
StdCharsetEncodingName ::=	STRING8–numeric part number of referenced standard
PrivCharsetEncodingName ::=	STRING8
StdOrganizationId ::=	STRING8–the registered name or acronym of the referenced standard organization
StdNumber ::=	STRING8–referenced standard number
OrganizationId ::=	STRING8–the registered name or acronym of the organization
Dot ::=	"."–ISO 8859-1 FULL STOP (Column/Row 2/14)
Year ::=	STRING8–numeric year (for example, 1989)

The X Consortium shall maintain and publish a registry of such character set names for use in X protocol font names and properties as specified in XLFD (see also appendix G, "X Consortium Standard Character Set Names").

The ISO Latin-1 character set shall be registered by the X Consortium as the CHARSET_REGISTRY-CHARSET_ENCODING value pair: "ISO8859-1".

3.1.3 Examples

The following examples of font names are derived from the screen fonts shipped with the MIT X distribution.

Font	*XFontName*
75 dpi Fonts	
Charter 12 pt	-Bitstream-Charter-Medium-R-Normal–12-120-75-75-P-68-ISO8859-1
Charter Bold 12 pt	-Bitstream-Charter-Bold-R-Normal–12-120-75-75-P-76-ISO8859-1
Charter Bold Italic 12 pt	-Bitstream-Charter-Bold-I-Normal–12-120-75-75-P-75-ISO8859-1
Charter Italic 12 pt	-Bitstream-Charter-Medium-I-Normal–12-120-75-75-P-66-ISO8859-1
Courier 8 pt	-Adobe-Courier-Medium-R-Normal–8-80-75-75-M-50-ISO8859-1
Courier 10 pt	-Adobe-Courier-Medium-R-Normal–10-100-75-75-M-60-ISO8859-1

Font	*XFontName*
Courier 12 pt	-Adobe-Courier-Medium-R-Normal–12-120-75-75-M-70-ISO8859-1
Courier 14 pt	-Adobe-Courier-Medium-R-Normal–14-140-75-75-M-90-ISO8859-1
Courier 18 pt	-Adobe-Courier-Medium-R-Normal–18-180-75-75-M-110-ISO8859-1
Courier 24 pt	-Adobe-Courier-Medium-R-Normal–24-240-75-75-M-150-ISO8859-1
Courier Bold 10 pt	-Adobe-Courier-Bold-R-Normal–10-100-75-75-M-60-ISO8859-1
Courier Bold Oblique 10 pt	-Adobe-Courier-Bold-O-Normal–10-100-75-75-M-60-ISO8859-1
Courier Oblique 10 pt	-Adobe-Courier-Medium-O-Normal–10-100-75-75-M-60-ISO8859-1
100 dpi Fonts	
Symbol 8 pt	-Adobe-Symbol-Medium-R-Normal–11-80-100-100-P-61-Adobe-FONTSPECIFIC
Symbol 10 pt	-Adobe-Symbol-Medium-R-Normal–14-100-100-100-P-85-Adobe-FONTSPECIFIC
Symbol 12 pt	-Adobe-Symbol-Medium-R-Normal–17-120-100-100-P-95-Adobe-FONTSPECIFIC
Symbol 14 pt	-Adobe-Symbol-Medium-R-Normal–20-140-100-100-P-107-Adobe-FONTSPECIFIC
Symbol 18 pt	-Adobe-Symbol-Medium-R-Normal–25-180-100-100-P-142-Adobe-FONTSPECIFIC
Symbol 24 pt	-Adobe-Symbol-Medium-R-Normal–34-240-100-100-P-191-Adobe-FONTSPECIFIC
Times Bold 10 pt	-Adobe-Times-Bold-R-Normal–14-100-100-100-P-76-ISO8859-1
Times Bold Italic 10 pt	-Adobe-Times-Bold-I-Normal–14-100-100-100-P-77-ISO8859-1
Times Italic 10 pt	-Adobe-Times-Medium-I-Normal–14-100-100-100-P-73-ISO8859-1
Times Roman 10 pt	-Adobe-Times-Medium-R-Normal–14-100-100-100-P-74-ISO8859-1

3.2 Font Properties

All font properties are optional but will generally include the font name fields and, on a font-by-font basis, any other useful font descriptive and use information that may be required to use the font intelligently. The XLFD specifies an extensive set of standard X font properties, their interpretation, and fallback rules when the property is not defined for a given font. The goal is to provide client applications with enough font information to be able to make automatic formatting and display decisions with good typographic results.

Additional standard X font property definitions may be defined in the future and private properties may exist in X fonts at any time. Private font properties should be defined to conform to the general mechanism defined in the X protocol to prevent overlap of name space and ambiguous property names, that is, private font property names are of the form: ISO8859-1 UNDERSCORE (Column/Row 05/15), followed by the organizational identifier, followed by UNDERSCORE, and terminated with the property name.

The Backus-Naur Form syntax description of X font properties is as follows:

Properties ::=	OptFontPropList
OptFontPropList ::=	NULL | OptFontProp OptFontPropList
OptFontProp ::=	PrivateFontProp | XFontProp
PrivateFontProp ::=	STRING8 | Underscore OrganizationId Underscore STRING8
XFontProp ::=	FOUNDRY | FAMILY_NAME | WEIGHT_NAME | SLANT | SETWIDTH_NAME | ADD_STYLE_NAME | PIXEL_SIZE | POINT_SIZE | RESOLUTION_X | RESOLUTION_Y | SPACING | AVERAGE_WIDTH | CHARSET_REGISTRY | CHARSET_ENCODING | QUAD_WIDTH | RESOLUTION | MIN_SPACE | NORM_SPACE | MAX_SPACE | END_SPACE | SUPERSCRIPT_X | SUPERSCRIPT_Y | SUBSCRIPT_X | SUBSCRIPT_Y | UNDERLINE_POSITION | UNDERLINE_THICKNESS | STRIKEOUT_ASCENT | STRIKEOUT_DESCENT | ITALIC_ANGLE | X_HEIGHT | WEIGHT | FACE_NAME | COPYRIGHT | AVG_CAPITAL_WIDTH | AVG_LOWERCASE_WIDTH | RELATIVE_SETWIDTH | RELATIVE_WEIGHT | CAP_HEIGHT | SUPERSCRIPT_ SIZE | FIGURE_WIDTH | SUBSCRIPT_SIZE | SMALL_CAP_SIZE | NOTICE | DESTINATION
Underscore ::=	OCTET–the value of ISO8859-1 UNDERSCORE character (Column/Row 05/15)
OrganizationId ::=	STRING8–the registered name of the organization

3.2.1 FOUNDRY

FOUNDRY is as defined in the `FontName` except that the property type is ATOM.

FOUNDRY cannot be calculated or defaulted if not supplied as a font property.

3.2.2 FAMILY_NAME

FAMILY_NAME is as defined in the `FontName` except that the property type is ATOM.

FAMILY_NAME cannot be calculated or defaulted if not supplied as a font property.

3.2.3 WEIGHT_NAME

WEIGHT_NAME is as defined in the `FontName` except that the property type is ATOM.

WEIGHT_NAME can be defaulted if not supplied as a font property, as follows:

```
if (WEIGHT_NAME undefined) then
  WEIGHT_NAME = ATOM(''Medium'')
```

3.2.4 SLANT

SLANT is as defined in the `FontName` except that the property type is ATOM.

SLANT can be defaulted if not supplied as a font property, as follows:

```
if (SLANT undefined) then
  SLANT = ATOM(''R'')
```

3.2.5 SETWIDTH_NAME

SETWIDTH_NAME is as defined in the `FontName` except that the property type is ATOM.

SETWIDTH_NAME can be defaulted if not supplied as a font property, as follows:

```
if (SETWIDTH_NAME undefined) then
  SETWIDTH_NAME = ATOM(''Normal'')
```

3.2.6 ADD_STYLE_NAME

ADD_STYLE_NAME is as defined in the `FontName` except that the property type is ATOM.

ADD_STYLE_NAME can be defaulted if not supplied as a font property, as follows:

```
if (ADD_STYLE_NAME undefined) then
  ADD_STYLE_NAME = ATOM("")
```

3.2.7 PIXEL_SIZE

PIXEL_SIZE is as defined in the `FontName` except that the property type is CARD32.

X clients requiring pixel values for the various typographic fixed spaces (em space, en space and thin space), can use the following algorithm for computing these values from other properties specified for a font:

```
DeciPointsPerInch = 722.7
EMspace = ROUND ((RESOLUTION_X * POINT_SIZE) /
          DeciPointsPerInch)
ENspace = ROUND (EMspace / 2)
THINspace = ROUND (EMspace / 3)
```

where a slash (/) denotes real division, the asterisk (*) denotes real multiplication, and ROUND denotes a function that rounds its real argument 'a' up or down to the next integer. This rounding is done according to X = FLOOR (a + 0.5), where FLOOR is a function that rounds its real argument down to the nearest integer.

PIXEL_SIZE can be approximated if not supplied as a font property, according to the following algorithm:

```
DeciPointsPerInch = 722.7
if (PIXEL_SIZE undefined) then
  PIXEL_SIZE = ROUND ((RESOLUTION_Y * POINT_SIZE) / DeciPointsPerInch)
```

3.2.8 POINT_SIZE

POINT_SIZE is as defined in the `FontName` except that the property type is CARD32.

X clients requiring device-independent values for em space, en space, and thin space can use the following algorithm:

EMspace = ROUND (POINT_SIZE / 10)
ENspace = ROUND (POINT_SIZE / 20)
THINspace = ROUND (POINT_SIZE / 30)

Design POINT_SIZE cannot be calculated or approximated.

3.2.9 RESOLUTION_X

RESOLUTION_X is as defined in the `FontName` except that the property type is CARD32.

RESOLUTION_X cannot be calculated or approximated.

3.2.10 RESOLUTION_Y

RESOLUTION_Y is as defined in the `FontName` except that the property type is CARD32.

RESOLUTION_X cannot be calculated or approximated.

3.2.11 SPACING

SPACING is as defined in the `FontName` except that the property type is ATOM.

SPACING can be calculated if not supplied as a font property, according to the definitions given above for the `FontName`.

3.2.12 AVERAGE_WIDTH

AVERAGE_WIDTH is as defined in the `FontName` except that the property type is CARD32.

AVERAGE_WIDTH can be calculated if not provided as a font property, according to the following algorithm:

```
if (AVERAGE_WIDTH undefined) then
  AVERAGE_WIDTH = ROUND (MEAN (all glyph widths in font) * 10)
```

where MEAN is a function that returns the arithmetic mean of its arguments.

X clients that require values for the number of characters per inch (pitch) of a monospaced font can use the following algorithm using the AVERAGE_WIDTH and RESOLUTION_X font properties:

```
if (SPACING not proportional) then
  CharPitch = (RESOLUTION_X * 10) / AVERAGE_WIDTH
```

3.2.13 CHARSET_REGISTRY

CHARSET_REGISTRY is as defined in the `FontName` except that the property type is ATOM.

CHARSET_REGISTRY cannot be defaulted if not supplied as a font property.

3.2.14 CHARSET_ENCODING

CHARSET_ENCODING is as defined in the `FontName` except that the property type is ATOM.

CHARSET_ENCODING cannot be defaulted if not supplied as a font property.

3.2.15 MIN_SPACE

MIN_SPACE is an unsigned integer value (of type CARD32) that gives the recommended minimum word-space value to be used with this font.

MIN_SPACE can be approximated if not provided as a font property, according to the following algorithm:

```
if (MIN_SPACE undefined) then
  MIN_SPACE = ROUND(0.75 * NORM_SPACE)
```

3.2.16 NORM_SPACE

NORM_SPACE is an unsigned integer value (of type CARD32) that gives the recommended normal word-space value to be used with this font.

NORM_SPACE can be approximated if not provided as a font property, according to the following algorithm:

```
DeciPointsPerInch = 722.7
if (NORM_SPACE undefined) then
  if (SPACE glyph exists) then
    NORM_SPACE = width of SPACE
  else NORM_SPACE =
      ROUND((0.33 * RESOLUTION_X * POINT_SIZE) / DeciPointsPerInch)
```

3.2.17 MAX_SPACE

MAX_SPACE is an unsigned integer value (of type CARD32) that gives the recommended maximum word-space value to be used with this font.

MAX_SPACE can be approximated if not provided as a font property, according to the following algorithm:

```
if (MAX_SPACE undefined) then
  MAX_SPACE = ROUND(1.5 * NORM_SPACE)
```

3.2.18 END_SPACE

END_SPACE is an unsigned integer value (of type CARD32) that gives the recommended spacing at the end of sentences.

END_SPACE can be approximated if not provided as a font property, according to the following algorithm:

```
if (END_SPACE undefined) then
  END_SPACE = NORM_SPACE
```

3.2.19 AVG_CAPITAL_WIDTH

AVG_CAPITAL_WIDTH is an integer value (of type INT32) that gives the unweighted arithmetic mean width of all the capital glyphs in the font, in tenths of pixels (applies to Latin and non-Latin fonts). For Latin fonts, capitals are the glyphs A through Z. This property is usually used for font matching or substitution.

AVG_CAPITAL_WIDTH can be calculated if not provided as a font property, according to the following algorithm:

```
if (AVG_CAPITAL_WIDTH undefined) then
  AVG_CAPITAL_WIDTH = ROUND (MEAN (capital glyph widths) * 10)
```

3.2.20 AVG_LOWERCASE_WIDTH

AVG_LOWERCASE_WIDTH is an integer value (of type INT32) that gives the unweighted arithmetic mean width of all the lowercase glyphs in the font in tenths of pixels. For Latin fonts, lowercase are the glyphs a through z. This property is usually used for font matching or substitution.

Where appropriate, AVG_LOWERCASE_WIDTH can be approximated if not provided as a font property, according to the following algorithm:

```
if (AVG_LOWERCASE_WIDTH undefined) then
  if (lowercase exists) then
    AVG_LOWERCASE_WIDTH = ROUND (MEAN (lowercase glyph widths) * 10)
  else AVG_LOWERCASE_WIDTH undefined
```

3.2.21 QUAD_WIDTH

QUAD_WIDTH is an integer typographic metric (of type INT32) that gives the width of a quad (em) space.

Note Because all typographic fixed spaces (em, en, and thin) are constant for a given font size (that is, they do not vary according to setwidth), the use of this font property has been deprecated. X clients that require typographic fixed space values are encouraged to discontinue use of QUAD_WIDTH and compute these values from other font properties (for example, PIXEL_SIZE). X clients that require a font-dependent width value should use either the FIGURE_WIDTH or one of the average character width font properties (AVERAGE_WIDTH, AVG_CAPITAL_WIDTH or AVG_LOWERCASE_WIDTH).

3.2.22 FIGURE_WIDTH

FIGURE_WIDTH is an integer typographic metric (of type INT32) that gives the width of the tabular figures and the dollar sign, if suitable for tabular setting (all widths equal). For Latin fonts, these tabular figures are the arabic numerals 0 through 9.

FIGURE_WIDTH can be approximated if not supplied as a font property, according to the following algorithm:

```
if (numerals and DOLLAR sign are defined & widths are equal) then
  FIGURE_WIDTH = width of DOLLAR
else FIGURE_WIDTH property undefined
```

3.2.23 SUPERSCRIPT_X

SUPERSCRIPT_X is an integer value (of type INT32) that gives the recommended horizontal offset in pixels from the position point to the X origin of synthetic superscript text. If the current position point is at [X,Y], then superscripts should begin at [X + SUPERSCRIPT_X, Y – SUPERSCRIPT_Y].

SUPERSCRIPT_X can be approximated if not provided as a font property, according to the following algorithm:

```
if (SUPERSCRIPT_X undefined) then
  if (TANGENT(ITALIC_ANGLE) defined) then
    SUPERSCRIPT_X = ROUND((0.40 * CAP_HEIGHT) / TANGENT(ITALIC_ANGLE))
  else SUPERSCRIPT_X = ROUND(0.40 * CAP_HEIGHT)
```

where TANGENT is a trigonometric function that returns the tangent of its argument (in degrees scaled by 64).

3.2.24 SUPERSCRIPT_Y

SUPERSCRIPT_Y is an integer value (of type INT32) that gives the recommended vertical offset in pixels from the position point to the Y origin of synthetic superscript text. If the current position point is at [X,Y], then superscripts should begin at [X + SUPERSCRIPT_X, Y – SUPERSCRIPT_Y].

SUPERSCRIPT_Y can be approximated if not provided as a font property, according to the following algorithm:

```
if (SUPERSCRIPT_Y undefined) then
  SUPERSCRIPT_Y = ROUND(0.40 * CAP_HEIGHT)
```

3.2.25 SUBSCRIPT_X

SUBSCRIPT_X is an integer value (of type INT32) that gives the recommended horizontal offset in pixels from the position point to the X origin of synthetic subscript text. If the current position point is at [X,Y], then subscripts should begin at [X + SUBSCRIPT_X, Y + SUBSCRIPT_Y].

SUBSCRIPT_X can be approximated if not provided as a font property, according to the following algorithm:

```
if (SUBSCRIPT_X undefined) then
  if (TANGENT(ITALIC_ANGLE) defined) then
    SUBSCRIPT_X = ROUND((0.40 * CAP_HEIGHT) / TANGENT(ITALIC_ANGLE))
  else SUBSCRIPT_X = ROUND(0.40 * CAP_HEIGHT)
```

3.2.26 SUBSCRIPT_Y

SUBSCRIPT_Y is an integer value (of type INT32) that gives the recommended vertical offset in pixels from the position point to the Y origin of synthetic subscript text. If the current position point is at [X,Y], then subscripts should begin at [X + SUBSCRIPT_X, Y + SUBSCRIPT_Y].

SUBSCRIPT_Y can be approximated if not provided as a font property, according to the following algorithm:

```
if (SUBSCRIPT_Y undefined) then
  SUBSCRIPT_Y = ROUND(0.40 * CAP_HEIGHT)
```

3.2.27 SUPERSCRIPT_SIZE

SUPERSCRIPT_SIZE is an unsigned integer value (of type CARD32) that gives the recommended body size of synthetic superscripts to be used with this font, in pixels. This will generally be smaller than the size of the current font; that is, superscripts are imaged from a smaller font offset according to SUPERSCRIPT_X and SUPERSCRIPT_Y.

SUPERSCRIPT_SIZE can be approximated if not provided as a font property, according to the following algorithm:

```
if (SUPERSCRIPT_SIZE undefined) then
  SUPERSCRIPT_SIZE = ROUND(0.60 * PIXEL_SIZE)
```

3.2.28 SUBSCRIPT_SIZE

SUBSCRIPT_SIZE is an unsigned integer value (of type CARD32) that gives the recommended body size of synthetic subscripts to be used with this font, in pixels. As with SUPERSCRIPT_SIZE, this will generally be smaller than the size of the current font; that is, subscripts are imaged from a smaller font offset according to SUBSCRIPT_X and SUBSCRIPT_Y.

SUBSCRIPT_SIZE can be approximated if not provided as a font property, according to the algorithm:

```
if (SUBSCRIPT_SIZE undefined) then
  SUBSCRIPT_SIZE = ROUND(0.60 * PIXEL_SIZE)
```

3.2.29 SMALL_CAP_SIZE

SMALL_CAP_SIZE is an unsigned integer value (of type CARD32) that gives the recommended body size of synthetic small capitals to be used with this font, in pixels. Small capitals are generally imaged from a smaller font of slightly more weight. No offset [X,Y] is necessary.

SMALL_CAP_SIZE can be approximated if not provided as a font property, according to the following algorithm:

```
if (SMALL_CAP_SIZE undefined) then
  SMALL_CAP_SIZE = ROUND(PIXEL_SIZE * ((X_HEIGHT
                          + ((CAP_HEIGHT - X_HEIGHT) / 3)) / CAP_HEIGHT))
```

3.2.30 UNDERLINE_POSITION

UNDERLINE_POSITION is an unsigned integer value (of type CARD32) that gives the recommended vertical offset in pixels from the baseline to the top of the underline. If the current position point is at [X,Y], the top of the baseline is given by [X, Y+ UNDERLINE_POSITION].

UNDERLINE_POSITION can be approximated if not provided as a font property, according to the following algorithm:

```
if (UNDERLINE_POSITION undefined) then
  UNDERLINE_POSITION = ROUND((maximum descent) / 2)
```

where maximum descent is the maximum descent (below the baseline) in pixels of any glyph in the font.

3.2.31 UNDERLINE_THICKNESS

UNDERLINE_POSITION is an unsigned integer value (of type CARD32) that gives the recommended underline thickness, in pixels.

UNDERLINE_THICKNESS can be approximated if not provided as a font property, according to the following algorithm:

```
CapStemWidth = average width of the stems of capitals
if (UNDERLINE_THICKNESS undefined) then
  UNDERLINE_THICKNESS = CapStemWidth
```

3.2.32 STRIKEOUT_ASCENT

STRIKEOUT_ASCENT is an integer value (of type INT32) that gives the vertical ascent for boxing or voiding glyphs in this font. If the current position is at [X,Y] and the string extent is EXTENT, the upper-left corner of the strikeout box is at [X, Y – STRIKEOUT_ASCENT] and the lower-right corner of the box is at [X + EXTENT, Y+ STRIKEOUT_DESCENT].

STRIKEOUT_ASCENT can be approximated if not provided as a font property, according to the following algorithm:

```
if (STRIKEOUT_ASCENT undefined)
  STRIKEOUT_ASCENT = maximum ascent
```

where maximum ascent is the maximum ascent (above the baseline) in pixels of any glyph in the font.

3.2.33 STRIKEOUT_DESCENT

STRIKEOUT_DESCENT is an integer value (of type INT32) that gives the vertical descent for boxing or voiding glyphs in this font. If the current position is at [X,Y] and the string extent is EXTENT, the upper-left corner of the strikeout box is at [X, Y – STRIKEOUT_ASCENT] and the lower-right corner of the box is at [X + EXTENT, Y + STRIKEOUT_DESCENT].

STRIKEOUT_DESCENT can be approximated if not provided as a font property, according to the following algorithm:

```
if (STRIKEOUT_DESCENT undefined)
  STRIKEOUT_DESCENT = maximum descent
```

where maximum descent is the maximum descent (below the baseline) in pixels of any glyph in the font.

3.2.34 ITALIC_ANGLE

ITALIC_ANGLE is an integer value (of type INT32) that gives the nominal posture angle of the typeface design, in 1/64 degrees, measured from the glyph origin counterclockwise from the three o'clock position.

ITALIC_ANGLE can be defaulted if not provided as a font property, according to the following algorithm:

```
if (ITALIC_ANGLE undefined) then
  ITALIC_ANGLE = (90 * 64)
```

3.2.35 CAP_HEIGHT

CAP_HEIGHT is an unsigned integer value (of type CARD32) that gives the nominal height of the capital letters contained in the font, as specified by the

FOUNDRY or typeface designer. Where applicable, it is defined to be the height of the Latin uppercase letter *X*.

Certain clients require CAP_HEIGHT to compute scale factors and positioning offsets for synthesized glyphs where this information or designed glyphs are not explicitly provided by the font (for example, small capitals, superiors, inferiors, and so on). CAP_HEIGHT is also a critical factor in font matching and substitution.

CAP_HEIGHT can be approximated if not provided as a font property, according to the following algorithm:

```
if (CAP_HEIGHT undefined) then
  if (latin font) then
    CAP_HEIGHT = XCharStruct.ascent[glyph X]
  else if (capitals exist) then
    CAP_HEIGHT = XCharStruct.ascent[some capital glyph]
  else CAP_HEIGHT undefined
```

3.2.36 X_HEIGHT

X_HEIGHT is an unsigned integer value (of type CARD32) that gives the nominal height above the baseline of the lowercase glyphs contained in the font, as specified by the FOUNDRY or typeface designer. Where applicable, it is defined to be the height of the Latin lowercase letter *x*.

As with CAP_HEIGHT, X_HEIGHT is required by certain clients to compute scale factors for synthesized small capitals where this information is not explicitly provided by the font resource. X_HEIGHT is a critical factor in font matching and substitution.

X_HEIGHT can be approximated if not provided as a font property, according to the following algorithm:

```
if (X_HEIGHT undefined) then
  if (latin font) then
    X_HEIGHT = XCharStruct.ascent[glyph x]
  else if (lowercase exists) then
    X_HEIGHT = XCharStruct.ascent[some lowercase glyph]
  else X_HEIGHT is undefined
```

3.2.37 RELATIVE_SETWIDTH

RELATIVE_SETWIDTH is an unsigned integer value (of type CARD32) that gives the coded proportionate width of the font, relative to all known fonts of the same typeface family, according to the type designer's or FOUNDRY's judgment.

The possible values are:

Code	*English Translation*	*Description*
0	Undefined	Undefined or unknown
10	UltraCondensed	The lowest ratio of average width to height
20	ExtraCondensed	
30	Condensed	Condensed, Narrow, Compressed, . . .
40	SemiCondensed	
50	Medium	Medium, Normal, Regular, . . .
60	SemiExpanded	SemiExpanded, DemiExpanded, . . .
70	Expanded	
80	ExtraExpanded	ExtraExpanded, Wide, . . .
90	UltraExpanded	The highest ratio of average width to height

RELATIVE_SETWIDTH can be defaulted if not provided as a font property, according to the following algorithm:

```
if (RELATIVE_SETWIDTH undefined) then
  RELATIVE_SETWIDTH = 50
```

X clients that want to obtain a calculated proportionate width of the font (that is, a font-independent way of identifying the proportionate width across all fonts and all font vendors) can use the following algorithm:

```
SETWIDTH = AVG_CAPITAL_WIDTH / (CAP_HEIGHT * 10)
```

where SETWIDTH is a real number with zero being the narrowest calculated setwidth.

3.2.38 RELATIVE_WEIGHT

RELATIVE_WEIGHT is an unsigned integer value (of type CARD32) that gives the coded weight of the font, relative to all known fonts of the same typeface family, according to the type designer's or FOUNDRY's judgment.

The possible values are:

Code	*English Translation*	*Description*
0	Undefined	Undefined or unknown

Code	*English Translation*	*Description*
10	UltraLight	The lowest ratio of stem width to height
20	ExtraLight	
30	Light	
40	SemiLight	SemiLight, Book, . . .
50	Medium	Medium, Normal, Regular, . . .
60	SemiBold	SemiBold, DemiBold, . . .
70	Bold	
80	ExtraBold	ExtraBold, Heavy, . . .
90	UltraBold	UltraBold, Black, . . ., the highest ratio of stem width to height

RELATIVE_WEIGHT can be defaulted if not provided as a font property, according to the following algorithm:

```
if (RELATIVE_WEIGHT undefined) then
  RELATIVE_WEIGHT = 50
```

3.2.39 WEIGHT

Calculated WEIGHT is an unsigned integer value (of type CARD32) that gives the calculated weight of the font, computed as the ratio of capital stem width to CAP_HEIGHT, in the range 0 to 1000, where 0 is the lightest weight.

WEIGHT can be calculated if not supplied as a font property, according to the following algorithm:

```
CapStemWidth = average width of the stems of capitals
if (WEIGHT undefined) then
  WEIGHT = ROUND ((CapStemWidth * 1000) / CAP_HEIGHT)
```

A calculated value for weight is necessary when matching fonts from different families because both the RELATIVE_WEIGHT and the WEIGHT_NAME are assigned by the typeface supplier, according to its tradition and practice, and therefore, are somewhat subjective. Calculated WEIGHT provides a font-independent way of identifying the weight across all fonts and all font vendors.

3.2.40 RESOLUTION

RESOLUTION is an integer value (of type INT32) that gives the resolution for which this font was created, measured in 1/100 pixels per point.

Note As independent horizontal and vertical design resolution components are required to accommodate displays with nonsquare aspect ratios, the use of this font property has been deprecated, and independent RESOLUTION_X and RESOLUTION_Y font name fields/properties have been defined (see sections 3.1.2.9 and 3.1.2.10). X clients are encouraged to discontinue use of the RESOLUTION property and are encouraged to use the appropriate X,Y resolution properties, as required.

3.2.41 FACE_NAME

FACE_NAME is a human-understandable string (of type ATOM) that gives the full device-independent typeface name, including the owner, weight, slant, set, and so on but not the resolution, size, and so on. This property may be used as feedback during font selection.

FACE_NAME cannot be calculated or approximated if not provided as a font property.

3.2.42 COPYRIGHT

COPYRIGHT is a human-understandable string (of type ATOM) that gives the copyright information of the legal owner of the digital font data.

This information is a required component of a font but is independent of the particular format used to represent it (that is, it cannot be captured as a comment that could later be thrown away for efficiency reasons).

COPYRIGHT cannot be calculated or approximated if not provided as a font property.

3.2.43 NOTICE

NOTICE is a human-understandable string (of type ATOM) that gives the copyright information of the legal owner of the font design or, if not applicable, the trademark information for the typeface FAMILY_NAME.

Typeface design and trademark protection laws vary from country to country, the USA having no design copyright protection currently while various countries in Europe offer both design and typeface family name trademark protection. As with COPYRIGHT, this information is a required component of a font but is independent of the particular format used to represent it.

NOTICE cannot be calculated or approximated if not provided as a font property.

3.2.44 DESTINATION

DESTINATION is an unsigned integer code (of type CARD32) that gives the font design destination, that is, whether it was designed as a screen proofing font to match printer font glyph widths (WYSIWYG), as an optimal video font (possibly with corresponding printer font) for extended screen viewing (video text), and so on.

The font design considerations are very different, and at current display resolutions, the readability and legibility of these two kinds of screen fonts are very different. DESTINATION allows publishing clients that use X to model the printed page and video text clients, such as on-line documentation browsers, to query for X screen fonts that suit their particular requirements.

The encoding is as follows:

Code	*English Translation*	*Description*
0	WYSIWYG	The font is optimized to match the typographic design and metrics of an equivalent printer font
1	Video text	The font is optimized for screen legibility and readability

3.3 Built-in Font Property Atoms

The following font property atom definitions were predefined in the initial version of the core protocol:

Font Property/Atom Name	*Property Type*
MIN_SPACE	CARD32
NORM_SPACE	CARD32
MAX_SPACE	CARD32
END_SPACE	CARD32
SUPERSCRIPT_X	INT32
SUPERSCRIPT_Y	INT32
SUBSCRIPT_X	INT32
SUBSCRIPT_Y	INT32
UNDERLINE_POSITION	INT32
UNDERLINE_THICKNESS	CARD32
STRIKEOUT_ASCENT	INT32
STRIKEOUT_DESCENT	INT32

Font Property/Atom Name	*Property Type*
FONT_ASCENT	INT32
FONT_DESCENT	INT32
FONT_ASCENT	INT32
FONT_DESCENT	INT32
ITALIC_ANGLE	INT32
X_HEIGHT	INT32
QUAD_WIDTH	INT32 – deprecated
WEIGHT	CARD32
POINT_SIZE	CARD32
RESOLUTION	CARD32 – deprecated
COPYRIGHT	ATOM
FULL_NAME	ATOM
FAMILY_NAME	ATOM
DEFAULT_CHAR	CARD32

SECTION 4. SCALABLE FONTS

The XLFD is designed to support scalable fonts. A scalable font is a font source from which instances of arbitrary size can be derived. A scalable font source might be one or more outlines together with zero or more hand-tuned bitmap fonts at specific sizes and resolutions, or it might be a programmatic description together with zero or more bitmap fonts or some other format (perhaps even just a single bitmap font).

The following definitions are useful for discussing scalable fonts:

- Well-formed XLFD pattern
  A pattern string containing 14 hyphens, one of which is the first character of the pattern. Wildcard characters are permitted in the fields of a well-formed XLFD pattern.
- Scalable font name
  A well-formed XLFD pattern containing no wildcards and containing the digit "0" in the PIXEL_SIZE, POINT_SIZE, and AVERAGE_WIDTH fields.
- Scalable fields
  The XLFD fields PIXEL_SIZE, POINT_SIZE, RESOLUTION_X, RESOLUTION_Y, and AVERAGE_WIDTH.
- Derived instance
  The result of replacing the scalable fields of a font name with values to yield a font name that could actually be produced from the font source. A scaling engine is permitted, but not required, to interpret the scalable fields in font names to support anamorphic scaling.

- Global list
  The list of names that would be returned by an X server for a `ListFonts` protocol request on the pattern "*" if there were no protocol restrictions on the total number of names returned.

The global list consists of font names derived from font sources. If a single font source can support multiple character sets (specified in the CHARSET_REGISTRY and CHARSET_ENCODING fields), each such character set should be used to form a separate font name in the list. For a nonscalable font source, the simple font name for each character set is included in the global list. For a scalable font source, a scalable font name for each character set is included in the list. In addition to the scalable font name, specific derived instance names may also be included in the list. The relative order of derived instances with respect to the scalable font name is not constrained. Finally, font name aliases may also be included in the list. The relative order of aliases with respect to the real font name is not constrained.

The values of the RESOLUTION_X and RESOLUTION_Y fields of a scalable font name are implementation dependent, but to maximize backward compatibility, they should be reasonable nonzero values, for example, a resolution close to that provided by the screen (in a single-screen server). Because some existing applications rely on seeing a collection of point and pixel sizes, server vendors are strongly encouraged in the near term to provide a mechanism for including, for each scalable font name, a set of specific, derived instance names. For font sources that contain a collection of hand-tuned bitmap fonts, including names of these instances in the global list is recommended and sufficient.

The X protocol request `OpenFont` on a scalable font name returns a font corresponding to an implementation dependent, derived instance of that font name.

The X protocol request `ListFonts` on a well-formed XLFD pattern returns the following. Starting with the global list, if the actual pattern argument has values containing no wildcards in scalable fields, then you should substitute each such field into the corresponding field in each scalable font name in the list. For each resulting font name, if the remaining scalable fields cannot be replaced with values to produce a derived instance, remove the font name from the list. Now take the modified list and perform a simple pattern match against the pattern argument. `ListFonts` returns the resulting list.

For example, given the global list:

-Linotype-Times-Bold-I-Normal--0-0-100-100-P-0-ISO8859-1
-Linotype-Times-Bold-R-Normal--0-0-100-100-P-0-ISO8859-1
-Linotype-Times-Medium-I-Normal--0-0-100-100-P-0-ISO8859-1
-Linotype-Times-Medium-R-Normal--0-0-100-100-P-0-ISO8859-1

a `ListFonts` request with the pattern:

-*-Times-*-R-Normal--*-120-100-100-P-*-ISO8859-1

would return:

-Linotype-Times-Bold-R-Normal--0-120-100-100-P-0-ISO8859-1
-Linotype-Times-Medium-R-Normal--0-120-100-100-P-0-ISO8859-1

`ListFonts` on a pattern containing wildcards that is not a well-formed XLFD pattern is only required to return the list obtained by performing a simple pattern match against the global list. X servers are permitted, but not required, to use a more sophisticated matching algorithm.

SECTION 5. AFFECTED ELEMENTS OF XLIB AND THE X PROTOCOL

The following X protocol requests must support the XLFD conventions:

- `OpenFont`—for the name argument
- `ListFonts`—for the pattern argument
- `ListFontsWithInfo`—for the pattern argument

In addition, the following Xlib functions must support the XLFD conventions:

- `XLoadFont`—for the name argument
- `XListFontsWithInfo`—for the pattern argument
- `XLoadQueryFont`—for the name argument
- `XListFonts`—for the pattern argument

SECTION 6. BDF CONFORMANCE

The bitmap font distribution and interchange format adopted by the X Consortium (BDF V2.1–see appendix H) provides a general mechanism for identifying the font name of an X font and a variable list of font properties, but it does not mandate the syntax or semantics of the font name or the semantics of the font properties that might be provided in a BDF font. This section identifies the requirements for BDF fonts that conform to XLFD.

6.1 XLFD Conformance Requirements

A BDF font conforms to the XLFD specification if and only if the following conditions are satisfied:

- The value for the BDF item **FONT** conforms to the syntax and semantic definition of a XLFD `FontName` string.
- The `FontName` begins with the X `FontNameRegistry` prefix: "—".
- All XLFD `FontName` fields are defined.
- Any FontProperties provided conform in name and semantics to the XLFD `FontProperty` definitions.

A simple method of testing for conformance would entail verifying that the `FontNameRegistry` prefix is the string "—", that the number of field delimiters in the string and coded field values are valid, and that each font property name either matches a standard XLFD property name or follows the definition of a private property.

6.2 FONT_ASCENT, FONT_DESCENT, and DEFAULT_CHAR

FONT_ASCENT, FONT_DESCENT, and DEFAULT_CHAR are provided in the BDF specification as properties that are moved to the `XFontStruct` by the BDF font compiler in generating the X server-specific binary font encoding. If present, these properties shall comply with the following semantic definitions.

6.2.1 FONT_ASCENT

FONT_ASCENT is an integer value (of type INT32) that gives the recommended typographic ascent above the baseline for determining interline spacing. Specific glyphs of the font may extend beyond this. If the current position point for line *n* is at [X,Y], then the origin of the next line *n+1* (allowing for a possible font change) is [X, Y+ $FONT\_DESCENT_n$ + $FONT\_ASCENT_{n+1}$].

FONT_ASCENT can be approximated if not provided as a font property, according to the following algorithm:

```
if (FONT_ASCENT undefined) then
  FONT_ASCENT = maximum ascent
```

where maximum ascent is the maximum ascent (above the baseline) in pixels of any glyph in the font.

6.2.2 FONT_DESCENT

FONT_DESCENT is an integer value (of type INT32) that gives the recommended typographic descent below the baseline for determining interline spacing. Specific glyphs of the font may extend beyond this. If the current position point for line *n* is at [X,Y], then the origin of the next line *n+1* (allowing for a possible font change) is [X, Y + $FONT\_DESCENT_n$ + $FONT\_ASCENT_{n+1}$].

The logical extent of the font is inclusive between the Y-coordinate values: Y – FONT_ASCENT and Y + FONT_DESCENT + 1.

FONT_DESCENT can be approximated if not provided as a font property, according to the following algorithm:

```
if (FONT_DESCENT undefined) then
  FONT_DESCENT = maximum descent
```

where maximum descent is the maximum descent (below the baseline) in pixels of any glyph in the font.

6.2.3 DEFAULT_CHAR

The DEFAULT_CHAR is an unsigned integer value (of type CARD32) that specifies the index of the default character to be used by the X server when an attempt is made to display an undefined or nonexistent character in the font. (For a font using 2-byte matrix format, the index bytes are encoded in the integer as byte1 * 65536 + byte2.) If the DEFAULT_CHAR itself specifies an undefined or nonexistent character in the font, then no display is performed.

DEFAULT_CHAR cannot be approximated if it is not provided as a font property.

Appendix A

Xlib Functions and Protocol Requests

This appendix provides two tables that relate to Xlib functions and the X protocol. The following table lists each Xlib function (in alphabetical order) and the corresponding protocol request that it generates.

Xlib Function	*Protocol Request*
XActivateScreenSaver	ForceScreenSaver
XAddHost	ChangeHosts
XAddHosts	ChangeHosts
XAddToSaveSet	ChangeSaveSet
XAllocColor	AllocColor
XAllocColorCells	AllocColorCells
XAllocColorPlanes	AllocColorPlanes
XAllocNamedColor	AllocNamedColor
XAllowEvents	AllowEvents
XAutoRepeatOff	ChangeKeyboardControl
XAutoRepeatOn	ChangeKeyboardControl
XBell	Bell
XChangeActivePointerGrab	ChangeActivePointerGrab
XChangeGC	ChangeGC
XChangeKeyboardControl	ChangeKeyboardControl
XChangeKeyboardMapping	ChangeKeyboardMapping
XChangePointerControl	ChangePointerControl
XChangeProperty	ChangeProperty

Xlib Function	*Protocol Request*
XChangeSaveSet	ChangeSaveSet
XChangeWindowAttributes	ChangeWindowAttributes
XCirculateSubwindows	CirculateWindow
XCirculateSubwindowsDown	CirculateWindow
XCirculateSubwindowsUp	CirculateWindow
XClearArea	ClearArea
XClearWindow	ClearArea
XConfigureWindow	ConfigureWindow
XConvertSelection	ConvertSelection
XCopyArea	CopyArea
XCopyColormapAndFree	CopyColormapAndFree
XCopyGC	CopyGC
XCopyPlane	CopyPlane
XCreateBitmapFromData	CreateGC
	CreatePixmap
	FreeGC
	PutImage
XCreateColormap	CreateColormap
XCreateFontCursor	CreateGlyphCursor
XCreateGC	CreateGC
XCreateGlyphCursor	CreateGlyphCursor
XCreatePixmap	CreatePixmap
XCreatePixmapCursor	CreateCursor
XCreatePixmapFromData	CreateGC
	CreatePixmap
	FreeGC
	PutImage
XCreateSimpleWindow	CreateWindow
XCreateWindow	CreateWindow
XDefineCursor	ChangeWindowAttributes
XDeleteProperty	DeleteProperty
XDestroySubwindows	DestroySubwindows
XDestroyWindow	DestroyWindow
XDisableAccessControl	SetAccessControl
XDrawArc	PolyArc
XDrawArcs	PolyArc
XDrawImageString	ImageText8
XDrawImageString16	ImageText16
XDrawLine	PolySegment

Xlib Function	*Protocol Request*
XDrawLines	PolyLine
XDrawPoint	PolyPoint
XDrawPoints	PolyPoint
XDrawRectangle	PolyRectangle
XDrawRectangles	PolyRectangle
XDrawSegments	PolySegment
XDrawString	PolyText8
XDrawString16	PolyText16
XDrawText	PolyText8
XDrawText16	PolyText16
XEnableAccessControl	SetAccessControl
XFetchBytes	GetProperty
XFetchName	GetProperty
XFillArc	PolyFillArc
XFillArcs	PolyFillArc
XFillPolygon	FillPoly
XFillRectangle	PolyFillRectangle
XFillRectangles	PolyFillRectangle
XForceScreenSaver	ForceScreenSaver
XFreeColormap	FreeColormap
XFreeColors	FreeColors
XFreeCursor	FreeCursor
XFreeFont	CloseFont
XFreeGC	FreeGC
XFreePixmap	FreePixmap
XGetAtomName	GetAtomName
XGetClassHint	GetProperty
XGetFontPath	GetFontPath
XGetGeometry	GetGeometry
XGetIconName	GetProperty
XGetIconSizes	GetProperty
XGetImage	GetImage
XGetInputFocus	GetInputFocus
XGetKeyboardControl	GetKeyboardControl
XGetKeyboardMapping	GetKeyboardMapping
XGetModifierMapping	GetModifierMapping
XGetMotionEvents	GetMotionEvents
XGetModifierMapping	GetModifierMapping
XGetNormalHints	GetProperty

Xlib Function	*Protocol Request*
XGetPointerControl	GetPointerControl
XGetPointerMapping	GetPointerMapping
XGetRGBColormaps	GetProperty
XGetScreenSaver	GetScreenSaver
XGetSelectionOwner	GetSelectionOwner
XGetSizeHints	GetProperty
XGetTextProperty	GetProperty
XGetTransientForHint	GetProperty
XGetWMClientMachine	GetProperty
XGetWMColormapWindows	GetProperty
	InternAtom
XGetWMHints	GetProperty
XGetWMIconName	GetProperty
XGetWMName	GetProperty
XGetWMNormalHints	GetProperty
XGetWMProtocols	GetProperty
	InternAtom
XGetWMSizeHints	GetProperty
XGetWindowAttributes	GetWindowAttributes
	GetGeometry
XGetWindowProperty	GetProperty
XGetZoomHints	GetProperty
XGrabButton	GrabButton
XGrabKey	GrabKey
XGrabKeyboard	GrabKeyboard
XGrabPointer	GrabPointer
XGrabServer	GrabServer
XIconifyWindow	InternAtom
	SendEvent
XInitExtension	QueryExtension
XInstallColormap	InstallColormap
XInternAtom	InternAtom
XKillClient	KillClient
XListExtensions	ListExtensions
XListFonts	ListFonts
XListFontsWithInfo	ListFontsWithInfo
XListHosts	ListHosts
XListInstalledColormaps	ListInstalledColormaps
XListProperties	ListProperties

Xlib Function	*Protocol Request*
XLoadFont	OpenFont
XLoadQueryFont	OpenFont
	QueryFont
XLookupColor	LookupColor
XLowerWindow	ConfigureWindow
XMapRaised	ConfigureWindow
	MapWindow
XMapSubwindows	MapSubwindows
XMapWindow	MapWindow
XMoveResizeWindow	ConfigureWindow
XMoveWindow	ConfigureWindow
XNoOp	NoOperation
XOpenDisplay	CreateGC
XParseColor	LookupColor
XPutImage	PutImage
XQueryBestCursor	QueryBestSize
XQueryBestSize	QueryBestSize
XQueryBestStipple	QueryBestSize
XQueryBestTile	QueryBestSize
XQueryColor	QueryColors
XQueryColors	QueryColors
XQueryExtension	QueryExtension
XQueryFont	QueryFont
XQueryKeymap	QueryKeymap
XQueryPointer	QueryPointer
XQueryTextExtents	QueryTextExtents
XQueryTextExtents16	QueryTextExtents
XQueryTree	QueryTree
XRaiseWindow	ConfigureWindow
XReadBitmapFile	CreateGC
	CreatePixmap
	FreeGC
	PutImage
XRecolorCursor	RecolorCursor
XReconfigureWMWindow	ConfigureWindow
	SendEvent
XRemoveFromSaveSet	ChangeSaveSet
XRemoveHost	ChangeHosts
XRemoveHosts	ChangeHosts

Xlib Function	*Protocol Request*
XReparentWindow	ReparentWindow
XResetScreenSaver	ForceScreenSaver
XResizeWindow	ConfigureWindow
XRestackWindows	ConfigureWindow
XRotateBuffers	RotateProperties
XRotateWindowProperties	RotateProperties
XSelectInput	ChangeWindowAttributes
XSendEvent	SendEvent
XSetAccessControl	SetAccessControl
XSetArcMode	ChangeGC
XSetBackground	ChangeGC
XSetClassHint	ChangeProperty
XSetClipMask	ChangeGC
XSetClipOrigin	ChangeGC
XSetClipRectangles	SetClipRectangles
XSetCloseDownMode	SetCloseDownMode
XSetCommand	ChangeProperty
XSetDashes	SetDashes
XSetFillRule	ChangeGC
XSetFillStyle	ChangeGC
XSetFont	ChangeGC
XSetFontPath	SetFontPath
XSetForeground	ChangeGC
XSetFunction	ChangeGC
XSetGraphicsExposures	ChangeGC
XSetIconName	ChangeProperty
XSetIconSizes	ChangeProperty
XSetInputFocus	SetInputFocus
XSetLineAttributes	ChangeGC
XSetModifierMapping	SetModifierMapping
XSetNormalHints	ChangeProperty
XSetPlaneMask	ChangeGC
XSetPointerMapping	SetPointerMapping
XSetRGBColormaps	ChangeProperty
XSetScreenSaver	SetScreenSaver
XSetSelectionOwner	SetSelectionOwner
XSetSizeHints	ChangeProperty
XSetStandardProperties	ChangeProperty
XSetState	ChangeGC

Xlib Function	*Protocol Request*
XSetStipple	ChangeGC
XSetSubwindowMode	ChangeGC
XSetTextProperty	ChangeProperty
XSetTile	ChangeGC
XSetTransientForHint	ChangeProperty
XSetTSOrigin	ChangeGC
XSetWMClientMachine	ChangeProperty
XSetWMColormapWindows	ChangeProperty
	InternAtom
XSetWMHints	ChangeProperty
XSetWMIconName	ChangeProperty
XSetWMName	ChangeProperty
XSetWMNormalHints	ChangeProperty
XSetWMProperties	ChangeProperty
XSetWMProtocols	ChangeProperty
	InternAtom
XSetWMSizeHints	ChangeProperty
XSetWindowBackground	ChangeWindowAttributes
XSetWindowBackgroundPixmap	ChangeWindowAttributes
XSetWindowBorder	ChangeWindowAttributes
XSetWindowBorderPixmap	ChangeWindowAttributes
XSetWindowBorderWidth	ConfigureWindow
XSetWindowColormap	ChangeWindowAttributes
XSetZoomHints	ChangeProperty
XStoreBuffer	ChangeProperty
XStoreBytes	ChangeProperty
XStoreColor	StoreColors
XStoreColors	StoreColors
XStoreName	ChangeProperty
XStoreNamedColor	StoreNamedColor
XSync	GetInputFocus
XSynchronize	GetInputFocus
XTranslateCoordinates	TranslateCoordinates
XUndefineCursor	ChangeWindowAttributes
XUngrabButton	UngrabButton
XUngrabKey	UngrabKey
XUngrabKeyboard	UngrabKeyboard
XUngrabPointer	UngrabPointer
XUngrabServer	UngrabServer

Xlib Function	*Protocol Request*
XUninstallColormap	UninstallColormap
XUnloadFont	CloseFont
XUnmapSubwindows	UnmapSubwindows
XUnmapWindow	UnmapWindow
XWarpPointer	WarpPointer
XWithdrawWindow	SendEvent
	UnmapWindow

The following table lists each X protocol request (in alphabetical order) and the Xlib functions that reference it.

Protocol Request	*Xlib Function*
AllocColor	XAllocColor
AllocColorCells	XAllocColorCells
AllocColorPlanes	XAllocColorPlanes
AllocNamedColor	XAllocNamedColor
AllowEvents	XAllowEvents
Bell	XBell
SetAccessControl	XDisableAccessControl
	XEnableAccessControl
	XSetAccessControl
ChangeActivePointerGrab	XChangeActivePointerGrab
SetCloseDownMode	XSetCloseDownMode
ChangeGC	XChangeGC
	XSetArcMode
	XSetBackground
	XSetClipMask
	XSetClipOrigin
	XSetFillRule
	XSetFillStyle
	XSetFont
	XSetForeground
	XSetFunction
	XSetGraphicsExposures
	XSetLineAttributes
	XSetPlaneMask
	XSetState
	XSetStipple

Protocol Request	*Xlib Function*
	XSetSubwindowMode
	XSetTile
	XSetTSOrigin
ChangeHosts	XAddHost
	XAddHosts
	XRemoveHost
	XRemoveHosts
ChangeKeyboardControl	XAutoRepeatOff
	XAutoRepeatOn
	XChangeKeyboardControl
ChangeKeyboardMapping	XChangeKeyboardMapping
ChangePointerControl	XChangePointerControl
ChangeProperty	XChangeProperty
	XSetClassHint
	XSetCommand
	XSetIconName
	XSetIconSizes
	XSetNormalHints
	XSetRGBColormaps
	XSetSizeHints
	XSetStandardProperties
	XSetTextProperty
	XSetTransientForHint
	XSetWMClientMachine
	XSetWMColormapWindows
	XSetWMHints
	XSetWMIconName
	XSetWMName
	XSetWMNormalHints
	XSetWMProperties
	XSetWMProtocols
	XSetWMSizeHints
	XSetZoomHints
	XStoreBuffer
	XStoreBytes
	XStoreName
ChangeSaveSet	XAddToSaveSet
	XChangeSaveSet
	XRemoveFromSaveSet

Protocol Request	*Xlib Function*
ChangeWindowAttributes	XChangeWindowAttributes
	XDefineCursor
	XSelectInput
	XSetWindowBackground
	XSetWindowBackgroundPixmap
	XSetWindowBorder
	XSetWindowBorderPixmap
	XSetWindowColormap
	XUndefineCursor
CirculateWindow	XCirculateSubwindowsDown
	XCirculateSubwindowsUp
	XCirculateSubwindows
ClearArea	XClearArea
	XClearWindow
CloseFont	XFreeFont
	XUnloadFont
ConfigureWindow	XConfigureWindow
	XLowerWindow
	XMapRaised
	XMoveResizeWindow
	XMoveWindow
	XRaiseWindow
	XReconfigureWMWindow
	XResizeWindow
	XRestackWindows
	XSetWindowBorderWidth
ConvertSelection	XConvertSelection
CopyArea	XCopyArea
CopyColormapAndFree	XCopyColormapAndFree
CopyGC	XCopyGC
CopyPlane	XCopyPlane
CreateColormap	XCreateColormap
CreateCursor	XCreatePixmapCursor
CreateGC	XCreateGC
	XCreateBitmapFromData
	XCreatePixmapFromData
	XOpenDisplay
	XReadBitmapFile
CreateGlyphCursor	XCreateFontCursor
	XCreateGlyphCursor

Protocol Request	*Xlib Function*
CreatePixmap	XCreatePixmap
	XCreateBitmapFromData
	XCreatePixmapFromData
	XReadBitmapFile
CreateWindow	XCreateSimpleWindow
	XCreateWindow
DeleteProperty	XDeleteProperty
DestroySubwindows	XDestroySubwindows
DestroyWindow	XDestroyWindow
FillPoly	XFillPolygon
ForceScreenSaver	XActivateScreenSaver
	XForceScreenSaver
	XResetScreenSaver
FreeColormap	XFreeColormap
FreeColors	XFreeColors
FreeCursor	XFreeCursor
FreeGC	XFreeGC
	XCreateBitmapFromData
	XCreatePixmapFromData
	XReadBitmapFile
FreePixmap	XFreePixmap
GetAtomName	XGetAtomName
GetFontPath	XGetFontPath
GetGeometry	XGetGeometry
	XGetWindowAttributes
GetImage	XGetImage
GetInputFocus	XGetInputFocus
	XSync
	XSynchronize
GetKeyboardControl	XGetKeyboardControl
GetKeyboardMapping	XGetKeyboardMapping
GetModifierMapping	XGetModifierMapping
GetMotionEvents	XGetMotionEvents
GetPointerControl	XGetPointerControl
GetPointerMapping	XGetPointerMapping
GetProperty	XFetchBytes
	XFetchName
	XGetClassHint
	XGetIconName

Protocol Request	*Xlib Function*
	XGetIconSizes
	XGetNormalHints
	XGetRGBColormaps
	XGetSizeHints
	XGetTextProperty
	XGetTransientForHint
	XGetWMClientMachine
	XGetWMColormapWindows
	XGetWMHints
	XGetWMIconName
	XGetWMName
	XGetWMNormalHints
	XGetWMProtocols
	XGetWMSizeHints
	XGetWindowProperty
	XGetZoomHints
GetSelectionOwner	XGetSelectionOwner
GetWindowAttributes	XGetWindowAttributes
GrabButton	XGrabButton
GrabKey	XGrabKey
GrabKeyboard	XGrabKeyboard
GrabPointer	XGrabPointer
GrabServer	XGrabServer
ImageText16	XDrawImageString16
ImageText8	XDrawImageString
InstallColormap	XInstallColormap
InternAtom	XGetWMColormapWindows
	XGetWMProtocols
	XIconifyWindow
	XInternAtom
	XSetWMColormapWindows
	XSetWMProtocols
KillClient	XKillClient
ListExtensions	XListExtensions
ListFonts	XListFonts
ListFontsWithInfo	XListFontsWithInfo
ListHosts	XListHosts
ListInstalledColormaps	XListInstalledColormaps
ListProperties	XListProperties

Protocol Request	*Xlib Function*
LookupColor	XLookupColor
	XParseColor
MapSubwindows	XMapSubwindows
MapWindow	XMapRaised
	XMapWindow
NoOperation	XNoOp
OpenFont	XLoadFont
	XLoadQueryFont
PolyArc	XDrawArc
	XDrawArcs
PolyFillArc	XFillArc
	XFillArcs
PolyFillRectangle	XFillRectangle
	XFillRectangles
PolyLine	XDrawLines
PolyPoint	XDrawPoint
	XDrawPoints
PolyRectangle	XDrawRectangle
	XDrawRectangles
PolySegment	XDrawLine
	XDrawSegments
PolyText16	XDrawString16
	XDrawText16
PolyText8	XDrawString
	XDrawText
PutImage	XPutImage
	XCreateBitmapFromData
	XCreatePixmapFromData
	XReadBitmapFile
QueryBestSize	XQueryBestCursor
	XQueryBestSize
	XQueryBestStipple
	XQueryBestTile
QueryColors	XQueryColor
	XQueryColors
QueryExtension	XInitExtension
	XQueryExtension
QueryFont	XLoadQueryFont
	XQueryFont

Protocol Request	*Xlib Function*
QueryKeymap	XQueryKeymap
QueryPointer	XQueryPointer
QueryTextExtents	XQueryTextExtents XQueryTextExtents16
QueryTree	XQueryTree
RecolorCursor	XRecolorCursor
ReparentWindow	XReparentWindow
RotateProperties	XRotateBuffers XRotateWindowProperties
SendEvent	XIconifyWindow XReconfigureWMWindow XSendEvent XWithdrawWindow
SetClipRectangles	XSetClipRectangles
SetCloseDownMode	XSetCloseDownMode
SetDashes	XSetDashes
SetFontPath	XSetFontPath
SetInputFocus	XSetInputFocus
SetModifierMapping	XSetModifierMapping
SetPointerMapping	XSetPointerMapping
SetScreenSaver	XGetScreenSaver XSetScreenSaver
SetSelectionOwner	XSetSelectionOwner
StoreColors	XStoreColor XStoreColors
StoreNamedColor	XStoreNamedColor
TranslateCoordinates	XTranslateCoordinates
UngrabButton	XUngrabButton
UngrabKey	XUngrabKey
UngrabKeyboard	XUngrabKeyboard
UngrabPointer	XUngrabPointer
UngrabServer	XUngrabServer
UninstallColormap	XUninstallColormap
UnmapSubwindows	XUnmapSubWindows
UnmapWindow	XUnmapWindow XWithdrawWindow
WarpPointer	XWarpPointer

Appendix B

X Font Cursors

The following are the available cursors that can be used with XCreateFont-Cursor.

XC_X_cursor	XC_clock
XC_arrow	XC_coffee_mug
XC_based_arrow_down	XC_cross
XC_based_arrow_up	XC_cross_reverse
XC_boat	XC_crosshair
XC_bogosity	XC_diamond_cross
XC_bottom_left_corner	XC_dot
XC_bottom_right_corner	XC_dot_box_mask
XC_bottom_side	XC_double_arrow
XC_bottom_tee	XC_draft_large
XC_box_spiral	XC_draft_small
XC_center_ptr	XC_draped_box
XC_circle	XC_exchange

XC_fleur
XC_gobbler
XC_gumby
XC_hand1
XC_hand2
XC_heart
XC_icon
XC_iron_cross
XC_left_ptr
XC_left_side
XC_left_tee
XC_leftbutton
XC_ll_angle
XC_lr_angle
XC_man
XC_middlebutton
XC_mouse
XC_pencil
XC_pirate
XC_plus
XC_question_arrow
XC_right_ptr
XC_right_side
XC_right_tee
XC_rightbutton
XC_rtl_logo
XC_sailboat
XC_sb_down_arrow
XC_sb_h_double_arrow
XC_sb_left_arrow
XC_sb_right_arrow
XC_sb_up_arrow
XC_sb_v_double_arrow
XC_shuttle
XC_sizing
XC_spider
XC_spraycan
XC_star
XC_target
XC_tcross
XC_top_left_arrow
XC_top_left_corner

XC_top_right_corner

XC_top_side

XC_top_tee

XC_trek

XC_ul_angle

XC_umbrella

XC_ur_angle

XC_watch

XC_xterm

Appendix C

Extensions

Because X can evolve by extensions to the core protocol, it is important that extensions not be perceived as second class citizens. At some point, your favorite extensions may be adopted as additional parts of the X Standard.

Therefore, there should be little to distinguish the use of an extension from that of the core protocol. To avoid having to initialize extensions explicitly in application programs, it is also important that extensions perform lazy evaluations, automatically initialize themselves when called for the first time.

This appendix describes techniques for writing extensions to Xlib that will run at essentially the same performance as the core protocol requests.

Note It is expected that a given extension to X consists of multiple requests. Defining ten new features as ten separate extensions is a bad practice. Rather, they should be packaged into a single extension and should use minor opcodes to distinguish the requests.

The symbols and macros used for writing stubs to Xlib are listed in `<X11/Xlibint.h>`.

Basic Protocol Support Routines

The basic protocol requests for extensions are `XQueryExtension` and `XListExtensions`.

```
Bool XQueryExtension( display, name, major_opcode_return, first_event_return,
                      first_error_return)
    Display *display;
    char *name;
```

```
      int *major_opcode_return;
      int *first_event_return;
      int *first_error_return;
```

display	Specifies the connection to the X server.
name	Specifies the extension name.
major_opcode_return	Returns the major opcode.
first_event_return	Returns the first event code, if any.
	Specifies the extension list.

The `XQueryExtension` function determines if the named extension is present. If the extension is not present, `XQueryExtension` returns `False`; otherwise, it returns `True`. If the extension is present, `XQueryExtension` returns the major opcode for the extension to major_opcode_return; otherwise, it returns zero. Any minor opcode and the request formats are specific to the extension. If the extension involves additional event types, `XQueryExtension` returns the base event type code to first_event_return; otherwise, it returns zero. The format of the events is specific to the extension. If the extension involves additional error codes, `XQueryExtension` returns the base error code to first_error_return; otherwise, it returns zero. The format of additional data in the errors is specific to the extension.

If the extension name is not in the Host Portable Character Encoding, the result is implementation dependent. Uppercase and lowercase matter; the strings "thing", "Thing", and "thinG" are all considered different names.

```
char **XListExtensions(display, nextensions_return)
      Display *display;
      int *nextensions_return;
```

display	Specifies the connection to the X server.
nextensions_return	Returns the number of extensions listed.

The `XListExtensions` functon returns a list of all extensions supported by the server. If the data returned by the server is in the Latin Portable Character Encoding, then the returned strings are in the Host Portable Character Encoding. Otherwise, the result is implementation dependent.

```
XFreeExtensionList(list)
      char **list;
```

list Specifies the list of extension names.

The XFreeExtensionList function frees the memory allocated by XListExtensions.

Hooking into Xlib

These functions allow you to hook into the library. They are not normally used by application programmers but are used by people who need to extend the core X protocol and the X library interface. The functions, which generate protocol requests for X, are typically called stubs.

In extensions, stubs first should check to see if they have initialized themselves on a connection. If they have not, they then should call XInitExtension to attempt to initialize themselves on the connection.

If the extension needs to be informed of GC/font allocation or deallocation or if the extension defines new event types, the functions described here allow the extension to be called when these events occur.

The XExtCodes structure returns the information from XInitExtension and is defined in <X11/Xlib.h>:

```
typedef struct _XExtCodes {     /* public to extension, cannot be changed */
    int extension;              /* extension number */
    int major_opcode;           /* major op-code assigned by server */
    int first_event;            /* first event number for the extension */
    int first_error;            /* first error number for the extension */
} XExtCodes;
```

```
XExtCodes *XInitExtension(display, name)
    Display *display;
    char *name;
```

display Specifies the connection to the X server.

name Specifies the extension name.

The XInitExtension function determines if the named extension exists. Then, it allocates storage for maintaining the information about the extension on the connection, chains this onto the extension list for the connection, and returns the information the stub implementor will need to access the extension. If the extension does not exist, XInitExtension returns NULL.

If the extension name is not in the Host Portable Character Encoding, the result is implementation dependent. Uppercase and lowercase matter; the strings "thing", "Thing", and "thinG" are all considered different names.

The extension number in the `XExtCodes` structure is needed in the other calls that follow. This extension number is unique only to a single connection.

```
XExtCodes *XAddExtension ( display)
      Display *display;
```

display Specifies the connection to the X server.

For local Xlib extensions, the `XAddExtension` function allocates the `XExtCodes` structure, bumps the extension number count, and chains the extension onto the extension list. (This permits extensions to Xlib without requiring server extensions.)

Hooks into the Library

These functions allow you to define procedures that are to be called when various circumstances occur. The procedures include the creation of a new GC for a connection, the copying of a GC, the freeing of a GC, the creating and freeing of fonts, the conversion of events defined by extensions to and from wire format, and the handling of errors.

All of these functions return the previous procedure defined for this extension.

```
int (*XESetCloseDisplay( display, extension, proc)) ()
      Display *display;
      int extension;
      int (*proc) ();
```

display Specifies the connection to the X server.
extension Specifies the extension number.
proc Specifies the procedure to call when the display is closed.

The `XESetCloseDisplay` function defines a procedure to be called whenever `XCloseDisplay` is called. It returns any previously defined procedure, usually NULL.

When `XCloseDisplay` is called, your procedure is called with these arguments:

```
(*proc) ( display, codes)
      Display *display;
      XExtCodes *codes;
```

```
int (*XESetCreateGC( display, extension, proc)) ()
      Display *display;
      int extension;
      int (*proc) ();
```

display Specifies the connection to the X server.

extension Specifies the extension number.

proc Specifies the procedure to call when a GC is closed.

The `XESetCreateGC` function defines a procedure to be called whenever a new GC is created. It returns any previously defined procedure, usually NULL.

When a GC is created, your procedure is called with these arguments:

```
(*proc) ( display, gc, codes)
      Display *display;
      GC gc;
      XExtCodes *codes;
```

```
int (*XESetCopyGC( display, extension, proc)) ()
      Display *display;
      int extension;
      int (*proc) ();
```

display Specifies the connection to the X server.

extension Specifies the extension number.

proc Specifies the procedure to call when GC components are copied.

The `XESetCopyGC` function defines a procedure to be called whenever a GC is copied. It returns any previously defined procedure, usually NULL.

When a GC is copied, your procedure is called with these arguments:

```
(*proc) ( display, gc, codes)
      Display *display;
      GC gc;
      XExtCodes *codes;
```

```
int (*XESetFreeGC( display, extension, proc)) ()
      Display *display;
      int extension;
      int (*proc) ();
```

display Specifies the connection to the X server.

extension Specifies the extension number.

proc Specifies the procedure to call when a GC is freed.

The `XESetFreeGC` function defines a procedure to be called whenever a GC is freed. It returns any previously defined procedure, usually NULL.

When a GC is freed, your procedure is called with these arguments:

```
(*proc) ( display, gc, codes)
      Display *display;
      GC gc;
      XExtCodes *codes;
```

```
int (*XESetCreateFont( display, extension, proc)) ( )
      Display *display;
      int extension;
      int (*proc) ( );
```

display	Specifies the connection to the X server.
extension	Specifies the extension number.
proc	Specifies the procedure to call when a font is created.

The `XESetCreateFont` function defines a procedure to be called whenever `XLoadQueryFont` and `XQueryFont` are called. It returns any previously defined procedure, usually NULL.

When `XLoadQueryFont` or `XQueryFont` is called, your procedure is called with these arguments:

```
(*proc) ( display, fs, codes)
      Display *display;
      XFontStruct *fs;
      XExtCodes *codes;
```

```
int (*XESetFreeFont( display, extension, proc)) ( )
      Display *display;
      int extension;
      int ( *proc) ( );
```

display	Specifies the connection to the X server.
extension	Specifies the extension number.
proc	Specifies the procedure to call when a font is freed.

The `XESetFreeFont` function defines a procedure to be called whenever `XFreeFont` is called. It returns any previously defined procedure, usually NULL.

When `XFreeFont` is called, your procedure is called with these arguments:

```
(*proc) ( display, fs, codes)
      Display *display;
      XFontStruct *fs;
      XExtCodes *codes;
```

The `XESetWireToEvent` and `XESetEventToWire` functions allow you to define new events to the library. An `XEvent` structure always has a type code (type `int`) as the first component. This uniquely identifies what kind of event it is. The second component is always the serial number (type `unsigned long`) of the last request processed by the server. The third component is always a Boolean (type `Bool`) indicating whether the event came from a `SendEvent` protocol request. The fourth component is always a pointer to the display the event was read from. The fifth component is always a resource ID of one kind or another, usually a window, carefully selected to be useful to toolkit dispatchers. The fifth component should always exist, even if the event does not have a natural destination; if there is no value from the protocol to put in this component, initialize it to zero.

Note There is an implementation limit such that your host event structure size cannot be bigger than the size of the `XEvent` union of structures. There also is no way to guarantee that more than 24 elements or 96 characters in the structure will be fully portable between machines.

```
int (*XESetWireToEvent( display, event_number, proc)) ()
      Display *display;
      int event_number;
      Status (*proc) ();
```

display Specifies the connection to the X server.
event_number Specifies the event code.
proc Specifies the procedure to call when converting an event.

The `XESetWireToEvent` function defines a procedure to be called when an event needs to be converted from wire format (`xEvent`) to host format (`XEvent`). The event number defines which protocol event number to install a conversion procedure for. `XESetWireToEvent` returns any previously defined procedure.

Note You can replace a core event conversion function with one of your own, although this is not encouraged. It would, however, allow you to intercept a core event and modify it before being placed in the queue or otherwise examined.

When Xlib needs to convert an event from wire format to host format, your procedure is called with these arguments:

```
Status (*proc) ( display, re, event)
      Display *display;
      XEvent *re;
      xEvent *event;
```

Your procedure must return status to indicate if the conversion succeeded. The re argument is a pointer to where the host format event should be stored, and the event argument is the 32-byte wire event structure. In the `XEvent` structure you are creating, you must fill in the five required members of the event structure. You should fill in the type member with the type specified for the `xEvent` structure. You should copy all other members from the `xEvent` structure (wire format) to the `XEvent` structure (host format). Your conversion procedure should return `True` if the event should be placed in the queue or `False` if it should not be placed in the queue.

To initialize the serial number component of the event, call `_XSetLastRequestRead` with the event and use the return value.

```
unsigned long _XSetLastRequestRead( display, rep)
      Display *display;
      xGenericReply *rep;
```

display Specifies the connection to the X server.
rep Specifies the wire event structure.

The `_XSetLastRequestRead` function computes and returns a complete serial number from the partial serial number in the event.

```
Status (*XESetEventToWire( display, event_number, proc)) ()
      Display *display;
      int event_number;
      int (*proc) ();
```

display Specifies the connection to the X server.
event_number Specifies the event code.
proc Specifies the procedure to call when converting an event.

The XESetEventToWire function defines a procedure to be called when an event needs to be converted from host format (XEvent) to wire format (xEvent) form. The event number defines which protocol event number to install a conversion procedure for. XESetEventToWire procedure returns any previously defined procedure. It returns zero if the conversion fails or nonzero otherwise.

Note You can replace a core event conversion function with one of your own, although this is not encouraged. It would, however, allow you to intercept a core event and modify it before being sent to another client.

When Xlib needs to convert an event from host format to wire format, your procedure is called with these arguments:

```
(*proc) ( display, re, event)
    Display *display;
    XEvent *re;
    xEvent *event;
```

The re argument is a pointer to the host format event, and the event argument is a pointer to where the 32-byte wire event structure should be stored. You should fill in the type with the type from the XEvent structure. All other members then should be copied from the host format to the xEvent structure.

```
Bool (*XESetWireToError( display, error_number, proc) ( )
    Display *display;
    int error_number;
    Bool (*proc) ( );
```

display Specifies the connection to the X server.
error_number Specifies the error code.
proc Specifies the procedure to call when an error is received.

The XESetWireToError function defines a procedure to be called when an extension error needs to be converted from wire format to host format. The error number defines which protocol error code to install the conversion procedure for. XESetWireToError returns any previously defined procedure.

Use this function for extension errors that contain additional error values beyond those in a core X error, when multiple wire errors must be combined into a single Xlib error, or when it is necessary to intercept an X error before it is otherwise examined.

When Xlib needs to convert an error from wire format to host format, the procedure is called with these arguments:

```
Bool (*proc) ( display, he, we)
     Display *display;
     XErrorEvent *he;
     xError *we;
```

The he argument is a pointer to where the host format error should be stored. The structure pointed at by he is guaranteed to be as large as an `XEvent` structure and so can be cast to a type larger than an `XErrorEvent` to store additional values. If the error is to be completely ignored by Xlib (for example, several protocol error structures will be combined into one Xlib error), then the function should return `False`; otherwise, it should return `True`.

```
int (*XESetError( display, extension, proc)) ( )
     Display *display;
     int extension;
     int (*proc) ( );
```

display Specifies the connection to the X server.
extension Specifies the extension number.
proc Specifies the procedure to call when an error is received.

Inside Xlib, there are times that you may want to suppress the calling of the external error handling when an error occurs. This allows status to be returned on a call at the cost of the call being synchronous (though most such functions are query operations, in any case, and are typically programmed to be synchronous).

When Xlib detects a protocol error in `_XReply`, it calls your procedure with these arguments:

```
int (*proc) (display, err, codes, ret_code)
     Display *display;
     xError *err;
     XExtCodes *codes;
     int *ret_code;
```

The err argument is a pointer to the 32-byte wire format error. The codes argument is a pointer to the extension codes structure. The ret_code argument is the return code you may want `_XReply` returned to.

If your procedure returns a zero value, the error is not suppressed, and the client's error handler is called. (For further information, see section 11.8.2 of part I, "Xlib — C Language X Interface.") If your procedure returns nonzero, the error is suppressed, and `_XReply` returns the value of ret_code.

```
char *(*XESetErrorString(display, extension, proc))()
      Display *display;
      int extension;
      char *(*proc)();
```

display Specifies the connection to the X server.
extension Specifies the extension number.
proc Specifies the procedure to call to obtain an error string.

The `XGetErrorText` function returns a string to the user for an error. `XESetErrorString` allows you to define a procedure to be called that should return a pointer to the error message. The following is an example.

```
(*proc)(display, code, codes, buffer, nbytes)
      Display *display;
      int code;
      XExtCodes *codes;
      char *buffer;
      int nbytes;
```

Your procedure is called with the error code for every error detected. You should copy nbytes of a null-terminated string containing the error message into buffer.

```
void (*XESetPrintErrorValues(display, extension, proc))()
      Display *display;
      int extension;
      void (*proc)();
```

display Specifies the connection to the X server.
extension Specifies the extension number.
proc Specifies the procedure to call when an error is printed.

The `XESetPrintErrorValues` function defines a procedure to be called when an extension error is printed, to print the error values. Use this function for extension errors that contain additional error values beyond those in a core X error. It returns any previously defined procedure.

When Xlib needs to print an error, the procedure is called with these arguments:

```
void (*proc) ( display, ev, fp)
    Display *display;
    XErrorEvent *ev;
    void *fp;
```

The structure pointed at by ev is guaranteed to be as large as an `XEvent` structure and so can be cast to a type larger than an `XErrorEvent` to obtain additional values set by using `XESetWireToError` . The underlying type of the fp argument is system dependent; on a POSIX-compliant system, fp should be cast to type FILE*.

```
int (*XESetFlushGC( display, extension, proc)) ()
    Display *display;
    int extension;
    int *(*proc) ();
```

display Specifies the connection to the X server.
extension Specifies the extension number.
proc Specifies the procedure to call when a GC is flushed.

The `XESetFlushGC` function is identical to `XESetCopyGC` except that `XESetFlushGC` is called when a GC cache needs to be updated in the server.

Hooks onto Xlib Data Structures

Various Xlib data structures have provisions for extension procedures to chain extension supplied data onto a list. These structures are `GC`, `Visual`, `Screen`, `ScreenFormat`, `Display`, and `XFontStruct`. Because the list pointer is always the first member in the structure, a single set of procedures can be used to manipulate the data on these lists.

The following structure is used in the functions in this section and is defined in `<X11/Xlib.h>`:

```
typedef struct _XExtData {
    int number;                     /* number returned by XInitExtension */
    struct _XExtData *next;         /* next item on list of data for structure */
    int (*free_private) ();         /* if defined, called to free private */
    XPointer private_data;          /* data private to this extension. */
} XExtData;
```

When any of the data structures listed above are freed, the list is walked, and the structure's free procedure (if any) is called. If free is NULL, then the library frees both the data pointed to by the private_data member and the structure itself.

```
union {Display *display;
    GC gc;
    Visual *visual;
    Screen *screen;
    ScreenFormat *pixmap_format;
    XFontStruct *font } XEDataObject;
```

XExtData **XEHeadOfExtensionList(*object*)
    XEDataObject *object*;

object Specifies the object.

The `XEHeadOfExtensionList` function returns a pointer to the list of extension structures attached to the specified object. In concert with `XAddToExtensionList`, `XEHeadOfExtensionList` allows an extension to attach arbitrary data to any of the structures of types contained in `XEDataObject`.

XAddToExtensionList(*structure, ext_data*)
    XExtData ***structure*;
    XExtData **ext_data*;

structure Specifies the extension list.
ext_data Specifies the extension data structure to add.

The structure argument is a pointer to one of the data structures enumerated above. You must initialize ext_data→number with the extension number before calling this function.

```
XExtData *XFindOnExtensionList(structure, number)
      struct _XExtData **structure;
      int number;
```

structure Specifies the extension list.
number Specifies the extension number from `XInitExtension`.

The `XFindOnExtensionList` function returns the first extension data structure for the extension numbered number. It is expected that an extension will add at most one extension data structure to any single data structure's extension data list. There is no way to find additional structures.

The `XAllocID` macro, which allocates and returns a resource ID, is defined in `<X11/Xlib.h>`.

```
XAllocID (display)
      Display *display;
```

display Specifies the connection to the X server.

This macro is a call through the `Display` structure to the internal resource ID allocator. It returns a resource ID that you can use when creating new resources.

GC Caching

GCs are cached by the library to allow merging of independent change requests to the same GC into single protocol requests. This is typically called a write-back cache. Any extension procedure whose behavior depends on the contents of a GC must flush the GC cache to make sure the server has up-to-date contents in its GC.

The `FlushGC` macro checks the dirty bits in the library's GC structure and calls `_XFlushGCCache` if any elements have changed. The `FlushGC` macro is defined as follows:

```
FlushGC ( display, gc)
      Display * display;
      GC gc;
```

display Specifies the connection to the X server.
gc Specifies the GC.

Note that if you extend the GC to add additional resource ID components, you should ensure that the library stub sends the change request immediately.

This is because a client can free a resource immediately after using it, so if you only stored the value in the cache without forcing a protocol request, the resource might be destroyed before being set into the GC. You can use the `_XFlushGCCache` procedure to force the cache to be flushed. The `_XFlushGCCache` procedure is defined as follows:

_XFlushGCCache (*display*, *gc*)
  Display * *display*;
  GC *gc*;

display Specifies the connection to the X server.
gc Specifies the GC.

Graphics Batching

If you extend X to add more poly graphics primitives, you may be able to take advantage of facilities in the library to allow back-to-back single calls to be transformed into poly requests. This may dramatically improve performance of programs that are not written using poly requests. A pointer to an `xReq`, called last_req in the display structure, is the last request being processed. By checking that the last request type, drawable, gc, and other options are the same as the new one and that there is enough space left in the buffer, you may be able to just extend the previous graphics request by extending the length field of the request and appending the data to the buffer. This can improve performance by five times or more in naive programs. For example, here is the source for the `XDrawPoint` stub. (Writing extension stubs is discussed in the next section.)

```
#include "Xlibint.h"
/* precompute the maximum size of batching request allowed */
static int size = sizeof(xPolyPointReq) + EPERBATCH * sizeof(xPoint);

XDrawPoint(dpy, d, gc, x, y)
  register Display *dpy;
  Drawable d;
```

```
    GC gc;
    int x, y; /* INT16 */
  {
    xPoint *point;
    LockDisplay(dpy);
    FlushGC(dpy, gc);
    {
    register xPolyPointReq *req = (xPolyPointReq *) dpy->last_req;
    /* if same as previous request, with same drawable, batch requests */
    if (
           (req->reqType == X_PolyPoint)
       &&  (req->drawable == d)
       &&  (req->gc == gc->gid)
       &&  (req->coordMode == CoordModeOrigin)
       &&  ((dpy->bufptr + sizeof (xPoint)) <= dpy->bufmax)
       &&  (((char *)dpy->bufptr - (char *)req) < size) ) {
           point = (xPoint *) dpy->bufptr;
           req->length += sizeof (xPoint) >> 2;
           dpy->bufptr += sizeof (xPoint);
           }

    else {
           GetReqExtra(PolyPoint, 4, req); /* 1 point = 4 bytes */
           req->drawable = d;
           req->gc = gc->gid;
           req->coordMode = CoordModeOrigin;
           point = (xPoint *) (req + 1);
           }
    point->x = x;
    point->y = y;
    }
    UnlockDisplay(dpy);
    SyncHandle();
  }
```

To keep clients from generating very long requests that may monopolize the server, there is a symbol defined in `<X11/Xlibint.h>` of EPERBATCH on the number of requests batched. Most of the performance benefit occurs in the first few merged requests. Note that `FlushGC` is called *before* picking up the value of last_req, because it may modify this field.

Writing Extension Stubs

All X requests always contain the length of the request, expressed as a 16-bit quantity of 32 bits. This means that a single request can be no more than 256K bytes in length. Some servers may not support single requests of such a length. The value of dpy->max_request_size contains the maximum length as defined by the server implementation. For further information, see part II, "X Window System Protocol."

Requests, Replies, and Xproto.h

The `<X11/Xproto.h>` file contains three sets of definitions that are of interest to the stub implementor: request names, request structures, and reply structures.

You need to generate a file equivalent to `<X11/Xproto.h>` for your extension and need to include it in your stub procedure. Each stub procedure also must include `<X11/Xlibint.h>`.

The identifiers are deliberately chosen in such a way that, if the request is called X_DoSomething, then its request structure is xDoSomethingReq, and its reply is xDoSomethingReply. The GetReq family of macros, defined in `<X11/Xlibint.h>`, takes advantage of this naming scheme.

For each X request, there is a definition in `<X11/Xproto.h>` that looks similar to this:

```
#define X_DoSomething  42
```

In your extension header file, this will be a minor opcode, instead of a major opcode.

Request Format

Every request contains an 8-bit major opcode and a 16-bit length field expressed in units of four bytes. Every request consists of four bytes of header (containing the major opcode, the length field, and a data byte) followed by zero or more additional bytes of data. The length field defines the total length of the request, including the header. The length field in a request must equal the minimum length required to contain the request. If the specified length is smaller or larger than the required length, the server should generate a `BadLength` error. Unused bytes in a request are not required to be zero. Extensions should be designed in such a way that long protocol requests can be split up into smaller requests, if it is possible to exceed the maximum request size of the server. The protocol guarantees the maximum request size to be no smaller than 4096 units (16384 bytes).

Major opcodes 128 through 255 are reserved for extensions. Extensions are intended to contain multiple requests, so extension requests typically have an additional minor opcode encoded in the second data byte in the request header, but the placement and interpretation of this minor opcode as well as all other fields in extension requests are not defined by the core protocol. Every request is implicitly assigned a sequence number (starting with one) used in replies, errors, and events.

To help but not cure portability problems to certain machines, the `B16` and `B32` macros have been defined so that they can become bitfield specifications on some machines. For example, on a Cray, these should be used for all 16-bit and 32-bit quantities, as discussed below.

Most protocol requests have a corresponding structure typedef in `<X11/Xproto.h>`, which looks like:

```
typedef struct _DoSomethingReq {
    CARD8 reqType;          /* X_DoSomething */
    CARD8 someDatum;        /* used differently in different requests */
    CARD16 length B16;      /* total # of bytes in request, divided by 4 */
    ...
    /* request-specific data */
    ...
} xDoSomethingReq;
```

If a core protocol request has a single 32-bit argument, you need not declare a request structure in your extension header file. Instead, such requests use `<X11/Xproto.h>`'s `xResourceReq` structure. This structure is used for any request whose single argument is a `Window`, `Pixmap`, `Drawable`, `GContext`, `Font`, `Cursor`, `Colormap`, `Atom`, or `VisualID`.

```
typedef struct _ResourceReq {
    CARD8 reqType;          /* the request type, e.g. X_DoSomething */
    BYTE pad;               /* not used */
    CARD16 length B16;      /* 2 (= total # of bytes in request, divided by 4) */
    CARD32 id B32;          /* the Window, Drawable, Font, GContext, etc. */
} xResourceReq;
```

If convenient, you can do something similar in your extension header file.

In both of these structures, the reqType field identifies the type of the request (for example, X_MapWindow or X_CreatePixmap). The length field tells how long the request is in units of 4-byte longwords. This length includes both the request structure itself and any variable length data, such as strings or lists, that follow the request structure. Request structures come in different sizes, but all requests are padded to be multiples of four bytes long.

A few protocol requests take no arguments at all. Instead, they use `<X11/Xproto.h>`'s `xReq` structure, which contains only a reqType and a length (and a pad byte).

If the protocol request requires a reply, then `<X11/Xproto.h>` also contains a reply structure typedef:

```
typedef struct _DoSomethingReply {
    BYTE type;                      /* always X_Reply */
    BYTE someDatum;                 /* used differently in different requests */
    CARD16 sequenceNumber B16;      /* # of requests sent so far */
    CARD32 length B32;              /* # of additional bytes, divided by 4 */
    ...
    /* request-specific data */
    ...
} xDoSomethingReply;
```

Most of these reply structures are 32 bytes long. If there are not that many reply values, then they contain a sufficient number of pad fields to bring them up to 32 bytes. The length field is the total number of bytes in the request minus 32, divided by 4. This length will be nonzero only if:

- The reply structure is followed by variable length data such as a list or string.
- The reply structure is longer than 32 bytes.

Only `GetWindowAttributes`, `QueryFont`, `QueryKeymap`, and `GetKeyboard-Control` have reply structures longer than 32 bytes in the core protocol.

A few protocol requests return replies that contain no data. `<X11/Xproto.h>` does not define reply structures for these. Instead, they use the `xGenericReply` structure, which contains only a type, length, and sequence number (and sufficient padding to make it 32 bytes long).

Starting to Write a Stub Procedure

An Xlib stub procedure should always start like this:

```
#include "Xlibint.h"
XDoSomething (arguments,...)
/* argument declarations */
{
register XDoSomethingReq *req;
...
```

If the protocol request has a reply, then the variable declarations should include the reply structure for the request. The following is an example:

```
xDoSomethingReply rep;
```

Locking Data Structures

To lock the display structure for systems that want to support multithreaded access to a single display connection, each stub will need to lock its critical section. Generally, this section is the point from just before the appropriate GetReq call until all arguments to the call have been stored into the buffer. The precise instructions needed for this locking depend upon the machine architecture. Two calls, which are generally implemented as macros, have been provided.

LockDisplay(*display*)
    Display **display*;

UnlockDisplay(*display*)
    Display **display*;

display Specifies the connection to the X server.

Sending the Protocol Request and Arguments

After the variable declarations, a stub procedure should call one of four macros defined in <X11/Xlibint.h>: `GetReq`, `GetReqExtra`, `GetResReq`, or `GetEmptyReq`. All of these macros take, as their first argument, the name of the protocol request as declared in <X11/Xproto.h> except with X_ removed. Each one declares a `Display` structure pointer, called dpy, and a pointer to a request structure, called req, which is of the appropriate type. The macro then appends the request structure to the output buffer, fills in its type and length field, and sets req to point to it.

If the protocol request has no arguments (for instance, X_GrabServer), then use `GetEmptyReq`.

```
GetEmptyReq (DoSomething, req);
```

If the protocol request has a single 32-bit argument (such as a `Pixmap`, `Window`, `Drawable`, `Atom`, and so on), then use `GetResReq`. The second argument to the macro is the 32-bit object. `X_MapWindow` is a good example.

```
GetResReq (DoSomething, rid, req);
```

The rid argument is the `Pixmap`, `Window`, or other resource ID.

If the protocol request takes any other argument list, then call `GetReq`. After the `GetReq`, you need to set all the other fields in the request structure, usually from arguments to the stub procedure.

```
GetReq (DoSomething, req);
/* fill in arguments here */
req->arg1 = arg1;
req->arg2 = arg2;
...
```

A few stub procedures (such as `XCreateGC` and `XCreatePixmap`) return a resource ID to the caller but pass a resource ID as an argument to the protocol request. Such procedures use the macro `XAllocID` to allocate a resource ID from the range of IDs that were assigned to this client when it opened the connection.

```
rid = req->rid = XAllocID();
...
return (rid);
```

Finally, some stub procedures transmit a fixed amount of variable length data after the request. Typically, these procedures (such as `XMoveWindow` and `XSetBackground`) are special cases of more general functions like `XMoveResizeWindow` and `XChangeGC`. These special case procedures use `GetReqExtra`, which is the same as `GetReq` except that it takes an additional argument (the number of extra bytes to allocate in the output buffer after the request structure). This number should always be a multiple of four.

Variable Length Arguments

Some protocol requests take additional variable length data that follow the `xDoSomethingReq` structure. The format of this data varies from request to request. Some requests require a sequence of 8-bit bytes, others a sequence of 16-bit or 32-bit entities, and still others a sequence of structures.

It is necessary to add the length of any variable length data to the length field of the request structure. That length field is in units of 32-bit longwords. If the data is a string or other sequence of 8-bit bytes, then you must round the length up and shift it before adding:

```
req->length += (nbytes+3)>>2;
```

To transmit variable length data, use the `Data` macros. If the data fits into the output buffer, then this macro copies it to the buffer. If it does not fit, however, the `Data` macro calls `_XSend`, which transmits first the contents of the buffer and then your data. The `Data` macros take three arguments: the display, a pointer to the beginning of the data, and the number of bytes to be sent.

Data(*display*, (char *) *data*, *nbytes*);

Data16(*display*, (short *) *data*, *nbytes*);

Data32(*display*, (long *) *data*, *nbytes*);

`Data`, `Data16`, and `Data32` are macros that may use their last argument more than once, so that argument should be a variable rather than an expression such as "nitems*sizeof(item)". You should do that kind of computation in a separate statement before calling them. Use the appropriate macro when sending byte, short, or long data.

If the protocol request requires a reply, then call the procedure `_XSend` instead of the `Data` macro. `_XSend` takes the same arguments, but because it sends your data immediately instead of copying it into the output buffer (which would later be flushed anyway by the following call on _XReply), it is faster.

Replies

If the protocol request has a reply, then call _XReply after you have finished dealing with all the fixed and variable length arguments. _XReply flushes the output buffer and waits for an xReply packet to arrive. If any events arrive in the meantime, _XReply places them in the queue for later use.

```
Status _XReply( display, rep, extra, discard)
      Display *display;
      xReply *rep;
      int extra;
      Bool discard;
```

display Specifies the connection to the X server.
rep Specifies the reply structure.
extra Specifies the number of 32-bit words expected after the replay.
discard Specifies if any data beyond that specified in the extra argument should be discarded.

The _XReply function waits for a reply packet and copies its contents into the specified rep. _XReply handles error and event packets that occur before the reply is received. _XReply takes four arguments:

- A Display * structure
- A pointer to a reply structure (which must be cast to an xReply *)
- The number of additional 32-bit words (beyond sizeof(xReply) = 32 bytes) in the reply structure
- A Boolean that indicates whether _XReply is to discard any additional bytes beyond those it was told to read

Because most reply structures are 32 bytes long, the third argument is usually 0. The only core protocol exceptions are the replies to GetWindow-Attributes, QueryFont, QueryKeymap, and GetKeyboardControl, which have longer replies.

The last argument should be False if the reply structure is followed by additional variable length data (such as a list or string). It should be True if there is not any variable length data.

Note This last argument is provided for upward-compatibility reasons to allow a client to communicate properly with a hypothetical later version of the server that sends more data than the client expected. For example, some later version of `GetWindowAttributes` might use a larger, but compatible, `xGetWindowAttributesReply` that contains additional attribute data at the end.

`_XReply` returns `True` if it received a reply successfully or `False` if it received any sort of error.

For a request with a reply that is not followed by variable length data, you write something like:

```
_XReply(display, (xReply *)&rep, 0, True);
*ret1 = rep.ret1;
*ret2 = rep.ret2;
*ret3 = rep.ret3;
...
UnlockDisplay(dpy);
SyncHandle();
return (rep.ret4);
}
```

If there is variable length data after the reply, change the `True` to `False`, and use the appropriate `_XRead` function to read the variable length data.

_XRead(*display*, *data_return*, *nbytes*)
  Display **display*;
  char **data_return*;
  long *nbytes*;

display	Specifies the connection to the X server.
data_return	Specifies the buffer.
nbytes	Specifies the number of bytes required.

The `_XRead` function reads the specified number of bytes into data_return.

_XRead16(*display*, *data_return*, *nbytes*)
  Display **display*;
  short **data_return*;
  long *nbytes*;

display	Specifies the connection to the X server.
data_return	Specifies the buffer.
nbytes	Specifies the number of bytes required.

The `_XRead16` function reads the specified number of bytes, unpacking them as 16-bit quantities, into the specified array as shorts.

```
_XRead32(display, data_return, nbytes)
      Display *display;
      long *data_return;
      long nbytes;
```

display Specifies the connection to the X server.
data_return Specifies the buffer.
nbytes Specifies the number of bytes required.

The `_XRead32` function reads the specified number of bytes, unpacking them as 32-bit quantities, into the specified array as longs.

```
_XRead16Pad(display, data_return, nbytes)
      Display *display;
      short *data_return;
      long nbytes;
```

display Specifies the connection to the X server.
data_return Specifies the buffer.
nbytes Specifies the number of bytes required.

The `_XRead16Pad` function reads the specified number of bytes, unpacking them as 16-bit quantities, into the specified array as shorts. If the number of bytes is not a multiple of four, `_XRead16Pad` reads and discards up to three additional pad bytes.

```
_XReadPad(display, data_return, nbytes)
      Display *display;
      char *data_return;
      long nbytes;
```

display Specifies the connection to the X server.
data_return Specifies the buffer.
nbytes Specifies the number of bytes required.

The `_XReadPad` function reads the specified number of bytes into data_return. If the number of bytes is not a multiple of four, `_XReadPad` reads and discards up to three additional pad bytes.

Each protocol request is a little different. For further information, see the Xlib sources for examples.

Synchronous Calling

To ease debugging, each procedure should have a call, just before returning to the user, to a procedure called `SyncHandle`, which generally is implemented as a macro. If synchronous mode is enabled (see `XSynchronize`), the request is sent immediately. The library, however, waits until any error the procedure could generate at the server has been handled.

Allocating and Deallocating Memory

To support the possible reentry of these procedures, you must observe several conventions when allocating and deallocating memory, most often done when returning data to the user from the window system of a size the caller could not know in advance (for example, a list of fonts or a list of extensions). The standard C library functions on many systems are not protected against signals or other multithreaded uses. The following analogies to standard I/O library functions have been defined:

`Xmalloc()`	Replaces `malloc()`
`XFree()`	Replaces `free()`
`Xcalloc()`	Replaces `calloc()`

These should be used in place of any calls you would make to the usual C library functions.

If you need a single scratch buffer inside a critical section (for example, to pack and unpack data to and from the wire protocol), the general memory allocators may be too expensive to use (particularly in output functions, which are performance critical). The following function returns a scratch buffer for your use:

char *_XAllocScratch(*display*, *nbytes*)
    Display **display*;
    unsigned long *nbytes*;

display Specifies the connection to the X server.
nbytes Specifies the number of bytes required.

This storage must only be used inside of the critical section of your stub.

Portability Considerations

Many machine architectures, including many of the more recent RISC architectures, do not correctly access data at unaligned locations; their compilers pad out structures to preserve this characteristic. Many other machines capable of unaligned references pad inside of structures as well to preserve alignment, because accessing aligned data is usually much faster. Because the library and the server use structures to access data at arbitrary points in a byte stream, all data in request and reply packets *must* be naturally aligned; that is, 16-bit data starts on 16-bit boundaries in the request and 32-bit data on 32-bit boundaries. All requests *must* be a multiple of 32 bits in length to preserve the natural alignment in the data stream. You must pad structures out to 32-bit boundaries. Pad information does not have to be zeroed unless you want to preserve such fields for future use in your protocol requests. Floating point varies radically between machines and should be avoided completely if at all possible.

This code may run on machines with 16-bit ints. So, if any integer argument, variable, or return value either can take only nonnegative values or is declared as a `CARD16` in the protocol, be sure to declare it as `unsigned int` and not as `int`. (This, of course, does not apply to Booleans or enumerations.)

Similarly, if any integer argument or return value is declared `CARD32` in the protocol, declare it as an `unsigned long` and not as `int` or `long`. This also goes for any internal variables that may take on values larger than the maximum 16-bit `unsigned int`.

The library currently assumes that a `char` is 8 bits, a `short` is 16 bits, an `int` is 16 or 32 bits, and a `long` is 32 bits. The `PackData` macro is a half-hearted attempt to deal with the possibility of 32 bit shorts. However, much more work is needed to make this work properly.

Deriving the Correct Extension Opcode

The remaining problem a writer of an extension stub procedure faces that the core protocol does not face is to map from the call to the proper major and minor opcodes. While there are a number of strategies, the simplest and fastest is outlined below.

1. Declare an array of pointers, _NFILE long (this is normally found in `<stdio.h>` and is the number of file descriptors supported on the system) of type `XExtCodes`. Make sure these are all initialized to NULL.

2. When your stub is entered, your initialization test is just to use the display pointer passed in to access the file descriptor and an index into the array. If the entry is NULL, then this is the first time you are entering the procedure for this display. Call your initialization procedure and pass it to the display pointer.
3. Once in your initialization procedure, call `XInitExtension`; if it succeeds, store the pointer returned into this array. Make sure to establish a close display handler to allow you to zero the entry. Do whatever other initialization your extension requires. (For example, install event handlers and so on.) Your initialization procedure would normally return a pointer to the `XExtCodes` structure for this extension, which is what would normally be found in your array of pointers.
4. After returning from your initialization procedure, the stub can now continue normally, because it has its major opcode safely in its hand in the `XExtCodes` structure.

Appendix D

Compatibility Functions

The X Version 11 and X Version 10 functions discussed in this appendix are obsolete, have been superseded by newer X Version 11 functions, and are maintained for compatibility reasons only.

X VERSION 11 COMPATIBILITY FUNCTIONS

You can use the X Version 11 compatibility functions to:

- Set standard properties
- Set and get window sizing hints
- Set and get an `XStandardColormap` structure
- Parse window geometry
- Get X environment defaults

Setting Standard Properties

To specify a minimum set of properties describing the simplest application, use `XSetStandardProperties`. This function has been superseded by `XSetWMProperties` and sets all or portions of the WM_NAME, WM_ICON_NAME, WM_HINTS, WM_COMMAND, and WM_NORMAL_HINTS properties.

```
XSetStandardProperties ( display, w, window_name, icon_name, icon_pixmap, argv,
                         argc, hints)
    Display *display;
    Window w;
```

```
    char *window_name;
    char *icon_name;
    Pixmap icon_pixmap;
    char **argv;
    int argc;
    XSizeHints *hints;
```

display Specifies the connection to the X server.
w Specifies the window.
window_name Specifies the window name, which should be a null-terminated string.
icon_name Specifies the icon name, which should be a null-terminated string.
icon_pixmap Specifies the bitmap that is to be used for the icon or `None`.
argv Specifies the application's argument list.
argc Specifies the number of arguments.
hints Specifies a pointer to the size hints for the window in its normal state.

The `XSetStandardProperties` function provides a means by which simple applications set the most essential properties with a single call. `XSetStandardProperties` should be used to give a window manager some information about your program's preferences. It should not be used by applications that need to communicate more information than is possible with `XSetStandardProperties`. (Typically, argv is the argv array of your main program.) If the strings are not in the Host Portable Character Encoding, the result is implementation dependent.

`XSetStandardProperties` can generate `BadAlloc` and `BadWindow` errors.

Setting and Getting Window Sizing Hints

Xlib provides functions that you can use to set or get window sizing hints. The functions discussed in this section use the flags and the `XSizeHints` structure, as defined in the `<X11/Xutil.h>` header file, and use the WM_NORMAL_HINTS property.

To set the size hints for a given window in its normal state, use `XSetNormalHints`. This function has been superseded by `XSetWMNormalHints`.

```
XSetNormalHints(display, w, hints)
    Display *display;
    Window w;
    XSizeHints *hints;
```

display	Specifies the connection to the X server.
w	Specifies the window.
hints	Specifies a pointer to the size hints for the window in its normal state.

The `XSetNormalHints` function sets the size hints structure for the specified window. Applications use `XSetNormalHints` to inform the window manager of the size or position desirable for that window. In addition, an application that wants to move or resize itself should call `XSetNormalHints` and specify its new desired location and size as well as making direct Xlib calls to move or resize. This is because window managers may ignore redirected configure requests, but they pay attention to property changes.

To set size hints, an application not only must assign values to the appropriate members in the hints structure but also must set the flags member of the structure to indicate which information is present and where it came from. A call to `XSetNormalHints` is meaningless, unless the flags member is set to indicate which members of the structure have been assigned values.

`XSetNormalHints` can generate `BadAlloc` and `BadWindow` errors.

To return the size hints for a window in its normal state, use `XGetNormalHints`. This function has been superseded by `XGetWMNormalHints`.

```
Status XGetNormalHints ( display, w, hints_return)
      Display *display;
      Window w;
      XSizeHints *hints_return;
```

display	Specifies the connection to the X server.
w	Specifies the window.
hints_return	Returns the size hints for the window in its normal state.

The `XGetNormalHints` function returns the size hints for a window in its normal state. It returns a nonzero status if it succeeds or zero if the application specified no normal size hints for this window.

`XGetNormalHints` can generate a `BadWindow` error.

The next two functions set and read the WM_ZOOM_HINTS property.

To set the zoom hints for a window, use `XSetZoomHints`. This function is no longer supported by part III, "Inter-Client Communication Conventions Manual."

```
XSetZoomHints ( display, w, zhints)
      Display *display;
      Window w;
      XSizeHints *zhints;
```

display Specifies the connection to the X server.

w Specifies the window.

zhints Specifies a pointer to the zoom hints.

Many window managers think of windows in one of three states: iconic, normal, or zoomed. The `XSetZoomHints` function provides the window manager with information for the window in the zoomed state.

`XSetZoomHints` can generate `BadAlloc` and `BadWindow` errors.

To read the zoom hints for a window, use `XGetZoomHints`. This function is no longer supported by part III, ''Inter-Client Communication Conventions Manual.''

```
Status XGetZoomHints ( display, w, zhints_return)
      Display *display;
      Window w;
      XSizeHints *zhints_return;
```

display Specifies the connection to the X server.

w Specifies the window.

zhints_return Returns the zoom hints.

The `XGetZoomHints` function returns the size hints for a window in its zoomed state. It returns a nonzero status if it succeeds or zero if the application specified no zoom size hints for this window.

`XGetZoomHints` can generate a `BadWindow` error.

To set the value of any property of type WM_SIZE_HINTS, use `XSetSizeHints`. This function has been superseded by `XSetWMSizeHints`.

```
XSetSizeHints ( display, w, hints, property)
      Display *display;
      Window w;
      XSizeHints *hints;
      Atom property;
```

display Specifies the connection to the X server.

w Specifies the window.

hints	Specifies a pointer to the size hints.
property	Specifies the property name.

The XSetSizeHints function sets the XSizeHints structure for the named property and the specified window. This is used by XSetNormalHints and XSetZoomHints, and can be used to set the value of any property of type WM_SIZE_HINTS. Thus, it may be useful if other properties of that type get defined.

XSetSizeHints can generate BadAlloc, BadAtom, and BadWindow errors.

To read the value of any property of type WM_SIZE_HINTS, use XGetSizeHints. This function has been superseded by XGetWMSizeHints.

```
Status XGetSizeHints( display, w, hints_return, property)
      Display *display;
      Window w;
      XSizeHints *hints_return;
      Atom property;
```

display	Specifies the connection to the X server.
w	Specifies the window.
hints_return	Returns the size hints.
property	Specifies the property name.

The XGetSizeHints function returns the XSizeHints structure for the named property and the specified window. This is used by XGetNormalHints and XGetZoomHints. It also can be used to retrieve the value of any property of type WM_SIZE_HINTS. Thus, it may be useful if other properties of that type get defined. XGetSizeHints returns a nonzero status if a size hint was defined or zero otherwise.

XGetSizeHints can generate BadAtom and BadWindow errors.

Getting and Setting an XStandardColormap Structure

To get the XStandardColormap structure associated with one of the described atoms, use XGetStandardColormap. This function has been superseded by XGetRGBColormap.

```
Status XGetStandardColormap( display, w, colormap_return, property)
      Display *display;
      Window w;
```

XStandardColormap **colormap_return*;
Atom *property*; /* RGB_BEST_MAP, etc. */

display	Specifies the connection to the X server.
w	Specifies the window.
colormap_return	Returns the colormap associated with the specified atom.
property	Specifies the property name.

The `XGetStandardColormap` function returns the colormap definition associated with the atom supplied as the property argument. `XGetStandardColormap` returns a nonzero status if successful and a zero otherwise. For example, to fetch the standard `GrayScale` colormap for a display, you use `XGetStandardColormap` with the following syntax:

```
XGetStandardColormap(dpy, DefaultRootWindow(dpy), &cmap,
                    XA_RGB_GRAY_MAP);
```

See section 14.3 of part I, "Xlib — C Language X Interface," for the semantics of standard colormaps.

`XGetStandardColormap` can generate `BadAtom` and `BadWindow` errors.

To set a standard colormap, use `XSetStandardColormap`. This function has been superseded by `XSetRGBColormap`.

XSetStandardColormap(*display, w, colormap, property*)
Display **display*;
Window *w*;
XStandardColormap **colormap*;
Atom *property*; /* RGB_BEST_MAP, etc. */

display	Specifies the connection to the X server.
w	Specifies the window.
colormap	Specifies the colormap.
property	Specifies the property name.

The `XSetStandardColormap` function usually is only used by window or session managers.

`XSetStandardColormap` can generate `BadAlloc`, `BadAtom`, `BadDrawable`, and `BadWindow` errors.

Parsing Window Geometry

To parse window geometry given a user-specified position and a default position, use `XGeometry`. This function has been superseded by `XWMGeometry`.

int XGeometry (*display, screen, position, default_position, bwidth, fwidth, fheight, xadder, yadder, x_return, y_return, width_return, height_return*)
    Display **display*;
    int *screen*;
    char **position*, **default_position*;
    unsigned int *bwidth*;
    unsigned int *fwidth*, *fheight*;
    int *xadder*, *yadder*;
    int **x_return*, **y_return*;
    int **width_return*, **height_return*;

display Specifies the connection to the X server.
screen Specifies the screen.
position
default_position Specify the geometry specifications.
bwidth Specifies the border width.
fheight
fwidth Specify the font height and width in pixels (increment size).
xadder
yadder Specify additional interior padding needed in the window.
x_return
y_return Return the x and y offsets.
width_return
height_return Return the width and height determined.

You pass in the border width (bwidth), size of the increments fwidth and fheight (typically font width and height), and any additional interior space (xadder and yadder) to make it easy to compute the resulting size. The `XGeometry` function returns the position the window should be placed given a position and a default position. `XGeometry` determines the placement of a window using a geometry specification as specified by `XParseGeometry` and the additional information about the window. Given a fully qualified default geometry specification and an incomplete geometry specification, `XParseGeometry` returns a bitmask value as defined above in the `XParseGeometry` call, by using the position argument.

The returned width and height will be the width and height specified by default_position as overridden by any user-specified position. They are not affected by fwidth, fheight, xadder, or yadder. The x and y coordinates are computed by using the border width, the screen width and height, padding as specified by xadder and yadder, and the fheight and fwidth times the width and height from the geometry specifications.

Obtaining the X Environment Defaults

The `XGetDefault` function provides a primitive interface to the resource manager facilities discussed in chapter 15 of part I, "Xlib — C Language X Interface." It is only useful in very simple applications.

```
char *XGetDefault(display, program, option)
      Display *display;
      char *program;
      char *option;
```

display Specifies the connection to the X server.

program Specifies the program name for the Xlib defaults (usually argv[0] of the main program).

option Specifies the option name.

The `XGetDefault` function returns the value of the resource *prog.option*, where *prog* is the program argument with the directory prefix removed and *option* must be a single component. Note that multilevel resources cannot be used with `XGetDefault`. The class "Program.Name" is always used for the resource lookup. If the specified option name does not exist for this program, `XGetDefault` returns NULL. The strings returned by `XGetDefault` are owned by Xlib and should not be modified or freed by the client.

If a database has been set with `XrmSetDatabase`, that database is used for the lookup. Otherwise, a database is created and is set in the display (as if by calling `XrmSetDatabase`). The database is created in the current locale. To create a database, `XGetDefault` uses resources from the RESOURCE_MANAGER property on the root window of screen zero. If no such property exists, a resource file in the user's home directory is used. On a POSIX-conformant system, this file is `$HOME/.Xdefaults`. After loading these defaults, `XGetDefault` merges additional defaults specified by the XENVIRONMENT environment variable. If XENVIRONMENT is defined, it contains a full path name for the additional resource file. If XENVIRONMENT is not defined, `XGetDefault` looks for `$HOME/.Xdefaults-`*name*, where *name* specifies the name of the machine on which the application is running.

X VERSION 10 COMPATIBILITY FUNCTIONS

You can use the X Version 10 compatibility functions to:

- Draw and fill polygons and curves
- Associate user data with a value

Drawing and Filling Polygons and Curves

Xlib provides functions that you can use to draw or fill arbitrary polygons or curves. These functions are provided mainly for compatibility with X Version 10 and have no server support. That is, they call other Xlib functions, not the server directly. Thus, if you just have straight lines to draw, using `XDrawLines` or `XDrawSegments` is much faster.

The functions discussed here provide all the functionality of the X Version 10 functions `XDraw`, `XDrawFilled`, `XDrawPatterned`, `XDrawDashed`, and `XDrawTiled`. They are as compatible as possible given X Version 11's new line drawing functions. One thing to note, however, is that `VertexDrawLastPoint` is no longer supported. Also, the error status returned is the opposite of what it was under X Version 10 (this is the X Version 11 standard error status). `XAppendVertex` and `XClearVertexFlag` from X Version 10 also are not supported.

Just how the graphics context you use is set up actually determines whether you get dashes or not, and so on. Lines are properly joined if they connect and include the closing of a closed figure (see `XDrawLines`). The functions discussed here fail (return zero) only if they run out of memory or are passed a `Vertex` list that has a `Vertex` with `VertexStartClosed` set that is not followed by a `Vertex` with `VertexEndClosed` set.

To achieve the effects of the X Version 10 `XDraw`, `XDrawDashed`, and `XDrawPatterned`, use `XDraw`.

```
#include <X11/X10.h>

Status XDraw(display, d, gc, vlist, vcount)
  Display *display;
  Drawable d;
  GC gc;
  Vertex *vlist;
  int vcount;
```

display Specifies the connection to the X server.
d Specifies the drawable.
gc Specifies the GC.
vlist Specifies a pointer to the list of vertices that indicate what to draw.
vcount Specifies how many vertices are in vlist.

The `XDraw` function draws an arbitrary polygon or curve. The figure drawn is defined by the specified list of vertices (vlist). The points are connected by lines as specified in the flags in the vertex structure.

Each Vertex, as defined in `<X11/X10.h>`, is a structure with the following members:

```
typedef struct _Vertex {
    short x,y;
    unsigned short flags; } Vertex;
```

The x and y members are the coordinates of the vertex that are relative to either the upper-left inside corner of the drawable (if `VertexRelative` is zero) or the previous vertex (if `VertexRelative` is one).

The flags, as defined in `<X11/X10.h>`, are as follows:

```
VertexRelative       0x0001    /* else absolute */
VertexDontDraw       0x0002    /* else draw */
VertexCurved         0x0004    /* else straight */
VertexStartClosed    0x0008    /* else not */
VertexEndClosed      0x0010    /* else not */
```

- If `VertexRelative` is not set, the coordinates are absolute (that is, relative to the drawable's origin). The first vertex must be an absolute vertex.
- If `VertexDontDraw` is one, no line or curve is drawn from the previous vertex to this one. This is analogous to picking up the pen and moving to another place before drawing another line.
- If `VertexCurved` is one, a spline algorithm is used to draw a smooth curve from the previous vertex through this one to the next vertex. Otherwise, a straight line is drawn from the previous vertex to this one. It makes sense to set `VertexCurved` to one only if a previous and next vertex are both defined (either explicitly in the array or through the definition of a closed curve).
- It is permissible for `VertexDontDraw` bits and `VertexCurved` bits both to be one. This is useful if you want to define the previous point for the smooth curve but do not want an actual curve drawing to start until this point.

- If `VertexStartClosed` is one, then this point marks the beginning of a closed curve. This vertex must be followed later in the array by another vertex whose effective coordinates are identical and that has a `VertexEndClosed` bit of one. The points in between form a cycle to determine predecessor and successor vertices for the spline algorithm.

This function uses these GC components: function, plane-mask, line-width, line-style, cap-style, join-style, fill-style, subwindow-mode, clip-x-origin, clip-y-origin, and clip-mask. It also uses these GC mode-dependent components: foreground, background, tile, stipple, tile-stipple-x-origin, tile-stipple-y-origin, dash-offset, and dash-list.

To achieve the effects of the X Version 10 `XDrawTiled` and `XDrawFilled`, use `XDrawFilled`.

```
#include <X11/X10.h>

Status XDrawFilled(display, d, gc, vlist, vcount)
      Display *display;
      Drawable d;
      GC gc;
      Vertex *vlist;
      int vcount;
```

display Specifies the connection to the X server.
d Specifies the drawable.
gc Specifies the GC.
vlist Specifies a pointer to the list of vertices that indicate what to draw.
vcount Specifies how many vertices are in vlist.

The `XDrawFilled` function draws arbitrary polygons or curves and then fills them.

This function uses these GC components: function, plane-mask, line-width, line-style, cap-style, join-style, fill-style, subwindow-mode, clip-x-origin, clip-y-origin, and clip-mask. It also uses these GC mode-dependent components: foreground, background, tile, stipple, tile-stipple-x-origin, tile-stipple-y-origin, dash-offset, dash-list, fill-style, and fill-rule.

Associating User Data with a Value

These functions have been superseded by the context management functions (see section 16.10 of part I, "Xlib — C Language X Interface"). It is often necessary to associate arbitrary information with resource IDs. Xlib provides the XAssocTable functions that you can use to make such an association. Application programs often need to be able to easily refer to their own data structures when an event arrives. The XAssocTable system provides users of the X library with a method for associating their own data structures with X resources (Pixmaps, Fonts, Windows, and so on).

An XAssocTable can be used to type X resources. For example, the user may want to have three or four types of windows, each with different properties. This can be accomplished by associating each X window ID with a pointer to a window property data structure defined by the user. A generic type has been defined in the X library for resource IDs. It is called an XID.

There are a few guidelines that should be observed when using an XAssocTable:

- All XIDs are relative to the specified display.
- Because of the hashing scheme used by the association mechanism, the following rules for determining the size of a XAssocTable should be followed. Associations will be made and looked up more efficiently if the table size (number of buckets in the hashing system) is a power of two and if there are not more than 8 XIDs per bucket.

To return a pointer to a new XAssocTable, use XCreateAssocTable.

```
XAssocTable *XCreateAssocTable (size)
      int size;
```

size Specifies the number of buckets in the hash system of XAssocTable.

The size argument specifies the number of buckets in the hash system of XAssocTable. For reasons of efficiency the number of buckets should be a power of two. Some size suggestions might be: use 32 buckets per 100 objects, and a reasonable maximum number of objects per buckets is 8. If an error allocating memory for the XAssocTable occurs, a NULL pointer is returned.

To create an entry in a given XAssocTable, use XMakeAssoc.

```
XMakeAssoc (display, table, x_id, data)
      Display *display;
      XAssocTable *table;
      XID x_id;
      char *data;
```

display Specifies the connection to the X server.

table Specifies the assoc table.
x_id Specifies the X resource ID.
data Specifies the data to be associated with the X resource ID.

The XMakeAssoc function inserts data into an XAssocTable keyed on an XID. Data is inserted into the table only once. Redundant inserts are ignored. The queue in each association bucket is sorted from the lowest XID to the highest XID.

To obtain data from a given XAssocTable, use XLookUpAssoc.

```
char *XLookUpAssoc ( display, table, x_id)
    Display *display;
    XAssocTable *table;
    XID x_id;
```

display Specifies the connection to the X server.
table Specifies the assoc table.
x_id Specifies the X resource ID.

The XLookUpAssoc function retrieves the data stored in an XAssocTable by its XID. If an appropriately matching XID can be found in the table, XLookUpAssoc returns the data associated with it. If the x_id cannot be found in the table, it returns NULL.

To delete an entry from a given XAssocTable, use XDeleteAssoc.

```
XDeleteAssoc ( display, table, x_id)
    Display *display;
    XAssocTable *table;
    XID x_id;
```

display Specifies the connection to the X server.
table Specifies the assoc table.
x_id Specifies the X resource ID.

The XDeleteAssoc function deletes an association in an XAssocTable keyed on its XID. Redundant deletes (and deletes of nonexistent XIDs) are ignored. Deleting associations in no way impairs the performance of an XAssocTable.

To free the memory associated with a given XAssocTable, use XDestroyAssocTable.

```
XDestroyAssocTable ( table)
    XAssocTable *table;
```

table Specifies the assoc table.

Appendix E

KEYSYM Encoding

For convenience, KEYSYM values are viewed as split into four bytes:

- Byte 1 (for the purposes of this encoding) is the most-significant 5 bits (because of the 29-bit effective values)
- Byte 2 is the next most-significant 8 bits
- Byte 3 is the next most-significant 8 bits
- Byte 4 is the least-significant 8 bits

There are two special KEYSYM values: `NoSymbol` and `VoidSymbol`. They are used to indicate the absence of symbols (see section 5 of part II, "X Window System Protocol").

Byte 1	*Byte 2*	*Byte 3*	*Byte 4*	*Name*
0	0	0	0	`NoSymbol`
0	255	255	255	`VoidSymbol`

All other standard KEYSYM values have zero values for bytes 1 and 2. Byte 3 indicates a character code set, and byte 4 indicates a particular character within that set.

Byte 3	*Byte 4*
0	Latin-1
1	Latin-2
2	Latin-3
3	Latin-4

Byte 3	*Byte 4*
4	Kana
5	Arabic
6	Cyrillic
7	Greek
8	Technical
9	Special
10	Publishing
11	APL
12	Hebrew
255	Keyboard

Each character set contains gaps where codes have been removed that were duplicates with codes in previous character sets (that is, character sets with lesser byte 3 value).

The 94 and 96 character code sets have been moved to occupy the right-hand quadrant (decimal 129 through 256), so the ASCII subset has a unique encoding across byte 4, which corresponds to the ASCII character code. However, this cannot be guaranteed with future registrations and does not apply to all of the Keyboard set.

To the best of our knowledge, the Latin, Kana, Arabic, Cyrillic, Greek, APL, and Hebrew sets are from the appropriate ISO and/or ECMA international standards. There are no Technical, Special, or Publishing international standards, so these sets are based on Digital Equipment Corporation standards.

The ordering between the sets (byte 3) is essentially arbitrary. National and international standards bodies were commencing deliberations regarding international 2-byte and 4-byte character sets at the time these keysyms were developed, but we did not know of any proposed layouts.

The order may be arbitrary, but it is important in dealing with duplicate coding. As far as possible, keysym values (byte 4) follow the character set encoding standards, except for the Greek and Cyrillic keysyms which are based on early draft standards. In the Latin-1 to Latin-4 sets, all duplicate glyphs occupy the same code position. However, duplicates between Greek and Technical do not occupy the same code position. Applications that wish to use the Latin-2, Latin-3, Latin-4, Greek, Cyrillic, or Technical sets may find it convenient to use arrays to transform the keysyms.

There is a difference between European and US usage of the names Pilcrow, Paragraph, and Section, as follows:

US name	*European name*	*code position in Latin-1*
Section sign	Paragraph sign	10/07
Paragraph sign	Pilcrow sign	11/06

We have adopted the US names (by accident rather than by design).

The Keyboard set is a miscellaneous collection of commonly occurring keys on keyboards. Within this set, the keypad symbols are generally duplicates of symbols found on keys on the main part of the keyboard, but they are distinguished here because they often have a distinguishable semantics associated with them.

Keyboards tend to be comparatively standard with respect to the alphanumeric keys, but they differ radically on the miscellaneous function keys. Many function keys are left over from early timesharing days or are designed for a specific application. Keyboard layouts from large manufacturers tend to have lots of keys for every conceivable purpose, whereas small workstation manufacturers often add keys that are solely for support of some of their unique functionality. There are two ways of thinking about how to define keysyms for such a world:

- The Engraving approach
- The Common approach

The Engraving approach is to create a keysym for every unique key engraving. This is effectively taking the union of all key engravings on all keyboards. For example, some keyboards label function keys across the top as F1 through Fn, and others label them as PF1 through PFn. These would be different keys under the Engraving approach. Likewise, Lock would differ from Shift Lock, which is different from the up-arrow symbol that has the effect of changing lowercase to uppercase. There are lots of other aliases such as Del, DEL, Delete, Remove, and so forth. The Engraving approach makes it easy to decide if a new entry should be added to the keysym set: if it does not exactly match an existing one, then a new one is created. One estimate is that there would be on the order of 300–500 Keyboard keysyms using this approach, without counting foreign translations and variations.

The Common approach tries to capture all of the keys present on an interesting number of keyboards, folding likely aliases into the same keysym. For example, Del, DEL, and Delete are all merged into a single keysym. Vendors would be expected to augment the keysym set (using the vendor-specific encoding space) to include all of their unique keys that were not included in the standard set. Each vendor decides which of its keys map into the standard keysyms, which presumably can be overridden by a user. It is more difficult to implement this approach, because judgment is required about when a sufficient set of keyboards implements an engraving to justify making it a keysym in the standard set and about which engravings should be merged into a single keysym. Under this scheme there are an estimated 100–150 keysyms.

Although neither scheme is perfect or elegant, the Common approach has been selected because it makes it easier to write a portable application. Having the Delete functionality merged into a single keysym allows an application to implement a deletion function and expect reasonable bindings on a wide set of workstations. Under the Common approach, application writers are still free to look for and interpret vendor-specific keysyms, but because they are in the extended set, the application developer is more conscious that they are writing the application in a nonportable fashion.

In the listings below, Code Pos is a representation of byte 4 of the KEYSYM value, expressed as most-significant/least-significant 4-bit values. The Code Pos numbers are for reference only and do not affect the KEYSYM value. In all cases, the KEYSYM value is

byte 3 * 256 + byte 4

Byte 3	Byte 4	Code Pos	Character	Name	Set
000	032	02/00		SPACE	Latin-1
000	033	02/01	!	EXCLAMATION POINT	Latin-1
000	034	02/02	"	QUOTATION MARK	Latin-1
000	035	02/03	#	NUMBER SIGN	Latin-1
000	036	02/04	$	DOLLAR SIGN	Latin-1
000	037	02/05	%	PERCENT SIGN	Latin-1
000	038	02/06	&	AMPERSAND	Latin-1
000	039	02/07	'	APOSTROPHE	Latin-1
000	040	02/08	(	LEFT PARENTHESIS	Latin-1
000	041	02/09	)	RIGHT PARENTHESIS	Latin-1
000	042	02/10	*	ASTERISK	Latin-1
000	043	02/11	+	PLUS SIGN	Latin-1
000	044	02/12	,	COMMA	Latin-1
000	045	02/13	-	MINUS SIGN	Latin-1
000	046	02/14	.	FULL STOP	Latin-1
000	047	02/15	/	SOLIDUS	Latin-1
000	048	03/00	0	DIGIT ZERO	Latin-1
000	049	03/01	1	DIGIT ONE	Latin-1
000	050	03/02	2	DIGIT TWO	Latin-1
000	051	03/03	3	DIGIT THREE	Latin-1
000	052	03/04	4	DIGIT FOUR	Latin-1
000	053	03/05	5	DIGIT FIVE	Latin-1
000	054	03/06	6	DIGIT SIX	Latin-1
000	055	03/07	7	DIGIT SEVEN	Latin-1
000	056	03/08	8	DIGIT EIGHT	Latin-1
000	057	03/09	9	DIGIT NINE	Latin-1
000	058	03/10	:	COLON	Latin-1
000	059	03/11	;	SEMICOLON	Latin-1
000	060	03/12	<	LESS THAN SIGN	Latin-1

Byte 3	*Byte 4*	*Code Pos*	*Character*	*Name*	*Set*
000	061	03/13	=	EQUALS SIGN	Latin-1
000	062	03/14	>	GREATER THAN SIGN	Latin-1
000	063	03/15	?	QUESTION MARK	Latin-1
000	064	04/00	@	COMMERCIAL AT	Latin-1
000	065	04/01	A	LATIN CAPITAL LETTER A	Latin-1
000	066	04/02	B	LATIN CAPITAL LETTER B	Latin-1
000	067	04/03	C	LATIN CAPITAL LETTER C	Latin-1
000	068	04/04	D	LATIN CAPITAL LETTER D	Latin-1
000	069	04/05	E	LATIN CAPITAL LETTER E	Latin-1
000	070	04/06	F	LATIN CAPITAL LETTER F	Latin-1
000	071	04/07	G	LATIN CAPITAL LETTER G	Latin-1
000	072	04/08	H	LATIN CAPITAL LETTER H	Latin-1
000	073	04/09	I	LATIN CAPITAL LETTER I	Latin-1
000	074	04/10	J	LATIN CAPITAL LETTER J	Latin-1
000	075	04/11	K	LATIN CAPITAL LETTER K	Latin-1
000	076	04/12	L	LATIN CAPITAL LETTER L	Latin-1
000	077	04/13	M	LATIN CAPITAL LETTER M	Latin-1
000	078	04/14	N	LATIN CAPITAL LETTER N	Latin-1
000	079	04/15	O	LATIN CAPITAL LETTER O	Latin-1
000	080	05/00	P	LATIN CAPITAL LETTER P	Latin-1
000	081	05/01	Q	LATIN CAPITAL LETTER Q	Latin-1
000	082	05/02	R	LATIN CAPITAL LETTER R	Latin-1
000	083	05/03	S	LATIN CAPITAL LETTER S	Latin-1
000	084	05/04	T	LATIN CAPITAL LETTER T	Latin-1
000	085	05/05	U	LATIN CAPITAL LETTER U	Latin-1
000	086	05/06	V	LATIN CAPITAL LETTER V	Latin-1
000	087	05/07	W	LATIN CAPITAL LETTER W	Latin-1
000	088	05/08	X	LATIN CAPITAL LETTER X	Latin-1
000	089	05/09	Y	LATIN CAPITAL LETTER Y	Latin-1

000	090	05/10	Z	LATIN CAPITAL LETTER Z	Latin-1
000	091	05/11	[	LEFT SQUARE BRACKET	Latin-1
000	092	05/12	\	REVERSE SOLIDUS	Latin-1
000	093	05/13	]	RIGHT SQUARE BRACKET	Latin-1
000	094	05/14	^	CIRCUMFLEX ACCENT	Latin-1
000	095	05/15	_	LOW LINE	Latin-1
000	096	06/00	`	GRAVE ACCENT	Latin-1
000	097	06/01	a	LATIN SMALL LETTER a	Latin-1
000	098	06/02	b	LATIN SMALL LETTER b	Latin-1
000	099	06/03	c	LATIN SMALL LETTER c	Latin-1
000	100	06/04	d	LATIN SMALL LETTER d	Latin-1
000	101	06/05	e	LATIN SMALL LETTER e	Latin-1
000	102	06/06	f	LATIN SMALL LETTER f	Latin-1
000	103	06/07	g	LATIN SMALL LETTER g	Latin-1
000	104	06/08	h	LATIN SMALL LETTER h	Latin-1
000	105	06/09	i	LATIN SMALL LETTER i	Latin-1
000	106	06/10	j	LATIN SMALL LETTER j	Latin-1
000	107	06/11	k	LATIN SMALL LETTER k	Latin-1
000	108	06/12	l	LATIN SMALL LETTER l	Latin-1
000	109	06/13	m	LATIN SMALL LETTER m	Latin-1
000	110	06/14	n	LATIN SMALL LETTER n	Latin-1
000	111	06/15	o	LATIN SMALL LETTER o	Latin-1
000	112	07/00	p	LATIN SMALL LETTER p	Latin-1
000	113	07/01	q	LATIN SMALL LETTER q	Latin-1
000	114	07/02	r	LATIN SMALL LETTER r	Latin-1
000	115	07/03	s	LATIN SMALL LETTER s	Latin-1
000	116	07/04	t	LATIN SMALL LETTER t	Latin-1
000	117	07/05	u	LATIN SMALL LETTER u	Latin-1
000	118	07/06	v	LATIN SMALL LETTER v	Latin-1
000	119	07/07	w	LATIN SMALL LETTER w	Latin-1
000	120	07/08	x	LATIN SMALL LETTER x	Latin-1
000	121	07/09	y	LATIN SMALL LETTER y	Latin-1

Byte 3	*Byte 4*	*Code Pos*	*Character*	*Name*	*Set*
000	122	07/10	z	LATIN SMALL LETTER z	Latin-1
000	123	07/11	{	LEFT CURLY BRACKET	Latin-1
000	124	07/12	|	VERTICAL LINE	Latin-1
000	125	07/13	}	RIGHT CURLY BRACKET	Latin-1
000	126	07/14	~	TILDE	Latin-1
000	160	10/00		NO-BREAK SPACE	Latin-1
000	161	10/01	¡	INVERTED EXCLAMATION MARK	Latin-1
000	162	10/02	¢	CENT SIGN	Latin-1
000	163	10/03	£	POUND SIGN	Latin-1
000	164	10/04	¤	CURRENCY SIGN	Latin-1
000	165	10/05	¥	YEN SIGN	Latin-1
000	166	10/06	¦	BROKEN VERTICAL BAR	Latin-1
000	167	10/07	§	SECTION SIGN	Latin-1
000	168	10/08	¨	DIAERESIS	Latin-1
000	169	10/09	©	COPYRIGHT SIGN	Latin-1
000	170	10/10	ª	FEMININE ORDINAL INDICATOR	Latin-1
000	171	10/11	«	LEFT ANGLE QUOTATION MARK	Latin-1
000	172	10/12	¬	NOT SIGN	Latin-1
000	173	10/13	-	HYPHEN	Latin-1
000	174	10/14	®	REGISTERED TRADEMARK SIGN	Latin-1
000	175	10/15	¯	MACRON	Latin-1
000	176	11/00	°	DEGREE SIGN, RING ABOVE	Latin-1
000	177	11/01	±	PLUS-MINUS SIGN	Latin-1
000	178	11/02	²	SUPERSCRIPT TWO	Latin-1
000	179	11/03	³	SUPERSCRIPT THREE	Latin-1
000	180	11/04	´	ACUTE ACCENT	Latin-1
000	181	11/05	µ	MICRO SIGN	Latin-1
000	182	11/06	¶	PARAGRAPH SIGN	Latin-1
000	183	11/07	·	MIDDLE DOT	Latin-1

000	184	11/08	¸	CEDILLA	Latin-1
000	185	11/09	¹	SUPERSCRIPT ONE	Latin-1
000	186	11/10	º	MASCULINE ORDINAL INDICATOR	Latin-1
000	187	11/11	»	RIGHT ANGLE QUOTATION MARK	Latin-1
000	188	11/12	¼	VULGAR FRACTION ONE QUARTER	Latin-1
000	189	11/13	½	VULGAR FRACTION ONE HALF	Latin-1
000	190	11/14	¾	VULGAR FRACTION THREE QUARTERS	Latin-1
000	191	11/15	¿	INVERTED QUESTION MARK	Latin-1
000	192	12/00	À	LATIN CAPITAL LETTER A WITH GRAVE ACCENT	Latin-1
000	193	12/01	Á	LATIN CAPITAL LETTER A WITH ACUTE ACCENT	Latin-1
000	194	12/02	Â	LATIN CAPITAL LETTER A WITH CIRCUMFLEX ACCENT	Latin-1
000	195	12/03	Ã	LATIN CAPITAL LETTER A WITH TILDE	Latin-1
000	196	12/04	Ä	LATIN CAPITAL LETTER A WITH DIAERESIS	Latin-1
000	197	12/05	Å	LATIN CAPITAL LETTER A WITH RING ABOVE	Latin-1
000	198	12/06	Æ	LATIN CAPITAL DIPHTHONG AE	Latin-1
000	199	12/07	Ç	LATIN CAPITAL LETTER C WITH CEDILLA	Latin-1
000	200	12/08	È	LATIN CAPITAL LETTER E WITH GRAVE ACCENT	Latin-1
000	201	12/09	É	LATIN CAPITAL LETTER E WITH ACUTE ACCENT	Latin-1
000	202	12/10	Ê	LATIN CAPITAL LETTER E WITH CIRCUMFLEX ACCENT	Latin-1
000	203	12/11	Ë	LATIN CAPITAL LETTER E WITH DIAERESIS	Latin-1
000	204	12/12	Ì	LATIN CAPITAL LETTER I WITH GRAVE ACCENT	Latin-1
000	205	12/13	Í	LATIN CAPITAL LETTER I WITH ACUTE ACCENT	Latin-1
000	206	12/14	Î	LATIN CAPITAL LETTER I WITH CIRCUMFLEX ACCENT	Latin-1
000	207	12/15	Ï	LATIN CAPITAL LETTER I WITH DIAERESIS	Latin-1
000	208	13/00	Ð	ICELANDIC CAPITAL LETTER ETH	Latin-1
000	209	13/01	Ñ	LATIN CAPITAL LETTER N WITH TILDE	Latin-1
000	210	13/02	Ò	LATIN CAPITAL LETTER O WITH GRAVE ACCENT	Latin-1
000	211	13/03	Ó	LATIN CAPITAL LETTER O WITH ACUTE ACCENT	Latin-1
000	212	13/04	Ô	LATIN CAPITAL LETTER O WITH CIRCUMFLEX ACCENT	Latin-1
000	213	13/05	Õ	LATIN CAPITAL LETTER O WITH TILDE	Latin-1
000	214	13/06	Ö	LATIN CAPITAL LETTER O WITH DIAERESIS	Latin-1
000	215	13/07	×	MULTIPLICATION SIGN	Latin-1

Byte 3	*Byte 4*	*Code Pos*	*Character*	*Name*	*Set*
000	216	13/08	Ø	LATIN CAPITAL LETTER O WITH OBLIQUE STROKE	Latin-1
000	217	13/09	Ù	LATIN CAPITAL LETTER U WITH GRAVE ACCENT	Latin-1
000	218	13/10	Ú	LATIN CAPITAL LETTER U WITH ACUTE ACCENT	Latin-1
000	219	13/11	Û	LATIN CAPITAL LETTER U WITH CIRCUMFLEX ACCENT	Latin-1
000	220	13/12	Ü	LATIN CAPITAL LETTER U WITH DIAERESIS	Latin-1
000	221	13/13	Ý	LATIN CAPITAL LETTER Y WITH ACUTE ACCENT	Latin-1
000	222	13/14	Þ	ICELANDIC CAPITAL LETTER THORN	Latin-1
000	223	13/15	ß	GERMAN SMALL LETTER SHARP s	Latin-1
000	224	14/00	à	LATIN SMALL LETTER a WITH GRAVE ACCENT	Latin-1
000	225	14/01	á	LATIN SMALL LETTER a WITH ACUTE ACCENT	Latin-1
000	226	14/02	â	LATIN SMALL LETTER a WITH CIRCUMFLEX ACCENT	Latin-1
000	227	14/03	ã	LATIN SMALL LETTER a WITH TILDE	Latin-1
000	228	14/04	ä	LATIN SMALL LETTER a WITH DIAERESIS	Latin-1
000	229	14/05	å	LATIN SMALL LETTER a WITH RING ABOVE	Latin-1
000	230	14/06	æ	LATIN SMALL DIPHTHONG ae	Latin-1
000	231	14/07	ç	LATIN SMALL LETTER c WITH CEDILLA	Latin-1
000	232	14/08	è	LATIN SMALL LETTER e WITH GRAVE ACCENT	Latin-1
000	233	14/09	é	LATIN SMALL LETTER e WITH ACUTE ACCENT	Latin-1
000	234	14/10	ê	LATIN SMALL LETTER e WITH CIRCUMFLEX ACCENT	Latin-1
000	235	14/11	ë	LATIN SMALL LETTER e WITH DIAERESIS	Latin-1
000	236	14/12	ì	LATIN SMALL LETTER i WITH GRAVE ACCENT	Latin-1
000	237	14/13	í	LATIN SMALL LETTER i WITH ACUTE ACCENT	Latin-1
000	238	14/14	î	LATIN SMALL LETTER i WITH CIRCUMFLEX ACCENT	Latin-1
000	239	14/15	ï	LATIN SMALL LETTER i WITH DIAERESIS	Latin-1
000	240	15/00	ð	ICELANDIC SMALL LETTER ETH	Latin-1
000	241	15/01	ñ	LATIN SMALL LETTER n WITH TILDE	Latin-1
000	242	15/02	ò	LATIN SMALL LETTER o WITH GRAVE ACCENT	Latin-1
000	243	15/03	ó	LATIN SMALL LETTER o WITH ACUTE ACCENT	Latin-1
000	244	15/04	ô	LATIN SMALL LETTER o WITH CIRCUMFLEX ACCENT	Latin-1

000	245	15/05	õ	LATIN SMALL LETTER o WITH TILDE	Latin-1
000	246	15/06	ö	LATIN SMALL LETTER o WITH DIAERESIS	Latin-1
000	247	15/07	÷	DIVISION SIGN	Latin-1
000	248	15/08	ø	LATIN SMALL LETTER o WITH OBLIQUE STROKE	Latin-1
000	249	15/09	ù	LATIN SMALL LETTER u WITH GRAVE ACCENT	Latin-1
000	250	15/10	ú	LATIN SMALL LETTER u WITH ACUTE ACCENT	Latin-1
000	251	15/11	û	LATIN SMALL LETTER u WITH CIRCUMFLEX ACCENT	Latin-1
000	252	15/12	ü	LATIN SMALL LETTER u WITH DIAERESIS	Latin-1
000	253	15/13	ý	LATIN SMALL LETTER y WITH ACUTE ACCENT	Latin-1
000	254	15/14	þ	ICELANDIC SMALL LETTER THORN	Latin-1
000	255	15/15	ÿ	LATIN SMALL LETTER y WITH DIAERESIS	Latin-1
001	161	10/01	Ą	LATIN CAPITAL LETTER A WITH OGONEK	Latin-2
001	162	10/02	˘	BREVE	Latin-2
001	163	10/03	Ł	LATIN CAPITAL LETTER L WITH STROKE	Latin-2
001	165	10/05	Ľ	LATIN CAPITAL LETTER L WITH CARON	Latin-2
001	166	10/06	Ś	LATIN CAPITAL LETTER S WITH ACUTE ACCENT	Latin-2
001	169	10/09	Š	LATIN CAPITAL LETTER S WITH CARON	Latin-2
001	170	10/10	Ş	LATIN CAPITAL LETTER S WITH CEDILLA	Latin-2
001	171	10/11	Ť	LATIN CAPITAL LETTER T WITH CARON	Latin-2
001	172	10/12	Ź	LATIN CAPITAL LETTER Z WITH ACUTE ACCENT	Latin-2
001	174	10/14	Ž	LATIN CAPITAL LETTER Z WITH CARON	Latin-2
001	175	10/15	Ż	LATIN CAPITAL LETTER Z WITH DOT ABOVE	Latin-2
001	177	11/01	ą	LATIN SMALL LETTER a WITH OGONEK	Latin-2
001	178	11/02	˛	OGONEK	Latin-2
001	179	11/03	ł	LATIN SMALL LETTER l WITH STROKE	Latin-2
001	181	11/05	ľ	LATIN SMALL LETTER l WITH CARON	Latin-2
001	182	11/06	ś	LATIN SMALL LETTER s WITH ACUTE ACCENT	Latin-2
001	183	11/07	ˇ	CARON	Latin-2
001	185	11/09	š	LATIN SMALL LETTER s WITH CARON	Latin-2
001	186	11/10	ş	LATIN SMALL LETTER s WITH CEDILLA	Latin-2

Byte 3	*Byte* 4	*Code* *Pos*	*Character*	*Name*	*Set*
001	187	11/11	ť	LATIN SMALL LETTER t WITH CARON	Latin-2
001	188	11/12	ź	LATIN SMALL LETTER z WITH ACUTE ACCENT	Latin-2
001	189	11/13	˝	DOUBLE ACUTE ACCENT	Latin-2
001	190	11/14	ž	LATIN SMALL LETTER z WITH CARON	Latin-2
001	191	11/15	ż	LATIN SMALL LETTER z WITH DOT ABOVE	Latin-2
001	192	12/00	Ŕ	LATIN CAPITAL LETTER R WITH ACUTE ACCENT	Latin-2
001	195	12/03	Ă	LATIN CAPITAL LETTER A WITH BREVE	Latin-2
001	197	12/05	Ĺ	LATIN CAPITAL LETTER L WITH ACUTE ACCENT	Latin-2
001	198	12/06	Ć	LATIN CAPITAL LETTER C WITH ACUTE ACCENT	Latin-2
001	200	12/08	Č	LATIN CAPITAL LETTER C WITH CARON	Latin-2
001	202	12/10	Ę	LATIN CAPITAL LETTER E WITH OGONEK	Latin-2
001	204	12/12	Ě	LATIN CAPITAL LETTER E WITH CARON	Latin-2
001	207	12/15	Ď	LATIN CAPITAL LETTER D WITH CARON	Latin-2
001	208	13/00	Đ	LATIN CAPITAL LETTER D WITH STROKE	Latin-2
001	209	13/01	Ń	LATIN CAPITAL LETTER N WITH ACUTE ACCENT	Latin-2
001	210	13/02	Ň	LATIN CAPITAL LETTER N WITH CARON	Latin-2
001	213	13/05	Ő	LATIN CAPITAL LETTER O WITH DOUBLE ACUTE ACCENT	Latin-2
001	216	13/08	Ř	LATIN CAPITAL LETTER R WITH CARON	Latin-2
001	217	13/09	Ů	LATIN CAPITAL LETTER U WITH RING ABOVE	Latin-2
001	219	13/11	Ű	LATIN CAPITAL LETTER U WITH DOUBLE ACUTE ACCENT	Latin-2
001	222	13/14	Ţ	LATIN CAPITAL LETTER T WITH CEDILLA	Latin-2
001	224	14/00	ŕ	LATIN SMALL LETTER r WITH ACUTE ACCENT	Latin-2
001	227	14/03	ă	LATIN SMALL LETTER a WITH BREVE	Latin-2
001	229	14/05	ĺ	LATIN SMALL LETTER l WITH ACUTE ACCENT	Latin-2
001	230	14/06	ć	LATIN SMALL LETTER c WITH ACUTE ACCENT	Latin-2
001	232	14/08	č	LATIN SMALL LETTER c WITH CARON	Latin-2
001	234	14/10	ę	LATIN SMALL LETTER e WITH OGONEK	Latin-2
001	236	14/12	ě	LATIN SMALL LETTER e WITH CARON	Latin-2
001	239	14/15	ď	LATIN SMALL LETTER d WITH CARON	Latin-2

001	240	15/00	đ	LATIN SMALL LETTER d WITH STROKE	Latin-2
001	241	15/01	ń	LATIN SMALL LETTER n WITH ACUTE ACCENT	Latin-2
001	242	15/02	ň	LATIN SMALL LETTER n WITH CARON	Latin-2
001	245	15/05	ő	LATIN SMALL LETTER o WITH DOUBLE ACUTE ACCENT	Latin-2
001	248	15/08	ř	LATIN SMALL LETTER r WITH CARON	Latin-2
001	249	15/09	ů	LATIN SMALL LETTER u WITH RING ABOVE	Latin-2
001	251	15/11	ű	LATIN SMALL LETTER u WITH DOUBLE ACUTE ACCENT	Latin-2
001	254	15/14	ţ	LATIN SMALL LETTER t WITH CEDILLA	Latin-2
001	255	15/15	˙	DOT ABOVE	Latin-2
002	161	10/01	Ħ	LATIN CAPITAL LETTER H WITH STROKE	Latin-3
002	166	10/06	Ĥ	LATIN CAPITAL LETTER H WITH CIRCUMFLEX ACCENT	Latin-3
002	169	10/09	İ	LATIN CAPITAL LETTER I WITH DOT ABOVE	Latin-3
002	171	10/11	Ğ	LATIN CAPITAL LETTER G WITH BREVE	Latin-3
002	172	10/12	Ĵ	LATIN CAPITAL LETTER J WITH CIRCUMFLEX ACCENT	Latin-3
002	177	11/01	ħ	LATIN SMALL LETTER h WITH STROKE	Latin-3
002	182	11/06	ĥ	LATIN SMALL LETTER h WITH CIRCUMFLEX ACCENT	Latin-3
002	185	11/09	ı	SMALL DOTLESS LETTER i	Latin-3
002	187	11/11	ğ	LATIN SMALL LETTER g WITH BREVE	Latin-3
002	188	11/12	ĵ	LATIN SMALL LETTER j WITH CIRCUMFLEX ACCENT	Latin-3
002	197	12/05	Ċ	LATIN CAPITAL LETTER C WITH DOT ABOVE	Latin-3
002	198	12/06	Ĉ	LATIN CAPITAL LETTER C WITH CIRCUMFLEX ACCENT	Latin-3
002	213	13/05	Ġ	LATIN CAPITAL LETTER G WITH DOT ABOVE	Latin-3
002	216	13/08	Ĝ	LATIN CAPITAL LETTER G WITH CIRCUMFLEX ACCENT	Latin-3
002	221	13/13	Ŭ	LATIN CAPITAL LETTER U WITH BREVE	Latin-3
002	222	13/14	Ŝ	LATIN CAPITAL LETTER S WITH CIRCUMFLEX ACCENT	Latin-3
002	229	14/05	ċ	LATIN SMALL LETTER c WITH DOT ABOVE	Latin-3
002	230	14/06	ĉ	LATIN SMALL LETTER c WITH CIRCUMFLEX ACCENT	Latin-3
002	245	15/05	ġ	LATIN SMALL LETTER g WITH DOT ABOVE	Latin-3
002	248	15/08	ĝ	LATIN SMALL LETTER g WITH CIRCUMFLEX ACCENT	Latin-3

Byte 3	Byte 4	Code Pos	Character	Name	Set
002	253	15/13	ŭ	LATIN SMALL LETTER u WITH BREVE	Latin-3
002	254	15/14	ŝ	LATIN SMALL LETTER s WITH CIRCUMFLEX ACCENT	Latin-3
003	162	10/02	ĸ	SMALL GREENLANDIC LETTER KRA	Latin-4
003	163	10/03	Ŗ	LATIN CAPITAL LETTER R WITH CEDILLA	Latin-4
003	165	10/05	Ĩ	LATIN CAPITAL LETTER I WITH TILDE	Latin-4
003	166	10/06	Ļ	LATIN CAPITAL LETTER L WITH CEDILLA	Latin-4
003	170	10/10	Ē	LATIN CAPITAL LETTER E WITH MACRON	Latin-4
003	171	10/11	Ģ	LATIN CAPITAL LETTER G WITH CEDILLA	Latin-4
003	172	10/12	Ŧ	LATIN CAPITAL LETTER T WITH OBLIQUE STROKE	Latin-4
003	179	11/03	ŗ	LATIN SMALL LETTER r WITH CEDILLA	Latin-4
003	181	11/05	ĩ	LATIN SMALL LETTER i WITH TILDE	Latin-4
003	182	11/06	ļ	LATIN SMALL LETTER l WITH CEDILLA	Latin-4
003	186	11/10	ē	LATIN SMALL LETTER e WITH MACRON	Latin-4
003	187	11/11	ģ	LATIN SMALL LETTER g WITH CEDILLA ABOVE	Latin-4
003	188	11/12	ŧ	LATIN SMALL LETTER t WITH OBLIQUE STROKE	Latin-4
003	189	11/13	Ŋ	LAPPISH CAPITAL LETTER ENG	Latin-4
003	191	11/15	ŋ	LAPPISH SMALL LETTER ENG	Latin-4
003	192	12/00	Ā	LATIN CAPITAL LETTER A WITH MACRON	Latin-4
003	199	12/07	Į	LATIN CAPITAL LETTER I WITH OGONEK	Latin-4
003	204	12/12	Ė	LATIN CAPITAL LETTER E WITH DOT ABOVE	Latin-4
003	207	12/15	Ī	LATIN CAPITAL LETTER I WITH MACRON	Latin-4
003	209	13/01	Ņ	LATIN CAPITAL LETTER N WITH CEDILLA	Latin-4
003	210	13/02	Ō	LATIN CAPITAL LETTER O WITH MACRON	Latin-4
003	211	13/03	Ķ	LATIN CAPITAL LETTER K WITH CEDILLA	Latin-4
003	217	13/09	Ų	LATIN CAPITAL LETTER U WITH OGONEK	Latin-4
003	221	13/13	Ũ	LATIN CAPITAL LETTER U WITH TILDE	Latin-4
003	222	13/14	Ū	LATIN CAPITAL LETTER U WITH MACRON	Latin-4

003	224	14/00	ā	LATIN SMALL LETTER a WITH MACRON	Latin-4
003	231	14/07	į	LATIN SMALL LETTER i WITH OGONEK	Latin-4
003	236	14/12	ė	LATIN SMALL LETTER e WITH DOT ABOVE	Latin-4
003	239	14/15	ī	LATIN SMALL LETTER i WITH MACRON	Latin-4
003	241	15/01	ņ	LATIN SMALL LETTER n WITH CEDILLA	Latin-4
003	242	15/02	ō	LATIN SMALL LETTER o WITH MACRON	Latin-4
003	243	15/03	ķ	LATIN SMALL LETTER k WITH CEDILLA	Latin-4
003	249	15/09	ų	LATIN SMALL LETTER u WITH OGONEK	Latin-4
003	253	15/13	ũ	LATIN SMALL LETTER u WITH TILDE	Latin-4
003	254	15/14	ū	LATIN SMALL LETTER u WITH MACRON	Latin-4
004	126	07/14	‾	OVERLINE	Kana
004	161	10/01	。	KANA FULL STOP	Kana
004	162	10/02	「	KANA OPENING BRACKET	Kana
004	163	10/03	」	KANA CLOSING BRACKET	Kana
004	164	10/04	、	KANA COMMA	Kana
004	165	10/05	・	KANA CONJUNCTIVE	Kana
004	166	10/06	ヲ	KANA LETTER WO	Kana
004	167	10/07	ァ	KANA LETTER SMALL A	Kana
004	168	10/08	ィ	KANA LETTER SMALL I	Kana
004	169	10/09	ゥ	KANA LETTER SMALL U	Kana
004	170	10/10	ェ	KANA LETTER SMALL E	Kana
004	171	10/11	ォ	KANA LETTER SMALL O	Kana
004	172	10/12	ャ	KANA LETTER SMALL YA	Kana
004	173	10/13	ュ	KANA LETTER SMALL YU	Kana
004	174	10/14	ョ	KANA LETTER SMALL YO	Kana
004	175	10/15	ッ	KANA LETTER SMALL TSU	Kana
004	176	11/00	ー	PROLONGED SOUND SYMBOL	Kana
004	177	11/01	ア	KANA LETTER A	Kana
004	178	11/02	イ	KANA LETTER I	Kana
004	179	11/03	ウ	KANA LETTER U	Kana

Byte 3	Byte 4	Code Pos	Character	Name	Set
004	180	11/04	ｴ	KANA LETTER E	Kana
004	181	11/05	ｵ	KANA LETTER O	Kana
004	182	11/06	ｶ	KANA LETTER KA	Kana
004	183	11/07	ｷ	KANA LETTER KI	Kana
004	184	11/08	ｸ	KANA LETTER KU	Kana
004	185	11/09	ｹ	KANA LETTER KE	Kana
004	186	11/10	ｺ	KANA LETTER KO	Kana
004	187	11/11	ｻ	KANA LETTER SA	Kana
004	188	11/12	ｼ	KANA LETTER SHI	Kana
004	189	11/13	ｽ	KANA LETTER SU	Kana
004	190	11/14	ｾ	KANA LETTER SE	Kana
004	191	11/15	ｿ	KANA LETTER SO	Kana
004	192	12/00	ﾀ	KANA LETTER TA	Kana
004	193	12/01	ﾁ	KANA LETTER CHI	Kana
004	194	12/02	ﾂ	KANA LETTER TSU	Kana
004	195	12/03	ﾃ	KANA LETTER TE	Kana
004	196	12/04	ﾄ	KANA LETTER TO	Kana
004	197	12/05	ﾅ	KANA LETTER NA	Kana
004	198	12/06	ﾆ	KANA LETTER NI	Kana
004	199	12/07	ﾇ	KANA LETTER NU	Kana
004	200	12/08	ﾈ	KANA LETTER NE	Kana
004	201	12/09	ﾉ	KANA LETTER NO	Kana
004	202	12/10	ﾊ	KANA LETTER HA	Kana
004	203	12/11	ﾋ	KANA LETTER HI	Kana
004	204	12/12	ﾌ	KANA LETTER FU	Kana
004	205	12/13	ﾍ	KANA LETTER HE	Kana
004	206	12/14	ﾎ	KANA LETTER HO	Kana
004	207	12/15	ﾏ	KANA LETTER MA	Kana
004	208	13/00	ﾐ	KANA LETTER MI	Kana

004	209	13/01	ム	KANA LETTER MU	Kana
004	210	13/02	メ	KANA LETTER ME	Kana
004	211	13/03	モ	KANA LETTER MO	Kana
004	212	13/04	ヤ	KANA LETTER YA	Kana
004	213	13/05	ユ	KANA LETTER YU	Kana
004	214	13/06	ヨ	KANA LETTER YO	Kana
004	215	13/07	ラ	KANA LETTER RA	Kana
004	216	13/08	リ	KANA LETTER RI	Kana
004	217	13/09	ル	KANA LETTER RU	Kana
004	218	13/10	レ	KANA LETTER RE	Kana
004	219	13/11	ロ	KANA LETTER RO	Kana
004	220	13/12	ワ	KANA LETTER WA	Kana
004	221	13/13	ン	KANA LETTER N	Kana
004	222	13/14	゛	VOICED SOUND SYMBOL	Kana
004	223	13/15	゜	SEMIVOICED SOUND SYMBOL	Kana
005	172	10/12	،	ARABIC COMMA	Arabic
005	187	11/11	؛	ARABIC SEMICOLON	Arabic
005	191	11/15	؟	ARABIC QUESTION MARK	Arabic
005	193	12/01	ء	ARABIC LETTER HAMZA	Arabic
005	194	12/02	آ	ARABIC LETTER MADDA ON ALEF	Arabic
005	195	12/03	أ	ARABIC LETTER HAMZA ON ALEF	Arabic
005	196	12/04	ؤ	ARABIC LETTER HAMZA ON WAW	Arabic
005	197	12/05	إ	ARABIC LETTER HAMZA UNDER ALEF	Arabic
005	198	12/06	ئ	ARABIC LETTER HAMZA ON YEH	Arabic
005	199	12/07	ا	ARABIC LETTER ALEF	Arabic
005	200	12/08	ب	ARABIC LETTER BEH	Arabic
005	201	12/09	ة	ARABIC LETTER TEH MARBUTA	Arabic
005	202	12/10	ت	ARABIC LETTER TEH	Arabic
005	203	12/11	ث	ARABIC LETTER THEH	Arabic
005	204	12/12	ج	ARABIC LETTER JEEM	Arabic
005	205	12/13	ح	ARABIC LETTER HAH	Arabic

Byte 3	Byte 4	Code Pos	Character	Name	Set
005	206	12/14	خ	ARABIC LETTER KHAH	Arabic
005	207	12/15	د	ARABIC LETTER DAL	Arabic
005	208	13/00	ذ	ARABIC LETTER THAL	Arabic
005	209	13/01	ر	ARABIC LETTER RA	Arabic
005	210	13/02	ز	ARABIC LETTER ZAIN	Arabic
005	211	13/03	س	ARABIC LETTER SEEN	Arabic
005	212	13/04	ش	ARABIC LETTER SHEEN	Arabic
005	213	13/05	ص	ARABIC LETTER SAD	Arabic
005	214	13/06	ض	ARABIC LETTER DAD	Arabic
005	215	13/07	ط	ARABIC LETTER TAH	Arabic
005	216	13/08	ظ	ARABIC LETTER ZAH	Arabic
005	217	13/09	ع	ARABIC LETTER AIN	Arabic
005	218	13/10	غ	ARABIC LETTER GHAIN	Arabic
005	224	14/00	ـ	ARABIC LETTER TATWEEL	Arabic
005	225	14/01	ف	ARABIC LETTER FEH	Arabic
005	226	14/02	ق	ARABIC LETTER QAF	Arabic
005	227	14/03	ك	ARABIC LETTER KAF	Arabic
005	228	14/04	ل	ARABIC LETTER LAM	Arabic
005	229	14/05	م	ARABIC LETTER MEEM	Arabic
005	230	14/06	ن	ARABIC LETTER NOON	Arabic
005	231	14/07	ه	ARABIC LETTER HA	Arabic
005	232	14/08	و	ARABIC LETTER WAW	Arabic
005	233	14/09	ى	ARABIC LETTER ALEF MAKSURA	Arabic
005	234	14/10	ي	ARABIC LETTER YEH	Arabic
005	235	14/11	ً	ARABIC LETTER FATHATAN	Arabic
005	236	14/12	ٌ	ARABIC LETTER DAMMATAN	Arabic
005	237	14/13	ٍ	ARABIC LETTER KASRATAN	Arabic
005	238	14/14	َ	ARABIC LETTER FATHA	Arabic
005	239	14/15	ُ	ARABIC LETTER DAMMA	Arabic

005	240	15/00	ِ	ARABIC LETTER KASRA	Arabic
005	241	15/01	ّ	ARABIC LETTER SHADDA	Arabic
005	242	15/02	ْ	ARABIC LETTER SUKUN	Arabic
006	161	10/01	ђ	SERBOCROATION CYRILLIC SMALL LETTER DJE	Cyrillic
006	162	10/02	ѓ	MACEDONIAN CYRILLIC SMALL LETTER GJE	Cyrillic
006	163	10/03	ё	CYRILLIC SMALL LETTER IO	Cyrillic
006	164	10/04	є	UKRAINIAN CYRILLIC SMALL LETTER IE	Cyrillic
006	165	10/05	ѕ	MACEDONIAN SMALL LETTER DSE	Cyrillic
006	166	10/06	і	BYELORUSSIAN/UKRAINIAN CYRILLIC SMALL LETTER I	Cyrillic
006	167	10/07	ї	UKRAINIAN SMALL LETTER YI	Cyrillic
006	168	10/08	ј	CYRILLIC SMALL LETTER JE	Cyrillic
006	169	10/09	љ	CYRILLIC SMALL LETTER LJE	Cyrillic
006	170	10/10	њ	CYRILLIC SMALL LETTER NJE	Cyrillic
006	171	10/11	ћ	SERBIAN SMALL LETTER TSHE	Cyrillic
006	172	10/12	ќ	MACEDONIAN CYRILLIC SMALL LETTER KJE	Cyrillic
006	174	10/14	ў	BYELORUSSIAN SMALL LETTER SHORT U	Cyrillic
006	175	10/15	џ	CYRILLIC SMALL LETTER DZHE	Cyrillic
006	176	11/00	№	NUMERO SIGN	Cyrillic
006	177	11/01	Ђ	SERBOCROATIAN CYRILLIC CAPITAL LETTER DJE	Cyrillic
006	178	11/02	Ѓ	MACEDONIAN CYRILLIC CAPITAL LETTER GJE	Cyrillic
006	179	11/03	Ё	CYRILLIC CAPITAL LETTER IO	Cyrillic
006	180	11/04	Є	UKRAINIAN CYRILLIC CAPITAL LETTER IE	Cyrillic
006	181	11/05	Ѕ	MACEDONIAN CAPITAL LETTER DSE	Cyrillic
006	182	11/06	І	BYELORUSSIAN/UKRAINIAN CYRILLIC CAPITAL LETTER I	Cyrillic
006	183	11/07	Ї	UKRAINIAN CAPITAL LETTER YI	Cyrillic
006	184	11/08	Ј	CYRILLIC CAPITAL LETTER JE	Cyrillic
006	185	11/09	Љ	CYRILLIC CAPITAL LETTER LJE	Cyrillic
006	186	11/10	Њ	CYRILLIC CAPITAL LETTER NJE	Cyrillic
006	187	11/11	Ћ	SERBIAN CAPITAL LETTER TSHE	Cyrillic
006	188	11/12	Ќ	MACEDONIAN CYRILLIC CAPITAL LETTER KJE	Cyrillic
006	190	11/14	Ў	BYELORUSSIAN CAPITAL LETTER SHORT U	Cyrillic

Byte 3	Byte 4	Code Pos	Character	Name	Set
006	191	11/15	Џ	CYRILLIC CAPITAL LETTER DZHE	Cyrillic
006	192	12/00	ю	CYRILLIC SMALL LETTER YU	Cyrillic
006	193	12/01	а	CYRILLIC SMALL LETTER A	Cyrillic
006	194	12/02	б	CYRILLIC SMALL LETTER BE	Cyrillic
006	195	12/03	ц	CYRILLIC SMALL LETTER TSE	Cyrillic
006	196	12/04	д	CYRILLIC SMALL LETTER DE	Cyrillic
006	197	12/05	е	CYRILLIC SMALL LETTER IE	Cyrillic
006	198	12/06	ф	CYRILLIC SMALL LETTER EF	Cyrillic
006	199	12/07	г	CYRILLIC SMALL LETTER GHE	Cyrillic
006	200	12/08	х	CYRILLIC SMALL LETTER HA	Cyrillic
006	201	12/09	и	CYRILLIC SMALL LETTER I	Cyrillic
006	202	12/10	й	CYRILLIC SMALL LETTER SHORT I	Cyrillic
006	203	12/11	к	CYRILLIC SMALL LETTER KA	Cyrillic
006	204	12/12	л	CYRILLIC SMALL LETTER EL	Cyrillic
006	205	12/13	м	CYRILLIC SMALL LETTER EM	Cyrillic
006	206	12/14	н	CYRILLIC SMALL LETTER EN	Cyrillic
006	207	12/15	о	CYRILLIC SMALL LETTER O	Cyrillic
006	208	13/00	п	CYRILLIC SMALL LETTER PE	Cyrillic
006	209	13/01	я	CYRILLIC SMALL LETTER YA	Cyrillic
006	210	13/02	р	CYRILLIC SMALL LETTER ER	Cyrillic
006	211	13/03	с	CYRILLIC SMALL LETTER ES	Cyrillic
006	212	13/04	т	CYRILLIC SMALL LETTER TE	Cyrillic
006	213	13/05	у	CYRILLIC SMALL LETTER U	Cyrillic
006	214	13/06	ж	CYRILLIC SMALL LETTER ZHE	Cyrillic
006	215	13/07	в	CYRILLIC SMALL LETTER VE	Cyrillic
006	216	13/08	ь	CYRILLIC SMALL SOFT SIGN	Cyrillic
006	217	13/09	ы	CYRILLIC SMALL LETTER YERU	Cyrillic
006	218	13/10	з	CYRILLIC SMALL LETTER ZE	Cyrillic
006	219	13/11	ш	CYRILLIC SMALL LETTER SHA	Cyrillic

006	220	13/12	э	CYRILLIC SMALL LETTER E	Cyrillic
006	221	13/13	щ	CYRILLIC SMALL LETTER SHCHA	Cyrillic
006	222	13/14	ч	CYRILLIC SMALL LETTER CHE	Cyrillic
006	223	13/15	ъ	CYRILLIC SMALL HARD SIGN	Cyrillic
006	224	14/00	Ю	CYRILLIC CAPITAL LETTER YU	Cyrillic
006	225	14/01	А	CYRILLIC CAPITAL LETTER A	Cyrillic
006	226	14/02	Б	CYRILLIC CAPITAL LETTER BE	Cyrillic
006	227	14/03	Ц	CYRILLIC CAPITAL LETTER TSE	Cyrillic
006	228	14/04	Д	CYRILLIC CAPITAL LETTER DE	Cyrillic
006	229	14/05	Е	CYRILLIC CAPITAL LETTER IE	Cyrillic
006	230	14/06	Ф	CYRILLIC CAPITAL LETTER EF	Cyrillic
006	231	14/07	Г	CYRILLIC CAPITAL LETTER GHE	Cyrillic
006	232	14/08	Х	CYRILLIC CAPITAL LETTER HA	Cyrillic
006	233	14/09	И	CYRILLIC CAPITAL LETTER I	Cyrillic
006	234	14/10	Й	CYRILLIC CAPITAL LETTER SHORT I	Cyrillic
006	235	14/11	К	CYRILLIC CAPITAL LETTER KA	Cyrillic
006	236	14/12	Л	CYRILLIC CAPITAL LETTER EL	Cyrillic
006	237	14/13	М	CYRILLIC CAPITAL LETTER EM	Cyrillic
006	238	14/14	Н	CYRILLIC CAPITAL LETTER EN	Cyrillic
006	239	14/15	О	CYRILLIC CAPITAL LETTER O	Cyrillic
006	240	15/00	П	CYRILLIC CAPITAL LETTER PE	Cyrillic
006	241	15/01	Я	CYRILLIC CAPITAL LETTER YA	Cyrillic
006	242	15/02	Р	CYRILLIC CAPITAL LETTER ER	Cyrillic
006	243	15/03	С	CYRILLIC CAPITAL LETTER ES	Cyrillic
006	244	15/04	Т	CYRILLIC CAPITAL LETTER TE	Cyrillic
006	245	15/05	У	CYRILLIC CAPITAL LETTER U	Cyrillic
006	246	15/06	Ж	CYRILLIC CAPITAL LETTER ZHE	Cyrillic
006	247	15/07	В	CYRILLIC CAPITAL LETTER VE	Cyrillic
006	248	15/08	Ь	CYRILLIC CAPITAL SOFT SIGN	Cyrillic
006	249	15/09	Ы	CYRILLIC CAPITAL LETTER YERU	Cyrillic
006	250	15/10	З	CYRILLIC CAPITAL LETTER ZE	Cyrillic
006	251	15/11	Ш	CYRILLIC CAPITAL LETTER SHA	Cyrillic

Byte 3	*Byte 4*	*Code Pos*	*Character*	*Name*	*Set*
006	252	15/12	Э	CYRILLIC CAPITAL LETTER E	Cyrillic
006	253	15/13	Щ	CYRILLIC CAPITAL LETTER SHCHA	Cyrillic
006	254	15/14	Ч	CYRILLIC CAPITAL LETTER CHE	Cyrillic
006	255	15/15	Ъ	CYRILLIC CAPITAL HARD SIGN	Cyrillic
007	161	10/01	Ά	GREEK CAPITAL LETTER ALPHA WITH ACCENT	Greek
007	162	10/02	Έ	GREEK CAPITAL LETTER EPSILON WITH ACCENT	Greek
007	163	10/03	Ή	GREEK CAPITAL LETTER ETA WITH ACCENT	Greek
007	164	10/04	Ί	GREEK CAPITAL LETTER IOTA WITH ACCENT	Greek
007	165	10/05	Ϊ	GREEK CAPITAL LETTER IOTA WITH DIAERESIS	Greek
007	167	10/07	Ό	GREEK CAPITAL LETTER OMICRON WITH ACCENT	Greek
007	168	10/08	Ύ	GREEK CAPITAL LETTER UPSILON WITH ACCENT	Greek
007	169	10/09	Ϋ	GREEK CAPITAL LETTER UPSILON WITH DIAERESIS	Greek
007	171	10/11	Ώ	GREEK CAPITAL LETTER OMEGA WITH ACCENT	Greek
007	174	10/14	΅	DIAERESIS AND ACCENT	Greek
007	175	10/15	―	HORIZONTAL BAR	Greek
007	177	11/01	ά	GREEK SMALL LETTER ALPHA WITH ACCENT	Greek
007	178	11/02	έ	GREEK SMALL LETTER EPSILON WITH ACCENT	Greek
007	179	11/03	ή	GREEK SMALL LETTER ETA WITH ACCENT	Greek
007	180	11/04	ί	GREEK SMALL LETTER IOTA WITH ACCENT	Greek
007	181	11/05	ϊ	GREEK SMALL LETTER IOTA WITH DIAERESIS	Greek
007	182	11/06	ΐ	GREEK SMALL LETTER IOTA WITH ACCENT+DIAERESIS	Greek
007	183	11/07	ό	GREEK SMALL LETTER OMICRON WITH ACCENT	Greek
007	184	11/08	ύ	GREEK SMALL LETTER UPSILON WITH ACCENT	Greek
007	185	11/09	ϋ	GREEK SMALL LETTER UPSILON WITH DIAERESIS	Greek
007	186	11/10	ΰ	GREEK SMALL LETTER UPSILON WITH ACCENT+DIAERESIS	Greek
007	187	11/11	ώ	GREEK SMALL LETTER OMEGA WITH ACCENT	Greek
007	193	12/01	Α	GREEK CAPITAL LETTER ALPHA	Greek

007	194	12/02	Β	GREEK CAPITAL LETTER BETA	Greek
007	195	12/03	Γ	GREEK CAPITAL LETTER GAMMA	Greek
007	196	12/04	Δ	GREEK CAPITAL LETTER DELTA	Greek
007	197	12/05	Ε	GREEK CAPITAL LETTER EPSILON	Greek
007	198	12/06	Ζ	GREEK CAPITAL LETTER ZETA	Greek
007	199	12/07	Η	GREEK CAPITAL LETTER ETA	Greek
007	200	12/08	Θ	GREEK CAPITAL LETTER THETA	Greek
007	201	12/09	Ι	GREEK CAPITAL LETTER IOTA	Greek
007	202	12/10	Κ	GREEK CAPITAL LETTER KAPPA	Greek
007	203	12/11	Λ	GREEK CAPITAL LETTER LAMDA	Greek
007	204	12/12	Μ	GREEK CAPITAL LETTER MU	Greek
007	205	12/13	Ν	GREEK CAPITAL LETTER NU	Greek
007	206	12/14	Ξ	GREEK CAPITAL LETTER XI	Greek
007	207	12/15	Ο	GREEK CAPITAL LETTER OMICRON	Greek
007	208	13/00	Π	GREEK CAPITAL LETTER PI	Greek
007	209	13/01	Ρ	GREEK CAPITAL LETTER RHO	Greek
007	210	13/02	Σ	GREEK CAPITAL LETTER SIGMA	Greek
007	212	13/04	Τ	GREEK CAPITAL LETTER TAU	Greek
007	213	13/05	ϒ	GREEK CAPITAL LETTER UPSILON	Greek
007	214	13/06	Φ	GREEK CAPITAL LETTER PHI	Greek
007	215	13/07	Χ	GREEK CAPITAL LETTER CHI	Greek
007	216	13/08	Ψ	GREEK CAPITAL LETTER PSI	Greek
007	217	13/09	Ω	GREEK CAPITAL LETTER OMEGA	Greek
007	225	14/01	α	GREEK SMALL LETTER ALPHA	Greek
007	226	14/02	β	GREEK SMALL LETTER BETA	Greek
007	227	14/03	γ	GREEK SMALL LETTER GAMMA	Greek
007	228	14/04	δ	GREEK SMALL LETTER DELTA	Greek
007	229	14/05	ϵ	GREEK SMALL LETTER EPSILON	Greek
007	230	14/06	ζ	GREEK SMALL LETTER ZETA	Greek
007	231	14/07	η	GREEK SMALL LETTER ETA	Greek
007	232	14/08	θ	GREEK SMALL LETTER THETA	Greek
007	233	14/09	ι	GREEK SMALL LETTER IOTA	Greek

Byte 3	*Byte 4*	*Code Pos*	*Character*	*Name*	*Set*
007	234	14/10	κ	GREEK SMALL LETTER KAPPA	Greek
007	235	14/11	λ	GREEK SMALL LETTER LAMDA	Greek
007	236	14/12	μ	GREEK SMALL LETTER MU	Greek
007	237	14/13	ν	GREEK SMALL LETTER NU	Greek
007	238	14/14	ξ	GREEK SMALL LETTER XI	Greek
007	239	14/15	ο	GREEK SMALL LETTER OMICRON	Greek
007	240	15/00	π	GREEK SMALL LETTER PI	Greek
007	241	15/01	ρ	GREEK SMALL LETTER RHO	Greek
007	242	15/02	σ	GREEK SMALL LETTER SIGMA	Greek
007	243	15/03	ς	GREEK SMALL LETTER FINAL SMALL SIGMA	Greek
007	244	15/04	τ	GREEK SMALL LETTER TAU	Greek
007	245	15/05	ν	GREEK SMALL LETTER UPSILON	Greek
007	246	15/06	φ	GREEK SMALL LETTER PHI	Greek
007	247	15/07	χ	GREEK SMALL LETTER CHI	Greek
007	248	15/08	ψ	GREEK SMALL LETTER PSI	Greek
007	249	15/09	ω	GREEK SMALL LETTER OMEGA	Greek
008	161	10/01	⎷	LEFT RADICAL	Technical
008	162	10/02	┌	TOP LEFT RADICAL	Technical
008	163	10/03	─	HORIZONTAL CONNECTOR	Technical
008	164	10/04	⌠	TOP INTEGRAL	Technical
008	165	10/05	⌡	BOTTOM INTEGRAL	Technical
008	166	10/06	│	VERTICAL CONNECTOR	Technical
008	167	10/07	⎡	TOP LEFT SQUARE BRACKET	Technical
008	168	10/08	⎣	BOTTOM LEFT SQUARE BRACKET	Technical
008	169	10/09	⎤	TOP RIGHT SQUARE BRACKET	Technical
008	170	10/10	⎦	BOTTOM RIGHT SQUARE BRACKET	Technical
008	171	10/11	⎛	TOP LEFT PARENTHESIS	Technical

008	172	10/12	⎩	BOTTOM LEFT PARENTHESIS	Technical
008	173	10/13	⎞	TOP RIGHT PARENTHESIS	Technical
008	174	10/14	⎠	BOTTOM RIGHT PARENTHESIS	Technical
008	175	10/15	⎨	LEFT MIDDLE CURLYBRACE	Technical
008	176	11/00	⎬	RIGHT MIDDLE CURLYBRACE	Technical
008	177	11/01	⎲	TOP LEFT SUMMATION	Technical
008	178	11/02	⎳	BOTTOM LEFT SUMMATION	Technical
008	179	11/03	\	TOP VERTICAL SUMMATION CONNECTOR	Technical
008	180	11/04	/	BOTTOM VERTICAL SUMMATION CONNECTOR	Technical
008	181	11/05	⌝	TOP RIGHT SUMMATION	Technical
008	182	11/06	⌟	BOTTOM RIGHT SUMMATION	Technical
008	183	11/07	⟩	RIGHT MIDDLE SUMMATION	Technical
008	188	11/12	≤	LESS THAN OR EQUAL SIGN	Technical
008	189	11/13	≠	NOT EQUAL SIGN	Technical
008	190	11/14	≥	GREATER THAN OR EQUAL SIGN	Technical
008	191	11/15	∫	INTEGRAL	Technical
008	192	12/00	∴	THEREFORE	Technical
008	193	12/01	∝	VARIATION, PROPORTIONAL TO	Technical
008	194	12/02	∞	INFINITY	Technical
008	197	12/05	∇	NABLA, DEL	Technical
008	200	12/08	∼	IS APPROXIMATE TO	Technical
008	201	12/09	≃	SIMILAR OR EQUAL TO	Technical
008	205	12/13	⇔	IF AND ONLY IF	Technical
008	206	12/14	⇒	IMPLIES	Technical
008	207	12/15	≡	IDENTICAL TO	Technical
008	214	13/06	√	RADICAL	Technical
008	218	13/10	⊂	IS INCLUDED IN	Technical
008	219	13/11	⊃	INCLUDES	Technical
008	220	13/12	∩	INTERSECTION	Technical
008	221	13/13	∪	UNION	Technical
008	222	13/14	∧	LOGICAL AND	Technical
008	223	13/15	∨	LOGICAL OR	Technical

Byte 3	Byte 4	Code Pos	Character	Name	Set
008	239	14/15	∂	PARTIAL DERIVATIVE	Technical
008	246	15/06	ƒ	FUNCTION	Technical
008	251	15/11	←	LEFT ARROW	Technical
008	252	15/12	↑	UPWARD ARROW	Technical
008	253	15/13	→	RIGHT ARROW	Technical
008	254	15/14	↓	DOWNWARD ARROW	Technical
009	223	13/15	(BLANK)	BLANK	Special
009	224	14/00	♦	SOLID DIAMOND	Special
009	225	14/01	▒	CHECKERBOARD	Special
009	226	14/02	␉	"HT"	Special
009	227	14/03	␌	"FF"	Special
009	228	14/04	␍	"CR"	Special
009	229	14/05	␊	"LF"	Special
009	232	14/08	␤	"NL"	Special
009	233	14/09	␋	"VT"	Special
009	234	14/10	┘	LOWER-RIGHT CORNER	Special
009	235	14/11	┐	UPPER-RIGHT CORNER	Special
009	236	14/12	┌	UPPER-LEFT CORNER	Special
009	237	14/13	└	LOWER-LEFT CORNER	Special
009	238	14/14	┼	CROSSING-LINES	Special
009	239	14/15	⎺ SCAN 1	HORIZONTAL LINE, SCAN 1	Special
009	240	15/00	⎻ SCAN 3	HORIZONTAL LINE, SCAN 3	Special
009	241	15/01	─ SCAN 5	HORIZONTAL LINE, SCAN 5	Special
009	242	15/02	⎼ SCAN 7	HORIZONTAL LINE, SCAN 7	Special
009	243	15/03	⎽ SCAN 9	HORIZONTAL LINE, SCAN 9	Special
009	244	15/04	├	LEFT "T"	Special
009	245	15/05	┤	RIGHT "T"	Special

009	246	15/06	⊥	BOTTOM "T"	Special
009	247	15/07	⊤	TOP "T"	Special
009	248	15/08	|	VERTICAL BAR	Special
010	161	10/01		EM SPACE	Publish
010	162	10/02		EN SPACE	Publish
010	163	10/03		3/EM SPACE	Publish
010	164	10/04		4/EM SPACE	Publish
010	165	10/05		DIGIT SPACE	Publish
010	166	10/06		PUNCTUATION SPACE	Publish
010	167	10/07		THIN SPACE	Publish
010	168	10/08		HAIR SPACE	Publish
010	169	10/09	—	EM DASH	Publish
010	170	10/10	–	EN DASH	Publish
010	172	10/12	␣	SIGNIFICANT BLANK SYMBOL	Publish
010	174	10/14	…	ELLIPSIS	Publish
010	175	10/15	..	DOUBLE BASELINE DOT	Publish
010	176	11/00	⅓	VULGAR FRACTION ONE THIRD	Publish
010	177	11/01	⅔	VULGAR FRACTION TWO THIRDS	Publish
010	178	11/02	⅕	VULGAR FRACTION ONE FIFTH	Publish
010	179	11/03	⅖	VULGAR FRACTION TWO FIFTHS	Publish
010	180	11/04	⅗	VULGAR FRACTION THREE FIFTHS	Publish
010	181	11/05	⅘	VULGAR FRACTION FOUR FIFTHS	Publish
010	182	11/06	⅙	VULGAR FRACTION ONE SIXTH	Publish
010	183	11/07	⅚	VULGAR FRACTION FIVE SIXTHS	Publish
010	184	11/08	℅	CARE OF	Publish
010	187	11/11	‒	FIGURE DASH	Publish
010	188	11/12	⟨	LEFT ANGLE BRACKET	Publish
010	189	11/13	.	DECIMAL POINT	Publish
010	190	11/14	⟩	RIGHT ANGLE BRACKET	Publish
010	191	11/15	▮	MARKER	Publish
010	195	12/03	⅛	VULGAR FRACTION ONE EIGHTH	Publish

Byte 3	*Byte 4*	*Code Pos*	*Character*	*Name*	*Set*
010	196	12/04	⅜	VULGAR FRACTION THREE EIGHTHS	Publish
010	197	12/05	⅝	VULGAR FRACTION FIVE EIGHTHS	Publish
010	198	12/06	⅞	VULGAR FRACTION SEVEN EIGHTHS	Publish
010	201	12/09	™	TRADEMARK SIGN	Publish
010	202	12/10	℠	SIGNATURE MARK	Publish
010	203	12/11	Ⓣ	TRADEMARK SIGN IN CIRCLE	Publish
010	204	12/12	◁	LEFT OPEN TRIANGLE	Publish
010	205	12/13	▷	RIGHT OPEN TRIANGLE	Publish
010	206	12/14	○	EM OPEN CIRCLE	Publish
010	207	12/15	□	EM OPEN RECTANGLE	Publish
010	208	13/00	‘	LEFT SINGLE QUOTATION MARK	Publish
010	209	13/01	’	RIGHT SINGLE QUOTATION MARK	Publish
010	210	13/02	“	LEFT DOUBLE QUOTATION MARK	Publish
010	211	13/03	”	RIGHT DOUBLE QUOTATION MARK	Publish
010	212	13/04	℞	PRESCRIPTION, TAKE, RECIPE	Publish
010	214	13/06	′	MINUTES	Publish
010	215	13/07	″	SECONDS	Publish
010	217	13/09	✝	LATIN CROSS	Publish
010	218	13/10	✡	HEXAGRAM	Publish
010	219	13/11	▬	FILLED RECTANGLE BULLET	Publish
010	220	13/12	◀	FILLED LEFT TRIANGLE BULLET	Publish
010	221	13/13	▶	FILLED RIGHT TRIANGLE BULLET	Publish
010	222	13/14	●	EM FILLED CIRCLE	Publish
010	223	13/15	■	EM FILLED RECTANGLE	Publish
010	224	14/00	◦	EN OPEN CIRCLE BULLET	Publish
010	225	14/01	▫	EN OPEN SQUARE BULLET	Publish
010	226	14/02	▭	OPEN RECTANGULAR BULLET	Publish
010	227	14/03	△	OPEN TRIANGULAR BULLET UP	Publish
010	228	14/04	▽	OPEN TRIANGULAR BULLET DOWN	Publish

010	229	14/05	☆	OPEN STAR	Publish
010	230	14/06	●	EN FILLED CIRCLE BULLET	Publish
010	231	14/07	■	EN FILLED SQUARE BULLET	Publish
010	232	14/08	▲	FILLED TRIANGULAR BULLET UP	Publish
010	233	14/09	▼	FILLED TRIANGULAR BULLET DOWN	Publish
010	234	14/10	◀	LEFT POINTER	Publish
010	235	14/11	▶	RIGHT POINTER	Publish
010	236	14/12	♣	CLUB	Publish
010	237	14/13	♦	DIAMOND	Publish
010	238	14/14	♥	HEART	Publish
010	240	15/00	✠	MALTESE CROSS	Publish
010	241	15/01	†	DAGGER	Publish
010	242	15/02	‡	DOUBLE DAGGER	Publish
010	243	15/03	✓	CHECK MARK, TICK	Publish
010	244	15/04	✕	BALLOT CROSS	Publish
010	245	15/05	♯	MUSICAL SHARP	Publish
010	246	15/06	♭	MUSICAL FLAT	Publish
010	247	15/07	♂	MALE SYMBOL	Publish
010	248	15/08	♀	FEMALE SYMBOL	Publish
010	249	15/09	☎	TELEPHONE SYMBOL	Publish
010	250	15/10	⌕	TELEPHONE RECORDER SYMBOL	Publish
010	251	15/11	℗	PHONOGRAPH COPYRIGHT SIGN	Publish
010	252	15/12	‸	CARET	Publish
010	253	15/13	‚	SINGLE LOW QUOTATION MARK	Publish
010	254	15/14	„	DOUBLE LOW QUOTATION MARK	Publish
010	255	15/15	▯	CURSOR	Publish
011	163	10/03	<	LEFT CARET	APL
011	166	10/06	>	RIGHT CARET	APL
011	168	10/08	∨	DOWN CARET	APL
011	169	10/09	∧	UP CARET	APL

Byte 3	*Byte 4*	*Code Pos*	*Character*	*Name*	*Set*
011	192	12/00	¯	OVERBAR	APL
011	194	12/02	⊥	DOWN TACK	APL
011	195	12/03	∪	UP SHOE (CAP)	APL
011	196	12/04	⌊	DOWN STILE	APL
011	198	12/06	_	UNDERBAR	APL
011	202	12/10	•	JOT	APL
011	204	12/12	⎕	QUAD	APL
011	206	12/14	⊤	UP TACK	APL
011	207	12/15	○	CIRCLE	APL
011	211	13/03	⌈	UP STILE	APL
011	214	13/06	∩	DOWN SHOE (CUP)	APL
011	216	13/08	⊃	RIGHT SHOE	APL
011	218	13/10	⊂	LEFT SHOE	APL
011	220	13/12	⊢	LEFT TACK	APL
011	252	15/12	⊣	RIGHT TACK	APL
012	223	13/15	‗	DOUBLE LOW LINE	Hebrew
012	224	14/00	א	HEBREW LETTER ALEPH	Hebrew
012	225	14/01	ב	HEBREW LETTER BET	Hebrew
012	226	14/02	ג	HEBREW LETTER GIMEL	Hebrew
012	227	14/03	ד	HEBREW LETTER DALET	Hebrew
012	228	14/04	ה	HEBREW LETTER HE	Hebrew
012	229	14/05	ו	HEBREW LETTER WAW	Hebrew
012	230	14/06	ז	HEBREW LETTER ZAIN	Hebrew
012	231	14/07	ח	HEBREW LETTER CHET	Hebrew
012	232	14/08	ט	HEBREW LETTER TET	Hebrew
012	233	14/09	י	HEBREW LETTER YOD	Hebrew
012	234	14/10	ך	HEBREW LETTER FINAL KAPH	Hebrew
012	235	14/11	כ	HEBREW LETTER KAPH	Hebrew

012	236	14/12	ל	HEBREW LETTER LAMED	Hebrew
012	237	14/13	ם	HEBREW LETTER FINAL MEM	Hebrew
012	238	14/14	מ	HEBREW LETTER MEM	Hebrew
012	239	14/15	ן	HEBREW LETTER FINAL NUN	Hebrew
012	240	15/00	נ	HEBREW LETTER NUN	Hebrew
012	241	15/01	ס	HEBREW LETTER SAMECH	Hebrew
012	242	15/02	ע	HEBREW LETTER A'YIN	Hebrew
012	243	15/03	ף	HEBREW LETTER FINAL PE	Hebrew
012	244	15/04	פ	HEBREW LETTER PE	Hebrew
012	245	15/05	ץ	HEBREW LETTER FINAL ZADE	Hebrew
012	246	15/06	צ	HEBREW LETTER ZADE	Hebrew
012	247	15/07	ק	HEBREW QOPH	Hebrew
012	248	15/08	ר	HEBREW RESH	Hebrew
012	249	15/09	ש	HEBREW SHIN	Hebrew
012	250	15/10	ת	HEBREW TAW	Hebrew
255	008	00/08		BACKSPACE, BACK SPACE, BACK CHAR	Keyboard
255	009	00/09		TAB	Keyboard
255	010	00/10		LINEFEED, LF	Keyboard
255	011	00/11		CLEAR	Keyboard
255	013	00/13		RETURN, ENTER	Keyboard
255	019	01/03		PAUSE, HOLD	Keyboard
255	020	01/04		SCROLL LOCK	Keyboard
255	027	01/11		ESCAPE	Keyboard
255	032	02/00		MULTI-KEY CHARACTER PREFACE	Keyboard
255	033	02/01		KANJI, KANJI CONVERT	Keyboard
255	034	02/02		MUHENKAN	Keyboard
255	035	02/03		HENKAN MODE	Keyboard
255	036	02/04		ROMAJI	Keyboard
255	037	02/05		HIRAGANA	Keyboard
255	038	02/06		KATAKANA	Keyboard

Byte 3	Byte 4	Code Pos	Character	Name	Set
255	039	02/07		HIRAGANA/KATAKANA TOGGLE	Keyboard
255	040	02/08		ZENKAKU	Keyboard
255	041	02/09		HANKAKU	Keyboard
255	042	02/10		ZENKAKU/HANKAKU TOGGLE	Keyboard
255	043	02/11		TOUROKU	Keyboard
255	044	02/12		MASSYO	Keyboard
255	045	02/13		KANA LOCK	Keyboard
255	046	02/14		KANA SHIFT	Keyboard
255	047	02/15		EISU SHIFT	Keyboard
255	048	03/00		EISU TOGGLE	Keyboard
255	080	05/00		HOME	Keyboard
255	081	05/01		LEFT, MOVE LEFT, LEFT ARROW	Keyboard
255	082	05/02		UP, MOVE UP, UP ARROW	Keyboard
255	083	05/03		RIGHT, MOVE RIGHT, RIGHT ARROW	Keyboard
255	084	05/04		DOWN, MOVE DOWN, DOWN ARROW	Keyboard
255	085	05/05		PRIOR, PREVIOUS	Keyboard
255	086	05/06		NEXT	Keyboard
255	087	05/07		END, EOL	Keyboard
255	088	05/08		BEGIN, BOL	Keyboard
255	096	06/00		SELECT, MARK	Keyboard
255	097	06/01		PRINT	Keyboard
255	098	06/02		EXECUTE, RUN, DO	Keyboard
255	099	06/03		INSERT, INSERT HERE	Keyboard
255	101	06/05		UNDO, OOPS	Keyboard
255	102	06/06		REDO, AGAIN	Keyboard
255	103	06/07		MENU	Keyboard
255	104	06/08		FIND, SEARCH	Keyboard
255	105	06/09		CANCEL, STOP, ABORT, EXIT	Keyboard
255	106	06/10		HELP, QUESTION MARK	Keyboard

255	107	06/11	BREAK	Keyboard
255	126	07/14	MODE SWITCH, SCRIPT SWITCH, CHARACTER SET SWITCH	Keyboard
255	127	07/15	NUM LOCK	Keyboard
255	128	08/00	KEYPAD SPACE	Keyboard
255	137	08/09	KEYPAD TAB	Keyboard
255	141	08/13	KEYPAD ENTER	Keyboard
255	145	09/01	KEYPAD F1, PF1, A	Keyboard
255	146	09/02	KEYPAD F2, PF2, B	Keyboard
255	147	09/03	KEYPAD F3, PF3, C	Keyboard
255	148	09/04	KEYPAD F4, PF4, D	Keyboard
255	170	10/10	KEYPAD MULTIPLICATION SIGN, ASTERISK	Keyboard
255	171	10/11	KEYPAD PLUS SIGN	Keyboard
255	172	10/12	KEYPAD SEPARATOR, COMMA	Keyboard
255	173	10/13	KEYPAD MINUS SIGN, HYPHEN	Keyboard
255	174	10/14	KEYPAD DECIMAL POINT, FULL STOP	Keyboard
255	175	10/15	KEYPAD DIVISION SIGN, SOLIDUS	Keyboard
255	176	11/00	KEYPAD DIGIT ZERO	Keyboard
255	177	11/01	KEYPAD DIGIT ONE	Keyboard
255	178	11/02	KEYPAD DIGIT TWO	Keyboard
255	179	11/03	KEYPAD DIGIT THREE	Keyboard
255	180	11/04	KEYPAD DIGIT FOUR	Keyboard
255	181	11/05	KEYPAD DIGIT FIVE	Keyboard
255	182	11/06	KEYPAD DIGIT SIX	Keyboard
255	183	11/07	KEYPAD DIGIT SEVEN	Keyboard
255	184	11/08	KEYPAD DIGIT EIGHT	Keyboard
255	185	11/09	KEYPAD DIGIT NINE	Keyboard
255	189	11/13	KEYPAD EQUALS SIGN	Keyboard
255	190	11/14	F1	Keyboard
255	191	11/15	F2	Keyboard
255	192	12/00	F3	Keyboard
255	193	12/01	F4	Keyboard
255	194	12/02	F5	Keyboard

Byte 3	*Byte 4*	*Code Pos*	*Character*	*Name*	*Set*
255	195	12/03		F6	Keyboard
255	196	12/04		F7	Keyboard
255	197	12/05		F8	Keyboard
255	198	12/06		F9	Keyboard
255	199	12/07		F10	Keyboard
255	200	12/08		F11, L1	Keyboard
255	201	12/09		F12, L2	Keyboard
255	202	12/10		F13, L3	Keyboard
255	203	12/11		F14, L4	Keyboard
255	204	12/12		F15, L5	Keyboard
255	205	12/13		F16, L6	Keyboard
255	206	12/14		F17, L7	Keyboard
255	207	12/15		F18, L8	Keyboard
255	208	13/00		F19, L9	Keyboard
255	209	13/01		F20, L10	Keyboard
255	210	13/02		F21, R1	Keyboard
255	211	13/03		F22, R2	Keyboard
255	212	13/04		F23, R3	Keyboard
255	213	13/05		F24, R4	Keyboard
255	214	13/06		F25, R5	Keyboard
255	215	13/07		F26, R6	Keyboard
255	216	13/08		F27, R7	Keyboard
255	217	13/09		F28, R8	Keyboard
255	218	13/10		F29, R9	Keyboard
255	219	13/11		F30, R10	Keyboard
255	220	13/12		F31, R11	Keyboard
255	221	13/13		F32, R12	Keyboard
255	222	13/14		F33, R13	Keyboard
255	223	13/15		F34, R14	Keyboard

255	224	14/00	F35, R15	Keyboard
255	225	14/01	LEFT SHIFT	Keyboard
255	226	14/02	RIGHT SHIFT	Keyboard
255	227	14/03	LEFT CONTROL	Keyboard
255	228	14/04	RIGHT CONTROL	Keyboard
255	229	14/05	CAPS LOCK	Keyboard
255	230	14/06	SHIFT LOCK	Keyboard
255	231	14/07	LEFT META	Keyboard
255	232	14/08	RIGHT META	Keyboard
255	233	14/09	LEFT ALT	Keyboard
255	234	14/10	RIGHT ALT	Keyboard
255	235	14/11	LEFT SUPER	Keyboard
255	236	14/12	RIGHT SUPER	Keyboard
255	237	14/13	LEFT HYPER	Keyboard
255	238	14/14	RIGHT HYPER	Keyboard
255	255	15/15	DELETE, RUBOUT	Keyboard

Appendix F

Protocol Encoding

Syntactic Conventions

All numbers are in decimal, unless prefixed with #x, in which case they are in hexadecimal (base 16).

The general syntax used to describe requests, replies, errors, events, and compound types is:

NameofThing
encode-form
. . .
encode-form

Each encode-form describes a single component.

For components described in the protocol as:

name: TYPE

the encode-form is:

N TYPE name

N is the number of bytes occupied in the data stream, and TYPE is the interpretation of those bytes. For example,

depth: CARD8

becomes:

1	CARD8	depth

For components with a static numeric value the encode-form is:

N	value	name

The value is always interpreted as an N-byte unsigned integer. For example, the first two bytes of a `Window` error are always zero (indicating an error in general) and three (indicating the `Window` error in particular):

1	0	Error
1	3	code

For components described in the protocol as:

name: { `Name1,...,NameI`}

the encode-form is:

N		name
	value1	Name1
	...	
	valueI	NameI

The value is always interpreted as an N-byte unsigned integer. Note that the size of N is sometimes larger than that strictly required to encode the values. For example:

class: {`InputOutput,InputOnly,CopyFromParent`}

becomes:

2		class
	0 `CopyFromParent`	
	1 `InputOutput`	
	2 `InputOnly`	

For components described in the protocol as:

NAME: TYPE or `Alternative1...` or `AlternativeI`

the encode-form is:

```
N    TYPE                          NAME
     value1   Alternative1
     ...
     valueI   AlternativeI
```

The alternative values are guaranteed not to conflict with the encoding of TYPE. For example:

destination: WINDOW or `PointerWindow` or `InputFocus`

becomes:

```
4    WINDOW                        destination
     0  PointerWindow
     1  InputFocus
```

For components described in the protocol as:

value-mask: BITMASK

the encode-form is:

```
N    BITMASK                       value-mask
     mask1   mask-name1
     ...
     maskI   mask-nameI
```

The individual bits in the mask are specified and named, and N is 2 or 4. The most-significant bit in a BITMASK is reserved for use in defining chained (multiword) bitmasks, as extensions augment existing core requests. The precise interpretation of this bit is not yet defined here, although a probable mechanism is that a 1-bit indicates that another N bytes of bitmask follows, with bits within the overall mask still interpreted from least-significant to most-significant with an N-byte unit, with N-byte units interpreted in stream order, and with the overall mask being byte-swapped in individual N-byte units.

For LISTofVALUE encodings, the request is followed by a section of the form:

VALUEs
encode-form . . .
encode-form

listing an encode-form for each VALUE. The NAME in each encode-form keys to the corresponding BITMASK bit. The encoding of a VALUE always occupies four bytes, but the number of bytes specified in the encoding-form indicates how many of the least-significant bytes are actually used; the remaining bytes are unused and their values do not matter.

In various cases, the number of bytes occupied by a component will be specified by a lowercase single-letter variable name instead of a specific numeric value, and often some other component will have its value specified as a simple numeric expression involving these variables. Components specified with such expressions are always interpreted as unsigned integers. The scope of such variables is always just the enclosing request, reply, error, event, or compound type structure. For example:

2	3+n	request length
4n	LISTofPOINT	points

For unused bytes (the values of the bytes are undefined and do no matter), the encode-form is:

N	unused

If the number of unused bytes is variable, the encode-form typically is:

p	unused, p=pad(E)

where E is some expression, and pad(E) is the number of bytes needed to round E up to a multiple of four.

pad(E) = (4 - (E mod 4)) mod 4

Common Types

LISTofFOO
In this document the LISTof notation strictly means some number of repetitions of the FOO encoding; the actual length of the list is encoded elsewhere.

SETofFOO

A set is always represented by a bitmask, with a 1-bit indicating presence in the set.

BITMASK: CARD32
WINDOW: CARD32
PIXMAP: CARD32
CURSOR: CARD32
FONT: CARD32
GCONTEXT: CARD32
COLORMAP: CARD32
DRAWABLE: CARD32
FONTABLE: CARD32
ATOM: CARD32
VISUALID: CARD32
BYTE: 8-bit value
INT8: 8-bit signed integer
INT16: 16-bit signed integer
INT32: 32-bit signed integer
CARD8: 8-bit unsigned integer
CARD16: 16-bit unsigned integer
CARD32: 32-bit unsigned integer
TIMESTAMP: CARD32

BITGRAVITY

0	`Forget`
1	`NorthWest`
2	`North`
3	`NorthEast`
4	`West`
5	`Center`
6	`East`
7	`SouthWest`
8	`South`
9	`SouthEast`
10	`Static`

WINGRAVITY

0	Unmap
1	NorthWest
2	North

3	NorthEast
4	West
5	Center
6	East
7	SouthWest
8	South
9	SouthEast
10	Static

BOOL

0	False
1	True

SETofEVENT

#x00000001	KeyPress
#x00000002	KeyRelease
#x00000004	ButtonPress
#x00000008	ButtonRelease
#x00000010	EnterWindow
#x00000020	LeaveWindow
#x00000040	PointerMotion
#x00000080	PointerMotionHint
#x00000100	Button1Motion
#x00000200	Button2Motion
#x00000400	Button3Motion
#x00000800	Button4Motion
#x00001000	Button5Motion
#x00002000	ButtonMotion
#x00004000	KeymapState
#x00008000	Exposure
#x00010000	VisibilityChange
#x00020000	StructureNotify
#x00040000	ResizeRedirect
#x00080000	SubstructureNotify
#x00100000	SubstructureRedirect
#x00200000	FocusChange
#x00400000	PropertyChange
#x00800000	ColormapChange
#x01000000	OwnerGrabButton
#xFE000000	unused but must be zero

SETofPOINTEREVENT
encodings are the same as for SETofEVENT, except with

#xFFFF8003	unused but must be zero

SETofDEVICEEVENT
encodings are the same as for SETofEVENT, except with

#xFFFFC0B0	unused but must be zero

KEYSYM: CARD32
KEYCODE: CARD8
BUTTON: CARD8
SETofKEYBUTMASK

#x0001	Shift
#x0002	Lock
#x0004	Control
#x0008	Mod1
#x0010	Mod2
#x0020	Mod3
#x0040	Mod4
#x0080	Mod5
#x0100	Button1
#x0200	Button2
#x0400	Button3
#x0800	Button4
#x1000	Button5
#xE000	unused but must be zero

SETofKEYMASK
encodings are the same as for SETofKEYBUTMASK, except with

#xFF00	unused but must be zero

STRING8: LISTofCARD8
STRING16: LISTofCHAR2B
CHAR2B

1	CARD8	byte1
1	CARD8	byte2

POINT

2	INT16	x
2	INT16	y

RECTANGLE

2	INT16	x
2	INT16	y
2	CARD16	width
2	CARD16	height

ARC

2	INT16	x
2	INT16	y
2	CARD16	width
2	CARD16	height
2	INT16	angle1
2	INT16	angle2

HOST

1		family
	0 `Internet`	
	1 `DECnet`	
	2 `Chaos`	
1		unused
2	n	length of address
n	LISTofBYTE	address
p		unused, p=pad(n)

STR

1	n	length of name in bytes
n	STRING8	name

Errors

Request

1	0	Error
1	1	code
2	CARD16	sequence number
4		unused

2	CARD16	minor opcode
1	CARD8	major opcode
21		unused

Value

1	0	Error
1	2	code
2	CARD16	sequence number
4	<32-bits>	bad value
2	CARD16	minor opcode
1	CARD8	major opcode
21		unused

Window

1	0	Error
1	3	code
2	CARD16	sequence number
4	CARD32	bad resource id
2	CARD16	minor opcode
1	CARD8	major opcode
21		unused

Pixmap

1	0	Error
1	4	code
2	CARD16	sequence number
4	CARD32	bad resource id
2	CARD16	minor opcode
1	CARD8	major opcode
21		unused

Atom

1	0	Error
1	5	code
2	CARD16	sequence number
4	CARD32	bad atom id
2	CARD16	minor opcode
1	CARD8	major opcode
21		unused

Cursor

1	0	Error
1	6	code
2	CARD16	sequence number
4	CARD32	bad resource id
2	CARD16	minor opcode
1	CARD8	major opcode
21		unused

Font

1	0	Error
1	7	code
2	CARD16	sequence number
4	CARD32	bad resource id
2	CARD16	minor opcode
1	CARD8	major opcode
21		unused

Match

1	0	Error
1	8	code
2	CARD16	sequence number
4		unused
2	CARD16	minor opcode
1	CARD8	major opcode
21		unused

Drawable

1	0	Error
1	9	code
2	CARD16	sequence number
4	CARD32	bad resource id
2	CARD16	minor opcode
1	CARD8	major opcode
21		unused

Access

1	0	Error
1	10	code

2	CARD16	sequence number
4		unused
2	CARD16	minor opcode
1	CARD8	major opcode
21		unused

Alloc

1	0	Error
1	11	code
2	CARD16	sequence number
4		unused
2	CARD16	minor opcode
1	CARD8	major opcode
21		unused

Colormap

1	0	Error
1	12	code
2	CARD16	sequence number
4	CARD32	bad resource id
2	CARD16	minor opcode
1	CARD8	major opcode
21		unused

GContext

1	0	Error
1	13	code
2	CARD16	sequence number
4	CARD32	bad resource id
2	CARD16	minor opcode
1	CARD8	major opcode
21		unused

IDChoice

1	0	Error
1	14	code
2	CARD16	sequence number
4	CARD32	bad resource id
2	CARD16	minor opcode

1	CARD8	major opcode
21		unused

Name

1	0	Error
1	15	code
2	CARD16	sequence number
4		unused
2	CARD16	minor opcode
1	CARD8	major opcode
21		unused

Length

1	0	Error
1	16	code
2	CARD16	sequence number
4		unused
2	CARD16	minor opcode
1	CARD8	major opcode
21		unused

Implementation

1	0	Error
1	17	code
2	CARD16	sequence number
4		unused
2	CARD16	minor opcode
1	CARD8	major opcode
21		unused

Keyboards

KEYCODE values are always greater than 7 (and less than 256).

KEYSYM values with the bit #x10000000 set are reserved as vendor-specific.

The names and encodings of the standard KEYSYM values are contained in appendix E.

Pointers

BUTTON values are numbered starting with one.

Predefined Atoms

PRIMARY	1
SECONDARY	2
ARC	3
ATOM	4
BITMAP	5
CARDINAL	6
COLORMAP	7
CURSOR	8
CUT_BUFFER0	9
CUT_BUFFER1	10
CUT_BUFFER2	11
CUT_BUFFER3	12
CUT_BUFFER4	13
CUT_BUFFER5	14
CUT_BUFFER6	15
CUT_BUFFER7	16
DRAWABLE	17
FONT	18
INTEGER	19
PIXMAP	20
POINT	21
RECTANGLE	22
RESOURCE_MANAGER	23
RGB_COLOR_MAP	24
RGB_BEST_MAP	25
RGB_BLUE_MAP	26
RGB_DEFAULT_MAP	27
RGB_GRAY_MAP	28
RGB_GREEN_MAP	29
RGB_RED_MAP	30
STRING	31
VISUALID	32
WINDOW	33
WM_COMMAND	34
WM_HINTS	35
WM_CLIENT_MACHINE	36
WM_ICON_NAME	37
WM_ICON_SIZE	38
WM_NAME	39
WM_NORMAL_HINTS	40
WM_SIZE_HINTS	41
WM_ZOOM_HINTS	42
MIN_SPACE	43
NORM_SPACE	44
MAX_SPACE	45
END_SPACE	46
SUPERSCRIPT_X	47
SUPERSCRIPT_Y	48
SUBSCRIPT_X	49
SUBSCRIPT_Y	50
UNDERLINE_POSITION	51
UNDERLINE_THICKNESS	52
STRIKEOUT_ASCENT	53
STRIKEOUT_DESCENT	54
ITALIC_ANGLE	55
X_HEIGHT	56
QUAD_WIDTH	57
WEIGHT	58
POINT_SIZE	59
RESOLUTION	60
COPYRIGHT	61
NOTICE	62
FONT_NAME	63
FAMILY_NAME	64
FULL_NAME	65
CAP_HEIGHT	66
WM_CLASS	67
WM_TRANSIENT_FOR	68

Connection Setup

For TCP connections, displays on a given host are numbered starting from 0, and the server for display N listens and accepts connections on port 6000 + N. For DECnet connections, displays on a given host are numbered starting from 0, and the server for display N listens and accepts connections on the object name obtained by concatenating "X$X" with the decimal representation of N, for example, X$X0 and X$X1.

Information sent by the client at connection setup:

1		byte-order
	#x42 MSB first	
	#x6C LSB first	
1		unused
2	CARD16	protocol-major-version
2	CARD16	protocol-minor-version
2	n	length of authorization-protocol-name
2	d	length of authorization-protocol-data
2		unused
n	STRING8	authorization-protocol-name
p		unused, p=pad(n)
d	STRING8	authorization-protocol-data
q		unused, q=pad(d)

Except where explicitly noted in the protocol, all 16-bit and 32-bit quantities sent by the client must be transmitted with the specified byte order, and all 16-bit and 32-bit quantities returned by the server will be transmitted with this byte order.

Information received by the client if authorization fails:

1	0	failed
1	n	length of reason in bytes
2	CARD16	protocol-major-version
2	CARD16	protocol-minor-version
2	(n+p)/4	length in 4-byte units of "additional data"
n	STRING8	reason
p		unused, p=pad(n)

Information received by the client if authorization is accepted:

1	1	success
1		unused
2	CARD16	protocol-major-version
2	CARD16	protocol-minor-version
2	8+2n+(v+p+m)/4	length in 4-byte units of "additional data"
4	CARD32	release-number
4	CARD32	resource-id-base
4	CARD32	resource-id-mask
4	CARD32	motion-buffer-size
2	v	length of vendor
2	CARD16	maximum-request-length
1	CARD8	number of SCREENs in roots
1	n	number for FORMATs in pixmap-formats
1		image-byte-order
	0 `LSBFirst`	
	1 `MSBFirst`	
1		bitmap-format-bit-order
	0 `LeastSignificant`	
	1 `MostSignificant`	
1	CARD8	bitmap-format-scanline-unit
1	CARD8	bitmap-format-scanline-pad
1	KEYCODE	min-keycode
1	KEYCODE	max-keycode
4		unused
v	STRING8	vendor
p		unused, p=pad(v)
8n	LISTofFORMAT	pixmap-formats
m	LISTofSCREEN	roots (m is always a multiple of 4)

FORMAT

1	CARD8	depth
1	CARD8	bits-per-pixel
1	CARD8	scanline-pad
5		unused

SCREEN

4	WINDOW	root
4	COLORMAP	default-colormap
4	CARD32	white-pixel
4	CARD32	black-pixel
4	SETofEVENT	current-input-masks
2	CARD16	width-in-pixels
2	CARD16	height-in-pixels
2	CARD16	width-in-millimeters
2	CARD16	height-in-millimeters
2	CARD16	min-installed-maps
2	CARD16	max-installed-maps
4	VISUALID	root-visual
1		backing-stores
	0 `Never`	
	1 `WhenMapped`	
	2 `Always`	
1	BOOL	save-unders
1	CARD8	root-depth
1	CARD8	number of DEPTHs in allowed-depths
n	LISTofDEPTH	allowed-depths (n is always a multiple of 4)

DEPTH

1	CARD8	depth
1		unused
2	n	number of VISUALTYPES in visuals
4		unused
24n	LISTofVISUALTYPE	visuals

VISUALTYPE

4	VISUALID	visual-id
1		class
	0 `StaticGray`	
	1 `GrayScale`	
	2 `StaticColor`	
	3 `PseudoColor`	

```
        4  TrueColor
        5  DirectColor
1       CARD8                               bits-per-rgb-value
2       CARD16                              colormap-entries
4       CARD32                              red-mask
4       CARD32                              green-mask
4       CARD32                              blue-mask
4                                           unused
```

Requests

CreateWindow

```
1       1                                   opcode
1       CARD8                               depth
2       8+n                                 request length
4       WINDOW                              wid
4       WINDOW                              parent
2       INT16                               x
2       INT16                               y
2       CARD16                              width
2       CARD16                              height
2       CARD16                              border-width
2                                           class
        0  CopyFromParent
        1  InputOutput
        2  InputOnly
4       VISUALID                            visual
        0  CopyFromParent
4       BITMASK                             value-mask (has n bits set to 1)
        #x00000001   background-pixmap
        #x00000002   background-pixel
        #x00000004   border-pixmap
        #x00000008   border-pixel
        #x00000010   bit-gravity
        #x00000020   win-gravity
        #x00000040   backing-store
        #x00000080   backing-planes
        #x00000100   backing-pixel
        #x00000200   override-redirect
        #x00000400   save-under
        #x00000800   event-mask
```

	#x00001000 do-not-propagate-mask	
	#x00002000 colormap	
	#x00004000 cursor	
4n	LISTofVALUE	value-list

VALUEs

4	PIXMAP	background-pixmap
	0 `None`	
	1 `ParentRelative`	
4	CARD32	background-pixel
4	PIXMAP	border-pixmap
	0 `CopyFromParent`	
4	CARD32	border-pixel
1	BITGRAVITY	bit-gravity
1	WINGRAVITY	win-gravity
1		backing-store
	0 `NotUseful`	
	1 `WhenMapped`	
	2 `Always`	
4	CARD32	backing-planes
4	CARD32	backing-pixel
1	BOOL	override-redirect
1	BOOL	save-under
4	SETofEVENT	event-mask
4	SETofDEVICEEVENT	do-not-propagate-mask
4	COLORMAP	colormap
	0 `CopyFromParent`	
4	CURSOR	cursor
	0 `None`	

ChangeWindowAttributes

1	2	opcode
1		unused
2	3+n	request length
4	WINDOW	window
4	BITMASK	value-mask (has n bits set to 1)
	encodings are the same as for `CreateWindow`	
4n	LISTofVALUE	value-list
	encodings are the same as for `CreateWindow`	

GetWindowAttributes

1	3	opcode
1		unused
2	2	request length
4	WINDOW	window
→		
1	1	Reply
1		backing-store
	0 NotUseful	
	1 WhenMapped	
	2 Always	
2	CARD16	sequence number
4	3	reply length
4	VISUALID	visual
2		class
	1 InputOutput	
	2 InputOnly	
1	BITGRAVITY	bit-gravity
1	WINGRAVITY	win-gravity
4	CARD32	backing-planes
4	CARD32	backing-pixel
1	BOOL	save-under
1	BOOL	map-is-installed
1		map-state
	0 Unmapped	
	1 Unviewable	
	2 Viewable	
1	BOOL	override-redirect
4	COLORMAP	colormap
	0 None	
4	SETofEVENT	all-event-masks
4	SETofEVENT	your-event-mask
2	SETofDEVICEEVENT	do-not-propagate-mask
2		unused

DestroyWindow

1	4	opcode
1		unused
2	2	request length
4	WINDOW	window

DestroySubwindows

1	5	opcode
1		unused
2	2	request length
4	WINDOW	window

ChangeSaveSet

1	6	opcode
1		mode
	0 Insert	
	1 Delete	
2	2	request length
4	WINDOW	window

ReparentWindow

1	7	opcode
1		unused
2	4	request length
4	WINDOW	window
4	WINDOW	parent
2	INT16	x
2	INT16	y

MapWindow

1	8	opcode
1		unused
2	2	request length
4	WINDOW	window

MapSubwindows

1	9	opcode
1		unused
2	2	request length
4	WINDOW	window

UnmapWindow

1	10	opcode
1		unused

2	2	request length
4	WINDOW	window

UnmapSubwindows

1	11	opcode
1		unused
2	2	request length
4	WINDOW	window

ConfigureWindow

1	12		opcode
1			unused
2	3+n		request length
4	WINDOW		window
2	BITMASK		value-mask (has n bits set to 1)
	#x0001	x	
	#x0002	y	
	#x0004	width	
	#x0008	height	
	#x0010	border-width	
	#x0020	sibling	
	#x0040	stack-mode	
2			unused
4n	LISTofVALUE		value-list

VALUEs

2	INT16		x
2	INT16		y
2	CARD16		width
2	CARD16		height
2	CARD16		border-width
4	WINDOW		sibling
1			stack-mode
	0	`Above`	
	1	`Below`	
	2	`TopIf`	
	3	`BottomIf`	
	4	`Opposite`	

CirculateWindow

1	13	opcode
1		direction
	0 RaiseLowest	
	1 LowerHighest	
2	2	request length
4	WINDOW	window

GetGeometry

1	14	opcode
1		unused
2	2	request length
4	DRAWABLE	drawable
→		
1	1	Reply
1	CARD8	depth
2	CARD16	sequence number
4	0	reply length
4	WINDOW	root
2	INT16	x
2	INT16	y
2	CARD16	width
2	CARD16	height
2	CARD16	border-width
10		unused

QueryTree

1	15	opcode
1		unused
2	2	request length
4	WINDOW	window
→		
1	1	Reply
1		unused
2	CARD16	sequence number
4	n	reply length
4	WINDOW	root
4	WINDOW	parent
	0 None	

2	n	number of WINDOWs in children
14		unused
4n	LISTofWINDOW	children

InternAtom

1	16	opcode
1	BOOL	only-if-exists
2	2+(n+p)/4	request length
2	n	length of name
2		unused
n	STRING8	name
p		unused, p=pad(n)
→		
1	1	Reply
1		unused
2	CARD16	sequence number
4	0	reply length
4	ATOM	atom
	0 None	
20		unused

GetAtomName

1	17	opcode
1		unused
2	2	request length
4	ATOM	atom
→		
1	1	Reply
1		unused
2	CARD16	sequence number
4	(n+p)/4	reply length
2	n	length of name
22		unused
n	STRING8	name
p		unused, p=pad(n)

ChangeProperty

1	18	opcode
1		mode

	0 Replace	
	1 Prepend	
	2 Append	
2	6+(n+p)/4	request length
4	WINDOW	window
4	ATOM	property
4	ATOM	type
1	CARD8	format
3		unused
4	CARD32	length of data in format units (= n for format = 8) (= n/2 for format = 16) (= n/4 for format = 32)
n	LISTofBYTE	data (n is a multiple of 2 for format = 16) (n is a multiple of 4 for format = 32)
p		unused, p=pad(n)

DeleteProperty

1	19	opcode
1		unused
2	3	request length
4	WINDOW	window
4	ATOM	property

GetProperty

1	20	opcode
1	BOOL	delete
2	6	request length
4	WINDOW	window
4	ATOM	property
4	ATOM	type
	0 AnyPropertyType	
4	CARD32	long-offset
4	CARD32	long-length

→

1	1	Reply
1	CARD8	format

2	CARD16	sequence number
4	(n+p)/4	reply length
4	ATOM	type
	0 None	
4	CARD32	bytes-after
4	CARD32	length of value in format units (= 0 for format = 0) (= n for format = 8) (= n/2 for format = 16) (= n/4 for format = 32)
12		unused
n	LISTofBYTE	value (n is zero for format = 0) (n is a multiple of 2 for format = 16) (n is a multiple of 4 for format = 32)
p		unused, p=pad(n)

ListProperties

1	21	opcode
1		unused
2	2	request length
4	WINDOW	window

→

1	1	Reply
1		unused
2	CARD16	sequence number
4	n	reply length
2	n	number of ATOMs in atoms
22		unused
4n	LISTofATOM	atoms

SetSelectionOwner

1	22	opcode
1		unused
2	4	request length
4	WINDOW	owner
	0 None	

4	ATOM	selection
4	TIMESTAMP	time
	0 `CurrentTime`	

GetSelectionOwner

1	23	opcode
1		unused
2	2	request length
4	ATOM	selection

→

1	1	Reply
1		unused
2	CARD16	sequence number
4	0	reply length
4	WINDOW	owner
	0 `None`	
20		unused

ConvertSelection

1	24	opcode
1		unused
2	6	request length
4	WINDOW	requestor
4	ATOM	selection
4	ATOM	target
4	ATOM	property
	0 `None`	
4	TIMESTAMP	time
	0 `CurrentTime`	

SendEvent

1	25	opcode
1	BOOL	propagate
2	11	request length
4	WINDOW	destination
	0 `PointerWindow`	
	1 `InputFocus`	
4	SETofEVENT	event-mask
32	standard event format (see the Events section)	event

GrabPointer

1	26	opcode
1	BOOL	owner-events
2	6	request length
4	WINDOW	grab-window
2	SETofPOINTEREVENT	event-mask
1		pointer-mode
	0 Synchronous	
	1 Asynchronous	
1		keyboard-mode
	0 Synchronous	
	1 Asynchronous	
4	WINDOW	confine-to
	0 None	
4	CURSOR	cursor
	0 None	
4	TIMESTAMP	time
	0 CurrentTime	

→

1	1	Reply
1		status
	0 Success	
	1 AlreadyGrabbed	
	2 InvalidTime	
	3 NotViewable	
	4 Frozen	
2	CARD16	sequence number
4	0	reply length
24		unused

UngrabPointer

1	27	opcode
1		unused
2	2	request length
4	TIMESTAMP	time
	0 CurrentTime	

GrabButton

1	28	opcode
1	BOOL	owner-events

2	6	request length
4	WINDOW	grab-window
2	SETofPOINTEREVENT	event-mask
1		pointer-mode
	0 Synchronous	
	1 Asynchronous	
1		keyboard-mode
	0 Synchronous	
	1 Asynchronous	
4	WINDOW	confine-to
	0 None	
4	CURSOR	cursor
	0 None	
1	BUTTON	button
	0 AnyButton	
1		unused
2	SETofKEYMASK	modifiers
	#x8000 AnyModifier	

UngrabButton

1	29	opcode
1	BUTTON	button
	0 AnyButton	
2	3	request length
4	WINDOW	grab-window
2	SETofKEYMASK	modifiers
	#x8000 AnyModifier	
2		unused

ChangeActivePointerGrab

1	30	opcode
1		unused
2	4	request length
4	CURSOR	cursor
	0 None	
4	TIMESTAMP	time
	0 CurrentTime	
2	SETofPOINTEREVENT	event-mask
2		unused

GrabKeyboard

```
1     31                         opcode
1     BOOL                       owner-events
2     4                          request length
4     WINDOW                     grab-window
4     TIMESTAMP                  time
      0   CurrentTime
1                                pointer-mode
      0   Synchronous
      1   Asynchronous
1                                keyboard-mode
      0   Synchronous
      1   Asynchronous
2                                unused
→
1     1                          Reply
1                                status
      0   Success
      1   AlreadyGrabbed
      2   InvalidTime
      3   NotViewable
      4   Frozen
2     CARD16                     sequence number
4     0                          reply length
24                               unused
```

UngrabKeyboard

```
1     32                         opcode
1                                unused
2     2                          request length
4     TIMESTAMP                  time
      0   CurrentTime
```

GrabKey

```
1     33                         opcode
1     BOOL                       owner-events
2     4                          request length
4     WINDOW                     grab-window
2     SETofKEYMASK               modifiers
      #x8000    AnyModifier
```

1	KEYCODE	key
	0 `AnyKey`	
1		pointer-mode
	0 `Synchronous`	
	1 `Asynchronous`	
1		keyboard-mode
	0 `Synchronous`	
	1 `Asynchronous`	
3		unused

UngrabKey

1	34	opcode
1	KEYCODE	key
	0 `AnyKey`	
2	3	request length
4	WINDOW	grab-window
2	SETofKEYMASK	modifiers
	#x8000 `AnyModifier`	
2		unused

AllowEvents

1	35	opcode
1		mode
	0 `AsyncPointer`	
	1 `SyncPointer`	
	2 `ReplayPointer`	
	3 `AsyncKeyboard`	
	4 `SyncKeyboard`	
	5 `ReplayKeyboard`	
	6 `AsyncBoth`	
	7 `SyncBoth`	
2	2	request length
4	TIMESTAMP	time
	0 `CurrentTime`	

GrabServer

1	36	opcode
1		unused
2	1	request length

UngrabServer

1	37	opcode
1		unused
2	1	request length

QueryPointer

1	38	opcode
1		unused
2	2	request length
4	WINDOW	window
→		
1	1	Reply
1	BOOL	same-screen
2	CARD16	sequence number
4	0	reply length
4	WINDOW	root
4	WINDOW	child
	0 None	
2	INT16	root-x
2	INT16	root-y
2	INT16	win-x
2	INT16	win-y
2	SETofKEYBUTMASK	mask
6		unused

GetMotionEvents

1	39	opcode
1		unused
2	4	request length
4	WINDOW	window
4	TIMESTAMP	start
	0 CurrentTime	
4	TIMESTAMP	stop
	0 CurrentTime	
→		
1	1	Reply
1		unused
2	CARD16	sequence number
4	2n	reply length

4	n	number of TIMECOORDs in events
20		unused
8n	LISTofTIMECOORD	events

TIMECOORD

4	TIMESTAMP	time
2	INT16	x
2	INT16	y

TranslateCoordinates

1	40	opcode
1		unused
2	4	request length
4	WINDOW	src-window
4	WINDOW	dst-window
2	INT16	src-x
2	INT16	src-y

→

1	1	Reply
1	BOOL	same-screen
2	CARD16	sequence number
4	0	reply length
4	WINDOW	child
	0 None	
2	INT16	dst-x
2	INT16	dst-y
16		unused

WarpPointer

1	41	opcode
1		unused
2	6	request length
4	WINDOW	src-window
	0 None	
4	WINDOW	dst-window
	0 None	
2	INT16	src-x
2	INT16	src-y
2	CARD16	src-width

2	CARD16	src-height
2	INT16	dst-x
2	INT16	dst-y

SetInputFocus

1	42	opcode
1		revert-to
	0 None	
	1 PointerRoot	
	2 Parent	
2	3	request length
4	WINDOW	focus
	0 None	
	1 PointerRoot	
4	TIMESTAMP	time
	0 CurrentTime	

GetInputFocus

1	43	opcode
1		unused
2	1	request length
→		
1	1	Reply
1		revert-to
	0 None	
	1 PointerRoot	
	2 Parent	
2	CARD16	sequence number
4	0	reply length
4	WINDOW	focus
	0 None	
	1 PointerRoot	
20		unused

QueryKeymap

1	44	opcode
1		unused
2	1	request length
→		
1	1	Reply

1		unused
2	CARD16	sequence number
4	2	reply length
32	LISTofCARD8	keys

OpenFont

1	45	opcode
1		unused
2	3+(n+p)/4	request length
4	FONT	fid
2	n	length of name
2		unused
n	STRING8	name
p		unused, p=pad(n)

CloseFont

1	46	opcode
1		unused
2	2	request length
4	FONT	font

QueryFont

1	47	opcode
1		unused
2	2	request length
4	FONTABLE	font

→

1	1	Reply
1		unused
2	CARD16	sequence number
4	7+2n+3m	reply length
12	CHARINFO	min-bounds
4		unused
12	CHARINFO	max-bounds
4		unused
2	CARD16	min-char-or-byte2
2	CARD16	max-char-or-byte2
2	CARD16	default-char
2	n	number of FONTPROPs in properties

1		draw-direction
	0 LeftToRight	
	1 RightToLeft	
1	CARD8	min-byte1
1	CARD8	max-byte1
1	BOOL	all-chars-exist
2	INT16	font-ascent
2	INT16	font-descent
4	m	number of CHARINFOs in char-infos
8n	LISTofFONTPROP	properties
12m	LISTofCHARINFO	char-infos

FONTPROP

4	ATOM	name
4	<32-bits>	value

CHARINFO

2	INT16	left-side-bearing
2	INT16	right-side-bearing
2	INT16	character-width
2	INT16	ascent
2	INT16	descent
2	CARD16	attributes

QueryTextExtents

1	48	opcode
1	BOOL	odd length, True if p = 2
2	2+(2n+p)/4	request length
4	FONTABLE	font
2n	STRING16	string
p		unused, p=pad(2n)

→

1	1	Reply
1		draw-direction
	0 LeftToRight	
	1 RightToLeft	
2	CARD16	sequence number
4	0	reply length

2	INT16	font-ascent
2	INT16	font-descent
2	INT16	overall-ascent
2	INT16	overall-descent
4	INT32	overall-width
4	INT32	overall-left
4	INT32	overall-right
4		unused

ListFonts

1	49	opcode
1		unused
2	2+(n+p)/4	request length
2	CARD16	max-names
2	n	length of pattern
n	STRING8	pattern
p		unused, p=pad(n)

→

1	1	Reply
1		unused
2	CARD16	sequence number
4	(n+p)/4	reply length
2	CARD16	number of STRs in names
22		unused
n	LISTofSTR	names
p		unused, p=pad(n)

ListFontsWithInfo

1	50	opcode
1		unused
2	2+(n+p)/4	request length
2	CARD16	max-names
2	n	length of pattern
n	STRING8	pattern
p		unused, p=pad(n)

→ (except for last in series)

1	1	Reply
1	n	length of name in bytes
2	CARD16	sequence number
4	7+2m+(n+p)/4	reply length

12	CHARINFO	min-bounds
4		unused
12	CHARINFO	max-bounds
4		unused
2	CARD16	min-char-or-byte2
2	CARD16	max-char-or-byte2
2	CARD16	default-char
2	m	number of FONTPROPs in properties
1		draw-direction
	0 LeftToRight	
	1 RightToLeft	
1	CARD8	min-byte1
1	CARD8	max-byte1
1	BOOL	all-chars-exist
2	INT16	font-ascent
2	INT16	font-descent
4	CARD32	replies-hint
8m	LISTofFONTPROP	properties
n	STRING8	name
p		unused, p=pad(n)

FONTPROP

encodings are the same as for QueryFont

CHARINFO

encodings are the same as for QueryFont

→ (last in series)

1	1	Reply
1	0	last-reply indicator
2	CARD16	sequence number
4	7	reply length
52		unused

SetFontPath

1	51	opcode
1		unused
2	2+(n+p)/4	request length
2	CARD16	number of STRs in path

2		unused
n	LISTofSTR	path
p		unused, p=pad(n)

GetFontPath

1	52	opcode
1		unused
2	1	request list
→		
1	1	Reply
1		unused
2	CARD16	sequence number
4	(n+p)/4	reply length
2	CARD16	number of STRs in path
22		unused
n	LISTofSTR	path
p		unused, p=pad(n)

CreatePixmap

1	53	opcode
1	CARD8	depth
2	4	request length
4	PIXMAP	pid
4	DRAWABLE	drawable
2	CARD16	width
2	CARD16	height

FreePixmap

1	54	opcode
1		unused
2	2	request length
4	PIXMAP	pixmap

CreateGC

1	55	opcode
1		unused
2	4+n	request length
4	GCONTEXT	cid
4	DRAWABLE	drawable

4	BITMASK		value-mask (has n bits set to 1)
	#x00000001	function	
	#x00000002	plane-mask	
	#x00000004	foreground	
	#x00000008	background	
	#x00000010	line-width	
	#x00000020	line-style	
	#x00000040	cap-style	
	#x00000080	join-style	
	#x00000100	fill-style	
	#x00000200	fill-rule	
	#x00000400	tile	
	#x00000800	stipple	
	#x00001000	tile-stipple-x-origin	
	#x00002000	tile-stipple-y-origin	
	#x00004000	font	
	#x00008000	subwindow-mode	
	#x00010000	graphics-exposures	
	#x00020000	clip-x-origin	
	#x00040000	clip-y-origin	
	#x00080000	clip-mask	
	#x00100000	dash-offset	
	#x00200000	dashes	
	#x00400000	arc-mode	
4n	LISTofVALUE		value-list

VALUEs

1			function
	0	`Clear`	
	1	`And`	
	2	`AndReverse`	
	3	`Copy`	
	4	`AndInverted`	
	5	`NoOp`	
	6	`Xor`	
	7	`Or`	
	8	`Nor`	
	9	`Equiv`	
	10	`Invert`	
	11	`OrReverse`	
	12	`CopyInverted`	

	13 `OrInverted`	
	14 `Nand`	
	15 `Set`	
4	CARD32	plane-mask
4	CARD32	foreground
4	CARD32	background
2	CARD16	line-width
1		line-style
	0 `Solid`	
	1 `OnOffDash`	
	2 `DoubleDash`	
1		cap-style
	0 `NotLast`	
	1 `Butt`	
	2 `Round`	
	3 `Projecting`	
1		join-style
	0 `Miter`	
	1 `Round`	
	2 `Bevel`	
1		fill-style
	0 `Solid`	
	1 `Tiled`	
	2 `Stippled`	
	3 `OpaqueStippled`	
1		fill-rule
	0 `EvenOdd`	
	1 `Winding`	
4	PIXMAP	tile
4	PIXMAP	stipple
2	INT16	tile-stipple-x-origin
2	INT16	tile-stipple-y-origin
4	FONT	font
1		subwindow-mode
	0 `ClipByChildren`	
	1 `IncludeInferiors`	
1	BOOL	graphics-exposures
2	INT16	clip-x-origin
2	INT16	clip-y-origin
4	PIXMAP	clip-mask
	0 `None`	

2	CARD16	dash-offset
1	CARD8	dashes
1		arc-mode
	0 `Chord`	
	1 `PieSlice`	

ChangeGC

1	56	opcode
1		unused
2	3+n	request length
4	GCONTEXT	gc
4	BITMASK	value-mask (has n bits set to 1)
	encodings are the same as for `CreateGC`	
4n	LISTofVALUE	value-list
	encodings are the same as for `CreateGC`	

CopyGC

1	57	opcode
1		unused
2	4	request length
4	GCONTEXT	src-gc
4	GCONTEXT	dst-gc
4	BITMASK	value-mask
	encodings are the same as for `CreateGC`	

SetDashes

1	58	opcode
1		unused
2	3+(n+p)/4	request length
4	GCONTEXT	gc
2	CARD16	dash-offset
2	n	length of dashes
n	LISTofCARD8	dashes
p		unused, p=pad(n)

SetClipRectangles

1	59	opcode
1		ordering

	0 `UnSorted`	
	1 `YSorted`	
	2 `YXSorted`	
	3 `YXBanded`	
2	3+2n	request length
4	GCONTEXT	gc
2	INT16	clip-x-origin
2	INT16	clip-y-origin
8n	LISTofRECTANGLE	rectangles

FreeGC

1	60	opcode
1		unused
2	2	request length
4	GCONTEXT	gc

ClearArea

1	61	opcode
1	BOOL	exposures
2	4	request length
4	WINDOW	window
2	INT16	x
2	INT16	y
2	CARD16	width
2	CARD16	height

CopyArea

1	62	opcode
1		unused
2	7	request length
4	DRAWABLE	src-drawable
4	DRAWABLE	dst-drawable
4	GCONTEXT	gc
2	INT16	src-x
2	INT16	src-y
2	INT16	dst-x
2	INT16	dst-y
2	CARD16	width
2	CARD16	height

CopyPlane

1	63	opcode
1		unused
2	8	request length
4	DRAWABLE	src-drawable
4	DRAWABLE	dst-drawable
4	GCONTEXT	gc
2	INT16	src-x
2	INT16	src-y
2	INT16	dst-x
2	INT16	dst-y
2	CARD16	width
2	CARD16	height
4	CARD32	bit-plane

PolyPoint

1	64	opcode
1		coordinate-mode
	0 Origin	
	1 Previous	
2	3+n	request length
4	DRAWABLE	drawable
4	GCONTEXT	gc
4n	LISTofPOINT	points

PolyLine

1	65	opcode
1		coordinate-mode
	0 Origin	
	1 Previous	
2	3+n	request length
4	DRAWABLE	drawable
4	GCONTEXT	gc
4n	LISTofPOINT	points

PolySegment

1	66	opcode
1		unused
2	3+2n	request length

4	DRAWABLE	drawable
4	GCONTEXT	gc
8n	LISTofSEGMENT	segments

SEGMENT

2	INT16	x1
2	INT16	y1
2	INT16	x2
2	INT16	y2

PolyRectangle

1	67	opcode
1		unused
2	3+2n	request length
4	DRAWABLE	drawable
4	GCONTEXT	gc
8n	LISTofRECTANGLE	rectangles

PolyArc

1	68	opcode
1		unused
2	3+3n	request length
4	DRAWABLE	drawable
4	GCONTEXT	gc
12n	LISTofARC	arcs

FillPoly

1	69	opcode
1		unused
2	4+n	request length
4	DRAWABLE	drawable
4	GCONTEXT	gc
1		shape
	0 Complex	
	1 Nonconvex	
	2 Convex	
1		coordinate-mode
	0 Origin	
	1 Previous	

2		unused
4n	LISTofPOINT	points

PolyFillRectangle

1	70	opcode
1		unused
2	3+2n	request length
4	DRAWABLE	drawable
4	GCONTEXT	gc
8n	LISTofRECTANGLE	rectangles

PolyFillArc

1	71	opcode
1		unused
2	3+3n	request length
4	DRAWABLE	drawable
4	GCONTEXT	gc
12n	LISTofARC	arcs

PutImage

1	72	opcode
1		format
	0 Bitmap	
	1 XYPixmap	
	2 ZPixmap	
2	6+(n+p)/4	request length
4	DRAWABLE	drawable
4	GCONTEXT	gc
2	CARD16	width
2	CARD16	height
2	INT16	dst-x
2	INT16	dst-y
1	CARD8	left-pad
1	CARD8	depth
2		unused
n	LISTofBYTE	data
p		unused, p=pad(n)

GetImage

1	73	opcode
1		format
	1 `XYPixmap`	
	2 `ZPixmap`	
2	5	request length
4	DRAWABLE	drawable
2	INT16	x
2	INT16	y
2	CARD16	width
2	CARD16	height
4	CARD32	plane-mask

→

1	1	Reply
1	CARD8	depth
2	CARD16	sequence number
4	(n+p)/4	reply length
4	VISUALID	visual
	0 `None`	
20		unused
n	LISTofBYTE	data
p		unused, p=pad(n)

PolyText8

1	74	opcode
1		unused
2	4+(n+p)/4	request length
4	DRAWABLE	drawable
4	GCONTEXT	gc
2	INT16	x
2	INT16	y
n	LISTofTEXTITEM8	items
p		unused, p=pad(n) (p is always 0 or 1)

TEXTITEM8

1	m	length of string (cannot be 255)
1	INT8	delta

m	STRING8	string
or		
1	255	font-shift indicator
1		font byte 3 (most-significant)
1		font byte 2
1		font byte 1
1		font byte 0 (least-significant)

PolyText16

1	75	opcode
1		unused
2	4+(n+p)/4	request length
4	DRAWABLE	drawable
4	GCONTEXT	gc
2	INT16	x
2	INT16	y
n	LISTofTEXTITEM16	items
p		unused, p=pad(n) (p must be 0 or 1)

TEXTITEM16

1	m	number of CHAR2Bs in string (cannot be 255)
1	INT8	delta
2m	STRING16	string
or		
1	255	font-shift indicator
1		font byte 3 (most-significant)
1		font byte 2
1		font byte 1
1		font byte 0 (least-significant)

ImageText8

1	76	opcode
1	n	length of string
2	4+(n+p)/4	request length

4	DRAWABLE	drawable
4	GCONTEXT	gc
2	INT16	x
2	INT16	y
n	STRING8	string
p		unused, p=pad(n)

ImageText16

1	77	opcode
1	n	number of CHAR2Bs in string
2	4+(2n+p)/4	request length
4	DRAWABLE	drawable
4	GCONTEXT	gc
2	INT16	x
2	INT16	y
2n	STRING16	string
p		unused, p=pad(2n)

CreateColormap

1	78	opcode
1		alloc
	0 None	
	1 All	
2	4	request length
4	COLORMAP	mid
4	WINDOW	window
4	VISUALID	visual

FreeColormap

1	79	opcode
1		unused
2	2	request length
4	COLORMAP	cmap

CopyColormapAndFree

1	80	opcode
1		unused
2	3	request length

4	COLORMAP	mid
4	COLORMAP	src-cmap

InstallColormap

1	81	opcode
1		unused
2	2	request length
4	COLORMAP	cmap

UninstallColormap

1	82	opcode
1		unused
2	2	request length
4	COLORMAP	cmap

ListInstalledColormaps

1	83	opcode
1		unused
2	2	request length
4	WINDOW	window

→

1	1	Reply
1		unused
2	CARD16	sequence number
4	n	reply length
2	n	number of COLORMAPs in cmaps
22		unused
4n	LISTofCOLORMAP	cmaps

AllocColor

1	84	opcode
1		unused
2	4	request length
4	COLORMAP	cmap
2	CARD16	red
2	CARD16	green
2	CARD16	blue
2		unused

→

1	1	Reply
1		unused
2	CARD16	sequence number
4	0	reply length
2	CARD16	red
2	CARD16	green
2	CARD16	blue
2		unused
4	CARD32	pixel
12		unused

AllocNamedColor

1	85	opcode
1		unused
2	3+(n+p)/4	request length
4	COLORMAP	cmap
2	n	length of name
2		unused
n	STRING8	name
p		unused, p=pad(n)

→

1	1	Reply
1		unused
2	CARD16	sequence number
4	0	reply length
4	CARD32	pixel
2	CARD16	exact-red
2	CARD16	exact-green
2	CARD16	exact-blue
2	CARD16	visual-red
2	CARD16	visual-green
2	CARD16	visual-blue
8		unused

AllocColorCells

1	86	opcode
1	BOOL	contiguous
2	3	request length
4	COLORMAP	cmap

```
     2     CARD16              colors
     2     CARD16              planes
→
     1     1                   Reply
     1                         unused
     2     CARD16              sequence number
     4     n+m                 reply length
     2     n                   number of CARD32s
                               in pixels
     2     m                   number of CARD32s
                               in masks
     20                        unused
     4n    LISTofCARD32        pixels
     4m    LISTofCARD32        masks
```

AllocColorPlanes

```
     1     87                  opcode
     1     BOOL                contiguous
     2     4                   request length
     4     COLORMAP            cmap
     2     CARD16              colors
     2     CARD16              reds
     2     CARD16              greens
     2     CARD16              blues
→
     1     1                   Reply
     1                         unused
     2     CARD16              sequence number
     4     n                   reply length
     2     n                   number of CARD32s
                               in pixels
     2                         unused
     4     CARD32              red-mask
     4     CARD32              green-mask
     4     CARD32              blue-mask
     8                         unused
     4n    LISTofCARD32        pixels
```

FreeColors

```
     1     88                  opcode
     1                         unused
```

2	3+n	request length
4	COLORMAP	cmap
4	CARD32	plane-mask
4n	LISTofCARD32	pixels

StoreColors

1	89	opcode
1		unused
2	2+3n	request length
4	COLORMAP	cmap
12n	LISTofCOLORITEM	items

COLORITEM

4	CARD32		pixel
2	CARD16		red
2	CARD16		green
2	CARD16		blue
1			do-red, do-green, do-blue
	#x01	do-red (1 is True, 0 is False)	
	#x02	do-green (1 is True, 0 is False)	
	#x04	do-blue (1 is True, 0 is False)	
	#xF8	unused	
1			unused

StoreNamedColor

1	90		opcode
1			do-red, do-green, do-blue
	#x01	do-red (1 is True, 0 is False)	
	#x02	do-green (1 is True, 0 is False)	
	#x04	do-blue (1 is True, 0 is False)	
	#xF8	unused	
2	4+(n+p)/4		request length
4	COLORMAP		cmap
4	CARD32		pixel
2	n		length of name
2			unused
n	STRING8		name
p			unused, p=pad(n)

QueryColors

1	91	opcode
1		unused
2	2+n	request length
4	COLORMAP	cmap
4n	LISTofCARD32	pixels
→		
1	1	Reply
1		unused
2	CARD16	sequence number
4	2n	reply length
2	n	number of RGBs in colors
22		unused
8n	LISTofRGB	colors

RGB

2	CARD16	red
2	CARD16	green
2	CARD16	blue
2		unused

LookupColor

1	92	opcode
1		unused
2	3+(n+p)/4	request length
4	COLORMAP	cmap
2	n	length of name
2		unused
n	STRING8	name
p		unused, p=pad(n)
→		
1	1	Reply
1		unused
2	CARD16	sequence number
4	0	reply length
2	CARD16	exact-red
2	CARD16	exact-green
2	CARD16	exact-blue
2	CARD16	visual-red
2	CARD16	visual-green

2	CARD16	visual-blue
12		unused

CreateCursor

1	93	opcode
1		unused
2	8	request length
4	CURSOR	cid
4	PIXMAP	source
4	PIXMAP	mask
	0 None	
2	CARD16	fore-red
2	CARD16	fore-green
2	CARD16	fore-blue
2	CARD16	back-red
2	CARD16	back-green
2	CARD16	back-blue
2	CARD16	x
2	CARD16	y

CreateGlyphCursor

1	94	opcode
1		unused
2	8	request length
4	CURSOR	cid
4	FONT	source-font
4	FONT	mask-font
	0 None	
2	CARD16	source-char
2	CARD16	mask-char
2	CARD16	fore-red
2	CARD16	fore-green
2	CARD16	fore-blue
2	CARD16	back-red
2	CARD16	back-green
2	CARD16	back-blue

FreeCursor

1	95	opcode
1		unused

2	2	request length
4	CURSOR	cursor

RecolorCursor

1	96	opcode
1		unused
2	5	request length
4	CURSOR	cursor
2	CARD16	fore-red
2	CARD16	fore-green
2	CARD16	fore-blue
2	CARD16	back-red
2	CARD16	back-green
2	CARD16	back-blue

QueryBestSize

1	97	opcode
1		class
	0 `Cursor`	
	1 `Tile`	
	2 `Stipple`	
2	3	request length
4	DRAWABLE	drawable
2	CARD16	width
2	CARD16	height

→

1	1	Reply
1		unused
2	CARD16	sequence number
4	0	reply length
2	CARD16	width
2	CARD16	height
20		unused

QueryExtension

1	98	opcode
1		unused
2	2+(n+p)/4	request length
2	n	length of name

```
     2                          unused
     n     STRING8              name
     p                          unused, p=pad(n)
→
     1     1                    Reply
     1                          unused
     2     CARD16               sequence number
     4     0                    reply length
     1     BOOL                 present
     1     CARD8                major-opcode
     1     CARD8                first-event
     1     CARD8                first-error
     20                         unused
```

ListExtensions

```
     1     99                   opcode
     1                          unused
     2     1                    request length
→
     1     1                    Reply
     1     CARD8                number of STRs in names
     2     CARD16               sequence number
     4     (n+p)/4              reply length
     24                         unused
     n     LISTofSTR            names
     p                          unused, p=pad(n)
```

ChangeKeyboardMapping

```
     1     100                  opcode
     1     n                    keycode-count
     2     2+nm                 request length
     1     KEYCODE              first-keycode
     1     m                    keysyms-per-keycode
     2                          unused
     4nm   LISTofKEYSYM         keysyms
```

GetKeyboardMapping

```
     1     101                  opcode
     1                          unused
     2     2                    request length
```

1	KEYCODE	first-keycode
1	m	count
2		unused

→

1	1	Reply
1	n	keysyms-per-keycode
2	CARD16	sequence number
4	nm	reply length (m = count field from the request)
24		unused
4nm	LISTofKEYSYM	keysyms

ChangeKeyboardControl

1	102		opcode
1			unused
2	2+n		request length
4	BITMASK		value-mask (has n bits set to 1)
	#x0001	key-click-percent	
	#x0002	bell-percent	
	#x0004	bell-pitch	
	#x0008	bell-duration	
	#x0010	led	
	#x0020	led-mode	
	#x0040	key	
	#x0080	auto-repeat-mode	
4n	LISTofVALUE		value-list

VALUEs

1	INT8		key-click-percent
1	INT8		bell-percent
2	INT16		bell-pitch
2	INT16		bell-duration
1	CARD8		led
1			led-mode
	0	Off	
	1	On	
1	KEYCODE		key
1			auto-repeat-mode
	0	Off	
	1	On	
	2	Default	

GetKeyboardControl

1	103	opcode
1		unused
2	1	request length
→		
1	1	Reply
1		global-auto-repeat
	0 Off	
	1 On	
2	CARD16	sequence number
4	5	reply length
4	CARD32	led-mask
1	CARD8	key-click-percent
1	CARD8	bell-percent
2	CARD16	bell-pitch
2	CARD16	bell-duration
2		unused
32	LISTofCARD8	auto-repeats

Bell

1	104	opcode
1	INT8	percent
2	1	request length

ChangePointerControl

1	105	opcode
1		unused
2	3	request length
2	INT16	acceleration-numerator
2	INT16	acceleration-denominator
2	INT16	threshold
1	BOOL	do-acceleration
1	BOOL	do-threshold

GetPointerControl

1	106	opcode
1		unused
2	1	request length

→

1	1	Reply
1		unused
2	CARD16	sequence number
4	0	reply length
2	CARD16	acceleration-numerator
2	CARD16	acceleration-denominator
2	CARD16	threshold
18		unused

SetScreenSaver

1	107	opcode
1		unused
2	3	request length
2	INT16	timeout
2	INT16	interval
1		prefer-blanking
	0 `No`	
	1 `Yes`	
	2 `Default`	
1		allow-exposures
	0 `No`	
	1 `Yes`	
	2 `Default`	
2		unused

GetScreenSaver

1	108	opcode
1		unused
2	1	request length

→

1	1	Reply
1		unused
2	CARD16	sequence number
4	0	reply length
2	CARD16	timeout
2	CARD16	interval
1		prefer-blanking
	0 `No`	
	1 `Yes`	

1		allow-exposures
	0 No	
	1 Yes	
18		unused

ChangeHosts

1	109	opcode
1		mode
	0 Insert	
	1 Delete	
2	2+(n+p)/4	request length
1		family
	0 Internet	
	1 DECnet	
	2 Chaos	
1		unused
2	n	length of address
n	LISTofCARD8	address
p		unused, p=pad(n)

ListHosts

1	110	opcode
1		unused
2	1	request length
→		
1	1	Reply
1		mode
	0 Disabled	
	1 Enabled	
2	CARD16	sequence number
4	n/4	reply length
2	CARD16	number of HOSTs in hosts
22		unused
n	LISTofHOST	hosts (n always a multiple of 4)

SetAccessControl

1	111	opcode
1		mode

	0 `Disable`	
	1 `Enable`	
2	1	request length

SetCloseDownMode

1	112	opcode
1		mode
	0 `Destroy`	
	1 `RetainPermanent`	
	2 `RetainTemporary`	
2	1	request length

KillClient

1	113	opcode
1		unused
2	2	request length
4	CARD32	resource
	0 `AllTemporary`	

RotateProperties

1	114	opcode
1		unused
2	3+n	request length
4	WINDOW	window
2	n	number of properties
2	INT16	delta
4n	LISTofATOM	properties

ForceScreenSaver

1	115	opcode
1		mode
	0 `Reset`	
	1 `Activate`	
2	1	request length

SetPointerMapping

1	116	opcode
1	n	length of map

2	1+(n+p)/4	request length
n	LISTofCARD8	map
p		unused, p=pad(n)
→		
1	1	Reply
1		status
	0 Success	
	1 Busy	
2	CARD16	sequence number
4	0	reply length
24		unused

GetPointerMapping

1	117	opcode
1		unused
2	1	request length
→		
1	1	Reply
1	n	length of map
2	CARD16	sequence number
4	(n+p)/4	reply length
24		unused
n	LISTofCARD8	map
p		unused, p=pad(n)

SetModifierMapping

1	118	opcode
1	n	keycodes-per-modifier
2	1+2n	request length
8n	LISTofKEYCODE	keycodes
→		
1	1	Reply
1		status
	0 Success	
	1 Busy	
	2 Failed	
2	CARD16	sequence number
4	0	reply length
24		unused

GetModifierMapping

1	119	opcode
1		unused
2	1	request length
→		
1	1	Reply
1	n	keycodes-per-modifier
2	CARD16	sequence number
4	2n	reply length
24		unused
8n	LISTofKEYCODE	keycodes

NoOperation

1	127	opcode
1		unused
2	1	request length

Events

KeyPress

1	2	code
1	KEYCODE	detail
2	CARD16	sequence number
4	TIMESTAMP	time
4	WINDOW	root
4	WINDOW	event
4	WINDOW	child
	0 None	
2	INT16	root-x
2	INT16	root-y
2	INT16	event-x
2	INT16	event-y
2	SETofKEYBUTMASK	state
1	BOOL	same-screen
1		unused

KeyRelease

1	3	code
1	KEYCODE	detail

2	CARD16	sequence number
4	TIMESTAMP	time
4	WINDOW	root
4	WINDOW	event
4	WINDOW	child
	0 None	
2	INT16	root-x
2	INT16	root-y
2	INT16	event-x
2	INT16	event-y
2	SETofKEYBUTMASK	state
1	BOOL	same-screen
1		unused

ButtonPress

1	4	code
1	BUTTON	detail
2	CARD16	sequence number
4	TIMESTAMP	time
4	WINDOW	root
4	WINDOW	event
4	WINDOW	child
	0 None	
2	INT16	root-x
2	INT16	root-y
2	INT16	event-x
2	INT16	event-y
2	SETofKEYBUTMASK	state
1	BOOL	same-screen
1		unused

ButtonRelease

1	5	code
1	BUTTON	detail
2	CARD16	sequence number
4	TIMESTAMP	time
4	WINDOW	root
4	WINDOW	event
4	WINDOW	child
	0 None	

2	INT16	root-x
2	INT16	root-y
2	INT16	event-x
2	INT16	event-y
2	SETofKEYBUTMASK	state
1	BOOL	same-screen
1		unused

MotionNotify

1	6	code
1		detail
	0 Normal	
	1 Hint	
2	CARD16	sequence number
4	TIMESTAMP	time
4	WINDOW	root
4	WINDOW	event
4	WINDOW	child
	0 None	
2	INT16	root-x
2	INT16	root-y
2	INT16	event-x
2	INT16	event-y
2	SETofKEYBUTMASK	state
1	BOOL	same-screen
1		unused

EnterNotify

1	7	code
1		detail
	0 Ancestor	
	1 Virtual	
	2 Inferior	
	3 Nonlinear	
	4 NonlinearVirtual	
2	CARD16	sequence number
4	TIMESTAMP	time
4	WINDOW	root
4	WINDOW	event
4	WINDOW	child
	0 None	

2	INT16	root-x
2	INT16	root-y
2	INT16	event-x
2	INT16	event-y
2	SETofKEYBUTMASK	state
1		mode
	0 Normal	
	1 Grab	
	2 Ungrab	
1		same-screen, focus
	#x01 focus (1 is True, 0 is False)	
	#x02 same-screen (1 is True, 0 is False)	
	#xFC unused	

LeaveNotify

1	8	code
1		detail
	0 Ancestor	
	1 Virtual	
	2 Inferior	
	3 Nonlinear	
	4 NonlinearVirtual	
2	CARD16	sequence number
4	TIMESTAMP	time
4	WINDOW	root
4	WINDOW	event
4	WINDOW	child
	0 None	
2	INT16	root-x
2	INT16	root-y
2	INT16	event-x
2	INT16	event-y
2	SETofKEYBUTMASK	state
1		mode
	0 Normal	
	1 Grab	
	2 Ungrab	
1		same-screen, focus
	#x01 focus (1 is True, 0 is False)	
	#x02 same-screen (1 is True, 0 is False)	
	#xFC unused	

FocusIn

1	9	code
1		detail
	0 `Ancestor`	
	1 `Virtual`	
	2 `Inferior`	
	3 `Nonlinear`	
	4 `NonlinearVirtual`	
	5 `Pointer`	
	6 `PointerRoot`	
	7 `None`	
2	CARD16	sequence number
4	WINDOW	event
1		mode
	0 `Normal`	
	1 `Grab`	
	2 `Ungrab`	
	3 `WhileGrabbed`	
23		unused

FocusOut

1	10	code
1		detail
	0 `Ancestor`	
	1 `Virtual`	
	2 `Inferior`	
	3 `Nonlinear`	
	4 `NonlinearVirtual`	
	5 `Pointer`	
	6 `PointerRoot`	
	7 `None`	
2	CARD16	sequence number
4	WINDOW	event
1		mode
	0 `Normal`	
	1 `Grab`	
	2 `Ungrab`	
	3 `WhileGrabbed`	
23		unused

KeymapNotify

1	11	code
31	LISTofCARD8	keys (byte for keycodes 0–7 is omitted)

Expose

1	12	code
1		unused
2	CARD16	sequence number
4	WINDOW	window
2	CARD16	x
2	CARD16	y
2	CARD16	width
2	CARD16	height
2	CARD16	count
14		unused

GraphicsExposure

1	13	code
1		unused
2	CARD16	sequence number
4	DRAWABLE	drawable
2	CARD16	x
2	CARD16	y
2	CARD16	width
2	CARD16	height
2	CARD16	minor-opcode
2	CARD16	count
1	CARD8	major-opcode
11		unused

NoExposure

1	14	code
1		unused
2	CARD16	sequence number
4	DRAWABLE	drawable
2	CARD16	minor-opcode
1	CARD8	major-opcode
21		unused

VisibilityNotify

1	15	code
1		unused
2	CARD16	sequence number
4	WINDOW	window
1		state
	0 Unobscured	
	1 PartiallyObscured	
	2 FullyObscured	
23		unused

CreateNotify

1	16	code
1		unused
2	CARD16	sequence number
4	WINDOW	parent
4	WINDOW	window
2	INT16	x
2	INT16	y
2	CARD16	width
2	CARD16	height
2	CARD16	border-width
1	BOOL	override-redirect
9		unused

DestroyNotify

1	17	code
1		unused
2	CARD16	sequence number
4	WINDOW	event
4	WINDOW	window
20		unused

UnmapNotify

1	18	code
1		unused
2	CARD16	sequence number
4	WINDOW	event

4	WINDOW	window
1	BOOL	from-configure
19		unused

MapNotify

1	19	code
1		unused
2	CARD16	sequence number
4	WINDOW	event
4	WINDOW	window
1	BOOL	override-redirect
19		unused

MapRequest

1	20	code
1		unused
2	CARD16	sequence number
4	WINDOW	parent
4	WINDOW	window
20		unused

ReparentNotify

1	21	code
1		unused
2	CARD16	sequence number
4	WINDOW	event
4	WINDOW	window
4	WINDOW	parent
2	INT16	x
2	INT16	y
1	BOOL	override-redirect
11		unused

ConfigureNotify

1	22	code
1		unused
2	CARD16	sequence number
4	WINDOW	event
4	WINDOW	window

4	WINDOW	above-sibling
	0 None	
2	INT16	x
2	INT16	y
2	CARD16	width
2	CARD16	height
2	CARD16	border-width
1	BOOL	override-redirect
5		unused

ConfigureRequest

1	23	code
1		stack-mode
	0 Above	
	1 Below	
	2 TopIf	
	3 BottomIf	
	4 Opposite	
2	CARD16	sequence number
4	WINDOW	parent
4	WINDOW	window
4	WINDOW	sibling
	0 None	
2	INT16	x
2	INT16	y
2	CARD16	width
2	CARD16	height
2	CARD16	border-width
2	BITMASK	value-mask
	#x0001 x	
	#x0002 y	
	#x0004 width	
	#x0008 height	
	#x0010 border-width	
	#x0020 sibling	
	#x0040 stack-mode	
4		unused

GravityNotify

1	24	code
1		unused

```
2     CARD16              sequence number
4     WINDOW              event
4     WINDOW              window
2     INT16               x
2     INT16               y
16                        unused
```

ResizeRequest

```
1     25                  code
1                         unused
2     CARD16              sequence number
4     WINDOW              window
2     CARD16              width
2     CARD16              height
20                        unused
```

CirculateNotify

```
1     26                  code
1                         unused
2     CARD16              sequence number
4     WINDOW              event
4     WINDOW              window
4     WINDOW              unused
1                         place
      0   Top
      1   Bottom
15                        unused
```

CirculateRequest

```
1     27                  code
1                         unused
2     CARD16              sequence number
4     WINDOW              parent
4     WINDOW              window
4                         unused
1                         place
      0   Top
      1   Bottom
15                        unused
```

PropertyNotify

1	28	code
1		unused
2	CARD16	sequence number
4	WINDOW	window
4	ATOM	atom
4	TIMESTAMP	time
1		state
	0 NewValue	
	1 Deleted	
15		unused

SelectionClear

1	29	code
1		unused
2	CARD16	sequence number
4	TIMESTAMP	time
4	WINDOW	owner
4	ATOM	selection
16		unused

SelectionRequest

1	30	code
1		unused
2	CARD16	sequence number
4	TIMESTAMP	time
	0 CurrentTime	
4	WINDOW	owner
4	WINDOW	requestor
4	ATOM	selection
4	ATOM	target
4	ATOM	property
	0 None	
4		unused

SelectionNotify

1	31	code
1		unused
2	CARD16	sequence number

4	TIMESTAMP	time
	0 `CurrentTime`	
4	WINDOW	requestor
4	ATOM	selection
4	ATOM	target
4	ATOM	property
	0 `None`	
8		unused

ColormapNotify

1	32	code
1		unused
2	CARD16	sequence number
4	WINDOW	window
4	COLORMAP	colormap
	0 `None`	
1	BOOL	new
1		state
	0 `Uninstalled`	
	1 `Installed`	
18		unused

ClientMessage

1	33	code
1	CARD8	format
2	CARD16	sequence number
4	WINDOW	window
4	ATOM	type
20		data

MappingNotify

1	34	code
1		unused
2	CARD16	sequence number
1		request
	0 `Modifier`	
	1 `Keyboard`	
	2 `Pointer`	
1	KEYCODE	first-keycode
1	CARD8	count
25		unused

Appendix G

X Consortium Standard Character Set Names

Font Names

The following CharSet names for the standard character set encodings are registered for use in font names under the X Logical Font Description:

Name	*Encoding Standard*
ISO8859-1	ISO 8859-1, Latin alphabet No. 1
ISO8859-2	ISO 8859-2, Latin alphabet No. 2
ISO8859-3	ISO 8859-3, Latin alphabet No. 3
ISO8859-4	ISO 8859-4, Latin alphabet No. 4
ISO8859-5	ISO 8859-5, Latin/Cyrillic alphabet
ISO8859-6	ISO 8859-6, Latin/Arabic alphabet
ISO8859-7	ISO 8859-7, Latin/Greek alphabet
ISO8859-8	ISO 8859-8, Latin/Hebrew alphabet
ISO8859-9	ISO 8859-9, Latin alphabet No. 5
JISX0201.1976-0	JIS X0201-1976 (reaffirmed 1984), 8-Bit Alphanumeric-Katakana Code
GB2312.1980-0	GB2312-1980, GL encoding, China (PRC) Hanzi
JISX0208.1983-0	JIS X0208-1983, GL encoding, Japanese Graphic Character Set
KSC5601.1987-0	KS C5601-1987, GL encoding, Korean Graphic Character Set

Appendix H

Bitmap Distribution Format Version 2.1

The Bitmap Distribution Format (BDF), Version 2.1, is an X Consortium standard for font interchange, intended to be easily understood by both humans and computers.

File Format

Character bitmap information will be distributed in an USASCII-encoded, human-readable form. Each file is encoded in the printable characters (octal 40 through 176) of USASCII plus carriage return and linefeed. Each file consists of a sequence of variable-length lines. Each line is terminated either by a carriage return (octal 015) and linefeed (octal 012) or by just a linefeed.

The information about a particular family and face at one size and orientation will be contained in one file. The file begins with information pertaining to the face as a whole, followed by the information and bitmaps for the individual characters.

A font bitmap description file has the following general form, where each item is contained on a separate line of text in the file. Tokens on a line are separated by spaces. Keywords are in uppercase and must appear in uppercase in the file.

1. The word STARTFONT followed by a version number indicating the exact file format used. The version described here is 2.1.
2. Lines beginning with the word COMMENT may appear anywhere between the STARTFONT line and the ENDFONT line. These lines are ignored by font compilers.
3. The word FONT followed by either the XLFD font name (as specified in part III) or some private font name. Creators of private font name syntaxes are encouraged to register unique font name prefixes with the X Consortium to prevent naming conflicts. Note that the name continues all the way to the end of the line and may contain spaces.
4. The word SIZE followed by the *point size* of the characters, the *x resolution*, and the *y resolution* of the device for which these characters were intended.
5. The word FONTBOUNDINGBOX followed by the *width in x, height in y*, and the x and y displacement of the lower left corner from the *origin.* (See the examples in the next section.)
6. Optionally, the word STARTPROPERTIES followed by the number of properties (*p*) that follow.
7. Then come *p* lines consisting of a word for the *property name* followed by either an integer or string surrounded by double-quote (octal 042). Internal double-quote characters are indicated by using two in a row.

   Properties named FONT_ASCENT, FONT_DESCENT, and DEFAULT_CHAR should be provided to define the logical font-ascent and font-descent and the default-char for the font. These properties will be removed from the actual font properties in the binary form produced by a compiler. If these properties are not provided, a compiler may reject the font or may compute (arbitrary) values for these properties.
8. The property section, if it exists, is terminated by ENDPROPERTIES.
9. The word CHARS followed by the number of character segments (*c*) that follow.
10. Then come *c* character segments of the form:
    a. The word STARTCHAR followed by up to 14 characters (no blanks) of descriptive *name* of the glyph.
    b. The word ENCODING followed by one of the following forms:
       i. <n> – the glyph index, that is, a positive integer representing the character code used to access the glyph in X requests, as defined by the encoded character set given by the CHARSET_REGISTRY-CHARSET_ENCODING font properties for XLFD conforming fonts. If these XLFD font properties are not defined, the encoding scheme is font-dependent.
       ii. –1 <n> – equivalent to form above. This syntax is provided for backward compatibility with previous versions of this specification and is not recommended for use with new fonts.
       iii. –1 – an unencoded glyph. Some font compilers may discard unencoded glyphs, but, in general, the glyph names may be used by font compilers and

X servers to implement dynamic mapping of glyph repertoires to character encodings as seen through the X protocol.

c. The word SWIDTH followed by the *scalable width* in x and y of character. Scalable widths are in units of 1/1000th of the size of the character. If the size of the character is *p* points, the width information must be scaled by *p*/1000 to get the width of the character in printer's points. This width information should be considered as a vector indicating the position of the next character's origin relative to the origin of this character. To convert the scalable width to the width in device pixels, multiply SWIDTH times *p*/1000 times *r*/72, where *r* is the device resolution in pixels per inch. The result is a real number giving the ideal print width in device pixels. The actual device width must of course be an integral number of device pixels and is given in the next entry. The SWIDTH y value should always be zero for a standard X font.
d. The word DWIDTH followed by the width in x and y of the character in device units. Like the SWIDTH, this width information is a vector indicating the position of the next character's origin relative to the origin of this character. Note that the DWIDTH of a given hand-tuned WYSIWYG glyph may deviate slightly from its ideal device-independent width given by SWIDTH in order to improve its typographic characteristics on a display. The DWIDTH y value should always be zero for a standard X font.
e. The word BBX followed by the width in x (*BBw*), *height* in y (*BBh*) and x and y displacement (*BBox, BBoy*) of the lower left corner from the *origin* of the character.
f. The optional word ATTRIBUTES followed by the attributes as 4 *hex-encoded* characters. The interpretation of these attributes is undefined in this document.
g. The word BITMAP.
h. *h* lines of *hex-encoded* bitmap, padded on the right with zeros to the nearest byte (that is, multiple of 8).
i. The word ENDCHAR.

11. The file is terminated with the word ENDFONT.

Metric Information

Figures H.1 and H.2 best illustrate the bitmap format and character metric information.

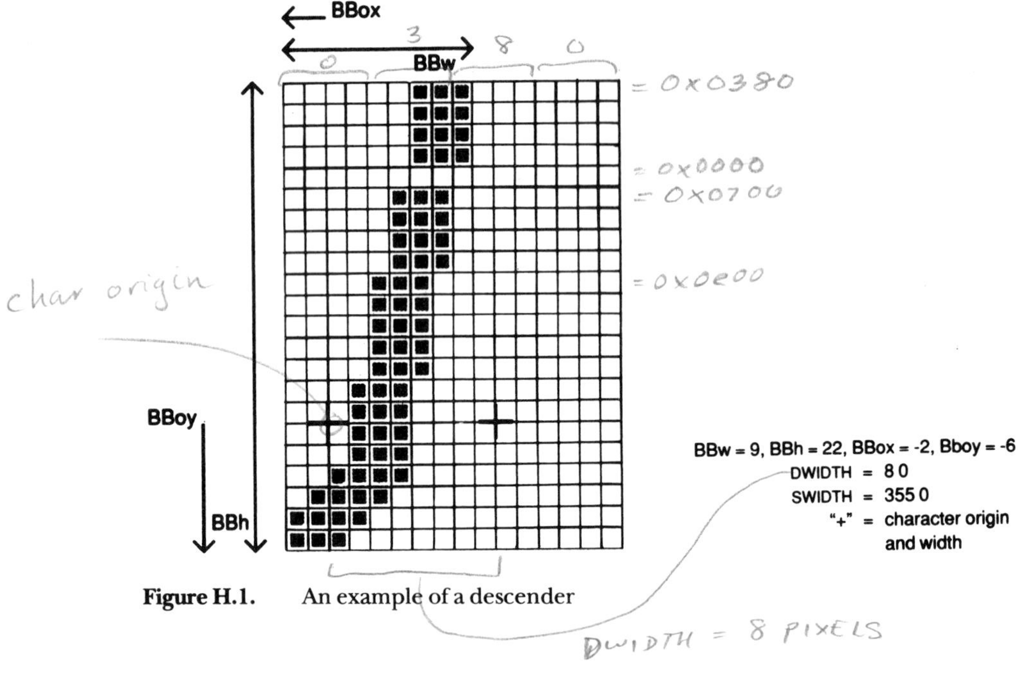

Figure H.1. An example of a descender

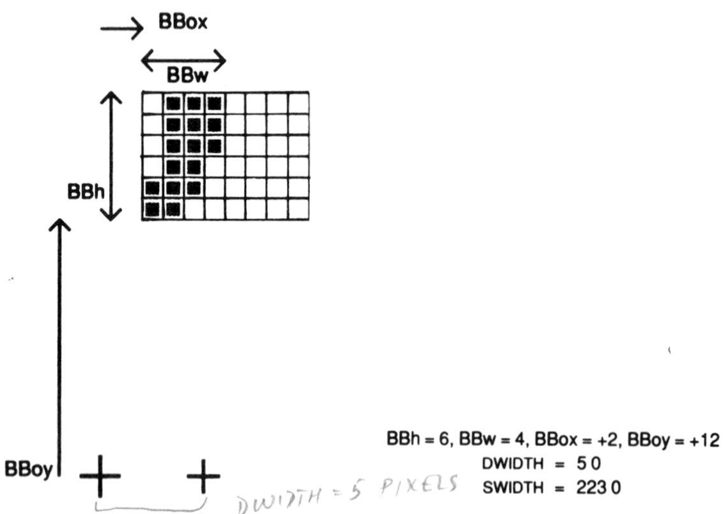

Figure H.2. An example with the origin outside the bounding box

An Example File

The following is an abbreviated example of a bitmap file containing the specification of two characters (the j and quoteright in figures H.1 and H.2).

```
STARTFONT 2.1
COMMENT This is a sample font in 2.1 format. FONT
-Adobe-Helvetica-Bold-R-Normal--24-240-75-75-P-65-ISO8859-1
SIZE 24 75 75
FONTBOUNDINGBOX 9 24 -2 -6
STARTPROPERTIES 19
FOUNDRY "Adobe"
FAMILY "Helvetica"
WEIGHT_NAME "Bold"
SLANT "R"
SETWIDTH_NAME "Normal"
ADD_STYLE_NAME ""
PIXEL_SIZE 24
POINT_SIZE 240
RESOLUTION_X 75
RESOLUTION_Y 75
SPACING "P"
AVERAGE_WIDTH 65
CHARSET_REGISTRY "ISO8859"
CHARSET_ENCODING "1"
MIN_SPACE 4
FONT_ASCENT 21
FONT_DESCENT 7
COPYRIGHT "Copyright (c) 1987 Adobe Systems, Inc."
NOTICE "Helvetica is a registered trademark of Linotype Inc."
ENDPROPERTIES
CHARS 2
STARTCHAR j
ENCODING 106
SWIDTH 355 0
DWIDTH 8 0
BBX 9 22 -2 -6
BITMAP
0380
0380
0380
0380
```

```
0000
0700
0700
0700
0700
0E00
0E00
0E00
0E00
0E00
1C00
1C00
1C00
1C00
3C00
7800
F000
E000
ENDCHAR
STARTCHAR quoteright
ENCODING 39
SWIDTH 223 0
DWIDTH 5 0
BBX 4 6 2 12
ATTRIBUTES 01C0
BITMAP
70
70
70
60
E0
C0
ENDCHAR
ENDFONT
```

Appendix I

Compound Text Encoding

Compound Text is a format for multiple character set data, such as multilingual text. The format is based on ISO standards for encoding and combining character sets. Compound Text is intended to be used in three main contexts: inter-client communication using selections (as defined in the ICCCM), window properties (for example, window manager hints as defined in the ICCCM), and resources (for example, as defined in Xlib and the Xt Intrinsics).

Compound Text is intended as an external representation, or interchange format, not as an internal representation. It is expected (but not required) that clients will convert Compound Text to some internal representation for processing and rendering and then convert from that internal representation to Compound Text when providing textual data to another client.

Values

The name of this encoding is "COMPOUND_TEXT". When text values are used in the ICCCM-compliant selection mechanism or are stored as window properties in the server, the type used should be the atom for "COMPOUND_TEXT".

Octet values are represented in this document as two decimal numbers in the form col/row. This means the value (col * 16) + row. For example, 02/01 means the value 33.

The octet encoding space is divided into four ranges:

C0	octets from 00/00 to 01/15
GL	octets from 02/00 to 07/15
C1	octets from 08/00 to 09/15
GR	octets from 10/00 to 15/15

C0 and C1 are control character sets, while GL and GR are graphic character sets. Only a subset of C0 and C1 octets are used in the encoding, and depending on the character set encoding defined as GL or GR, a subset of GL and GR octets may be used. See the following sections for details. All octets (00/00 to 15/15) may appear inside the text of extended segments.

[For those familiar with ISO 2022, Compound Text uses only an 8-bit environment and always uses G0 for GL and G1 for GR.]

Control Characters

In C0, only the following values will be used:

00/09	HT	HORIZONTAL TABULATION
00/10	NL	NEW LINE
01/11	ESC	(ESCAPE)

In C1, only the following value will be used:

09/11	CSI	CONTROL SEQUENCE INTRODUCER

[Compound Text does not use the alternate 7-bit CSI encoding 01/11 05/11.]

Compound Text does not define control sequences for changing the C0 and C1 sets.

A horizontal tab can be represented with the octet 00/09. Specification of tabulation width settings is not part of Compound Text and must be obtained from context (in an unspecified manner).

[Inclusion of horizontal tab is for consistency with the STRING type currently defined in the ICCCM.]

A newline (line separator/terminator) can be represented with the octet 00/10.

[Note that 00/10 is normally LINEFEED, but is being interpreted as NEWLINE. This can be thought of as using the (deprecated) NEW LINE mode,

E.1.3, in ISO 6429. Use of this value instead of 08/05 (NEL, NEXT LINE) is for consistency with the STRING type currently defined in the ICCCM.]

The remaining C0 and C1 values (01/11 and 09/11) are only used in the control sequences defined in the following sections.

Standard Character Set Encodings

The default GL and GR sets in Compound Text correspond to the left and right halves of ISO 8859-1 (Latin-1). As such, any legal instance of a STRING type (as defined in the ICCCM) is also a legal instance of type COMPOUND_TEXT.

[The implied initial state in ISO 2022 is defined with the sequence:

01/11	02/00	04/03	G0 and G1 in an 8-bit environment only. Designation also invokes.
01/11	02/00	04/07	In an 8-bit environment, C1 is represented as 8-bits.
01/11	02/00	04/09	Graphic character sets can be 94 or 96.
01/11	02/00	04/11	8-bit code is used.
01/11	02/08	04/02	Designate ASCII into G0.
01/11	02/13	04/01	Designate the right-hand part of ISO Latin-1 into G1.

]

To define one of the approved standard character set encodings to be the GL set, use one of the following control sequences:

01/11 02/08 {I} F	94 character set
01/11 02/04 02/08 {I} F	94^N character set

To define one of the approved standard character set encodings to be the GR set, use one of the following control sequences:

01/11 02/09 {I} F	94 character set
01/11 02/13 {I} F	96 character set
01/11 02/04 02/09 {I} F	94^N character set

The F in the control sequences stands for Final character, which is always in the range 04/00 to 07/14. The {I} stands for zero or more intermediate characters, which are always in the range 02/00 to 02/15, with the first intermediate character always in the range 02/01 to 02/03. The registration authority has defined an {I} F sequence for each registered character set encoding.

[Final characters for private encodings (in the range 03/00 to 03/15) are not permitted in Compound Text.]

For GL, octet 02/00 is always defined as SPACE, and octet 07/15 (usually DELETE) is never used. For a 94-character set defined as GR, octets 10/00 and 15/15 are never used. [This is consistent with ISO 2022.]

A 94^N character set uses N octets ($N > 1$) for each character. The value of N is derived from the column value for F:

column 04 or 05	2 octets
column 06	3 octets
column 07	4 or more octets

In a 94^N encoding, the octet values 02/00 and 07/15 (in GL) and 10/00 and 15/15 (in GR) are never used.

[The column definitions come from ISO 2022.]

Once a GL or GR set has been defined, all further octets in that range (except within control sequences and extended segments) are interpreted with respect to that character set encoding until the GL or GR set is redefined. GL and GR sets can be defined independently; they do not have to be defined in pairs.

Note that when actually using a character set encoding as the GR set, you must force the most-significant bit (08/00) of each octet to be a 1 so that it falls in the range 10/00 to 15/15.

[Control sequences to specify character set encoding revisions (as in section 6.3.13 of ISO 2022) are not used in Compound Text. Revision indicators do not appear to provide useful information in the context of Compound Text. The most recent revision can always be assumed, because revisions are upwardly compatible.]

Approved Standard Encodings

The following are the approved standard encodings to be used with Compound Text. None have intermediate characters; however, a good parser will still deal with intermediate characters in the event that additional encodings are later added to this list.

{I} F	*94/96*	*Description*
04/02	94	7-bit ASCII graphics (ANSI X3.4-1968), Left half of ISO 8859 sets
04/09	94	Right half of JIS X0201-1976 (reaffirmed 1984), 8-Bit Alphanumeric-Katakana Code
04/10	94	Left half of JIS X0201-1976 (reaffirmed 1984), 8-Bit Alphanumeric-Katakana Code
04/01	96	Right half of ISO 8859-1, Latin alphabet No. 1
04/02	96	Right half of ISO 8859-2, Latin alphabet No. 2
04/03	96	Right half of ISO 8859-3, Latin alphabet No. 3
04/04	96	Right half of ISO 8859-4, Latin alphabet No. 4
04/06	96	Right half of ISO 8859-7, Latin/Greek alphabet
04/07	96	Right half of ISO 8859-6, Latin/Arabic alphabet
04/08	96	Right half of ISO 8859-8, Latin/Hebrew alphabet
04/12	96	Right half of ISO 8859-5, Latin/Cyrillic alphabet
04/13	96	Right half of ISO 8859-9, Latin alphabet No. 5
04/01	94^2	GB2312-1980, China (PRC) Hanzi
04/02	94^2	JIS X0208-1983, Japanese Graphic Character Set
04/03	94^2	KS C5601-1987, Korean Graphic Character Set

The sets listed as "Left half of . . ." should always be defined as GL. The sets listed as "Right half of . . ." should always be defined as GR. Other sets can be defined either as GL or GR.

Nonstandard Character Set Encodings

Character set encodings that are not in the list of approved standard encodings can be included using extended segments. An extended segment begins with one of the following sequences:

01/11 02/05 02/15 03/00 M L	variable number of octets per character
01/11 02/05 02/15 03/01 M L	1 octet per character
01/11 02/05 02/15 03/02 M L	2 octets per character
01/11 02/05 02/15 03/03 M L	3 octets per character
01/11 02/05 02/15 03/04 M L	4 octets per character

[This uses the "other coding system" of ISO 2022, using private final characters.]

The M and L octets represent a 14-bit unsigned value giving the number of octets that appear in the remainder of the segment. The number is computed as ((M - 128) * 128) + (L - 128). The most-significant bit M and L are always set to 1. The remainder of the segment consists of two parts, the name of the character set encoding and the actual text. The name of the encoding comes first and is separated from the text by the octet 00/02 (STX, START OF TEXT). The length defined by M and L includes the encoding name and separator.

[The encoding of the length is chosen to avoid having zero octets in Compound Text when possible, because embedded NUL values are problematic in many C language routines. The use of zero octets cannot be ruled out entirely, however, because some octets in the actual text of the extended segment may have to be zero.]

The name of the encoding should be registered with the X Consortium to avoid conflicts and should, when appropriate, match the CharSet Registry and Encoding registration used in the X Logical Font Description. The name itself should be encoded using ISO 8859-1 (Latin-1), should not use question mark (03/15) or asterisk (02/10), and should use hyphen (02/13) only in accordance with the X Logical Font Description.

Extended segments should not be used for any character set encoding that can be constructed from a GL/GR pair of approved standard encodings. For example, it is incorrect to use an extended segment for any of the ISO 8859 family of encodings.

It should be noted that the contents of an extended segment are arbitrary; for example, they may contain octets in the C0 and C1 ranges, including 00/00, and octets comprising a given character may differ in their most-significant bit.

[ISO registered "other coding systems" are not used in Compound Text; extended segments are the only mechanism for non-2022 encodings.]

Directionality

If desired, horizontal text direction can be indicated using the following control sequences:

09/11 03/01 05/13	begin left-to-right text
09/11 03/02 05/13	begin right-to-left text
09/11 05/13	end of string

[This is a subset of the SDS (START DIRECTED STRING) control in the Draft Bidirectional Addendum to ISO 6429.]

Directionality can be nested. Logically, a stack of directions is maintained. Each of the first two control sequences pushes a new direction on the stack, and the third sequence (revert) pops a direction from the stack. The stack starts out empty at the beginning of a Compound Text string. When the stack is empty, the directionality of the text is unspecified.

Directionality applies to all subsequent text, whether in GL, GR, or an extended segment. If the desired directionality of GL, GR, or extended segments differs, then directionality control sequences must be inserted when switching between them.

The definition of GL and GR sets is independent of directionality. Defining a new GL or GR set does not change the current directionality, and pushing or popping a directionality does not change the current GL and GR definitions.

Specification of directionality is entirely optional; text direction should be clear from the context in most cases. However, it must be the case that either all characters in a Compound Text string have explicitly specified direction or that all characters have unspecified direction. That is, if directionality control sequences are used, the first such control sequence must precede the first graphic character in a Compound Text string, and graphic characters are not permitted whenever the directionality stack is empty.

Resources

To use Compound Text in a resource, you can simply treat all octets as if they were ASCII/Latin-1 and replace all "\" octets (05/12) with the two octets "\\", all newline octets (00/10) with the two octets "\n", and all zero octets with the four octets "\000". It is up to the client making use of the resource to interpret the data as Compound Text; the policy by which this is ascertained is not constrained by the Compound Text specification.

Font Names

The following CharSet names for the standard character set encodings are registered for use in font names under the X Logical Font Description:

Name	*Encoding Standard*
ISO8859-1	ISO 8859-1
ISO8859-2	ISO 8859-2
ISO8859-3	ISO 8859-3
ISO8859-4	ISO 8859-4
ISO8859-5	ISO 8859-5
ISO8859-6	ISO 8859-6
ISO8859-7	ISO 8859-7
ISO8859-8	ISO 8859-8
ISO8859-9	ISO 8859-9
JISX0201.1976-0	JIS X0201-1976 (reaffirmed 1984)
GB2312.1980-0	GB2312-1980, GL encoding
JISX0208.1983-0	JIS X0208-1983, GL encoding
KSC5601.1987-0	KS C5601-1987, GL encoding

Extensions

There is no absolute requirement for a parser to deal with anything but the particular encoding syntax defined in this specification. However, it is possible that Compound Text may be extended in the future, and therefore, it may be desirable to construct the parser to handle 2022/6429 syntax more generally.

There are two general formats covering all control sequences that are expected to appear in extensions:

01/11 {I} F
: For this format, I is always in the range 02/00 to 02/15, and F is always in the range 03/00 to 07/14.

09/11 {P} {I} F
: For this format, P is always in the range 03/00 to 03/15, I is always in the range 02/00 to 02/15, and F is always in the range 04/00 to 07/14.

In addition, new (singleton) control characters (in the C0 and C1 ranges) might be defined in the future. Finally, new kinds of "segments" might be defined in the future using syntax similar to extended segments:

01/11 02/05 02/15 F M L
: For this format, F is in the range 03/05 to 3/15. M and L are as defined in extended segments. Such a segment will always be followed by the number of octets defined by

M and L. These octets can have arbitrary values and need not follow the internal structure defined for current extended segments.

If extensions to this specification are defined in the future, then any string incorporating instances of such extensions must start with one of the following control sequences:

01/11 02/03 V 03/00	ignoring extensions is OK
01/11 02/03 V 03/01	ignoring extensions is not OK

In either case, V is in the range 02/00 to 02/15 and indicates the major version minus one of the specification being used. These version control sequences are for use by clients that implement earlier versions but have implemented a general parser. The first control sequence indicates that it is acceptable to ignore all extension control sequences; no mandatory information will be lost in the process. The second control sequence indicates that it is unacceptable to ignore any extension control sequences; mandatory information would be lost in the process. In general, it will be up to the client generating the Compound Text to decide which control sequence to use.

Errors

If a Compound Text string does not match the specification here (for example, uses undefined control characters, undefined control sequences, or incorrectly formatted extended segments), it is best to treat the entire string as invalid, except as indicated by a version control sequence.

Glossary

Access control list X maintains a list of hosts from which client programs can be run. By default, only programs on the local host and hosts specified in an initial list read by the server can use the display. This access control list can be changed by clients on the local host. Some server implementations can also implement other authorization mechanisms in addition to or in place of this mechanism. The action of this mechanism can be conditional based on the authorization protocol name and data received by the server at connection setup.

Active grab A grab is active when the pointer or keyboard is actually owned by the single grabbing client.

Ancestors If W is an inferior of A, then A is an ancestor of W.

Atom An atom is a unique ID corresponding to a string name. Atoms are used to identify properties, types, and selections.

Background An `InputOutput` window can have a background, which is defined as a pixmap. When regions of the window have their contents lost or invalidated, the server automatically tiles those regions with the background.

Backing store When a server maintains the contents of a window, the pixels saved off-screen are known as a backing store.

Base font name A base font name is used to select a family of fonts whose members may be encoded in various charsets. The `CharSetRegistry` and `CharSetEncoding` fields of an XLFD name identify the charset of the font. A base font name may be a full XLFD name, with all fourteen — delimiters, or it may be an abbreviated XLFD name containing only the first 13 fields of an XLFD name, up to but not including `CharSetRegistry`, with or without the thirteenth —, or a non-XLFD name. Any XLFD fields may contain wildcards.

When creating an `XFontSet`, Xlib accepts from the client a list of one or more base font names that select one or more font families. They are combined with charset names obtained from the encoding of the locale to load the fonts required to render text.

Bit gravity When a window is resized, the contents of the window are not necessarily discarded. It is possible to request that the server relocate the previous contents to some region of the window (though no guarantees are made). This attraction of window contents for some location of a window is known as bit gravity.

Bit plane When a pixmap or window is thought of as a stack of bitmaps, each bitmap is called a bit plane or plane.

Bitmap A bitmap is a pixmap of depth one.

Border An `InputOutput` window can have a border of equal thickness on all four sides of the window. The contents of the border are defined by a pixmap, and the server automatically maintains the contents of the border. Exposure events are never generated for border regions.

Button grabbing Buttons on the pointer can be passively grabbed by a client. When the button is pressed, the pointer is then actively grabbed by the client.

Byte order For image (pixmap/bitmap) data, the server defines the byte order, and clients with different native byte ordering must swap bytes as necessary. For all other parts of the protocol, the client defines the byte order, and the server swaps bytes as necessary.

Character A character is a member of a set of elements used for the organization, control, or representation of text (ISO2022, as adapted by XPG3). In ISO2022 terms, a character is not bound to a coded value until it is identified as part of a coded character set.

Character glyph A character glyph is the abstract graphical symbol for a character. Character glyphs may or may not map one-to-one to font glyphs and may be context-dependent, varying with the adjacent characters. Multiple characters may map to a single character glyph.

Character set A character set is a collection of characters.

Charset A charset is an encoding with a uniform, state-independent mapping from characters to codepoints, or a coded character set.

For display in X, there can be a direct mapping from a charset to one font, if the width of all characters in the charset is either one or two bytes. A text string encoded in an encoding such as Shift-JIS cannot be passed directly to the X server, because the text imaging requests accept only single-width charsets (either 8 or 16 bits). Charsets that meet these restrictions can serve as font charsets. Font charsets, strictly speaking, map font indices to font glyphs, not characters to character glyphs.

Note that a single font charset is sometimes used as the encoding of a locale, for example, ISO8859-1.

Children The children of a window are its first-level subwindows.

Class Windows can be of different classes or types. See the entries for `InputOnly` and `InputOutput` windows for further information about valid window types.

Client An application program connects to the window system server by some interprocess communication (IPC) path, such as a TCP connection or a shared memory buffer. This program is referred to as a client of the window system server. More precisely, the client is the IPC path itself. A program with multiple paths open to the server is viewed as multiple clients by the protocol. Resource lifetimes are controlled by connection lifetimes, not by program lifetimes.

Clipping region In a graphics context, a bitmap or list of rectangles can be specified to restrict output to a particular region of the window. The image defined by the bitmap or rectangles is called a clipping region.

Coded character A character bound to a codepoint is considered a coded character.

Coded character set A coded character set is a set of unambiguous rules that establishes that character set and the one-to-one relationship between each character of the set and its bit representation (ISO2022, as adapted by

XPG3). It is a definition of a one-to-one mapping of a set of characters to a set of codepoints.

Codepoint The coded representation of a single character in a coded character set is a codepoint.

Colormap A colormap consists of a set of entries defining color values. The colormap associated with a window is used to display the contents of the window; each pixel value indexes the colormap to produce an RGB value that drives the guns of a monitor. Depending on hardware limitations, one or more colormaps can be installed at one time so that windows associated with those maps display with true colors.

Connection The IPC path between the server and client program is known as a connection. A client program typically (but not necessarily) has one connection to the server over which requests and events are sent.

Containment A window contains the pointer if the window is viewable and the hotspot of the cursor is within a visible region of the window or a visible region of one of its inferiors. The border of the window is included as part of the window for containment. The pointer is in a window if the window contains the pointer but no inferior contains the pointer.

Coordinate system The coordinate system has X horizontal and Y vertical, with the origin [0, 0] at the upper-left corner. Coordinates are integral and coincide with pixel centers. Each window and pixmap has its own coordinate system. For a window, the origin is inside the border at the inside, upper-left corner.

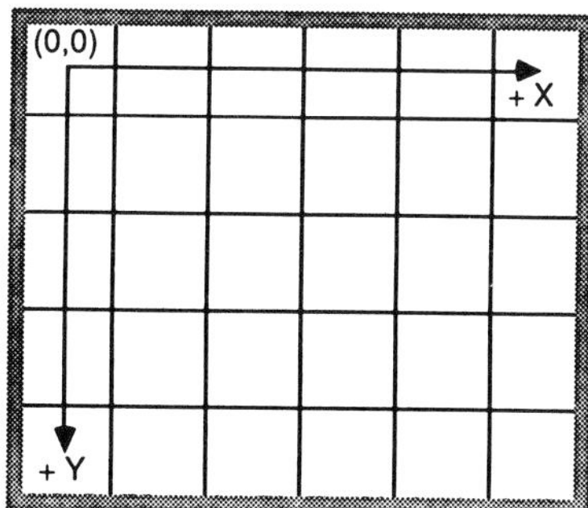

Coordinates Are Pixel Centers

Figure G.1. Coordinate system

Cursor A cursor is the visible shape of the pointer on a screen. It consists of a hotspot, a source bitmap, a shape bitmap, and a pair of colors. The cursor defined for a window controls the visible appearance when the pointer is in that window.

Depth The depth of a window or pixmap is the number of bits per pixel it has. The depth of a graphics context is the depth of the drawables it can be used in conjunction with graphics output.

Device Keyboards, mice, tablets, track-balls, button boxes, and so on are all collectively known as input devices. Pointers can have one or more buttons (the most common number is three). The core protocol only deals with two devices: the keyboard and the pointer.

DirectColor `DirectColor` is a class of colormap in which a pixel value is decomposed into three separate subfields for indexing. The first subfield indexes an array to produce red intensity values. The second subfield indexes a second array to produce blue intensity values. The third subfield indexes a third array to produce green intensity values. The RGB (red, green, and blue) values in the colormap entry can be changed dynamically.

Display A server, together with its screens and input devices, is called a display. The Xlib `Display` structure contains all information about the particular display and its screens as well as the state that Xlib needs to communicate with the display over a particular connection.

Drawable Both windows and pixmaps can be used as sources and destinations in graphics operations. These windows and pixmaps are collectively known as drawables. However, an `InputOnly` window cannot be used as a source or destination in a graphics operation.

Encoding An encoding is a set of unambiguous rules that establishes a character set and a relationship between the characters and their representations. The character set does not have to be fixed to a finite predefined set of characters. The representations do not have to be of uniform length. Examples are an ISO2022 graphic set, a state-independent or state-dependent combination of graphic sets, possibly including control sets, and the X Compound Text encoding.

In X, encodings are identified by a string that appears as the `CharSetRegistry` and `CharSetEncoding` components of an XLFD name, the name of a charset of the locale for which a font could not be found, or an atom that identifies the encoding of a text property or that names an encoding for a text selection target type. Encoding names should be composed of characters from the X Portable Character Set.

Escapement The escapement of a string is the distance in pixels in the primary draw direction from the drawing origin to the origin of the next character (that is, the one following the given string) to be drawn.

Event Clients are informed of information asynchronously by means of events. These events can be either asynchronously generated from devices or generated as side effects of client requests. Events are grouped into types. The server never sends an event to a client unless the client has specifically asked to be informed of that type of event. However, clients can force events to be sent to other clients. Events are typically reported relative to a window.

Event mask Events are requested relative to a window. The set of event types a client requests relative to a window is described by using an event mask.

Event propagation Device-related events propagate from the source window to ancestor windows until some client has expressed interest in handling that type of event or until the event is discarded explicitly.

Event source The deepest viewable window that the pointer is in is called the source of a device-related event.

Event synchronization There are certain race conditions possible when demultiplexing device events to clients (in particular, deciding where pointer and keyboard events should be sent when in the middle of window management operations). The event synchronization mechanism allows synchronous processing of device events.

Exposure event Servers do not guarantee to preserve the contents of windows when windows are obscured or reconfigured. Exposure events are sent to clients to inform them when contents of regions of windows have been lost.

Extension Named extensions to the core protocol can be defined to extend the system. Extensions to output requests, resources, and event types are all possible and expected.

Font A font is an array of glyphs (typically characters). The protocol does no translation or interpretation of character sets. The client simply indicates values used to index the glyph array. A font contains additional metric information to determine interglyph and interline spacing.

Font glyph The abstract graphical symbol for an index into a font is called a font glyph.

Frozen events Clients can freeze event processing during keyboard and pointer grabs.

GC GC is an abbreviation for graphics context. See **Graphics context**.

Glyph A glyph is an identified abstract graphical symbol independent of any actual image (ISO/IEC/DIS 9541-1) or an abstract visual representation of a graphic character not bound to a codepoint.

Glyph image A glyph image is an image of a glyph, as obtained from a glyph representation displayed on a presentation surface (ISO/IEC/DIS 9541-1).

Grab Keyboard keys, the keyboard, pointer buttons, the pointer, and the server can be grabbed for exclusive use by a client. In general, these facilities are not intended to be used by normal applications but are intended for various input and window managers to implement various styles of user interfaces.

Graphics context Various information for graphics output is stored in a graphics context (GC), such as foreground pixel, background pixel, line width, clipping region, and so on. A graphics context can only be used with drawables that have the same root and the same depth as the graphics context.

Gravity The contents of windows and windows themselves have a gravity, which determines how the contents move when a window is resized. See **Bit gravity** and **Window gravity**.

GrayScale `GrayScale` can be viewed as a degenerate case of `PseudoColor`, in which the red, green, and blue values in any given colormap entry are equal and thus, produce shades of gray. The gray values can be changed dynamically.

Host Portable Character Encoding The encoding of the X Portable Character Set on the host is the Host Portable Character Encoding. The encoding itself is not defined by this standard, but the encoding must be the same in all locales supported by Xlib on the host. If a string is said to be in the Host Portable Character Encoding, then it only contains characters from the X Portable Character Set in the host encoding.

Hotspot A cursor has an associated hotspot, which defines the point in the cursor corresponding to the coordinates reported for the pointer.

Identifier An identifier is a unique value associated with a resource that clients use to name that resource. The identifier can be used over any connection to name the resource.

Inferiors The inferiors of a window are all of the subwindows nested below it: the children, the children's children, and so on.

Input focus The input focus is usually a window defining the scope for processing of keyboard input. If a generated keyboard event usually would be reported to this window or one of its inferiors, the event is reported as usual. Otherwise, the event is reported with respect to the focus window. The input focus also can be set such that all keyboard events are discarded and such that the focus window is dynamically taken to be the root window of whatever screen the pointer is on at each keyboard event.

Input manager Control over keyboard input is typically provided by an input manager client, which usually is part of a window manager.

InputOnly window An `InputOnly` window is a window that cannot be used for graphics requests. `InputOnly` windows are invisible and are used to control such things as cursors, input event generation, and grabbing. `InputOnly` windows cannot have `InputOutput` windows as inferiors.

InputOutput window An `InputOutput` window is the normal kind of window that is used for both input and output. `InputOutput` windows can have both `InputOutput` and `InputOnly` windows as inferiors.

Internationalization Internationalization is the process of making software adaptable to the requirements of different native languages, local customs, and character string encodings or of making a computer program adaptable to different locales without program source modifications or recompilation.

ISO2022 ISO2022 is the ISO standard for code extension techniques for 7-bit and 8-bit coded character sets.

Keyboard grabbing A client can actively grab control of the keyboard, and key events will be sent to that client rather than the client the events would normally have been sent to.

Key grabbing Keys on the keyboard can be passively grabbed by a client. When the key is pressed, the keyboard is then actively grabbed by the client.

Keysym An encoding of a symbol on a keycap on a keyboard.

Latin-1 Latin-1 is the coded character set defined by the ISO8859-1 standard.

Latin Portable Character Encoding Latin Portable Character Encoding is the encoding of the X Portable Character Set using the Latin-1 codepoints plus ASCII control characters. If a string is said to be in the Latin Portable Character Encoding, then it only contains characters from the X Portable Character Set, not all of Latin-1.

Locale A locale is the international environment of a computer program defining the localized behavior of that program at runtime. This information can be established from one or more sets of localization data. ANSI C defines locale-specific processing by C system library calls. See ANSI C and the X/Open Portability Guide specifications for more details. In Xlib, on implementations that conform to the ANSI C library, the current locale is the current setting of the LC_CTYPE `setlocale` category. Associated with each locale is a text encoding. When text is processed in the context of a locale, the text must be in the encoding of the locale. The current locale affects Xlib in its:

- Encoding and processing of input method text
- Encoding of resource files and values
- Encoding and imaging of text strings
- Encoding and decoding for inter-client text communication

Locale name The identifier used to select the desired locale for the host C library and X library functions is the locale name, which, on ANSI C library compliant systems, is the locale argument to the `setlocale` function.

Localization The process of establishing information within a computer system specific to the operation of particular native languages, local customs and coded character sets (XPG3) is called localization.

Mapped A window is said to be mapped if a map call has been performed on it. Unmapped windows and their inferiors are never viewable or visible.

Modifier keys Shift, Control, Meta, Super, Hyper, Alt, Compose, Apple, CapsLock, ShiftLock, and similar keys are called modifier keys.

Monochrome Monochrome is a special case of `StaticGray` in which there are only two colormap entries.

Multibyte Multibyte describes a character whose codepoint is stored in more than one byte, any encoding that can contain multibyte characters, text in a multibyte encoding, or the "char *" null-terminated string datatype in ANSI C. Note that all references in this book to multibyte strings imply only that the strings may contain multibyte characters.

Obscure A window is obscured if some other window obscures it. A window can be partially obscured and so still have visible regions. Window A obscures window B if both are viewable `InputOutput` windows, if A is higher in the global stacking order, and if the rectangle defined by the outside edges of A intersects the rectangle defined by the outside edges of B. Note the distinction between obscures and occludes. Also note that window borders are included in the calculation.

Occlude A window is occluded if some other window occludes it. Window A occludes window B if both are mapped, if A is higher in the global stacking order, and if the rectangle defined by the outside edges of A intersects the rectangle defined by the outside edges of B. Note the distinction between occludes and obscures. Also note that window borders are included in the calculation and that `InputOnly` windows never obscure other windows but can occlude other windows.

Padding Some padding bytes are inserted in the data stream to maintain alignment of the protocol requests on natural boundaries. This increases ease of portability to some machine architectures.

Parent window If C is a child of P, then P is the parent of C.

Passive grab Grabbing a key or button is a passive grab. The grab activates when the key or button is actually pressed.

Pixel value A pixel is an N-bit value, where N is the number of bit planes used in a particular window or pixmap (that is, is the depth of the window or pixmap). A pixel in a window indexes a colormap to derive an actual color to be displayed.

Pixmap A pixmap is a three-dimensional array of bits. A pixmap is normally thought of as a two-dimensional array of pixels, where each pixel can be a value from 0 to $2^N–1$, and where N is the depth (z axis) of the pixmap. A pixmap can also be thought of as a stack of N bitmaps. A pixmap can only be used on the screen that it was created in.

Plane When a pixmap or window is thought of as a stack of bitmaps, each bitmap is called a plane or bit plane.

Plane mask Graphics operations can be restricted to only affect a subset of bit planes of a destination. A plane mask is a bit mask describing which planes are to be modified. The plane mask is stored in a graphics context.

Pointer The pointer is the pointing device currently attached to the cursor and tracked on the screens.

Pointer grabbing A client can actively grab control of the pointer. Then button and motion events will be sent to that client rather than the client the events would normally have been sent to.

Pointing device A pointing device is typically a mouse, tablet, or some other device with effective dimensional motion. The core protocol defines only one visible cursor, which tracks whatever pointing device is attached as the pointer.

POSIX POSIX is the Portable Operating System Interface, ISO/IEC 9945-1 (IEEE Std 1003.1).

POSIX Portable Filename Character Set The POSIX Portable Filename Character Set is the set of 65 characters that can be used in naming files on a POSIX-compliant host that are correctly processed in all locales. The set is:

a..z A..Z 0..9 ._-

Property Windows can have associated properties that consist of a name, a type, a data format, and some data. The protocol places no interpretation on properties. They are intended as a general-purpose naming mechanism for clients. For example, clients might use properties to share information such as resize hints, program names, and icon formats with a window manager.

Property list The property list of a window is the list of properties that have been defined for the window.

PseudoColor `PseudoColor` is a class of colormap in which a pixel value indexes the colormap entry to produce an independent RGB value; that is, the colormap is viewed as an array of triples (RGB values). The RGB values can be changed dynamically.

Rectangle A rectangle specified by [x,y,w,h] has an infinitely thin outline path with corners at [x,y], [x+w,y], [x+w,y+h], and [x, y+h]. When a rectangle is filled, the lower-right edges are not drawn. For example, if w = h = 0, nothing would be drawn. For w = h = 1, a single pixel would be drawn.

Redirecting control Window managers (or client programs) may enforce window layout policy in various ways. When a client attempts to change the size or position of a window, the operation may be redirected to a specified client rather than the operation actually being performed.

Reply Information requested by a client program using the X protocol is sent back to the client with a reply. Both events and replies are multiplexed on the same connection. Most requests do not generate replies, but some requests generate multiple replies.

Request A command to the server is called a request. It is a single block of data sent over a connection.

Resource Windows, pixmaps, cursors, fonts, graphics contexts, and colormaps are known as resources. They all have unique identifiers associated with them for naming purposes. The lifetime of a resource usually is bounded by the lifetime of the connection over which the resource was created.

RGB values RGB values are the red, green, and blue intensity values that are used to define a color. These values are always represented as 16-bit, unsigned numbers, with 0 the minimum intensity and 65535 the maximum intensity. The X server scales these values to match the display hardware.

Root The root of a pixmap or graphics context is the same as the root of whatever drawable was used when the pixmap or GC was created. The root of a window is the root window under which the window was created.

Root window Each screen has a root window covering it. The root window cannot be reconfigured or unmapped, but otherwise it acts as a full-fledged window. A root window has no parent.

Save set The save set of a client is a list of other clients' windows that, if they are inferiors of one of the client's windows at connection close, should not be destroyed and that should be remapped if currently unmapped. Save sets are typically used by window managers to avoid lost windows if the manager should terminate abnormally.

Scanline A scanline is a list of pixel or bit values viewed as a horizontal row (all values having the same y coordinate) of an image, with the values ordered by increasing the x coordinate.

Scanline order An image represented in scanline order contains scanlines ordered by increasing the y coordinate.

Screen A server can provide several independent screens, which typically have physically independent monitors. This would be the expected configuration when there is only a single keyboard and pointer shared among the screens. A `Screen` structure contains the information about that screen and is linked to the `Display` structure.

Selection A selection can be thought of as an indirect property with dynamic type. That is, rather than having the property stored in the X server, it is maintained by some client (the owner). A selection is global and is thought of as belonging to the user and being maintained by clients, rather than being private to a particular window subhierarchy or a particular set of clients. When a client asks for the contents of a selection, it specifies a selection target type, which can be used to control the transmitted representation of the contents. For example, if the selection is "the last thing the user clicked on," and that is currently an image, then the target type might specify whether the contents of the image should be sent in XY format or Z format.

The target type can also be used to control the class of contents transmitted; for example, asking for the "looks" (fonts, line spacing, indentation, and so forth) of a paragraph selection, rather than the text of the paragraph. The target type can also be used for other purposes. The protocol does not constrain the semantics.

Server The server, which is also referred to as the X server, provides the basic windowing mechanism. It handles IPC connections from clients, multiplexes graphics requests onto the screens, and demultiplexes input back to the appropriate clients.

Server grabbing The server can be grabbed by a single client for exclusive use. This prevents processing of any requests from other client connections until the grab is completed. This is typically only a transient state for such things as rubber-banding, pop-up menus, or executing requests indivisibly.

Shift sequence ISO2022 defines control characters and escape sequences that temporarily (single shift) or permanently (locking shift) cause a different character set to be in effect (invoking a character set).

Sibling Children of the same parent window are known as sibling windows.

Stacking order Sibling windows, similar to sheets of paper on a desk, can stack on top of each other. Windows above both obscure and occlude lower windows. The relationship between sibling windows is known as the stacking order.

State-dependent encoding An encoding in which an invocation of a charset can apply to multiple characters in sequence is a state-dependent encoding. A state-dependent encoding begins in an initial state and enters other shift states when specific shift sequences are encountered in the byte sequence. In ISO2022 terms, this means the use of locking shifts, not single shifts.

State-independent encoding Any encoding in which the invocations of the charsets are fixed or span only a single character is a state-independent encoding. In ISO2022 terms, this means the use of at most single shifts, not locking shifts.

StaticColor `StaticColor` can be viewed as a degenerate case of `PseudoColor` in which the RGB values are predefined and read-only.

StaticGray `StaticGray` can be viewed as a degenerate case of `GrayScale` in which the gray values are predefined and read-only. The values are typically linear or near-linear increasing ramps.

Status Many Xlib functions return a success status. If the function does not succeed, however, its arguments are not disturbed.

Stipple A stipple pattern is a bitmap that is used to tile a region to serve as an additional clip mask for a fill operation with the foreground color.

STRING encoding String encoding consists of Latin-1, plus tab and newline.

String equivalence Two ISO Latin-1 STRING8 values are considered equal if they are the same length and if corresponding bytes are either equal or are equivalent as follows: decimal values 65 to 90 inclusive (characters "A" to "Z") are pairwise equivalent to decimal values 97 to 122 inclusive (characters "a" to "z"), decimal values 192 to 214 inclusive (characters "A grave" to "O diaeresis") are pairwise equivalent to decimal values 224 to 246 inclusive (characters "a grave" to "o diaeresis"), and decimal values 216 to 222 inclusive (characters "O oblique" to "THORN") are pairwise equivalent to decimal values 246 to 254 inclusive (characters "o oblique" to "thorn").

Tile A pixmap can be replicated in two dimensions to tile a region. The pixmap itself is also known as a tile.

Timestamp A timestamp is a time value expressed in milliseconds. It is typically the time since the last server reset. Timestamp values wrap around (after about 49.7 days). The server, given its current time is represented by timestamp T, always interprets timestamps from clients by treating half of the timestamp space as being earlier in time than T and half of the timestamp space as being later in time than T. One timestamp value, represented by the constant `CurrentTime`, is never generated by the server. This value is reserved for use in requests to represent the current server time.

TrueColor `TrueColor` can be viewed as a degenerate case of `DirectColor` in which the subfields in the pixel value directly encode the corresponding RGB values. That is, the colormap has predefined read-only RGB values. The values are typically linear or near-linear increasing ramps.

Type A type is an arbitrary atom used to identify the interpretation of property data. Types are completely uninterpreted by the server. They are solely for the benefit of clients. X predefines type atoms for many frequently used types, and clients also can define new types.

Viewable A window is viewable if it and all of its ancestors are mapped. This does not imply that any portion of the window is actually visible. Graphics requests can be performed on a window when it is not viewable, but output will not be retained unless the server is maintaining backing store.

Visible A region of a window is visible if someone looking at the screen can actually see it; that is, the window is viewable and the region is not occluded by any other window.

White space White space is any spacing character. On implementations that conform to the ANSI C library, white space is any character for which `isspace` returns true.

Window gravity When windows are resized, subwindows may be repositioned automatically relative to some position in the window. This attraction of a subwindow to some part of its parent is known as window gravity.

Window manager Manipulation of windows on the screen and much of the user interface (policy) is typically provided by a window manager client.

X Portable Character Set The X Portable Character Set is a basic set of 97 characters that are assumed to exist in all locales supported by Xlib. This set contains the following characters:

a..z A..Z 0..9
!"#$%&'()*+,-./:;<=>?@[ ]^_'{|}~
<space>, <tab>, and <newline>

This is the left/lower half (also called the G0 set) of the graphic character set of ISO8859-1 plus space, tab, and newline. It is also the set of graphic characters in 7-bit ASCII plus the same three control characters. The actual encoding of these characters on the host is system dependent. See **Host Portable Character Encoding**.

XLFD The X Logical Font Description Conventions that define a standard syntax for structured font names.

XY format The data for a pixmap is said to be in XY format if it is organized as a set of bitmaps representing individual bit planes with the planes appearing from most-significant to least-significant bit order.

Z format The data for a pixmap is said to be in Z format if it is organized as a set of pixel values in scanline order.

References

ANSI Programming Language – C: ANSI X3.159-1989, December 14, 1989.

Draft Proposed Multibyte Extension of ANSI C, Draft 1.1, November 30, 1989. SC22/C WG/SWG IPSJ/ITSCJ Japan.

X/Open Portability Guide, Issue 3, December 1988 (XPG3), X/Open Company, Ltd, Prentice-Hall, Inc. 1989. ISBN 0-13-685835-8. (See especially Volume 3: XSI Supplementary Definitions.)

POSIX: Information Technology – Portable Operating System Interface (POSIX) – Part 1: System Application Program Interface (API) [C Language], ISO/IEC 9945-1.

ISO2022: Information processing – ISO 7-bit and 8-bit coded character sets – Code extension techniques.

ISO8859-1: Information processing – 8-bit single-byte coded graphic character sets – Part 1: Latin alphabet No. 1.

Text of ISO/IEC/DIS 9541-1, Information Processing – Font Information Interchange – Part 1: Architecture.

Index

Trademarks

Credits

Design: David Ford
Manuscript editor: Christie Williams
Index: Marilyn Rowland
Production: Editorial Inc.; Kathryn S. Daniel, Production manager
Composition: Chiron, Inc.
Printing: Hamilton Printing